ADVANCED TEXTS IN ECONOMETRICS

Editors

Other Advanced Texts in Econometrics

ARCH: Selected Readings
Edited by Robert F. Engle

Asymptotic Theory for Integrated Processes
By H. Peter Boswijk

Bayesian Inference in Dynamic Econometric Models
By Luc Bauwens, Michel Lubrano, and Jean-François Richard

Co-integration, Error Correction, and the Econometric Analysis of Non-Stationary Data
By Anindya Banerjee, Juan J. Dolado, John W. Galbraith, and David Hendry

Dynamic Econometrics
By David F. Hendry

Finite Sample Econometrics
By Aman Ullah

Generalized Method of Moments
By Alastair Hall

Likelihood-Based Inference in Cointegrated Vector Autoregressive Models
By Søren Johansen

Long-Run Econometric Relationships: Readings in Cointegration
Edited by R. F. Engle and C. W. J. Granger

Micro-Econometrics for Policy, Program, and Treatment Effect
By Myoung-jae Lee

Modelling Econometric Series: Readings in Econometric Methodology
Edited by C. W. J. Granger

Modelling Non-Linear Economic Relationships
By Clive W. J. Granger and Timo Teräsvirta

Modelling Seasonality
Edited by S. Hylleberg

Non-Stationary Times Series Analysis and Cointegration
Edited by Colin P. Hargeaves

Outlier Robust Analysis of Economic Time Series
By André Lucas, Philip Hans Franses, and Dick van Dijk

Panel Data Econometrics
By Manuel Arellano

Periodicity and Stochastic Trends in Economic Time Series
By Philip Hans Franses

Progressive Modelling: Non-nested Testing and Encompassing
Edited by Massimiliano Marcellino and Grayham E. Mizon

Readings in Unobserved Components
Edited by Andrew Harvey and Tommaso Proietti

Stochastic Limit Theory: An Introduction for Econometricians
By James Davidson

Stochastic Volatility
Edited by Neil Shephard

Testing Exogeneity
Edited by Neil R. Ericsson and John S. Irons

The Econometrics of Macroeconomic Modelling
By Gunnar Bårdsen, Øyvind Eitrheim, Eilev S. Jansen, and Ragnar Nymoen

Time Series with Long Memory
Edited by Peter M. Robinson

Time-Series-Based Econometrics: Unit Roots and Co-integrations
By Michio Hatanaka

Workbook on Cointegration
By Peter Reinhard Hansen and Søren Johansen

READINGS IN UNOBSERVED COMPONENTS MODELS

Edited by
ANDREW C. HARVEY
and
TOMMASO PROIETTI

OXFORD
UNIVERSITY PRESS

OXFORD
UNIVERSITY PRESS

Great Clarendon Street, Oxford OX2 6DP

Oxford University Press is a department of the University of Oxford.
It furthers the University's objective of excellence in research, scholarship,
and education by publishing worldwide in

Oxford New York

Auckland Cape Town Dar es Salaam Hong Kong Karachi
Kuala Lumpur Madrid Melbourne Mexico City Nairobi
New Delhi Shanghai Taipei Toronto

With offices in

Argentina Austria Brazil Chile Czech Republic France Greece
Guatemala Hungary Italy Japan Poland Portugal Singapore
South Korea Switzerland Thailand Turkey Ukraine Vietnam

Oxford is a registered trade mark of Oxford University Press
in the UK and in certain other countries

Published in the United States
by Oxford University Press Inc., New York

British Library Cataloguing in Publication Data
Data available

Library of Congress Cataloging in Publication Data
Data available

Typeset by Newgen Imaging Systems (P) Ltd., Chennai, India
Printed in Great Britain
on acid-free paper by
Biddles Ltd., King's Lynn, Norfolk

ISBN 0-19-927865-2 (hbk.)
ISBN 0-19-927869-5 (pbk.)

1 3 5 7 9 10 8 6 4 2

Foreword

The aim of this volume is to present a collection of papers, many recent, which give the reader an idea of the nature and scope of unobserved components (UC) models and the methods used to deal with them.

The volume is divided into four parts, three of which deal with theoretical developments in classical and Bayesian estimation of linear, nonlinear, and non-Gaussian UC models, signal extraction and testing, and one is devoted to selected econometric applications.

More specifically, part I focuses on the linear state space model; the proposed readings provide insight on prediction theory for non stationary and non invertible processes, signal extraction and inference in linear Gaussian state space models, diagnostic checking, and the use of state space methods for spline smoothing.

Part II focuses on applications of linear UC models to various estimation problems concerning economic time series: the decomposition of a time series into a trend a cycle components, the seasonal adjustment of weekly time series, and the modelling of the serial correlation induced by survey sample design.

Part III considers the issues involved in testing in linear UC models; in particular, it deals with tests concerned with whether or not certain variance parameters are zero, with special reference to stationarity tests.

The final part (part IV) is devoted to the advances concerning classical and Bayesian inference for non-linear and non-Gaussian state space models, an area that has been evolving very rapidly during the last decade, paralleling the advances in computational inference using stochastic simulation techniques.

Each part has an introductory chapter whose primary aim is that of providing an overview of the main recent developments and to unify the notation.

A thorough presentation of the main ideas and methodological aspects underlying UC models is contained in the monographs by Harvey (1989), West and Harrison (1997), Kitagawa and Gersch (1996) and Durbin and Koopman (2001); a good reference for early developments and applications is Nerlove, Grether and Carvalho (1979).

Availability of Software

Most of the state space methods presented in this volume can be implemented in practice. General routines for filtering and smoothing are available in statistical and econometric software (SAS, Eviews, Rats, etc.).

SsfPack (Koopman, Shephard and Doornik, 1999) is a suite of C routines for filtering, smoothing, simulation smoothing, likelihood evaluation, forecasting and signal extraction in the general linear Gaussian state space model. The routines are linked to Ox, the object-oriented matrix programming language by Doornik (1998), and to S+FinMetrics, and S-PLUS module for modelling financial data; see Zivot, Wang and Koopman (2002). Contributed software using Ssfpack for stochastic volatility models and for non-Gaussian and non-linear models is also available.

Other software specialised on a particular class of unobserved components models. Captain, developed by the Centre for Research on Environmental Systems at Lancaster University (UK), is a Matlab toolbox for signal extraction and forecasting for various dynamic regression models. Software for applied Bayesian Analysis of Time Series (BATS) based on the book by Pole, West and Harrison (1994) is also available. Finally, Stamp, by Koopman, Harvey, Shephard and Doornik (2000), is a menu driven package for modelling and forecasting time series based on univariate and multivariate structural time series models (see Harvey, 1989).

Contents

Part I

Signal Extraction and Likelihood Inference for Linear UC Models

1
Introduction

1 The Linear State Space Form

The statistical framework for unobserved components models is the state space representation, which is made up of a *measurement equation* and a *transition equation*. The former relates the $N \times 1$ vector time series y_t to an $m \times 1$ vector of unobservable components or state vector, α_t:

$$y_t = Z_t \alpha_t + G_t \varepsilon_t, \quad t = 1, 2, \ldots, T, \tag{1.1}$$

where Z_t is an $N \times m$ matrix, G_t is $N \times g$ and ε_t is a $g \times 1$ vector of random disturbances that we assume $\mathsf{NID}(0, I_g)$, or, more weakly, uncorrelated standard white noise. The *transition equation* is a dynamic linear model for the states α_t, taking the form of a first order vector autoregression:

$$\alpha_{t+1} = T_t \alpha_t + H_t \varepsilon_t, \tag{1.2}$$

where T_t and H_t are $m \times m$ and $m \times g$ matrices, respectively.

The system matrices, Z_t, G_t, T_t, and H_t, are non-stochastic, i.e. they are allowed to vary over time, but in a deterministic fashion, and are functionally related to a set of parameters, θ, which usually will have to be estimated. A state space model is *time invariant* if the system matrices are constant, that is $Z_t = Z$, $G_t = G$, $T_t = T$, and $H_t = H$. Moreover, UC models are usually specified in a way that the measurement and transition equation disturbances are uncorrelated, i.e. $H_t G_t' = 0, \forall t$.

The state space model is completed by the specification of initial conditions, concerning the distribution of α_1: this turns out to be a relevant issue when non-stationary components are present, as it will be seen shortly. When the system is time-invariant and α_t is stationary (the eigenvalues of the transition matrix, T, are inside the unit circle), the initial conditions are provided by the unconditional mean and covariance matrix of the state vector, $\mathsf{E}(\alpha_1) = 0$ and $\mathsf{Var}(\alpha_1) = P$, satisfying the matrix equation $P = TPT' + HH'$.

2 Alternative State Space Representations and Extensions

The reader will soon realise that the notation changes across the various chapters. Perhaps it is useful to comment on the representation chosen for the transition equation and to explain how to derive equivalent parameterisations.

Equation (1.2) has been specified in the so-called *future* form; often, as in Harvey (1989) and West and Harrison (1996), the *contemporaneous* form of the model is adopted, with (1.2) replaced by $\alpha_t = T_t\alpha_{t-1} + H_t\varepsilon_t$. This makes some difference for filtering and prediction, and we can always translate it into the future form by replacing α_t in the measurement equation by the right hand side of the transition equation and setting $y_t = Z_t^*\alpha_t^* + G_t^*\varepsilon_t$, $\alpha_{t+1}^* = T_t\alpha_t^* + H_t\varepsilon_t$, with $\alpha_t^* = \alpha_{t-1}$, $Z_t^* = Z_t T_t$, $G_t^* = G_t + Z_t H_t$. Notice that if the contemporaneous form has uncorrelated disturbances, $H_t G_t' = 0$, in the future form $H_t G_t^{*'}$ is not necessarily equal to a zero matrix.

When $H_t G_t' \neq 0$, the state space form can also be rewritten with uncorrelated measurement and transition disturbances, as in Burridge and Wallis (Chapter 2), Section 3.2,

$$y_t = Z\alpha_t + G_t\varepsilon_t, \qquad \alpha_{t+1} = T_t^*\alpha_t + B_t y_t + H_t^*\varepsilon_t,$$

where $B_t = H_t G_t'(G_t G_t')^{-1}G_t$, $T_t^* = T_t - B_t Z_t$; $H_t^* = H_t - B_t$; $H_t^*\varepsilon_t$ is the residual from the linear projection of $H_t\varepsilon_t$ on $G_t\varepsilon_t$ and $H_t^* G_t' = 0$.

The linear state space model can be extended to introduce fixed and regression effects. If we let X_t and W_t denote fixed and known matrices of dimension $N \times k$ and $m \times k$, respectively, the state space form can be generalised as follows:

$$y_t = Z_t\alpha_t + X_t\beta + G_t\varepsilon_t, \qquad \alpha_{t+1} = T_t\alpha_t + W_t\beta + H_t\varepsilon_t.$$

Alternatively, β is included in the state vector and the state space model becomes:

$$y_t = Z_t^\dagger\alpha_t^\dagger + G_t\varepsilon_t, \qquad \alpha_{t+1}^\dagger = T_t^\dagger\alpha_t^\dagger + H_t^\dagger\varepsilon_t,$$

where

$$\alpha_t^\dagger = \begin{bmatrix} \alpha_t \\ \beta_t \end{bmatrix}, \quad Z_t^\dagger = [Z_t \quad X_t], \quad T_t^\dagger = \begin{bmatrix} T_t & W_t \\ 0 & I_k \end{bmatrix}, \quad H_t^\dagger = \begin{bmatrix} H_t \\ 0 \end{bmatrix}.$$

Doran (1992) discusses how contemporaneous (time-varying) constraints imposed on the state variables of the form $c_t = C_t\alpha_t$ can be dealt with by a suitable augmentation of the measurement equation, treating each constraint as a pseudo-observation (free of measurement error).

3 The Kalman Filter

The Kalman filter (KF, Kalman, 1960; Kalman and Bucy, 1961) is a fundamental algorithm for the statistical treatment of a state space model. Under the Gaussian assumption it produces the minimum mean square estimator (MMSE) of the state vector conditional on past information, $\tilde{\alpha}_{t|t-1} = \mathsf{E}(\alpha_t|Y_{t-1})$, along with its mean square error (MSE) matrix, $P_{t|t-1} = \mathsf{MSE}(\tilde{\alpha}_{t|t-1})$, where $Y_t = \{y_1, \ldots, y_t\}$ is the information set available at time t.

For a standard state space model with initial conditions $\alpha_1 \sim \mathsf{N}(\tilde{\alpha}_{1|0}, P_{1|0})$, with $\tilde{\alpha}_{1|0}$ and $P_{1|0}$ known and finite, it consists of the following recursive formulae and definitions ($t = 1, \ldots, T$):

$$v_t = y_t - Z_t \tilde{\alpha}_{t|t-1},$$

$$F_t = Z_t P_{t|t-1} Z_t' + G_t G_t',$$
$$K_t = (T_t P_{t|t-1} Z_t' + H_t G_t') F_t^{-1},$$
$$\tilde{\alpha}_{t+1|t} = T_t \tilde{\alpha}_{t|t-1} + K_t v_t, \qquad P_{t+1|t} = T_t P_{t|t-1} T_t' + H_t H_t' - K_t F_t K_t'; \qquad (1.3)$$

as $\tilde{y}_{t|t-1} = \mathsf{E}(y_t|Y_{t-1}) = Z_t \tilde{\alpha}_{t|t-1}$, v_t represent the one-step-ahead prediction error, or innovation at time t, and F_t is its variance matrix.

When the Gaussianity assumption is removed the KF still yields the minimum mean square linear estimator (MMSLE) of the state vector. Proofs of the KF are available from different perspectives: best linear prediction (Duncan and Horn, 1972; Anderson and Moore, 1979), minimum mean square prediction (Harvey, 1989), Bayesian estimation (Meinhold and Singpurwalla, 1983; West and Harrison, 1997). Chapter 2 provides a step by step illustration of the KF computations with reference to an ARMA(1,1) model and to an AR(1) plus noise model.

4 Prediction

The prediction problem has two fundamental aspects: *forecasting* deals with optimal estimation of future observations conditional on past and current observations. If the optimality criterion is the mean square error, then the MMSE of y_{t+l} given Y_t is the conditional expectation $\tilde{y}_{t+l} = \mathsf{E}(y_{t+l}|Y_t)$. *Signal extraction* deals with the estimation of an unobserved component; related problems are interpolation and cross-validation, aiming at determining the expected value of y_t conditional on the information set excluding y_t.

The classical Wiener-Kolmogorov prediction theory provides a solution (the optimal linear predictor) for stationary processes. Letting ς_t denote some stationary process and y_t an indeterministic linear process with Wold representation $y_t = \psi(L)\xi_t, \sum|\psi_j| < \infty$, where ξ_t is a white noise process with variance σ^2, the MMSLE of ς_{t+l} based on a semi-infinite sample y_t is:

$$\tilde{\varsigma}_{t+l|t} = \frac{1}{\sigma^2 \psi(L)} \left[\frac{g_{\varsigma y}(L)}{\psi(L^{-1})} L^{-l} \right]_+ y_t; \qquad (1.4)$$

here $g_{\varsigma y}(L)$ denotes the cross covariance generating function of ς_t and y_t, and for $h(L) = \sum_{j=-\infty}^{\infty} h_j L^j$, $[h(L)]_+ = \sum_{j=0}^{\infty} h_j L^j$, i.e. a polynomial containing only nonnegative powers of L; see Whittle (1983, p. 42).

The pure prediction case arises when $\varsigma_{t+l} = y_{t+l}$, $l > 0$, and formula (1.4) specialises as follows:

$$\tilde{y}_{t+l|t} = \frac{1}{\psi(L)} \left[\frac{\psi(L)}{L^l} \right]_+ y_t.$$

If ς_{t+l} is a signal, the formula for $l \leq 0$ provides the weights for signal extraction (contemporaneous filtering for $l = 0$). If a doubly infinite sample of y_t

is available the signal extraction filter is

$$\tilde{\varsigma}_{t|\infty} = \frac{g_{\varsigma y}(L)}{g_y(L)} y_t;$$

when the decomposition $y_t = \varsigma_t + \epsilon_t$ is orthogonal, $g_{\varsigma y}(L) = g_{\varsigma}(L)$; see Whittle (1983, ch. 5).

Chapter 2 is concerned with establishing a rigorous prediction theory for non stationary and non invertible processes. It shows the equivalence and the connections between the Wiener-Kolmogorov theory and the recursive filtering techniques based upon the Kalman filter. Drawing from basic results from control theory, Burridge and Wallis establish the conditions under which signals are estimable with finite MSE and the forecast errors follow a stationary process.

Assuming a time invariant system, and given initial conditions $\tilde{a}_{1|0}$ and $P_{1|0}$, from (1.1), (1.2), and (1.3), it can be seen that the innovations and the state one-step-ahead prediction error, $x_t = \alpha_t - \tilde{\alpha}_{t|t-1}$, can be written as

$$v_t = Zx_t + G\varepsilon_t, \qquad x_{t+1} = L_t x_t + (H - K_t G)\varepsilon_t,$$

where $L_t = T - K_t Z$. Thus, x_t follows a VAR(1) process that is (asymptotically) stationary if the autoregressive matrix L_t, known as the *closed loop matrix* in system theory, converges to a matrix $L = T - KZ$, whose eigenvalues lie all inside the unit circle.

The basic properties that ensure convergence to such a stabilising solution are *detectability* and *stabilisability*, formally stated in Section 3.2. They imply that, independently of initial conditions, $P_{t+1|t}$ converges at an exponential rate to a steady state solution P, satisfying the Riccati equation $P = TPT' + HH' - KFK'$, with $K = (TPZ' + HG')F^{-1}$ and $F = ZPZ' + GG'$, and the Kalman gain matrix K is such that the eigenvalues of L all lie inside the unit circle.

A well known case where detectability fails is the trend plus seasonal decomposition $y_t = \mu_t + \gamma_t + \epsilon_t$, where $\mu_{t+1} = \mu_t + \eta_t$, $\gamma_{t+s} = \gamma_t + \omega_t$, s is the seasonal period, and the disturbances ϵ_t, η_t and ω_t are mutually and serially uncorrelated. Detectability failure is due to the presence of the common nonstationary root $(1 - L)$ in the trend and the seasonal components.

As far as ARMA processes are concerned, it should be noticed that the authors refer to the Pearlman (1980) state space representation, such that the dimension of the state vector is the greatest between the AR and MA orders, p and q, respectively, and the measurement and state disturbances are correlated. Other representations are possible with no measurement noise, but with $m = \max(p, q + 1)$. Along with providing the minimal state dimension the Pearlman representation has amenable properties for statistical discussion, after an orthogonalisation of the disturbances.

The prediction theory presented in Chapter 2 is conditional upon starting values $\tilde{a}_{1|0}$ and $P_{1|0}$. Further developments, illustrated in the following sections, have led to establishing a prediction theory unconditional on the initialisation. Also, it is mainly set up in a time invariant framework; the derivation of weighting functions for prediction in time varying and multivariate state space models is dealt with in Harvey and Koopman (2000) and Koopman and Harvey (2003).

5 Initialisation and Likelihood Inference

When $\tilde{\alpha}_{1|0}$ and $P_{1|0}$ are known and finite, the KF enables the likelihood function to be written in prediction error decomposition form (Schweppe, 1965). Apart from a constant term the log-likelihood is:

$$L(y_1, \ldots, y_T; \theta) = \sum_{t=1}^{T} L(y_t | Y_{t-1}; \theta) = -\frac{1}{2}\left(\sum_{t=1}^{T} \ln|F_t| + \sum_{t=1}^{T} v_t' F_t^{-1} v_t\right),$$

(1.5)

and can be maximised numerically with respect to the unknown parameters, θ, by a quasi-Newton optimisation routine.

The KF and the definition of the likelihood need to be amended when non-stationary effects are present. This is the topic of Chapter 3, in which Koopman (1997) provides an elegant and computationally efficient solution to the initialisation problem. The paper reviews other solutions to the same problem. Here we discuss maximum likelihood estimation and the notion of a diffuse likelihood.

Let us assume that d nonstationary state elements are present; the initial state vector can be expressed as $\alpha_1 = a + B\eta + D\delta$, where a and B are respectively an $m \times 1$ known vector and an $m \times (m - d)$ known matrix, and D is a $m \times d$ selection matrix assigning the appropriate elements of δ to the states. The vectors $\eta \sim N(0, I_N)$ and δ are used to initialise respectively the stationary and nonstationary elements of α_t and are mutually independent and independent of ε_t, for all t.

Two assumptions can be made: (i) δ is considered as a fixed, but unknown vector, this being suitable if it is deemed that the transition process (1.2) governing the states has started at time $t = 1$; (ii) δ is a diffuse random vector, i.e. it has an improper distribution with a mean of zero and an arbitrarily large variance matrix: $\delta \sim N(0, \kappa I_d)$, $\kappa \to \infty$. This is suitable if the process has started in the indefinite past.

Case (i) has been considered by Rosenberg (1973), who shows that δ can be estimated by maximum likelihood. Initial conditions are thus $\tilde{\alpha}_{1|0} = a + D\delta$ and $P_{1|0} = BB'$ and for a given value of δ the KF, here written as a function of δ, KF(δ), delivers the the innovation and the conditional mean of the state vector as $v_t = v_t^* - V_t\delta$ and $\tilde{\alpha}_{t+1|t} = \tilde{\alpha}_{t+1|t}^* - A_{t+1|t}\delta$. The starred quantities, v_t^* and $\tilde{\alpha}_{t+1|t}^*$, are produced by the KF run with $\delta = 0$, i.e. with initial conditions $\tilde{\alpha}_{1|0}^* = a$ and $P_{1|0}^* = BB'$, hereby denoted KF(0). Notice that the matrices F_t, K_t and $P_{t+1|t}$, $t = 1, \ldots, T$, are invariant to δ and thus are delivered by KF(0). The matrices V_t and $A_{t+1|t}$ are generated by the following recursions, that are run in parallel to KF(0):

$$V_t = -Z_t A_{t|t-1}, \qquad A_{t+1|t} = T_t A_{t|t-1} + K_t V_t, \qquad t = 1, \ldots, T, \qquad (1.6)$$

with initial value $A_{1|0} = -D$. Then, replacing $v_t = v_t^* - V_t\delta$ into (1.5), yields:

$$-\frac{1}{2}\left(\sum_{t=1}^{T}\ln|F_t| + \sum_{t=1}^{T}v_t^{*'}F_t^{-1}v_t^* - 2\delta's_T + \delta'S_T\delta\right), \qquad (1.7)$$

where $s_T = \sum_1^T V_t'F_t^{-1}v_t^*$ and $S_T = \sum_1^T V_t'F_t^{-1}V_t$. Hence, the maximum likelihood estimate of δ is $\hat{\delta} = S_T^{-1}s_T$ and the concentrated likelihood is

$$\mathsf{L}_\delta(y_1, \ldots, y_T; \theta) = -\frac{1}{2}\left(\sum_{t=1}^{T}\ln|F_t| + \sum_{t=1}^{T}v_t^{*'}F_t^{-1}v_t^* - s_T'S_T^{-1}s_T\right). \qquad (1.8)$$

When δ is diffuse, the definition of the likelihood needs to be amended; the argument set forth by de Jong (1991) stems from the decomposition

$$\mathsf{L}(y_1, \ldots, y_T; \theta) = \mathsf{L}(y_1, \ldots, y_T; \theta|\delta) + \mathsf{L}(\delta; \theta) - \mathsf{L}(\delta; \theta|y_1, \ldots, y_T). \qquad (1.9)$$

The first term, $\mathsf{L}(y_1, \ldots, y_T; \theta|\delta)$, is given by (1.7), which is reinterpreted as the likelihood of the observed series, conditional on δ; also, $\mathsf{L}(\delta; \theta) = -\frac{1}{2}(d\ln\kappa + \kappa^{-1}\delta'\delta)$; moreover, it can be shown (De Jong, 1988a) that the mean and the variance of δ conditional on $y_1, \ldots, y_T$ are $(\kappa^{-1}I_d + S_T)^{-1}s_T$ and $(\kappa^{-1}I_d + S_T)$, respectively, so that $\mathsf{L}(\delta; \theta|y_1, \ldots, y_T)$ can be written

$$-\frac{1}{2}\{\ln|\kappa^{-1}I_d + S_T| + [\delta - (\kappa^{-1}I_d + S_T)^{-1}s_T]'(\kappa^{-1}I_d + S_T)$$
$$\times [\delta - (\kappa^{-1}I_d + S_T)^{-1}s_T]\}.$$

Substituting into (1.9) and rearranging gives:

$$\mathsf{L}(y_1, \ldots, y_T; \theta) = -\frac{1}{2}\left\{\sum\ln|F_t| + \ln|\kappa I_d| + \ln|\kappa^{-1}I_d + S_T|\right.$$
$$\left. + \sum v_t^{*'}F_t^{-1}v_t^* - s_T'(\kappa^{-1}I_d + S_T)^{-1}s_T\right\}. \qquad (1.10)$$

This shows that only $\mathsf{L}(Y_T; \theta, \delta) + (d/2)\ln\kappa$ is a proper likelihood and that its limiting expression for $\kappa \to \infty$ is

$$\mathsf{L}_\infty(y_1, \ldots, y_T; \theta) = -\frac{1}{2}\left(\sum\ln|F_t| + \ln|S_T| + \sum v_t^{*'}F_t^{-1}v_t^* - s_T'S_T^{-1}s_T\right). \qquad (1.11)$$

The notion of a diffuse likelihood is close to that of a marginal likelihood, being based on a rank $T - d$ linear transformation of the series that eliminates dependence on δ. Comparing (1.11) with (1.8), it turns out that $\mathsf{L}_\infty(Y_T; \theta)$ differs from $\mathsf{L}_\delta(Y_T; \theta)$ because of the presence of the term $\ln|S_T|$, which could have significant effects on the estimation of θ, especially when the data generating process is close to nonstationarity and noninvertibility. In this situation, as shown by Tunnicliffe-Wilson (1986) and Shephard and Harvey (1990), the estimators based on (1.11) exhibit better small sample properties.

De Jong and Chu-Chun-Lin (1994) show that the additional recursions (1.6) can be dropped after the d-th update, at which a collapse to the ordinary KF occurs. Chapter 3 provides an exact analytic solution to the initialisation and likelihood inference problems that is computationally more efficient than the augmentation approach. Koopman's approach entails the derivation of a modified KF, the *exact initial KF*, hinging on the fundamental idea, adopted by Ansley and Kohn (1985, 1989), of expressing the KF quantities explicitly in terms of κ and letting $\kappa \to \infty$ to get the exact solution. Illustrations are provided with respect to some standard univariate and bivariate structural time series models; issues such as the treatment of missing values, exact initial smoothing, and the computational and numerical performance of the filter are also discussed.

6 Smoothing Algorithms

The Wiener-Kolmogorov signal extraction formulae discussed in Section 1.4 are useful for theoretical discussion on the nature of model-based filters. Computationally efficient smoothing algorithms for the general state space model (1.1)–(1.2), with possibly time-varying system matrices and nonstationary state components, are discussed in Chapter 4, which reproduces de Jong (1989).

Smoothing refers to optimal estimation of the unobserved components based also on future observations. *Fixed-interval smoothing* is concerned with computing the full set of smoothed estimates $\tilde{a}_{t|T} = \mathsf{E}(\alpha_t|Y_T)$, along with their covariance matrix $P_{t|T}$ for the entire sample, $t = 1, \ldots, T$; *fixed-point smoothing* computes smoothed estimates with reference to a fixed point in time, $\tilde{\alpha}_{t|j}, j > t$, whereas *fixed-lag smoothing* computes $\tilde{\alpha}_{t-j|t}$, where j is fixed and t varies.

Anderson and Moore (1979, ch. 7) provide a comprehensive account of the classic algorithms. Chapter 4 derives new smoothing results that lead to greater computational efficiency with respect to classic algorithms. As far as fixed-interval smoothing is concerned, the algorithm proposed by de Jong consists of the following backwards recursions starting at $t = T$, with initial values $r_T = 0$ and $N_T = 0$:

$$r_{t-1} = Z_t' F_t^{-1} v_t + L_t' r_t, \qquad N_{t-1} = Z_t' F_t^{-1} Z_t + L_t' N_t L_t,$$
$$\tilde{\alpha}_{t|T} = \tilde{\alpha}_{t|t-1} + P_{t|t-1} r_{t-1}, \qquad P_{t|T} = P_{t|t-1} - P_{t|t-1} N_{t-1} P_{t|t-1}. \tag{1.12}$$

A preliminary forward KF pass is required to store the quantities $\tilde{\alpha}_{t|t-1}$, $P_{t|t-1}$, v_t, F_t, and K_t, but compared with classic fixed-interval smoother, it avoids the inversion of the possibly very large and singular matrix $P_{t+1|t}$.

De Jong also deals with the modifications to introduce under diffuse initial conditions, and de Jong and Chu-Chun-Lin (2003) further illustrate the adjustment to be made to the initial stretch $t = d, \ldots, 1$, when the augmented Kalman filter is collapsed to enhance computational speed. Alternatively, using the exact initial KF of Koopman (Chapter 3), (1.12) still apply for $t = T, \ldots, d+1$ and an adjustment can be made for the initial stretch $t = d, \ldots, 1$.

6.1 Cross-validatory and auxiliary residuals

In the state space framework two other sets of residuals can be defined, complementing the KF innovations in providing further diagnostic quantities.

The *smoothing errors* (de Jong, 1988b; Kohn and Ansley, 1989) $u_t = F_t^{-1}v_t - K_t'r_t$, with variance $M_t = F_t^{-1} + K_t'N_tK_t$, play a role in interpolation and cross-validation. As a matter of fact, the residuals arising from deletion of the observation at time t (cross-validatory, or jacknifed, or deletion residuals) are related to them by:

$$y_t - \mathsf{E}(y_t|y_1, \ldots, y_{t-1}, y_{t+1}, \ldots, y_T) = M_t^{-1}u_t;$$

their covariance matrix is given by M_t^{-1}.

The estimation of the disturbances ε_t associated with the the various components, referred to as *disturbance smoothing*, is built upon the smoothing errors: Koopman (1993) shows that $\tilde{\varepsilon}_{t|T} = \mathsf{E}(\varepsilon_t|Y_T) = G_t'u_t + H_t'r_t$ and $\mathsf{Var}(\tilde{\varepsilon}_{t|T}) = G_t'D_tG_t + H_t'N_tH_t$. The standardised smoothed estimates of the disturbances are known as *auxiliary residuals*.

When the measurement and the transition equation disturbances are uncorrelated ($H_tG_t' = 0$), the irregular auxiliary residual,

$$y_t - Z_t\tilde{\alpha}_{t|T} = G_tG_t'u_t$$

standardised by the square root of the diagonal elements in $G_tG_t'M_tG_tG_t'$, corresponds to what is known in the regression literature as an internally studentised residuals (Kohn and Ansley, 1989). Also, the auxiliary residuals associated with the unobserved components in α_t are the elements of $H_tH_t'r_t$, scaled by the square root of the diagonal elements of $H_tH_t'N_tH_tH_t'$.

In Harvey and Koopman (1992, Chapter 5) the auxiliary residuals are employed to provide test statistics for outliers and structural change in the various components of interest. Unlike the innovations, the auxiliary residuals are serially correlated and Harvey and Koopman derive their autocorrelation structure and show how they can be employed to form appropriate tests of normality. The theoretical autocovariance generating function is derived from the Wiener-Kolmogorov filter.

6.2 Smoothing splines and non parametric regression

Suppose we have observations on a stock variable $y(t_i)$ at times $0 < t_1 < \cdots < t_i < \cdots < t_n$; we assume that the underlying process is continuous in t and the observations are contaminated by random error, $\epsilon(t_i) \sim \mathsf{NID}(0, \sigma^2)$. The model $y(t_i) = \varsigma(t_i) + \epsilon(t_i)$, where $\varsigma(t)$ is a deterministic, but possibly unknown, function of t, has a long tradition in time series analysis and in cross-sectional regression. When $\varsigma(t)$ represents a trend component, it has traditionally been represented as a polynomial of t of adequate degree.

To achieve more flexibility local rather than global polynomial approximations to $\varsigma(t)$ are employed, see for instance Anderson (1971) and Fan and Gijbels (1996); if interest lies in estimating the signal at a specific point in time τ, $\varsigma(t)$ is approximated by a Taylor series expansion in a neighbourhood of τ, giving $\varsigma(t) = \sum_{j=0}^{m} \alpha_j (t - \tau)^j$, where $\alpha_j = \varsigma^{(j)}(\tau)/(j!)$, and $\varsigma^{(j)}(\tau)$ is the j-th derivative evaluated at τ. The unknown α_j's are determined by minimising

$$\sum_{i=1}^{n} [y(t_i) - \sum_{j=0}^{m} \alpha_j (t_i - \tau)^j]^2 K_h(t_i - \tau),$$

where $K(\cdot)$ denotes a kernel function and h is the bandwidth. The estimate of the signal at time τ is then $\hat{\varsigma}(\tau) = \hat{\alpha}_0$. When the observations are equally spaced and the uniform kernel is adopted the equivalent kernel for $\hat{\varsigma}(\tau)$ is known as Macaulay's moving average. Some of the most popular filters employed for signal extraction can be derived from this principle: the Henderson filter, that represents the trend extraction filter within the X-11 seasonal adjustment filter (see Ladiray and Quenneville, 2001) arises for $m = 3$ with the kernel as given in Kenny and Durbin (1982, p. 28).

An alternative approach is to postulate that $\varsigma(t)$ is a flexible and smooth function of time, e.g. a spline of degree k, which is a piecewise polynomial of degree k in each of the intervals (t_i, t_{i+1}), $i = 1, \ldots, n - 1$, such that the first $k - 1$ derivatives are continuous. In the sequel we take $k = 2m - 1$, where the positive integer m is the order of the spline. The smoothing spline of order m is the unique minimiser of the penalised least square criterion (Green and Silverman, 1994):

$$\sum_{i=1}^{n} [y(t_i) - \varsigma(t_i)]^2 + \lambda \int_{t_1}^{t_n} [\varsigma^{(m)}(t)]^2 \, dt$$

for a given smoothness parameter λ. The cubic smoothing spline arises for $m = 2$: it can be described as the smoothest function (minimising $\int_{t_1}^{t_n} [\varsigma^{(2)}(t)]^2 dt$) that achieves a specified degree of fidelity.

Wahba (1978) showed that smoothing with a spline of order m is equivalent to signal extraction when $\varsigma(t)$ is an $(m-1)$-fold integrated Wiener process. Wecker and Ansley (1983) further established the state space formulation of the problem, which opens the way to efficient computation and estimation of λ via the KF and associated smoothing algorithms in $O(n)$ operations.

The j-fold integrated Wiener process is defined recursively as (see Tanaka, 1996, sec. 2.4):

$$\varsigma_j(t) = \int_0^t \varsigma_{j-1}(s)ds = \varsigma_j(t_i) + \int_{t_i}^t \varsigma_{j-1}(s)ds, \qquad \varsigma_0(t) = \sqrt{q}\sigma w(t),$$

where $t > t_i$. Here q denotes the signal-noise ratio and $\{w(t)\}$ is a standard Wiener process, with $w(0) = 0$, independent increments, $w(t_{i+1}) - w(t_i)$, $i = 1, \ldots, n$, and $w(t) - w(s) \sim \mathsf{N}(0, (t - s))$, for $t > s$.

Writing $\varsigma_0(t) = \varsigma_0(t_i) + \sqrt{q}\sigma \int_{t_i}^t dw(s)$ and replacing into $\varsigma_1(t) = \varsigma_1(t_i) + \int_{t_i}^t \varsigma_0(s)ds$, we have

$$\varsigma_1(t) = \varsigma_1(t_i) + (t - t_i)\varsigma_0(t_i) + \sqrt{q}\sigma \int_{t_i}^t (s - t_i)dw(s);$$

proceeding recursively we have

$$\varsigma_j(t) = \sum_{k=0}^{j} \frac{(t - t_i)^k}{k!}\varsigma_{j-k}(t_i) + \sqrt{q}\sigma \int_{t_i}^t \frac{(s - t_i)^j}{j!}dw(s). \tag{1.13}$$

The stochastic integral equation (1.13) is at the basis of the state space representation: defining

$$\alpha(t) = [\varsigma_{m-1}(t), \varsigma_{m-2}(t), \ldots, \varsigma_0(t)]',$$

$$\omega(t) = [\omega_{m-1}(t), \omega_{m-2}(t), \ldots, \omega_0(t)]',$$

with $\omega_j(t) = \sqrt{q}\sigma \int_{t_i}^t ((s - t_i)^j/j!)dw(s)$, $j = 0, \ldots, m - 1$, we can write $\alpha(t) = T(t, t_i)\alpha(t_i) + \omega(t)$, where $T(t, t_i)$ is an upper triangular matrix with unit diagonal elements and, for $h < k$, $T_{hk}(t, t_i) = (t - t_i)^{k-h}/[(k - h)!]$ is the row h – column k element of the transition matrix. Moreover,

$$\mathsf{Cov}(\omega_j(t), \omega_h(t)) = q\sigma^2 \int_{t_i}^t \int_{t_i}^t \frac{(s - t_i)^j(r - t_i)^h}{j!h!}\mathsf{E}[dw(s)dw(r)]$$

$$= q\sigma^2 \frac{(t - t_i)^{j+h+1}}{(j + h + 1)j!h!}.$$

Specialising results with respect to cubic spline smoothing ($m = 2$), the exact discrete time state space model has measurement equation $y(t_i) = [1, 0]\alpha(t_i) + \epsilon(t_i)$, $\alpha(t_i) = [\varsigma_1(t_i), \varsigma_0(t_i)]'$, and transition equation $\alpha(t_{i+1}) = T(t_{i+1}, t_i) \times \alpha(t_i) + \omega(t_{i+1})$, such that

$$T(t_{i+1}, t_i) = \begin{bmatrix} 1 & (t_{i+1} - t_i) \\ 0 & 1 \end{bmatrix},$$

$$\mathsf{Var}[\omega(t_{i+1})] = q\sigma^2 \begin{bmatrix} \frac{1}{3}(t_{i+1} - t_i)^3 & \frac{1}{2}(t_{i+1} - t_i)^2 \\ \frac{1}{2}(t_{i+1} - t_i)^2 & (t_{i+1} - t_i) \end{bmatrix}.$$

The paper by Kohn, Ansley and Wong (1992, Chapter 6) generalises the signal extraction approach to spline smoothing when $\epsilon(t_i)$ is a stationary ARMA process. This is suitable if the observations are equally spaced or the gaps between observations, $t_{i+1} - t_i$, are a multiple of a standard interval. The more general case in which $\epsilon(t)$ is a stationary continuous time process is also discussed.

A simulation study is conducted to judge the performance of maximum like-lihood estimation of the parameters (which include the smoothness parameter $\lambda = q^{-1}$) relative to cross-validation (CV) and generalised cross-validation (GCV). Parameter estimation according to the latter is performed by minimising respectively:

$$CV(\theta) = \sum_{i=1}^{n} \{y(t_i) - \mathsf{E}[y(t_i)|y(t_1), \ldots, y(t_{i-1}), y(t_{i+1}), \ldots, y(t_n)]\}^2$$

$$= \sum_{i=1}^{n} u(t_i)'[M(t_i)]^{-2} u(t_i),$$

and

$$GCV(\theta) = \frac{\sum_{i=1}^{n} u(t_i)'u(t_i)}{[\sum_t \mathrm{tr}(M(t_i))]^2}.$$

Interestingly, Kohn, Ansley and Wong find that there is some scope for GCV only "when the generating model for the error process is unknown but we take it to be an ARMA process of a given order", that is in the presence of model misspecification. Similar evidence is found for alternative estimation methods such as "adaptive forecasting" (also known as dynamic or multi-step estimation), where the sum of squares of multi-step forecast errors is the criterion function, see for instance Tiao and Xu (1993) and Tiao and Tsay (1994). The overall conclusion, though, is that maximum likelihood works best.

2

Prediction Theory for Autoregressive-Moving Average Processes*

PETER BURRIDGE

University of Birmingham

AND

KENNETH F. WALLIS

University of Warwick

This paper reviews statistical prediction theory for autoregressive-moving average processes using techniques developed in control theory. It demonstrates explicitly the connections between the statistical and control theory literatures. Both the forecasting problem and the signal extraction problem are considered, using linear least squares methods. Whereas the classical statistical theory developed by Wiener and Kolmogorov is restricted to stationary stochastic processes, the recursive techniques known as the Kalman filter are shown to provide a satisfactory treatment of the difference-stationary case and other more general cases. Complete results for non-invertible moving averages are also obtained.

1 Introduction

In the statistical time series literature, the dominant approach to prediction theory is that developed by Wiener and Kolmogorov and exposited, for example, by Whittle (1963). This "classical" statistical theory relates to purely non-deterministic stationary processes, and is based on the autocovariance function of the relevant variables. Both in theoretical work and in practical implementation, the autocovariance function is commonly specified by postulating models for the relevant processes, and so is expressed as a function of model parameters. Most often, linear autoregressive-moving average (ARMA) models are chosen. Attention is usually restricted to linear least squares (l.l.s.) methods, and the theory delivers the linear combination of observed values that minimizes the mean square error of prediction. The set of observed values is usually assumed to extend from the indefinite past, that is, to comprise a semi-infinite sample.

Two branches of the prediction problem are typically distinguished. In the forecasting or pure prediction problem the objective is to estimate a future value of a variable, given its current and past observed values. In the signal extraction problem the variable to be predicted or estimated is not directly observed, but

* This work was previously published as P. Burridge and K. F. Wallis (1988), 'Prediction Theory for Autoregressive-Making Average Processes', *Econometric Reviews*, 1988, 7(1), 65–95. Reproduced by permission of Taylor & Francis, Inc.

may be a "signal" observed with superimposed "noise" or, more generally, one component of a process comprising several unobserved components. Here the requirement may be for an estimate of the signal for a future period, as in the forecasting problem, or alternatively an estimate for some past or present period. Both problems have a wide range of applications in economics and econometrics. Theoretical models of optimal behaviour in dynamic and uncertain environments draw on the Wiener-Kolmogorov theory, as indicated, for example, in Sargent's foreword to the second edition of Whittle's book (Whittle, 1983), or in his own macroeconomics text (Sargent, 1979). Empirical applications of the forecasting results are legion, following their popularization by Box and Jenkins (1970) and others. Applications of the signal extraction results range from permanent income theory to the seasonal adjustment of economic time series.

This paper reviews statistical prediction theory for ARMA processes using techniques developed in control theory. There the emphasis has been on recursive methods, in which estimates or forecasts formed from information available at a given point in time are sequentially updated as each successive observation becomes available. These techniques, familiarly known as Kalman filtering, are well adapted to on-line or real-time prediction, and have been utilized in economics and econometrics in models of learning behaviour and methods of recursive parameter estimation. The techniques have not been widely exploited in statistical prediction theory, however, and one objective of this paper is to demonstrate explicitly the connections between the statistical and control theory literatures.

The classical statistical theory is limited to stationary processes, as noted above, yet applications often concern non-stationary processes variously termed accumulated, integrated, or difference-stationary processes. For example, theoretical economic models may deliver propositions that certain variables follow random walks, and in empirical analysis of economic time series it is a common finding that series must be differenced at least once before appearing stationary. In such circumstances the usual approach is to apply to the differenced series the theory relevant to stationary processes. This neglects theoretical difficulties that have not been properly treated; for example, with a semi-infinite sample the observed series has unbounded variance. Of course, in practical applications only a finite record is available, and we show that the recursive techniques, with appropriate attention to initial conditions, yield a satisfactory treatment of the difference-stationary case. Indeed, in the context of the finite-degree ARMA model with known and time-invariant parameters, the results require no restriction on the autoregressive parameters, such as those associated with stationarity. Likewise, the approach we adopt requires no restriction on the moving average parameters, hence a complete account of the non-invertible case is obtained.

The paper proceeds as follows. Section 2 considers two examples that are well known in the time series literature, namely forecasting the first-order ARMA process and extracting a first-order autoregressive signal from noise-contaminated observations. In each case we develop recursions for the l.l.s. forecasts or signal estimates from first principles, and show their equivalence to Wiener-Kolmogorov theory in the case that this is applicable. Section 3 surveys some results in the control theory literature, first presenting the state-space representation of a linear dynamic system and the l.l.s. recursions known in that context as the Kalman filter. These time-varying recursions may achieve a form which has constant coefficients, and we collect together a number of theorems dealing with the convergence of the recursions to such a steady state. In Sections 4 and 5 the forecasting and signal extraction problems for general ARMA models are dealt with in turn. In each case we first present a convenient state-space representation of the time series model, and then investigate the applicability of the apparatus of Section 3. The l.l.s. recursions are shown to converge to a steady state from given initial conditions in circumstances more general than those considered in the time series literature: as with the simple examples of Section 2, the results cover non-stationary and non-invertible cases of the underlying models. For stationary models, to which the Wiener-Kolmogorov theory applies, we show explicitly that the steady state of the Kalman filter coincides with the classical time series formulae. Finally in Section 6 we discuss the relationship between the results of this paper and other treatments of the same, or closely related, problems in the time series literature, and present some concluding comments.

2 Two Leading Examples

2.1 Forecasting the ARMA(1,1) process
In this section we develop from first principles recursive methods of forecasting a variable y which obeys the ARMA(1,1) process

$$y_t = \phi y_{t-1} + \epsilon_t - \theta \epsilon_{t-1}, \tag{2.1}$$

where ϵ_t is white noise with constant variance σ_ϵ^2. It is assumed that $\phi \neq \theta$, but these parameters are otherwise unrestricted. At time t the observed history is $\{y_\tau; 0 \leq \tau \leq t\}$, and the problem is to construct the l.l.s. forecast of y_{t+1}, denoted $\hat{y}_{t+1,t}$, together with quantities such as the mean square error or innovation variance $E\{(y_{t+1} - \hat{y}_{t+1,t})^2\} = \Sigma_{t+1}$. It is convenient to express y as the sum of two random variables, one of which, x, is forecastable while the other, ϵ, is not (other than at a value of zero). Thus we write (2.1) as

$$\begin{aligned} x_t &= \phi y_{t-1} - \theta \epsilon_{t-1} \\ y_t &= x_t + \epsilon_t. \end{aligned} \tag{2.2}$$

Then x obeys the stochastic difference equation

$$x_t = \phi x_{t-1} + (\phi - \theta)\epsilon_{t-1}, \tag{2.3}$$

and forecasts of x and y coincide.

The recursive procedure is started off at time 0. Before any observations are made, our state of knowledge about x_0 is assumed to comprise its expectation $\hat{x}_{0,-1}$ and variance $p_{0,-1} = E\{(x_0 - \hat{x}_{0,-1})^2\}$. Since ϵ is serially uncorrelated, the l.l.s. forecast of y_0 is simply $\hat{x}_{0,-1}$, with variance $\Sigma_0 = p_{0,-1} + \sigma_\epsilon^2$, and the covariance between y_0 and x_0 is equal to $p_{0,-1}$. On observing y_0 we first update our initial estimate of x_0 by projection on y_0, giving the l.l.s. estimate

$$\hat{x}_{0,0} = \hat{x}_{0,-1} + p_{0,-1}\Sigma_0^{-1}(y_0 - \hat{y}_{0,-1})$$
$$= \hat{x}_{0,-1} + p_{0,-1}\Sigma_0^{-1}\tilde{y}_0, \qquad (2.4)$$

where $\tilde{y}_0$ is the innovation in y, and $p_{0,-1}\Sigma_0^{-1}$ is the least squares regression coefficient. The corresponding estimate of the unobserved ϵ_0 is

$$\hat{\epsilon}_{0,0} = y_0 - \hat{x}_{0,0} = \sigma_\epsilon^2 \Sigma_0^{-1}\tilde{y}_0, \qquad (2.5)$$

using $\Sigma_0 - p_{0,-1} = \sigma_\epsilon^2$. Since $\epsilon_0 - \hat{\epsilon}_{0,0} = -(x_0 - \hat{x}_{0,0})$ their variances are equal, to $p_{0,0}$ say, which from the projection (2.4) is given as

$$p_{0,0} = p_{0,-1} - p_{0,-1}^2\Sigma_0^{-1} = \sigma_\epsilon^2 p_{0,-1}\Sigma_0^{-1}. \qquad (2.6)$$

Turning to the one-step-ahead forecast, from (2.2) we have

$$\hat{x}_{1,0} = \phi y_0 - \theta\hat{\epsilon}_{0,0}, \qquad (2.7)$$

with variance $p_{1,0} = E\{(x_1 - \hat{x}_{1,0})^2\} = \theta^2 p_{0,0}$, so from (2.6) we have the recursion

$$p_{1,0} = \theta^2\sigma_\epsilon^2 p_{0,-1}\Sigma_0^{-1}. \qquad (2.8)$$

Finally, since the forecasts of x and y coincide, from (2.5) and (2.7) the l.l.s. forecast recursion for y is obtained as

$$\hat{y}_{1,0} = \phi y_0 - \theta\sigma_\epsilon^2\Sigma_0^{-1}(y_0 - \hat{y}_{0,-1}), \qquad (2.9)$$

with mean square error $\Sigma_1 = p_{1,0} + \sigma_\epsilon^2$.

The sequence of steps leading from (2.4) to (2.9) may be repeated as each new observation arrives, yielding the general recursions, valid for $t = 0, 1, 2, \ldots,$

$$\hat{y}_{t+1,t} = \phi y_t - \theta\sigma_\epsilon^2\Sigma_t^{-1}(y_t - \hat{y}_{t,t-1}) \qquad (2.10a)$$

$$\Sigma_t = p_{t,t-1} + \sigma_\epsilon^2 \qquad (2.10b)$$

$$p_{t+1,t} = \theta^2\sigma_\epsilon^2 p_{t,t-1}\Sigma_t^{-1}. \qquad (2.10c)$$

This system of equations provides the l.l.s. forecasts of y, irrespective of the stationarity or otherwise of the process, or of the invertibility of its moving average component, no assumption about the values of ϕ and θ having been made, except that they are distinct.

The coefficient of the innovation in the forecasting rule (2.10a) varies over time, and it is of interest to study its evolution, as described by equations (b) and (c). We note, however, that these are independent of the data, so there is no necessary connection between the coefficient sequence and the observation sequence: the coefficients can be calculated "off-line". Combining equations (2.10b, c), their evolution is described by the non-linear difference equation

$$p_{t+1,t} = \theta^2 \sigma_\epsilon^2 p_{t,t-1}(\sigma_\epsilon^2 + p_{t,t-1})^{-1} = h(p_{t,t-1}), \text{ say.} \quad (2.11)$$

This has fixed points at $p = 0$ and $p = (\theta^2 - 1)\sigma_\epsilon^2$, furthermore $h'(p_{t,t-1}) > 0$ and $h''(p_{t,t-1}) < 0$ for $p_{t,t-1} \geq 0$. In consequence

(i) if $|\theta| \leq 1$, then $p_{t+1,t}$ converges monotonically to zero and the innovation variance to σ_ϵ^2 for all $p_{0,-1} \geq 0$, the second fixed point being non-positive,

(ii) if $|\theta| > 1$, then $p_{t+1,t}$ converges monotonically to $(\theta^2 - 1)\sigma_\epsilon^2$ and the innovation variance to $\theta^2 \sigma_\epsilon^2$ for all $p_{0,-1} > 0$; if, on the other hand, $p_{0,-1} = 0$, then $p_{t+1,t} = 0$ for all t.

Thus in all cases, again irrespective of the value of ϕ, the recursions (2.10) deliver a steady-state forecasting rule. In case (i), this is

$$\hat{y}_{t+1,t} = \phi y_t - \theta(y_t - \hat{y}_{t,t-1}) \quad (2.12)$$

whereas in case (ii), with $|\theta| > 1$, unless $p_{0,-1} = 0$, we have

$$\hat{y}_{t+1,t} = \phi y_t - \theta^{-1}(y_t - \hat{y}_{t,t-1}). \quad (2.13)$$

With respect to invertibility, we note that this is immaterial to the existence of the steady-state forecasting rule. If the process is non-invertible, with $|\theta| > 1$, the recursions deliver an "invertible" steady-state rule (2.13), in which the coefficient of the innovation $\tilde{y}_t$ is θ^{-1}, corresponding to the moving average coefficient in the observationally equivalent invertible process. Such a process may be written

$$y_t = \phi y_{t-1} + \eta_t - \theta^{-1}\eta_{t-1}, \quad (2.14)$$

whereupon the innovation $\tilde{y}_t$ coincides with the driving random variable η_t, whose variance is $\sigma_\eta^2 = \theta^2 \sigma_\epsilon^2$. The choice of invertible or non-invertible representation is more apparent than real, since whatever choice is made, the result is the same steady state forecasting rule with the same forecast mean square error. The only case in which this is not so is $|\theta| > 1$ and $p_{0,-1} = 0$. The latter requirement represents perfect knowledge of x_0, and is unrealistic: in practical situations it is customary to assign a relatively large value to $p_{0,-1}$, reflecting uncertainty about the initial state.

The equivalence to the Wiener-Kolmogorov theory is readily analysed. That theory is usually restricted to stationary invertible processes, and the forecast is expressed as a function of observations extending from the indefinite past. Accordingly we consider the limit of the steady-state forecasting rule (2.12), which by repeated substitution can be written as the linear filter (with lag operator L)

$$\hat{y}_{t+1,t} = f_1(L)y_t, \quad (2.15)$$

where the generating function of the coefficients of the observations is

$$f_1(z) = \frac{\phi - \theta}{1 - \theta z}. \qquad (2.16)$$

Simple manipulation of this function yields

$$f_1(z) = \frac{z^{-1}(1 - \theta z) - z^{-1}(1 - \phi z)}{1 - \theta z}$$

$$= \frac{1 - \phi z}{1 - \theta z} \left\{ \frac{z^{-1}(1 - \theta z)}{1 - \phi z} - z^{-1} \right\} = \frac{1 - \phi z}{1 - \theta z} \left[\frac{z^{-1}(1 - \theta z)}{1 - \phi z} \right]_+,$$

where $[a(z)]_+$ denotes that part of the polynomial $a(z)$ containing non-negative powers of z, the operator $[.]_+$ being sometimes termed an "annihilation" operator. This last expression is the form in which the Wiener-Kolmogorov predictor is usually given (Whittle, 1963, Ch. 3; Nerlove et al., 1979, Ch. V). It is derived under the assumption that $|\phi| < 1$, and there are clearly difficulties with the term $(1 - \phi z)^{-1}$ if this is not so. But this assumption has no bearing on the form in which $f_1(z)$ is given in (2.16), which thus represents a more convenient device for calculating the coefficients, nor has it any bearing on our derivation. So, in addition to an equivalence to the Wiener-Kolmogorov predictor in the case for which it is defined, we see that the same expression, interpreted as the limit of our l.l.s. forecast recursions, applies to non-stationary cases of the same process. Vice versa, when the Wiener-Kolmogorov predictor is expressed in recursive form,[1] it coincides with the steady-state l.l.s. recursion (2.12), again valid more generally. The particular case $\phi = 1$ has been treated, somewhat informally, in much discussion; here (2.12) can be rearranged to give the familiar "adaptive expectations" formula

$$\hat{y}_{t+1,t} - \hat{y}_{t,t-1} = (1 - \theta)(y_t - \hat{y}_{t,t-1}).$$

Forecasting j steps ahead ($j > 1$) is straightforward in the present framework, since $\hat{y}_{t+j,t}$ is simply $\hat{x}_{t+j,t}$. Returning to the general case, this together with its forecast error is obtained from (2.3) as

$$\hat{x}_{t+j,t} = \phi^{j-1}\hat{x}_{t+1,t}, \quad j = 2, 3, \ldots$$

$$x_{t+j} - \hat{x}_{t+j,t} = (\phi - \theta)(\epsilon_{t+j-1} + \phi\epsilon_{t+j-2} + \cdots + \phi^{j-2}\epsilon_{t+1})$$

$$+ \phi^{j-1}(x_{t+1} - \hat{x}_{t+1,t}).$$

Thus the j-step-ahead forecast $\hat{y}_{t+j,t} = \phi^{j-1}\hat{y}_{t+1,t}$ has mean square error

$$E\{(y_{t+j} - \hat{y}_{t+j,t})^2\} = (\phi - \theta)^2 \sum_{i=0}^{j-2} \phi^{2i}\sigma_\epsilon^2 + \phi^{2j-2}p_{t+1,t} + \sigma_\epsilon^2.$$

If $|\phi| < 1$, we see that as j increases the forecast $\hat{y}_{t+j,t}$, tends to zero, the unconditional mean, the observed history summarized in $\hat{x}_{t+1,t}$, becoming less informative; similarly the forecast error variance tends to the variance of y, namely $\sigma_\epsilon^2(1 - 2\phi\theta + \theta^2)/(1 - \phi^2)$. Conversely, if $|\phi| > 1$, neither the forecast nor its error variance approach limits, while if $\phi = 1$ the forecast is constant, with error variance which increases linearly in j, as is well known. In all cases, the steady-state forecasting rule can be expressed as a function of past observations, corresponding to (2.15) and (2.16), giving

$$\hat{y}_{t+j,t} = f_j(L)y_t$$

$$f_j(z) = \phi^{j-1} f_1(z) = \frac{\phi^{j-1}(\phi - \theta)}{1 - \theta z}.$$

It is then easily seen that this again corresponds to the usual result for the stationary case, namely (Nerlove et al., 1979, p. 92)

$$f_j(z) = \frac{1 - \phi z}{1 - \theta z} \left[\frac{(1 - \theta z)z^{-j}}{1 - \phi z} \right]_+,$$

sustaining the same interpretation as in the previous paragraph.

2.2 Extracting an AR(1) signal masked by white noise

In this section we consider a simple signal extraction problem and again develop from first principles recursive methods of calculating the l.l.s. signal estimate. The signal s is assumed to follow an AR(1) process, and represents the variable of principal interest, but it is observed subject to a superimposed white noise error, η. Thus the model, for $t = 0, 1, 2, \ldots$, is

$$y_t = s_t + \eta_t$$
$$s_{t+1} = \phi s_t + \epsilon_{t+1}, \tag{2.17}$$

where η and ϵ are contemporaneously and serially uncorrelated, with variances σ_η^2 and σ_ϵ^2 respectively. The problem is to estimate s_t from observations on y.

In advance of the first observation, y_0, knowledge about s_0 is summarized in its expectation $\hat{s}_{0,-1}$ and variance $p_{0,-1} \geq 0$. The corresponding mean and variance of y_0 are then

$$\hat{y}_{0,-1} = \hat{s}_{0,-1}, \qquad \Sigma_0 = p_{0,-1} + \sigma_\eta^2$$

and the covariance between y_0 and s_0 is $p_{0,-1}$. Once the observation y_0 is available, the signal estimate is updated by the projection

$$\hat{s}_{0,0} = \hat{s}_{0,-1} + p_{0,-1}\Sigma_0^{-1}(y_0 - \hat{y}_{0,-1}),$$

and its mean square error correspondingly updated as

$$E\{(s_0 - \hat{s}_{0,0})^2\} = p_{0,-1} - p_{0,-1}^2 \Sigma_0^{-1}.$$

The l.l.s. forecast of the next value s_1 is now simply

$$\hat{s}_{1,0} = \phi \hat{s}_{0,0},$$

and since the error in this forecast is

$$s_1 - \hat{s}_{1,0} = \phi(s_0 - \hat{s}_{0,0}) + \epsilon_1$$

its mean square error is given as

$$p_{1,0} = \mathrm{E}\{(s_1 - \hat{s}_{1,0})^2\} = \phi^2(p_{0,-1} - p_{0,-1}^2 \Sigma_0^{-1}) + \sigma_\epsilon^2.$$

This procedure may be repeated as the observations $y_1, y_2, \ldots$ in turn become available, giving the general recursions

$$\hat{s}_{t,t} = \phi \hat{s}_{t-1,t-1} + p_{t,t-1} \Sigma_t^{-1}(y_t - \phi \hat{s}_{t-1,t-1}) \tag{2.18a}$$

$$\Sigma_t = p_{t,t-1} + \sigma_\eta^2 \tag{2.18b}$$

$$p_{t+1,t} = \phi^2(p_{t,t-1} - p_{t,t-1}^2 \Sigma_t^{-1}) + \sigma_\epsilon^2. \tag{2.18c}$$

Equation (2.18a) gives a recursion for the current estimate of the signal, with coefficients that vary over time, but again independently of the observations.

As in the previous example, we are interested in the possibility that the error variance $p_{t,t-1}$ and hence the time-varying coefficient in (2.18a) approaches a limit. From (2.18b, c) we obtain the nonlinear difference equation

$$p_{t+1,t} = \phi^2 p_{t,t-1} \sigma_\eta^2 (p_{t,t-1} + \sigma_\eta^2)^{-1} + \sigma_\epsilon^2 = h(p_{t,t-1}), \text{ say} \tag{2.19}$$

and on setting $p = h(p)$ we see that the fixed points are the solutions of the quadratic equation

$$f(p) = p^2 + \{\sigma_\eta^2(1 - \phi^2) - \sigma_\epsilon^2\}p - \sigma_\epsilon^2 \sigma_\eta^2 = 0. \tag{2.20}$$

This has real solutions of opposite sign, since $f(0) < 0$, and choosing the positive solution we also have $p > \sigma_\epsilon^2$, since $f(\sigma_\epsilon^2) < 0$. Moreover, $h'(p_{t,t-1}) > 0$ and $h''(p_{t,t-1}) < 0$ guarantee convergence of the iteration (2.19) to p for any $p_{0,-1} \geq 0$. As in the first example, convergence of the error variance does not depend on stationarity, that is, on the value of ϕ.

The steady-state signal estimate recursion obtained by setting $p_{t,t-1}$ equal to p in (2.18) can be rearranged as

$$\hat{s}_{t,t} = b \hat{s}_{t-1,t-1} + \left(1 - \frac{b}{\phi}\right) y_t,$$

where $b = \phi \sigma_\eta^2/(p + \sigma_\eta^2)$. Repeated substitutions then give the current estimate as a function of the observed history and the initial estimate, namely

$$\hat{s}_{t,t} = \left(1 - \frac{b}{\phi}\right) \sum_{j=0}^{t} b^j y_{t-j} + b^{t+1} \hat{s}_{0,-1}/\phi. \tag{2.21}$$

The steady state of the variance recursion (2.19) gives an alternative expression for the coefficient b, namely

$$b = \frac{\phi\sigma_\eta^2}{p + \sigma_\eta^2} = \frac{p - \sigma_\epsilon^2}{\phi p},$$

and from one or the other we see that $|b| < 1$ irrespective of the value of ϕ. The expression (2.21) may be compared with the classical formula obtained when $|\phi| < 1$ and a semi-infinite sample is available, which is (Whittle, 1963, §6.3; Nerlove et al., 1979, §V.5)

$$\hat{s}_{t,t} = (1 - \beta/\phi)(1 - \beta L)^{-1} y_t. \tag{2.22}$$

Here β is found from the unique invertible factorization of the covariance generating function of $(y_t - \phi y_{t-1})$; that is, β satisfies

$$g(z) = \sigma_\epsilon^2 + \sigma_\eta^2 (1 - \phi z)(1 - \phi z^{-1}) = \sigma^2 (1 - \beta z)(1 - \beta z^{-1}), \tag{2.23}$$

and is the moving average coefficient in the ARMA(1,1) representation of y. The quadratic equation to be solved for β, which has a reciprocal pair of solutions, is obtained by setting $z = \beta$ in (2.23), whence

$$\sigma_\epsilon^2 + \sigma_\eta^2 (1 - \phi\beta)(1 - \phi/\beta) = 0. \tag{2.24}$$

Making a change of variable from β to p by substituting $\phi\sigma_\eta^2/(p + \sigma_\eta^2)$ for β in (2.24) and rearranging yields the quadratic equation (2.20), and it is clear that the positive solution for p corresponds to the invertible solution for β, so b and β in (2.21) and (2.22) coincide. Thus the classical result, derived under a stationarity assumption, again coincides with the limiting case of the l.l.s. recursion, which is valid more generally.

The principal case of this model discussed in the literature occurs when $\phi = 1$, so that the signal follows a random walk. For example, s_t might then represent the "persisting" or "permanent" component of income, and observed income y_t comprises this together with a purely random "transitory" component, η_t. Permanent income is then estimated from current and past observed income via (2.22), which in this case gives the familiar exponentially weighted moving average (Muth, 1960). Its classical derivation is unsatisfactory, however, since apparatus developed for stationary processes is being applied to a non-stationary process.[2] Nevertheless we have seen that l.l.s. recursions can be readily developed in this case, with proper attention to initial conditions, and the sense in which the same apparatus can be applied is made precise.

In some situations it may be desirable to update the estimate of s_t as further data arrive, that is, to obtain a sequence $\hat{s}_{t,t}, \hat{s}_{t,t+1}, \hat{s}_{t,t+2}, \ldots$ of increasingly accurate l.l.s. estimates of s_t. This can be generalized, and we return to this problem, known as the "smoothing" problem, below.

Summarizing the lessons of the two examples, we first note the similar roles of x_t in the first example and s_t in the second. Both variables follow first-order auto-regressions, and neither is observed directly. Secondly, the fundamental quantity required to calculate successive estimates is in each case the error variance of the l.l.s. estimate of this variable, $p_{t,t-1}$. In effect, each of these examples has been analysed in *state-space form* and, as discussed below, the recursions developed from first principles are scalar versions of the Kalman filter. The ease with which the behaviour of $p_{t,t-1}$ is analysed results from the fact that the relevant *state variable* (x_t or s_t) is a scalar. To consider more general forecasting and signal extraction problems we introduce representations in which the state variable is a vector, with the error covariance matrix $P_{t,t-1}$ replacing the scalar variance. These representations, and the appropriate generalizations of the l.l.s. recursions, are presented next.

3 State-Space Methods and Convergence Conditions

3.1 The state-space form and the Kalman filter

We consider linear dynamic systems in which a first-order vector autoregression describes the evolution of intermediate "state" or "process" variables x_t and a contemporaneous equation expresses the observations y_t as a linear combination of state variables, possibly with measurement error. The state transition and measurement equations are, respectively,

$$x_{t+1} = Fx_t + Gw_t \tag{3.1}$$

$$y_t = H'x_t + v_t. \tag{3.2}$$

The random input w_t and the observation noise v_t are serially uncorrelated random variables with zero mean and finite covariance matrix

$$\text{cov}\begin{pmatrix} w_t \\ v_t \end{pmatrix} = \begin{pmatrix} Q & S \\ S' & R \end{pmatrix};$$

this matrix, together with the coefficient matrices F, G and H are assumed known and time-invariant. In our use of this model to analyse univariate ARMA processes, y_t is a scalar.

The representation (3.1)–(3.2) (or "realization" in control theory parlance) of the relation between w_t, v_t and the output, y_t, is not unique since this relation is invariant to non-singular transformations of the states. Indeed, in many situations the order of the state vector is not uniquely determined either, and these features of the set-up can be exploited to improve the tractability of the analysis in particular situations. In some circumstances it is convenient to date the input, w, at $t + 1$ rather than t, but this makes no essential difference to the Kalman filtering equations. In this paper we are concerned with the *filtering* problem, that is, the recovery of x_t from observations on y. A dual problem is that of *controlling* x_t by varying the input, w_t, and a number of the concepts we employ take their names from this duality; the duality is discussed by numerous authors including, in an economic context, Preston and Pagan (1982). An earlier survey of Kalman filtering techniques and their application to forecasting is given by Mehra (1979).

We seek the l.l.s. estimator of x_t, say, given information up to and including y_{t+k}. To solve this problem we need the covariances of x_t and y_τ ($\tau = 0, 1, \ldots, t+k$). These are rendered well-defined by the model (3.1)–(3.2) and the assumed *initial conditions* that, in advance of any observations, x_0 is known to be randomly distributed with mean $\hat{x}_{0,-1}$ and variance $P_{0,-1}$. Thus the information available at time τ is $\Omega_\tau \equiv \{\hat{x}_{0,-1}, P_{0,-1}, y_0, \ldots, y_\tau\}$. We write the l.l.s. estimate of a random variable u_t given Ω_τ as $\hat{u}_{t,\tau}$, and the *innovation* in u_t is defined as the error in the one-step-ahead l.l.s. forecast: $\tilde{u}_t = u_t - \hat{u}_{t,t-1}$. (We note that the information sets Ω_τ and $\tilde{\Omega}_\tau \equiv \{\hat{x}_{0,-1}, P_{0,-1}, \tilde{y}_0, \ldots, \tilde{y}_\tau\}$ are identical, since each can be constructed from the other.) In the statistical time series literature, it has been commonplace not to indicate explicitly the dependence of Ω_τ on initial conditions, since the lack of dependence is implicit in stationarity assumptions. In the present context, where stationarity is not assumed, the nature of the initial conditions is important not only practically, but also theoretically, to define the underlying sigma fields (cf. Florens and Mouchart, 1982).

The l.l.s. estimates of the state vector and their covariances

$$P_{t+j,t} = \mathrm{E}\{(x_{t+j} - \hat{x}_{t+j,t})(x_{t+j} - \hat{x}_{t+j,t})'\}$$

for $j = 0, 1$ may be obtained recursively from the following Kalman filter equations:

$$\hat{x}_{t,t} = \hat{x}_{t,t-1} + C_{t,t}\tilde{y}_t \tag{3.3a}$$

$$\hat{x}_{t+1,t} = F\hat{x}_{t,t} + GS\Sigma_t^{-1}\tilde{y}_t \tag{3.3b}$$

$$C_{t,t} = P_{t,t-1}H\Sigma_t^{-1} \tag{3.3c}$$

$$\Sigma_t = \mathrm{E}\{\tilde{y}_t\tilde{y}_t'\} = H'P_{t,t-1}H + R. \tag{3.3d}$$

Equation (3.3a) expresses the fact that the innovation in x_t, which is not observed, is estimated by its orthogonal projection on that in y_t. Similarly, the second term on the right-hand side of equation (b) is the projection of Gw_t on $\tilde{y}_t$; equations (c) and (d) are definitional. The covariance update is the Riccati difference equation

$$P_{t+1,t} = FP_{t,t-1}F' + GQG' - K_t\Sigma_t K_t' \tag{3.3e}$$

$$K_t = FC_{t,t} + GS\Sigma_t^{-1}. \tag{3.3f}$$

The final term of equation (e) is the reduction in the conditional variance of x_{t+1} attributable to the information in $\tilde{y}_t$, and K_t is the Kalman gain, so called because it gives the amount by which the new information affects the one-step-ahead forecast of the state: combining (a) and (b) we have

$$\hat{x}_{t+1,t} = F\hat{x}_{t,t-1} + K_t\tilde{y}_t. \tag{3.3g}$$

Finally, some intermediate quantities are defined as follows:

$$P_{t,t} = P_{t,t-1}(I - HC'_{t,t}) \tag{3.3h}$$

$$\tilde{y}_t = y_t - H'\hat{x}_{t,t-1} \tag{3.3i}$$

$$\tilde{F}_t = F - K_t H'. \tag{3.3j}$$

Equation (j) defines the "closed loop system matrix" $\tilde{F}_t$, which is important in the filtering context because it determines the properties of the error process, $e_t = x_t - \hat{x}_{t,t-1}$. Subtracting (3.3g) from the state transition equation and substituting (3.3i) and the measurement equation gives a first-order vector difference equation for e, namely

$$e_{t+1} = \tilde{F}_t e_t - K_t v_t + G w_t. \tag{3.4}$$

Thus if the error variance is to remain bounded as t increases then it is necessary in general that there exist gain matrices, K_t, such that the closed loop system matrix is stable (has eigenvalues inside the unit circle). That this condition is also sufficient to guarantee that the error variance, $P_{t+1,t}$, converges to a steady state, P, given as a fixed point of (3.3e), is less obvious, however, and is discussed below in the context of our applications. Equation (3.4) indicates that, unlike the one-step-ahead forecast errors for the observed series, y_t, which form an innovation sequence, the errors in the one-step-ahead estimates of the unobserved state vector follow a first-order autoregression. The difference is essentially that observing y_t allows the previous estimate to be fully corrected before the forecast of y_{t+1} is made, but only partial correction to the state forecast is possible, resulting in the persistence of errors.

Forecasting the state vector more than one period ahead is very simple in the present framework. Since w_{t+j}, $j > 0$, is uncorrelated with all variables in Ω_t, we have $\hat{w}_{t+j,t} = 0$, so that

$$\hat{x}_{t+j,t} = F\hat{x}_{t+j-1,t}, \quad j = 2, 3, \ldots \tag{3.5a}$$

with error variance given by the auxiliary recursion

$$P_{t+j,t} = F P_{t+j-1,t} F' + GQG'. \tag{3.5b}$$

Forecasts of y are then obtained as

$$\hat{y}_{t+j,t} = H'\hat{x}_{t+j,t} \tag{3.5c}$$

with error variance $H'P_{t+j,t}H + R$, which reduces to the innovation variance Σ_{t+1} when $j = 1$. Notice that the sequence of j-step-ahead forecast errors $\ldots$, $(y_{t+j} - \hat{y}_{t+j,t})$, $(y_{t+j+1} - \hat{y}_{t+j+1,t+1})$, $\ldots$ is not an innovation sequence when $j > 1$, but exhibits autocorrelation of order $j - 1$.

Once the concurrent estimate of the state is available at time t, say, it may be improved as further observations arrive. This is achieved by the smoothing recursions[3]

$$\hat{x}_{t,t+k} = \hat{x}_{t,t+k-1} + C_{t,t+k}\tilde{y}_{t+k}, \quad k = 0, 1, \ldots \qquad (3.6a)$$

$$P_{t,t+k} = P_{t,t+k-1} - C_{t,t+k}\Sigma_{t+k}C'_{t,t+k} \qquad (3.6b)$$

$$C_{t,t+k} = \bar{P}'_{t,t+k-1}H\Sigma^{-1}_{t+k} \qquad (3.6c)$$

$$\bar{P}_{t,t+k} = \tilde{F}_{t+k}\bar{P}_{t,t+k-1} \qquad (3.6d)$$

initializing (3.6d) by $\bar{P}_{t,t-1} = P_{t,t-1}$ from (3.3), with the first three equations corresponding at $k = 0$ to (3.3a, c, h). Here $\bar{P}_{t,t+k}$ is the covariance of the error in the current one-step forecast of the state and that in the estimate of x_t:

$$\bar{P}_{t,t+k} = E\{(x_{t+k+1} - \hat{x}_{t+k+1,t+k})(x_t - \hat{x}_{t,t+k})'\}$$

so that $C_{t,t+k}\tilde{y}_{t+k}$ appearing in (3.6a) has a similar interpretation to $C_{t,t}\tilde{y}_t$ of equation (3.3a). Furthermore, $P_{t,t+k}$, the error variance of the smoothed estimate, is monotonically non-increasing in k (that is, $P_{t,t+k} - P_{t,t+k+1}$ is positive semi-definite) and bounded below by zero, so that $C_{t,t+k}$ tends to zero and revisions to the state estimate eventually die out. Finally, (3.6b) reflects the fact that the error in $\hat{x}_{t,t+k}$ is orthogonal to the $(t + k)$th innovation (were this not so, $\hat{x}_{t,t+k}$ would not be the l.l.s. estimate).

That the forecasting and signal extraction problems considered in Section 2 are examples of the application of the Kalman filter is clear once notational equivalences are established. First, with x_t scalar and $F = \phi$, $G = \phi - \theta$, $H = 1$, $w_t = \epsilon_t$ and $Q = S = R = \sigma^2_\epsilon$ the state-space form gives the ARMA(1,1) model (2.2) and (2.3); the l.l.s. recursions (2.10) then correspond to (the relevant parts of) the Kalman filter equations (3.3). Secondly, with scalar state variable $x_t = s_t$ and $F = \phi$, $G = 1$, $H = 1$, $w_t = \epsilon_{t+1}$, $v_t = \eta_t$, $Q = \sigma^2_\epsilon$, $R = \sigma^2_\eta$ and $S = 0$, the state-space form gives the AR(1)-plus-noise model (2.17), and the l.l.s. recursions (2.18) may again be obtained as a special case of (3.3).

In our discussion of these examples and in consideration of the Kalman filter more generally an important aspect of the recursions is their time-varying nature, and an important question concerns their possible convergence to a steady state. In applied work it is clearly more convenient computationally if the recursions have fixed coefficients, and in studying the relations with the statistical time series literature this is a central question, since in that literature most attention is given to time-invariant forecasting or filtering formulae. In the examples and more generally, a key role is played by the forecast error covariance matrix $P_{t+1,t}$ (written $p_{t+1,t}$ in the scalar examples): if this converges, possibly rapidly, to a fixed point P of the recursion (3.3e), or takes such a value from the beginning, then the complete recursions (3.3) are in steady state (are time-invariant), as are the extended forecast recursions (3.5) and the smoothing recursions (3.6). Conditions under which this occurs are described in the next section.

3.2 Conditions for convergence of the covariance sequence

In this section we state without proof a number of theorems concerning the behaviour of the covariance of the one-step-ahead state-estimation error, $P_{t+1,t}$, associated with the system (3.1)–(3.2). In subsequent sections these results are specialized and extended to cover forecasting and signal extraction in ARMA processes. Proofs of the theorems, and an indication of their antecedents in the control literature, may be found in the papers by Caines and Mayne (1970, 1971), Hager and Horowitz (1976), Chan, Goodwin and Sin (1984), and De Souza, Gevers and Goodwin (1986) to which we refer below. The behaviour of the filter covariance is determined by two properties of the system, first identified by Kalman (1960), which relate to the extent to which changes in the state vector, x_t, affect the measurements or output, y_t, and the extent to which variations in the input, w_t, affect the state vector. We begin by defining these system properties.

Definition 1 The pair (F, H) is said to be *detectable* if F has no eigenvalue λ with corresponding non-zero eigenvector b such that $|\lambda| \geq 1$ and $H'b = 0$. If $H'b \neq 0$ for all λ the pair is said to be *observable*.

Definition 2 The pair $(F, GQ^{1/2})$ is said to be *stabilizable* if F has no eigenvalue λ with corresponding non-zero left eigenvector a' such that $|\lambda| \geq 1$ and $a'GQ^{1/2} = 0$. If $a'GQ^{1/2} \neq 0$ for all λ the pair is said to be *controllable*.

Observability and controllability are frequently expressed as the condition that the range space of F^n is contained in those of the matrices

$$\mathcal{O}(F, H) \equiv (H \vdots FH \vdots \cdots \vdots F^{n-1}H)$$

$$\mathcal{C}(F, GQ^{1/2}) \equiv (GQ^{1/2} \vdots FGQ^{1/2} \vdots \cdots \vdots F^{n-1}GQ^{1/2}).$$

These conditions are implied by Definitions 1 and 2 (Kailath, 1980, p. 135). In the context of ARMA models the eigenvalues and eigenvectors of F are easily obtained, and so it is convenient to work with the definitions in the form given. As noted above, these concepts take their names from the dual control problem (see Preston and Pagan, 1982, chs. 5, 6). Controllability is the ability to move the state in finite time from an arbitrary initial point to an arbitrary terminal point by manipulation of the input (control instruments); stabilizability, or asymptotic controllability, is the asymptotic version of this capability. Whereas controllability is an existence property, observability is a uniqueness property. Interpreted as a property of the dynamic structure of the model, it specifies that all the natural modes of the state dynamics are contained in, or observed by, the output dynamics. When observability fails, detectability rules out instability of the unobserved modes. In the filtering problem, detectability holds when movements in the state vector along directions which do not affect the measurement have bounded variance whenever the input, w, has bounded variance. An important implication of detectability is that there exist column vectors $\bar{K}$ such that the matrix $\{F - \bar{K}H'\}$ has eigenvalues inside the unit circle.

If the covariance possesses a steady state, P, then there exists a corresponding steady-state closed-loop system matrix, $\tilde{F}$, which from (3.3) is a function of P, F, G, H, S and R. Chan, Goodwin and Sin (1984) define a *strong* steady-state solution, P, of (3.3e) as one for which the eigenvalues of $\tilde{F}$ lie *inside or on* the unit circle, and a *stabilizing* solution as one for which these eigenvalues lie *strictly inside* the unit circle. Usually no other steady state exists, as is clear from the form of the error process (3.4), but exceptions are possible, as discussed in Section 4.4 later.

Before giving the theorem statements, we note that a system in which the input and measurement noises are correlated may be converted to one in which they are not, with considerable notational savings in the ensuing analysis of the covariance recursions. On replacing w_t by the residual in its projection on v_t, and incorporating the matrix G into the definition, so that $w_t^* = G(w_t - SR^{-1}v_t)$, the state transition equation (3.1) may be rearranged as

$$x_{t+1} = (F - GSR^{-1}H')x_t + w_t^* + GSR^{-1}y_t$$
$$= F^*x_t + w_t^* + GSR^{-1}y_t,$$

also using the measurement equation. Since at time t, $GSR^{-1}y_t$ is known, the covariance $P_{t+1,t}$ is unaffected by the presence of this term, and its properties may be obtained by reference to those of the system

$$x_{t+1} = F^*x_t + w_t^*$$
$$y_t = H'x_t + v_t \tag{3.7}$$

in which w_t^* and v_t are uncorrelated. For convenience we factorize the positive semi-definite covariance of w_t^* in the form $G(Q - SR^{-1}S')G' \equiv DD'$. The following results now relate to the model (3.7). The first characterizes the steady states of P (and $\tilde{F}$) in the detectable case.

Theorem 3.1 (Chan, Goodwin and Sin, 1984; De Souza, Gevers and Goodwin, 1986)

If the pair (F^*, H) is detectable then

(1) there exists a unique strong solution
(2) if the pair (F^*, D) has no uncontrollable eigenvalue outside the unit circle, then the strong solution is the only non-negative definite solution
(3) if the pair (F^*, D) has no uncontrollable eigenvalue on the unit circle, then the strong solution is also stabilizing

(4) if the pair (F^*, D) has an uncontrollable eigenvalue on the unit circle, then there is no stabilizing solution
(5) if the pair (F^*, D) has an uncontrollable eigenvalue inside or on the unit circle, then the strong solution is not positive definite
(6) if the pair (F^*, D) has an uncontrollable eigenvalue outside the unit circle, then there is at least one other solution besides the strong solution.

The proof of this theorem requires application of the theory of simplectic matrix pencils to give fixed points of the Riccati equation (3.3e), and is thus algebraic rather than statistical in nature. The implications of the theorem are implicit in the discussion of the steady-state forecasting rule for the ARMA(1, 1) process following equation (2.11), and emerge more fully in the treatment of the ARMA(p, q) process in Section 4.

Sufficient conditions for convergence of the covariance $P_{t+1,t}$ to the strong solution are given in the following theorems. The first, due to Hager and Horowitz (1976), generalizes a result for controllable systems, obtained by Caines and Mayne (1970), to the stabilizable case.[4]

Theorem 3.2 (after Hager and Horowitz, 1976, who give the dual control result)
If (F^*, D) is stabilizable and (F^*, H) is detectable, then the sequence of covariance matrices $P_{0,-1}, \ldots, P_{t+1,t}, \ldots$ converges (exponentially fast) to the unique stabilizing solution, P, from all initial conditions $P_{0,-1} \geq 0$.

Theorem 3.3 (De Souza, Gevers and Goodwin, 1986)
If $P_{0,-1} - P \geq 0$, then the sequence of covariance matrices $P_{0,-1}, \ldots, P_{t+1,t}, \ldots$ converges to the strong solution, P, if and only if (F^*, H) is detectable.

Theorem 3.4 (Caines and Mayne, 1970, 1971)
If $R > 0, DD' \geq 0, (F^*, D)$ is controllable and (F^*, H) is detectable, then the sequence $P_{0,-1}, \ldots, P_{t+1,t}, \ldots$ converges to the unique positive semi-definite stabilizing solution, P, from all $P_{0,-1} \geq 0$.

These convergence results allow us to focus attention on the steady-state recursions in the following two sections.

4 Forecasting the ARMA(p, q) Process

4.1 Setting up the problem
We consider a scalar variable y which is generated by the ARMA(p, q) process

$$\phi(L)y_t = \theta(L)\epsilon_t, \tag{4.1}$$

where $\phi(L)$ and $\theta(L)$ are polynomials in the lag operator L of degrees p and q respectively, and ϵ_t is white noise. A state-space representation in which the first element of the state vector is the forecastable part of y_t, that is $x(1)_t = y_t - \epsilon_t$, is obtained from the following equivalences. Define $r = \max(p, q)$, and

$\phi_{p+1} = \cdots = \phi_r = 0$ if $p < q$, or $\theta_{q+1} = \cdots = \theta_r = 0$ if $p > q$. Let

$$
F = \begin{pmatrix}
\phi_1 & 1 & 0 & \cdots & 0 & 0 \\
\phi_2 & 0 & 1 & & 0 & 0 \\
\vdots & \vdots & & \ddots & \vdots & \vdots \\
\phi_{r-2} & 0 & 0 & \cdots & 1 & 0 \\
\phi_{r-1} & 0 & 0 & \cdots & 0 & 1 \\
\phi_r & 0 & 0 & \cdots & 0 & 0
\end{pmatrix}, \qquad
F_\theta = \begin{pmatrix}
\theta_1 & 1 & 0 & \cdots & 0 & 0 \\
\theta_2 & 0 & 1 & & 0 & 0 \\
\vdots & \vdots & & \ddots & \vdots & \vdots \\
\theta_{r-2} & 0 & 0 & \cdots & 1 & 0 \\
\theta_{r-1} & 0 & 0 & \cdots & 0 & 1 \\
\theta_r & 0 & 0 & \cdots & 0 & 0
\end{pmatrix}
$$

$$
G = (\phi_1 - \theta_1, \phi_2 - \theta_2, \ldots, \phi_r - \theta_r)'
$$
$$
H = (1, 0, \ldots, 0)'.
$$

Then defining the state transition and measurement equations as

$$
x_t = F x_{t-1} + G \epsilon_{t-1} \tag{4.2}
$$

$$
y_t = H' x_t + \epsilon_t, \tag{4.3}
$$

the latter gives $x(1)_t = y_t - \epsilon_t$ as above. Using this repeatedly, and substituting in turn from the rth, $(r-1)$th, ... rows of (4.2) to the first gives

$$
x(1)_t = \sum_{j=1}^{r} \phi_j y_{t-j} - \sum_{k=1}^{r} \theta_k \epsilon_{t-k}
$$

as required. A simple relation between the transition matrices and the ARMA coefficient polynomials is $|I - Fz| = \phi(z)$, $|I - F_\theta z| = \theta(z)$. The system (4.2)–(4.3) corresponds to (3.1)–(3.2), with $w_t = v_t = \epsilon_t$ and $Q = S = R = \sigma_\epsilon^2$ (all scalars). In the alternative form (3.7) the matrix $F^* = F - GSR^{-1}H'$ is equal to F_θ, defined above, in this case, and $\mathrm{cov}(w_t^*) = G(Q - SR^{-1}S')G' = 0$.

To express the forecast as a function of the observations and to consider the steady-state filter we examine the form taken by equations (3.3) in the present case. First, the covariance recursion can be greatly simplified. From (3.3c, e, f) applied to the alternative form (3.7), as specialized in the preceding paragraph, we obtain

$$
P_{t+1,t} = F_\theta \{ P_{t,t-1} - P_{t,t-1} H \Sigma_t^{-1} H' P_{t,t-1} \} F_\theta'. \tag{4.4}
$$

Furthermore, the closed-loop system matrix is now

$$
\tilde{F}_t = F_\theta \{ I - P_{t,t-1} H \Sigma_t^{-1} H' \}. \tag{4.5}
$$

We note that these expressions do not involve the autoregressive parameters so that, for example, in computing the one-step-ahead forecast error variance we need only consider the initial conditions and the moving average operator; specifically, the stationarity or otherwise of the process is irrelevant. The limiting behaviour of (4.4) depends on the location of the eigenvalues of F_θ, which are the roots of $\theta(z)$. We consider the various possibilities case by case, using the convergence and existence theorems given in Section 3.2. To apply these to the ARMA(p, q) form (4.2)–(4.3) we note first that (F^*, H) is observable since for any vector b, $F^*b = \lambda b$ and $H'b = 0$ together imply $b = 0$. Secondly, (F^*, D) is not controllable since $D = 0$; it is stabilizable if and only if all roots of $\theta(z)$, the eigenvalues of F^*, lie inside the unit circle.

4.2 The invertible moving average case

If the roots of $\theta(z)$ lie inside the unit circle, it follows from Theorems 3.1 and 3.2 that the sequence of covariance matrices $P_{0,-1}, \ldots, P_{t,t-1}, P_{t+1,t}, \ldots$ converges to the unique non-negative definite fixed point P of (4.4) from all bounded non-negative definite $P_{0,-1}$. Since, as is clear by inspection, $P = 0$ is such a fixed point, and the associated steady-state gain (K), innovation variance (Σ) and closed loop system matrix $(\tilde{F})$ are G, R and F_θ respectively, the steady-state filter takes the simple form

$$\hat{x}_{t+1,t} = F_\theta \hat{x}_{t,t-1} + G y_t.$$

Repeated substitution in this equation gives

$$\hat{x}_{t+1,t} = \sum_{i=0}^{t} F_\theta^i G y_{t-i} + F_\theta^t \hat{x}_{0,-1} \tag{4.6}$$

and from (3.5) the j-step-ahead forecast of y is given as

$$\hat{y}_{t+j,t} = H' F^{j-1} \hat{x}_{t+1,t}, \quad j = 1, 2, \ldots . \tag{4.7}$$

The forecast error variance is

$$V_j = H' P_{t+j,t} H + R$$

where, using (3.5b) and noting that $Q = R$,

$$P_{t+j,t} = \sum_{i=0}^{j-2} F^i G R G' (F')^i.$$

If the eigenvalues of F (that is, the roots of $\phi(z)$) lie inside the unit circle, we see from (4.7) that as the forecast horizon, j, increases so the observed history ceases to be informative, and the forecast $\hat{y}_{t+j,t}$ tends to the unconditional mean, zero. Similarly, V_j tends to the variance of y. Conversely, if $\phi(L)$ is not invertible, neither the forecast nor its error variance in general approach limits as j increases. We note further that since $P = 0$, we must have $e_t = 0$, and $\hat{x}_{t+1,t} = x_{t+1}$, hence $\tilde{y}_{t+1}$, the innovation, is equal to ϵ_{t+1}; comparing (3.4) we have $K v_t = G w_t$ since $K = G$ and $v_t = w_t = \epsilon_t$.

To relate the l.l.s. recursions to the classical results, which assume a semi-infinite sample, we consider the limit of the recursions (4.6)–(4.7) and obtain a generating function for the weight on y_{t-i} in the forecast of y_{t+j} as

$$f_j(z) = H' F^{j-1} (I - z F_\theta)^{-1} G, \quad j = 1, 2, \ldots . \tag{4.8}$$

The equivalence of (4.8) to the classical formulae, which rest additionally on a stationarity assumption, may be demonstrated as follows. First, an expression appearing in (4.8) can be written in terms of the ARMA polynomial operators as

$$H'(I - zF_\theta)^{-1}G = z^{-1}\theta^{-1}(z)\{\theta(z) - \phi(z)\},$$

hence we also have

$$\{1 - zH'(I - zF_\theta)^{-1}G\} = \phi(z)\theta^{-1}(z).$$

Next, since $F_\theta = F - GH'$ we may write

$$I - zF = \{I - zGH'(I - zF_\theta)^{-1}\}(I - zF_\theta),$$

and, if $\phi(L)$ is invertible, so that $(I - zF)^{-1}$ exists for $|z| = 1$, this gives

$$(I - zF_\theta)^{-1}G = (I - zF)^{-1}\{I - zGH'(I - zF_\theta)^{-1}\}G$$
$$= (I - zF)^{-1}G\{I - zH'(I - zF_\theta)^{-1}G\}.$$

On substituting these expressions into (4.8) we obtain

$$f_j(z) = H'F^{j-1}(I - zF)^{-1}G\phi(z)\theta^{-1}(z).$$

Since $(I - zF)^{-1}$ may be expanded as a power series, we may write the right-hand side as

$$H'[z^{-(j-1)}(I - zF)^{-1}G]_+\phi(z)\theta^{-1}(z)$$

which, using results above, may be written

$$[z^{-j}\phi^{-1}(z)\{\theta(z) - \phi(z)\}]_+\phi(z)\theta^{-1}(z)$$

to give, finally, the formula to be found in Whittle (1963, Ch. 3), namely

$$f_j(z) = \left[z^{-j}\frac{\theta(z)}{\phi(z)}\right]_+ \phi(z)\theta^{-1}(z). \tag{4.9}$$

It is clear from its definition at (4.8) that $f_j(z)$ has a convergent power series expansion even when $(I - zF)^{-1}$ does not exist, and for this reason (4.8) is to be preferred to (4.9), in general, as a basis for calculating the coefficients.

4.3 Moving average with roots on the unit circle
If $\theta(z)$ has roots inside and on the unit circle, then by Theorems 3.1 and 3.3, the covariance sequence again converges to $P = 0$, the unique non-negative definite fixed point of (4.4). In this case, however, the closed loop system matrix $\tilde{F} = F_\theta$ has at least one unit eigenvalue if $\theta(z)$ has any unit roots. Then (4.8) no longer holds in the usual sense, that is $\sum_{i=0}^{\infty} z^i F_\theta^i \neq (I - zF_\theta)^{-1}$ for $|z| = 1$, but if

it is regarded primarily as shorthand for the power series in F_θ, we may think of taking $|z| < 1$ and deriving (4.9) as before. Such heuristic devices could be avoided by writing the generating function of the coefficients on past observations in the forecast of y_{t+j} in the explicit form

$$f_j(z) = H' F^{j-1} \left(\sum_{i=0}^{t} z^i F_\theta^i \right) G. \tag{4.10}$$

In this case, however, the second term on the right-hand side of (4.6) cannot be neglected.

4.4 Moving average with roots outside the unit circle

If $\theta(z)$ has any roots outside the unit circle, it follows from Theorem 3.1 that there are at least two steady states, but that only one of these is the strong solution. With $P_{0,\ 1}$ positive definite, the case of practical relevance, it follows from Theorem 3.3 that the sequence of covariance matrices tends to this strong solution. We show that the eigenvalues of $\tilde{F}$ are then the roots of $\theta(z)$ inside or on the unit circle together with the complex conjugate inverses of those roots outside $|z| = 1$.

Obviously, $P = 0$ is again a solution of (4.4) with a filter z-transform again given by (4.10), but it is not the strong solution. To find the strong solution we first note that $\tilde{F} = F_\theta \{ I - PH\Sigma^{-1}H' \}$ is of the same form as F_θ. To see this, note that the matrix $PH\Sigma^{-1}H'$ has a single non-zero column followed by $r - 1$ columns of zeros, so that $\tilde{F}$ differs from F_θ only in the first column. Thus if we let $\theta^*(L)$ denote the lag operator which corresponds to $\tilde{F}$ in the same way that $\theta(L)$ corresponds to F_θ, the steady-state filter in question has z-transform

$$f_j(z) = H' \left(F^{j-1} \sum_{i=0}^{t} z^i F_{\theta*}^i \right) G. \tag{4.11}$$

This filter has one-step-ahead variance Σ (the innovation variance) which is given by the solution to the invertible factorization of the covariance generating function of $\phi(L)y_t$, namely

$$\Sigma \theta^*(z)\theta^*(z^{-1}) = R\theta(z)\theta(z^{-1}). \tag{4.12}$$

To establish this result, first observe that since Σ is independent of the autoregressive operator, we can take this to be invertible without loss of generality. Since $Q = R = S$, the covariance generating function of y_t is then

$$g_{yy}(z) = \{ 1 + z H'(I - zF)^{-1}G \} R \{ G'(I - z^{-1}F')^{-1}Hz^{-1} + 1 \}, \tag{4.13}$$

and, as shown in the Appendix, this may be written

$$g_{yy}(z) = \{ 1 + z H'(I - zF)^{-1}K \} \Sigma \{ K'(I - z^{-1}F')^{-1}Hz^{-1} + 1 \}. \tag{4.14}$$

Now $g_{yy}(z)$ is a scalar, and is thus equal to its determinant, and using the result that if T_1 is $n \times m$ and T_2 is $m \times n$, then $|I_n + T_1 T_2| = |I_m + T_2 T_1|$, we have, for example

$$|1 + zH'(I - zF)^{-1}G| = |I + z(I - zF)^{-1}GH'|$$

$$= |(I - zF)^{-1}||I - zF + zGH'|$$

$$= |(I - zF)^{-1}||I - zF_\theta|.$$

Similarly, $|1 + zH'(I - zF)^{-1}K| = |(I - zF)^{-1}||I - z\tilde{F}|$; hence equating (4.13) and (4.14) and cancelling common factors gives

$$|I - zF_\theta|R|I - z^{-1}F_\theta'| = |I - z\tilde{F}|\Sigma|I - z^{-1}\tilde{F}'|.$$

But $|I - zF_\theta| = \theta(z)$, and $|I - z\tilde{F}| = \theta^*(z)$, so this gives (4.12), as asserted.

This treatment provides a generalization of the discussion of the ARMA(1,1) example in Section 2.1, and the same general considerations apply. As in the example of equation (2.13), and now seen to be true more generally, for a non-invertible moving average process the l.l.s. recursions deliver a steady-state forecasting rule of an "invertible" form, automatically parameterized in terms of the coefficients of the observationally equivalent invertible moving average process. This coincides with the Wiener-Kolmogorov predictor in the case in which the latter is defined, but is also valid if the process is non-stationary.

5 Signal Extraction in Unobserved-Component ARMA Models

5.1 Setting up the problem

We now assume that the observations, y_t, are the sum of two or more unobserved components, each of which is an ARMA process of known form. Such specifications are frequently employed in studies of seasonal adjustment, where we find decompositions of time series into either two components (one seasonal, the other not) or three components (seasonal, cyclical, irregular), one of which is white noise. In either case the problem of interest is to estimate the seasonal component, in order to subtract it from the observed series to give a "seasonally adjusted" series. A three-component specification can always be reduced to two components by absorbing the white noise into one of the other components. Since the converse is not true unless at least one of the (non-white) processes has MA order greater than or equal to its AR order, the two-component specification is more general. From the point of view of state-space representations, however, it is more natural to think of the two-component specification as a special case of three components that arises when the noise in the measurement equation, v_t, has zero variance ($R = 0$). Since results for two-component processes can be recovered from those for three components by taking $R = 0$, we prefer to work with the three-component specification.

We consider the following three-component model

$$y_t = S_t + C_t + I_t, \quad t = 0, 1, 2, \ldots, \tag{5.1}$$

where S_t and C_t are ARMA processes, and I_t is white noise. That is, $\phi^S(L)S_t = \theta^S(L)w_{1t}$, $\phi^C(L)C_t = \theta^C(L)w_{2t}$, and $I_t = v_t$, where the four lag polynomials are of degree m, n, p and q respectively, and the uncorrelated white noise variables w_{1t}, w_{2t} and v_t have variances $\sigma_{w_1}^2, \sigma_{w_2}^2$ and σ_v^2. We further assume that there is no common factor in the pair $\{\phi^S(L), \theta^S(L)\}$, nor in the pair $\{\phi^C(L), \theta^C(L)\}$. We seek the l.l.s. estimate of S_t given observations on y and appropriate initial conditions. A formal solution to this problem is the projection

$$\hat{S}_{t,t+k} = \hat{S}_{t,-1} + \text{cov}(S_t, y|\Omega_{-1})[\text{var}(y|\Omega_{-1})]^{-1}(y - E(y|\Omega_{-1})) \tag{5.2}$$

where y denotes the vector $(y_0, y_1, \ldots, y_{t+k})$. The essence of the classical approach is then to set $\hat{S}_{t,-1}$ equal to zero (the unconditional mean), and to replace dependence on Ω_{-1} by the assumption of joint stationarity of S_t and y_t, in order to define $\text{cov}(S_t, y)$ and $\text{var}(y)$ given the ARMA component specifications set out above. The $(t + k + 1) \times (t + k + 1)$ matrix, $\text{var}(y)$, may then be inverted by transforming y_t into an innovation sequence, that is, by finding the invertible ARMA representation for y_t. Finally, the coefficients on past observations in (5.2) can be compactly represented when $t \to \infty$ using the generating functions given by Whittle (1963, Ch. 6).

In contrast, the Kalman filter implements (5.2) recursively. To connect the two approaches, in the stationary case, we show that solving the Riccati equation in steady state yields the unique invertible ARMA representation for y_t. This generalizes the demonstration of the equivalence of the two approaches given, for a simple example, in Section 2.2. That the implied coefficients in (5.2) then coincide with their classical counterparts, as they must, is shown algebraically in the Appendix. No stationarity assumption need be invoked in order to solve (5.2) recursively, however, and we conclude by describing circumstances in which the classical approach may be extended to cover difference-stationary or explosively non-stationary cases.

A suitable state-space form for the present problem which, although not of the smallest possible order, has the merit of retaining the original variables of (5.1) in the state vector, is given in (5.3). An empirical application of this representation is given by Burridge and Wallis (1985).

$$x_t = (x'_{1t}, x'_{2t})'$$

$$x_{1t} = (S_t, S_{t-1}, \ldots, S_{t-m+1}, w_{1,t}, w_{1,t-1}, \ldots, w_{1,t-n+1})'$$

$$x_{2t} = (C_t, C_{t-1}, \ldots, C_{t-p+1}, w_{2,t}, w_{2,t-1}, \ldots, w_{2,t-q+1})'$$

$$F = \text{block diagonal } (F_1, F_2)$$

$$
F_1 = \begin{pmatrix}
\phi_{s,1} & \phi_{s,2} & \cdots & \phi_{s,m-1} & \phi_{s,m} & -\theta_{s,1} & -\theta_{s,2} & \cdots & -\theta_{s,n-1} & -\theta_{s,n} \\
1 & 0 & \cdots & 0 & 0 & 0 & 0 & \cdots & 0 & 0 \\
0 & 1 & \cdots & 0 & 0 & 0 & 0 & \cdots & 0 & 0 \\
\vdots & & \ddots & & \vdots & \vdots & \vdots & \ddots & \vdots & \vdots \\
0 & 0 & \cdots & 1 & 0 & 0 & 0 & \cdots & 0 & 0 \\
0 & 0 & \cdots & 0 & 0 & 0 & 0 & \cdots & 0 & 0 \\
0 & 0 & \cdots & 0 & 0 & 1 & 0 & \cdots & 0 & 0 \\
0 & 0 & \cdots & 0 & 0 & 0 & 1 & \cdots & 0 & 0 \\
\vdots & \vdots & \ddots & \vdots & \vdots & \vdots & & \ddots & & \vdots \\
0 & 0 & \cdots & 0 & 0 & 0 & 0 & \cdots & 1 & 0
\end{pmatrix}
$$

F_2 similarly matches coefficients in the model for C_t to elements of x_{2t}

$$
G' = \begin{pmatrix}
1 & 0 & \cdots & 0 & 1 & 0 & \cdots & 0 & 0 & 0 & \cdots & 0 & 0 & 0 & \cdots & 0 \\
0 & 0 & \cdots & 0 & 0 & 0 & \cdots & 0 & 1 & 0 & \cdots & 0 & 1 & 0 & \cdots & 0
\end{pmatrix}
$$

$$
H' = (1 \quad 0 \quad \cdots \quad 0 \quad 0 \quad 0 \quad \cdots \quad 0 \quad 1 \quad 0 \quad \cdots \quad 0 \quad 0 \quad 0 \quad \cdots \quad 0)
$$

$$
w_t = (w_{1t}, w_{2t})'
$$

$$
Q = \text{diag}(\sigma_{w_1}^2, \sigma_{w_2}^2)
$$

$$
R = \sigma_v^2 \text{ (scalar)}
$$

$$
S = 0. \tag{5.3}
$$

Our first concern is to establish conditions under which the covariance generated by (3.3e) goes to a steady state. Before applying relevant theorems from Section 3.2 we need to check the detectability and controllability of the system (5.3). Since $S = 0$, the matrices defined in (3.7) are $F^* = F$ and $DD' = GQG'$. The eigenvalues of F are the union of those of F_1 and F_2, which are obtained from the characteristic equations $|F_1 - \lambda I| = (-\lambda)^{n+m} \phi^S(\lambda^{-1})$ and $|F_2 - \lambda I| = (-\lambda)^{p+q} \phi^C(\lambda^{-1})$. Thus, writing

$$
\phi^S(L) - \prod_{i=1}^{m}(1 - \lambda_{si} L), \qquad \psi^C(L) = \prod_{j=1}^{p}(1 - \lambda_{cj} L)
$$

the eigenvalues of F are $\{\lambda_{si}\}$ and $\{\lambda_{cj}\}$ together with $n + q$ zeros.

Detectability In the system (5.3), the pair (F^*, H) is detectable if and only if the polynomials $\phi^S(L)$ and $\phi^C(L)$ contain no unstable common factor.

Proof Suppose b is a right eigenvector of F. Now $H'b = b_1 + b_{m+n+1}$, and if λ is an eigenvalue of either F_1 or F_2, but not of both, then either b_{m+n+1} or b_1 must be zero. However, it is easy to check that since the top left blocks of F_1 and F_2 are companion matrices, their corresponding nontrivial eigenvectors cannot have zero first elements. Thus if F_1 and F_2 have no eigenvalues in common, then $H'b \neq 0$ for all λ and the pair (F, H) is observable. Conversely, if λ is an eigenvalue of *both* F_1 and F_2, the vector $b = \{1, \lambda^{-1}, \ldots, \lambda^{-(m-1)}, 0, \ldots, 0, -1, -\lambda^{-1}, \ldots, -\lambda^{-(p-1)}, 0, \ldots, 0\}'$ is a right eigenvector of F, and satisfies $H'b = 0$. Finally, F_1 and F_2 have a common eigenvalue λ if and only if $(1 - \lambda L)$ is a factor of both $\phi^S(L)$ and $\phi^C(L)$.

Controllability In the system (5.3), the pair (F^*, D) is controllable if and only if neither $\{\phi^S(L), \theta^S(L)\}$ nor $\{\phi^C(L), \theta^C(L)\}$ contains a redundant common factor.

Proof Noting that $D = GQ^{1/2}$ has the form

$$D = \begin{pmatrix} \sigma_{w_1} & 0 & \cdots & 0 & \sigma_{w_1} & 0 & \cdots & 0 & 0 & 0 & \cdots & 0 & 0 & 0 & \cdots & 0 \\ 0 & 0 & \cdots & 0 & 0 & 0 & \cdots & 0 & \sigma_{w_2} & 0 & \cdots & 0 & \sigma_{w_2} & 0 & \cdots & 0 \end{pmatrix}'$$

we see that $a'D = 0$ implies that $a_1 + a_{m+1} = 0$ and $a_{m+n+1} + a_{m+n+p+1} = 0$. On writing out the equations $a'F = \lambda a'$, it is readily seen that these equalities hold if and only if either $\phi^S(\lambda^{-1}) = \theta^S(\lambda^{-1}) - 0$ or $\phi^C(\lambda^{-1}) = \theta^C(\lambda^{-1}) - 0$.

From Theorem 3.4 it thus follows that the covariance, $P_{t+1,t}$, converges to the unique positive semi-definite stabilizing solution to (3.3) from all $P_{0,-1} \geq 0$ if and only if $\phi^S(L)$ and $\phi^C(L)$ have no common factor $(1 - \lambda L)$ with $|\lambda| \geq 1$. Furthermore, this convergence is exponentially fast, by Theorem 3.2, and so the result is of practical use in the non-stationary case, as in the examples of Burridge and Wallis (1985). The ensuing discussion of the steady-state filters falls naturally into three parts, dealing with first the case in which $\phi^S(L)$ and $\phi^C(L)$ are both invertible, then the general detectable case, and finally the non-detectable case in which a common factor of $(1 - L)$ is present.

5.2 The stationary case
If S_t and C_t are stationary processes, the classical solution to (5.2) may be written

$$\hat{S}_{t,t+k} = f_k^S(L)y_t,$$

where the coefficient of y_{t-j}, $j \geq -k$, is the coefficient of z^j in the first element of the power series expansion of

$$f_k(z) = \left[g_{xy}(z)\{g_{yy}^-(z)\}^{-1} \right]_{-k} \{g_{yy}^+(z)\}^{-1}. \tag{5.4}$$

This expression utilizes the unique invertible ("canonical") factorization of the covariance generating function of y, written as a symmetric product of polynomials in z and z^{-1}, namely

$$g_{yy}(z) = g_{yy}^+(z)g_{yy}^-(z);$$

$g_{yy}(z)$ is obtained directly from (3.1)–(3.2) with $S = 0$ as

$$g_{yy}(z) = R + H'(I - zF)^{-1}GQG'(I - z^{-1}F')^{-1}H. \tag{5.5}$$

To approach this from the Kalman filter, we substitute repeatedly in the steady-state version of (3.3g), then the definition (3.3i) yields y_t in terms of the innovations and the initial conditions as

$$y_t = \tilde{y}_t + \sum_{i=0}^{t-1} H' F^i K \tilde{y}_{t-1-i} + H' F^t \hat{x}_{0,-1}. \tag{5.6}$$

Since $\tilde{y}_t$ is a white noise process with constant variance Σ, and F has eigenvalues inside the unit circle, the limit of (5.6) gives the covariance generating function of y_t as

$$g_{yy}(z) = \{1 + z H'(I - zF)^{-1} K\} \Sigma \{1 + z^{-1} K'(I - z^{-1} F')^{-1} H\}. \tag{5.7}$$

We show algebraically that (5.5) and (5.7) are identical in the Appendix, and (5.7) supplies the required factorization.

To show that (5.7) corresponds to the unique invertible factorization, it is sufficient to show that $\{1 + z H'(I - zF)^{-1} K\}^{-1}$ has a power series expansion on $|z| = 1$. Rather than employ a purely algebraic argument, we proceed indirectly by writing the innovation, $\tilde{y}_t$, as a function of the observations. Repeated substitution of (3.3i) into (3.3g) yields

$$\hat{x}_{t+1,t} = \sum_{i=0}^{t} \tilde{F}^i K y_{t-i} + \tilde{F}^t \hat{x}_{0,-1}, \tag{5.8}$$

and, as $\tilde{F}$ has eigenvalues strictly inside the unit circle, by Theorem 3.4, we obtain the generating function for the coefficients of y_{t-i}, in the limit, as

$$f_{-1}(z) = (I - z\tilde{F})^{-1} K. \tag{5.9}$$

It follows that $\tilde{y}_t$ may be expressed as a linear combination of the observations with generating function

$$\tilde{w}(z) = 1 - z H'(I - z\tilde{F})^{-1} K, \tag{5.10}$$

but this is, by construction, the inverse of the first factor in (5.7), and hence yields the required power series expansion. That is, we may write

$$g_{yy}(z) = \tilde{w}^{-1}(z) \Sigma \tilde{w}^{-1}(z^{-1}),$$

which can also be checked algebraically.

The remaining quantity in (5.4), the covariance of x_t and y_t, is again obtained directly from (3.1)–(3.2) as

$$g_{xy}(z) = (I - zF)^{-1} GQG'(I - z^{-1} F')^{-1} H. \tag{5.11}$$

Since $g_{yy}^-(z)$ is a scalar, attention can be restricted to the first element of $g_{xy}(z)$, which is obtained, after a little algebra, as

$$g_{sy}(z) = \sigma_{w_1}^2 \{\phi^S(z)\phi^S(z^{-1})\}^{-1} \theta^S(z)\theta^S(z^{-1}). \qquad (5.12)$$

Using this expression in (5.4), and writing (5.7) as $\sigma^2 \beta(z)\beta(z^{-1})$, we obtain (5.4) in the form of Whittle's (6.1.13), and equation (4.5) of Pierce (1979), whose treatment admits difference-stationary components. Substituting from (5.10) and (5.11) gives the classical solution (5.4) in terms of the system matrices as

$$f_k(z) = [(I - zF)^{-1}GQG'(I - z^{-1}F')^{-1}H\tilde{w}'(z^{-1})]_{-k}\Sigma^{-1}\tilde{w}(z). \qquad (5.13)$$

The limit of the l.l.s. recursion obtained via repeated use of (3.6a) and (5.8)–(5.10) is

$$f_k(z) = zf_{-1}(z) + \sum_{i=0}^{k} z^{-i}C_i\tilde{w}(z), \qquad (5.14)$$

in which $C_i = P(\tilde{F}')^i H\Sigma^{-1}$. We show in the Appendix that (5.13) and (5.14) coincide, and hence that the classical and steady-state Kalman filters are identical. Other authors have considered this equivalence, but so far as we are aware the precise connection between expressions such as (5.13) and (5.14) has not been made explicit (cf. Anderson and Moore, 1979, p. 257; Whittle, 1983, p. 151). The discussion in Section 2.2 concerns the same equivalence in respect of the filter $f_0(z)$, in a simple two-component example of the unobserved-component ARMA model.

5.3 The non-stationary detectable case

If $\phi^C(L)$ and/or $\phi^S(L)$ are not invertible, but contain no non-invertible common factor, then the covariance $P_{t+1,t}$ attains a steady state, P, and $\tilde{F}$ has all eigenvalues inside the unit circle. In this case, therefore, there is still a steady-state filter of the form (5.14), and the question that then arises is how much of the analysis in the preceding section survives? In particular, is there an expression corresponding to (5.13) in this case? To make progress, it is necessary to be clear about the practical significance of the various z-transforms manipulated above. Although we replace the series $I + z\tilde{F} + z^2\tilde{F}^2 + \cdots$ by its limit $(I - z\tilde{F})^{-1}$ at (5.9), and also $I + zF + z^2F^2 + \cdots$ by $(I - zF)^{-1}$ at various points, the practical reality is that only a finite record is ever analysed, so that we could equally proceed with, for example, (5.9) written as

$$f_{-1,t}(z) = \sum_{i=0}^{t} z^i \tilde{F}^i K$$

and (5.10) as

$$\tilde{w}_t(z) = 1 - zH'\left\{\sum_{i=0}^{t} z^i \tilde{F}^i K\right\}.$$

Now an "inverse" of $\tilde{w}_t(z)$ could be defined as

$$w(z) = 1 + zH' \left\{ \sum_{i=0}^{\infty} z^i F^i K \right\}.$$

This is the z-transform for the coefficient on $\tilde{y}_{t-i}$ when y_t is written as a linear combination of the innovations, as in (5.6). It is the inverse of $\tilde{w}_t(z)$ in the sense that

$$w(z)\tilde{w}_t(z) = 1 + \text{terms resulting from truncation at any finite power of } z.$$

However, in order to apply (5.14) in practice, all we need ensure is that coefficients on powers of z from $-k$ to t are correct. With this in mind (5.14) can be written as

$$f_k(z) = \left\{ z(I + z\tilde{F} + z^2\tilde{F}^2 + \cdots)Kw(z) \right.$$

$$\left. + P \sum_{j=0}^{k} z^{-j}(\tilde{F}')^j H \Sigma^{-1} \right\} \tilde{w}(z) + U(z), \tag{5.15}$$

where $U(z)$ is a remainder involving powers of z greater than t (it is assumed that the first term inside the braces is expanded far enough to give the first term of (5.14) exactly, before the remainder is taken). Now by direct calculation the first term inside the braces of (5.15) can be seen to be $z(I + zF + z^2F^2 + \cdots)K$ plus a remainder due to truncation; the same argument applies, however, and so we can write

$$f_k(z) = \left\{ z(I + zF + z^2F^2 + \cdots)FPH \right.$$

$$\left. + P \sum_{i=0}^{k} z^{-i}(\tilde{F}')^i H \right\} \Sigma^{-1}\tilde{w}(z) + U^*(z). \tag{5.16}$$

Pursuing the same line of reasoning, we might seek to obtain $f_k(z)$ by expanding the following z-transform, obtained from (5.13) by replacing $(I - zF)^{-1}$ and $(I - z^{-1}F')^{-1}$ by the divergent power series $(I + zF + z^2F^2 + \cdots)$ and $(I + z^{-1}F' + z^{-2}(F')^2 + \cdots)$ respectively:

$$f_k^*(z) = [\{I + zF + \cdots\} GQG'\{I + z^{-1}F' + z^{-2}(F')^2 + \cdots\} H\tilde{w}'(z^{-1})]_{-k}$$

$$\times \Sigma^{-1}\tilde{w}(z). \tag{5.17}$$

The requirement here is that the polynomial in negative powers of z inside the annihilation operator converges more rapidly than F^j diverges. Recall that

$$\tilde{w}'(z^{-1}) = 1 - z^{-1}K'\{I + z^{-1}\tilde{F}' + z^{-2}(\tilde{F}')^2 + \cdots\}H.$$

By direct calculation $f_k^*(z)$ can thus be written (cf. A.5) as

$$f_k^*(z) = [\{I + zF + z^2 F^2 + \cdots\} GQG'\{I + z^{-1}\tilde{F}' + z^{-2}(\tilde{F}')^2 + \cdots\} H]_{-k}$$
$$\times \, \Sigma^{-1}\tilde{w}(z) \qquad (5.18)$$

in which the coefficients on finite powers of z inside the annihilation operator are as follows:

$$\text{coefficient of } z^0: \quad \sum_{i=0}^{\infty} F^i GQG'(\tilde{F}')^i H$$

$$\text{coefficient of } z^{-j}: \quad \sum_{i=0}^{\infty} F^i GQG'(\tilde{F}')^{i+j} H$$

$$\text{coefficient of } z^j: \quad \sum_{i=0}^{\infty} F^{i+j} GQG'(\tilde{F}')^i H.$$

That these coefficients are bounded if F has eigenvalues on or inside the unit circle follows from the fact that those of $\tilde{F}$ are strictly inside the unit circle. A simple rearrangement of (3.3e) in steady state gives $GQG' = P - FP\tilde{F}'$, so the coefficient of z^0 is then PH, and so on. We thus see that $f_k^*(z)$ coincides with $f_k(z)$ in (5.16) up to any desired power of z. The interest in this result is that formulae analogous to (5.17) for the case in which F has eigenvalues on or inside the unit circle have appeared in the literature, and although these provide a means of correctly calculating the coefficients, as we have shown, they have not been derived directly, as here. As a basis for calculating the coefficients, (5.14) is obviously to be preferred, however, since the intervention of rounding errors is thereby minimized. Whether any meaning can be attached to (5.18) in the explosive case remains an open question.

5.4 The non-detectable case
The model of (5.1) and (5.3) fails the detectability condition if the polynomials $\phi^S(\text{L})$ and $\phi^C(\text{L})$ have a common factor $(1 - \lambda\text{L})$ with $|\lambda| \geq 1$. Although cases with $|\lambda| > 1$ might be considered to be coincidental situations of little practical relevance, in the seasonal adjustment literature cases with $\lambda = 1$ arise, through specifications in which $\phi^S(\text{L})$ has a factor $(1 - \text{L}^d)$ where d is the seasonal period, and $\phi^C(\text{L})$ has a factor $(1 - \text{L})$, and we briefly consider this case here.

Burridge and Hall (1987) show that convergence of the filter gain to a steady state, K, does occur when a common factor of $(1 - \text{L})$ is present. The matrix $\tilde{F}$ has an eigenvalue of unity, however, and so we must consider carefully what meaning, if any, is to be attached to expressions such as (5.16) and (5.18) in these circumstances. The time-invariant Kalman filter can still be written as

$$f_{k,t}(z) = z f_{-1,t}(z) + \sum_{i=0}^{k} z^{-i} C_i \tilde{w}_{t+k}(z), \qquad (5.19)$$

with power series interpreted as in the previous section, namely

$$f_{-1,t}(z) = \sum_{i=0}^{t} z^i \tilde{F}^i K$$

$$\tilde{w}_{t+k}(z) = 1 - zH' \sum_{i=0}^{t+k} z^i \tilde{F}^i K,$$

and $C_i = P_{t,t-1}(\tilde{F}')^i H \Sigma^{-1}$. That C_i is time-invariant when K is follows from the use of the transformation employed in the convergence proof of Burridge and Hall (1987). Now exactly the same argument can be applied as in the previous section, except that $GQG' = P_{t+1,t} - FP_{t,t-1}\tilde{F}'$ and a time subscript on P needs to be retained in obtaining the equivalence of (5.18) and (5.16), since $P_{t+1,t}$ does not approach a limit in this case, and in particular is not equal to $P_{t,t-1}$.

That the coefficients displayed below (5.18) are finite follows from the fact that F^i converges to a constant matrix, while $(\tilde{F}')^i H$ converges to the zero vector. Again it is clear that (5.19) provides a better means of calculating the coefficients than (5.18). In the limit this filter coincides with that considered by Pierce (1979), who shows that the estimation error is non-stationary in the presence of a common factor $(1 - L)$. Pierce's result corresponds to the fact that $P_{t+1,t}$ diverges in this case. The possibility that K_t converges while $P_{t+1,t}$ increases without limit, as in this case, is scarcely considered in the control literature.

6 Discussion

In the preceding sections we have reviewed the classical statistical theory of forecasting and signal extraction for ARMA processes using techniques developed in control theory. These techniques have not been widely used in statistical prediction theory, and our first objective has been to demonstrate explicitly the connections between the two literatures. In this analysis, it is necessary to give careful attention to initial conditions, and we show that, if this is done, then the results readily extend to non-stationary and non-invertible processes. Soundly-based results for the non-stationary case are not available in the statistical literature, and it remains to comment briefly on a number of earlier treatments of this case.

The prediction of a difference-stationary process, possibly masked by stationary noise, is discussed by Whittle (1963, §8.5). He obtains the z-transform of the l.l.s. predictor in the case where the AR operator contains a (possibly repeated) factor of $(1 - \phi L)$, with $|\phi| < 1$, and then allows $\phi \to 1$ in this z-transform. Whittle (p. 95) does not claim that the resulting predictor is the l.l.s. predictor, but that this is true, with appropriate assumptions on initial conditions, is shown above.

The extraction of non-stationary signals with roots on the unit circle, observed in stationary noise, where an infinite sample is available, is also considered by Hannan (1967) and Sobel (1967). These two papers are closely related in that they address the same problem, but they use different methods. Hannan finds that filter in the class of linear filters which pass a polynomial trend generated by the same

mth order difference equation as the signal, which minimizes the m.s.e. His result is a straightforward generalization of Whittle's. Sobel, on the other hand, proves by Hilbert space arguments that in this class of process the projection of S_t on $\{y_t = S_t + N_t\}$ tends to a limit as given by Hannan. Sobel's argument requires the noise to be stationary, and the variance of S_t to be bounded at time τ, say, by taking as "initial" conditions $S_{\tau-m}, \ldots, S_{\tau-2}, S_{\tau-1}$ with finite variance. This device, which is used also by Bell (1984), makes the resulting estimates sensitive to the choice of τ, a fact which neither of these authors discuss. Sobel was aware of Kalman's work, but seems to have dismissed it on the (mistaken) grounds that only autoregressive processes could be handled—with the benefit of hindsight this seems to have been unfortunate, perhaps contributing to the slow diffusion of state-space methods into statistical time series analysis.

Cleveland and Tiao (1976) consider the extension of Whittle's result to situations in which signal and noise processes may have shared and repeated unit roots. That is, $\phi^S(L)$ may have a factor $(1 - L^d)$ and $\phi^N(L)$ a factor of $(1 - L)$, giving a non-detectable model as discussed in Section 5.4. They assert that the l.l.s. estimator (in their case, the conditional expectation) takes the same form as in the stationary case. However, their argument allows no proof of convergence of the filter to steady state, and no initial conditions which would bound the variance of S_t, N_t or y_t at some point in the sample are given.

More recently, Bell (1984) extends Sobel's result to situations in which the signal and noise processes have unrestricted autoregressive operators of finite order. As noted above, his results depend on the arbitrary treatment of some part of the record as "initial" conditions. In particular, his claim (pp. 660–661) that the signal extraction error in the non-detectable case discussed by Pierce (see Section 5.4) has finite variance, contrary to Pierce's result, rests on the use of initial conditions *in the middle of an infinite record*, which seems to conflict with what is usually intended when writers in this field discuss such a record. Bell suggests that the Kalman filter, which he does not use, is a convenient device for solving the data processing problem in finite samples, to which his results do not apply.

That a variety of signal extraction problems may be usefully cast in the state-space framework is recognized by several authors. For example, Pagan (1975) displays the steady-state filter for a simple unobserved-components model with autoregressive components, and Engle (1978) and Kitagawa (1981) discuss both practical signal extraction and parameter estimation for various ARMA components models. In fact, the most common applications of Kalman filtering in econometrics are to be found in the estimation context, where the prediction error decomposition facilitates evaluation of the likelihood function for models with state structure (Harvey, 1984; Engle and Watson, 1985). Parameter estimation problems are not discussed in the present paper; rather the emphasis is on the use of state-space methods in prediction theory. In that context, the techniques applied above have been seen to be powerful and direct, and their application to further problems, such as those of specification error and parameter uncertainty, will undoubtedly be equally rewarding.

Acknowledgements

Early versions of parts of this work were presented at the Rencontre Franco-Belgé de Statisticiens, Rouen, 1982, and the European Meetings of the Econometric Society, Pisa, 1983 and Madrid, 1984, and circulated as Warwick Economics Research Papers Nos. 234 (August 1983) and 274 (October 1986). The helpful comments of Peter Crouch, Graham Goodwin, Mark Salmon, anonymous referees, and participants in numerous seminars on three continents are gratefully acknowledged. This research was supported by a grant from the Economic and Social Research Council.

Appendix

Alternative forms for the covariance generating function of y_t

In Sections 4.4 and 5.2 the c.g.f. of y_t, defined only in the stationary case, is expressed in two different forms. In this Appendix we show their equivalence by a direct algebraic argument.

First, from the general system (3.1)–(3.2) we obtain

$$g_{yy}(z) = R + H'(I - zF)^{-1}GQG'(I - z^{-1}F')^{-1}H + zH'(I - zF)^{-1}GS$$
$$+ z^{-1}S'G'(I - z^{-1}F')^{-1}H. \tag{A.1}$$

The second form is obtained from the steady-state relationship between y_t and current and past innovations as

$$g_{yy}(z) = \{1 + zH'(I - zF)^{-1}K\} \Sigma \{1 + z^{-1}K'(I - z^{-1}F')^{-1}H\}. \tag{A.2}$$

In this expression we have

$$\Sigma = H'PH + R,$$
$$K = (FPH + GS)\Sigma^{-1},$$
$$P = FPF' + GQG' - K\Sigma K'.$$

Expanding (A.2) and substituting for K and Σ then gives

$$g_{yy}(z) = H'PH + R + zH'(I - zF)^{-1}(FPH + GS)$$
$$+ z^{-1}(H'PF' + S'G')(I - z^{-1}F')^{-1}H$$
$$+ H'(I - zF)^{-1}(FPF' + GQG' - P)(I - z^{-1}F')^{-1}H. \tag{A.3}$$

Subtracting (A.1) from (A.3) leaves the remainder

$$H'PH + zH'(I - zF)^{-1}FPH + z^{-1}H'PF'(I - z^{-1}F')^{-1}H$$
$$+ H'(I - zF)^{-1}(FPF' - P)(I - z^{-1}F')^{-1}H,$$

and on rearranging this in the form $H'(I - zF)^{-1}\Delta(I - z^{-1}F')^{-1}H$ it is readily seen that $\Delta = 0$, as required. This algebra both generalizes and simplifies the discussion of Anderson and Moore (1979, §4.5), who treat the case $S = 0$.

In the state-space representation of the ARMA model that is used in Section 4 we have $Q = S = R$, and using this in (A.1) gives equation (4.13) of the main text. In the representation used in Section 5 we have $S = 0$, and again specializing (A.1) gives equation (5.5); the alternative form (A.2) is obtained as (5.7) of the main text.

Equivalence of (5.13) and (5.14)

Substituting for $f_{-1}(z)$ and C_i in (5.14) and using the invertibility of $\tilde{w}(z)$ we obtain

$$f_k(z) = [z\{I - z\tilde{F}\}^{-1}K\tilde{w}^{-1}(z)\Sigma + P\{I - z^{-1}\tilde{F}'\}^{-1}H]_{-k}\,\Sigma^{-1}\tilde{w}(z). \quad \text{(A.4)}$$

Using (5.7), the first term in the annihilation operator of (A.4) is

$$z\{I - z\tilde{F}\}^{-1}K\{1 + zH'(I - zF)^{-1}K\}\Sigma$$

$$= z\{I - z\tilde{F}\}^{-1}\{I + zKH'(I - zF)^{-1}\}K\Sigma$$

$$= z\{I - zF\}^{-1}K\Sigma$$

$$= z\{I - zF\}^{-1}FPH.$$

Taking out a left factor of $(I - zF)^{-1}$ and a right factor of $(I - z^{-1}\tilde{F}')^{-1}H$ then gives

$$f_k(z) = [(I - zF)^{-1}\{zFP(I - z^{-1}\tilde{F}')$$

$$+ (I - zF)P\}(I - z^{-1}\tilde{F}')^{-1}H]_{-k}\Sigma^{-1}\tilde{w}(z)$$

$$= [(I - zF)^{-1}GQG'(I - z\tilde{F}')^{-1}H]_{-k}\,\Sigma^{-1}\tilde{w}(z). \quad \text{(A.5)}$$

Finally, noting that algebra similar to that above gives

$$H\tilde{w}'(z^{-1}) = \{I - z^{-1}F'\}\{I - z^{-1}\tilde{F}'\}^{-1}H$$

we see that (5.13) coincides with (A.5), and thus with (5.14), as required.

Notes

1. For the present model this is given (with a typographical error) as Exercise 3.3.12 of Whittle (1963, p. 35).
2. In his presentation and discussion of Muth's result Sargent (1979, p. 310) notes "... a technical difficulty that arises because our $\{Y_i\}$ process is (borderline) nonstationary. In particular, the variance of Y is not finite, making application of least squares projection theory a touchy matter."

3. For a derivation see Anderson and Moore (1979, Ch. 7) or, for the Gaussian case from a slightly different perspective, Jazwinski (1970, pp. 215–218).
4. This result is sometimes incorrectly attributed to Caines and Mayne, whose original proof of their theorem was in error. The confusion arises because in a subsequent correction (Caines and Mayne, 1971) the condition that (F^*, D) be stabilizable had to be strengthened to controllability, and this change has been overlooked by some authors.

References

Anderson, B.D.O. and Moore, J.B. (1979). *Optimal Filtering*. Englewood Cliffs, NJ: Prentice-Hall.

Bell, W.R. (1984). Signal extraction for nonstationary time series. *Annals of Statistics*, 12, 646–664.

Box, G.E.P. and Jenkins, G.M. (1970). *Time Series Analysis: Forecasting and Control*. San Francisco: Holden-Day.

Burridge, P. and Hall, A.R. (1987). Convergence of the Kalman filter gain for a class of non-detectable signal extraction problems. *IEEE Transactions on Automatic Control*, 32, 1036–1039.

Burridge, P. and Wallis, K.F. (1985). Calculating the variance of seasonally adjusted series. *Journal of the American Statistical Association*, 80, 541–552.

Caines, P.E. and Mayne, D.Q. (1970). On the discrete time matrix Riccati equation of optimal control. *International Journal of Control*, 12, 785–794.

Caines, P.E. and Mayne, D.Q. (1971). On the discrete time matrix Riccati equation of optimal control: a correction. *International Journal of Control*, 14, 205–207.

Chan, S.W., Goodwin, G.C. and Sin, K.S. (1984). Convergence properties of the Riccati difference equation in optimal filtering of non-stabilizable systems. *IEEE Transactions on Automatic Control*, 29, 110–118.

Cleveland, W.P. and Tiao, G.C. (1976). Decomposition of seasonal time series: a model for the Census X-11 program. *Journal of the American Statistical Association*, 71, 581–587.

De Souza, C.E., Gevers, M.R. and Goodwin, G.C. (1986). Riccati equations in optimal filtering of nonstabilizable systems having singular state transition matrices. *IEEE Transactions on Automatic Control*, 31, 831–838.

Engle, R.F. (1978). Estimating structural models of seasonality. In *Seasonal Analysis of Economic Time Series* (A. Zellner, ed.), pp. 281–297. Washington, DC: Bureau of the Census.

Engle, R.F. and Watson, M. (1985). Applications of Kalman filtering in econometrics. Presented at the Econometric Society World Congress, Cambridge, Mass., August 1985.

Florens, J.P. and Mouchart, M. (1982). A note on non-causality. *Econometrica*, 50, 583–591.

Granger, C.W.J. and Newbold, P. (1977). *Forecasting Economic Time Series*. New York: Academic Press.

Hager, W.W. and Horowitz, L.L. (1976). Convergence and stability properties of the discrete Riccati operator equation and the associated optimal control and filtering problems. *SIAM Journal of Control and Optimization*, 14, 295–312.

Hannan, E.J. (1967). Measurement of a wandering signal amid noise. *Journal of Applied Probability*, 4, 90–102.

Harvey, A.C. (1981). *Time Series Models*. Oxford: Philip Allan.

Harvey, A.C. (1984). Dynamic models, the prediction error decomposition and state space. In *Econometrics and Quantitative Economics* (D.F. Hendry and K.F. Wallis, eds.), pp. 37–59. Oxford: Basil Blackwell.

Jazwinski, A.H. (1970). *Stochastic Processes and Filtering Theory*. New York: Academic Press.

Kailath, T. (1980). *Linear Systems*. Englewood Cliffs, NJ: Prentice-Hall.

Kalman, R.E. (1960). A new approach to linear filtering and prediction problems. *Transactions ASME, Journal of Basic Engineering*, 85, 35–45.

Kitagawa, G. (1981). A nonstationary time series model and its fitting by a recursive filter. *Journal of Time Series Analysis*, 2, 103 116.

Mehra, R.K. (1979). Kalman filters and their applications to forecasting. In *TIMS Studies in the Management Sciences* vol. 12 (S. Makridakis and S.C. Wheelwright, eds.), pp. 75–99. Amsterdam: North Holland.

Muth, J.F. (1960). Optimal properties of exponentially weighted forecasts. *Journal of the American Statistical Association*, 55, 299–305.

Nerlove, M., Grether, D.M. and Carvalho, J.L. (1979). *Analysis of Economic Time Series*. New York: Academic Press.

Pagan, A.R. (1975). A note on the extraction of components from time series. *Econometrica*, 43, 163–168.

Pierce, D.A. (1979). Signal extraction error in nonstationary time series. *Annals of Statistics*, 7, 1303–1320.

Preston, A.J. and Pagan, A.R. (1982). *The Theory of Economic Policy*. Cambridge: Cambridge University Press.

Sargent, T.J. (1979). *Macroeconomic Theory*. New York: Academic Press.

Sobel, E. (1967). Prediction of a noise-distorted, multivariate, non-stationary signal. *Journal of Applied Probability*, 4, 330–342.

Whittle, P. (1963). *Prediction and Regulation by Linear Least-Square Methods*. London: English Universities Press. Second edition, Minneapolis: University of Minnesota Press, 1983.

3

Exact Initial Kalman Filtering and Smoothing for Nonstationary Time Series Models*

SIEM JAN KOOPMAN[†]

This article presents a new exact solution for the initialization of the Kalman filter for state space models with diffuse initial conditions. For example, the regression model with stochastic trend, seasonal, and other nonstationary autoregressive integrated moving average components requires a (partially) diffuse initial state vector. The proposed analytical solution is easy to implement and computationally efficient. The exact solution for smoothing is also given. Missing observations are handled in a straightforward manner. All proofs rely on elementary results.

1 Introduction

Assume that a vector of observations $\mathbf{y}_t$ is generated by the Gaussian state-space model

$$\mathbf{y}_t = \mathbf{Z}_t \boldsymbol{\alpha}_t + \mathbf{G}_t \boldsymbol{\varepsilon}_t, \qquad \boldsymbol{\varepsilon}_t \sim \mathrm{N}(0, I), \quad t = 1, \ldots, n,$$

$$\boldsymbol{\alpha}_{t+1} = \mathbf{T}_t \boldsymbol{\alpha}_t + \mathbf{H}_t \boldsymbol{\varepsilon}_t, \qquad \boldsymbol{\alpha}_1 \sim \mathrm{N}(\mathbf{a}, \mathbf{P}), \tag{1}$$

where $p \times 1$ vector $\boldsymbol{\alpha}_t$ is the state vector. The system matrices, $\mathbf{Z}_t, \mathbf{T}_t, \mathbf{G}_t$, and $\mathbf{H}_t$, for $t = 1, \ldots, n$, are assumed to be fixed and known. The former equation of (1) is referred to as the observation equation, whereas the latter equation is called the transition equation. A normally distributed random vector $\mathbf{x}$ with mean μ and variance matrix $\boldsymbol{\Lambda}$ is denoted by $\mathbf{x} \sim \mathrm{N}(\mu, \boldsymbol{\Lambda})$. The disturbance vector $\boldsymbol{\varepsilon}_t$ is serially uncorrelated. The appearance of $\boldsymbol{\varepsilon}_t$ in both equations is general rather than restrictive. The special case $\mathbf{H}_t \mathbf{G}_t' = 0$, for $t = 1, \ldots, n$, implies mutual independence between the two sets of disturbances. The mean vector $\mathbf{a}$ and variance matrix $\mathbf{P}$ of the initial state vector are assumed to be known.

The state-space model (1) is often used as a framework for representing linear time series models such as autoregressive integrated moving average (ARIMA)

* Reprinted from *Journal of the American Statistical Association*, "Exact Initial Kalman Filtering and Smoothing for Non-stationary Time Series Models" by S. J. Koopman, pp. 1630–1638, Vol. 92, No. 456, December 1997. Reproduced here with the permission of the American Statistical Association.

[†] Siem Jan Koopman is Assistant Professor, CentER, Tilburg University, 5000 LE Tilburg, The Netherlands. This work was carried out while the author was a lecturer at the Department of Statistics of the London School of Economics and Political Science and it was supported by ESRC grant R000235330. The author thanks J. Durbin, A. C. Harvey, J. R. Magnus, the associate editor, and a referee for their help and support in this research project.

models, regression models with stochastic trend, seasonal or other ARIMA components, and models with time-varying regression parameters. The state space representation may contain some unknown elements in the system matrices. These hyperparameters are estimated by maximizing the likelihood function via some quasi-Newton optimization routine; see Section 4.

The Kalman filter produces the minimum mean squared linear estimator of the state vector α_{t+1} using the set of observations $Y_t = \{y_1, \ldots, y_t\}$—that is, $a_{t+1} = E(\alpha_{t+1}|Y_t)$—and the corresponding variance matrix of the estimator a_{t+1}—that is, $P_{t+1} = \text{var}(\alpha_{t+1}|Y_t)$—for $t = 1, \ldots, n$. The Kalman filter is given by

$$\mathbf{v}_t = \mathbf{y}_t - \mathbf{Z}_t \mathbf{a}_t, \qquad \mathbf{F}_t = \mathbf{Z}_t \mathbf{P}_t \mathbf{Z}_t' + \mathbf{G}_t \mathbf{G}_t',$$

$$\mathbf{M}_t = \mathbf{T}_t \mathbf{P}_t \mathbf{Z}_t' + \mathbf{H}_t \mathbf{G}_t, \qquad \mathbf{a}_{t+1} = \mathbf{T}_t \mathbf{a}_t + \mathbf{K}_t \mathbf{v}_t,$$

$$\mathbf{P}_{t+1} = \mathbf{T}_t \mathbf{P}_t \mathbf{T}_t' + \mathbf{H}_t \mathbf{H}_t' - \mathbf{C}_t, \tag{2}$$

where $\mathbf{K}_t = \mathbf{M}_t \mathbf{F}_t^{-1}$ and $\mathbf{C}_t = \mathbf{M}_t \mathbf{F}_t^{-1} \mathbf{M}_t'$ for $t = 1, \ldots, n$. The Kalman filter is initialized by $\mathbf{a}_1 = \mathbf{a}$ and $\mathbf{P}_1 = \mathbf{P}$. (The proof of the Kalman filter can be found in Anderson and Moore 1979.) The one-step-ahead prediction error of the observation vector is $\mathbf{v}_t = \mathbf{y}_t - E(\mathbf{y}_t|Y_{t-1})$ with variance matrix $\mathbf{F}_t = \text{var}(\mathbf{y}_t|Y_{t-1}) = \text{var}(\mathbf{v}_t)$. Furthermore, matrix $\mathbf{M}_t$ is defined as the covariance matrix $\mathbf{M}_t = \text{cov}(\alpha_{t+1}, \mathbf{y}_t|Y_t)$. The matrix $\mathbf{K}_t$ is called the Kalman gain matrix. The output of the Kalman filter can be used to compute the likelihood function of the state-space model (1) via the prediction error decomposition; see Section 4.

Minimum mean squared linear estimators using all observations Y_n are evaluated by a smoothing algorithm; that is, a set of backwards recursions that requires output generated by the Kalman filter. The basic smoothing algorithm of de Jong (1988) and Kohn and Ansley (1989) is given by

$$\mathbf{r}_{t-1} = \mathbf{Z}_t' \mathbf{F}_t' \mathbf{v}_t + \mathbf{L}_t' \mathbf{r}_t, \qquad \mathbf{N}_{t-1} = \mathbf{Z}_t' \mathbf{F}_t^{-1} \mathbf{Z}_t + \mathbf{L}_t' \mathbf{N}_t \mathbf{L}_t, \tag{3}$$

where $\mathbf{L}_t = \mathbf{T}_t - \mathbf{K}_t \mathbf{Z}_t$, $\mathbf{r_n} = \mathbf{0}$, and $\mathbf{N_n} = \mathbf{0}$, for $t = 1, \ldots, n$. The vector $\mathbf{r}_t$ and matrix $\mathbf{N}_t$ can be used for different purposes. For example, (a) de Jong (1988) and Kohn and Ansley (1989) applied (3) to obtain the smoothed estimator for α_t—that is, $E(\alpha_t|Y_n) = \mathbf{a}_t + \mathbf{P}_t \mathbf{r}_{t-1}$, for $t = 1, \ldots, n$; (b) Koopman (1993) used it to obtain the smoothed estimator for ε_t, that is $E(\varepsilon_t|Y_n) = \mathbf{H}_t' \mathbf{r}_t + \mathbf{G}_t' \mathbf{e}_t$ where $\mathbf{e}_t = \mathbf{F}_t^{-1} \mathbf{v}_t - \mathbf{K}_t' \mathbf{r}_t$, for $t = 1, \ldots, n$; (c) Koopman and Shephard (1992) get the exact score function of the hyperparameter vector using (3); see Section 4.

The Kalman filter provides a general tool to handle missing observations in time series. When the vector of observations $\mathbf{y}_t$ is missing, the matrices $\mathbf{Z}_t$ and $\mathbf{G}_t$ are set equal to 0. When only some entries of $\mathbf{y}_t$ are missing, the matrices $\mathbf{Z}_t$ and $\mathbf{G}_t$ are adjusted appropriately by eliminating the rows corresponding to the missing entries in $\mathbf{y}_t$. The Kalman filter and the basic smoothing algorithm deal straightforwardly with different matrix dimensions of $\mathbf{Z}_t$ and $\mathbf{G}_t$.

The Kalman filter for a stationary time series model is initialized by the unconditional mean and variance matrix of α_1; that is, $\mathbf{a}_1 = \mathbf{a}$ and $\mathbf{P}_1 = \mathbf{P}$. Stationarity implies a time-invariant state space model [i.e., (1)], for which the system matrices are constant over time. We obtain $\text{var}(\boldsymbol{\alpha}_t) = \text{var}(\boldsymbol{\alpha}_1) = \mathbf{P} = \mathbf{TPT'} + \mathbf{HH'}$, which can be solved easily with respect to $\mathbf{P}$ (see Magnus and Neudecker 1988, chap. 2). Nonstationary time series models such as regression models with stochastic trend, seasonal, or other ARIMA components require noninformative prior conditions for the initial state vector $\boldsymbol{\alpha}_1$. In this article I consider the problem of initializing the Kalman filter for any nonstationary model in state-space form.

The initial state vector $\boldsymbol{\alpha}_t$ can generally be specified as

$$\boldsymbol{\alpha}_1 = \mathbf{a} + \mathbf{A}\boldsymbol{\eta} + \mathbf{B}\boldsymbol{\delta}, \qquad \boldsymbol{\eta} \sim \text{N}(0, \mathbf{I}), \quad \boldsymbol{\delta} \sim \text{N}(0, \kappa\mathbf{I}), \tag{4}$$

where matrices $\mathbf{A}$ and $\mathbf{B}$ are fixed and known. The $m \times 1$ vector $\boldsymbol{\delta}$ is referred to as the *diffuse* vector as $\kappa \to \infty$. This leads to

$$\boldsymbol{\alpha}_1 \sim \text{N}(\mathbf{a}, \mathbf{P}), \qquad \mathbf{P} = \mathbf{P}_* + \kappa\mathbf{P}_\infty, \tag{5}$$

where $\mathbf{P}_* = \mathbf{AA'}$ and $\mathbf{P}_\infty = \mathbf{BB'}$. This specification implies that some elements of the initial state vector are not well defined. The Kalman filter (2) cannot be applied in cases where $\mathbf{P}_\infty$ is a nonzero matrix, because no real value can represent κ as $\kappa \to \infty$.

A numerical device for dealing with the diffuse initial state vector is to replace the scalar κ be some large value k; for example, 10^7 (see Burridge and Wallis 1985 and Harvey and Phillips 1979). This numerical solution is not exact and may generate inaccuracies due to numerical rounding errors. In this article I pursue an analytical approach where I express the Kalman filter quantities in terms of κ explicitly and then let $\kappa \to \infty$ to obtain the exact solution. Ansley and Kohn (1985, 1990; hereafter referred to as AK) first solved the initialization problem using an analytical approach. Their solution is general and deals with missing observations in the initial period. However, the general algorithm of AK is difficult to implement, standard software cannot be used, and the proof is long and complex. This article presents a new analytical solution that uses a trivial initialization. The proof is based on elementary results in calculus and matrix algebra.

An alternative exact approach was taken by de Jong (1991), which he labelled as the diffuse Kalman filter, hereafter referred to as DKF. The DKF augments the Kalman filter quantities $\mathbf{v}_t$ and $\mathbf{a}_{t \mid 1}$ by m columns to get $\mathbf{V}_t$ and $\mathbf{A}_{t+1}$, with the initialization $\mathbf{A}_1 = (\mathbf{a}, \mathbf{B})$ and $\mathbf{P}_1 = \mathbf{P}_*$. Also, the DKF includes the matrix recursion $\mathbf{S}_{t+1} = \mathbf{S}_t + \mathbf{V}_t'\mathbf{F}_t^{-1}\mathbf{V}_t$ with $\mathbf{S}_1 = 0$. When the lower $m \times m$ block of $\mathbf{S}_d$ can be inverted, the appropriate corrections for $\mathbf{a}_{d+1}$ and $\mathbf{P}_{d+1}$ are made, for some $d < n$, and the augmented part disappears. The DKF is computationally inefficient due to the additional matrix operations and the inversion of a $m \times m$ matrix. Moreover, the corrections for the basic smoothing algorithm (3) are complicated and difficult to implement (see Chu-Chun-Lin and de Jong 1993).

Other solutions for the initialization problem of the Kalman filter are as follows:

- Anderson and Moore (1979) and Kitagawa (1981) discussed the information filter that evaluates the inverse of $\mathbf{P}_t$ recursively. This straightforward solution avoids the infinite case because $\kappa^{-1} \to 0$ as $\kappa \to \infty$. However, the information approach is not general because it cannot be applied to all cases.

- Harvey and Pierse (1984) treated the initial vector δ as an unknown parameter and included it in the state vector. This approach is computationally inefficient due to the increased size of the state vector.

- Bell and Hillmer (1991) suggested applying the transformation approach of Ansley and Kohn (1985) directly to the initial dataset. This approach provides the appropriate initialization of the Kalman filter for the remaining dataset but needs modification when missing observations occur in the initial dataset. Gomez and Maravall (1994) rediscovered this approach for the specific application of ARIMA models.

- A specific square root algorithm based on fast Givens transformations can deal explicitly with $\mathbf{P}_t$ when it depends on $\kappa \to \infty$ (see Snyder and Saligari 1996). It is known that square root algorithms are numerically stable but have high computational costs. Moreover, it is not clear how to implement smoothing algorithms in this approach.

The article is organized as follows. Section 2 presents the exact initial Kalman filter, and Section 3 presents the exact initial smoothing algorithm. Section 4 applies the new results to compute the diffuse likelihood function and the score vector of the hyperparameter vector for nonstationary time series models. Section 5 gives some examples of how to implement the algorithm for univariate and multivariate cases, and Section 6 discusses some related issues and it gives an assessment of the computational efficiency of the new algorithms. Section 7 concludes.

2 The Exact Initial Kalman Filter

The formulation of the initial state variance matrix $\mathbf{P} = \mathbf{P}_* + \kappa \mathbf{P}_\infty$ implies a similar formulation for the Kalman filter quantities $\mathbf{F}_t = \mathbf{F}_{*,t} + \kappa \mathbf{F}_{\infty,t}$ and $\mathbf{M}_t = \mathbf{M}_{*,t} + \kappa \mathbf{M}_{\infty,t}$, where

$$\mathbf{F}_{*,t} = \mathbf{Z}_t \mathbf{P}_{*,t} \mathbf{Z}_t' + \mathbf{G}_t \mathbf{G}_t', \qquad \mathbf{F}_{\infty,t} = \mathbf{Z}_t \mathbf{P}_{\infty,t} \mathbf{Z}_t',$$

$$\mathbf{M}_{*,t} = \mathbf{T}_t \mathbf{P}_{*,t} \mathbf{Z}_t' + \mathbf{H}_t \mathbf{G}_t', \qquad \mathbf{M}_{\infty,t} = \mathbf{T}_t \mathbf{P}_{\infty,t} \mathbf{Z}_t'. \tag{6}$$

The Kalman update equations for $\mathbf{a}_{t+1}$ and $\mathbf{P}_{t+1} = \mathbf{P}_{*,t+1} + \kappa \mathbf{P}_{\infty,t+1}$ rely on the matrices $\mathbf{K}_t = \mathbf{M}_t \mathbf{F}_t^{-1}$ and $\mathbf{C}_t = \mathbf{M}_t \mathbf{F}_t^{-1} \mathbf{M}_t'$. In developing expressions for $\mathbf{K}_t$ and $\mathbf{C}_t$, we temporarily drop the time index t for notational convenience. For a properly defined model (1), the $N \times N$ matrix $\mathbf{F} = \mathbf{F}_* + \kappa \mathbf{F}_\infty$ is nonsingular, but matrices $\mathbf{F}_*$ and $\mathbf{F}_\infty = \mathbf{Z}\mathbf{P}_\infty \mathbf{Z}'$ are not necessarily nonsingular and can be partially diagonalized as shown in Lemma 2 of the Appendix; that is,

$$(\mathbf{J}_1, \mathbf{J}_2)' \mathbf{F}_\infty (\mathbf{J}_1, \mathbf{J}_2) = \begin{bmatrix} \mathbf{I} & 0 \\ 0 & 0 \end{bmatrix},$$

$$(\mathbf{J}_1, \mathbf{J}_2)' \mathbf{F}_* (\mathbf{J}_1, \mathbf{J}_2) = \begin{bmatrix} \mathbf{V}_* & 0 \\ 0 & \mathbf{I}_{N-r} \end{bmatrix}, \tag{7}$$

where $\mathbf{J} = (\mathbf{J}_1, \mathbf{J}_2)$ is a nonsingular matrix, $r = r(\mathbf{F}_\infty)$, and $r(\mathbf{V}_*) \leq r$. Theorem 2 of the Appendix shows that the inverse of $\mathbf{F}$ can be expanded as

$$\mathbf{F}^{-1} = \mathbf{F}_*^- + \frac{1}{\kappa}\mathbf{F}_\infty^- - \frac{1}{\kappa^2}\mathbf{F}_\infty^-\mathbf{F}_*\mathbf{F}_\infty^- + O\left(\frac{1}{\kappa^3}\right), \qquad (8)$$

where $\mathbf{F}_\infty^- = \mathbf{J}_1\mathbf{J}_1'$ and $\mathbf{F}_*^- = \mathbf{J}_2\mathbf{J}_2'$. It follows from (7) that $\mathbf{J}_2'\mathbf{Z}\mathbf{P}_\infty = 0$, so that $\mathbf{M}_\infty\mathbf{J}_2 = 0$ and $\mathbf{M}_\infty\mathbf{F}_*^- = 0$. Then the Kalman gain matrix $\mathbf{K}$ is

$$\mathbf{K} = (\mathbf{M}_* + \kappa\mathbf{M}_\infty)\mathbf{F}^{-1}$$
$$= \mathbf{M}_*\mathbf{F}_*^- + \mathbf{M}_\infty\mathbf{F}_\infty^- + O\left(\frac{1}{\kappa}\right), \qquad (9)$$

and matrix $\mathbf{C}$ is

$$\mathbf{C} = (\mathbf{M}_* + \kappa\mathbf{M}_\infty)\mathbf{F}^{-1}(\mathbf{M}_* + \kappa\mathbf{M}_\infty)'$$
$$= \mathbf{M}_*\mathbf{F}_*^-\mathbf{M}_*' + \mathbf{M}_\infty\mathbf{F}_\infty^-\mathbf{M}_*' + \mathbf{M}_*\mathbf{F}_\infty^-\mathbf{M}_\infty' + \kappa\mathbf{M}_\infty\mathbf{F}_\infty^-\mathbf{M}_\infty'$$
$$- \mathbf{M}_\infty\mathbf{F}_\infty^-\mathbf{F}_*\mathbf{F}_\infty^-\mathbf{M}_\infty' + O\left(\frac{1}{\kappa}\right). \qquad (10)$$

By reintroducing the time indices, the exact initial Kalman filter update equations of $\mathbf{a}_{t+1}$ and $\mathbf{P}_{t+1} = \mathbf{P}_{*,t+1} + \kappa\mathbf{P}_{\infty,t+1}$, when $\kappa \to \infty$, are given by

$$\mathbf{a}_{t+1} = \mathbf{T}_t\mathbf{a}_t + \mathbf{K}_{*,t}\mathbf{v}_t, \qquad \mathbf{P}_{*,t+1} = \mathbf{T}_t\mathbf{P}_{*,t}\mathbf{T}_t' - \mathbf{C}_{*,t} + \mathbf{H}_t\mathbf{H}_t',$$
$$\mathbf{P}_{\infty,t+1} = \mathbf{T}_t\mathbf{P}_{\infty,t}\mathbf{T}_t' - \mathbf{C}_{\infty,t}, \qquad (11)$$

where $\mathbf{v}_t = \mathbf{y}_t - \mathbf{Z}_t\mathbf{a}_t$ and

$$\mathbf{K}_{*,t} = \mathbf{M}_{*,t}\mathbf{F}_{*,t}^- + \mathbf{M}_{\infty,t}\mathbf{F}_{\infty,t}^-,$$
$$\mathbf{C}_{*,t} = \mathbf{M}_{*,t}\mathbf{K}_{*,t}' + \mathbf{M}_{\infty,t}\mathbf{F}_{\infty,t}^-(\mathbf{M}_{*,t} - \mathbf{M}_{\infty,t}\mathbf{F}_{\infty,t}^-\mathbf{F}_{*,t})',$$

and

$$\mathbf{C}_{\infty,t} = \mathbf{M}_{\infty,t}\mathbf{F}_{\infty,t}^-\mathbf{M}_{\infty,t}'. \qquad (12)$$

The update of $\mathbf{a}_{t+1}$ in (11) follows from (2) and (9), because $\mathbf{v}_t$ does not depend on κ and the terms associated with $1/\kappa$ in (9) disappear when $\kappa \to \infty$. The update of $\mathbf{P}_{t+1}$ has two parts: $\mathbf{P}_{*,t+1}$ represents the part that does not rely on κ, whereas $\mathbf{P}_{\infty,t+1}$ is the part associated with κ. The specification for $\mathbf{C}_{*,t}$ in (12) follows from rearranging the terms not associated with κ in (10) and using the definition of $\mathbf{K}_{*,t}$. The remaining part of (10) is found in $\mathbf{C}_{\infty,t}$ as the terms associated with $1/\kappa$ disappear when $\kappa \to \infty$.

It is noted that the dimension N is generally small, and the usual Kalman filter requires the inversion of $\mathbf{F}_t$, for which some diagonalization routine is required. Thus diagonalization of matrices $\mathbf{F}_{\infty,t}$ and $\mathbf{F}_{*,t}$ in (7) does not impose an excessive additional computational burden compared to the usual Kalman filter. Moreover, the diagonalization (7) does not apply to univariate time series models, because $N = 1$. The remaining computations for (12) can be done very efficiently; see Section 6.

2.1 The nonsingular and univariate case

The general solution can be simplified for cases where $\mathbf{F}_{\infty,t}$ is either a zero matrix or a nonsingular matrix for $t = 1, \ldots, n$. If $\mathbf{F}_{\infty,t}$ is a zero matrix, then $\mathbf{J}_{2,t} = \mathbf{J}_t$ and $\mathbf{J}_{1,t} = 0$, so $\mathbf{F}_{*,t}^- = \mathbf{F}_{*,t}^{-1}$ and $\mathbf{F}_{\infty,t}^- = 0$. If $\mathbf{F}_{\infty,t}$ is a nonsingular matrix, then $\mathbf{J}_{1,t} = \mathbf{J}_t$ and $\mathbf{J}_{2,t} = 0$ so $\mathbf{F}_{*,t}^- = 0$ and $\mathbf{F}_{\infty,t}^- = \mathbf{F}_{\infty,t}^{-1}$. For the cases (a) $\mathbf{F}_{\infty,t} = 0$ and (b) $r(\mathbf{F}_{\infty,t}) = N$, the matrices $\mathbf{K}_{*,t}$, $\mathbf{C}_{*,t}$, and $\mathbf{C}_{\infty,t}$ are given by

(a) $\mathbf{K}_{*,t} = \mathbf{M}_{*,t}\mathbf{F}_{*,t}^{-1}$,
$\mathbf{C}_{*,t} = \mathbf{M}_{*,t}\mathbf{K}_{*,t}'$,
$\mathbf{C}_{\infty,t} = 0$,　　　　　　　　　　　　　　　　　　　(13)
(b) $\mathbf{K}_{*,t} = \mathbf{M}_{\infty,t}\mathbf{F}_{\infty,t}^{-1}$,
$\mathbf{C}_{*,t} = \mathbf{M}_{*,t}\mathbf{K}_{*,t}' + \mathbf{K}_{*,t}(\mathbf{M}_{*,t} - \mathbf{K}_{*,t}\mathbf{F}_{*,t})'$,
$\mathbf{C}_{\infty,t} = \mathbf{M}_{\infty,t}\mathbf{F}_{\infty,t}^{-1}\mathbf{M}_{\infty,t}'$.

The expansion (8) for a nonsingular matrix $\mathbf{F}_{\infty,t}$ is given by Theorem 1 of the Appendix. Case (a) is the usual Kalman update (2). The modified Kalman filter of Ansley and Kohn (1990) for univariate models can be reformulated similar to (13).

These special cases are specifically relevant for univariate state-space models. When $N = 1$, $\mathbf{F}_{\infty,t}$ is a scalar that is 0 or positive. Thus the relevant equations for the univariate exact Kalman filter are (6), (11), and (13). The number of extra flops for case (b) of (13) compared to case (a) is limited to $p^2 + 2p$ in the univariate case.

2.2 Automatic collapse to Kalman filter

In the following it is shown that generally the rank of matrix $\mathbf{P}_{\infty,t+1}$ is equal to the rank of $\mathbf{P}_{\infty,t}$ minus the rank of $\mathbf{F}_{\infty,t}$. Specifically,

$$r(\mathbf{P}_{\infty,t+1}) \le \min\{r(\mathbf{P}_{\infty}, t) - r(\mathbf{F}_{\infty,t}), r(\mathbf{T}_t)\}. \qquad (14)$$

The update for $\mathbf{P}_{\infty,t+1}$ in (11) can be rewritten as

$$\mathbf{P}_{\infty,t+1} = \mathbf{T}_t\mathbf{P}_{\infty,t}^{\dagger}\mathbf{T}_t', \qquad (15)$$

where $\mathbf{P}_{\infty,t}^{\dagger} = \mathbf{P}_{\infty,t} - \mathbf{P}_{\infty,t}\mathbf{Z}_t'\mathbf{F}_{\infty,t}^-\mathbf{Z}_t\mathbf{P}_{\infty,t} = \mathbf{P}_{\infty,t} - \mathbf{P}_{\infty,t}\mathbf{U}_{+,t}\mathbf{U}_{+,t}'\mathbf{P}_{\infty,t}$ with $\mathbf{F}_{\infty,t}^- = \mathbf{J}_{1,t}\mathbf{J}_{1,t}'$ and $\mathbf{U}_{+,t} = \mathbf{Z}_t'\mathbf{J}_{1,t}$; see also Equations (7) and (8). Matrix $\mathbf{P}_{\infty,t}$ is positive semidefinite and can be diagonalized so that matrix $\mathbf{U}_t'\mathbf{P}_{\infty,t}\mathbf{U}_t$ is diagonal with 0 and unity values for some nonsingular matrix $\mathbf{U}_t$. It is clear from (7) that $\mathbf{U}_{+,t}$ is a subset of the columns of $\mathbf{U}_t$. By noting that $r(\mathbf{F}_{\infty,t}) = r(\mathbf{U}_{+,t})$ and applying Lemma 4 of the Appendix to matrix $\mathbf{P}_{\infty,t}$ it follows that $r(\mathbf{P}_{\infty,t}^{\dagger}) = r(\mathbf{P}_{\infty,t}) - r(\mathbf{F}_{\infty,t})$. The proof of (14) is complete, because $r(\mathbf{AB}) \le \min\{r(\mathbf{A}), r(\mathbf{B})\}$ for any matrix $\mathbf{A}$ and $\mathbf{B}$. Finally, it can be easily verified that $m = r(\mathbf{P}_\infty) = \sum_{t=1}^{n} r(\mathbf{F}_{\infty,t})$ for a properly defined state-space model (1) where $r(\mathbf{T}_t) \geq r(\mathbf{P}_{\infty,t}^\dagger)$, for $t = 1, \ldots, n$.

Result (14) ensures that matrix $\mathbf{P}_{\infty,d+1}$ for some time period $d < n$ is 0 and that $\mathbf{P}_t = \mathbf{P}_{*,t}$, for $t = d + 1, \ldots, n$. Thus the Kalman update equations (2) are exact for $t = d + 1, \ldots, n$, because the dependency of $\mathbf{P}_t$ on κ is eliminated after time $t = d$. The set of update equations (11) is termed the exact initial Kalman filter: a relatively simple but general algorithm for computing the exact initialization of the Kalman filter at time $t = d + 1$.

For univariate cases, the initialization period length d is equal to m when no missing observations are present in the initial dataset. When some data points or systematic sequences of data points are missing at the beginning of the dataset (e.g., all January observations are missing in the first 10 years of a monthly dataset), the initialization period d is larger than m. Under these circumstances, cases where $\mathbf{F}_{\infty,t} = \mathbf{Z}_t \mathbf{P}_{\infty,t} \mathbf{Z}_t' = 0$ but with $\mathbf{P}_{\infty,t} \neq 0$ occur, for $t = 1, \ldots, d$.

3 Exact Initial Smoothing

The backward smoothing algorithm (3) is valid for $t = n, \ldots, d + 1$, because the Kalman quantities do not depend on κ. Adjustments for dealing with κ in the initial period $t = d, \ldots, 1$, are derived as follows. The matrices $\mathbf{K}_t$ and $\mathbf{F}_t^{-1}$ in (3) are not multiplied by matrices depending on κ, so it follows from (8) and (12) that they are equal to $\mathbf{K}_{*,t}$ and $\mathbf{F}_{*,t}^-$, as $\kappa \to \infty$. This leads to the exact solution for smoothing; that is,

$$\mathbf{r}_{*,t-1} = \mathbf{Z}_t' \mathbf{F}_{*,t}^- \mathbf{v}_t + \mathbf{L}_{*,t}' \mathbf{r}_{*,t},$$

$$\mathbf{N}_{*,t-1} = \mathbf{Z}_t' \mathbf{F}_{*,t}^- \mathbf{Z}_t + \mathbf{L}_{*,t}' \mathbf{N}_{*,t} \mathbf{L}_{*,t}, \tag{16}$$

with $\mathbf{L}_{*,t} = \mathbf{T}_t - \mathbf{K}_{*,t} \mathbf{Z}_t$, for $t = d, \ldots, 1$. The backward recursions (16) are initialized by $\mathbf{r}_{*,d} = \mathbf{r}_d$ and $\mathbf{N}_{*,d} = \mathbf{N}_d$. It is surprising that the exact initial smoother (16) is the same as the usual smoother (3), as it requires no extra storage or computing.

On the other hand, the smoother adjustments for the diffuse Kalman filter of de Jong (1991) are difficult to implement and are computationally inefficient (see Chu-Chun-Lin and de Jong 1993). This is a strong argument for using the exact initial Kalman filter of Section 2 when dealing with nonstationary time series models. The next section sets out the importance of Kalman filtering and smoothing for maximum likelihood estimation of state-space models.

4 Log-Likelihood Function and Score Vector

The diffuse likelihood function is the likelihood function of $\mathbf{y}$ invariant to the diffuse vector $\boldsymbol{\delta}$, where $\boldsymbol{\delta} \sim \mathrm{N}(0, \kappa \mathbf{I})$ and $\kappa \to \infty$. Specifically, it is the likelihood function of $\mathbf{My}$, where the rank of M is $r(\mathbf{M}) = Nn - m$, $\mathrm{cov}(\mathbf{My}, \boldsymbol{\delta}) = 0$, and $\log |\mathrm{var}(\mathbf{My})| = \sum_{t=1}^{n} \log |\mathbf{F}_t| - m \log |\kappa|$ (see Ansley and Kohn 1985, thm. 5.1, and de Jong 1991, thm. 4.2). The diffuse log-likelihood is formally defined as

$$\log L_\infty(\mathbf{y}) = \log L(\mathbf{y}) + \frac{m}{2} \log |\kappa|, \tag{17}$$

where

$$\log L(\mathbf{y}) = \text{constant} - \frac{1}{2} \sum_{t=1}^{n} \log |\mathbf{F}_t| - \frac{1}{2} \sum_{t=1}^{n} \mathbf{v}_t' \mathbf{F}_t^{-1} \mathbf{v}_t. \tag{18}$$

The likelihood function for state-space models with $\mathbf{P}_\infty = 0$ is given by (18), which follows from the prediction error decomposition (see Schweppe 1965). The exact diffuse log-likelihood function (17) is relevant for nonstationary time series models and, as $\kappa \to \infty$, it can be expressed directly in terms of the initial Kalman filter quantities. First, it follows from (8) that $\sum_{t=1}^{n} \mathbf{v}_t' \mathbf{F}_t^{-1} \mathbf{v}_t = \sum_{t=1}^{n} \mathbf{v}_t' \mathbf{F}_{*,t}^{-} \mathbf{v}_t$ as $\kappa \to \infty$. Also, note that $m = \sum_{t=1}^{n} r(\mathbf{F}_{\infty,t})$ for a properly defined state-space model (1). Applying Theorem 3 of the Appendix to $|\mathbf{F}_t| = |\mathbf{F}_{*,t} + \kappa \mathbf{F}_{\infty,t}|$ and taking logs yields

$$\log |\mathbf{F}_t| - r(\mathbf{F}_{\infty,t}) \log \kappa = -\log |\mathbf{F}_{*,t}^{-} + \mathbf{F}_{\infty,t}^{-}|,$$

so that

$$\log L_\infty(\mathbf{y}) = \text{constant} + \frac{1}{2} \sum_{t=1}^{n} \log |\mathbf{F}_{*,t}^{-} + \mathbf{F}_{\infty,t}^{-}| - \frac{1}{2} \sum_{t=1}^{n} \mathbf{v}_t' \mathbf{F}_{*,t}^{-} \mathbf{v}_t. \tag{19}$$

The definitions of $\mathbf{F}_{*,t}^{-}$ and $\mathbf{F}_{\infty,t}^{-}$ are given below Equation (8), and for the special cases $\mathbf{F}_t^\infty = 0$ and $r(\mathbf{F}_t^\infty) = N$, they are given above Equation (13).

Unknown elements of the system matrices are placed in the hyperparameter vector $\boldsymbol{\psi}$. Maximum likelihood estimation of $\boldsymbol{\psi}$ involves numerical maximization of the diffuse log-likelihood function (19). Quasi-Newton optimization methods require score information (see Gill, Murray and Wright 1981). Koopman and Shephard (1992) showed that the score vector with respect to $\boldsymbol{\psi}$ can be obtained by using an appropriate smoothing algorithm. For example, when the ith element of the hyperparameter vector $\boldsymbol{\psi}$ relates only to entries in $\mathbf{H}_t$ and $\mathbf{H}_t \mathbf{G}_t' = 0$, for $t = 1, \ldots, n$, its score value, evaluated at $\boldsymbol{\psi} = \boldsymbol{\psi}^*$, is given by

$$q_i(\boldsymbol{\psi}^*) = \left. \frac{\partial \log L_\infty(\mathbf{y})}{\partial \boldsymbol{\psi}_i} \right|_{\boldsymbol{\psi} = \boldsymbol{\psi}^*} = \text{tr} \sum_{t=1}^{n} \frac{\partial \mathbf{H}_t}{\partial \boldsymbol{\psi}_i} \mathbf{H}_t' (\mathbf{r}_t \mathbf{r}_t' - \mathbf{N}_t), \tag{20}$$

where $\mathbf{r}_t$ and $\mathbf{N}_t$ are obtained from the smoother (3). System matrix $\mathbf{H}_t$ does not depend on κ, so $\mathbf{r}_t$ and $\mathbf{N}_t$ in (20) can be directly replaced by $\mathbf{r}_{*,t}$ and $\mathbf{N}_{*,t}$ of (16) for $t = d, \ldots, 1$, as $\kappa \to \infty$. It is convenient that nonstationary time series models do not impose a huge computational burden on exact likelihood and score evaluation.

5 Some Examples

5.1 Local-level component model

The univariate time series model with a local level component belongs to the class of unobserved components time series models (see Harrison and Stevens 1976 and Harvey 1989). The model is given by

$$y_t = \mu_t + [\sigma_y \quad 0]\varepsilon_t, \quad \varepsilon_t \sim \text{NID}(0, \mathbf{I}_2),$$
$$\mu_{t+1} = \mu_t + [0 \quad \sigma_\mu]\varepsilon_t, \quad t = 1, \ldots, n, \tag{21}$$

where μ_t is the stochastic time-varying level component and ε_t is the 2×1 vector of disturbances. It is straightforward to represent the local level model as a time-invariant state-space model (1): the (scalar) system matrices $\mathbf{Z}$ and $\mathbf{T}$ are set equal to unity, and $\mathbf{GG}' = \sigma_y^2$ and $\mathbf{HH}' = \sigma_\mu^2$. The initial state is $\alpha_1 \sim \text{N}(0, \kappa)$, where $\kappa \to \infty$. The exact initial Kalman filter starts off with $a_1 = 0$, $P_{*,1} = 0$, and $P_{\infty,1} = 1$. Then the first update is given by

$$v_1 = y_1, \qquad F_{*,1} = \sigma_y^2, \qquad F_{\infty,1} = 1,$$
$$K_{*,1} = 1, \qquad C_{*,1} = -\sigma_y^2, \qquad C_{\infty,1} = 1,$$
$$a_2 = y_1, \qquad P_{*,2} = \sigma_y^2 + \sigma_\mu^2, \qquad P_{\infty,2} = 0.$$

This example for model (21) shows that the initial Kalman filter allows the Kalman filter (2) to start off at $t = 2$ with $a_2 = y_1$ and $P_2 = \sigma_y^2 + \sigma_\mu^2$ (see also Harvey 1989, example 3.2.1).

5.2 Local linear trend component model

The time series model with a local linear trend component is given by

$$y_t = \mu_t + [\sigma_y \quad 0 \quad 0]\varepsilon_t, \quad \varepsilon_t \sim \text{NID}(0, \mathbf{I}_3),$$
$$\mu_{t+1} = \mu_t + \beta_t + [0 \quad \sigma_\mu \quad 0]\varepsilon_t,$$
$$\beta_{t+1} = \beta_t + [0 \quad 0 \quad \sigma_\beta]\varepsilon_t, \quad t = 1, \ldots, n, \tag{22}$$

where the stochastic process μ_t represents a time-varying trend with a time-varying slope term β_t and ε_t is a 3×1 vector of disturbances (see Harvey 1989, sec. 2.3.2). The stochastic trend model (22) can be represented as a time-invariant state-space model, where the state vector is given by $\alpha_t = (\mu_t, \beta_t)'$ and the system matrices are given by

$$\mathbf{Z} = [1 \quad 0], \qquad \mathbf{T} = \begin{bmatrix} 1 & 1 \\ 0 & 1 \end{bmatrix}, \qquad \mathbf{GG}' = \sigma_y^2,$$

$$\mathbf{HH}' = \begin{bmatrix} \sigma_\mu^2 & 0 \\ 0 & \sigma_\beta^2 \end{bmatrix},$$

with $\mathbf{HG}' = 0$. The initial Kalman filter starts off with $\mathbf{a}_1 = 0, \mathbf{P}_{*,1} = 0$, and $\mathbf{P}_{\infty,1} = \mathbf{I}_2$, and the first update is

$$
\mathbf{K}_{*,1} = \begin{bmatrix} 1 \\ 0 \end{bmatrix}, \qquad \mathbf{C}_{*,1} = -\sigma_y^2 \begin{bmatrix} 1 & 0 \\ 0 & 0 \end{bmatrix},
$$

$$
\mathbf{C}_{\infty,1} = \begin{bmatrix} 1 & 0 \\ 0 & 0 \end{bmatrix}, \qquad \mathbf{a}_2 = \begin{bmatrix} y_1 \\ 0 \end{bmatrix},
$$

$$
\mathbf{P}_{*,2} = \sigma_y^2 \begin{bmatrix} 1+q_\mu & 0 \\ 0 & q_\beta \end{bmatrix}, \qquad \mathbf{P}_{\infty,2} = \begin{bmatrix} 1 & 1 \\ 1 & 1 \end{bmatrix},
$$

where $q_\mu = \sigma_\mu^2/\sigma_y^2$ and $q_\beta = \sigma_\beta^2/\sigma_y^2$. Note that the rank of $\mathbf{P}_{\infty,2}$ equals 1. The next update is

$$
\mathbf{K}_{*,2} = \begin{bmatrix} 2 \\ 1 \end{bmatrix}, \qquad \mathbf{C}_{*,2} = -\sigma_y^2 \begin{bmatrix} 4 & 3+q_\mu \\ 3+q_\mu & 2+q_\mu \end{bmatrix},
$$

$$
\mathbf{C}_{\infty,2} = \begin{bmatrix} 4 & 2 \\ 2 & 1 \end{bmatrix}, \qquad \mathbf{a}_3 = \begin{bmatrix} 2y_2 - y_1 \\ y_2 - y_1 \end{bmatrix},
$$

$$
\mathbf{P}_{*,3} = \sigma_y^2 \begin{bmatrix} 5+2q_\mu+q_\beta & 3+q_\mu+q_\beta \\ 3+q_\mu+q_\beta & 2+q_\mu+2q_\beta \end{bmatrix},
$$

$$
\mathbf{P}_{\infty,3} = \begin{bmatrix} 0 & 0 \\ 0 & 0 \end{bmatrix},
$$

such that $\mathbf{P}_3 = \mathbf{P}_{*,3}$. It is shown that the initial Kalman filter lets the usual Kalman filter (2) start at $t = 3$ with the initializations $\mathbf{a}_3$ and $\mathbf{P}_3 = \mathbf{P}_{*,3}$ as given.

5.3 Common-level component model
Consider the bivariate common-level component model

$$
\mathbf{y}_t = \begin{pmatrix} y_{1,t} \\ y_{2,t} \end{pmatrix} = \begin{pmatrix} 0 \\ \bar\mu \end{pmatrix} + \begin{pmatrix} 1 \\ \theta \end{pmatrix} \mu_t + \begin{bmatrix} \sigma_1 & 0 & 0 \\ \sigma_{12} & \sigma_2 & 0 \end{bmatrix} \boldsymbol\varepsilon_t,
$$

$$
\boldsymbol\varepsilon_t \sim \text{NID}(0, \mathbf{I}_3),
$$

$$
\mu_{t+1} = \mu_t + [0 \ \ 0 \ \ \sigma_\mu]\boldsymbol\varepsilon_t, \qquad t = 1, \ldots, n, \tag{23}
$$

where $\boldsymbol\varepsilon_t$ is the 3×1 disturbance vector and $\bar\mu$ is a fixed constant. This model lets both series in $\mathbf{y}_t$ depend on the same underlying trend. The state-space form of the bivariate model is based on the state vector $\boldsymbol\alpha_t = (\mu_t, \bar\mu)'$ with the initial state $\boldsymbol\alpha_1 \sim N(0, \kappa\mathbf{I}_2)$, where $\kappa \to \infty$. Note that the constant $\bar\mu$ is treated as a diffuse random vector. The exact Kalman filter initialization is $\mathbf{a}_1 = 0, \mathbf{P}_{*,1} = 0$, and $\mathbf{P}_{\infty,1} = \mathbf{I}_2$. For simplicity, we set $\sigma_1 = \sigma_2 = 1$ and $\sigma_{12} = 0$ such that $\mathbf{GG}' = \mathbf{I}_2$.

The initial Kalman step is

$$\mathbf{v}_1 = \begin{bmatrix} y_{1,1} \\ y_{2,1} \end{bmatrix}, \qquad \mathbf{F}_{*,1} = \mathbf{I}_2,$$

$$\mathbf{F}_{\infty,1} = \begin{bmatrix} 1 & \theta \\ \theta & 1+\theta^2 \end{bmatrix}, \qquad \mathbf{K}_{*,1} = \begin{bmatrix} 1 & 0 \\ -\theta & 1 \end{bmatrix},$$

$$\mathbf{C}_{*,1} = -\begin{bmatrix} 1 & -\theta \\ -\theta & 1+\theta^2 \end{bmatrix}, \qquad \mathbf{C}_{\infty,1} = \mathbf{I}_2,$$

$$\mathbf{a}_2 = \begin{bmatrix} y_{1,1} \\ y_{2,1} - \theta y_{1,1} \end{bmatrix},$$

$$\mathbf{P}_{*,2} = \begin{bmatrix} 1+\sigma_\mu^2 & -\theta \\ -\theta & 1+\theta^2 \end{bmatrix}, \qquad \mathbf{P}_{\infty,2} = 0.$$

This shows that the Kalman filter (2) can start from $t = 2$ onward.

The restriction $\bar{\mu} = 0$ enforces the ratio of both levels to be constant for all time periods $t = 1, \ldots, n$. The state-space form of the restricted model is given by

$$\mathbf{y}_t = \begin{bmatrix} 1 \\ \theta \end{bmatrix} \alpha_t + \begin{bmatrix} \alpha_1 & 0 & 0 \\ \sigma_{12} & \sigma_2 & 0 \end{bmatrix} \boldsymbol{\varepsilon}_t,$$

$$\alpha_{t+1} = \alpha_t + \begin{bmatrix} 0 & 0 & \sigma_\mu \end{bmatrix} \boldsymbol{\varepsilon}_t, \tag{24}$$

with the scalar state $\alpha_t = \mu_t$ and the initial state $\alpha_1 \sim N(0, \kappa)$, where $\kappa \to \infty$. The intialization is $a_1 = 0$, $P_{*,1} = 0$, and $P_{\infty,1} = 1$. For this case, matrix $\mathbf{F}_{\infty,1}$ is singular; that is, $r(\mathbf{F}_{\infty,1}) = 1$. The initial Kalman step, when $\mathbf{GG}' = \mathbf{I}_2$, is given by

$$\mathbf{v}_1 = \begin{bmatrix} y_{1,1} \\ y_{2,1} \end{bmatrix}, \qquad \mathbf{F}_{*,1} = \mathbf{I}_2, \qquad \mathbf{F}_{\infty,1} = \begin{bmatrix} 1 & \theta \\ \theta & \theta^2 \end{bmatrix},$$

$$\mathbf{J} = \begin{bmatrix} \varphi & -\theta\sqrt{\varphi} \\ \theta\varphi & \sqrt{\varphi} \end{bmatrix}, \qquad \mathbf{F}_{*,1}^- = \varphi \begin{bmatrix} \theta^2 & -\theta \\ -\theta & 1 \end{bmatrix},$$

$$\mathbf{F}_{\infty,1}^- = \varphi^2 \begin{bmatrix} 1 & \theta \\ \theta & \theta^2 \end{bmatrix},$$

$$\mathbf{K}_{*,1} = \varphi[1 \quad \theta], \qquad C_{*,1} = -\varphi, \qquad C_{\infty,1} = 1,$$

$$a_2 = \varphi(y_{1,1} + \theta y_{2,1}), \qquad P_{*,2} = \varphi + \sigma_\mu, \qquad P_{\infty,2} = 0,$$

where $\varphi = (1+\theta^2)^{-1}$. Note that $\mathbf{F}_{\infty,1}\mathbf{F}_{*,1}^- = 0$. Again, the Kalman filter (2) is applied from $t = 2$ onward. (More details on the common trend components model can be found in Harvey and Koopman 1997.)

6 Miscellaneous Issues

This section discusses some practical issues: computational costs, numerical performance of the usual Kalman filter and missing values. These matters are illustrated by using the following unobserved components time series models:

1. Local level model (see Sec. 5 or Harvey 1989, p. 102)
2. Local linear trend model (see Sec. 5 or Harvey 1989, p. 170)
3. Trend model with quarterly seasonals (see Harvey 1989, p. 172)
4. Trend model with monthly seasonals (see Harvey 1989, p. 172)
5. Trend model with stochastic cycle (see Harvey 1989, p. 171)
6. Bivariate local level model (see Harvey and Koopman 1997)
7. Bivariate local linear trend model (see Harvey and Koopman 1997).

6.1 Computational costs

The exact initial Kalman filter requires more computations than the usual Kalman filter. However, after a limited number of updates, the initial Kalman filter reduces to the usual Kalman filter, and no extra computations are required. The additional computations for the initial Kalman filter are caused by the updating of matrix $\mathbf{P}_{\infty,t}$ and the computing of matrices $\mathbf{K}_{*,t}$ and $\mathbf{C}_{*,t}$ when $r(\mathbf{F}_t^{\infty}) \neq 0$, for $t = 1, \ldots, d$. For many practical state-space models, the system matrices $\mathbf{Z}_t$ and $\mathbf{T}_t$ are sparse selection matrices containing many 0s and ones such that the updating of matrix $\mathbf{P}_{\infty,t}$ is computationally cheap. Table 1 reports the number of extra flops (compared to the usual Kalman filter) required for likelihood evaluation using the approach of Section 2 and using the DKF approach of de Jong (1991) as described in Section 1.

The results in Table 1 show that on average, the additional number of computations for the initial Kalman filter is 50% less compared to the additional computational effort for the DKF when the set of models 1–7 is considered. Regarding computation of the score vector, the results in Table 1 for the approach of Section 3 are even more favorable. The initial smoothing algorithm requires no additional computing, whereas the DKF smoothing algorithm needs additional computing for the initial period (see Chu-Chun-Lin and de Jong 1993).

Table 1. Number of extra flops

Model	Initial	Diffuse
Likelihood evaluation		
1. Local level ($N = 1$)	3	7
2. Local linear trend ($N = 1$)	18	46
3. Trend plus cycle ($N = 1$)	60	100
4. Basic seasonal ($s = 4$, $N = 1$)	225	600
5. Basic seasonal ($s = 12$, $N = 1$)	3,549	9,464
7. Local level ($N = 2$)	44	76
8. Local linear trend ($N = 2$)	272	488
Score vector calculation		
1. Local level ($N = 1$)	0	11
2. Local linear trend ($N = 1$)	0	105
4. Basic seasonal ($s = 4$, $N = 1$)	0	1,800

For example, DKF smoothing requires an additional 1,800 flops when it is used to calculate the score vector for a trend model with quarterly seasonals; see Table 1. This will slow down the maximum likelihood estimation of such models considerably.

6.2 Missing values

The initial Kalman filter can deal with any pattern of missing data in the set of observations. For example, the strategy of initializing the Kalman filter for the local linear trend model in Section 5 is still valid when observation 2 is missing. In this case, the Kalman filter (2) starts at $t = 4$ with the initialization

$$\mathbf{a}_4 = \begin{bmatrix} 1.5y_3 - .5y_1 \\ .5y_3 - .5y_1 \end{bmatrix},$$

$$\mathbf{P}_4 = \sigma_y^2 \begin{bmatrix} 2.5 + 1.5q_\mu + 1.25q_\beta & 1 + .5q_\mu + 1.25q_\beta \\ 1 + .5q_\mu + 1.25q_\beta & .5 + .5q_\mu + 2.25q_\beta \end{bmatrix},$$

where $q_\mu = \sigma_\mu^2/\sigma_y^2$ and $q_\beta = \sigma_\beta^2/\sigma_y^2$. The solution can be verified by applying the initial Kalman filter (11). Note that when the full observation vector $\mathbf{y}_t$ is missing, the initial Kalman quantities $\mathbf{K}_t$, $\mathbf{C}_{*,t}$, and $\mathbf{C}_{\infty,t}$ are set to 0.

To illustrate how the initialization deals with missing data, Table 2 considers a univariate time series and a bivariate time series. Missing entries in the time series are indicated by "y." The rank of the matrices $\mathbf{F}_{\infty,t}$ and $\mathbf{P}_{\infty,t}$ for $t = 1, \ldots, n$, are reported for a selection of time series models. Note that $\mathbf{F}_{\infty,t}$ is a scalar in the univariate case.

Table 2 confirms that the initial Kalman filter must be applied as long as the rank of covariance matrix $\mathbf{P}_{\infty,t}$ is larger than 0. The rank of matrix $\mathbf{F}_{\infty,t}$ determines the rank reduction of $\mathbf{P}_{\infty,t+1}$; see Section 2. The conclusion is that the presence of missing values in the initial period does not alter our strategy of initializing the Kalman filter.

6.3 Numerical performance

The initial Kalman filter requires an extra computational effort. It would be computationally more efficient to apply the usual Kalman filter and replace k by some large value k, though this strategy may give numerical inaccuracies and is not an exact solution. Bell and Hillmer (1991) assessed the performance of the large k initialization by comparing the innovation variance of the numerical approach and the exact approach. The performance of the numerical approach can be measured by the statistic

$$\log k \|\mathbf{F}_t^{(k)} - \mathbf{F}_{\infty,t}\|, \quad t = d + 1, \ldots n,$$

where $\mathbf{F}_{\infty,t}$ is the variance matrix $\mathbf{F}_t$ of the Kalman filter with the exact initialization and $\mathbf{F}_t^{(k)}$ is the corresponding $\mathbf{F}_t$ matrix of the Kalman filter with the large k initialization for $t = d + 1, \ldots, n$. Note that $\|\mathbf{A}\|$ denotes the absolute value of the determinant of square matrix $\mathbf{A}$. The statistic should be as negative as possible to

Table 2. Rank reduction when missing observations are present

Univariate Kalman filter

t	1	2	3	4	5	6	7	8	9	10	11	12	13	14	15
Missing	n	y	n	y	n	y	n	n	n	y	n	n	n	n	n
Model 2, 5															
$r(\mathbf{F}_{\infty,t})$	1	0	1	0	0	0	0	0	0	0	0	0	0	0	0
$r(\mathbf{P}_{\infty,t})$	2	1	1	0	0	0	0	0	0	0	0	0	0	0	0
Model 3															
$r(\mathbf{F}_{\infty,t})$	1	0	1	0	1	0	0	1	0	0	0	0	0	1	0
$r(\mathbf{P}_{\infty,t})$	5	4	4	3	3	2	2	2	1	1	1	1	1	1	0

Bivariate Kalman filter

t	1	2	3	4	5
Missing Y_1	n	y	n	n	n
Missing Y_2	y	n	y	n	n
Model 6					
$r(\mathbf{F}_{\infty,t})$	1	1	0	0	0
$r(\mathbf{P}_{\infty,t})$	2	1	0	0	0
Model 7					
$r(\mathbf{F}_{\infty,t})$	1	1	1	1	0
$r(\mathbf{P}_{\infty,t})$	4	3	2	1	0

achieve numerical precision for the usual Kalman filter. The statistic depends on the numerical accuracy of the computer; the most negative value obtained on my Pentium computer was -22.5.

The statistic is calculated for models 1, 2, and 3 with variance matrix $\mathbf{HH}'$ equal to $q\mathbf{I}$, where q is some predetermined value. Figure 1 plots the statistic for model 1 and three different values of q. The choice of k is 10^7, but the statistic is almost invariant to k when $k > 10^4$. Similarly, Figs 2 and 3 are constructed for models 2 and 3. They show that the numerical performance of the usual Kalman filter is unsatisfactory, because most values are too far away from the computer accuracy level of -22.5. Also, the statistic depends very much on the choice of the value q.

7 Conclusions

This article has presented an analytical solution for the initialization of the Kalman filter for state-space models with diffuse initial conditions. The univariate initial Kalman filter is similar to the modified Kalman filter of Ansley and Kohn (1990). However, more efficient and straightforward methods are developed for univariate and multivariate state-space models. The proofs are simple and transparent. Also, it is shown that likelihood and score evaluation for nonstationary time series models

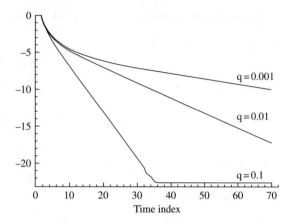

Fig. 1. Numerical accuracy of the Kalman filter for the local level model.

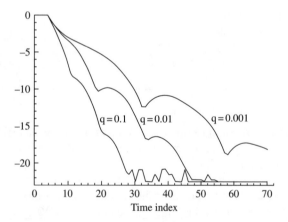

Fig. 2. Numerical accuracy of the Kalman filter for the local trend model.

requires only a small number of extra computations. The new results have important implications for the computational efficiency of statistical algorithms dealing with univariate and multivariate time series models.

Other findings of this article are as follows:

- The alternative solution of de Jong (1991) is computationally less efficient when applied to a wide class of time series models with ARIMA components.
- The performance of the Kalman filter with the diffuse prior replaced by some large value is numerically unsatisfactory.
- The exact initial filtering and smoothing algorithms deal with any pattern of missing data entries in the time series.

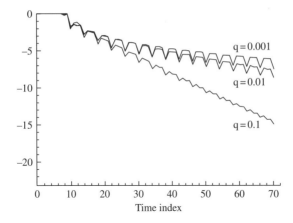

Fig. 3. Numerical accuracy of the Kalman filter for the local level model.

Appendix: Technical Proofs

Notation The dimensionality of vectors or matrices is not given when it is obvious or when it is not relevant. Most of the notation in this article is standard, but a selection is summarized here for convenience:

- The identity matrix is $\mathbf{I}$ and the $m \times m$ identity matrix is $\mathbf{I}_m$.
- The rank of matrix $\mathbf{A}$ is $r(\mathbf{A})$, its determinant is $|\mathbf{A}|$, and its inverse is $\mathbf{A}^{-1}$.
- A block diagonal matrix is denoted by diag $\{\mathbf{A}, \mathbf{B}\}$ with $\mathbf{A}$ and $\mathbf{B}$ both square; psd refers to a symmetric positive (semi) definite matrix.

Lemma 1 Simultaneous Diagonalization of a psd matrix $\mathbf{A}$ and a pd matrix $\mathbf{M}$. Let $\mathbf{A}$ be a $p \times p$ psd matrix and let $\mathbf{M}$ be a $p \times p$ pd matrix. A nonsingular matrix $\mathbf{P}$ and a diagonal positive semidefinite matrix $\mathbf{\Lambda}$ exist so that

$$\mathbf{A} = \mathbf{P}'\mathbf{\Lambda}\mathbf{P}, \qquad \mathbf{M} = \mathbf{P}'\mathbf{P}.$$

It follows that

$$\mathbf{Q}'\mathbf{A}\mathbf{Q} = \mathbf{\Lambda}, \qquad \mathbf{Q}'\mathbf{M}\mathbf{Q} = \mathbf{I}, \qquad \mathbf{M}^{-1} = \mathbf{Q}\mathbf{Q}',$$

where $\mathbf{Q} = \mathbf{P}^{-1}$ (see Magnus and Neudecker 1988, sec. 1.18, them. 23).

Lemma 2 Partial Diagonalization of two psd matrices $\mathbf{A}$ and $\mathbf{B}$. Let $\mathbf{A}$ and $\mathbf{B}$ be two $p \times p$ psd matrices for which $\mathbf{A} + \mathbf{B}$ is pd and $r(\mathbf{B}) = q \leq p$. Then

$$\mathbf{Q}'\mathbf{B}\mathbf{Q} = \begin{bmatrix} \mathbf{I}_q & 0 \\ 0 & 0 \end{bmatrix}, \qquad \mathbf{Q}'\mathbf{A}\mathbf{Q} = \begin{bmatrix} \mathbf{C}_1 & 0 \\ 0 & \mathbf{I}_{p-q} \end{bmatrix},$$

where $\mathbf{Q}$ is nonsingular and $r(\mathbf{C}_1) \leq q$.

Proof Matrix **B** is diagonalized using nonsingular matrix **K**, so

$$\mathbf{K}'\mathbf{BK} = \begin{bmatrix} \mathbf{I}_q & 0 \\ 0 & 0 \end{bmatrix}, \qquad \mathbf{K}'\mathbf{AK} = \begin{bmatrix} \mathbf{E}_1 & \mathbf{E}_{12} \\ \mathbf{E}'_{12} & \mathbf{E}_2 \end{bmatrix},$$

where $r(\mathbf{E}_2) = p - q$ because $r(\mathbf{A} + \mathbf{B}) = p$. Also,

$$\mathbf{L}'\mathbf{K}'\mathbf{AKL} = \begin{bmatrix} \mathbf{C}_1 & 0 \\ 0 & \mathbf{I}_{p-q} \end{bmatrix},$$

where $\mathbf{C}_1$ is a $q \times q$ matrix. The operations with respect to the nonsingular matrix **L** apply only to the last $p - q$ columns and rows of matrix $\mathbf{K}'\mathbf{AK}$, so that matrix **L** has no effect on $\mathbf{K}'\mathbf{BK}$, because the last $p - q$ columns and rows of $\mathbf{K}'\mathbf{BK}$ are 0. Setting $\mathbf{Q} = \mathbf{KL}$ completes the proof (see also Searle (1982), appendix to chap. 11, sec. 2.c, thm. 3).

Lemma 3 Expansion of ratio $1/(1 + y)$. The infinite geometric progression formula is

$$\frac{1}{1 - x} = \sum_{n=0}^{\infty} x^n, \quad |x| < 1.$$

An expansion for

$$\frac{1}{1 + y}, \quad y > 1,$$

is obtained through the identities

$$\frac{1}{1 + y} = 1 + \left(\frac{1}{1 + y} - 1 \right) = 1 - \left(\frac{y}{1 + y} \right) = 1 - \left(\frac{1}{1 + 1/y} \right).$$

Setting $x = -1/y$, it follows that

$$\frac{1}{1 + y} = \frac{1}{y} - \frac{1}{y^2} + \frac{1}{y^3} - \cdots, \quad y > 1.$$

Lemma 4 Rank reduction of a psd matrix **A**. Let **A** be a $p \times p$ psd matrix that can be diagonalized such that $\mathbf{Q}'\mathbf{AQ} = \mathbf{D}$, where **Q** is nonsingular and **D** is diagonal with unity and zero values. Then

$$r(\mathbf{A} - \mathbf{AQ}_+\mathbf{Q}'_+\mathbf{A}) = r(\mathbf{A}) - q,$$

where matrix $\mathbf{Q}_+$ is a subset of columns of **Q** such that $\mathbf{Q}'_+\mathbf{AQ}_+ = \mathbf{I}_q$ and $q \le r(\mathbf{A})$.

Proof Matrix **A** is diagonable, and its rank equals the number of nonzero eigenvalues (see Searle 1982, Appendix to chap. 11, sec. 2b). It follows that $r(\mathbf{A}) = r(\mathbf{Q}'\mathbf{AQ}) = r(\mathbf{D})$, because **Q** is nonsingular. Matrix **Q** can be scaled such that matrix **D** contains only unity and zero values. The rank of **A** is equal to the number of unity values of **D**. The proof is complete, because the diagonal matrix $\mathbf{Q'AQ} - \mathbf{Q'AQ_+Q'_+AQ}$ has q unity values less compared to matrix $\mathbf{D} = \mathbf{Q'AQ}$.

Theorem 1 Expansion of $(\mathbf{A} + \kappa\mathbf{M})^{-1}$ where **A** is a psd matrix and **M** is a pd matrix. Let **A** be a $p \times p$ psd matrix, and let **M** be a $p \times p$ pd matrix. Then

$$(\mathbf{A} + \kappa\mathbf{M})^{-1} = \frac{1}{\kappa}\mathbf{M}^{-1} - \frac{1}{\kappa^2}\mathbf{M}^{-1}\mathbf{AM}^{-1} + O\left(\frac{1}{\kappa^3}\right),$$

with κ large enough.

Proof It follows from Lemma 1 that the inverse of $(\mathbf{A} + \kappa\mathbf{M})$ can be written as

$$(\mathbf{A} + \kappa\mathbf{M})^{-1} = (\mathbf{P'\Lambda P} + \kappa\mathbf{P'P})^{-1}$$
$$= \{\mathbf{P'(\Lambda + \kappa I)P}\}^{-1}$$
$$= \mathbf{Q(\Lambda + \kappa I)}^{-1}\mathbf{Q'},$$

where **P** is nonsingular and $\mathbf{Q} = \mathbf{P}^{-1}$. The diagonal matrix $\mathbf{\Lambda} = \text{diag}(\lambda_1, \ldots, \lambda_p)$ may contain 0s, as it is a psd matrix. Any element $1/(\lambda + \kappa)$ of matrix $(\mathbf{\Lambda} + \kappa\mathbf{I})^{-1}$ can be expanded by using Lemma 3 as

$$\frac{1}{\lambda + \kappa} = \frac{1}{\lambda}\left(\frac{1}{1+y}\right) = \frac{1}{\lambda}\left(\frac{1}{y} - \frac{1}{y^2} = \frac{1}{y^3} - \cdots\right),$$

where $y = \kappa/\lambda$ and $\kappa > \lambda$. Resubstituting y back leads to

$$\frac{1}{\lambda + \kappa} = \frac{1}{\kappa} - \frac{\lambda}{\kappa^2} + \frac{\lambda^2}{\kappa^3} - \cdots,$$

so that

$$(\mathbf{\Lambda} + \kappa\mathbf{I})^{-1} = \frac{1}{k}\mathbf{I} - \frac{1}{\kappa^2}\mathbf{\Lambda} + \frac{1}{\kappa^3}\mathbf{\Lambda}^2 - \cdots.$$

By writing

$$(\mathbf{A} + \kappa\mathbf{M})^{-1} = \mathbf{Q}\left[\frac{1}{\kappa}\mathbf{I} - \frac{1}{\kappa^2}\mathbf{\Lambda} + O\left(\frac{1}{\kappa^3}\right)\right]\mathbf{Q'}$$

and by applying Lemma 1, which states that $\mathbf{QQ'} = \mathbf{M}^{-1}$ and $\mathbf{\Lambda} = \mathbf{Q'AQ}$, the proof is completed. Note that scalar κ must be subject to $\kappa > \max(\lambda_1, \ldots, \lambda_p)$.

Theorem 2 Expansion of $(\mathbf{A}+\kappa\mathbf{B})^{-1}$ where **A** and **B** are psd matrices. Let **A** and **B** be two $p \times p$ psd matrices such that $\mathbf{A}+\kappa\mathbf{B}$ is pd as $\kappa > 0$ and $r(\mathbf{B}) = q \leq p$. Then

$$(\mathbf{A} + \kappa\mathbf{B})^{-1} = \mathbf{A}^- + \frac{1}{\kappa}\mathbf{B}^{-1} - \frac{1}{\kappa^2}\mathbf{B}^-\mathbf{AB}^- + O\left(\frac{1}{\kappa^3}\right),$$

where $\mathbf{A}^- = \mathbf{Q}_2\mathbf{Q}_2'$, $\mathbf{B}^- = \mathbf{Q}_1\mathbf{Q}_1'$, and $\mathbf{Q} = [\mathbf{Q}_1 \quad \mathbf{Q}_2]$ is the partial diagonalization matrix of Lemma 2 so that $r(\mathbf{Q}_1'\mathbf{A}\mathbf{Q}_1) = q$.

Proof Lemma 2 shows that matrix $\mathbf{A} + \mathbf{B}$ can be partially diagonalized by the nonsingular matrix $\mathbf{Q} = [\mathbf{Q}_1 \quad \mathbf{Q}_2]$, where $\mathbf{Q}_1$ is a $p \times q$ matrix and $\mathbf{Q}_2$ is a $p \times p - q$ matrix, so that $r(\mathbf{Q}_1'\mathbf{A}\mathbf{Q}_1) = q$, $\mathbf{Q}_2'\mathbf{A}\mathbf{Q}_2 = \mathbf{I}_{p-q}$, $\mathbf{Q}_1'\mathbf{B}\mathbf{Q}_1 = \mathbf{I}_q$, and

$$\mathbf{Q}\mathbf{Q}' = [\mathbf{Q}_1 \quad \mathbf{Q}_2]\begin{bmatrix} \mathbf{Q}_1' \\ \mathbf{Q}_2' \end{bmatrix} = \mathbf{B}^- + \mathbf{A}^-,$$

with $\mathbf{A}^-$ and $\mathbf{B}^-$ as defined earlier. Define the partial diagonal matrix $\mathbf{C} = \mathbf{Q}'(\mathbf{A} + \kappa\mathbf{B})\mathbf{Q}$, and define the nonsingular matrix $\mathbf{C}_1 = \mathbf{Q}_1'\mathbf{A}\mathbf{Q}_1$. It follows from Lemma 2 that $\mathbf{C} = \mathrm{diag}\{\mathbf{C}_1 + \kappa\mathbf{I}_q, \mathbf{I}_{p-q}\}$, and by applying Theorem 1 to matrix $\mathbf{C}_1 + \kappa\mathbf{I}_q$, we obtain that $\mathbf{C}^{-1} = \mathrm{diag}\{[(1/\kappa)\mathbf{I}_q] - [(1/\kappa^2)\mathbf{C}_1] + O(1/\kappa^3), \mathbf{I}_{p-q}\}$ or

$$\mathbf{C}^{-1} = \begin{bmatrix} 0 & 0 \\ 0 & \mathbf{I}_{p-q} \end{bmatrix} + \frac{1}{\kappa}\begin{bmatrix} \mathbf{I}_q & 0 \\ 0 & 0 \end{bmatrix} - \frac{1}{\kappa^2}\begin{bmatrix} \mathbf{C}_1 & 0 \\ 0 & 0 \end{bmatrix} + O\left(\frac{1}{\kappa^3}\right),$$

with κ large enough. The definition of $\mathbf{C}$ implies that $(\mathbf{A} + \kappa\mathbf{B})^{-1} = \mathbf{Q}\mathbf{C}^{-1}\mathbf{Q}'$, which completes the proof. Note that $\mathbf{Q}_1\mathbf{C}_1\mathbf{Q}_1' = \mathbf{Q}_1\mathbf{Q}_1'\mathbf{A}\mathbf{Q}_1\mathbf{Q}_1' = \mathbf{B}^-\mathbf{A}\mathbf{B}^-$.

Theorem 3 Determinant of $\mathbf{A} + \kappa\mathbf{B}$ where $\mathbf{A}$ and $\mathbf{B}$ are psd matrices. Let $\mathbf{A}$ and $\mathbf{B}$ be two $p \times p$ psd matrices such that $\mathbf{A} + \kappa\mathbf{B}$ is pd as $\kappa > 0$ and $r(\mathbf{B}) = q \leq p$. Then

$$\kappa^{-q}|\mathbf{A} + \kappa\mathbf{B}| \to |\mathbf{A}^- + \mathbf{B}^-|^{-1}, \quad \text{as } \kappa \to \infty,$$

where $\mathbf{A}^- = \mathbf{Q}_2\mathbf{Q}_2'$ and $\mathbf{B}^- = \mathbf{Q}_1\mathbf{Q}_1'$ with matrix $\mathbf{Q} = [\mathbf{Q}_1 \quad \mathbf{Q}_2]$ from Lemma 2 so that $\mathbf{Q}_1'\mathbf{B}\mathbf{Q}_1 = \mathbf{I}_q$.

Proof This result follows from the proof of Theorem 2, because $\mathbf{C} = \mathbf{Q}'(\mathbf{A} + \kappa\mathbf{B})\mathbf{Q} = \mathrm{diag}\{\mathbf{C}_1 + \kappa\mathbf{I}_q, \mathbf{I}_{p-q}\}$ and $\mathbf{Q}\mathbf{Q}' = \mathbf{A}^- + \mathbf{B}^-$, so that

$$\kappa^{-q}|\mathbf{A} + \kappa\mathbf{B}| = \kappa^{-q}|\mathbf{C}||\mathbf{Q}\mathbf{Q}'|^{-1}$$

$$= \kappa^{-q}|\mathbf{C}_1 + \kappa\mathbf{I}_q||\mathbf{A}^- + \mathbf{B}^-|^{-1}$$

$$= |\kappa^{-1}\mathbf{C}_1 + \mathbf{I}_q||\mathbf{A}^- + \mathbf{B}^-|^{-1}.$$

Letting $\kappa \to \infty$ completes the proof.

References

Anderson, B. D. O., and Moore, J. B. (1979), *Optimal Filtering*, Englewood Cliffs, NJ: Prentice-Hall.

Ansley, C. F., and Kohn, R. (1985), "Estimation, Filtering and Smoothing in State Space Models With Incompletely Specified Initial Conditions," *The Annals of Statistics*, 13, 1286–1316.

—— (1990), "Filtering and Smoothing in State Space Models With Partially Diffuse Initial Conditions," *Journal of Time Series Analysis*, 11, 275–293.

Bell, W., and Hillmer, S. (1991), "Initializing the Kalman Filter for Nonstationary Time Series Models," *Journal of Time Series Analysis*, 12, 283–300.

Burridge, P., and Wallis, K. F. (1985), "Calculating the Variance of Seasonally Adjusted Series," *Journal of the American Statistical Association*, 80, 541–552.

Chu-Chun-Lin, S., and de Jong, P. (1993), "A Note on Fast Smoothing," unpublished paper, University of British Columbia, Vancouver.

de Jong, P. (1988), "A Cross-Validation Filter for Time Series Models," *Biometrika*, 75, 594–600.

—— (1991),"The Diffuse Kalman Filter," *The Annals of Statistics*, 19, 1073–1083.

Gill, P. E., Murray, W., and Wright, M. H. (1981), *Practical Optimization*, New York: Academic Press.

Gomez, V., and Maravall, A. (1994), "Estimation, Prediction and Interpolation for Nonstationary Series With the Kalman Filter," *Journal of the American Statistical Association*, 89, 611–624.

Harrison, P. J., and Stevens, C. F. (1976), "Bayesian Forecasting," *Journal of the Royal Statistical Society*, Ser. B, 38, 205–247.

Harvey, A. C. (1989), *Forecasting, Structural Time Series Models and the Kalman Filter*, Cambridge, U.K.: Cambridge University Press.

Harvey, A. C., and Koopman, S. J. (1997), "Multivariate Structural Time Series Models," in *Systematic Dynamics in Economic and Financial Models*, C. Heij, H. Schumacher, B. Hanzon, and C. Praagman (eds.), Chichester, U.K.: Wiley.

Harvey, A. C., and Phillips, G. D. A. (1979), "Maximum Likelihood Estimation of Regression Models With Autoregressive-Moving Average Disturbances," *Biometrika*, 66, 49–58.

Harvey, A. C., and Pierse, R. G. (1984), "Estimating Missing Observations in Economic Time Series," *Journal of the American Statistical Association*, 79, 125–131.

Kitagawa, G. (1981), "A Nonstationary Time Series Model and Its Fitting by a Recursive Filter," *Journal of Time Series Analysis*, 2, 103–116.

Kohn, R., and Ansley, C. F. (1989), "A Fast Algorithm for Signal Extraction, Influence and Cross-Validation in State Space Models," *Biometrika*, 76, 65–79.

Koopman, S. J. (1993), "Disturbance Smoother for State Space Models," *Biometrika*, 80, 117–126.

Koopman, S. J., and Shephard, N. (1992), "Exact Score for Time Series Model in State Space Form," *Biometrika*, 79, 823–826.

Magnus, J. R., and Neudecker, H. (1988), *Matrix Differential Calculus With Applications in Statistics and Econometrics*, Chichester, U.K.: Wiley.

Searle, S. R. (1982), *Matrix Algebra Useful for Statistics*, New York: Wiley.

Schweppe, C. F. (1965), "Evaluation of Likelihood Functions for Gaussian Signals," *IEEE Transactions on Information Theory*, 11, 61–70.

Snyder, R. D., and Saligari, G. R. (1996), "Initialization of the Kalman Filter With Partially Diffuse Initial Conditions," *Journal of Time Series Analysis*, 17, 409–424.

4

Smoothing and Interpolation with the State-Space Model*

PIET DE JONG[†]

A new result dealing with smoothing and interpolation in the state-space model is developed and explored. The result simplifies the derivation of existing smoothing algorithms and provides alternate forms that have analytic and practical computing advantages. The connection to signal extraction and interpolation is explored, and diffuse specifications are considered.

1 Introduction

This article develops and explores a new result dealing with smoothing for state-space models. Smoothing for state-space models arises in areas such as signal extraction (Kohn and Ansley 1987a), maximum likelihood estimation of parameters in the state-space model (Shumway and Stoffer 1982), cross-validation (Ansley and Kohn 1987), and missing-value estimation and interpolation (Kohn and Ansley 1986). Kitagawa (1987) dealt with smoothing for nonlinear processes. A good survey of smoothing results was given by Anderson and Moore (1979).

The advantages of the new smoothing result are as follows.

1. *Statistical.* The result leads to new and practically valuable methods for smoothing, signal extraction, interpolation of data, computation of residuals, deleted residuals, and leverage statistics in the state-space model. The methods apply to all models that can be cast into the state-space form, including autoregressive integrated moving average (ARIMA), structural, multiple ARIMA, and regression models with autoregressive moving average disturbances.
2. *Analytic.* The result leads to substantially improved derivations of existing algorithms and associated expressions.
3. *Computational.* The new algorithms implied by the result are computationally efficient. No matrix inversions are required once the Kalman-filter pass

* Reprinted from *Journal of the American Statistical Association*, "Smoothing and Interpolation with the State Space Model" by P. de Jong, pp. 1085–1088, Vol. 84, No. 408, December 1989. Reproduced here with the permission of the American Statistical Association.

† Piet de Jong is Associate Professor, Faculty of Commerce and Business Administration, University of British Columbia, Vancouver, BC V6T 1Y8, Canada. This research was supported by a grant from the Natural Sciences and Engineering Research Council of Canada.

has been completed. In particular, inverses of the state error covariance matrix are not required.

4. *Degenerate cases are covered.* The case where state error covariance matrices are singular can be handled without modification. The other extreme case, where the state error covariance matrix is arbitrarily large, is handled with minor modifications.

The recursion at the heart of the new result occurs in the work by Bryson and Ho (1969), who provided a variant and used it in fixed-interval smoothing. Kohn and Ansley (1987b) considered a scalar version of the recursion in the context of signal estimation. De Jong (1988a) explores the connection of the recursion to fixed-interval smoothing and cross-validation.

The layout of this article is as follows. Section 2 reviews the state-space model, notation, and the Kalman-filter algorithm. Section 3 presents the new result and some of its consequences. Section 4 considers signal extraction, and Section 5 deals with interpolation. Finally, Section 6 covers smoothing under diffuse specifications. Proofs are contained in the Appendix.

2 The State-Space Model, Kalman Filtering, and Smoothing

The state-space model asserts that observation (column) vectors $y_1, y_2, \ldots, y_n$ are generated according to $y_t = X_t\beta + Z_t\alpha_t + u_t$ and $\alpha_{t+1} = W_t\beta + T_t\alpha_t + v_t$, where for $1 \leq t \leq n$, the u_t and v_t are mutually and serially uncorrelated zero-mean random-noise vectors with finite covariance matrices $\sigma^2 U_t$ and $\sigma^2 V_t$, respectively. The X_t, Z_t, W_t, and T_t are nonrandom matrices. In addition, $\alpha_1 = W_0\beta + v_0$, where W_0 is nonrandom and v_0 has mean 0 and finite covariance matrix $\sigma^2 V_0$, and v_0 is uncorrelated with u_t and v_t ($1 \leq t \leq n$). The vector β is a vector of fixed parameters.

The notation $[y_1, y_2, \ldots, y_n]$ denotes the space of all linear combinations of the components of $y_1, y_2, \ldots, y_n$ and the degenerate random variable 1. The minimum mean square linear estimator, or projection, of a random variable x, given $y_1, y_2, \ldots, y_n$, is the element $\tilde{x}$ of $[y_1, y_2, \ldots, y_n]$ such that $E\{(x - \tilde{x})^2\}$ is minimum. The vector of the projections of the components of a random vector x onto a space is denoted by $\tilde{x}$, whereas $\text{MSE}(\tilde{x}) \equiv \text{cov}(x - \tilde{x}) = E[(x - \tilde{x})(x - \tilde{x})']$, where (as throughout this article) expectations and covariances are unconditional. More generally, if $\tilde{x}$ and $\tilde{z}$ are two vectors of projections, then $\text{MSE}(\tilde{x}, \tilde{z}) \equiv \text{cov}\{(x - \tilde{x})(z - \tilde{z})'\}$; $E\{(x - \tilde{x})\tilde{x}'\} = 0$, and hence $\text{MSE}(\tilde{x}) = E\{(x - \tilde{x})x'\}$.

The Kalman filter is the recursion

$$e_t = y_t - X_t\beta - Z_t\hat{\alpha}_t, \quad D_t = Z_t P_t Z_t' + U_t, \quad K_t = T_t P_t Z_t' D_t^{-1},$$

$$\hat{\alpha}_{t+1} = W_t\beta + T_t\hat{\alpha}_t + K_t e_t, \quad L_t = T_t - K_t Z_t,$$

$$P_{t+1} = T_t P_t L_t' + V_t, \tag{2.1}$$

where $\hat{\alpha}_1 = W_0\beta$ and $P_1 = V_0$. Here $\hat{\alpha}_t$ is the projection of α_t onto $[y_1, y_2, \ldots, y_{t-1}]$, $\text{MSE}(\hat{\alpha}_t) = \sigma^2 P_t$, $e_t = y_t - \hat{y}_t$ is the error of the projection of y_t onto $[y_1, y_2, \ldots, y_{t-1}]$, and $\sigma^2 D_t = \text{cov}(e_t) \equiv \text{MSE}(\hat{y}_t)$. See Anderson and

Table 1. Projection notation for α_t

Projection	Space projected on
$\tilde{\alpha}_{t\mid m}$	$[y_1, y_2, \ldots, y_m]$
$\hat{\alpha}_t \equiv \tilde{\alpha}_{t\mid t-1}$	$[y_1, y_2, \ldots, y_{t-1}]$
$\tilde{\alpha}_t \equiv \tilde{\alpha}_{t\mid n}$	$[y_1, y_2, \ldots, y_n]$
$\mathring{\alpha}_t$	$[y_1, y_2, \ldots, y_{t-1}, y_{t+1}, \ldots, y_n]$

Moore (1979) for proof. It is assumed that the covariance matrix of the stack of the vectors $y_1, y_2, \ldots, y_n$ is non-singular. This implies that the D_t matrices are nonsingular and that all of the quantities in (2.1) are well defined.

Smoothing refers to constructing the projection of α_t onto $[y_1, y_2, \ldots, y_n]$, where $1 \leq t \leq n$. The fixed-interval smoothing algorithm supposes that n is fixed and t varies. With fixed-point smoothing t remains fixed and n increases. With fixed-lag smoothing t and n both vary, but in such a way that the difference, or lag, $n - t$ remains fixed. Signal extraction deals with constructing projections of the signal $x_t \equiv X_t\beta + Z_t\alpha_t$. Interpolation deals with constructing the projection α_t, y_t, or x_t onto $[y_1, \ldots, y_{t-1}, y_{t+1}, \ldots, y_n]$.

Table 1 indicates projection notation used throughout. The notation displayed is for α_t but applies equally to y_t or the signal x_t.

A well-known intermediate result used in this article is as follows.

Lemma 1 For $1 \leq t \leq s$, $\text{MSE}(\hat{\alpha}_t, \hat{\alpha}_s) = \text{MSE}(\tilde{\alpha}_{t\mid s-1}, \hat{\alpha}_s) = \sigma^2 P_t L'_{s-1,t}$, where $L_{t-1,t} \equiv I$ and $L_{st} \equiv L_s \cdots L_t$.

3 A New Smoothing Result

The next result is crucial. Despite its usefulness, and the simplicity of both its statement and proof, the general case appears not to have been noticed in the literature before.

Theorem 1 Suppose that $1 \leq t, s \leq m + 1$, where $m \leq n$. Then,

$$\tilde{\alpha}_t = \tilde{\alpha}_{t\mid m} + P_t L'_{mt} r_m$$

$$\text{MSE}(\tilde{\alpha}_t, \tilde{\alpha}_s) = \text{MSE}(\tilde{\alpha}_{t\mid m}, \tilde{\alpha}_{s\mid m}) - \sigma^2 P_t L'_{mt} R_m L_{ms} P_s, \tag{3.1}$$

where $r_n = 0$, $R_n = 0$, and for $1 \leq t \leq n$,

$$r_{t-1} = Z'_t D_t^{-1} e_t + L'_t r_t,$$

$$R_{t-1} = Z'_t D_t^{-1} Z_t + L'_t R_t L_t. \tag{3.2}$$

The proof (given in the Appendix) is short and direct. The expression for $\tilde{\alpha}_t$ can be put together from material of Anderson and Moore (1979, pp. 121, 189) after noting the recursive nature of r_t. Immediate consequences of Theorem 1 are detailed in Sections 3.1–3.5.

3.1 Fixed-interval smoothing

Suppose that in Theorem 1 $m = t - 1$ and $t = s$. Then, (3.1) becomes

$$\tilde{\alpha}_t = \hat{\alpha}_t + P_t r_{t-1}, \qquad \mathrm{MSE}(\tilde{\alpha}_t) = \sigma^2 (P_t - P_t R_{t-1} P_t), \qquad (3.3)$$

since $L_{t-1,t} \equiv I$. Bryson and Ho (1969) stated a related result without proof, whereas De Jong (1988a) proves (3.3) by involved arguments.

A further specialization is to assume $m = t - 1$ and $t = s = n$, which proves the well-known relations $\hat{\alpha}_{t|t} = \hat{\alpha}_t + P_t Z_t' D_t^{-1} e_t$ and $\mathrm{MSE}(\hat{\alpha}_{t|t}) = \sigma^2 (P_t - P_t Z_t' D_t^{-1} Z_t P_t)$.

3.2 Classic fixed-interval smoothing

Suppose that in Theorem 1 $m = t = s$. Then, (3.1) reduces to

$$\tilde{\alpha}_t = \tilde{\alpha}_{t|t} + P_t L_t' r_t, \qquad \mathrm{MSE}(\tilde{\alpha}_t) = \mathrm{MSE}(\tilde{\alpha}_{t|t}) - \sigma^2 P_t L_t' R_t L_t P_t, \qquad (3.4)$$

where $P_t L_t' = P_t (T_t - K_t Z_t)' = (P_t - P_t Z_t' D_t^{-1} Z_t P_t) T_t'$. From (3.3), $r_t = P_{t+1}^{-1}(\tilde{\alpha}_{t+1} - \hat{\alpha}_{t+1})$ and $R_t = P_{t+1}^{-1}\{P_{t+1} - \mathrm{MSE}(\tilde{\alpha}_{t+1})\} P_{t+1}^{-1}$, and after defining $C_t = \sigma^{-2} \mathrm{MSE}(\tilde{\alpha}_{t|t}) T_t' P_{t+1}^{-1}$, substituting yields

$$\tilde{\alpha}_t = \tilde{\alpha}_{t|t} + C_t (\tilde{\alpha}_{t+1} - \hat{\alpha}_{t+1}),$$

$$\mathrm{MSE}(\tilde{\alpha}_t) = \mathrm{MSE}(\tilde{\alpha}_{t|t}) + C_t \{\mathrm{MSE}(\tilde{\alpha}_{t+1}) - \sigma^2 P_{t+1}\} C_t'. \qquad (3.5)$$

The equations in (3.5) constitute the classic fixed-interval smoothing algorithm. Note that the expression for C_t assumes that P_{t+1} is nonsingular.

Original proofs of (3.5) were long and messy until Ansley and Kohn (1982) gave a clever proof. The previous proof is even more straightforward.

A comparison of (3.3) with (3.5) shows that (3.3) requires no matrix inversions once the forward Kalman-filter pass has been completed. Thus the algorithm in (3.3) avoids the inversion of possibly very large matrices and can handle the practically important case where P_t is singular. The disadvantage of (3.3) compared with (3.5) is that it makes slightly higher storage demands. Thus in addition to $\hat{\alpha}_t$ and P_t, the quantities e_t, D_t^{-1}, and L_t are stored on the forward pass. If y_t is scalar, then these additional quantities are two scalars and a vector, with dimension equal to that of the state vector.

3.3 Fixed-point smoothing

Suppose that it Theorem 1 $m = n - 1$ and $t = s$. Then,

$$\tilde{\alpha}_t = \tilde{\alpha}_{t|n-1} + P_t L_{n-1,t}' Z_n' D_n^{-1} e_n$$

and

$$\mathrm{MSE}(\tilde{\alpha}_t) = \mathrm{MSE}(\tilde{\alpha}_{t|n-1}) - \sigma^2 P_t L_{n-1,t}' Z_n' D_n^{-1} Z_n L_{n-1,t} P_t.$$

This is the fixed-point smoothing algorithm, where t is fixed but the sample size n is increasing. Implementation requires the concurrent calculation of e_n, D_n, and L_n via (2.1), and the accumulation of the factor $L_{n-1,t} P_t$.

3.4 Fixed-lag smoothing

From (3.2), it follows that

$$r_{t|n+1} = r_{t-1} - Z_t' D_t^{-1} e_t + L_{n,t+1}' Z_{n+1}' D_{n+1}^{-1} e_{n+1}$$

and

$$R_{t|n+1} = R_{t-1} - Z_t' D_t^{-1} Z_t + L_{n,t+1}' Z_{n+1}' D_{n+1}^{-1} Z_{n+1} L_{n,t+1},$$

where the second subscripts on r_t and R_t emphasize dependence on the sample size. These two equations update r_{t-1} and R_{t-1} as both n and t increase. The quantities $r_{t|n+1}$ and $R_{t|n+1}$ in turn are used to compute $\tilde{\alpha}_{t+1|n+1}$ and $\text{MSE}(\tilde{\alpha}_{t+1|n+1})$ via (3.3).

The equations perform fixed-lag smoothing, since n and t vary in such a way that their difference, or lag, $n - t$ remains fixed. Implementation requires the concurrent calculation and storage of $\hat{\alpha}_{n+1}$, P_{n+1}, e_{n+1}, and D_{n+1}, and the successive computation of the factors $L_{n,t+1}$. If L_t is nonsingular, then this can be done recursively, since $L_{n,t+1} = L_n L_{n-1,t} L_t^{-1}$.

3.5 Covariances between smoothed estimates

If $m = s - 1$, the MSE expression in (3.1) yields for $1 \leq t, s \leq n + 1$, where $t < s$,

$$\text{MSE}(\tilde{\alpha}_t, \tilde{\alpha}_s) = \text{MSE}(\hat{\alpha}_t, \hat{\alpha}_s) - \text{MSE}(\hat{\alpha}_t, \hat{\alpha}_s) R_{s-1} \text{MSE}(\hat{\alpha}_s)$$
$$= \sigma^2 P_t L_{s-1,t}' (I - R_{s-1} P_s).$$

This formula is more efficient then the one given in De Jong and MacKinnon (1988). When $s = n + 1$, the expression yields the result of Lemma 1, since $R_n = 0$. When $s = t - 1$, then $\text{MSE}(\tilde{\alpha}_t, \tilde{\alpha}_{t-1}) = \sigma^2 P_t (I - R_{t-2} P_{t-1})$.

Further applications of Theorem 1 are to signal extraction, interpolation, and smoothing where β has an arbitrarily large covariance matrix. These applications are dealt with in Sections 4–6. These sections employ the notation and results of the following lemma.

Lemma 2 For $1 \leq t \leq n$, define $n_t \equiv D_t^{-1} e_t - K_t' r_t$, $N_t \equiv D_t^{-1} + K_t' R_t K_t$, and $M_t \equiv L_t' R_t K_t - Z_t' D_t^{-1}$. Then, for $1 \leq t, s \leq n$ with $t < s$, $\text{cov}(n_t) = \sigma^2 N_t$, $\text{cov}(\alpha_t, n_t) = -\sigma^2 P_t M_t$, and $\text{cov}(n_t, n_s) = \sigma^2 K_t' L_{s-1,t+1}' M_s \equiv \sigma^2 N_{ts}$.

4 Signal Extraction

Signal extraction refers to estimating the signal $x_t \equiv X_t \beta + Z_t \alpha_t$ ($1 \leq t \leq n$). The projection $\tilde{x}_t$ of x_t onto $[y_1, y_2, \ldots, y_n]$ is clearly $X_t \beta + Z_t \tilde{\alpha}_t$. For many models, the dimension of x_t is less than that of α_t, in which case there is a more efficient way of computing $\tilde{x}_t$ than first finding $\tilde{\alpha}_t$ and then $X_t\beta + Z_t\tilde{\alpha}_t$. This is important for computing regression-type diagnostics for state-space models where the residual $y_t - \tilde{x}_t$ is required.

Theorem 2 Using the notation of Lemma 2, for $1 \le t, s \le n$ with $t < s$, $\tilde{x}_t = y_t - U_t n_t$, $\text{MSE}(\tilde{x}_t) = \sigma^2(U_t - U_t N_t U_t)$, and $\text{MSE}(\tilde{x}_t, \tilde{x}_s) = -\sigma^2(U_t N_{ts} U_s)$.

Kohn and Ansley (1987b) stated a scalar version of Theorem 2 together with the recursion (3.2). De Jong (1988a) proves a similar result by less direct methods.

Theorem 3 Define a matrix A with diagonal blocks $I - U_t N_t (1 \le t \le n)$ and off-diagonal blocks (t, s) equal to $-U_t N_{ts}$, and suppose that $\tilde{x}$ and y are (respectively) the stacks of $\tilde{x}_t$ and $y_t (1 \le t \le n)$. Then, $\tilde{x} = Ay + (I - A)E(y)$ and $\text{MSE}(\tilde{x}) = AU$, where U is block diagonal with diagonal blocks $U_t (1 \le t \le n)$.

The matrix A is called the *influence matrix* and displays the weights of the components of y in the signal estimate $\tilde{x}$. Diagonal elements of A, and hence $I - U_t N_t (1 \le t \le n)$, are called *leverages*, as in regression. In an article that appeared after this article was submitted, Kohn and Ansley (1989) developed and discussed a similar result for scalar time series.

5 Interpolation

Interpolation is the procedure where y_t, x_t, or α_t are projected onto the space $[y_1, y_2, \ldots, y_{t-1}, y_{t+1}, \ldots, y_n]$. Denote these projections $\grave{y}_t$, $\grave{\alpha}_t$, and $\grave{x}_t$. A deleted residual is of the form $y_t - \grave{y}_t$ and indicates the error when predicting a given data point from all other data. Deleted residuals are important for regression-type diagnostics.

Theorem 4 For $1 \le t \le r \le n$, $\grave{y}_t = y_t - N_t^{-1} n_t$, $\text{MSE}(\grave{y}_t) = \sigma^2 N_t^{-1}$, and $\text{MSE}(\grave{y}_t, \grave{y}_s) = \sigma^2 N_t^{-1} N_{ts} N_s^{-1}$.

A related scalar version of this result was displayed by Kohn and Ansley (1987), whereas De Jong (1988a) proves the aforementioned result in a less direct manner. It follows from Theorem 4 that $\grave{x}_t = \grave{y}_t$ and $\text{MSE}(\grave{x}_t) = \sigma^2(N_t^{-1} - U_t)$. Theorems 3 and 4 combine to show that the ordinary and deleted residual are related as $y_t - \tilde{x}_t = U_t N_t (y_t - \grave{y}_t)$. Theorem 4 and its proof also imply the relation

$$\{y - E(y)\}' W^{-2} \{y - E(y)\} / \{\text{tr}(W^{-1})\}^2 = \sum_{t=1}^{n} n_t' n_t \bigg/ \left\{ \sum_{t=1}^{n} \text{tr}(N_t) \right\}^2,$$

where $\sigma^2 W = \text{cov}(y)$. The expression is called the *cross-validation criterion*.

Theorem 5 For $1 \le t, s \le n$, $\grave{\alpha}_t = \tilde{\alpha}_t + P_t M_t N_t^{-1} n_t$, and $\text{MSE}(\grave{\alpha}_t, \grave{\alpha}_s) = \text{MSE}(\tilde{\alpha}_t, \tilde{\alpha}_s) + \sigma^2 P_t M_t N_t^{-1} N_{ts} N_s^{-1} M_s' P_s$.

6 Diffuse Smoothing

Smoothing algorithms such as the Kalman filter depend on $\hat{\alpha}_1 = W_0\beta$ and $P_1 = V_0$. This section deals with a diffuse specification for β; that is, the case where β is assumed random with an arbitrarily large covariance matrix. This specification arises when the model is nonstationary or β is unknown.

To model diffuseness, suppose that $\beta = b + B\delta$, where b is a fixed vector, B is a fixed matrix of full column rank, and δ is a random vector unrelated to the v_t and u_t, and with nonsingular covariance matrix $\sigma^2 \Sigma$. A diffuse specification results when $\Sigma \to \infty$, meaning that Σ^{-1} converges to a 0 matrix in the Euclidean norm. A *diffuse projection* is the Euclidean limit (if it exists) of a projection as $\Sigma \to \infty$.

Diffuse projections and their associated limiting mean squared errors can be constructed using a slightly extended form of the Kalman filter, called the *diffuse Kalman filter*. The diffuse Kalman filter differs from (2.1) in that the vector recursion for e_t and $\hat{\alpha}_t$ are replaced by matrix recursions $E_t = (y_t - X_t b, X_t B) - Z_t A_t$ and $A_{t+1} = W_t(b, -B) + T_t A_t + K_t E_t$, and the addition of the matrix recursion $Q_t = Q_{t-1} + E_t' D_t^{-1} E_t$. Here $A_1 = W_0(b, -B)$, $P_1 = V_0$, and $Q_0 = 0$ is a square matrix of dimension equal to that of δ. The matrix Q_t, for $1 \leq t \leq n$, is partitioned as follows:

$$Q_t = \begin{vmatrix} q_t & s_t' \\ s_t & S_t \end{vmatrix},$$

where q_t is scalar.

In terms of the previously given notation, the diffuse projections of δ and β onto the space $[y_1, y_2, \ldots, y_n]$ are (respectively) $S_n^{-1} s_n \equiv \tilde{\delta}$ and $b + B\tilde{\delta}$, where it is assumed that S_n is nonsingular, which is a sufficient condition for the existence of diffuse projections onto the space $[y_1, y_2, \ldots, y_n]$. Details are in De Jong (1988b). Diffuse projection formulas for α_t, y_t, and the signal x_t are directly derived from Theorems 1–5, combined with the results in De Jong (1988b). The following is a typical result.

Theorem 6 Assume that S_n is nonsingular, and put $\tilde{\delta} \equiv S_n^{-1} s_n$. Suppose that $1 \leq t \leq n$. Then, as $\Sigma \to \infty$ the Euclidean limits of $\tilde{\alpha}_t$ and $\text{MSE}(\tilde{\alpha}_t, \tilde{\alpha}_s)$, where $1 \leq t \leq s \leq n + 1$, are (respectively) $(A_t + P_t G_t)(1, -\tilde{\delta}')'$ and $P_t L_{s-1,t}'(I - R_{s-1} P_s) + G_{t2} S_n^{-1} G_{s2}'$, where G_t is the matrix extension of the recursion for r_t in (3.2), namely $G_{t-1} \equiv Z_t' D_t^{-1} E_t + L_t' G_t$ with $G_n = 0$, and G_{t2} is all but the first column of G_t.

Appendix: Proofs

Lemma 1 The first equality follows directly. The second follows since $\alpha_s - \hat{\alpha}_s = L_{s-1}(\alpha_{s-1} - \hat{\alpha}_{s-1}) + v_{s-1} - K_{s-1} u_{s-1}$, where $\alpha_t - \hat{\alpha}_t$, v_{s-1}, and u_{s-1} are uncorrelated. Hence $\text{MSE}(\hat{\alpha}_t, \hat{\alpha}_s) = \text{cov}(\alpha_t - \hat{\alpha}_t, \alpha_{s-1} - \hat{\alpha}_{s-1}) L_{s-1}' = \text{MSE}(\hat{\alpha}_t, \hat{\alpha}_{s-1}) L_{s-1}'$. Iterating this expression yields the required result.

Theorem 1 Since $[y_1, y_2, \ldots, y_n] = [y_1, \ldots, y_m, e_{m+1}, \ldots, e_n]$,

$$\tilde{\alpha}_t = \tilde{\alpha}_{t|m} + \sigma^{-2} \sum_{s=m+1}^{n} \text{cov}(\alpha_t, e_s) D_s^{-1} e_s,$$

$$= \tilde{\alpha}_{t|m} + P_t(L_m \cdots L_t)'(Z'_{m+1} D_{m+1}^{-1} e_{m+1}$$

$$+ L'_{m+1} Z'_{m+2} D_{m+2}^{-1} e_{m+2} + \cdots)$$

$$= \tilde{\alpha}_{t|m} + P_t L'_{mt} r_m,$$

as required. To prove the MSE formula, note that $\text{cov}(r_m) = \sigma^2 R_m$, and from the just-established relation, $\text{MSE}(\tilde{\alpha}_t, \tilde{\alpha}_s) = \text{cov}(\alpha_t, \alpha_s - \tilde{\alpha}_{s|m}) - \text{cov}(\alpha_t, r_m) L_{ms} P_s$, with $\text{cov}(\alpha_t, r_m) = \text{cov}(\alpha_t - \tilde{\alpha}_t + \tilde{\alpha}_t, r_m) = \text{cov}(\tilde{\alpha}_{t|m} + P_t L'_{mt} r_m, r_m) = \sigma^2 P_t L'_{mt} R_m$. Substituting back into the expression for $\text{MSE}(\tilde{\alpha}_t, \tilde{\alpha}_s)$ yields the stated result.

Lemma 2 $\text{cov}(n_t) = \sigma^2 N_t$, follows since e_t and r_t are uncorrelated. If $t < s$, then $\text{cov}(n_t, n_s) = \text{cov}(D_t^{-1} e_t - K'_t r_t, D_s^{-1} e_s - K'_s r_s) = -K'_t \text{cov}(r_t, e_s) D_s^{-1} + K'_t \text{cov}(r_t, r_s) K_s = -\sigma^2 K'_t L'_{s-1,t+1}(Z'_s D_s^{-1} - L'_s R_s K_s)$. Finally, $\text{cov}(\alpha_t, n_t) = \text{cov}(\alpha_t, e_t) D_t^{-1} - \text{cov}(\alpha_t, r_t) K_t = \sigma^2 P_t(Z'_t D_t^{-1} - L'_t R_t K_t)$.

Theorem 2 From the first relation in (3.3), $y_t - X_t \beta - Z_t \tilde{\alpha}_t = e_t - Z_t P_t r_{t-1} = U_t n_t$, where the final equality follows after manipulation. Thus $U_t n_t - (x_t - \tilde{x}_t) = u_t$ and $\text{cov}(u_t, u_s) = \text{cov}\{U_t n_t - (x_t - \tilde{x}_t), U_s n_s - (x_s - \tilde{x}_s)\} = U_t \text{cov}(n_t, n_s) U_s + \text{MSE}(\tilde{x}_t, \tilde{x}_s)$. Applying Lemma 2 completes the proof.

Theorem 3 Put $\text{cov}(y) = \sigma^2 W$ and $B = I - U W^{-1}$. Then, $\tilde{x} = E(x) + \sigma^{-2}\text{cov}(x, y)W^{-1}\{y - E(y)\} = E(y) + (W - U)W^{-1}\{y - E(y)\} = By + (I - B)E(y)$, and $\text{MSE}(\tilde{x}) = \text{cov}(x, x - \tilde{x}) = \sigma^2(W - U) - \text{cov}(x, y)B' = \sigma^2(W - U)(I - B') = \sigma^2(U - U W^{-1} U) = \sigma^2 B U$. From Theorem 2, the diagonal and off-diagonal blocks of $\text{MSE}(\tilde{x})$ are $\sigma^2(U_t - U_t N_t U_t)$ and $-\sigma^2 U_t N_{ts} U_s$ $(1 \le t \le s \le n)$, respectively, implying $B = A$.

Theorem 4 As in the proof of Theorem 3, $\tilde{x} = y - U W^{-1}\{y - E(y)\}$. It is well known that $W^{-1}\{y - E(y)\}$ has vector component t equal to $\sigma^2\{\text{MSE}(\tilde{y}_t)\}^{-1}(y_t - \tilde{y}_t)$. Thus $\tilde{x}_t = y_t - \sigma^2 U_t\{\text{MSE}(\tilde{y}_t)\}^{-1}(y_t - \tilde{y}_t)$, which together with Theorem 2 yields $\tilde{y}_t = y_t - \sigma^{-2}\text{MSE}(\tilde{y}_t)n_t$. Thus $\text{MSE}(\tilde{y}_t, \tilde{y}_s) = \sigma^{-4}\text{MSE}(\tilde{y}_t)\text{cov}(n_t, n_s)\text{MSE}(\tilde{y}_s)$ which, using Lemma 2, completes the proof.

Theorem 5 Since $[y_1, y_2, \ldots, y_n] = [y_1, \ldots, y_{t-1}, y_{t+1}, \ldots, y_n, y_t - \tilde{y}_t]$, it follows that $\tilde{\alpha}_t = \grave{\alpha}_t + \sigma^{-2}\text{cov}(\alpha_t, y_t - \grave{y}_t)N_t(y_t - \grave{y}_t) = \grave{\alpha}_t + \sigma^{-2}\text{cov}(\alpha_t, n_t)N_t^{-1}n_t = \grave{\alpha}_t - P_t M_t N_t^{-1}n_t$. The expression for $\text{MSE}(\grave{\alpha}_t, \grave{\alpha}_s)$ follows by noting that a $\alpha_t - \tilde{\alpha}_t$ and n_s are uncorrelated.

References

Anderson, B. D. O., and Moore, J. B. (1979), *Optimal Filtering*, Englewood Cliffs, NJ: Prentice-Hall.

Ansley, C. F., and Kohn, R. (1982), "A Geometrical Derivation of the Fixed Interval Smoothing Algorithm," *Biometrika*, 69, 486–487.

—— (1987), "Efficient Generalized Cross-Validation for State Space Models," *Biometrika*, 74, 139–148.

Bryson, A. E., and Ho, Y. (1969), *Applied Optimal Control*, Waltham, MA: Blaisdell.

De Jong, P. (1988a), "A Cross Validation Filter for Time Series Models," *Biometrika*, 75, 594–600.

—— (1988b), "The Diffuse Kalman Filter," unpublished manuscript.

De Jong, P., and MacKinnon, M. (1988), "Covariances for Smoothed Estimates in State Space Models," *Biometrika*, 75, 601–602.

Kitagawa, G. (1987), "Non-Gaussian State-Space Modeling of Nonstationary Time Series" (with discussion), *Journal of the American Statistical Association*, 82, 1032–1063.

Kohn, R., and Ansley, C. F. (1986), "Estimation, Prediction, and Interpolation for ARIMA Models With Missing Data," *Journal of the American Statistical Association*, 81, 751-761.

—— (1987a), "Signal Extraction for Finite Nonstationary Time Series," *Biometrika*, 74, 411–421.

—— (1987b), "A Fast Algorithm for Smoothing, Cross-Validation and Influence in State Space Models," in *Proceedings of the Business and Economic Statistics Section, American Statistical Association,* pp. 106–112.

—— (1989), "A Fast Algorithm for Signal Extraction, Influence and Cross-Validation in State Space Models," *Biometrika*, 76, 65–79.

Shumway, R. H., and Stoffer, D. S. (1982), " An Approach to Time Series Smoothing and Forecasting Using the EM Algorithm," *Journal of Time Series Analysis*, 3, 253–264.

5

Diagnostic Checking of Unobserved-Components Time Series Models*

ANDREW C. HARVEY AND SIEM JAN KOOPMAN
Department of Statistics, London School of Economics

Diagnostic checking of the specification of time series models is normally carried out
using the innovations—that is, the one-step-ahead prediction errors. In an unobserved-
components model, other sets of residuals are available. These auxiliary residuals are
estimators of the disturbances associated with the unobserved components. They can
often yield information that is less apparent from the innovations, but they suffer from
the disadvantage that they are serially correlated even in a correctly specified model
with known parameters. This article shows how the properties of the auxiliary residuals
may be obtained, how they are related to each other and to the innovations, and how
they can be used to construct test statistics. Applications are presented showing how
residuals can be used to detect and distinguish between outliers and structural change.

Diagnostic checking of the specification of a time series model is normally carried out using the innovations—that is, the one-step-ahead prediction errors. In an unobserved-components model, other residuals are available. These *auxiliary residuals* are estimators of the disturbances associated with the unobserved components. The auxiliary residuals are functions of the innovations, but they present the information in a different way. This can lead to the discovery of features of a fitted model that are not apparent from the innovations themselves. Unfortunately, the auxiliary residuals suffer from the disadvantage that they are serially correlated, even in a correctly specified model with known parameters. The purpose of this article is to show how the properties of auxiliary residuals may be obtained, how they are related to each other and to the innovations, and how they can be used to construct test statistics. The methods extend straightforwardly to models containing observed explanatory variables.

Section 1 derives the properties of the auxiliary residuals using the classical approach based on a doubly infinite sample. This follows Maravall (1987), except that in his article attention is restricted to the irregular component in the decomposition of an autoregressive integrated moving average (ARIMA) model. Although we initially give general results, our main interest lies in structural time series models since, in our view, these models provide the most satisfactory framework for exploring issues concerning outliers and structural change. Structural time

* Reprinted from *The Journal of Business and Economic Statistics*, "Diagnostic checking of unobserved components time series models" by A. C. Harvey, and S. J. Koopman, pp. 377–89, Vol. 10,
No. 4, October 1992. Reproduced here with the permission of the American Statistical Association.

series models are now quite widely used, and a full description can be found in the work of Harvey (1989).

Section 2 derives various relationships between the auxiliary residuals in finite samples. We then discuss a general algorithm that can be used to compute the auxiliary residuals in finite samples in any linear state-space model. This algorithm, the full details of which were given by Koopman (in press), is a development of earlier work by De Jong (1989) and Kohn and Ansley (1989). The efficiency and speed of the algorithm makes the computation of diagnostic procedures based on the auxiliary residuals a viable proposition.

The interpretation of the auxiliary residuals means that they are potentially useful, not only for detecting outliers and structural changes in components but for distinguishing between them. Thus we extend the work of Kohn and Ansley (1989), which was concerned only with the residuals that are estimators of the irregular disturbances and the way in which these residuals may be used to detect outliers. Sections 3 and 4 discuss diagnostics. It is shown how the Bowman–Shenton test can be modified to take account of the serial correlation in the auxiliary residuals, and Section 5 applies it to several data sets. Related modifications can also be made to certain tests for heteroscedasticity, but this particular issue is not pursued here.

1 Properties of Residuals in Large Samples

Classical results in signal extraction can be used to derive the properties of various auxiliary residuals in a doubly infinite sample. Let the observed series, y_t, be the sum of $m + 1$ mutually uncorrelated ARIMA processes μ_{it}; that is,

$$y_t = \sum_{i=0}^{m} \mu_{it} = \sum_{i=0}^{m} \frac{\theta_i(L)}{\phi_i(L)} \xi_{it}, \tag{1.1}$$

where $\theta_i(L)$ and $\phi_i(L)$ are polynomials in the lag operator and the ξ_{it} are mutually and serially uncorrelated random variables with zero means and constant variances $\sigma_i^2 (i = 0, \ldots, m)$. The autoregressive polynomials may contain unit roots. The minimum mean squared linear estimator (MMSLE) of μ_{it} is

$$\hat{\mu}_{it} = \left\{ |\phi_i(L)|^{-2} |\theta_i(L)|^2 \sigma_i^2 \Big/ \sum_{j=0}^{m} |\phi_j(L)|^{-2} |\theta_j(L)|^2 \sigma_j^2 \right\} y_t; \tag{1.2}$$

see Bell (1984). If the reduced form is

$$y_t = \phi^{-1}(L) \theta(L) \xi_t, \tag{1.3}$$

where ξ_t is white noise, with variance σ^2, then

$$\hat{\mu}_{it} = \{ |\phi_i(L)|^{-2} |\theta_i(L)|^2 \sigma_i^2 / |\phi(L)|^{-2} |\theta(L)|^2 \sigma^2 \} y_t. \tag{1.4}$$

Since the MMSLE of ξ_{it} is given by $\hat{\xi}_{it} = \phi_i(L)\theta_i^{-1}(L)\hat{\mu}_{it}$, we have, from (1.2), (1.3), and (1.4),

$$\hat{\xi}_{it} = \left\{ \phi_i^{-1}(L^{-1})\theta_i(L^{-1})\sigma_i^2 \Big/ \sum_{j=0}^{m} |\phi_j(L)|^{-2}|\theta_j(L)|^2 \sigma_j^2 \right\} y_t$$

$$= \{\phi_i^{-1}(L^{-1})\theta_i(L^{-1})\sigma_i^2 / |\phi(L)|^{-2}|\theta(L)|^2 \sigma^2\} y_t$$

$$= \{\phi_i^{-1}(L^{-1})\theta_i(L^{-1})\sigma_i^2 / \phi^{-1}(L^{-1})\theta(L^{-1})\sigma^2\} \xi_t. \tag{1.5}$$

The last expression may be written as

$$\hat{\xi}_{it} = \frac{\phi(F)\theta_i(F)}{\phi_i(F)\theta(F)} \frac{\sigma_i^2}{\sigma^2} \xi_t, \quad i = 0, \dots, m, \tag{1.6}$$

where $F = L^{-1}$ is the lead operator. Unit roots in $\phi_i(F)$ will cancel with unit roots in $\phi(F)$, so, if time is reversed, $\hat{\xi}_{it}$ is seen to be an autoregressive moving average (ARMA) process, driven by the innovations ξ_t. The process is stationary but, due to the possibility of unit roots in $\phi(F)$, not necessarily strictly invertible.

The autocovariance function (ACF) of $\hat{\xi}_{it}$ may be evaluated from a knowledge of the ARMA process implied by (1.6). Alternatively, we may note that the autocovariance generating function of $\hat{\xi}_{it}$ is

$$\hat{g}_i(L) = \frac{|\phi(L)\theta_i(L)|^2}{|\theta_i(L)\theta(L)|^2} \frac{\sigma_i^4}{\sigma^4} = \frac{|\phi_i(L)|^{-2}|\theta_i(L)|^2}{g(L)} \frac{\sigma_i^4}{\sigma^2},$$

where $g(L) = \Sigma|\phi_i(L)|^{-2}|\theta_i(L)|^2\sigma_i^2$. Given a method of computing $\hat{g}_i(L)$, the autocovariances may be obtained.

We now apply these results to some of the principal structural time series models.

1.1 Local level
The local-level model is

$$y_t = \mu_t + \varepsilon_t \tag{1.7a}$$

and

$$\mu_t = \mu_{t-1} + \eta_t, \tag{1.7b}$$

where ε_t and η_t are mutually uncorrelated white-noise processes with variance σ_ε^2 and σ_η^2. The reduced form is the ARIMA(0,1,1) model

$$\Delta y_t = (1 + \theta L)\xi_t, \quad -1 \le \theta \le 0, \tag{1.8}$$

with

$$\theta = \left(\sqrt{(q^2 + 4q)} - 2 - q\right)\Big/2, \tag{1.9}$$

where $q = \sigma_\eta^2/\sigma_\varepsilon^2$.

Writing the model as

$$y_t = \frac{\eta_t}{\Delta} + \varepsilon_t,$$

and applying (1.6) gives

$$\hat{\varepsilon}_t = \frac{(1 - F)}{1 + \theta F} \frac{\sigma_\varepsilon^2}{\sigma^2} \xi_t \qquad (1.10)$$

and

$$\hat{\eta}_t = \frac{1}{1 + \theta F} \frac{\sigma_\eta^2}{\sigma^2} \xi_t. \qquad (1.11)$$

Thus both $\hat{\varepsilon}_t$ and $\hat{\eta}_t$ depend on future innovations and, if time is reversed, it can be seen that $\hat{\eta}_t$ follows an (autoregressive) AR(1) process with parameter minus θ, whereas $\hat{\varepsilon}_t$ follows a strictly noninvertible ARMA(1,1) process. Note that the effect of serial correlation is to make the variance of $\hat{\varepsilon}_t$ less than that of ε_t. In fact, it can be shown that $\mathrm{var}(\hat{\varepsilon}_t)/\sigma_\varepsilon^2 = -2\theta/(1 - \theta) \leq 1$ for $-1 \leq \theta < 0$.

On comparing (1.10) and (1.11), we see that

$$\hat{\eta}_t = \hat{\eta}_{t+1} + q\hat{\varepsilon}_t, \quad 0 \leq q \leq \infty. \qquad (1.12)$$

The theoretical cross-correlation function, $\rho_{\varepsilon\eta}(\tau)$, can be evaluated from the preceding equation. The cross-covariance is $\gamma_{\varepsilon\eta}(\tau) = E\{(\hat{\eta}_t - \hat{\eta}_{t+1})\hat{\eta}_{t-\tau}/q\}$ $(\tau = 0, \pm1, \pm2, \ldots)$, so, for $-1 < \theta < 0$,

$$\rho_{\varepsilon\eta}(\tau) = (-\theta)^\tau \sqrt{(1 + \theta)/2}, \quad \tau \geq 0, \qquad (1.13)$$

and

$$\rho_{\varepsilon\eta}(-\tau) = -\rho_{\varepsilon\eta}(\tau - 1), \quad \tau > 0. \qquad (1.14)$$

As σ_ε^2 becomes smaller, θ tends toward 0 and $\rho_{\varepsilon\eta}(0)$ tends towards .707. Thus, although ε_t and η_t are assumed to be uncorrelated, their estimators may be quite highly correlated.

1.2 Local linear trend
The local-linear-trend model consists of Equation (1.7a) with the trend having a slope. Thus

$$\mu_t = \mu_{t-1} + \beta_{t-1} + \eta_t \qquad (1.15a)$$

and

$$\beta_t = \beta_{t-1} + \zeta_t, \qquad (1.15b)$$

where η_t and ζ_t are mutually uncorrelated white-noise processes with variances σ_η^2 and σ_ζ^2. The reduced form is the ARIMA(0,2,2) model

$$\Delta^2 y_t = (1 + \theta_1 L + \theta_2 L^2)\xi_t. \tag{1.16}$$

If the structural form is expressed as

$$y_t = \frac{\eta_t}{\Delta} + \frac{\zeta_{t-1}}{\Delta^2} + \varepsilon_t, \tag{1.17}$$

we find that

$$\hat{\varepsilon}_t = \frac{(1-F)^2}{1 + \theta_1 F + \theta_2 F^2} \frac{\sigma_\varepsilon^2}{\sigma^2}\xi_t, \tag{1.18}$$

$$\hat{\eta}_t = \frac{1-F}{1 + \theta_1 F + \theta_2 F^2} \frac{\sigma_\eta^2}{\sigma^2}\xi_t, \tag{1.19}$$

and

$$\hat{\zeta}_t = \frac{F}{1 + \theta_1 F + \theta_2 F^2} \frac{\sigma_\zeta^2}{\sigma^2}\xi_t. \tag{1.20}$$

Thus $\hat{\varepsilon}_t$, $\hat{\eta}_t$, and $\hat{\zeta}_t$ are ARMA(2,2), ARMA(2,1) and AR(2), with $\hat{\varepsilon}_t$ and $\hat{\eta}_t$ being strictly noninvertible. The three processes are stationary provided that $\sigma_\zeta^2 > 0$.
  As in the local-level model, Expression (1.12) holds, and in addition

$$\hat{\zeta}_t = \hat{\zeta}_{t+1} + q_\zeta^* \hat{\eta}_{t+1}, \quad 0 < q_\zeta^* < \infty, \tag{1.21}$$

$$= 2\hat{\zeta}_{t+1} - \hat{\zeta}_{t+2} + q_\zeta \hat{\varepsilon}_{t+1}, \quad 0 < q_\zeta < \infty, \tag{1.22}$$

where $q_\zeta^* = \sigma_\zeta^2/\sigma_\eta^2$ and $q_\zeta = \sigma_\zeta^2/\sigma_\varepsilon^2$.
  In typical applications, the variance of σ_ζ^2 is relatively small. As a result, the moving average polynomial in (1.16) will have one, and possibly two, of its roots close to unity. The $\hat{\zeta}_t$'s will therefore tend to exhibit very strong positive serial correlation. This effect is counteracted in the other auxiliary residuals by the presence of unit roots in the moving average.

1.3 Basic structural model

The three methods of modeling a seasonal component γ_t were described by Harvey (1989, chap. 2). All can be expressed in the form

$$\sum_{j=0}^{s-1} \gamma_{t-j} = \theta_\omega(L)\omega_t, \tag{1.23}$$

where ω_t denotes a white-noise disturbance with variance σ_ω^2, s is the number of seasons, and $\theta_\omega(L)$ is a polynomial of order at most $s-2$. The simplest such model has $\theta_\omega(L)$ equal to 1. Combining with a trend component of the form (1.15) and an irregular yields the basic structural model (BSM). This may be written

$$y_t = \frac{\eta_t}{\Delta} + \frac{\zeta_{t-1}}{\Delta^2} + \frac{\theta_\omega(L)\omega_t}{S(L)} + \varepsilon_t, \tag{1.24}$$

where $S(L) = 1 + L + \cdots + L^{s-1}$. The reduced form is such that

$$\Delta\Delta_s y_t = \theta(L)\xi_t, \tag{1.25}$$

where $\theta(L)$ is of order $s + 1$. Then, from (1.6),

$$\hat{\varepsilon}_t = \frac{(1 - F)(1 - F^s)}{\theta(F)} \frac{\sigma_\varepsilon^2}{\sigma^2} \xi_t, \tag{1.26}$$

$$\hat{\eta}_t = \frac{(1 - F^s)}{\theta(F)} \frac{\sigma_\eta^2}{\sigma^2} \xi_t, \tag{1.27}$$

$$\hat{\zeta}_t = \frac{S(F)F}{\theta(F)} \frac{\sigma_\zeta^2}{\sigma^2} \xi_t, \tag{1.28}$$

and

$$\hat{\omega}_t = \frac{(1 - F)^2}{\theta(F)} \frac{\theta_\omega(F)\sigma_\omega^2}{\sigma^2} \xi_t. \tag{1.29}$$

The residuals $\hat{\varepsilon}_t$, $\hat{\eta}_t$, and $\hat{\zeta}_t$ bear exactly the same relationship to each other as in the local-linear-trend model. In addition, note that

$$S(F)\hat{\omega}_t = q_\omega \theta_\omega(F)\hat{\varepsilon}_t, \quad 0 < q_\omega < \infty, \tag{1.30}$$

where $q_\omega = \sigma_\omega^2/\sigma_\varepsilon^2$.

Explicit expressions for the autocorrelation functions of the ARMA processes followed by the auxiliary residuals are not easy to obtain in this case. Numerical values, however, can be computed for specific parameter values using the algorithm described in Subsection 2.2. As an example, for a quarterly BSM where $\theta_\omega(L) = 1$, $q_\eta = 1$, $q_\zeta = .1$, and $q_\omega = .1$, the first 10 autocorrelations are as shown in Table 1. The ACF's of the irregular and level residuals are not too dissimilar to what one might expect in a local-level model with $q = 1$, although, if anything, the serial correlation in the level is somewhat reduced by the presence of the other components. The high positive serial correlation in the slope residual, to which attention was drawn at the end of the previous subsection, is clearly apparent, but the seasonal residual shows a strong pattern of serial correlation, the most prominent feature of which is the high values at the seasonal lags 4 and 8. As regards cross-correlations (see Table 2) the relatively pronounced patterns for $\hat{\varepsilon}\hat{\eta}$ and $\hat{\eta}\hat{\zeta}$ suggested by the analysis for the local-linear-trend model are still apparent, but the relationships involving $\hat{\omega}$ show seasonal effects.

Table 1. Theoretical autocorrelations for the
auxiliary residuals of a quarterly basic structural
model with $q_\eta = 1$, $q_\zeta = .1$, and $q_\omega = .1$

Lag	$\hat{\varepsilon}$	$\hat{\eta}$	$\hat{\zeta}$	$\hat{\omega}$
0	1	1	1	1
1	−.29	.28	.88	−.44
2	−.14	−.02	.70	−.14
3	.02	−.12	.52	−.24
4	−.18	−.24	.37	.65
5	.07	−.09	.28	−.25
6	.03	−.05	.21	−.14
7	.04	−.05	.15	−.14
8	−.11	−.11	.10	.42
9	.05	−.02	.07	−.14
10	.03	.00	.06	−.13

Table 2. Theoretical cross-correlations for the auxiliary residuals of a quarterly basic structural model with
$q_\eta = 1$, $q_\zeta = .1$, and $q_\omega = .1$

Lag	$\hat{\varepsilon}\hat{\eta}$	$\hat{\varepsilon}\hat{\zeta}$	$\hat{\varepsilon}\hat{\omega}$	$\hat{\eta}\hat{\zeta}$	$\hat{\eta}\hat{\omega}$	$\hat{\zeta}\hat{\omega}$
0	.60	.11	.06	.24	−.07	.07
1	.25	−.01	.06	.38	−.00	.03
2	.08	−.05	−.32	.37	.07	.03
3	.10	−.10	.35	.31	−.31	.07
4	−.12	−.04	−.02	.19	.11	−.08
5	−.03	−.02	−.02	.15	.09	−.03
6	−.00	−.02	−.22	.13	.06	.01
7	.05	−.05	.22	.10	−.20	.05
8	−.08	.01	.01	.05	.06	−.05
9	−.02	.00	−.03	.04	.07	−.02
10	.01	−.00	−.14	.04	.04	.01

2 Finite Samples

Relationships between auxiliary residuals, such as (1.12), are valid for doubly
infinite samples. However, exact relationships can be derived for finite samples.
The following subsection shows how this may be done using a very simple approach
based on an idea of Whittle (1991). Unfortunately this approach does not lead to
a viable algorithm for computing the auxiliary residuals and associated statistics
such as variances and autocovariances. The ideas underlying a stable algorithm
are sketched out in Subsection 2.2.

We will use a tilde to denote finite-sample auxiliary residuals, thereby distinguishing them from the corresponding infinite-sample residuals of Section 1.

The properties of the finite-sample residuals in the middle of the sample will be the same as the properties derived for the infinite-sample residuals. Note that both finite- and infinite-sample residuals can be regarded as minimum mean squared estimators of the corresponding disturbances under Gaussianity.

2.1 Relationship between auxiliary residuals

Consider the local-level model (1.7) defined for $t = 1$ to T, and suppose that the disturbances ε_t and η_t are normally distributed. Suppose also that the initial state is Gaussian with zero mean and a finite variance, p_0; that is, $\mu_0 \sim N(0, p_0)$ and it is independent of the disturbances. The logarithm of the joint density of the observations $y_1, \ldots, y_T$ and the states $\mu_0, \ldots, \mu_T$ is, neglecting constants,

$$J = -\frac{1}{2\sigma_\eta^2} \sum_{t=1}^{T} (\mu_t - \mu_{t-1})^2 - \frac{1}{2\sigma_\varepsilon^2} \sum_{t=1}^{T} (y_t - \mu_t)^2 - \frac{1}{2p_0} \mu_0^2. \tag{2.1}$$

Partially differentiating J with respect to each of the states, $\mu_0, \mu_1, \ldots, \mu_T$ provides a means of evaluating the smoothed estimators, which are, by definition, the expected values (and therefore the modes) of the states conditional on the observations. The result is the backward recursion

$$\tilde{\mu}_{t-1} = 2\tilde{\mu}_t - \tilde{\mu}_{t+1} - q(y_t - \tilde{\mu}_t), \quad t = T - 1, \ldots, 2. \tag{2.2}$$

The initialization, given from $\partial J/\partial \mu_T$, is

$$\tilde{\mu}_{T-1} = \tilde{\mu}_T - q(y_T - \tilde{\mu}_T), \tag{2.3}$$

so (2.2) can be started at $t = T$ by setting $\tilde{\mu}_{T+1}$ equal to $\tilde{\mu}_T$. Letting $p_0 \to \infty$ gives the end condition for a diffuse prior—namely,

$$\tilde{\mu}_2 = \tilde{\mu}_1 - q(y_1 - \tilde{\mu}_1). \tag{2.4}$$

Although (2.2) looks, at first sight, to be an extremely attractive way of computing the smoothed estimators of the μ_t's, it is, unfortunately, numerically unstable, and the $\tilde{\mu}_2$ and $\tilde{\mu}_1$ computed in this way are almost certain to violate (2.4). Nevertheless (2.2) is useful for the theoretical insight it provides. Noting that $\tilde{\eta}_t = \tilde{\mu}_t - \tilde{\mu}_{t-1}$, (2.2) can be rewritten as in (1.12)—namely,

$$\tilde{\eta}_t = \tilde{\eta}_{t+1} + q\tilde{\varepsilon}_t, \quad t = T, \ldots, 2, \tag{2.5}$$

but with starting value $\tilde{\eta}_{T+1} = 0$. Thus $\tilde{\eta}_t$ is a backward cumulative sum of the $\tilde{\varepsilon}_t$'s; that is,

$$\tilde{\eta}_t = q \sum_{j=t}^{T} \tilde{\varepsilon}_j, \quad t = 2, \ldots, T. \tag{2.6}$$

Furthermore, from (2.4), $\tilde{\eta}_2 = -q\tilde{\varepsilon}_1$, so, on setting $t = 2$ in (2.6), it can be seen that

$$\sum_{j=1}^{T} \tilde{\varepsilon}_j = 0. \tag{2.7}$$

It will be recalled that the ordinary least squares regression residuals have this property when a constant term is included.

A similar approach can be used in the local-linear-trend model to show that in a finite sample (2.3) holds and that (1.21) can be initialized with $\tilde{\zeta}_T = 0$. In addition, (2.5) holds, and if $q_\zeta^* > 0$,

$$\tilde{\zeta}_t = q_\zeta^* \sum_{j=t+1}^{T} \tilde{\eta}_j, \quad t = 3, \ldots, T-1, \tag{2.8}$$

and, provided that $q_\zeta > 0$,

$$\tilde{\zeta}_t = q_\zeta \sum_{j=t+1}^{T} \sum_{i=j}^{T} \tilde{\varepsilon}_i. \tag{2.9}$$

Finally, both (2.6) and (2.7) hold if $\sigma_\varepsilon^2 > 0$.

2.2 Algorithm

Calculation of the auxiliary residuals is carried out by putting the model in state-space form and applying the Kalman filter and smoother. The algorithm described by Koopman (in press) enables the computations to be carried out relatively quickly in a numerically stable manner; see the Appendix. Structural time series models generally contain nonstationary components, and these are handled by means of a diffuse prior on the state. In Koopman's algorithm, the calculations associated with the diffuse prior are carried out exactly.

The theoretical variances of the auxiliary residuals near the middle of the series can be obtained directly from the large-sample theory of Section 1. The variances at the beginning and end of a finite sample are different, however. The exact algorithm is therefore used to standardize all of the residuals before they are plotted.

The theoretical autocorrelations and cross-correlations of the auxiliary residuals can be calculated exactly at any point in time, but for the purposes of the test statistics employed in Section 3 only the autocorrelations appropriate for the middle of the series need be used.

3 Diagnostics

Within the context of a structural time series model, an outlier arises at time t if the value taken by y_t is not consistent with what might reasonably be expected given the model specification and the way in which this fits the other observations. The best indicator of an outlier should be $\tilde{\varepsilon}_t$; compare Kohn and Ansley (1989). Note that an outlier at time t will not affect the innovations before time t. Therefore, it makes sense that $\tilde{\varepsilon}_t$ depends only on the innovations that are affected by the outlier.

The simplest kind of structural change is a permanent shift in the level of a series that is of a greater magnitude than might reasonably be expected given the model specification and the other observations. Within the context of the local-level model, (1.7), such a shift might be best detected by an outlying value of $\tilde{\eta}_t$. Again, only the innovations at time t and beyond are affected by such a shift, and $\tilde{\eta}_t$ combines these innovations in the most appropriate way.

A sudden change in the slope is likely to be more difficult to detect than a shift in the level. As already noted, the $\tilde{\zeta}_t$'s will typically be very strongly correlated, so a break will spread its effect over several $\tilde{\zeta}_t$'s. Furthermore, the high serial correlation means that the variances of the normality and kurtosis statistics that will be discussed will need to be increased considerably, giving the tests rather low power. The seasonal residuals suffer a similar drawback. Furthermore, it may be difficult to associate a sudden change in the seasonal pattern with a particular disturbance in (1.23). Nevertheless, there may still be some value in using the seasonal auxiliary residuals to detect changes of this kind.

The basic detection procedure is to plot the auxiliary residuals after they have been standardized. (As pointed out in Section 2, the residuals at the end and the beginning will tend to have a higher variance.) In a Gaussian model, indications of outliers and/or structural change arise for values greater than 2 in absolute value. The standardized innovations may also indicate outliers and structural change but will not normally give a clear indication as to the source of the problem.

A more formal procedure for detecting the unusually large residuals is to carry out a test for excess kurtosis. If this test is combined with a test for skewness, we have the Bowman–Shenton test for normality. For such tests to be asymptotically valid, it is necessary to make an allowance for serial correlation.

3.1 Tests based on skewness and kurtosis

Let x_t be a stationary, Gaussian time series with autocorrelations ρ_τ ($\tau = 0, 1, 2, \ldots$) and variance σ_x^2. Following Lomnicki (1961), consider the estimated moments about the sample mean

$$m_\alpha = T^{-1} \sum_{t=1}^{T} (x_t - \bar{x})^\alpha, \quad \alpha = 2, 3, 4, \tag{3.1}$$

and define

$$\kappa(\alpha) = \sum_{\tau=-\infty}^{\infty} \rho_\tau^\alpha, \quad \alpha = 2, 3, 4. \tag{3.2}$$

Then, if μ_α denotes the theoretical αth moment,

$$\sqrt{T}(m_\alpha - \mu_\alpha) \xrightarrow{L} N[0, \alpha! \, \kappa(\alpha)\sigma_x^{2\alpha}]. \tag{3.3}$$

This result enables asymptotically valid test statistics based on higher order moments to be constructed as follows:

1. *Excess kurtosis test*. The measure of kurtosis is

$$b_2 = m_4/m_2^2. \tag{3.4}$$

Since m_2 is a consistent estimator of σ_x^2, it follows that the excess kurtosis test statistic

$$K = (b_2 - 3)/\sqrt{24\,\kappa(4)/T} \tag{3.5}$$

is asymptotically $N(0, 1)$ under the null hypothesis. An outlier test is carried out as a one-sided test on the upper tail.

2. *Normality test*. The measure of skewness is $\sqrt{b_1} = m_3/m_2^{3/2}$. Combining this with b_2 gives the Bowman–Shenton normality test, which when corrected for serial correlation takes the form

$$N = \frac{Tb_1}{6\kappa(3)} + \frac{T(b_2 - 3)^2}{24\,\kappa(4)}. \tag{3.6}$$

Under the null hypothesis, N is asymptotically χ_2^2; see Lomnicki (1961).

The normality and excess kurtosis tests may be applied to the innovations and auxiliary residuals. In contrast to serial-correlation tests, no amendments are needed to allow for the estimation of unknown parameters; compare Subsection 4.1. The serial-correlation correction terms, the $\kappa(\alpha)$'s, needed for the auxiliary residuals can be computed using the general algorithm of Subsection 2.2. The results in Section 1 are useful in that they enable one to get some idea of the likely size of $\kappa(\alpha)$. In the case of the local-level model (1.7) we find that for $\tilde{\eta}_t$

$$\kappa(\alpha) = \frac{1 + (-\theta)^\alpha}{1 - (-\theta)^\alpha}. \tag{3.7}$$

This is unity for a random walk—that is, $\theta = 0$—and goes monotonically toward infinity as q tends toward 0; that is, θ tends to minus one. On the other hand, for $\tilde{\varepsilon}_t$,

$$\kappa(\alpha) = 1 + \frac{-(1 + \theta)^\alpha}{2^{\alpha-1}\{1 - (-\theta)^\alpha\}}, \tag{3.8}$$

which is greater than or equal to unity for $\alpha = 4$ but less than or equal to unity for $\alpha = 3$. When θ is minus one, it takes the values $-.75$ and 1.125 for $\alpha = 3$ and 4. The kurtosis test statistic, therefore, always becomes smaller after being corrected for serial correlation, and this is also true for the normality statistic when applied to the level residual. The normality test statistic for the irregular may, however, increase. For the irregular, the correction factors are relatively small. The high correction factors for the level residual when θ is close to minus one

Table 3. Correlation factors for basic structural model with $q_\eta = 1, q_\zeta = .1$, and $q_\omega = .1$

	$\kappa(3)$	$\kappa(4)$
Irregular	.93	1.02
Level noise	1.01	1.02
Slope noise	3.53	2.90
Seasonal noise	1.49	1.53

may appear to make the detection of structural change difficult. If level shifts are introduced into an otherwise well-behaved series, however, the effect is likely to be an increase in the estimate of the relative variance of η_t and hence a corresponding increase in θ.

For more complex models, the correction factors can be computed numerically using the algorithm of Subsection 2.2. Table 3 shows the $\kappa(\alpha)$'s for the four sets of auxiliary residuals from the BSM of Tables 1 and 2, calculated using the first 20 autocorrelations.

3.2 Monte Carlo experiments

A series of simulation experiments were run to examine the performance of the test statistics discussed in Section 3.1. The experiments were conducted on the local-level model, using a sample size of $T = 150$ and different values of the signal noise ratio, q. The white-noise disturbances, ε_t and η_t, were generated using the Box–Muller algorithm of Knuth (1981). The results presented in Table 4 are based on 1,000 replications and show the estimated probabilities of rejection for tests at a nominal 5% level of significance.

Table 4(a) gives the estimated sizes of the tests. It is known that, for independent observations, the size of the Bowman–Shenton test can be some way from the nominal size for small samples, and Granger and Newbold (1977, pp. 314–315) cited evidence that suggests that serial correlation may make matters even worse. Their remarks, however, are concerned with a test statistic in which the correction factors are based on the correlogram, whereas in our case the correction factor is based on the estimator of a single parameter θ. The figures in Table 4(a) indicate that the estimated type I errors are not too far from the nominal values for both the innovations and the auxiliary residuals.

Table 4(b) shows the estimated powers of the tests when an outlier was inserted three-quarters of the way along the series. The magnitude of the outlier was five times σ_ε^2. As can be seen, the powers of the tests based on the irregular residual are higher than those based on the innovation. As we had hoped, the power of the tests based on the level residual are much lower. The kurtosis test is slightly more powerful than the normality test.

A shift in the level, up by five times σ_ε^2, was introduced three-quarters of the way along the series to generate the results in Table 4(c). The tests based on the level residual are now more powerful.

Table 4. Estimated rejection probability for tests at a nominal 5% level of significance for a local-level model with $T = 150$

| | | $q = 2.0$ | | $q = .5$ | |
		N	K	N	K
(a) No	Innovations	.062	.077	.055	.077
misspecification*	Irregular	.038 (.036)	.058 (.062)	.039 (.039)	.060 (.062)
	Level	.034 (.038)	.061 (.062)	.037 (.064)	.053 (.065)
(b) Single	Innovations	.49	.56	.87	.90
outlier at $t = 112$	Irregular	.76	.79	.97	.97
	Level	.25	.30	.26	.31
(c) Structural	Innovations	.42	.45	.83	.85
shift on level	Irregular	.15	.19	.27	.34
at $t = 112$	Level	.47	.49	.94	.95

* Uncorrected tests in parentheses.

Overall, the results are very encouraging. They suggest that the tests have acceptable sizes for moderate samples even when serial correlation corrections have to be made. Furthermore, the tests based on auxiliary residuals are reasonably effective in detecting and distinguishing between outliers and structural change.

4 Miscellaneous Issues

Several other issues arise in connection with diagnostic checking.

4.1 Tests for serial correlation

In a correctly specified model, the standardized innovations are normally and independently distributed (NID) when the parameters are known, and hence a portmanteau test for serial correlation is straightforward to carry out. In the more usual case when parameters have to be estimated, a correction to the degrees of freedom of the relevant χ^2 distribution can be made along the lines suggested by Box and Pierce (1970). As we have seen, the auxiliary residuals are serially correlated even for a correctly specified model with known parameters. We may be alerted to misspecification by the fact that the correlograms of the auxiliary residuals are very different to their implied ACF's; see Maravall (1987). If a formal test of serial correlation is to be based on residuals, however, it would seem that we have no alternative but to *prewhiten* the auxiliary residuals, which, in view of (1.6), means going back to the innovations.

It should perhaps be stressed that if the reduced form of an unobserved-components model is correctly specified, the serial and cross-correlations in the auxiliary residuals tell us nothing whatsoever about the validity of the assumptions underlying the particular unobserved-components model being employed; compare Garcia-Ferrer and del Hoyo (in press). When we talk about misspecification in the previous paragraph, this is to be understood as meaning misspecification of the reduced form. When a particular unobserved-components decomposition is consistent with a correctly specified reduced form, the question of whether the decomposition is a sensible one can only be resolved by an appeal to theoretical arguments concerning the type of properties one wishes components such as trends and seasonals to possess; see Harvey (1989, secs. 6.1 and 6.2).

4.2 Residuals from the canonical decomposition

In structural time series modeling, the components are specified explicitly, and the reduced form follows as a result of this specification. This contrasts with the initial specification of an ARIMA model and the subsequent decomposition of this model into unobserved components. The usual way in which this is done is via the canonical decomposition of Pierce (1979) and Hillmer and Tiao (1982), the aim of which is to maximize the variance of the irregular term.

This subsection examines the relationship between the properties of the structural and canonical decomposition auxiliary residuals for observations following an ARIMA(0,1,1) process. It is shown that the standardized residuals associated with the irregular term are the same, but the residuals associated with the trend are different. It is then argued that the structural residuals are likely to be more useful for detecting a structural change in the level.

The canonical decomposition of an ARIMA(0,1,1) process is such that

$$y_t = \mu_t^* + \varepsilon_t^*, \tag{4.1}$$

where

$$\mu_t^* = \mu_{t-1}^* + \eta_t^* + \eta_{t-1}^*, \tag{4.2}$$

with ε_t^* and η_t^* mutually uncorrelated white-noise processes. The residual estimating ε_t^*, denoted $\tilde{\varepsilon}_t^*$, follows exactly the same process as $\tilde{\varepsilon}_t$, except that its variance is at least as great as that of ε_t, since $\sigma_\varepsilon^2/\sigma^2 (= -\theta)$ in (1.10) is replaced by $(1-\theta)^2/4$; see Maravall (1987, p. 116). The standardized residuals are obviously the same, however. The residuals associated with η_t^*, $\tilde{\eta}t^*$, on the other hand, follow an ARMA(1,1) process,

$$\tilde{\eta}_t^* = \frac{1+F}{1+\theta F} \frac{\sigma_\eta^{*2}}{\sigma^2} \xi_t, \tag{4.3}$$

where $\sigma_\eta^{*2} = \mathrm{var}(\eta_t^*)$. Comparing this with (1.11), we see that

$$\tilde{\eta}_t^* = (\tilde{\eta}_t + \tilde{\eta}_{t+1})\sigma_\eta^{*2}/\sigma_\eta^2. \tag{4.4}$$

The fact that $\tilde{\eta}_t^*$ is an average of the corresponding structural residuals in the current and next period means that it may provide a less sharply defined tool for detecting structural change.

4.3 Explanatory variables

Explanatory variables can be added to a structural time series model. Thus we might have

$$y_t = \mu_t + x_t'\delta + \varepsilon_t, \quad t = 1, \ldots, T, \tag{4.5}$$

where μ_t is a stochastic trend (1.15) and x_t is a $k \times 1$ vector of exogenous explanatory variables with associated $k \times 1$ vector of coefficients, δ. If δ is fixed and known, residuals are constructed exactly as in the corresponding univariate model by treating $y_t - x_t'\delta$ ($t = 1, \ldots, T$) as the observed values. If δ is unknown, the main issue that arises is that two sets of innovations may be calculated, depending on whether or not δ is included in the state vector. If it is, the standardized prediction errors are known as generalized recursive residuals; see Harvey (1989, chap. 7). The distinction between these two sets of residuals is somewhat peripheral to the discussion here since the auxiliary residuals are unaffected. In the example in Section 5, the innovations are calculated by including δ in the state vector.

5 Applications

The following examples illustrate the way in which outliers and structural changes may be detected. In all cases, parameter estimation was carried out in the frequency domain, using the method of scoring described by Harvey (1989, chap. 4, sec. 3).

5.1 U.S. exports to Latin America

The monthly series of U.S. exports to Latin America contains a number of outliers that are easily detected by examining the irregular components $\tilde{\varepsilon}_t$ from a BSM; see the comments by Harvey (1989) on Bruce and Martin (1989). In fact, the principal outliers, which turn out to be due to dock strikes, are easily seen in a plot of the series and also appear quite clearly in the innovations. We therefore aggregated the data to the quarterly level and fitted a BSM of the form described in Subsection 1.3. The outliers are now less apparent in the innovations, though they still emerge clearly in the irregular component; see Fig. 1. The kurtosis statistic for the innovations is $K = 2.00$, and the normality statistic is $N = 4.52$. The normality statistic is therefore not statistically significant at the 5% level, whereas the kurtosis is significant on a one-sided test at the 5% level, but not at the 1% level. For the irregular, on the other hand, the raw K and N statistics are 7.92 and 90.73. After correction for serial correlation, these become $K = 7.85$ and $N = 91.55$, both of which are highly significant.

Since σ_η^2 is estimated to be 0, all of the movements in the trend stem from the slope disturbance. The (corrected) K and N statistics for the associated auxiliary residuals are only .18 and .03. The auxiliary residual diagnostics therefore point clearly to the presence of outliers.

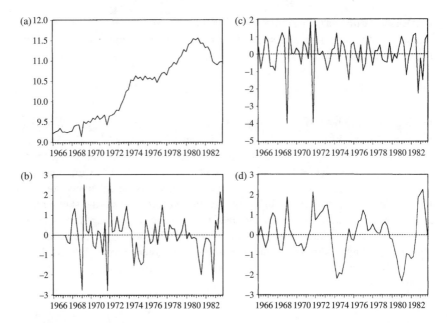

Fig. 1. U.S. exports to Latin America: (a) observations (in logarithms); (b) innovations; (c) irregular; (d) slope residual.

5.2 Car drivers killed and seriously injured in Great Britain

Monthly observations of car drivers killed and seriously injured in Great Britain were used by Harvey and Durbin (1986) in their study of the effects of the seat-belt legislation that took effect at the beginning of February 1983. The seat-belt law led to a drop in the level of the series. We now show how this structural change would be detected by the auxiliary residuals.

To avoid the large fluctuations associated with the oil crisis of 1974, a BSM was estimated using data from 75 M7 to the end of the series in 84 M12. The slope and seasonal variances were both estimated to be 0, so the fitted model is basically a random walk plus noise, with a fixed slope and seasonal; see Table 5. The theory at the end of Subsection 3.1 therefore applies directly, with $q = .118$ and $\theta = -.710$. The correction factors for the irregular are $\kappa(3) = .99$ and $\kappa(4) = 1.00$, but for the level they are $\kappa(3) = 2.12$ and $\kappa(4) = 1.69$.

The kurtosis and normality statistics are shown in Table 6. The innovation statistics clearly indicate excess kurtosis, and the auxiliary residual diagnostics point to this as emanating from a change in level, with the K and N statistics both being statistically significant at the 1% level. The plot of the innovations in Fig. 2(b) shows large values in 81 M12 and 83 M2 at -3.28 and -3.97. In the irregular residuals, shown in Fig. 2(c), both of these months are -2.84, but such a value is not excessively large compared with those for some of the other months. In the level residuals, on the other hand, 83 M2 is -4.46, but 81 M12 is only -1.76.

Table 5. Estimated hyperparameters $(\times 10^{-5})$ for U.S. exports to Latin America and car drivers killed and seriously injured in Great Britain

Parameters	Exports	Car drivers
σ_ε^2	314	425
σ_η^2	0	49.5
σ_ζ^2	84	0
σ_ω^2	1	0

Table 6. Diagnostic statistics for car drivers

Residual	K	N
Innovation	2.51*	12.61*
Irregular	.50	.86
Level	4.80*	38.04*

* Significant at 1% level.

The residuals therefore point clearly to a structural break at the beginning of 1983. The role of 81 M12 is less clear. It could be treated as an outlier; in fact, Harvey and Durbin (1986) noted that December 1981 was a very cold month. Even when the model is reestimated with an intervention variable for the seat-belt law, however, it does not give rise to a particularly large irregular residual, though curiously enough the corresponding innovation is still quite high.

A final point with respect to this example concerns checks for serial correlation. For the innovations, the Box–Ljung statistic based on the first 10 sample autocorrelations is $Q(10) = 8.58$. Thus no serial correlation is indicated. As expected from the argument in Subsection 4.1, the correlograms and theoretical ACF's for the irregular and level residuals are quite similar and hence give no further hint of model misspecification. Nor do the sample and theoretical cross-correlations. Of course, evidence of dynamic misspecification can be masked by outliers and structural breaks, but in this instance there was still no evidence of serial correlation after the inclusion of interventions.

5.3 Consumption of spirits in the United Kingdom

The per capita consumption of spirits in the United Kingdom for 1870 to 1938 can be explained, at least partly, by income per capita and relative price. A regression formulated in this way, however, shows significant serial correlation even if a time trend is included. Indeed the data set is a classic one and was used as one of the testbeds for the d statistic in the work of Durbin and Watson (1951).

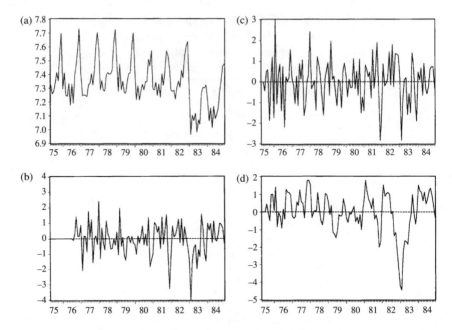

Fig. 2. Car drivers killed and seriously injured in Great Britain: (a) observations (in logarithms); (b) innovations; (c) irregular; (d) level residual.

A regression model with a stochastic trend component, as in (4.5), provides a good fit in many respects. It is more parsimonious than the regression model with a quadratic time trend and a first-order autoregressive disturbance reported by Fuller (1976, p. 426), and the stochastic trend can be interpreted as reflecting changes in tastes.

The estimates reported in Table 7 are for the period 1870–1930. As can be seen, the slope is stochastic, so there are three sets of auxiliary residuals. The associated test statistics are in Table 8. Kohn and Ansley (1989) estimated the model without a slope component, so μ_t is just a random walk. Indeed, estimating such a model might not be unreasonable for preliminary data analysis if we wish to focus attention on structural changes that affect the level. In this particular case, however, the kurtosis statistics in Table 8 are high for both the irregular and level residuals, and the presence of the slope makes very little difference.

The plots shown in Fig. 3 indicate a shift in the level in 1909, with several candidates for outliers during World War I. We fitted a level intervention first. The 1918 outlier then stood out most clearly in the irregular. On estimating with a 1918 intervention, 1915 stood out most clearly. This led to a model with a 1909 level intervention together with outlier interventions at 1918 and 1915. All of the diagnostics in this model are satisfactory. Table 7 shows the estimated coefficients of the explanatory variables and compares them with the coefficients obtained from the model without interventions. There is a clear improvement in goodness of fit, and this is reflected in the t statistics shown in parentheses.

Table 7. Parameters, diagnostics and goodness-of-fit statistics for spirits model before and after interventions

Parameters/statistics	No interventions	Interventions	
Income	.69 (5.28)	.66 (7.82)	.58 (6.45)
Price	.95 (−13.6)	−.73 (−15.2)	−.53 (−6.31)
1909 level	—	−.09 (−7.90)	−.09 (−8.69)
1915 outlier	—	.05 (5.33)	.06 (4.34)
1916 outlier	—	—	.004 (.30)
1917 outlier	—	—	−.05 (−2.79)
1918 outlier	—	−.06 (−7.47)	−.10 (−6.41)
1919 outlier	—	—	−.01 (−1.25)
σ_ε^2	161×10^{-6}	0	0
σ_η^2	69×10^{-6}	117×10^{-6}	79×10^{-6}
σ_ζ^2	37×10^{-6}	14×10^{-6}	30×10^{-6}
Prediction error SD, σ	229×10^{-4}	166×10^{-4}	144×10^{-4}
R_D^2	.71	.91	.93
Box–Ljung, $Q(10)$	13.06	5.25	4.93
N	5.87	1.53	.73
K	2.21	1.23	.84
H	2.47	.83	.75

Note: Figures in parentheses are t statistics, R_D^2 is the coefficient of determination with respect to the differenced observations as in Harvey (1989, chapter 5), and $Q(P)$ is the Box–Ljung statistic based on the first P residual autocorrelations.

Table 8. Diagnostic statistics for spirits

Residual	K	N
Innovation	2.21	5.87
Irregular	7.53	69.76
Level	5.19	31.65
Slope	.32	.45

The innovation diagnostics in the intervention model are entirely satisfactory. It is particularly interesting to note the reduction in the value of the Box–Ljung Q statistic based on the first 10 residual autocorrelations, $Q(10)$; in the original model there were high autocorrelations at lags 8, 9, and 10, which had no obvious explanation.

Referring back to Prest (1949), who originally assembled the spirits data set, reveals that the figures for 1915–1919 were estimates based on consumption in the British army. Thus they may be considerably less reliable than the other observations, and taking them all out by intervention variables may not be unreasonable. On the basis of Fig. 3(e), there is a case for a structural change in 1919. The general

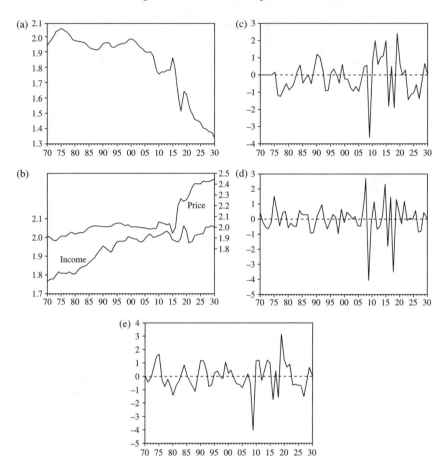

Fig. 3. Consumption of spirits in the United Kingdom, 1870–1930: (a) observations (in logarithms); (b) explanatory variables; (c) innovations; (d) irregular; (e) level residual.

unreliability of the observations in 1915 to 1919, however, makes it difficult to estimate such a change with any degree of confidence. None of the other results change significantly when the 1919 outlier intervention is replaced by a level shift intervention. The results are shown in the last column of Table 7. The changes in the coefficients of income and price are due to the influence of the observations corresponding to the additional interventions rather than the fact that they may be outliers; see Kohn and Ansley (1989).

The fall in the level in 1909 is highly significant in both of our intervention models and indicates a permanent reduction, other things being equal, of about 9%. It is this feature that is detected by our techniques and that is the prime source of the difference between our model and that of Kohn and Ansley (1989). They identified 1909 as a possible outlier. Their preferred model has outlier interventions for the years 1915–1919 and 1909. Fitting this model, including variations such as the inclusion of a stochastic slope and using time-domain instead of frequency-domain estimation, resulted in a poorer fit than our model and somewhat different coefficients for the explanatory variables. A possible explanation for the shift in 1909 may lie in the program of social reforms begun in that year by Lloyd George; see Tsay (1986, p. 137).

6 Conclusions

The auxiliary residuals are serially correlated with each other even when the model is correctly specified. Nevertheless, it seems that they are a useful tool for detecting outliers and shifts in the level in structural time series models. Plots of the auxiliary residuals can be very informative, and these can be supplemented with tests for normality and kurtosis corrected to allow for the implied serial correlation. The examples and Monte Carlo experiments illustrate that the techniques work quite well in practice.

Acknowledgments

We thank Neil Shephard, Peter Robinson, a referee, and an associate editor for helpful comments. All opinions, and any errors, are our responsibility. Support from the Economic and Social Research Council and the Tinbergen Institute is gratefully acknowledged.

Appendix: Smoothing Algorithm for Computation of the Auxiliary Residuals

The unobserved-components time series models discussed in this article can be cast in the state-space form $y_t = z_t'\alpha_t + x_t'\beta + \varepsilon_t$, $\varepsilon_t \sim \text{NID}(0, h_t)$, $\alpha_t = T_t\alpha_{t-1} + W_t\beta + \eta_t$, $\eta_t \sim \text{NID}(0, Q_t)$, $(t = 1, \ldots, T)$, where $\alpha_0 = a + A\delta$, $\beta = b + B\delta$, and δ can be regarded as fixed or diffuse; see the discussion by De Jong (1991). The disturbances ε_t and η_t are assumed to be uncorrelated, but this restriction can be relaxed. A structural time series model is placed in state-space form, with the system vector z_t and system matrix T_t being time-invariant; see Harvey (1989). Regression effects and outlier and structural change interventions are modeled by use of the system vector x_t and system matrix W_t.

Following De Jong (1991), we set up an augmented Kalman filter that gives $a_{t|t-1}$, the estimator, made at time $t - 1$, of the state vector at time t when δ is assumed to be 0, together with a matrix $A_{t|t-1}$ that allows for the correction when δ is not 0. Thus the actual estimator of the state vector α_t, made at time $t - 1$, is $a_{t|t-1} + A_{t|t-1}\delta = A_{t|t-1}^\dagger(1, \delta')'$, where $A_{t|t-1}^\dagger$ is the partitioned matrix $(a_{t|t-1}, A_{t|t-1})$. The one-step-ahead prediction errors associated with $A_{t|t-1}^\dagger$ are contained in the row vector $v_t^\dagger = (v_t, v_t^*)$ so that the scalar v_t and row vector v_t^*

correspond to $a_{t|t-1}$ and $A_{t|t-1}$. Thus

$$v_t^\dagger = (y_t, \mathbf{0}) - z_t' A_{t|t-1}^\dagger - x_t' B^\dagger, \quad t = 1, \ldots, T,$$

where $B^\dagger$ is (b, B) and $\mathbf{0}$ is a row vector of zeros. The filter for $A_{t|t-1}^\dagger$ is the recursion

$$A_{t+1|t}^\dagger = T_{t+1} A_{t|t-1}^\dagger + W_{t+1} B^\dagger + k_t v_t^\dagger, \quad t = 1, \ldots, T,$$

where $k_t = T_{t+1} P_{t|t-1} z_t'/f_t$ and $f_t = z_t P_{t|t-1} z_t' + h_t$. The mean squared error matrix of the estimated state vector at time $t - 1$, $P_{t|t-1}$, is evaluated by the matrix recursion $P_{t+1|t} = T_{t+1} P_{t|t-1} L_t' + Q_t$, where $L_t = T_{t+1} - k_t z_t'$. The starting values of the recursions are $A_{1|0}^\dagger = (a, A)$ and $P_{1|0} = 0$.

In addition, we have the following recursion: $M_t = M_{t-1} + v_t^\dagger v_t^{\dagger'}/f_t$, $(t = 1, \ldots, T)$, where M_t is partitioned as

$$M_t = \begin{bmatrix} q_t & s_t' \\ s_t & S_t \end{bmatrix}$$

and $M_0 = 0$. From this recursion, we obtain the estimator of δ at time t; that is, $m_t = S_t^{-1} s_t$ with mean squared error matrix S_t^{-1}. We also obtain the log-likelihood as $\log L = -\frac{1}{2} T \log 2\pi - \frac{1}{2} \sum_{t=1}^{T} \log f_t - \frac{1}{2}(q_T - s_T' S_T^{-1} s_T)$.

The smoothed estimator of the disturbances and the corresponding mean squared error matrices are obtained by the following algorithm derived by Koopman (1992): $\bar{\varepsilon}_t = h_t(e_t + e_t^* m_T)$, $\mathrm{MSE}(\bar{\varepsilon}_t) = h_t - h_t^2(d_t - e_t^* S_t^{-1} e_t^{*'})$, and $\tilde{\eta}_t = Q_t(r_{t-1} + R_{t-1} m_T)$, $\mathrm{MSE}(\tilde{\eta}_t) = Q_t - Q_t(N_{t-1} - R_{t-1} S_t^{-1} R_{t-1}')Q_t$ $(t = T, \ldots, 1)$, where the row vector $e_t^\dagger = (e_t, e_t^*)$, the scalar d_t, the matrices $R_t^\dagger = (r_t, R_t)$, and N_t are calculated by the backward recursions $e_t^\dagger = v_t^\dagger/f_t - k_t' R_t^\dagger$, $d_t = 1/f_t + k_t' N_t k_t$, and $R_{t-1}^\dagger = z_t' v_t^\dagger/f_t + L_t' R_t^\dagger$, $N_{t-1} = z_t' z_t/f_t + L_t' N_t L_t$ $(t = T, \ldots, 1)$, started off with $R_T^\dagger = 0$ and $N_T = 0$. The auxiliary residuals are obtained by standardizing $\bar{\varepsilon}_t$ and $\tilde{\eta}_t$ using their mean squared errors.

The disturbance smoother requires, for a typical structural time series model, about the same number of computations as for the Kalman filter. The storage requirement is limited to $v_t^\dagger$, f_t, and k_t. Koopman (in press) also discussed a more general disturbance smoother, efficient methods of calculation, and a quick-state smoother.

References

Bell, W. R. (1984), "Signal Extraction for Nonstationary Time Series," *The Annals of Statistics*, 13, 646–664.

Box, G. E. P., and Pierce, D. A. (1970), "Distribution of Residual Autocorrelations in Autoregressive-Integrated-Moving Average Time Series Models," *Journal of the American Statistical Association*, 65, 1509–1526.

Bruce, A. G., and Martin, R. D. (1989), "Leave-k-out Diagnostics for Time Series," *Journal of the Royal Statistical Society*, Ser. B, 51, 363–424.

De Jong, P. (1989), "Smoothing and Interpolation With the State-Space Model," *Journal of the American Statistical Association*, 84, 1085–1088.

—— (1991), "The Diffuse Kalman Filter," *The Annals of Statistics*, 19, 1073–1083.

Durbin, J., and Watson, G. S. (1951), "Testing for Serial Correlation in Least Squares Regression II," *Biometrika*, 56, 1–15.

Fuller, W. A. (1976), *Introduction to Statistical Time Series*, New York: John Wiley.

Garcia-Ferrer, A., and del Hoyo, J. (in press), "On Trend Extraction Models: Interpretation, Empirical Evidence and Forecasting Performance" (with discussion), *Journal of Forecasting*, 11.

Granger, C. W. J., and Newbold, P. (1977), *Forecasting Economic Time Series*, New York: Academic Press.

Harvey, A. C. (1989), *Forecasting, Structural Time Series Models and the Kalman Filter*, Cambridge, U.K.: Cambridge University Press.

Harvey, A. C., and Durbin, J. (1986), "The Effects of Seat Belt Legislation on British Road Casualties: A Case Study in Structural Time Series Modelling," *Journal of the Royal Statistical Society*, Ser. A, 149, 187–227.

Hillmer, S. C., and Tiao, G. C. (1982), "An ARIMA-Model-Based Approach to Seasonal Adjustment," *Journal of the American Statistical Association*, 77, 63–70.

Knuth, D. E. (1981), *The Art of Computer Programming* (Vol. II), Reading, MA: Addison-Wesley.

Kohn, R., and Ansley, C. F. (1989), "A Fast Algorithm for Signal Extraction, Influence and Cross-validation in State Space Models," *Biometrika*, 76, 65–79.

Koopman, S. J. (in press), "Disturbance Smoother for State Space Models," *Biometrika*, 79.

Lomnicki, Z. A. (1961), "Tests for Departure From Normality in the Base of Linear Stochastic Processes," *Metrika*, 4, 37–62.

Maravall, A. (1987), "Minimum Mean Squared Errors Estimation of the Noise in Unobserved Components Models," *Journal of Business & Economic Statistics*, 5, 115–120.

Pierce, D. A. (1979), "Signal Extraction Error in Nonstationary Time Series," *The Annals of Statistics*, 7, 1303–1320.

Prest, A. R. (1949), "Some Experiments in Demand Analysis," *Review of Economics and Statistics*, 31, 33–49.

Tsay, R. S. (1986), "Time Series Model Specification in the Presence of Outliers," *Journal of the American Statistical Association*, 81, 132–141.

Whittle, P. (1991), "Likelihood and Cost as Path Integrals" (with discussion), *Journal of the Royal Statistical Society*, Ser. B, 53, 505–538.

6

Nonparametric Spline Regression with Autoregressive Moving Average Errors*

ROBERT KOHN

Australian Graduate School of Management, University of New South Wales

CRAIG F. ANSLEY

Department of Accounting and Finance, University of Auckland

AND

CHI-MING WONG

Australian Graduate School of Management, University of New South Wales

SUMMARY

We estimate by spline nonparametric regression an unknown function observed with autocorrelated errors when the errors are modelled by an autoregressive moving average model. Unknown parameters are estimated by either maximum likelihood, cross-validation or generalized cross-validation. By expressing the problem in state space form we obtain $O(n)$ algorithms to estimate the function and its derivatives and evaluate the marginal likelihood and cross-validation functions. The finite sample properties of the function estimates are evaluated by an extensive simulation study and examples are given.

1 Introduction

Suppose we observe a function with noise. When the noise is independent, spline or kernel nonparametric regression is a popular way of estimating the function which does not require specifying its functional form. If the data are collected in time order then the noise is likely to be correlated and the usual nonparametric regression estimators may perform poorly. See for example Diggle & Hutchinson (1989), Altman (1990) and Hart (1991).

We estimate the unknown function by spline smoothing assuming that the noise is generated by a stationary autoregressive-moving average, ARMA, model. The smoothing problem is expressed as a signal extraction problem and the resulting stochastic model is written in state space form. The unknown function is then obtained by state space filtering and smoothing algorithms. Both the smoothing parameter and the parameters of the ARMA model are estimated by marginal likelihood or by modifications of cross-validation or generalized cross-validation

* This work was previously published as R. Kohn, C. F. Ansley and D. Wong, "Nonparametric Spline Regression with Autoregressive Moving Average Errors", *Biometrika*, 1992, Vol. 79, pp. 335–346. Reproduced by permission of the Biometrika Trustees.

which take into account the correlation structure of the residuals. Algorithms are obtained to compute the function estimate and evaluate the likelihood and cross-validation criterion functions in $O(n)$ operations for both equally and unequally spaced data. We illustrate our approach using two examples previously discussed in the literature. Because it is difficult to obtain the finite sample properties of the function estimates we summarize the results of an extensive simulation study of the performance of the marginal likelihood and cross-validation estimators. We took the square root of the integrated squared error of the function estimate as the performance criterion and found that if the order of the ARMA model is assumed known then the marginal likelihood estimator of the parameters using quintic splines performed better than the marginal likelihood estimator using cubic splines and also outperformed the generalized cross-validation estimators using cubic and quintic splines. We also found that when the noise is independent there is little loss in efficiency in estimating the noise by an autoregressive process of order 2 or 3. This suggests that if we suspect that the errors are autocorrelated then we should carry out spline smoothing with the errors modelled by an autoregressive, AR, model of order 2 or 3 or a low order ARMA model. Although we found that the marginal likelihood estimator performed better than the generalized cross-validation estimator when the order of the ARMA process is known, the generalized cross-validation estimators may prove to be important when the generating model for the error process is unknown but we take it to be an ARMA process of a given order.

Wahba (1978) shows that the spline smoothing problem could be expressed as a signal extraction problem. Diggle & Hutchinson (1989) extend her result to the correlated residuals case and our state space representation is based on their stochastic model. Diggle & Hutchinson (1989) obtain the spline estimate of the function and estimate the unknown parameters in $O(n)$ operations for an AR(1) error model and estimate the smoothing parameter and the autoregressive parameter by a mixture of maximum likelihood and generalized cross-validation. Their approach does not generalize to higher order ARMA models and seems computationally demanding. Altman (1990) and Hart (1991) use kernel regression to estimate the unknown function when the errors are correlated and Hurvich & Zeger (1990) propose a frequency domain cross-validation approach to estimate the parameters.

Our approach is also related to the structural time series models proposed by Harvey & Todd (1983) and Kitagawa & Gersch (1984) but their aims are somewhat different. In nonparametric regression the aim is to estimate an unknown function and possibly also its derivatives assuming only that the function is sufficiently smooth, whereas the aim of structural modelling is to estimate components of a time series given stochastic models for the components.

The paper is organized as follows. In Section 2 we describe function estimation by penalized least squares, and the equivalent signal extraction problem and the state space representation of the stochastic model. In Section 3 we discuss parameter estimation by both marginal likelihood and cross-validation and Section 4 generalizes the treatment in Sections 2 and 3 to handle unequally spaced data. Section 5 summarizes the results of a simulation study and Section 6 discusses two examples.

2 Penalized Least Squares and Signal Extraction

We define the penalized least squares problem which gives the smoothing spline estimate of the function and present the stochastic model from which the spline estimate can be obtained by signal extraction. The model is then expressed in state space form.

Suppose we observe

$$y(i) = f(t_i) + v(t_i) \quad (i = 1, \ldots, n), \tag{2.1}$$

where $y(i)$ is the ith observation, $f(.)$ is the unknown regression function and $v(t_i)$ is the ith residual. Suppose that $0 < t_1 < \cdots < t_n$. Let

$$y = \{y(1), \ldots, y(n)\}', \qquad f = \{f(t_1), \ldots, f(t_n)\}', \qquad v = \{v(t_1), \ldots, v(t_n)\}'$$

and suppose that $v \sim N(0, \sigma^2 \Omega)$. Given Ω, Diggle & Hutchinson (1989) propose estimating $f(t)$ by minimizing the penalized least squares criterion function

$$(y - f)' \Omega^{-1} (y - f) + \frac{1}{\lambda} \int_0^{t_n} \{f^{(m)}(t)\}^2 \, dt \tag{2.2}$$

over all functions f having square integrable mth derivative. The smoothing parameter λ controls the tradeoff between the least squares fit and the smoothness of the function estimate. It follows from Diggle & Hutchinson (1989) and Kohn & Ansley (1988) that the penalized least squares criterion function (2.2) has a unique minimum and from the results below and Kohn & Ansley (1983) that the resulting function estimate is a spline of order m, that is a polynomial of degree $2m - 1$ having $2m - 2$ continuous derivatives throughout. For $\Omega = I_n$, Wahba (1978) shows that the spline estimate can be obtained equivalently by signal extraction. This result is extended to general matrices Ω by Diggle & Hutchinson (1989) and Kohn & Ansley (1988). Specifically, suppose that $f(t)$ is generated by the stochastic differential equation

$$d^m f(t)/dt^m = \sigma \lambda^{1/2} dW(t)/dt, \tag{2.3}$$

where $W(t)$ is a zero mean Wiener process and $f(t)$ has initial conditions

$$\tilde{f}_0 = \{f(0), f^{(1)}(0), \ldots, f^{(m-1)}(0)\}' \sim N(0, kI_m). \tag{2.4}$$

Let $\hat{f}(t; k) = E\{f(t)|y; k\}$ be the signal extraction estimate of $f(t)$. Then Kohn & Ansley (1988) show that $\hat{f}(t) = \lim \hat{f}(t; k)$, as $k \to \infty$, exists and is the spline smoothing estimate of $f(t)$ which minimizes (2.2).

To simplify the discussion we assume for the rest of the paper, with the exception of Section 4, that the observations are equally spaced with a unit spacing between them so that without loss of generality we take $t_0 = 0$ and $t_i = i$ for $i = 1, \ldots, n$. The errors $v(t)$ are generated by the discrete time stationary ARMA (p, q)

model

$$v(i) = \phi_1 v(i-1) + \cdots + \phi_p v(i-p) + e(i) + \theta_1 e(i-1) + \cdots + \theta_q e(i-q),$$
$$(2.5)$$

with the $e(i)$ being $N(0, \sigma^2)$ and independent of the Wiener process $W(t)$.

It follows from Kohn & Ansley (1987) that the stochastic model (2.3) and (2.4) for $f(t)$ can be written in state space form as

$$z(i) = F_1(i)z(i-1) + u^{(1)}(i) \quad (i \geqslant 1). \qquad (2.6)$$

The state vector $z(i) = \{f(t_i), f^{(1)}(t_i), \ldots, f^{(m-1)}(t_i)\}'$ and the error $u^{(1)}(i)$ are independent $N\{0, \sigma^2 \lambda U^{(1)}(i)\}$. For $i \geqslant 1$ let $\delta_i = t_i - t_{i-1}$. Then $F_1(i)$ is an upper triangular $m \times m$ matrix having ones on the diagonal and (j, k)th element $\delta_i^{k-j}/(k-j)!$ for $k > j$ and $U^{(1)}(i)$ is an $m \times m$ matrix with (j, k)th element

$$\delta_i^{2m-j-k+1}/\{(2m-i-j+1)(m-k)!(m-j)!\}.$$

Following Harvey (1981, p. 103) we can write the ARMA model (2.5) in state space form as

$$v(i) = w_1(i), \qquad w(i) = F_2 w(i-1) + u^{(2)}(i), \qquad (2.7)$$

where the state vector $w(i)$ is $m' \times 1$ with $m' = \max(p, q+1)$. The vector $u^{(2)}(i) = g e(i)$ with $g = (1, \theta_1, \ldots, \theta_{m'})'$. The $m' \times m'$ matrix F_2 has first column $(\phi_1, \phi_2, \ldots, \phi_{m'})'$, $F_2(i, i+1) = 1$ for $i = 1, \ldots, m'-1$ and the rest of the elements of F_2 are equal to zero. Combining (2.1), (2.6) and (2.7) we have that

$$y(i) = h'x(i), \qquad x(i) = F(i)x(i-1) + u(i), \qquad (2.8)$$

where

$$x(i) = \{z(i)', w(i)'\}', \qquad u(i) = \{u^{(1)}(i)', u^{(2)}(i)'\}',$$

the vector h has a 1 in the first and $(m+1)$st positions and zeros elsewhere and $F(i)$ is a block diagonal matrix with block submatrices $F_1(i)$ and F_2. The vector $x(1)$ is normal with mean zero and variance matrix

$$\text{var}\{x(1)\} = \begin{bmatrix} k I_m & 0 \\ 0 & \sigma^2 V \end{bmatrix},$$

where $\sigma^2 V = \text{var}\{w(i)\}$. Given $\phi_1, \ldots, \phi_p$ and $\theta_1, \ldots, \theta_q$ the matrix V is obtained by solving $V = F_2 V F_2' + g g'$.

We now explain how to estimate the function $f(t)$ and its first derivative by state space filtering and smoothing algorithms. Let

$$x(i|j; k) = E\{x(i)|y(1), \ldots, y(j); k\},$$

$$\sigma^2 S(i|j; k) = \text{var}\{x(i)|y(1), \ldots, y(j); k\}.$$

By Ansley & Kohn (1985) we have that

$$x(i|j; k) = x^{(0)}(i|j) + O(1/k),$$

$$S(i|j; k) = kS^{(1)}(i|j) + S^{(0)}(i|j) + O(1/k),$$

where $x^{(0)}(i|j)$, $S^{(1)}(i|j)$ and $S^{(0)}(i|j)$ are independent of σ^2 and k; furthermore $S^{(1)}(i|j) = 0$ for $j \geqslant m$. We can now use the filtering and smoothing algorithms of Ansley & Kohn (1990) to obtain $x^{(0)}(i|n)$ for $i = 1, \ldots, n$, and hence the spline estimate $\hat{f}(i) = x_1^{(0)}(i|n)$ and its first derivative $\hat{f}^{(1)} = x_2^{(0)}(i|n)$.

3 Parameter Estimation

3.1 Maximum likelihood parameter estimation

In Section 2 we assumed that $\tau = (\lambda, \phi_1, \ldots, \phi_m, \theta_1, \ldots, \theta_q)'$ is known. Usually it is not and has to be estimated from the data. In this section we show how to estimate τ and σ^2 by both marginal likelihood and cross-validation methods.

Maximum likelihood estimation of the smoothing parameter was proposed by Wecker & Ansley (1983) for ordinary spline smoothing and later modified to marginal likelihood by Wahba (1985) and Ansley & Kohn (1985). Let $g(y; \tau, \sigma^2; k)$ be the density of y for given $k > 0$. Then, following Wahba (1985) the marginal likelihood for τ and σ^2 is defined as the limit of $k^{m/2}g(y; \tau, \sigma^2; k)$ as $k \rightarrow \infty$. To compute the marginal likelihood first define

$$\varepsilon(i; k) = y(i) - E\{y(i)|y(1), \ldots, y(i - 1); k\}, \qquad R(i; k) = \text{var}\{\varepsilon(i; k)/\sigma\}.$$

By Ansley & Kohn (1985) we have that

$$\varepsilon(i; k) = \varepsilon^{(0)}(i) + O(1/k), \qquad R(i; k) = kR^{(1)}(i) + R^{(0)}(i) + O(1/k),$$

with $\varepsilon^{(0)}(i)$, $R^{(0)}(i)$ and $R^{(1)}(i)$ functionally independent of k and σ^2; $R^{(1)}(i) = 0$ for $i > m$ and $R^{(1)}(i)$ is functionally independent of τ for all i. Then (Ansley & Kohn, 1985), minus twice the log marginal likelihood with σ^2 concentrated out is

$$L(\tau) = \prod_{i=m+1}^{n} \frac{\{\varepsilon^{(0)}(i)\}^2}{R^{(0)}(i)} \left\{ \prod_{i=m+1}^{n} R^{(0)}(i) \right\}^{1/(n-m)},$$

and the marginal likelihood estimate of σ^2 is

$$\hat{\sigma}^2 = \sum_{i=m+1}^{n} \{\varepsilon^{(0)}(i)\}^2 \Big/ (n - m).$$

The innovations $\varepsilon^{(0)}(i)$ and the innovation variance $R^{(0)}(i)$ are obtained using the modified Kalman filter (Ansley & Kohn, 1990).

3.2 Parameter estimation by cross-validation

When the errors $v(i)$ are independent two popular and effective ways of estimating the smoothing parameter λ are cross-validation and generalized cross-validation with generalized cross-validation introduced by Craven & Wahba (1979) to improve the performance of cross-validation for unequally spaced data. It is shown by Diggle & Hutchinson (1989), Altman (1990) and Hart (1991) that ordinary cross-validation and generalized cross-validation perform poorly when the $v(i)$ are correlated. We now generalize cross-validation and generalized cross-validation to take into account the correlation in the $v(i)$. For the stochastic model (2.8) let

$$\hat{y}^{(-i)}(i;\tau) = \lim_{k\to\infty} E\{y(i)|y(1),\ldots,y(i-1),y(i+1),\ldots,y(n);k;\tau\}$$

be the estimate of $y(i)$ based on all the other observations. The cross-validation function $C(\tau)$ is defined as

$$C(\tau) = \sum_{i=1}^{n}\{y(i) - \hat{y}^{(-i)}(i;\tau)\}^2. \tag{3.1}$$

We now present an efficient $O(n)$ algorithm for computing $C(\tau)$. Its motivation and derivation are given in the Appendix. First define the $(m+m')\times 1$ vectors $a(i)$ and the $(m+m')\times(m+m')$ matrices $b(i)$ for $i = 1,\ldots,n+1$ by the following recursions. Set $a(n+1) = 0$ and $b(n+1) = 0$ and for $i = n,\ldots,m+1$,

$$a(i) = h\varepsilon^{(0)}(i)/R^{(0)}(i) + M(i)'a(i+1), \tag{3.2}$$

$$b(i) = hh'/R^{(0)}(i) + M(i)'b(i+1)M(i), \tag{3.3}$$

$$M(i) = F(i+1)\{I - s(i)h'/R^{(0)}(i)\}, \tag{3.4}$$

with $s(i) = S^{(0)}(i|i-1)h$ the sum of the first and $(m+1)$st columns of $S^{(0)}(i|i-1)$. For $i \leqslant m$

$$a(i) = M(i)'a(i+1), \tag{3.5}$$

$$b(i) = M(i)'b(i+1)M(i), \tag{3.6}$$

$$M(i) = F(i+1)\{I - s(i)h'/R^{(1)}(i)\}, \tag{3.7}$$

with $s(i) = S^{(1)}(i|i-1)h$.

Now define the scalars $\xi(i)$ and $\eta(i)$, for $i = 1,\ldots,n$, as follows. For $i = n,\ldots,m+1$, let

$$\xi(i) = \varepsilon^{(0)}(i)/R^{(0)}(i) - s(i)'F(i+1)'a(i+1)/R^{(0)}(i), \tag{3.8}$$

$$\eta(i) = 1/R^{(0)}(i) + s(i)'F(i+1)'b(i+1)F(i+1)s(i)/\{R^{(0)}(i)\}^2. \tag{3.9}$$

For $i \leqslant m$,

$$\xi(i) = -s(i)'F(i+1)'a(i+1)/R^{(1)}(i), \tag{3.10}$$

$$\eta(i) = s(i)'F(i+1)'b(i+1)F(i+1)s(i)/\{R^{(1)}(i)\}^2. \tag{3.11}$$

Then the cross-validation function (3.1) can be written as

$$C(\tau) = \sum_{i=1}^{n} \xi(i)^2 \Big/ \eta(i)^2.$$

By analogy with the definition of generalized cross-validation when the errors are independent (Craven & Wahba, 1979), we define the generalized cross-validation function $G(\tau)$ as

$$G(\tau) = \sum_{i=1}^{n} \xi(i)^2 \Big/ \sum_{i=1}^{n} \eta(i)^2.$$

Then $C(\tau)$ and $G(\tau)$ are obtained in $O(n)$ operations using (3.2)–(3.11).

4 Unequally Spaced Observations

If the increments $t_i - t_{i-1}$ are a multiple of some basic length then it is straight-forward to extend the algorithms in Section 3. This happens, for example, if the observations are equally spaced but there are some missing observations. Other-wise we model the errors $v(t_i)$ as a continuous time stationary autoregressive, AR, or ARMA process. To simplify notation it is sufficient to discuss the autoregressive case. Thus suppose that $v(t)$ is generated by the pth order AR model

$$d^p v(t)/dt^p = \phi_1 d^{p-1} v(t)/dt^{p-1} + \cdots + \phi_p v(t) + \sigma dW_v(t)/dt, \qquad (4.1)$$

with $W_v(t)$ a Wiener process which is independent of the $e(i)$ and $W(t)$.

Define the state vector $w(t) = \{v(t), v^{(1)}(t), \ldots, v^{(p-1)}(t)\}'$. Then we can rewrite (4.1) as

$$dw(t)/dt = \Phi w(t) + \sigma g \, dW_v(t)/dt, \qquad (4.2)$$

where Φ is a $p \times p$ matrix such that $\Phi(i, i+1) = 1$ for $i = 1, \ldots, p-1$, the last row of Φ is $(\phi_1, \ldots, \phi_{p-1})$ and the rest of the elements of Φ are zero. The vector $g = (0, \ldots, 0, 1)'$. Following Harvey & Stock (1986) we can rewrite (4.2) as

$$v(t_i) = w_1(t_i), \qquad w(t_i) = F_2(i)w(t_{i-1}) + u^{(2)}(i),$$

where $F_2(i) = e^{\Phi \delta_i}$ and

$$u^{(2)}(i) = \sigma \int_{t_{i-1}}^{t_i} e^{\Phi(t_i - s)} g \, dW_v(s).$$

We can now estimate the signal and evaluate the likelihood as in Sections 2 and 3. To do so practically we need to evaluate $V = \text{var}\{w(t)\}/\sigma^2$, $F_2(i)$ and $U^{(2)}(i) = \text{var}\{u^{(2)}(i)\}/\sigma^2$ efficiently and accurately. We now show briefly how to do so.

Given $(\phi_1, \ldots, \phi_p)'$ we use $\Phi V + V \Phi' = -gg'$ (Bryson & Ho, 1975, p. 334) to solve for V. The matrix $F_2(i) = e^{\Phi \delta_i}$ is obtained using a Pade approximation

(Golub & Van Loan, 1983, pp. 396–400). Once $F_2(i)$ is obtained we evaluate $U^{(2)}(i)$ as $V - F_2(i)VF_2(i)'$ because $v(t)$ is stationary and hence so is $w(t)$. If $p = 1$ then Φ is a scalar and it is straightforward to compute $F_2(i)$ and $U^{(2)}(i)$ directly.

The estimation of a continuous time stationary autoregressive model using a state space approach is discussed by Harvey & Stock (1986) and Jones (1981) who use a Jordan decomposition of Φ to evaluate $e^{\Phi\delta}$ when Φ has distinct eigenvalues. However, this approach does not allow coincident eigenvalues and will be unstable if the eigenvalues are close together. See Moler & Van Loan (1978). In contrast our approach for computing V, $F_2(i)$ and $U^{(2)}(i)$ is both fast and accurate.

5 Performance of Function Estimators: Simulation Results

Because it is very difficult to determine theoretically the finite sample properties of the regression function estimates we carried out a simulation study using the square root of integrated squared error

$$\text{ISE}(\tau; p, q) = \sum_{i=1}^{n} \{f(t_i) - \hat{f}(t_i; \tau)\}^2$$

as the performance criterion when an ARMA (p, q) model is fitted to the errors and τ is the parameter vector defined in Section 3. In her simulations Wahba (1985) also compared estimators using integrated squared error. Our study consisted of three parts. In the first and major part we studied the performance of the function estimates using cross-validation and marginal likelihood estimates of τ assuming that the errors are generated by an autoregression of known order. To motivate the second and third parts of the study we note that unlike ordinary time series analysis we do not have at present adequate methods for identifying the ARMA error structure in nonparametric regression. If the objective is to estimate the regression function and we suspect the errors are autocorrelated then we suggest fitting a low order autoregressive, $p = 2$ or 3, or ARMA model to the errors. We base this suggestion on our experience that such models are adequate for most nonseasonal time series. See, for example, the data sets analyzed by Box & Jenkins (1976). The next two parts investigated the implications of such a strategy. In the second part we looked at the loss in efficiency in estimating the function by fitting a low-order autoregressive model to the errors when they are independent. The third part of the study considered the loss in efficiency when the errors are generated by a moving average process but estimated as a second or third order autoregression.

We present only a small part of our results and summarize the rest. Full details are available from the authors on request. By an AR (p) model we mean an autoregressive model of order p.

To study the performance of the cross-validation, generalized cross-validation and marginal likelihood estimators of τ the regression function was estimated using cubic and quintic splines with the errors generated by an AR process of known order. In addition we also considered a fourth 'estimator' called the true squared error estimator which minimizes ISE $(\tau; p, q)$ over all τ for given p, q and regression function f. Although the true squared error estimator is not a feasible estimator because the regression function $f(.)$ is unknown, it provides an upper bound on the performance of the other three estimators. Figures 1(a) and 1(b) present results for quintic splines with the errors $v(t)$ generated by an AR (1) process and with the autoregressive parameter ϕ_1 taking the values 0.2, 0.4, 0.6 and 0.8 so that the residuals are positively correlated. We looked at eleven test functions, sample sizes $n = 50$, 100 and 150 and 0.05, 0.1 and 0.2 values of the error standard deviation, σ_v. One hundred replications were performed for each spline order, test function, sample size n, value of σ_v and value of ϕ_1. We aggregate Figs 1(a) and 1(b) over the eleven test functions, three values of σ_v and the four values of ϕ_1 to summarize the results concisely and because the test function, the standard deviation of the errors and the correlation structure of the errors are unknown in practice. When the errors $v(t)$ are negatively correlated we found from a more limited set of simulations than those reported in the paper that all estimators perform better than in the positively correlated case, but the negative correlation case is of limited interest and we omit details.

The eleven test functions used are

$$f_1(t) = \{\beta_{10,5}(t) + \beta_{5,10}(t) + \beta_{7,7}(t)\}/3, \qquad f_2(t) = 0.6\beta_{30,17} + 0.4\beta_{3,11}(t),$$

$$f_3(t) = \{\beta_{20,5}(t) + \beta_{12,12}(t) + \beta_{7,30}(t)\}/3,$$

$$f_4(t) = 4.26e^{-3.25t} + 4.0e^{-6.5t} + 3.0e^{-9.75t},$$

$$f_5(t) = \{2.0 - 5t + e^{-(t-0.5)^2/0.04}\}/3.77, \qquad f_6(t) = 5e^{-5t},$$

$$f_7(t) = \{1 + e^{-7(t-0.5)}\}^{-1}, \qquad f_8(t) = \exp(-3e^{-3t}), \qquad f_9(t) = t,$$

$$f_{10}(t) = t^2, \qquad f_{11}(t) = \sin(4\pi t),$$

where in f_1, f_2 and f_3,

$$\beta_{p,q}(t) = \frac{\Gamma(p+q)}{\Gamma(p)\Gamma(q)} t^{p-1}(1-t)^{q-1}.$$

Functions f_1, f_2 and f_3 were used by Wahba (1985) in her simulations and f_4 is used by Eubank (1988). The functions f_5 and f_6 are used by Gasser, Sroka & Jennen-Steinmetz (1986) in their simulations. The functions f_7 and f_8 are the logistic and Gompertz functions respectively which are often used to model growth curves. The functions f_9 and f_{10} are linear and quadratic respectively. Finally, the function f_{11} is similar to that used by Diggle & Hutchinson (1989), Altman (1990) and Hart (1991) in their simulations.

Let $\hat{\tau}_{\mathrm{GCV}}$, $\hat{\tau}_{\mathrm{ML}}$ and $\hat{\tau}_{\mathrm{TSE}}$ be the generalized cross-validation, marginal likelihood and true squared error estimators of τ. Figure 1(a) is a plot of the percentage of times that

$$\mathrm{ISE}(\hat{\tau}_{\mathrm{ML}}; p = 1, q = 0)^{1/2}/\mathrm{ISE}(\hat{\tau}_{\mathrm{TSE}}; p = 1, q = 0)^{1/2} \leqslant t$$

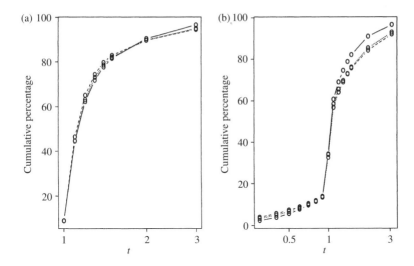

Fig. 1. Plot of the percentage of times ISE $(\hat{\tau}_1; p = 1, q = 0)^{1/2}/\text{ISE}(\hat{\tau}_2; p = 1, q = 0)^{1/2} \leqslant t$ as a function of t using splines of order $m = 3$ for all eleven test functions, three values of σ_n and four values of ϕ_1. The t axis is on a log scale. Solid line, $n = 50$; dotted line, $n = 100$; dashed line, $n = 150$. (a) $\hat{\tau}_1 = \hat{\tau}_{\text{ML}}$ and $\hat{\tau}_2 = \hat{\tau}_{\text{TSE}}$; circles placed at $t = 1$, 1.1, 1.2, 1.3, 1.4, 1.5, 2.0 and 3.0. (b) $\hat{\tau}_1 = \hat{\tau}_{\text{GCV}}$ and $\hat{\tau}_2 = \hat{\tau}_{\text{ML}}$; circles are placed at $t = 0.3$, 0.4, 0.5, 0.6, 0.7, 0.8, 0.9, 1, 1.1, 1.2, 1.3, 1.4, 1.5, 2.0 and 3.0.

as a function of t for sample sizes $n = 50$, 100 and 150 and shows that the marginal likelihood estimator performs well relative to the true squared error estimator, being within 20% of the true squared error estimator 63% of the time and being within 40% of the true squared error 79% of the time. The percentages were virtually the same for sample size $n = 50$, 100 and 150. Figure 1(b) is a plot of the percentage of times that

$$\text{ISE}(\hat{\tau}_{\text{GCV}}; p = 1, q = 0)^{1/2}/\text{ISE}(\hat{\tau}_{\text{ML}}; p = 1, q = 0)^{1/2} \leqslant t$$

and shows that the marginal likelihood estimator performed as well as or better than the generalized cross-validation estimator 67% of the time for all three sample sizes.

We now summarize some of the other results obtained in our study but not reported in detail. We found that for errors generated by AR (2) and AR (3) models of known order the marginal likelihood estimator again performed as well as or better than the generalized cross-validation estimator. We also found that for the generalized cross-validation, cross-validation, marginal likelihood and true squared error estimators, quintic splines performed a little better than cubic splines and that the generalized cross-validation estimator is at least as good as the cross-validation estimator. We also found that there is little loss in efficiency in fitting a low order

AR model to the errors when they are independent. For example, the ratio

$$\text{ISE}(\hat{\tau}_{\text{ML}}; p = 2, q = 0)^{1/2}/\text{ISE}(\hat{\tau}_{\text{TSE}}; p = 0, q = 0)^{1/2}$$

was less than or equal to one approximately 46% of the time for the three sample sizes $n = 50$, 100 and 150 when the errors are independent. Finally, we found that there is little loss in efficiency in fitting a low order autoregressive process to the errors when the errors are actually generated by a first order moving average. Although our results suggest that the marginal likelihood performs better than generalized cross-validation if the order of the ARMA process is known we need further experience with ARMA models of unknown order and with stationary errors not generated by ARMA models before we can say that the marginal likelihood estimator is superior to the generalized cross-validation estimator.

The simulations repeated above were performed as follows. Independent Gaussian random variables were generated by IMSL subroutine GGNML and the ARMA errors were then obtained using (2.7). The cross-validation, generalized cross-validation, marginal likelihood and true squared error functions were minimized using subroutine LMDIF in the MINPACK subroutine library; see More, Garbow & Hillstrom (1980). The simulations were carried out on the IBM 3090 at the University of New South Wales.

6 Examples

We illustrate our approach with two examples. The first is from Pandit & Wu (1983) who estimate the profile of a block of wood after it was subjected to a grinding process. There are 320 equally spaced observations and Pandit & Wu carry out a nonlinear regression with ARMA errors with the unobserved profile estimated as an arc of a circle by $f(t) = a + \{c^2 - (t - b)^2\}^{1/2}$, where the parameters a, b and c are estimated from the data. We estimate $f(t)$ nonparametrically using cubic and quintic splines and AR (1) errors with the parameters estimated by marginal likelihood. The dashed and solid lines in Fig. 2 correspond to the cubic and quintic spline estimates and the dots correspond to the observations. For the quintic spline the estimate of the smoothing parameter was very small giving effectively a quadratic estimate of the regression curve. The cubic spline estimate was similar although a little less smooth. Figure 2 shows that our data only covers a small arc of the circle so that the parametric model fitted by Pandit & Wu is approximately a quadratic. This implies that the parametric and quintic spline estimates are consistent. For both cubic and quintic splines similar estimates to those in Fig. 2 are obtained for errors modelled by an AR (2) and an ARMA (2, 1) process.

The second example consists of a data set of 4380 daily sea surface temperature observations collected daily at Granite Canyon, California (Breaker & Lewis, 1988). Figure 3(a) is a plot of the data and Fig. 3(b) presents the cubic, shown by dotted line, and quintic, solid line, spline estimates with the error in both cases modelled by an AR (2) process. Both spline estimates display the seasonality in the data with the quintic estimate being a little smoother. Altman (1990) also analyzed these data and her estimates are a little less smooth than the cubic spline estimate.

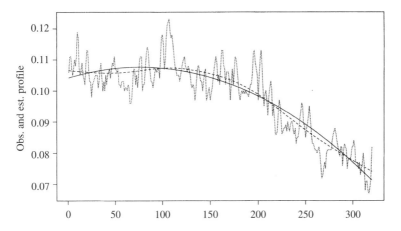

Fig. 2. Analysis of profile of a block of wood using AR (1) model for errors and marginal likelihood estimation. There are 320 equally spaced observations. Dotted line, observations; dashed line, cubic spline estimate; solid line, quintic spline estimate.

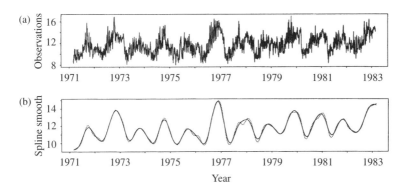

Fig. 3. Analysis of sea surface temperature using AR (2) model for errors and marginal likelihood estimation. (a) Observations. (b) Dotted line, cubic spline estimate; solid line, quintic spline estimate.

Acknowledgements

The research for this paper was partially supported by an ARC grant and Hewlett Packard. We would like to thank Naomi Altman and Jeff Hart for providing pre-prints of their work, to Professor P. A. W. Lewis for permission to use the data in Fig. 3 and to Geoff Eagleson for useful comments.

Appendix

Derivation of the cross-validation algorithm

To derive the algorithm in Section 3.2 for the computation of the cross-validation function $C(\tau)$ and the generalized cross-validation function $G(\tau)$ we temporarily extend the observation equation (2.8) so that

$$y(i) = h'x(i) + \zeta(i) \tag{A.1}$$

with $\zeta(i)$ independent $N(0, \kappa\sigma^2)$. If $\kappa = 0$ then (A.1) becomes (2.8). The state transition equation is described in Section 2. For notational convenience we do not indicate dependence on τ below. We now proceed as Kohn & Ansley (1989). Let $g(i) = h'x(i)$ be the signal in (A.1). For $k > 0$ and $\kappa > 0$ let

$$\hat{g}(i; k, \kappa) = E\{g(i)|y(1), \ldots, y(n); k, \kappa\},$$

$$\hat{g}^{(-i)}(i; k, \kappa) = E\{g(i)|y(1), \ldots, y(i-1), y(i+1), \ldots, y(n); k, \kappa\},$$

$$\hat{\zeta}(i; k, \kappa) = y(i) - \hat{g}(i; k, \kappa).$$

Then by an argument similar to that of Kohn & Ansley (1989, p. 72)

$$y(i) - \hat{g}^{(-i)}(i; k, \kappa) = \kappa\hat{\zeta}(i; k, \kappa)/\text{var}\{\hat{\zeta}(i; k, \kappa)\}. \tag{A.2}$$

Below we find the limits of $\hat{\zeta}(i; k, \kappa)/\kappa$ and $\text{var}\{\hat{\zeta}(i; k, \kappa)/\kappa\}$ as $k \to \infty$ and $\kappa \to 0$.

First we define the $(m + m') \times 1$ vectors $a(i; k, \kappa)$ and the sequence of $(m + m') \times (m + m')$ matrices $b(i; k, \kappa)$ $(i = 1, \ldots, n + 1)$ recursively. Initialize $a(n + 1; k, \kappa) = 0$ and $b(n + 1; k, \kappa) = 0$. For $i = n, \ldots, 1$, define

$$a(i; k, \kappa) = h\varepsilon(i; k, \kappa)/R(i; k, \kappa) + M'(i; k, \kappa)a(i + 1; k, \kappa),$$

$$b(i; k, \kappa) = hh'/R(i; k, \kappa) + M'(i; k, \kappa)b(i + 1; k, \kappa)M(i; k, \kappa),$$

where

$$M(i; k, \kappa) = F\{I - S(i|i - 1; k, \kappa)hh'/R(i; k, \kappa)\}.$$

Let $a(i)$, $b(i)$ and $M(i)$ be the limits as $k \to \infty$ and $\kappa \to 0$ of $a(i; k, \kappa)$, $b(i; k, \kappa)$ and $M(i; k, \kappa)$. It is not difficult to verify that these limits exist and are given by (3.2)–(3.7). As Kohn & Ansley (1989, p. 67) we can show that

$$\hat{\zeta}(i; k, \kappa) = \varepsilon(i; k, \kappa)/R(i; k, \kappa) - h'S(i|i - 1; k, \kappa)F'a(i + 1; k, \kappa).$$

Let $\xi(i)$ be the limit as $k \to \infty$ and $\kappa \to 0$ of $\hat{\zeta}(i; k, \kappa)/\kappa$ and let $\eta(i) = \text{var}\{\xi(i)\}$. Then $\xi(i)$ and $\eta(i)$ are given by (3.8)–(3.11) and the expression for $C(\tau)$ follows from (A.2) because $\hat{y}^{(-i)}(i; k, \kappa) = \hat{g}^{(-i)}(i; k, \kappa)$.

References

Altman, N. S. (1990). Kernel smoothing of data with correlated errors. *J. Am. Statist. Assoc.* 85, 749–59.

Ansley, C. F. & Kohn, R. (1985). Estimation, filtering and smoothing in state space models with incompletely specified initial conditions. *Ann. Statist.* 13, 1286–316.

Ansley, C. F. & Kohn, R. (1990). Filtering and smoothing in state space models with partially diffuse initial conditions. *J. Time Ser. Anal.* 11, 275–93.

Box, G. E. P. & Jenkins, G. M. (1976). *Time Series Analysis: Forecasting and Control.* San Francisco, CA: Holden-Day.

Breaker, L. C. & Lewis, P. A. W. (1988). On the detection of a 40 to 50 day oscillation in sea surface temperature along the central California coast. *Estuarine Coastal and Shelf Sci.* 26, 395–408.

Bryson, A. E. & Ho, Y. (1975). *Applied Optimal Control.* New York: Wiley.

Craven, P. & Wahba, G. (1979). Smoothing noisy data with spline functions. *Numer. Math.* 31, 377–403.

Diggle, P. J. & Hutchinson, M. F. (1989). On spline smoothing with autocorrelated errors. *Aust. J. Statist.* 31, 166–82.

Eubank, R. L. (1988). *Spline Smoothing and Nonparametric Regression.* New York: Marcel Dekker.

Gasser, T., Sroka, L. & Jennen-Steinmetz, C. (1986). Residual variance and residual pattern in nonlinear regression. *Biometrika* 73, 625–33.

Golub, G. & Van Loan, C. F. (1983). *Matrix Computations.* Baltimore: Johns Hopkins University Press.

Hart, J. D. (1991). Kernel regression estimation with time series errors. *J. R. Statist. Soc.* B 53, 173–87.

Harvey, A. C. (1981). *Time Series Models.* New York: Wiley.

Harvey, A. C. & Stock, J. H. (1986). The estimation of higher order continuous time autoregressive models. *Econometric Theory* 1, 97–118.

Harvey, A. C. & Todd, P. H. J. (1983). Forecasting economic time series with structural and Box–Jenkins models: a case study. *J. Bus. Econ. Statist.* 1, 299–315.

Hurvich, C. M. & Zeger, S. L. (1990). A frequency domain selection criterion for regression with autocorrelated errors. *J. Am. Statist. Assoc.* 85, 705–14.

Jones, R. H. (1981). Fitting a continuous time autoregression to discrete data. In *Applied Time Series Analysis II*, D. F. Findley (ed.), pp. 651–82. New York: Academic Press.

Kitagawa, G. & Gersch, W. (1984). A smoothness priors-state space modeling of time series with trend and seasonality. *J. Am. Statist. Assoc.* 79, 378–89.

Kohn, R. & Ansley, C. F. (1983). On the smoothness properties of the best linear unbiased estimate of a stochastic process observed with noise. *Ann. Statist.* 11, 1011–7.

Kohn, R. & Ansley, C. F. (1987). A new algorithm for spline smoothing based on smoothing a stochastic process. *SIAM J. Sci. Statist. Comput.* 8, 33–48.

Kohn, R. & Ansley, C. F. (1988). The equivalence between Bayesian smoothness priors and optimal smoothing for function estimation. In *Bayesian Analysis of Time Series and Dynamic Models*, J. C. Spall (ed.), pp. 393–430. New York: Dekker.

Kohn, R. & Ansley, C. F. (1989). A fast algorithm for signal extraction, influence and cross-validation in state space models. *Biometrika* 76, 65–79.

Moler, C. B. & Van Loan, C. F. (1978). Nineteen dubious ways to compute the exponential of a matrix. *SIAM Rev.* 20, 801–36.

More, J. J., Garbow, B. S. & Hillstrom, K. E. (1980). *User Guide for Minpack*. Argonne, Illinois: Argonne National Laboratory.

Pandit, S. M. & Wu, S. M. (1983). *Time Series and System Analysis with Applications*. New York: Wiley.

Wahba, G. (1978). Improper priors, spline smoothing and the problem of guarding against model errors in regression. *J. R. Statist. Soc.* B 40, 364–72.

Wahba, G. (1985). A comparison of GCV and GML for choosing the smoothing parameter in the generalized spline smoothing problem. *Ann. Statist.* 11, 1378–402.

Wecker, W. E. & Ansley, C. F. (1983). The signal extraction approach to linear regression and spline smoothing. *J. Am. Statist. Assoc.* 78, 81–9.

Part II

Unobserved Components in Economic Time Series

7

Introduction

The articles reproduced in this part specialise in the extraction of signals in economic time series. Chapters 8–10 deal with the characterisation of trends and cycles, a controversial topic in macroeconomics. Chapter 11 shows how to incorporate the serial correlation induced by survey sample design into time series models. This is particularly important for data obtained from labour force surveys and the method illustrates the power of the state space approach. Finally, Chapter 12 deals with seasonal adjustment of weekly time series, with an application to U.K. money supply. Again state space methods are able to deal with a problem difficult to solve by other techniques.

1 Trends and Cycles in Economic Time Series

The decomposition of economic time series into trend and cyclical components has a long tradition. Along with providing a description of the salient features of a series, the distinction between what is permanent and what is transitory in economic dynamics has important implications for monetary and fiscal policy. The measurement of *potential output*, *output gaps*, *core inflation* and the *natural* rate of unemployment are all facets of the same problem.

Needless to say, the formulation of a dynamic model for the components turns out to be a highly controversial issue; this is the general message conveyed by the first three articles reproduced in this part. Even when attention is restricted to the class of linear Gaussian time series models, where it is generally acknowledged that the trend should be nonstationary and the cycle stationary, several points have been the topic of an interesting and ongoing debate.

The first issue is whether the kind of nonstationary behaviour displayed by economic time series is best captured by deterministic or stochastic trends. In the former case it is also said that the series is trend-stationary, implying that it can be decomposed into a deterministic function of time and a stationary cycle; in the second the series can be made stationary after suitable differencing and so it is said to be difference-stationary or integrated order of order d (or I(d)), where d denotes the power of the stationary inducing transformation, $(1 - L)^d$. The characterisation of the nature of the series was addressed in a seminal paper by Nelson and Plosser (1982), who adopted the (augmented) Dickey-Fuller test for testing the hypothesis that the series is I(1) versus the alternative that it is trend-stationary. Using a set of annual U.S. macroeconomic time series they were unable to reject the null for most series and discuss the implications for economic interpretation.

A second issue deals with the specification of a time series model for the trend component for difference-stationary processes and is nicely exposited in Chapter 8, on stochastic detrending. The difficulties stem from the fundamental fact that commonly agreed definitions of the trend component as "the value the series would take if it were on its long-run path" (Beveridge and Nelson, 1981), leading e.g. to a random walk representation of the trend for I(1) processes, are consistent with any assumption on the (usually unidentifiable) correlation between the transitory and the permanent disturbances.

Watson considers the implications of three decompositions of a *given* ARIMA(p,1,q) process. The (identifying) assumption of orthogonal trend and cycle disturbances (Model 1) means that the spectral density of Δy_t is a global minimum at the zero frequency (see also Lippi and Reichlin, 1993), which in turn implies that persistence (the long-run effect of a trend disturbance) cannot be greater than one.

The Beveridge-Nelson (BN) decomposition, with perfectly correlated disturbances (Model 2), is always admissible, but may yield trends which are as or more variable than the observations; this occurs for instance for an ARIMA(1,1,0) with positive AR parameter (see also Proietti and Harvey, 2000). When the true model is $\Delta y_t = \beta + \psi(L)\xi_t$, and $\psi(L) = \theta(L)/\phi(L)$, the BN decomposition is

$$y_t = \mu_t^{BN} + c_t^{BN}, \quad t = 1, \dots, T,$$

where the trend, μ_t^{BN}, is defined as the long run prediction of the series (eventual forecast function) at time t, that is $\lim_{l \to \infty} \tilde{y}_{t+l|t} - l\beta$. This is easily shown to give

$$\mu_t^{BN} = \mu_{t-1}^{BN} + \beta + \psi(1)\xi_t.$$

Correspondingly the representation of the cyclical component is a stationary ARMA$(p, \max(p, q) - 1)$ model, with

$$\phi(L)c_t^{BN} = \{\vartheta(L)/\phi(1)\}\xi_t,$$

where the MA polynomial $\vartheta(L)$ satisfies: $\psi(1)\theta(L) - \theta(1)\psi(L) - \Delta\vartheta(L)$. Computational algorithms based on the state representation and the Kalman filter are given in Proietti (1995). It should be noticed that the sign of the correlation between the trend and cycle disturbances is determined by the parameters of the ARIMA process. As shown in Chapter 8, the μ_t^{BN} and c_t^{BN} are coincident with the filtered or real time estimates (i.e. using current and past observations) of the components of the UC orthogonal decomposition, when the ARIMA reduced form is the same.

UC models with perfectly correlated components were also considered by Godolphin (1976) with the explicit intent of extending the parameter range yielding decomposable models. Snyder (1985) and Ord, Koehler and Snyder (1997) propose unobserved components models with only one source of random disturbances, arguing that models with multiple disturbances are unnecessarily complex.

The third decomposition (Model 3) arises when a less than perfect nonzero correlation is assumed. This is usually unidentified unless one imposes an a priori value on the correlation or uses untestable restrictions on the dynamic model for the cyclical components; for instance, for an ARIMA(2,1,2) process one may specify the cycle as an AR(2) process as in Morley, Nelson and Zivot (2003), which leaves one degree of freedom for estimating the correlation between the trend and cycle disturbances.

The three decompositions yield the same trend forecasts. Indeed the filtered estimates of the components for Model 1 and 2 coincide (assuming the first is admissible), although their MSEs differ, as the MSE for the BN decomposition is zero (as the components are observable at time t). Watson shows that when UC models with uncorrelated disturbances are estimated on real time series, without conditioning on a particular ARIMA reduced form, they lead to models with different long-run properties compared to ARIMA models; the latter tend to favour highly persistent processes, such that most variation in the data is accounted for by trend movements. These differences are a direct consequence of model specification and the likelihood is rather uninformative on the long-run properties of the series. This is highlighted in Watson's discussion of U.S. GDP.

2 The Hodrick–Prescott Filter

The specification of a model for the trend often embodies the analyst's smoothness prior on this component (see Kitagawa and Gersch, 1996). One popular example is the *ad hoc* trend extraction filter proposed by Hodrick and Prescott (1997, HP henceforth), on the following grounds: "Our prior knowledge is that the growth component varies 'smoothly' over time". Undoubtedly, its popularity stems from its capability of producing trends resembling the curve that a relatively unexperienced user would draw through the time plot of the series (Kydland and Prescott, 1990).

HP define the estimator of the trend as the minimiser of the penalised least square criterion:

$$PLS = \sum_{t=1}^{T}(y_t - \mu_t)^2 + \lambda \sum_{t=3}^{T}(\Delta^2 \mu_t)^2, \tag{7.1}$$

where the first summand measures fidelity and the second roughness; λ is the *smoothness parameter* governing the trade-off between them.

In vector notation, setting $y = (y_1, \ldots, y_T)'$ and $\mu = (\mu_1, \ldots, \mu_T)'$,

$$PLS = (y - \mu)'(y - \mu) + \lambda \mu' D^{2'} D^2 \mu,$$

where $D = \{d_{ij}\}$ denotes the $T \times T$ matrix corresponding to first differences, with $d_{ii} = 1, d_{i,i-1} = -1$ and zero otherwise. Differentiating with respect to μ, the first order conditions yield: $\tilde{\mu} = (I_T + \lambda D^2)^{-1} y$, but the component is more efficiently computed by the Kalman filter and smoother, thereby avoiding the inversion of a potentially very large matrix.

As a matter of fact, the HP filter is coincident with the smoothed estimator of the trend component of local linear trend model:

$$
\begin{aligned}
y_t &= \mu_t + \epsilon_t, & \epsilon_t &\sim \text{NID}(0, \sigma_\epsilon^2), & t = 1, 2, \ldots, T, \\
\mu_t &= \mu_{t-1} + \beta_{t-1} + \eta_t, & \eta_t &\sim \text{NID}(0, \sigma_\eta^2), & \text{(7.2)} \\
\beta_t &= \beta_{t-1} + \zeta_t, & \zeta_t &\sim \text{NID}(0, \sigma_\zeta^2),
\end{aligned}
$$

with the restrictions $\sigma_\eta^2 = 0$ and $\sigma_\epsilon^2 / \sigma_\zeta^2 = \lambda$.

This is so since the fixed-interval smoother under Gaussianity will provide the mode of the distribution of μ conditional on y, whose kernel takes exactly the form (7.1), as $f(\mu|y) \propto f(y|\mu) f(\mu) = \prod_t f(y_t|\mu_t) \prod_t (\mu_t|\mu_{t-1}, \mu_{t-2})$. Notice also that the PLS problem (7.1) is a discrete version of the cubic spline smoothing problem dealt with in Part I.

The HP detrended or cyclical component is the smoothed estimate of the irregular component in (7.2) and, although the maintained representation for the deviations from the trend is a purely irregular component, the filter has been one of the most widely employed tools in macroeconomics to extract measures of the business cycle.

The connection with the signal-noise ratio makes clear that the Lagrange multiplier, λ, measures the variability of the (noise) cyclical component relative to that of the trend, and regulates the smoothness of the long-term component. As σ_η^2 approaches zero, λ tends to infinity, and the limiting representation of the trend is a straight line.

HP purposively select the value $\lambda = 1600$ for quarterly time series; some recent papers (Gómez, 2001; Maravall and Del Rio, 2001) have dealt with the design of this parameter using frequency domain arguments, that we briefly review. Assuming the availability of a doubly infinite sample, the minimum mean square linear estimator of the trend is:

$$
\tilde{\mu}_{t|\infty} - w_{HP}(L) y_t, \qquad w_{HP}(L) = \frac{1}{1 + \lambda |1 - L|^4}
$$

with $|1 - L|^2 = (1 - L)(1 - L^{-1})$. Note that $w_{HP}(1) = 1$, i.e. the weights sum to 1.

The gain of the filter $w_{HP}(L)$ is:

$$
G_{HP}(\omega) = \frac{1}{1 + 4\lambda(1 - \cos \omega)^2}, \qquad \omega \in [0, \pi];
$$

notice that this is 1 at the zero frequency and decreases monotonically to zero as ω approaches π. Its behaviour enforces the interpretation of $w_{HP}(L)$ as a low-pass filter, and the corresponding detrending filter, $1 - w_{HP}(L)$, as the high-pass filter derived from it.

The implicit cut-off frequency is the value ω_c corresponding to a gain $G_{HP}(\omega) = 1/2$. This satisfies the equation

$$\lambda = [4(1 - \cos \omega_c)^2]^{-1} = [2 \sin(\omega_c/2)]^{-4}; \tag{7.3}$$

for a given smoothness parameter (7.3) can be solved with respect to the cut-off frequency ω_c, giving $\omega_c = \arccos(1 - 0.5\lambda^{-1/2})$. For instance, setting $\lambda = 1600$ we get that the HP filter for quarterly data is a low-pass filter with $\omega_c = 0.158$ corresponding to a period of 39.69 e.g. 10 years. Solving equation (7.3) for λ given a specific cut-off ω_c, provides a way of designing the HP filter as a low-pass filter.

Harvey and Jaeger (1993, Chapter 9) show that for I(1) and I(2) series the detrended series can display spurious cyclical behaviour, thereby providing another example of the Slutzky-Yule effect. The transfer function will in fact display a distinctive peak at business cycle frequencies. In Section 5.4 the possibility of generating spurious comovements among detrended series is also shown. Having pointed out the potential dangers of mechanical detrending by the HP filter, Harvey and Jaeger propose characterising the stylised facts by a structural time series model capable of interpreting the cyclical dynamics in the series, which can be estimated by maximum likelihood and for which data coherency can be assessed by suitable diagnostics and goodness of fit statistics.

3 Canonical Decomposition

Maravall (1993, Chapter 10) describes the *ARIMA model based* (AMB) or *canonical* approach to the decomposition of a time series, with a particular emphasis on the characterisation of the trend component. Unlike the structural approach, the starting point is the ARIMA model fitted to the series according to the Box and Jenkins methodology; the series is then decomposed into trends, seasonals, etc., using representations for the components that are consistent with the ARIMA model and that are balanced with respect to the AR and MA orders; this leads to the specification of trend models of the kind IMA(1,1), IMA(2,2), etc. (whereas in the structural framework the MA order is one less, e.g. IMA(1,0), IMA(2,1), etc.). Different components are taken to be orthogonal. The canonical principle, according to which the variance of the irregular component is maximised, ensures that the decomposition is uniquely identified. This induces the noninvertible root -1 in the MA representation of the differenced trend, so that its spectral density is zero at the Nyquist frequency.

Maravall illustrates the relationships with the structural approach and other *ad hoc* filters. He also provides a thorough discussion of the time series properties of the optimal estimator of the trend component, highlighting the differences with the theoretical model specified for it. As a natural consequence of signal extraction the model for the estimator will not be invertible at specific frequencies and the author stresses the implications for econometric modelling (e.g. unit root testing and autoregressive modelling applied to seasonally adjusted data).

We now elaborate a little further on the relationships between the canonical and structural approaches, concentrating on the decomposition of the

IMA(1,1) model: $\Delta y_t = \xi_t + \xi_{t-1}, \xi_t \sim \text{WN}(0, \sigma^2)$. In the structural framework, the local level model is formulated as follows:

$$
\begin{aligned}
y_t &= \mu_t + \epsilon_t, & t = 1, 2, \ldots, T, & \quad \epsilon_t \sim \text{WN}(0, \sigma_\epsilon^2), \\
\mu_{t+1} &= \mu_t + \eta_t, & & \quad \eta_t \sim \text{WN}(0, \sigma_\eta^2),
\end{aligned}
\tag{7.4}
$$

where the disturbances are mutually uncorrelated; equating the autocovariance generating functions of Δy_t we find that $\sigma_\eta^2 = (1+\theta)^2\sigma^2$ and $\sigma_\epsilon^2 = -\theta\sigma^2$; hence the structural model requires $\theta \leq 0$.

Initialising μ_t with a diffuse prior amounts to starting off the KF at $t = 2$ with $\tilde{\mu}_{2|1} = y_1$ and $P_{2|1} = \sigma_\eta^2 + \sigma_\epsilon^2$. If $\sigma_\eta^2 > 0$ the model is detectable and stabilisable and its steady state solution (see Chapter 2) has $P = \sigma_\epsilon^2(q + \sqrt{q^2 + 4q})/2$, where $q = \sigma_\eta^2/\sigma_\epsilon^2$, $F = P + \sigma_\epsilon^2$, and gain $K = P/(P + \sigma_\epsilon^2)$. In terms of the reduced form parameters, $P = (1 + \theta)\sigma^2$, $F = \sigma^2$ and $K = 1 + \theta$. Notice that $K \leq 1$.

The forecast function is a horizontal straight line, being given by $\tilde{y}_{t+l|t} = \tilde{\mu}_{t+1|t}, l = 1, 2, \ldots$, where $\tilde{\mu}_{t+1|t} = \tilde{\mu}_{t|t-1} + Kv_t$. Hence, the forecasts are an *exponentially weighted moving average* of the available observation: $\tilde{y}_{t+l|t} = Ky_t + (1 - K)Ky_{t-1} + (1 - K)^2 Ky_{t-2} + \cdots + (1 - K)^j Ky_{t-j} + \cdots$.

Let us consider now the canonical decomposition of y_t: $y_t = \mu_t^* + \epsilon_t^*$, where $\mu_{t+1}^* = \mu_t^* + \eta_t^* + \eta_{t-1}^*$ where the disturbances ϵ_t^* and η_t^* are mutually and serially uncorrelated with variances $\sigma_{\epsilon*}^2$ and $\sigma_{\eta*}^2$, respectively. Equating the autocovariance generating functions of Δy_t gives

$$
\sigma_{\eta*}^2 = \tfrac{1}{4}(1 + \theta)^2, \qquad \sigma_{\epsilon*}^2 = \tfrac{1}{4}(1 - \theta)^2,
$$

from which it is seen that the decomposition is admissible for all values of θ.

The model can be cast in state space form defining the state vector $\alpha_t = [\mu_t^*, \eta_{t-1}^*]'$, and system matrices

$$
Z = [1, 0], \qquad G = \sigma_{\epsilon*}, \qquad T = \begin{bmatrix} 1 & 1 \\ 0 & 0 \end{bmatrix}, \qquad H = \sigma_{\eta*}[1, 1]'.
$$

The steady state KF can be shown to have

$$
P = \begin{bmatrix} \sigma_{\eta*}^2 + 2\sigma_{\eta*}\sigma_{\epsilon*} & \sigma_{\eta*}^2 \\ \sigma_{\eta*}^2 & \sigma_{\eta*}^2 \end{bmatrix}, \qquad F = (\sigma_{\eta*} + \sigma_{\epsilon*})^2,
$$

$$
K = \begin{bmatrix} 2\sigma_{\eta*}/(\sigma_{\eta*} + \sigma_{\epsilon*}) \\ 0 \end{bmatrix}.
$$

The last two quantities are expressed in terms of the reduced form parameters as $F = \sigma^2$ and $K_1 = (1 + \theta)$, where we have written $K = [K_1, 0]'$.

The forecast function is $\tilde{y}_{t+l|t} = \tilde{\mu}_{t+1|t}^*$, $l = 1, 2, \ldots$, where $\tilde{\mu}_{t+1|t}^* = \tilde{\mu}_{t|t-1}^* + \tilde{\eta}_{t-1|t-1}^* + K_1 v_t$; and $\tilde{\eta}_{t|t}^* = 0$. Since initialising the KF with a diffuse prior on the first state element and the stationary distribution for the second amounts to start-off the KF at $t = 2$ with $\tilde{\mu}^*_{2|1} = y_1$, the one-step-ahead state (and observation) forecast are identical to the local level model, when this is admissible ($\theta \leq 0$). This simply shows that the two decomposition are observationally equivalent, as the innovations and their variance are identical. In this case the canonical decomposition produces forecasts according to EWMA; the same cannot be said when $\theta > 0$ since in the forecast revision the forecast error is assigned a weight greater than one, the weight being $(1 + \theta)$.

The differences arise with respect to contemporaneous filtering and smoothing: as a matter of fact, it is immediately shown that the updated estimate of the canonical trend is $\tilde{\mu}^*_{t|t} = \tilde{\mu}^*_{t|t-1} + (1 + \theta)((3 - \theta)/4)v_t$ (also, for the second state component, $\tilde{\eta}^*_{t-1|t} = (1 + \theta)^2 v_t/4$), whereas for the local level model, $\tilde{\mu}_{t|t} = \tilde{\mu}_{t|t-1} + (1 + \theta)v_t$; the canonical trend will integrate a smaller fraction of the innovation at time t, hence will tend to be smoother. The estimators of the two components based on a doubly infinite sample are related by:

$$\tilde{\mu}_{t|\infty} = \frac{(1 + \theta)^2}{|\theta(L)|^2} y_t = \frac{1}{1 + q^{-1}|1 - L|^2} y_t, \qquad \tilde{\mu}^*_{t|\infty} = \frac{1}{4}|1 + L|^2 \tilde{\mu}_{t|\infty},$$

which shows that the canonical trend estimator is a symmetric moving average of the structural trend with weights $(0.25L^{-1} + 0.5 + 0.25L)$. All the formulae continue to hold when y_t is random walk ($\theta = 0$), in which case the structural trend is coincident with the observations, $\tilde{\mu}_{t+1|t} = \tilde{\mu}_{t|t} = \tilde{\mu}_{t|\infty} = y_t$, whereas $\tilde{\mu}^*_{t+1|t} = y_t$, $\tilde{\mu}^*_{t|t} = 0.75 y_t + 0.25 y_{t-1}$, and finally $\tilde{\mu}^*_{t|\infty} = 0.25 y_{t-1} + 0.5 y_t + 0.25 y_{t+1}$.

The chapter also includes a nice discussion of the I(1) versus I(2) controversy on the nature of trends.

4 Estimation and Seasonal Adjustment in Panel Surveys

Chapter 11 proposes a time series approach to the estimation of population means from repeated surveys, making an important contribution towards the use of model based estimation techniques in official statistics, and the integration of micro and macro data in economics.

In Pfefferman's approach, population means are considered as random variables, which evolve stochastically over time (according to a trend plus seasonal structural model), rather than fixed parameters, as in classic analysis. Moreover, important features of the statistical data generating process, arising from the adoption of a rotational scheme, and in particular the correlation between the panel estimates induced by the partial overlapping of the same units, can be properly incorporated within the model.

The author shows, both by simulation and by an empirical application to the Israel Labour Force Survey, that his model based approach leads to substantial improvements in the accuracy of the estimates, especially in the case of primary analysis.

In primary analysis the population means arise as the optimal estimates of the common signal in the individual panel estimates t (see equation 2.4), which usually contains a trend plus a seasonal component. Rotation group bias (considered by the author as a time invariant feature of the panels) can also be estimated subject to either identification constraints: i) it is absent from any one panel, ii) it satisfies a linear constraint, e.g. a zero sum constraint.

Significant improvements arise also from modelling the correlation of the panel estimates. Here the reference model for the panel survey error is a first order autoregression. If $\bar{\epsilon}_t^{t-j}$ denotes the sampling error in the panel which entered the sample at time $t - j$, $\bar{\epsilon}_t^{t-j} = \rho\bar{\epsilon}_{t-1}^{t-j} + \bar{v}_t$, $\bar{v}_t \sim \text{WN}(0, \sigma_v^2/M)$, where M is the number of units in the panel; referring to the 2-2-2 Israel Labour Force Survey rotational scheme, and rearranging the components of the survey error in Pfefferman's equation (2.5) as $\alpha_t^{(2)} = [\bar{\epsilon}_t^t, \bar{\epsilon}_t^{t-1}, \bar{\epsilon}_t^{t-2}, \ldots, \bar{\epsilon}_t^{t-6}]$, the vector of survey errors follow the recursion (see Harvey and Chung, 2000): $\alpha_t^{(2)} = T_{22} + \eta_t^{(2)}$, where T_{22} has zero elements except on the first leading subdiagonal, where it takes the constant value ρ; correspondingly, $\eta_t^{(22)}$ has diagonal covariance matrix, $\text{Var}(\eta_t^{(22)}) = (\sigma_v^2/M)\text{diag}((1 - \rho^2)^{-1}, 1, \ldots, 1)$. For secondary analysis the total survey error would be $[1/4, 1/4, 0, 0, 1/4, 1/4]\alpha_t^{(2)}$, and is equivalent to an MA(5) process with gaps (more generally the survey error component yields an MA(m) model, where m is the number of periods between the first and the last time that units are retained in the sample). For primary analysis the measurement equation selects the first two and last two elements of $\alpha_t^{(2)}$.

A relevant issue for secondary data users is whether one should be concerned at all with the survey error component. The author responds positively in his conclusive remarks, but it must be stressed that in the absence of a priori knowledge on the stochastic process governing the survey errors, the analyst must rely on unverifiable model assumptions, e.g. a first order autoregression (whereas, as the author shows, for primary analysis the panel contrasts are informative on the specification of the survey error model), the available information may give rise to imprecise estimates of ρ, and the component may be impossible to disentangle from other short run effects.

Also, in the case of designs with a relatively large number of panels the survey error component requires the addition of a corresponding large number (16 in the U.S. Labour Force Survey) of state elements, imposing a very high computational burden.

5 Seasonality in Weekly Data

The primary concern of Harvey, Koopman and Riani (1997, Chapter 12) is modelling seasonality for weekly data, with application to monetary time series. The availability of weekly measurements on a stock variable, such as U.K. money supply (M0), poses some difficulties: a new problem (with respect to monthly and quarterly data) is that the seasonal cycle is "sampled" at different points from year to year; moreover, the seasonal period, s, is not an integral number, oscillating between 52 and 53, and is relatively large, which calls for parsimony in modelling the seasonal pattern. Finally, leap years and moving festivals need to be handled, the latter with the necessary flexibility, as their effect depends on their position in the year.

The authors propose to model the seasonal pattern as the sum of a purely periodic component (adjusted for leap years) and a moving festival component. The model for the periodic component is specified at the daily frequency of observation; the full pattern resulting from $s = 365$ effects is expressed as a linear combination of a much smaller set of representative points, called knots. The coefficients of the linear combination (weights) are provided by cubic spline interpolation embodying the periodicity constraint. Time-varying periodic effects are then allowed for by letting the parameters evolve according to a multivariate random walk with one cointegration constraint which is a reflection of periodicity.

A yearly pattern can also be represented in the frequency domain by a trigonometric seasonal model based on stochastic cycles at the seasonal frequencies, but the authors point out that the main virtue of the periodic spline model in their application is the flexibility to handle a seasonal pattern that changes more rapidly around Christmas.

Another application can be found in Harvey and Koopman (1993), where periodic splines are employed to model and forecast hourly electricity demand; Proietti (1998) deals with modelling seasonal heteroscedasticity with an application to the Italian industrial production series.

8
Univariate Detrending Methods with Stochastic Trends*

MARK W. WATSON[†]
Harvard University and NBER

This paper discusses detrending economic time series, when the trend is modelled as a stochastic process. It considers unobserved components models in which the observed series is decomposed into a trend (a random walk with drift) and a residual stationary component. Optimal detrending methods are discussed, as well as problems associated with using these detrended data in regression models. The methods are applied to three time series: GNP, disposable income, and consumption expenditures. The detrended data are used to test a version of the Life Cycle consumption model.

1 Introduction

Most macroeconomic time series exhibit a clear tendency to grow over time and can be characterized as 'trending'. The statistical theory underlying most modern time series analysis relies on the assumption of covariance stationarity, an assumption that is clearly violated by most macroeconomic time series. In applied econometric work it is usually assumed that this statistical theory can be applied to deviations of the observed time series from their trend value. Since it is often the case that these deviations or economic fluctuations are of primary interest, modern time series techniques are often applied to 'detrended' economic time series.

   Much recent work has been devoted to issues involving trends or long-run components in economic series. Some of this work has devoted itself to the proper characterization of 'trends' in economic data. A notable contribution on this topic is the paper by Nelson and Plosser (1982) which considers the use of deterministic and stochastic trends. Other work [e.g., Nelson and Kang (1981, 1984)] has been concerned with the econometric consequences of misspecification in the model for the trend component. Still more work has addressed the issue of detecting long-run relations [e.g., Geweke (1983)] or incorporating long-run relationships in short-run dynamic relations [e.g., the work on 'error correction models' begun in Davidson et al. (1978) and the co-integrated processes introduced in Granger (1983) and discussed further in Engle and Granger (1984)].

* Reprinted from *Journal of Monetary Economics*, Vol. 18, M. W. Watson, "Univariate Detrending Methods with Stochastic Trends", pp. 49–75, © 1986, with permission from Elsevier.

† I would like to thank Andy Abel, Olivier Blanchard, Rob Engle, Charles Plosser, Charles Nelson, and Jim Stock for useful comments and discussions. I would also like to thank the National Science Foundation for financial support.

Research concerning the proper characterization of long-run trend behavior in economic time series is important for a variety of reasons. First, the work of Nelson and Kang and others shows that misspecification in the model for the trend can seriously affect the estimated dynamics in an econometric model. Proper estimation of these dynamic relations is important if they are to be used to test modern theories of economic behavior. These theories put very tight restrictions on the dynamic interrelations between economic variables. Misspecification of trend components will often lead the analyst to incorrect inferences concerning the validity of these theories. The proper specification of long-run relations is also critical for long-term forecasting.

This paper makes two points. The first point concerns the theory of stochastic detrending, and the second concerns its empirical implementation. We first propose a method for removing stochastic trends from economic time series. The method is similar to the one originally proposed by Beveridge and Nelson (1981), but differs in one important respect. The problem is cast in an unobserved components framework, in which the trend is modelled as a random walk with drift, and the residual 'cyclical' component is modelled as a covariance stationary process. This framework allows us to discuss and construct optimal detrending methods. One of the optimal methods corresponds to the (negative of the) Beveridge and Nelson transitory component. Our theoretical work shows that, in principle, our unobserved components (UC)[1] representation of the process describing the data will give exactly the same results as the usual ARIMA representation. That is, both models imply exactly the same long-run behavior of the data.

The second point of this paper is that *estimated* ARIMA and UC models imply very different long-run behavior of economic time series. For example, we estimate UC and ARIMA models for post-war US GNP. Both models yield essentially identical values of the likelihood function and short-run forecasts. However, estimated long-run behavior of the models is quite different. The ARIMA model implies that an innovation of one unit in GNP is expected to eventually increase the level of GNP by 1.68 units, the UC model implies that the same innovation will eventually increase GNP by only 0.57 units. These results suggest that it is a dangerous practice to use the estimated time series models such as ARIMA or UC models to make inferences about long-run characteristics of economic time series.

The paper is organized as follows. The next section specifies the model for the observed series, the trend component, and the residual 'cyclical' component. We begin with a general ARIMA formulation for the observed series and describe how the stochastic process can be 'factored' into the two processes for the components. Identification issues are also addressed in this section. Section 3 discusses methods for estimating and eliminating the stochastic trends. The properties of the detrended series are addressed, and special attention is paid to the use of these series in constructing econometric models. The final two sections contain empirical examples. Three post-war US macroeconomic time series – GNP, disposable income, and consumption of non-durables – are analysed. Section 4 looks at each of these series in isolation, and presents and compares various estimates of the detrended series. Section 5 uses the data for non-durable consumption and disposable income to test the 'consumption follows a random walk' implication of one version of the life cycle consumption model. The final section contains a short summary and some concluding remarks.

2 The Model

This section will introduce three models that additively decompose an observed time series, x_t, into a trend and cyclical component. Each of these models will assume, or imply, that the change in x_t is a covariance stationary process. We begin with the Wold representation for the change in x_t, which we write as

$$(1 - B)x_t = \delta + \theta^x(B)e_t^x, \qquad \text{var}(e_t^x) = \sigma_{ex}^2, \tag{2.1}$$

where $\theta^x(B)$ is a polynomial in the backshift operator B, and e_t^x is white noise. The assumption that $(1 - B)x_t$ is stationary is appropriate for most non-seasonal macroeconomic time series. Seasonal series often require a differencing operator of the form $(1 - B^s)$ where s is the seasonal span (12 for monthly, 4 for quarterly, etc.). Our assumption is not adequate to handle these series, and therefore, we are assuming that the series are non-seasonal.

The representation for the level of the series x_t that we consider in this paper is

$$x_t = \tau_t + c_t, \tag{2.2}$$

where

$$\tau_t = \delta + \tau_{t-1} + e_t^\tau, \qquad \text{var}(e_t^\tau) = \sigma_{e\tau}^2, \tag{2.3}$$

and (c_t, e_t^τ) is a jointly stationary process. A variety of specific assumptions about this process will be discussed below. The component τ_t corresponds to the trend component in the variable x_t; the 'detrending' will attempt to eliminate this component. Equation (2.3) represents this trend as a random walk with drift, which can be viewed as a flexible linear trend. The linear trend is a special case of (2.3) and corresponds to the restriction $\sigma_{e\tau}^2 = 0$. The forecast function of (2.3) is linear with a constant slope of δ and a level that varies with the realization of e_t^τ. More general formulations are certainly possible. Harvey and Todd (1983) consider a model in which the drift term, δ_t, evolves as a random walk. This allows the slope as well as the level of the forecast function of τ_t to vary through time. This formulation implies that x_t must be differenced twice to induce stationarity, and therefore is ruled out by our assumption that $(1 - B)x_t$ is stationary.

To complete the specification of the model we must list our assumptions concerning the covariance properties of c_t and the cross-covariances between c_t and e_t^τ. We consider three sets of assumptions. The assumptions will differ in the way that c_t and e^τ_{t-k} are correlated. We consider each model in turn:

Model 1

In this model the component c_t evolves independently of the τ_t component, and follows the process

$$c_t = \theta^c(B)e^c_t, \tag{2.4.1}$$

where e^c_t and e^τ_{t-k} are uncorrelated for all k. The parameters of the UC model given by (2.2), (2.3), and (2.4.1) are econometrically identifiable. To see this, equate the representations for $(1 - B)x_t$ corresponding to (2.1) and the UC model given in (2.2), (2.3), and (2.4.1). This implies

$$\theta^x(B)e^x_t = e^\tau_t + (1 - B)\theta^c(B)e^c_t,$$

so that

$$|\theta^x(1)|^2\sigma^2_{ex} = \sigma^2_{e\tau}. \tag{2.5}$$

The coefficients in $\theta^c(B)$ can be found by forming the factorization of

$$\theta^x(z)\theta^x(z^{-1})\sigma^2_{ex} - \sigma^2_{e\tau} = (1 - z)(1 - z^{-1})\theta^c(z)\theta^c(z^{-1})\sigma^2_{ec}, \tag{2.6}$$

subject to the usual identifying normalizations [e.g., $\theta^c_0 = 1$ and the roots of $\theta^c(z)$ are on or outside the unit circle].

Equation (2.6) can be used to show that (2.2)–(2.4.1) place testable restrictions on the x_t process given in (2.1). To see this, set $z = e^{-i\omega}$, so that the right-hand side of (2.6) is the spectrum of $(1 - B)c_t$. Since the spectrum is non-negative, the left-hand side of (2.6) must be non-negative for all ω. This implies that $\theta^x(e^{-i\omega})\theta^x(e^{i\omega})\sigma^2_{ex} \geq \sigma^2_{e\tau}$ for all ω, with equality guaranteed at $\omega = 0$ by (2.5). We conclude that the spectrum of $(1 - B)x_t$, $\theta^x(e^{-i\omega})\theta^x(e^{i\omega})\sigma^2_{ex}$, has a global minimum at $\omega = 0$. Only processes with this feature can be represented by Model 1. [As discussed in Nelson and Plosser (1981), this rules out many common processes such as the ARIMA(1,1,0) with positive autoregressive coefficient.] The restrictiveness of this assumption will be investigated empirically for three macroeconomic time series in Section 4.

Most of the discussion in the remainder of the paper will be devoted to Model 1. The restrictiveness of the model, however, suggests that other models are needed if the UC model is to be useful in describing all models of the form given in (2.1). Because of this we briefly discuss two other models. These differ from Model 1 in the assumptions they make about the covariance between c_t and e^τ_{t-k}. The first of these is:

Model 2

The model for c_t is

$$c_t = \theta^\tau(B)e^\tau_t, \tag{2.4.2}$$

where $\theta^{\tau}(B)$ is a one-sided polynomial in the backshift operator. In this model, the innovations in the trend and cyclical components are perfectly correlated. The advantage of this model is that there is a one-to-one correspondence between models of the form (2.1) and models characterized by (2.2), (2.3), and (2.4.2). This implies that the parameters of the UC formulation (2.3) and (2.4.2) are econometrically identifiable, and that unlike Model 1, this UC formulation places no constraints on the model (2.1). [A proof of this assertion can be found in an earlier version of this paper, Watson (1985).]

The perfect correlation between the innovations in the components is an assumption that some might find objectionable on *a priori* grounds. Some correlation is needed, however, to give the UC model enough flexibility to capture all of the dynamic behavior possible in the model (2.1). Our final model is a mix of Models 1 and 2, in which the c_t and τ_t are partially correlated.

Model 3

The component c_t is represented as

$$c_t = \phi^c(B)e_t^c + \phi^{\tau}(B)e_t^{\tau}, \tag{2.4.3}$$

where $\phi^c(B)$ and $\phi^{\tau}(B)$ are one-sided polynomials in B. This model can be viewed as a mixture of Models 1 and 2. Since both of those models are individually identifiable, Model 3 is not.

3 Estimation Issues

The models presented in the last section suggest that 'detrending' should be viewed as a method for estimating and removing the component τ_t from the observed series x_t. If we denote the estimated trend by $\hat{\tau}_t$, then the detrended series is given by $\hat{c}_t = x_t - \hat{\tau}_t$. Different detrending methods correspond to different methods for estimating τ. A variety of criteria can be used to choose among competing estimation methods. We will consider linear minimum mean square error (LMSE) estimators constructed using information sets $X_0^h = (x_0, x_1, \ldots, x_h)$. We concentrate on these estimators for a variety of reasons. In addition to the usual reasons, including ease of computation and optimality for quadratic loss, the use of LMSE estimators guarantee certain orthogonality properties involving the estimation errors $\tau_t - \hat{\tau}_t = \hat{c}_t - c_t$. These properties play a key role in the formation of instrumental variable estimators that are discussed below. We concentrate on a univariate information set for computational ease. In general, multivariate methods will produce more accurate estimates. The univariate methods considered in this paper can serve as a benchmark to measure the marginal gains from considering more general, multivariate models.

We will discuss detrending in the context of the general model – Model 3. The results for Model 1 can be found by setting $\phi^{\tau}(B) = 0$ and $\theta^c(B) = \phi^c(B)$, and the results for Model 2 can be found by setting $\phi^c(B) = 0$ and $\theta^{\tau}(B) = \phi^{\tau}(B)$. A convenient starting point for the discussion is the LMSE of using the information set $(\ldots, x_{-1}, x_0, x_1, \ldots)$. In this case the standard Wiener filter for stationary processes [see, e.g., Whittle (1963)] can be extended to this non-stationary case [see Bell (1984)] to yield

$$\hat{\tau}_t = V(B)x_t = \sum v_i x_{t-i}, \qquad (3.1)$$

where the coefficients in the two-sided polynomial $V(B)$ can be found from

$$V(x) = \sigma_{e\tau}^2 [1 + (1 - z^{-1})\phi^\tau(z^{-1})][\theta^*(z)\theta^*(z^{-1})\sigma_{ex}^2]^{-1}. \qquad (3.2)$$

We denote $E(w_t|X_0^h)$ by $w_{t/h}$ for any variable w (where E is used to denote the projection operator). From eq. (3.1),

$$\tau_{t/h} = E(\hat{\tau}_t|X_0^h) = \sum v_i E(x_{t-i}|X_0^h), \qquad (3.3)$$

so that the estimates of the trend using the information set X_0^h can be formed from the Wiener filter with unknown values of x replaced by forecasts or backcasts constructed from the set X_0^h.

The form of the filter $V(B)$ given in (3.2) makes it clear that the LMSE estimate depends on $\phi^\tau(z)$. Different $V(B)$ polynomials will be associated with Models 1, 2, and 3, so that different LMSE estimates of c_t will be constructed. Equation (3.2) makes it clear, however, that the difference arises from the way in which future data is used in the construction of $\tau_{t/h}$. All models produce the identical values of $\tau_{t/h}$ for $h \leq t$. This is easily demonstrated. From (2.2),

$$x_{t/h} = \tau_{t/h} + c_{t/h}.$$

For $h \leq t$,

$$\tau_{t+k/h} = \tau_{t/h} + k\delta \quad \text{for} \quad k = 1, 2, \ldots,$$

so that

$$x_{t+k/h} - k\delta = \tau_{t/h} + c_{t+k/h}.$$

Since all of the models imply that c_t is stationary (with mean zero),

$$\lim(k \to \infty)c_{t+k/h} = 0,$$

so that

$$\lim(k \to \infty)[x_{t+k/h} - k\delta] = \tau_{t/h}.$$

This result shows that, in principle, the estimates $c_{t/t}$ (which will be called the filtered estimates) can be formed without access to any specialized software. To calculate the filtered estimates one merely constructs an ARIMA model for x_t and then forecasts the series (less the deterministic increases $k\delta$) into the distant future. This forecast corresponds to the filtered estimate, $\tau_{t/t}$, and $c_{t/t} = x_t - \tau_{t/t}$. This estimate of a permanent component was first suggested by Beveridge and Nelson (1981) in their permanent/transitory decomposition of economic time series. They define their transitory component as $\tau_{t/t} - x_t = -c_{t/t}$, in the notation above. This discussion shows that their estimate of the permanent component corresponds to an optimal one-sided estimator for the trend in the models under consideration in this paper.

While the optimal filtered estimate $c_{t/t}$ is identified – is not model-dependent – its precision is not identified. That is, the mean square of $(c_t - c_{t/t})$ will depend on the assumed model. If Model 2 is used to describe the decomposition of the data, then $c_{t/t} = c_t$, so that the mean square error is zero. For the other models, x_t is made up of both noises e^τ and e^c so that it is impossible to perfectly disentangle τ_t and c_t when only their sum, x_t, is observed. Since the Models 1, 2, and 3 are observationally equivalent, the mean square of $(c_t - c_{t/t})$ is not identified.

The remainder of this section will focus on the use of estimated values of c_t in linear regression models. Replacing c_t by $c_{t/h}$ in regression models leads to problems similar to those in the classic errors-in-variables model. As the examples below will demonstrate, OLS estimates of regression coefficients will quite often be inconsistent.

We will begin our discussion by writing the orthogonal decomposition of c_t as

$$c_t = c_{t/h} + a_{t/h},$$

where $a_{t/h}$ is the signal extraction error that arises from the use of information set X_0^h. Ordinary least square regression estimates rely on sample covariances between observable variables, and the consistency of OLS estimates follows from the consistency of these sample covariances. Consider then the covariance between an arbitrary variable w and c. From the decomposition of c, we have

$$\text{cov}(w_t c_t) = \text{cov}(w_t c_{t/h}) + \text{cov}(w_t a_{t/h}).$$

The $\text{cov}(w_t c_t)$ will be consistently estimated by the sample covariance between w_t and $c_{t/h}$ if $\text{cov}(w_t a_{t/h}) = 0$. In general this will not be true, so that $\text{cov}(w_t c_t) \neq \text{cov}(w_t c_{t/h})$. Recall, however, that $a_{t/h}$ is a projection error, so that it is uncorrelated with linear combinations of data in X_0^h. By constructing w_t as a linear combination of the elements in X_0^h, we can guarantee that $\text{cov}(w_t c_t) = \text{cov}(w_t c_{t/h})$. We will use this fact in construction of instrumental variable estimators. It will be convenient to discuss a variety of estimation issues in the context of some specific models.

The first model has current and lagged values of c_t as independent variables, so that

$$y_t = \sum_{i=1}^{k} c_{t-i}\beta_i + z_t'\gamma + \xi_t,$$

where z_t is a j vector of unobserved variables, and we will assume (without loss of generality) that ξ_t is white noise. We can rewrite this model in terms of unobserved variables as

$$y_t = \sum_{i=1}^{k} c_{t-i/h}\beta_i + z_t'\gamma + \xi_t + \sum_{i=1}^{k} a_{t-i/h}\beta_i$$

$$= \sum_{i=1}^{k} c_{t-i/h}\beta_i + z_t'\gamma + u_t,$$

where u_t is the composite error term $(\xi_t + \sum_{i=1}^{k} a_{t-i/h}\beta_i)$. The unknown parameters $\beta_1, \beta_2, \ldots, \beta_k$ and $\gamma_1, \ldots, \gamma_j$ will be consistently estimated by OLS if the regressors $c_{t-i/h}$ and z_t are uncorrelated with the error term u_t. This may not be true for a variety of reasons.

Two sources of correlation are immediately apparent. First, consider the correlation between $c_{t-i/h}$ and ξ_t. In many models it will be reasonable to assume that ξ_t is uncorrelated with current and lagged values of c_t, but unreasonable to assume that ξ_t is uncorrelated with future values of c_t. (Correlation between ξ_t and c_{t+i} will exist if there is feedback from y_t to c_t.) But when $h > t$, $c_{t-i/h}$ will contain future x_t's, and therefore $c_{t-i/h}$ will contain linear combinations of future c_t's. This may induce a correlation between $c_{t-i/h}$ and ξ_t even though c_{t-i} and ξ_t are uncorrelated. The second source of correlation between the regressors and the disturbance arises from the possible correlation between z_t and $a_{t-i/h}$. These variables will be correlated when z_t contains useful information about c_t not contained in X_0^h.

These problems can be circumvented by the use of instrumental variables. In particular, the variables in X_0^t can be used as instruments to estimate the model. When constructing instrumental variable estimates, it is useful to make use of the fact that, for $h > t$, $c_{t/t} = E(c_{t/h}|X_0^t)$, so that IV estimates can be formed by regressing y_t on the filtered values, $c_{t/t}$, and $\hat{z}_t$, the fitted values from the regression of z_t onto the set of instruments. Finally, it should be pointed out that the error terms, u_t, may be serially correlated so that standard errors may have to be calculated using the procedures outlined in Cumby, Huizinga and Obstfeld (1983) or Hayashi and Sims (1983).

The second regression model that we consider is

$$c_t = \sum_{i=1}^{k} c_{t-i}\beta_i + z_t'\gamma + \xi_t.$$

This model should be interpreted as the true generating equation for c_t, so that ξ_t is uncorrelated with all variables dated $t - 1$ or earlier. Models 1–3 described in the last section can be viewed as reduced forms of this model, where the z_t's have been solved out as in Zellner and Palm (1976). Writing the model in terms of observables, we have

$$c_{t/h} = \sum_{i=1}^{k} c_{t-i/h}\beta_i + z_t'\gamma + \xi_t + \sum_{i=1}^{k} a_{t-i/h}\beta_i - a_{t/h}$$

$$= \sum_{i=1}^{k} c_{t-i/h}\beta_i + z_t'\gamma + u_t.$$

As in the previous model, the observed regressors $c_{t-i/h}$ and z_t may be correlated with the error term, u_t, leading to inconsistency of the OLS estimates. When $h \geq t$, the estimates $c_{t-i/h}$ contain future c_t's and therefore will be correlated with ξ_t. The variables z_t can be viewed as 'causes' of c_t and will therefore contain useful information about the c's, which is not contained in the univariate information set X_0^h. This will induce a correlation between z_t and $a_{t-i/h}$. Instrumental variables can again be used to estimate the model. The data in X_0^{t-1} are valid instruments.

In the discussion above, we replaced the true values of c_{t-i} by the estimates $c_{t-i/h}$. Since these estimates depend crucially on the model for c_t, a useful altern- ative is to replace them by the estimates $c_{t-i/t-i}$, which do not depend on the model assumed for c_t. To see the implications of this procedure, rewrite the first regression example as

$$y_t = \sum_{i=1}^{k} c_{t-i/t-i}\beta_i + z_t'\gamma - \xi_t + \sum_{i=1}^{k} a_{t-i/t-i}\beta_i.$$

This differs from the formulation above in that each c_{t-i} is estimated using a dif- ferent information set. Since $\text{cov}(c_{t-i/t-i}a_{t-j/t-j}) \neq 0$ for $i > j$, care must be taken in choosing instruments. Since $X_0^t \supset X_0^{t-1} \supset \cdots \supset X_0^{t-k}$, data in X_0^{t-k} are valid instruments, and this set can be used.

Finally, it is important to keep in mind that the inconsistency in OLS estimates will depend on the magnitude of the error in the estimate of c_t. When c_t is estimated very precisely, the inconsistencies from OLS have no practical importance.

4 Univariate Examples

In this section we will analyze three US macroeconomic time series – real GNP, real disposable income, and real consumption of non-durables. We begin by apply- ing the univariate detrending methods outlined in the last section to the logs of these series, using quarterly data from 1949 through 1984. The estimated univariate models and corresponding trend and cyclical components will be discussed in this section. In the next section, we will investigate the relation between the cyclical components of disposable income and consumption using regression methods.

Two univariate models have been estimated for each series. The first is the usual ARIMA model. The second is an unobserved components (UC) model suggested by the independent trend/cycle decomposition in Model 1. For each time series, we will present and compare the models and their corresponding trend/cycle decomposition. The analysis in the last section indicated that, *given the Wold decomposition* of the observed series, the optimal one-sided estimates of the components could be formed using any of the observationally equivalent representations of the data. In principle then, it should not matter whether we form the one-sided estimates from the ARIMA model or from the UC model. The results below show that, in practice, it matters a great deal which representation is used. This apparent contradiction arises from the fact that the Wold representation for the data is not known. The ARIMA model and the UC model correspond to different parsimonious approximations to the Wold representation. Given a finite amount of data it is very difficult to discriminate between these alternative representations for the data sets that we consider.

4.1 GNP

The estimated autocorrelations for log GNP suggested that the data were non-stationary (the first estimated autocorrelation was 0.98). The correlogram for the change in the series suggested that an ARIMA(1,1,0) model was appropriate. [An ARIMA(0,1,1) was also possible and yields very similar results.] The estimated model was

$$(1 - B)x_t = 0.005 + 0.406\,(1 - B)x_{t-1},$$
$$\quad\quad\quad\quad (0.001)\quad (0.077)$$

$$SE = 0.0103, \quad\quad L(1) = 0.73, \quad\quad L(3) = 6.3,$$

$$Q(23) = 14.9, \quad\quad LLF = 292.07.$$

SE is the estimated standard error, $L(1)$ and $L(3)$ are LM statistics for serial correlation in the error term of order 1 and 3, respectively, and $Q(df)$ is the Box–Pierce statistic of the residuals. Under the null hypothesis of no serial correlation, the LM test statistics are distributed as X_1^2 and X_3^2, respectively. The final statistic reported, *LLF*, is the value of the log likelihood function.

Interestingly, this estimated model suggests that the spectrum for $(1 - B)x_t$ has a global maximum at the zero frequency, so that decomposition of $(1 - B)x_t$ into an independent random walk and stationary component is not possible. (Recall that this decomposition required that the spectrum had a global minimum at the zero frequency.) This means, as was pointed out in Nelson and Plosser (1981), that the trend/cyclical decomposition in Model 1 is inappropriate. Nevertheless, we estimated a model of the form given into Model 1.[2] The result were

$$x_t = \tau_t - c_t,$$

$$(1 - B)\tau_t = 0.008 , \quad\quad \sigma = 0.0057,$$
$$\quad\quad\quad (0.001)$$

$$c_t = 1.501\,c_{t-1} - 0.577\,c_{t-2}, \quad\quad \sigma = 0.0076,$$
$$\quad\quad (0.121)\quad\quad\quad (0.125)$$

$$SE = 0.0099, \quad\quad Q(17) = 10.4, \quad\quad LLF = 294.42.$$

The values for σ next to each equation refer to the standard deviation of the disturbance in that equation. The value for *SE* is the standard error of the innovation in x_t, i.e., the one-step-ahead forecast standard error. It is comparable to the *SE* reported for the ARIMA model.[3]

Both the ARIMA model and the UC model are special cases of the general Wold representation for $(1 - B)x_t$ given in (2.1). In the Wold representation the moving average polynomial $\theta^x(B)$ is, in general, an infinite-degree polynomial. Both the ARIMA and UC models can be viewed as ways of approximating this infinite-degree polynomial. The ARIMA model uses a ratio of finite-order polynomials, while the UC model uses a (restricted) sum of ratios of finite-order polynomials. Presumably neither of these approximations is entirely correct. One may be better at approximating certain characteristics of the $\theta^x(B)$ polynomial and the other may provide a better approximation to other characteristics. With this in mind we will now discuss some of the similarities and differences in the estimated ARIMA and UC models.

The UC model performs slightly better than the ARIMA model in terms of (within-sample) one-step-ahead forecasting, or equivalently, in terms of the value of the likelihood function. Indeed, both models imply very similar behavior for the short-run behavior of the series. To see this, notice that the UC model implies that

$$(1 - 1.501B + 0.577B^2)(1 - B)x_t$$
$$= (1 - 1.501B + 0.577B^2)e_t^\tau + (1 - B)e_t^c. \qquad (4.1)$$

By Granger's Lemma the right-hand side of (4.1) can be represented as a MA(2) and solving for the implied coefficients yields

$$(1 - 1.501B = 0.577B^2)(1 - B)x_t = (1 - 1.144B + 0.189B^2)a_t,$$
$$\sigma_a = 0.0099.$$

The autoregressive representation for the model is

$$(1 - 1.144B + 0.189B^2)^{-1}(1 - 1.501B + 0.577B^2)(1 - B)x_t = a_t.$$

Carrying out the polynomial division we have, approximately,

$$(1 - 0.36B - 0.05B^2)(1 - B)x_t \approx a_t,$$

which is very close to the estimated ARIMA model.

While the short-run behavior of the UC and ARIMA models are very similar, their long-run properties are quite different. This shows itself in a variety of ways. The spectra implied by the models are quite different at the low frequencies (so that sums of the implied moving average coefficients θ_i^x are quite different), the models produce markedly different long-run forecasts and give quite different one-sided estimates of the trend and cyclical components. Figure 1a compares the two implied spectra. The ARIMA model implies a spectra with a maximum at

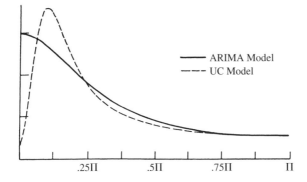

Fig. 1a. Spectra for change in log GNP.

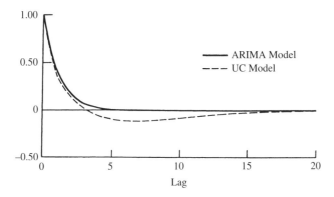

Fig. 1b. Moving average coefficients for change in log GNP.

the zero frequency, while the UC model implies a model with a minimum at that frequency. Unfortunately, with only 142 data points there are very few periodogram points corresponding to the low frequencies, so that direct frequency domain estimation methods help little in discriminating between the models.

Many readers may be more comfortable comparing moving average coefficients rather than spectra. In Fig. 1b, we have plotted the coefficients on the moving average processes for $(1-B)x_t$ implied by the two models. The plots are very similar for the first few lags; they differ for longer lags. The ARIMA(1,1,0) model has moving average coefficients that follow $\theta_i^x = (0.406)^i$, and therefore die off exponentially, but are always positive. The moving average coefficients in the UC model become negative at lag 4 and remain negative until lag 24. The differences in these moving average representations can lead to significantly different conclusions about the long-run behavior of x_t. In the ARIMA model, for example, the sum of the moving average coefficients is 1.68, while in the UC model the sum of the moving average coefficients is 0.59. This means that using the ARIMA model, a one-unit innovation in x will eventually increase log GNP by 1.68, while in the UC model

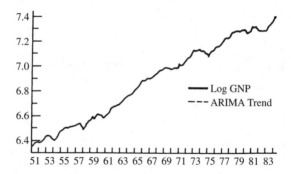

Fig. 2a. Trend decomposition for the log of GNP.

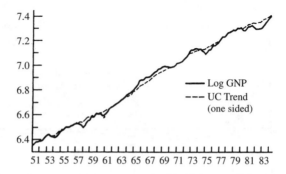

Fig. 2b. Trend decomposition for the log of GNP.

the same innovation is predicted to give rise to a 0.57 increase in GNP. Hypotheses concerning the effects of innovations on permanent income, defined as the discounted expected future sum of x_t, are also quite different. The ARIMA model predicts an impact nearly three times as large, and therefore has fundamentally different implications for permanent income. [The relationship between the moving average coefficients in measured income and the permanent income hypothesis is discussed in Deaton (1985).]

In Figs 2a and 2b, we present the actual series and the optimal one-sided estimate of the trend using the two models. The trend in the ARIMA model is very close to the actual series, whereas the trend in the UC model smoothes the series considerably. In Fig. 2d we compare the (one-sided) estimates of the cyclical component. Here again the differences are substantial. The estimates constructed from the ARIMA model are difficult to interpret; interestingly, the estimates corresponding to the UC model correspond closely to conventional chronologies of post-war cyclical behavior. This correspondence can be seen in Fig. 2e, where we have plotted the UC one-sided estimates, and the shade and peak to trough business cycle periods as calculated by the NBER.

The one-sided estimates of the trend correspond to the long-run forecasts of the series. Since these estimates differ markedly between the ARIMA and UC models,

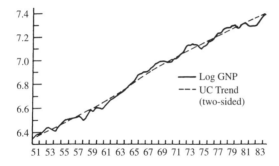

Fig. 2c. Trend decomposition for the log of GNP.

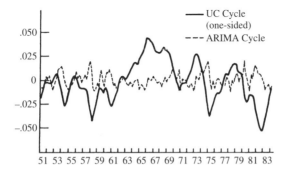

Fig. 2d. Cycle decomposition for the log of GNP.

the long-run forecasts are also quite different. One way to discriminate between the competing specifications is to compare their long-run forecasting ability. Within the sample, the UC model produces more accurate forecasts for all forecast horizons up to forty quarters, but within-sample comparisons can be misleading. A true out-of-sample experiment would be much more convincing.

As we pointed out in the last section, conditional on the estimated model for x_t, the one-sided LMSE estimates of c_t are unique, i.e., do not depend on the choice of Model 1, 2, or 3. In addition, if we accept Model 2 as the appropriate decomposition, then conditional on the parameters of the ARIMA model, the one-sided estimates are exact, i.e., they have a root mean square error of zero. If, however, we assume that Model 1 or 3 is the correct representation for the cyclical component, then more precise estimates can be constructed. These estimates use future as well as past data to improve the one-sided LMSE estimates. Using the estimated UC model, which assumes that Model 1 is the correct representation for c_t, we have constructed the optimal two-sided estimates. The estimate of the trend is plotted in Fig. 2c, and Fig. 2e compares the optimal one-sided and two-sided estimates of the trend component.

Conditional on the parameter estimates, it is also possible to obtain estimates of the precision of the estimates $c_{t/t}$ and $c_{t/T}$ (the two-sided estimate). Using

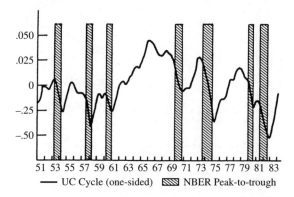

Fig. 2e. Cycle decomposition for the log of GNP.

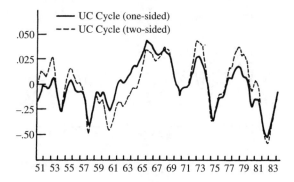

Fig. 2f. Cycle decomposition for the log of GNP.

the estimates from the UC model, the root mean square of $(c_t - c_{t/t}) = 0.020$. The root mean square of $(c_t - c_{t/T})$ depends on the amount of future data available. For t near the middle of the sample, the root mean square of $(c_t - c_{t/T}) = 0.017$. Both estimates are reasonably precise. Using the orthogonal decomposition of $c_t = c_{t/h} + a_{t/h}$, we see that $\text{var}(c_t) = \text{var}(c_{t/h}) + \text{var}(a_{t/h})$, so that a unit-free measure of precision is $R^2(h) = \text{var}(c_{t/h})/\text{var}(c_t)$, which shows the proportion of the variance of c_t explained by $c_{t/h}$. For this model $R^2(t) = 0.54$ and $R^2(T) = 0.71$ (for data near the center of the sample).

4.2 Disposable income
The estimated ARIMA model for disposable income was

$$(1 - B)x_t = 0.011 - 0.210\,(1 - B)x_{t-4},$$
$$\qquad\quad (0.001) \quad (0.080)$$

$$SE = 0.010, \qquad L(1) = 0.01, \qquad L(3) = 1.7,$$

$$Q(23) = 22.9, \qquad LLF = 297.1.$$

The corresponding UC model was

$$x_t = \tau_t + c_t,$$

$$(1 - B)\tau_t = \underset{(0.001)}{0.009}, \qquad \sigma = 0.0057,$$

$$c_t = \underset{(0.073)}{1.029}\, c_{t-1} - \underset{(0.094)}{0.024}\, c_{t-2} + \underset{(0.084)}{0.051}\, c_{t-3} - \underset{(0.058)}{0.152}\, c_{t-4}$$

$$+ \underset{(0.017)}{0.055}\, c_{t-5}, \qquad \sigma = 0.0076,$$

$$SE = 0.009, \qquad Q(14) = 10.4, \qquad LLF = 299.6.$$

We can compare the two models for disposable income, using the same procedures discussed in the comparison of the models for GNP. First, the UC model produces a larger likelihood, but at the cost of six additional parameters. While the models produce similar likelihood values and hence have similar short-run forecasting ability, their long-run forecasts are markedly different. These long-run forecasts – the one-sided trend estimates – are compared in Figs 3a and 3b.

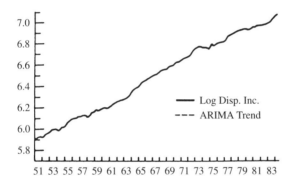

Fig. 3a. Trend decomposition for the log of disposable income.

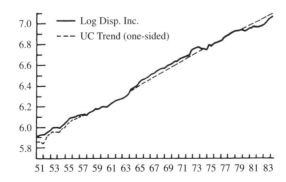

Fig. 3b. Trend decomposition for the log of disposable income.

In Fig. 3e, we compare the optimal one-sided and two-sided estimates of the cycle, where the two-sided estimates are calculated assuming that the UC model is correct. The plots are similar for data after 1954, but differ from 1951 to 1954. The one-sided estimates are rather volatile during this early period, reflecting the small number of data points used in their construction. For one-sided estimates constructed with a moderately large amount of data the root mean square of $(c_t - c_{t/t}) = 0.019$. The root mean square of $(c_t - c_{t/T})$ is only slightly smaller.[4] The corresponding $R^2(t)$ is 0.68.

4.3 Non-durable consumption

The ARIMA model for non-durable consumption is a random walk. The estimated model and associated statistics are

$$(1 - B)x_t = 0.0065 ,$$
$$(0.0007)$$

$$SE = 0.0086, \qquad L(4) = 1.04, \qquad Q(24) = 21.7, \qquad LLF = 314.0.$$

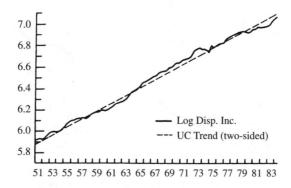

Fig. 3c. Trend decomposition for the log of disposable income.

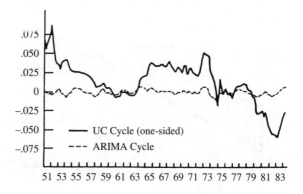

Fig. 3d. Cycle decomposition for the log of disposable income.

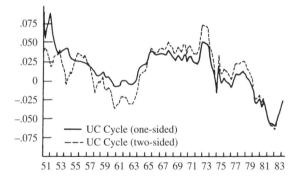

.075
.050
.025
0
−.025
−.050
−.075

—— UC Cycle (one-sided)
---- UC Cycle (two-sided)

51 53 55 57 59 61 63 65 67 69 71 73 75 77 79 81 83

Fig. 3e. Cycle decomposition for the log of disposable income.

The estimated UC model was

$$x_t = \tau_t + c_t,$$

$$(1 - B)\tau_t = \underset{(0.0003)}{0.0067}, \qquad \sigma = 0.0018,$$

$$c_t = \underset{(0.036)}{0.940\, c_{t-1}}, \qquad \sigma = 0.0082,$$

$$SE = 0.0085, \qquad Q(20) = 14.9, \qquad LLF = 314.3.$$

The models are clearly very close to one another in terms of their one-step-ahead forecast ability and likelihood values. If we set the variance of the cyclical component to zero, the UC model implies that x_t is a random walk, so that the random walk model is nested within the UC model. It is therefore possible, in principle, to test the competing models, using a likelihood ratio test. Unfortunately, the test is complicated by the fact that the AR coefficient in the model for c_t is not identified under the random walk hypothesis, but it is identified in the more general model. This complicates the distribution of the likelihood ratio statistic; it will not have the usual asymptotic distribution. This problem has been discussed in detail in Watson and Engle (1985) and Davies (1977). They show that the correct (asymptotic) critical value for carrying out the test (using the square root of the likelihood ratio statistic) is bounded below by the critical value for the standard normal distribution. In this example, the square root of the likelihood ratio statistic is 0.77, which implies a lower bound of the (asymptotic) prob-value of 0.27. This suggests that the random walk hypothesis cannot be rejected at levels of 27% or less.

The examples in this section tell a consistent story. The short-run forecasting performance of the ARIMA and UC models are very similar. At longer forecast horizons, the forecasts from the models differ markedly. This difference in the long-run properties of the estimated models, leads to very different estimates of the underlying trend components and cyclical components.

5 Regression Examples

In this section we investigate the relationship between non-durable consumption expenditures and the cyclical component of disposable income. We test the proposition that the change in consumption from period t to $t + 1$ is uncorrelated with the cyclical component of disposable income dated t or earlier. The empirical validity of this proposition, first tested in Hall (1978), has been the subject of ongoing controversy. [See, for example, the papers by Flavin (1981), and Mankiw and Shapiro (1985).] The model that we consider implies that the change in log consumption from period t to period $t + 1$ should be unpredictable using information available at time t. We test this implication using the cyclical component of disposable income at time t. The importance of using a stationary variable (like the cyclical component of income) rather than a non-stationary variable (like the level of income) has been pointed out by Mankiw and Shapiro (1985). We begin by motivating the empirical specification that is used in this paper.

Assume that a consumer is choosing consumption to maximize a time-separable utility function, subject to an intertemporal budget constraint, i.e., the consumer solves

$$\max_{\{C_t\}} \mathrm{E}\left(\sum_{i=0}^{\infty}(1 + \delta)^{-i}u(C_{t+i})|I_t \right), \tag{5.1}$$

subject to

$$\mathrm{E}\left(\sum_{i=0}^{\infty}(1 + r)^{-i}C_{t+i}|I_t \right) \leq W_t,$$

where W_t is wealth at time t (which includes the expected discounted value of future earning), δ is a time-invariant subjective discount factor, I_t is the information set at time t, and r is the constant one-period interest rate. The first-order conditions for utility maximization imply

$$\mathrm{E}(Z_{t+1}|I_t) = (1 + \delta)(1 + r)^{-1}, \tag{5.2}$$

where $Z_{t+1} = u'(C_{t+1})/u'(C_t)$ is the marginal rate of substitution for consumption between periods t and $t + 1$. An empirical specification follows from an assumption concerning the functional form of the utility function and the probability distribution for Z_t. Here, we follow Hansen and Singleton (1983). Let $z_t = \log Z_t$, and assume that $z_{t+1}|I_t \sim \mathrm{N}(\mu_t, \sigma^2)$. The log normality of Z_{t+1} implies that $\mathrm{E}(Z_{t+1}|I_t) = \exp(\mu_t + \sigma^2/2)$. But (5.2) implies that $\mathrm{E}(Z_{t+1}|I_t)$ is constant, so that $\mu_t = \mu$ for all t. If we now assume that $u(C)$ is of the constant relative risk aversion form, so that $u(C) = (1-\beta)^{-1}C^{1-\beta}$, then $z_t = -\beta(c_{t+1}-c_t)$, with $c_t = \log C_t$. When c_t is in the information set I_t, this implies

$$\mathrm{E}(c_{t+1}|I_t) = c_t + \alpha,$$

with $\alpha \approx \beta^{-1}[(\sigma^2/2) + r - \delta]$, so that

$$c_{t+1} = c_t + \alpha + e_{t+1}, \tag{5.3}$$

where e_{t+1} is uncorrelated with information available at time t. We will test this proposition by investigating the correlation between $(1 - B)c_t$ and lagged values of the cyclical component of disposable income.

The analysis of the last section casts some light on the hypothesis embodied in (5.3). There we showed that the hypothesis that c_t was a univariate random walk was consistent with the data. We calculated a 't-statistic' associated with this hypothesis that had a value of 0.77. In this section we ask whether $(1 - B)c_t$ can be predicted by linear combinations of disposable income. The models that we will estimate in this section all have the form

$$(1 - B)c_t = \alpha + \rho(B)y_{t-1}^c + e_t, \tag{5.4}$$

where y_t^c is the cyclical component in disposable income, and $\rho(B)$ is a one-sided polynomial in B. Under the assumption of the life cycle consumption model outlined above, $\rho(B) = 0$ for any choice of a (one-sided) polynomial. Since y_t^c is not directly observed, the model (5.4) cannot be estimated by OLS. We will estimate the model using various proxies for the unobserved y_t^c data. The sample period is 1954:1 to 1984:2.[5]

Before proceeding to a test of this hypothesis using the data described in the last section, one issue concerning the data should be addressed. When this random walk hypothesis is tested using macro data, the consumption and income figures are usually deflated by population before the analysis begins. This expresses all variables in per-capita terms, so that the data are loosely consistent with a representative consumer notion. We have chosen not to follow this course. While we agree that this transformation is useful in principle, in practice it can lead to serious problems. These problems arise from the errors in the quarterly population series. While the underlying trend in the population estimate is probably close to the trend in the true series, the quarter-to-quarter changes in the estimates series is, most likely, almost entirely noise. Indeed, over 50% of the sample variation in quarterly post-war population growth rates can be attributed to three large outliers in the data series.[6] Since our specification is in quarterly changes (for c_t) or deviations from a stochastic trends (for y_t^c), this increase in the noise-to-signal ratio will lead to serious inconsistencies. Rather than introduce this additional noisy series into the analysis, we will use the raw log differences of the non-durable consumption data and the stochastically detrended estimates of the log of disposable income.

The first model we estimate regresses $(1 - B)c_t$ on four lags of $y_{t/t}^c$ (i.e., $y_{t-1/t-1}^c, y_{t-2/t-2}^c, \ldots, y_{t-4/t-4}^c$). Since each of these constructed variables is a linear combination of data at time $t - 1$ or earlier, the population OLS coefficients should be zero. The results of this regression are shown in the first column of Table 1. Individually, the coefficients are large and have t-statistics ranging from 1.7 to 2.6. The last entry in the table shows the F-statistic, which tests that all

Table 1. Consumption and income regressions

	Equation 1[a]	Equation 2[b]	Equation 3[c]
Constant	0.007	0.007	0.008
	(0.001)	(0.001)	(0.001)
y^c_{t-1}	0.201	0.203	0.115
	(0.101)	(0.075)	(0.131)
y^c_{t-2}	−0.264	−0.289	−0.201
	(0.151)	(0.111)	(0.169)
y^c_{t-3}	0.231	0.108	0.479
	(0.128)	(0.111)	(0.261)
y^c_{t-4}	−0.192	−0.074	−0.445
	(0.075)	(0.076)	(0.218)
DW	1.6	1.8	1.7
F	2.7	3.8	2.3

[a] $y^c_{t/t}$ used as a proxy for u^c_t; coefficients estimated by OLS.

[b] $y^c_{t/T}$ used as a proxy for y^c_t; coefficients estimated by OLS.

[c] $y^c_{t/T}$ used as a proxy for y^c_t; coefficients estimated by IV.

of the coefficients are equal to zero. It takes on the value 2.7, larger than the 5% critical value.

In the next column, the results are presented for the same model, but with $y^c_{t/T}$, the two-sided estimates, used as proxies for y^c_t. The results are similar. The F-statistic is now 3.8, which is significant at any reasonable level. The results in this column, however, are perfectly consistent with the theory. Recall that the two-sided estimates contain future values of disposable income. Since future values of disposable income are not included in I_{t-1}, $(1 - B)c_t$ may be correlated with these variables. (Indeed we would expect innovations in consumption to be correlated with innovations in income.) If we proxy the components y^c_t by the smoothed values and estimate the coefficients using data in I_{t-1} as instruments, then the coefficients should not be significantly different from zero. The results of this exercise are shown in the third column. Only the last coefficient is now significant and the F-statistic has fallen to 2.3, significant at the 10% but not the 5% levels.

The results of this section suggest that aggregate post-war US data are not consistent with the life cycle model outlined above.

6 Concluding Remarks

This paper was motivated by the desire for a flexible method to eliminate trends in economic time series. The method that was developed in this paper was predicated on the assumption that deterministic trend models were too rigid and not appropriate for most economic time series. The alternative – modelling economic time series as non-stationary stochastic processes of the ARIMA class – confused long-run and cyclical movements in the series. The useful, fictitious decomposition of a time series into trend and cyclical components could not be used when modelling series as ARIMA processes. The method described in this paper maintains the convenient trend/cycle decomposition, while allowing flexibility in the models for both of the components.

In addition to discussing a new method for 'detrending' economic time series, this paper makes an important empirical point. The paper compares two empirical approximations to the Wold representation for the changes in GNP, disposable income, and non-durable consumption expenditures. These two empirical approximations correspond to ARIMA and UC models. The models imply very similar short-run behavior for the series: the one-step-ahead forecasts from the models are nearly identical. The implied long-run behavior of the models are quite different. The UC models imply that innovations in the process have a much smaller impact on the long-run level of the series than is implied by the ARIMA model. It is very difficult to discriminate between the competing models on statistical grounds: their log-likelihoods are nearly identical. Since both competing models describe the data equally well, we are left with the conclusion that the data are not very informative about the long-run characteristics of the process. While this may seem to an obvious conclusion, one must keep in mind that very different conclusions would be reached using the implied large-sample confidence intervals constructed from either the UC or the ARIMA models. The difference arises because these large-sample confidence intervals are conditional on the specific parameterization of the Wold representation.

The paper also discussed the use of stochastically detrended data in the construction of econometric models. Here we demonstrated that care has to be taken to avoid inconsistencies arising from complications similar to errors-in-variables. Our empirical example investigated the relation between the change in consumption of non-durables and lags of the cyclical component of disposable income. Here we found a significant relation, which indicates that the simple life cycle model, with its maintained assumptions of constant discount rates, no liquidity constraints, and time-separable utility, is not consistent with aggregate post-war US data.

Notes

1. Unobserved component models of the kind used in this paper have been advocated in Harvey and Todd (1983) and more recently in Harvey (1985). These two references contain excellent discussions of the similarities and differences between dynamic behavior of models parameterized as parsimonious ARIMA models and those parameterized as UC models.
2. The UC models were estimated by maximum likelihood methods. Details concerning the methods can be found in Watson and Engle (1983). For those familiar with varying parameter regression (VPR) models, notice that the UC model described in the text can be viewed as a VPR model with serially

correlated errors and a time-varying intercept. This allowed us to use previously written VPR computer programs to carry out the estimation.

3. There are a variety of interesting features of the estimated UC model that one might want to test. For example, the sum of the autoregressive coefficients for the cyclical component is 0.92, which implies substantial persistence in c_t. Roots this close to unity can be troublesome, and one might want to test the hypothesis that the AR process for c_t contains a unit root (and hence the c_t process was misspecified). In addition, conditional on no unit roots in the c_t process, a zero variance for e_t^τ implies that the trend is deterministic rather than stochastic. This too would be an interesting hypothesis to test. Unfortunately, standard tests cannot be carried out, as the usual asymptotic normal approximations for test statistics are not valid for the reasons discussed in Fuller (1976) and elsewhere. Construction of test statistics for these sorts of hypotheses is an interesting area for future research.

4. Those familiar with recursive signal extraction methods will recognize the mean square of $(c_t - c_{t/t})$ is a time-varying quantity that, for the model under consideration, will converge to a fixed quantity as t grows large. [See Burridge and Wallis (1983).] Since one root of the AR process for c_t is close to the unit circle, and is therefore close to the roots of the AR polynomial for τ_t, the convergence of the mean square of $(c_t - c_{t/t})$ is very slow. The value of the root mean square of $(c_t - c_{t/t})$ reported in the text corresponds to the value for 1984:2. The recursive algorithm, the Kalman filter, was initialized with a vague prior, so that the root mean square errors for earlier dates are larger. For example, the value for 1966 is 0.028. The root mean square of $(c_t - c_{t/T})$ is approximately 0.019 over the entire sample period.

5. We have started the sample period in 1954 to eliminate the observations in which the estimates $y_{t/t}^c$ are very imprecise. See the discussion in note 3.

6. The quarterly population data (published by the Department of Commerce, Bureau of Economic Analysis) are very close to a deterministic trend. The trend is interrupted by three very large quarterly outliers. Over the period 1948:1 to 1980:4, the average quarterly population growth rate was 0.34%, with a sample standard deviation of 0.12%. The data show a 0.85% population growth rate in 1959:1, a 0.79% growth rate in 1971:4, and a -0.23% growth rate in 1972:1. These three data points are responsible for most of the sample variance in post-war population growth rates. They account for 51% of the sample sum of squares. When these data are used to deflate the consumption and income series used in the regressions, the results are dominated by these three data points.

References

Bell, W., 1984, Signal extraction for nonstationary time series, *Annals of Statistics*, 12, 646–684.

Beveridge, S. and C.R. Nelson, 1981, A new approach to decomposition of economic time series, into permanent and transitory components with particular attention to measurement of the 'business cycle', *Journal of Monetary Economics*, 7, 151–174.

Burridge, P. and K.F. Wallis, 1983, Signal extraction in nonstationary time series, University of Warwick working paper no. 234.

Cumby, R.E., J. Huizinga and M. Obstfeld, 1983, Two-step two-stage least squares estimation in models with rational expectations, *Journal of Econometrics*, 21, 333–355.

Davidson, J.E.H., David F. Hendry, Frank Srba and Steven Yeo, 1978, Econometric modelling of the aggregate time-series relationship between consumer's expenditure and income in the United Kingdom, *Economic Journal*, 88, 661–692.

Davies, R.B., 1977, Hypothesis testing when a nuisance parameter is present only under the alternative, *Biometrika*, 64, 247–254.

Deaton, Angus, 1985, Consumer behavior: Tests of the life cycle model, Invited paper delivered at the World Congress of the Econometric Society, Cambridge, MA.

Flavin, M., 1981, The adjustment of consumption to changing expectations about future income, *Journal of Political Economy*, 89, 974–1009.

Fuller, W.A., 1976, *Introduction to statistical time series* (Wiley, New York).

Geweke, John, 1983, The superneutrality of money in the United States: An interpretation of the evidence, Carnegie-Mellon University discussion paper, May.

Granger, C.W.J., 1983, Co-integrated and error-correcting models, UCSD discussion paper no. 83-13a.

Granger, C.W.J. and R.F. Engle, 1984, Dynamic model specification with equilibrium constraints: Co-integration and error-correction, UCSD discussion paper, Aug.

Hansen, L. and K. Singleton, 1983, Stochastic consumption, risk aversion, and the temporal behavior of asset returns, *Journal of Political Economy*, 91, 249–265.

Hall, R.E., 1978, The stochastic implications of the life-cycle permanent income hypothesis: Theory and evidence, *Journal of Political Economy*, 86, 971–987.

Harvey, A.C., 1985, Trends and cycles in macroeconomic time series, *Journal of Business and Economic Statistics*, 3, 216–227.

Harvey, A.C. and P.H.J. Todd, 1983, Forecasting economic time series with structural and Box–Jenkins models: A case study (with discussion), *Journal of Business and Economic Statistics*, 1, 299–315.

Hayashi, F. and C. Sims, 1983, Efficient estimation of time series models with predetermined, but not exogenous, instruments, *Econometrica*, 51, 783–798.

Mankiw, N.G. and M.D. Shapiro, 1984, Trends, random walks, and tests of the permanent income hypothesis, *Journal of Monetary Economics*, 16, 141–164.

Nelson, C.R. and H. Kang, 1981, Spurious periodicity in inappropriately detrended time series, *Econometrica*, 49, 741–751.

Nelson, C.R. and H. Kang, 1984, Pitfalls in the use of time as an explanatory variable in regression, *Journal of Business and Economic Statistics*, 2, 73–82.

Nelson, C.R. and C.I. Plosser, 1981, Trends and random walks in macroeconomic time series: Some evidence and implications, *Journal of Monetary Economics*, 10, 139–162.

Watson, M.W., 1985, Univariate detrending methods with stochastic trends, H.I.E.R. discussion paper no. 1158.

Watson, M.W. and R.F. Engle, 1983, Alternative algorithms for the estimation of dynamic factor, MIMIC, and varying coefficient regression models, *Journal of Econometrics*, 23, 485–500.

Watson, M.W. and R.F. Engle, 1985, Testing for regression coefficient stability with a stationary AR(1) alternative, *Review of Economics and Statistics* LXVII, 341–346.

Whittle, P., 1963, Prediction and regulation (English Universities Press, London).

Zellner, A. and F. Palm, 1976, Time-series analysis and simultaneous equation econometric models, *Journal of Econometrics*, 2, 17–54.

9

Detrending, Stylized Facts and the Business Cycle*

A. C. HARVEY

Department of Statistics, London School of Economics

AND

A. JAEGER

Austrian Institute of Economic Research

SUMMARY

The stylized facts of macroeconomic time series can be presented by fitting structural time series models. Within this framework, we analyse the consequences of the widely used detrending technique popularised by Hodrick and Prescott (1980). It is shown that mechanical detrending based on the Hodrick–Prescott filter can lead investigators to report spurious cyclical behaviour, and this point is illustrated with empirical examples. Structural time-series models also allow investigators to deal explicitly with seasonal and irregular movements that may distort estimated cyclical components. Finally, the structural framework provides a basis for exposing the limitations of ARIMA methodology and models based on a deterministic trend with a single break.

1 Introduction

Establishing the 'stylized facts' associated with a set of time series is widely considered a crucial step in macroeconomic research (see e.g. Blanchard and Fischer, 1989, chapter 1). For such facts to be useful they should (1) be consistent with the stochastic properties of the data and (2) present meaningful information. Nevertheless, many stylized facts reported in the literature do not fulfil these criteria. In particular, information based on mechanically detrended series can easily give a spurious impression of cyclical behaviour. Analysis based on autoregressive-integrated-moving average (ARIMA) models can also be misleading if such models are chosen primarily on grounds of parsimony.

We argue here that structural time-series models provide the most useful framework within which to present stylized facts on time series. These models are explicitly based on the stochastic properties of the data. We illustrate how, when these models are fitted to various macroeconomic time series, they provide meaningful information and serve as a basis for exposing the limitations of other

* Reprinted from *Journal of Applied Econometrics*, "Detrending, Stylized Facts and the Business Cycle", 1993, Vol. 8, pp. 231–241, A. C. Harvey and A. Jaeger. Copyright 1993 ©John Wiley & Sons Limited. Reproduced with permission.

techniques. These arguments have, to some extent, been made before (Harvey 1985, 1989; Clark 1987). They are further elaborated here. In addition, we examine the consequences of the mechanical detrending method suggested by Hodrick and Prescott (1980), which has recently started to become popular in macroeconomics (see e.g. Danthine and Girardin 1989; Backus and Kehoe 1989; Kydland and Prescott 1990; Brandner and Neusser 1992). We show that the uncritical use of mechanical detrending can lead investigators to report spurious cyclical behaviour. This point has also been made by Cogley (1990). We argue that the structural framework provides further insights and that trends and cycles should be fitted simultaneously to avoid such pitfalls.

The plan of the paper is as follows. In Section 2 we lay out the basic framework of structural time-series modelling in this context. Section 3 provides an analysis of the consequences of detrending using the Hodrick–Prescott filter approach. Section 4 considers modelling and detrending of several macroeconomic time series. Section 5 discusses several issues including seasonal adjustment, trends with deterministic break points, and spurious cross-correlations between inappropriately detrended series. Section 6 draws together the main conclusions.

2 The Trend Plus Cycle Model

Structural time-series models are set up explicitly in terms of components that have a direct interpretation (see Harvey 1989). In the present context we postulate the appropriate model to be

$$y_t = \mu_t + \psi_t + \varepsilon_t, \quad t = 1, \dots, T \tag{1}$$

where y_t is the observed series, μ_t is the trend, ψ_t is the cycle, and ε_t is the irregular component. The trend is a local linear trend defined as

$$\mu_t = \mu_{t-1} + \beta_{t-1} + \eta_t, \quad \eta_t \sim \text{NID}(0, \sigma_\eta^2) \tag{2}$$

$$\beta_t = \beta_{t-1} + \zeta_t, \quad \zeta_t \sim \text{NID}(0, \sigma_\zeta^2) \tag{3}$$

where β_t is the slope and the normal white-noise disturbances, η_t and ζ_t, are independent of each other. The stochastic cycle is generated as

$$\psi_t = \rho \cos \lambda_c \psi_{t-1} + \rho \sin \lambda_c \psi_{t-1}^* + x_t \tag{4}$$

$$\psi_t^* = -\rho \sin \lambda_c \psi_{t-1} + \rho \cos \lambda_c \psi_{t-1}^* + x_t^* \tag{5}$$

where ρ is a damping factor such that $0 \leqslant \rho \leqslant 1$, λ_c is the frequency of the cycle in radians, and x_t and x_t^* are both $\text{NID}(0, \sigma_x^2)$. The irregular component is $\text{NID}(0, \sigma_\varepsilon^2)$ and the disturbances in all three components are taken to be independent of each other.

The trend is equivalent to an ARIMA(0,2,1) process. However, if $\sigma_\zeta^2 = 0$, it reduces to a random walk with drift. If, furthermore, $\sigma_\eta^2 = 0$ it becomes deterministic, that is, $\mu_t = \mu_0 + \beta t$. When $\sigma_\eta^2 = 0$, but $\sigma_\zeta^2 > 0$, the trend is still a process integrated of order two, abbreviated $I(2)$, that is, stationary in second differences. A trend component with this feature tends to be relatively smooth. An important issue is therefore whether or not the constraint $\sigma_\eta^2 = 0$ should be imposed at the outset. We argue that there are series where it is unreasonable to assume a smooth trend *a priori* and therefore the question whether or not σ_η^2 is set to zero is an empirical one. The examples in Section 4 illustrate this point.

The cyclical component, ψ_t, is stationary if ρ is strictly less than one. It is equivalent to an ARMA(2,1) process in which both the MA and the AR parts are subject to restrictions (see Harvey 1985, p. 219). The most important of these is that the AR parameters are constrained to lie within the region corresponding to complex roots. Since the purpose is to model the possible occurrence of stochastic cycles, imposing this constraint *a priori* is desirable.

Estimation of the hyperparameters, $(\sigma_\eta^2, \sigma_\zeta^2, \sigma_x^2, \rho, \lambda_c, \sigma_\varepsilon^2)$, can be carried out by maximum likelihood either in the time domain or the frequency domain. Once this has been done, estimates of the trend, cyclical, and irregular components are obtained from a smoothing algorithm. These calculations may be carried out very rapidly on a PC using the STAMP package.

The model in equation (1) can be extended to deal with seasonal data. Thus there is no need to use data that may have been distorted by a seasonal adjustment procedure. Furthermore, if we are interested in stylized facts relating to seasonal components, structural time-series models provide a ready tool to determine these components without imposing a deterministic structure on the seasonal pattern (see e.g. Barsky and Miron 1989).

3 The Hodrick–Prescott Filter

Nelson and Kang (1981) have drawn attention to the distortions that can arise from fitting deterministic trends to series actually driven by stochastic trends. Similarly, it has long been known that the mechanical use of moving average filters can create a wide range of undesirable effects in the data (see Fishman 1969). The filter adopted by Hodrick and Prescott (1980), hereafter denoted HP filter, has a long tradition as a method of fitting a smooth curve through a set of points. It may be rationalized as the optimal estimator of the trend component in a structural time-series model

$$y_t = \mu_t + \varepsilon_t, \quad t = 1, \ldots, T \tag{6}$$

where μ_t is defined by equation (2) and (3) but with σ_η^2 set equal to zero.[1]

Of course, the reason for estimating the trend in the present context is to detrend the data. The optimal filter which gives the detrended observations, y_t^d, is, for large samples and t not near the beginning or end of the series

$$y_t^d = \left[\frac{(1-L)^2(1-L^{-1})^2}{q_\zeta + (1-L)^2(1-L^{-1})^2} \right] y_t, \quad q_\zeta > 0 \tag{7}$$

where $q_\zeta = \sigma_\zeta^2/\sigma_\varepsilon^2$ and L is the lag operator. This expression can be obtained as the optimal estimator of ε_t in equation (6) by means of the standard signal extraction formulae which, as shown by Bell (1984), apply to non-stationary, as well as stationary, time series.[2]

If equation (6) was believed to be the true model, q_ζ could be estimated by maximum likelihood as outlined in the previous section. However, the whole reason for applying the HP filter is the belief that detrended data consist of something more than white noise. Thus, a value of q_ζ is imposed, rather than estimated. We will denote this value of q_ζ by $\bar{q}_\zeta$. From the point of view of structural time-series modelling, HP filtering is therefore equivalent to postulating model (1) and imposing the restrictions $\sigma_\zeta^2/\sigma_\varepsilon^2 = \bar{q}_\zeta$, $\sigma_\eta^2 = 0$, and $\psi_t = 0$. The HP estimate of the cyclical component is then simply given by the smoothed irregular component.

Given a particular model for y_t, the process followed by the HP detrended series, y_t^{HP}, and hence its dynamic properties, may be determined by substituting for y_t in equation (7). Suppose that we specify y_t as an ARIMA (p,d,q) process, possibly representing the reduced form of a structural time-series model such as equation (1). That is,

$$(1 - L)^d y_t = \varphi^{-1}(L)\theta(L)\xi_t, \quad \xi_t \sim \text{NID}(0, \sigma^2) \tag{8}$$

where $\varphi(L)$ and $\theta(L)$ denote the AR and MA polynomials in the lag operator. Then

$$y_t^{\text{HP}} = \left[\frac{(1 - L)^{2-d}(1 - L^{-1})^2}{\bar{q}_\zeta + (1 - L)^2(1 - L^{-1})^2} \right] \frac{\theta(L)}{\varphi(L)} \xi_t \tag{9}$$

As noted by King and Rebelo (1989), y_t^{HP} is a stationary process for $d \leqslant 4$.

The autocovariance generating function (a.c.g.f.) of y_t^{HP} is given by

$$g_{\text{HP}}(L) = \left[\frac{(1 - L)^{4-d}(1 - L^{-1})^{4-d}}{[\bar{q}_\zeta + (1 - L)^2(1 - L^{-1})^2]^2} \right] g_y(L) \tag{10}$$

where $g_y(L)$ is the a.c.g.f. of $\Delta^d y_t$ and $\Delta = 1 - L$.

Note that if y_t is specified in terms of unobserved components, $g_y(L)$ may be obtained directly without solving for the ARIMA reduced form. Setting $L = \exp(i\lambda)$ gives the spectrum of y_t^{HP}, $f_{\text{HP}}(\lambda)$.[3] The spectrum may be calculated straightforwardly and it provides particularly useful information if we wish to study the possible creation of spurious cycles.

Specifying y_t to be a structural time-series model of the form (1) gives insight into the effects of detrending, since the contribution of each of the unobserved components to the overall spectrum, $f_{\text{HP}}(\lambda)$, can be assessed. To this end, rewrite model (1) in the single-equation form

$$y_t = \frac{\zeta_{t-1}}{\Delta^2} + \frac{\eta_t}{\Delta} + \psi_t + \varepsilon_t \tag{11}$$

The first term is integrated of order two, abbreviated as $I(2)$, the second term is $I(1)$, and the last two terms are stationary or $I(0)$. From model (10) we have

$$f_{\text{HP}}(\lambda) = \tau(\lambda)\{\sigma_\zeta^2 + 2(1 - \cos\lambda)\sigma_\eta^2 + 4(1 - \cos\lambda)^2[g_\psi(\lambda) + \sigma_\varepsilon^2]\} \tag{12}$$

where

$$\tau(\lambda) = \frac{1}{2\pi} \frac{4(1 - \cos \lambda)^2}{[\bar{q}_\zeta + 4(1 - \cos \lambda)^2]^2}$$

and $g_\psi(\lambda)$ is the spectral generating function of ψ_t.

More generally, suppose we have any unobserved components model with $I(2)$, $I(1)$, and $I(0)$ components. Then the transfer function for an $I(d)$ component is

$$\tau_d(\lambda) = 2^{(2-d)}(1 - \cos \lambda)^{2-d}\tau(\lambda), \quad d = 0, 1, 2 \qquad (13)$$

The transfer function tells us the effect of the filter on the spectrum of the dth difference of an $I(d)$ component. Note that $\tau_2(\lambda) = \tau(\lambda)$.

For the macroeconomic series they study, Kydland and Prescott (1990) set $\bar{q}_\zeta = 0.000625$. Figures 1(a) to 1(c) show the transfer functions for $I(0)$, $I(1)$, and $I(2)$ components assuming this value for $\bar{q}_\zeta$ plotted against a period over the range $0 \leqslant 2\pi/\lambda \leqslant 4$. The filter for $I(0)$ components removes the very low frequency components, but frequencies corresponding to periods of less than 20 are virtually unaffected. Multiplying $\tau(\lambda)$ by $2(1 - \cos(\lambda))$, on the other hand, produces a transfer function $\tau_1(\lambda)$, with a peak at

$$\lambda_{\max} = \arccos[1 - \sqrt{0.75\bar{q}_\zeta}] \qquad (14)$$

which for $\bar{q}_\zeta = 0.000625$ corresponds to a period of about 30. Thus applying the standard HP filter to a random walk produces detrended observations which have the characteristics of a business cycle for quarterly observations. Such cyclical behaviour is spurious and is a classic example of the Yule–Slutzky effect.

Spurious cycles can also emanate from the $I(2)$ component. The transfer function in Fig. 1(c) has a peak at a frequency corresponding to a period of about 40. The nature of any spurious cyclical behaviour in the detrended observations depends on the relative importance of $I(1)$ and $I(2)$ components. For data generated by (1) the peaks created in the spectrum are of similar height if $\sigma_\zeta^2/\sigma_\eta^2 \approx 25$. In this case they tend to merge together, and the overall effect is of a transfer function with a single peak corresponding to a period between 30 and 40.

4 Macroeconomic Time Series

We now examine the stylized facts that can be produced by different techniques when applied to quarterly macroeconomic time series (all in logarithms). The series are US, real GNP, Austrian real GDP, the implicit deflator for US GNP, and the nominal value of the US monetary base.[4] All four series were seasonally adjusted by some variant of the Census X-11 program.

The HP filter was always applied with $\bar{q}_\zeta = 0.000625$. Attempts to estimate this ratio by applying maximum likelihood to model (6) usually produced a very high value of q_ζ, leading to the trend effectively picking up most of the movements in the stationary part of the series. Thus unless model (1) is a reasonable model for the series in question, q_ζ must be fixed in order to obtain sensible results.

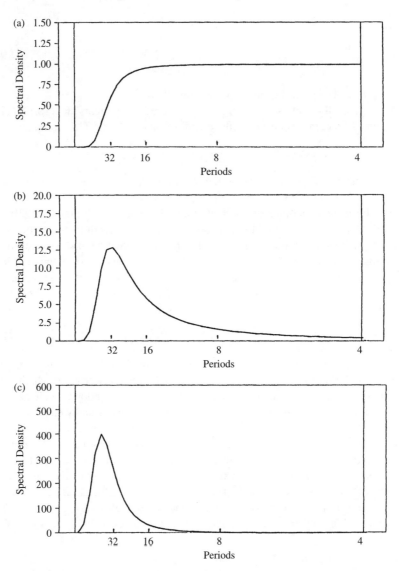

Fig. 1. Transfer functions of HP filter. (a) $I(0)$ component; (b) $I(1)$ component; (c) $I(2)$ component.

Details of the results of fitting structural time-series model (1) are shown in Table I. Estimation was carried out in the frequency domain. Estimation in the time domain gave similar results and so these are not reported. Goodness of fit can be assessed by means of the estimated prediction error variance (σ^2), or, equivalently, by R_D^2 which is the coefficient of determination with respect to first differences. The Box–Ljung statistic, $Q(P)$, is based on the first P residual

Table I. Estimates of structural time-series models

Series	Time range	Restrictions	σ_ζ^2	σ_η^2	σ_x^2	ρ	$2\pi/\lambda_c$	σ_ε^2	σ^2	R_D^2	$Q(P)$
US GNP	1954 : 1—89:4	None	8	0	625	0.92	22.2	0	937	0.05	8.01
Austrian GDP	1964 : 1—88:4	None	9	578	0	—	—	244	1126	0.05	13.63
		$\sigma_\eta^2 = 0$	21	—	36	0.97	13.0	438	1071	0.09	7.46
US Prices	1954 : 1—89:4	None	28	94	0	—	—	0	161	0.64	5.78
		$\sigma_\eta^2 = 0$	19	—	79	0.94	27.5	3	160	0.65	4.27
US monetary base	1959 : 1—89:4	None	40	63	3	0.98	5.6	0	151	0.64	7.89
		$\sigma_\eta^2 = 0$	47	—	25	0.73	5.0	0	153	0.64	10.68

Notes: All variance estimates have been multiplied by 10^7. $2\pi/\lambda_c$ is period (in quarters). $Q(P)$ is Box–Ljung statistic based on first P residual autocorrelations. $P = 12$ for US Series and $P = 10$ for Austrian GDP.

autocorrelations. The degrees of freedom for the resulting χ^2 statistic should be taken to be $P + 1$ minus the number of estimated hyperparameters (see Harvey 1989, chapter 5). Tests for normality and heteroscedasticity were also carried out. They are not reported in Table I and are only mentioned in the text if they were significant.

Estimating model (1) for real US GNP gives $\tilde{\sigma}_\eta^2 = 0$. Thus the result of unrestricted estimation is a relatively smooth trend. Furthermore, since $\tilde{\sigma}_\varepsilon^2 = 0$, the series effectively decomposes into a smooth trend plus a cycle (see Fig. 2(a)). This is not surprising since $\tilde{\sigma}_\zeta^2$ is small and, coupled with the zero for $\tilde{\sigma}_\eta^2$, this means there is little contamination from nonstationary components in the series. Application of the HP filter yields a detrended series which is difficult to distinguish from the cycle extracted from the structural model (see Fig. 2(b)). Thus applying the HP filter to real US GNP data is practically equivalent to estimating the structural time-series model (1). The striking coincidence between the estimated business

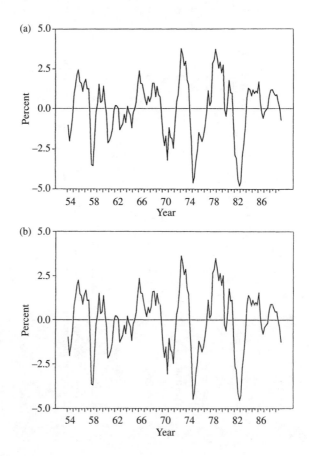

Fig. 2. Business cycles in US GNP. (a) Estimated cyclical component; (b) Hodrick–Prescott cycle.

cycle component and the HP cycle suggests that the HP filter is tailor-made for extracting the business cycle component from US GNP.

The close similarity between estimated and HP cycle reported for US GNP may not necessarily obtain for output series from other countries. To illustrate this point, we estimated model (1) using real Austrian GDP. Attempting to estimate the full model, (1), leads to the cyclical component virtually disappearing and we are led to a local linear trend model. On the other hand, if we impose $\sigma_\eta^2 = 0$ on (1) we obtain a smooth trend and a cycle. A graph of the cycle shows it to be relatively small (see Fig. 3(a)); it rarely deviates from the trend by more than 2 per cent. However, the cycles do coincide with the Austrian experience of somewhat muted booms and recessions. The cyclical component obtained from HP filtering, shown in Fig. 3(b), is more volatile and quite erratic because it includes the irregular movements in the series which appear to be substantial.

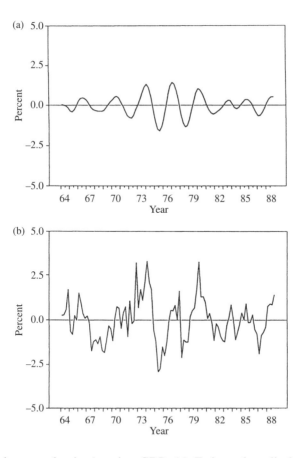

Fig. 3. Business cycles in Austrian GDP. (a) Estimated cyclical component; (b) Hodrick–Prescott cycle.

The cyclical model obtained by imposing a smooth trend by setting $\sigma_\eta^2 = 0$ has a slightly better fit than the local linear trend model. The explanation lies in the fact that the local linear trend model emerges as a limiting case of the smooth trend and cycle model as $\rho \to 0$ and $\lambda_c \to 0$. Thus, when σ_x^2 is quite small, as it is here, it is difficult to pick out the cycle in an unrestricted model since the likelihood function is very flat. The fact that the cycle model would be rejected on grounds of parsimony does not mean that it does not provide a valid description of the data. Furthermore, if we feel *a priori* that the underlying trend should be smooth then the cycle model is to be preferred over the more parsimonious local linear trend.

The two examples considered so far are based on real output series. Next we look at a price series and a nominal money stock series. Unrestricted estimation of model (1) for the implicit US GNP deflator leads quite clearly to a random walk plus noise model in first differences. This very simple model is also consistent with the correlogram of the second differences which is -0.47 at lag 1 and $-0.07, 0.04,$ $0.05, -0.01$ for lags 2 to 5. Thus Box–Jenkins methodology would almost certainly select an equivalent model, namely ARIMA(0,2,1). Nevertheless, setting $\sigma_\eta^2 = 0$ does give a cycle and the model has essentially the same fit. It would clearly be rejected on grounds of parsimony, but it is consistent with the data and so cannot be dismissed, just as we could not dismiss the smooth trend/cycle model for Austrian GDP. However, while it may be reasonable to argue that a real series, such as GDP, contains a smooth trend, such an argument is less convincing for prices. Abrupt upwards or downwards movements in the price level can easily arise from indirect tax changes or oil price shocks, suggesting that the underlying trend is not smooth and contains an $I(1)$ component.

Applying the HP filter to the US price series yields what Kydland and Prescott (1990) identify as cyclical movements. While we cannot rule out the possibility that the price level contains cycles, we note that the transfer function for our preferred model, the random walk plus noise in first differences, has a peak since it is a combination of the $\tau_2(\lambda)$ and $\tau_1(\lambda)$ filters shown in Figs. 1(b) and 1(c). It is therefore possible that the price cycle identified by Kydland and Prescott (1990) is spurious.

For the US monetary base series, the unrestricted structural model is a local linear trend with a very small cycle. Setting $\sigma_\eta^2 = 0$ gives a model with basically the same fit and a cycle with a somewhat larger amplitude (see Fig. 4(a)). The HP filter procedure imposes a smaller variance on the trend component and gives rise to a large cycle (see Fig. 4(b)). This provides an illustration of how HP filtering may change substantially the volatility and periodicity properties of an estimated cyclical component.

5 Further Issues

5.1 Seasonality

In common with most studies, the results reported above used seasonally adjusted data. Such data may not always have desirable properties, particularly if the seasonality pattern changes in some way, and is not of a kind that a standard adjustment method, such as the Bureau of the Census X-11, handles well. Data on real GDP for

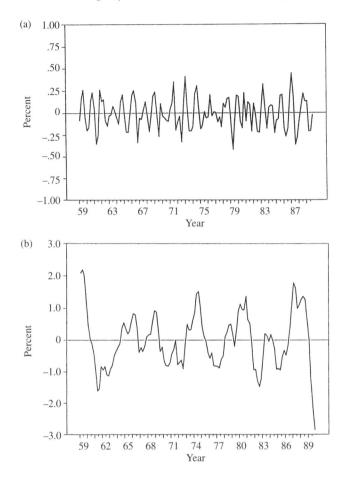

Fig. 4. Business cycles in US monetary base. (a) Estimated cyclical component;
(b) Hodrick–Prescott cycle.

the United Kingdom provide a good example.[5] With the seasonally adjusted data
and the restriction $\sigma_\eta^2 = 0$ imposed we estimated the cyclical component given in
Fig. 5(b). This cycle is not well defined and does not coincide particularly well with
the known booms and recessions in the UK. On the other hand, seasonally unadjusted data produce much better results when a seasonal component[6] is added to
model (1) (compare Fig. 5(a) with 5(b)). The estimated seasonality pattern given
in Fig. 5(c) changes quite noticeably and the adjustment procedure presumably
creates distortions in the series in attempting to cope with it.

5.2 ARIMA methodology and smooth trends
ARIMA methodology usually results in the stylized fact that real output series
are $I(1)$. Informal Box–Jenkins identification as well as formal root tests support

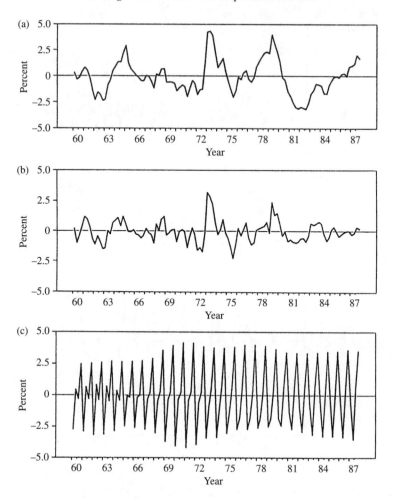

Fig. 5. Business cycles in UK GDP. (a) Estimated cycle in seasonally unadjusted data; (b) estimated cycle in seasonally adjusted data; (c) estimated seasonal component

this notion. For example, the first five autocorrelations of the first differences of real US GNP are 0.29, 0.19, −0.02, −0.10, −0.01. These autocorrelations show no need for second differencing of the data. A standard augmented Dickey–Fuller test rejects the null hypothesis of a second unit root in US GNP quite clearly. The relevant t-statistic is around −6.0, the precise value depending on the number of lags included. Thus, an ARIMA model of order (0,1,2) with a constant might be a reasonable selection. If we restrict attention to pure autoregressions and test down from a high number of lags an ARIMA(1,1,0) model with constant is obtained.

Neither of the above models is consistent with the structural time-series model (1) which has an ARIMA(2,2,4) reduced form. However, since σ_ζ^2 is

Table II. Autocorrelations of first differences of $I(2)$ process

Sample	Autocorrelation at lag							
	1	2	3	4	5	6	7	8
100	0.41	0.30	0.19	0.09	0.01	−0.05	−0.09	−0.11
	(0.12)	(0.12)	(0.11)	(0.12)	(0.13)	(0.13)	(0.14)	(0.14)
500	0.58	0.50	0.42	0.34	0.28	0.23	0.18	0.18
	(0.11)	(0.13)	(0.15)	(0.17)	(0.18)	(0.20)	(0.20)	(0.20)

Notes: This table presents the results of a Monte Carlo experiment. The data generating process is given by the estimated structural time-series model for US GNP. The table reports the mean of the autocorrelations of the first differences, and, in parentheses, standard deviations of the estimates. The results are based on 500 replications.

relatively small, the $I(2)$ component may be difficult to detect by ARIMA methodology given typical sample sizes. To verify this conjecture we conducted two small Monte Carlo experiments. The data generating process for both experiments is the estimated structural time series model for real US GNP reported in Table I. Table II reports the sample autocorrelations up to lag eight for the first differences of the generated series using sample sizes 100 and 500, respectively. Table III reports the empirical size of augmented Dickey–Fuller tests at the 5 per cent level for the null hypothesis that the first difference of the generated data has a unit root. The numbers of lags included in the Dickey–Fuller regression is fixed at 4, 8, and 16. experiments are based on 500 replications. The results for $T = 100$ in Table II, confirm that much longer time series would be needed than commonly available to detect small but persistent changes in growth rates using ARIMA methodology. As regards the results for unit root tests reported in Table III, the findings of Schwert (1989) and Pantula (1991) are clearly applicable. They demonstrate that if, after first differencing, we have an MA process which is close to being non-invertible, standard unit root tests will tend to reject the null hypothesis that a unit root is present with much higher frequency than the nominal test size. This tendency appears to be even more pronounced in a situation where a smooth local linear trend model (6) is appropriate since the reduced-form ARIMA (0,2,2) model will then have two roots close to the unit circle. For example, the results in Table III show that with a sample size of 100 and the number of lags in the Dickey–Fuller regression fixed at 8, the empirical size of the test is 0.74, exceeding the nominal 5 per cent size of the test substantially.

For purposes of short-term forecasting a parsimonious ARIMA model, such as ARIMA (1,1,0), may well be perfectly adequate compared with a trend plus cycle model. But as a descriptive device it may have little meaning and may even be misleading. For example, it may lead to a rejection of cyclical behaviour when such behaviour is, in fact, quite consistent with the data (see Harvey 1985). Perhaps more important is the concept of 'persistence' associated with the identification of $I(1)$ models. A trend plus cycle model of the form (1) with $\sigma_\eta^2 = 0$ has stationary components with no persistence and a smooth $I(2)$ trend with infinite persistence. But since the trend is reflecting slow long-term changes in growth rates, perhaps

Table III. Empirical size of 5 per cent
ADF-test for unit root in first differences
of $I(2)$ process

Sample size	Empirical size		
	$k = 4$	$k = 8$	$k = 16$
100	0.90	0.74	0.25
500	0.99	0.94	0.38

Notes: This table presents the results of a Monte
Carlo experiment. The data generating process is
given by the estimated structural time-series model
for US GNP. The table reports the empirical size of
the 5 per cent level augmented Dickey–Fuller test of
the null hypothesis of a unit root in the first differences. k denotes the numbers of lags included in the
Dickey–Fuller regressions. The results are based on
500 replications.

arising from demographic changes, innovations in technology, changes in savings
behaviour, or increasing integration of capital and goods markets, the shocks which
drive the smooth trend may have no connection with short-term economic policy.
Following the extensive literature on the productivity slowdown phenomenon, we
may well argue that understanding the reasons for persistent changes in growth
rates is one of the key problems in macroeconomics.

5.3 Segmented trends
It is sometimes argued that the trend component in economic time series is deterministic, but with a break at one or more points. We do not find the arguement for
such a trend particularly persuasive but if the data were really generated in this way,
it is worth noting that a smooth trend within a structural time series model would
adapt to it. Thus the structural time series model would still give a good indication
of the appropriate stylized facts. Indeed it is interesting to note that the trend
component we estimated for US GNP shows a slowdown in the underlying growth
rate in the late 1960s (see Fig. 6(b)) and not in the first quarter of 1973 as maintained
by Perron (1989) (see Fig. 6(a)).[7] The imposition of exogenously determined
breakpoints could therefore be potentially misleading and subject to many of the
pitfalls associated with fitting deterministic trends to the series as a whole.

Making segmented trends more flexible by allowing several endogenously
determined breaks also has a limited appeal. Such an approach is unnecessarily complicated and the conclusions could be very sensitive to the method used to
choose the breaks. Structural models are not only likely to be more robust, but are
also easier to fit.

5.4 Spurious cross-correlations between detrended series
The illustrative examples in Section 4 cast serious doubt on the validity of the
cycles in the detrended price and monetary base series obtained using the HP

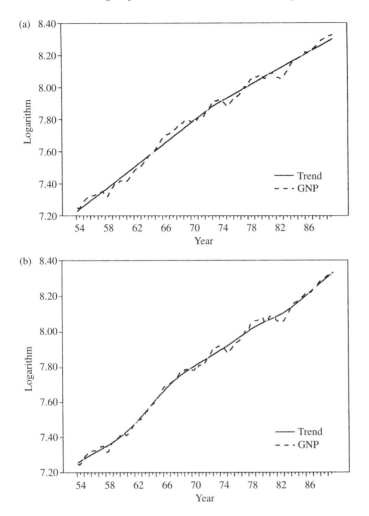

Fig. 6. Segmented trends in US GNP. (a) Deterministic trend with break in 1973 : 1; (b) estimated trend component.

filter. For US data, Kydland and Prescott (1990) draw wide-ranging conclusions about macroeconomic behaviour based on such data by examining sample cross-correlations. In particular, they argue that mainstream macroeconomic theory is inconsistent with a negative contemporaneous correlation of about −0.50 for US data between HP detrended prices and real GNP.

In this section we use some of the results developed in Section 3 to study the possibility of spurious sample cross-correlations between spurious cycles. From the point of view of the structural time-series model (1), arbitrary cross-correlations can arise if one or both of the cyclical components is absent and the shocks of the trend components are correlated across series. In the following, we focus our attention on the analytically tractable case where spurious HP cycles are imposed on two series and the two series are independent by construction. First, note that the asymptotic distribution of the sample cross-correlations between two independent stationary series is asymptotically normal (AN) and given by (see e.g. Brockwell and Davis 1987, p. 400)

$$\hat{r}_{12}(h) \sim \text{AN}\left(0, T^{-1}\left(1 + 2\sum_{j=1}^{\infty} r_1(j)r_2(j)\right)\right) \tag{15}$$

where $\hat{r}_{12}(h)$ is the sample cross-correlation at lag h between two series with sample size T and $r_1(j)$ and $r_2(j)$ are the autocorrelations of the two stationary processes at lag j, respectively. The standard deviation of $\hat{r}_{12}(h)$ can be used to evaluate the probability of finding large spurious sample cross correlations between spurious cycles imposed on independent series. To evaluate the standard deviation of the sample cross-correlations we need the autocorrelations of the spurious HP cycles. As a benchmark case, assume we have two independent random walk processes

$$(1 - L)y_{i,t} = \xi_{i,t}, \quad \xi_{i,t} \sim \text{NID}(0, \sigma_i^2) \tag{16}$$

where $i = 1, 2$ and the $\xi_{i,t}$ are uncorrelated with each other. From equation (12), the spectra of the two HP filtered random walk processes are

$$f_{c,i}(\lambda) = \frac{8(1 - \cos \lambda)^3}{[\bar{q}_\zeta + 4(1 - \cos \lambda)^2]^2} \frac{\sigma_i^2}{2\pi} \tag{17}$$

The autocovariances of the HP-filtered processes may be calculated by taking the inverse Fourier transform of equation (17)

$$c(j) = \frac{\sigma_i^2}{2\pi} \int_{-\pi}^{\pi} \frac{\cos(\lambda j)8(1 - \cos \lambda)^3}{[\bar{q}_\zeta + 4(1 - \cos \lambda)^2]^2} d\lambda, \quad j = 0, 1, \dots \tag{18}$$

and the autocorrelations are therefore given as $r(j) = c(j)/c(0)$ for $j = 1, \dots$. Setting $\sigma_i^2 = 1.0$, the autocorrelations can be calculated by numerical integration up to some maximum lag $j_{\max}$.

Line 1 in Table IV reports the asymptotic standard deviations for the chosen benchmark case. Sample sizes T are 25, 100, and 500; $\bar{q}_\zeta$ is fixed at 0.000625; and the first 100 autocorrelations are used to approximate the infinite sum for the asymptotic variance defined in equation (15). If the sample size T is 100, the standard deviation for the sample cross-correlations $\hat{r}_{12}(h)$ is 0.20. Thus, given a normal distribution there is about a 30 per cent chance of finding spurious cross-correlations exceeding 0.20 in absolute value. To reduce the chance of finding spurious cross-correlations to about 5 per cent, cross-correlations have to exceed 0.40 in absolute value. If the sample size is as low as $T = 25$, the standard deviation increases to 0.41.[8] Even if the sample size is as large as 500, there is still a chance

Table IV. Asymptotic standard deviation of sample cross-correlations

Process	Standard deviation		
	$T = 25$	$T = 100$	$T = 500$
$(1 - L)y_{i,t} = \xi_{i,t}$	0.41	0.20	0.09
$(1 - L)^2 y_{i,t} = \xi_{i,t}$	0.67	0.34	0.15

Notes: This table reports the asymptotic standard deviations for the sample cross-correlations between two independent spurious HP cycles. $\bar{q}_\zeta$ is fixed at 0.000625.

of about 5 per cent that the sample cross-correlations will exceed 0.18 in absolute value. If the two independent processes are specified as doubly integrated random walks, $(1 - L)^2 y_{i,t} = \xi_{i,t}$, appropriately modified versions of equations (17) and (18) give the standard deviations reported in line 2 of Table IV. For $T = 100$, the standard deviation is 0.34 and so values of sample cross-correlations which are quite high in absolute value may easily arise under this specification for the two independent processes. These examples illustrate that the danger of finding large sample cross-correlations between independent but spurious HP cycles is not negligible. Furthermore, they strongly indicate that research on stylized business cycle facts should report standard errors in addition to point estimates of cross-correlations.[9]

6 Conclusions

Given the nature of macroeconomic time series, it is almost impossible to unambiguously obtain stylized facts from a single series. Instead we must be content with the less ambitious objective of extracting sets of stylized facts that are consistent with the data. It will often be possible to obtain several sets of stylized facts for a series and these may have very different implications. In such cases it is necessary to look for corroborating evidence from other sources.

We have argued in this article that because structural time-series models are formulated in terms of components that have a direct interpretation, they are a particularly useful way of presenting stylized facts. Furthermore, they provide a framework for assessing the limitations of stylized facts obtained by other methods. Our principal conclusions are as follows:

(1) ARIMA models fitted on the basis of parsimony may be uninformative and are sometimes misleading. A process integrated of order 2, or $I(2)$, is unlikely to be chosen in small samples using correlogram and standard unit root tests. The net result are simple $I(1)$ representations which are not consistent with a smooth trend plus cycle representation. If the latter representation is believed to be appropriate, measures of persistence associated with $I(1)$ models have little meaning.

(2) Pure autoregressive models are even more unlikely than ARIMA models to be consistent with trend plus cycle models. Furthermore, they have virtually no hope of adequately modelling the kind of changing seasonality that is to be found in the UK GDP series. These points need to be borne in mind when making inferences from vector autoregressions.

(3) The Hodrick–Prescott filter may create spurious cycles and/or distort unrestricted estimates of the cyclical component. This property of the Hodrick–Prescott filter may lead to misleading conclusions being drawn on the relationship between short-term movements in macroeconomic time series. A proper presentation of the stylized facts associated with a trend plus cycle view needs to be done within the framework of a model that fits both components at the same time.

Acknowledgements

We would like to thank Robert Kunst, Klaus Neusser, George Tiao, and Mark Watson for helpful comments on the original draft of this paper.

Notes

1. The continuous time version of this model can be used to rationalize a cubic spline fitted to data which may not be regularly spaced. See Wecker and Ansley (1983).
2. The exact solution is given by the smoother obtained from the state space model. A fast algorithm is given in Koopman (1991). Such a smoother is valid even if the trend is deterministic, that is, $q_\zeta = 0$.
3. Neglecting factors of proportionality.
4. The US series are taken from Citibase data bank. Austrian GDP data are taken from the data bank of the Austrian Institute of Economic Research.
5. The series run from 1960 : 1 1987 : 4. The seasonally adjusted series is taken from the OECD Main Economic Indicator data bank whereas the seasonally unadjusted series from the OECD Quarterly National data bank.
6. The estimated seasonal component is modelled using the trigonometric formulation described in Harvey (1989, pp. 42–3).
7. In fact, Nordhaus (1972) published a paper entitled 'The recent productivity slowdown' before the assumed breakpoint.
8. Monte Carlo experiments indicate that the asymptotic distribution in equation (15) approximates the actual small sample distribution well for sample sizes as low as $T = 25$.
9. As an exception, Brandner and Neusser (1992) suggest the rule of thumb that cross-correlations between detrended series exceeding $2/\sqrt{T}$ in absolute value are significant at the 5 per cent level. From equation (15), however, this rule of thumb is misleading because it implicitly assumes that at least one of the detrended series is white noise.

References

Backus, D. K., and P. J. Kehoe (1989), 'International evidence on the historical properties of business cycles', Working Paper 402R, Federal Reserve Bank of Minneapolis.

Barsky, R. B., and J. A. Miron (1989), 'The seasonal cycle and the business cycle', *Journal of Political Economy*, 97, 503–35.

Blanchard, O. J., and S. Fischer (1989), *Lectures in Macroeconomics*, MIT Press, Cambridge.

Bell, W. (1984), 'Signal extraction for nonstationary time series', *The Annals of Statistics*, 12, 646–664.

Brandner, P., and K. Neusser (1992), 'Business cycles in open economies: Stylized facts for Austria and Germany', *Weltwirtschaftliches Archiv*, 128, 67–87.

Brockwell, P. J., and R. A. Davis (1987), *Time Series: Theory and Methods*, Springer, New York.

Clark, P. (1987), 'The cyclical component of U.S. economic activity', *Quarterly Journal of Economics*, 102, 797–814.

Cogley, T. (1990), 'Spurious business cycle phenomena in HP filtered time series', Mimeo, University of Washington.

Danthine, J. P., and M. Girardin (1989), 'Business cycles in Switzerland. A comparative study', *European Economic Review*, 33, 31–50.

Fishman, G. S. (1969), *Spectral Methods in Econometrics*, Harvard University Press, Cambridge.

Harvey, A. C. (1985), 'Trends and cycles in macroeconomic time series', *Journal of Business and Economic Statistics*, 3, 216–27.

Harvey, A. C. (1989), *Forecasting, Structural Time Series Models and the Kalman Filter*, Cambridge University Press, Cambridge.

Hodrick, R. J., and E. C. Prescott (1980), 'Postwar U.S. business cycles: An empirical investigation', Discussion Paper No. 451, Carnegie-Mellon University.

King, R. G., and S. T. Rebelo (1989), 'Low frequency filtering and real business cycles', Working Paper No. 205, University of Rochester.

Koopman, S. (1991), 'Efficient smoothing algorithms for time series models', Mimeo, London School of Economics.

Kydland, F. E., and E. C. Prescott (1990), 'Business cycles: Real facts and a monetary myth', *Federal Reserve Bank of Minneapolis Quarterly Review*, 14, 3–18.

Nelson C. R., and H. Kang (1981), 'Spurious periodicity in inappropriately detrended time series', *Econometrica*, 49, 741–51.

Nordhaus, W. D. (1972), 'The recent productivity slowdown', *Brookings Papers on Economic Activity*, 3, 493–546.

Pantula, S. G. (1991), 'Asymptotic ditributions of unit-root tests when the process is nearly stationary', *Journal of Business and Economic Statistics*, 9, 63–71.

Perron, P. (1989), 'The great crash, the oil shock, and the unit root hypothesis', *Econometrica*, 57, 1361–1401.

Schwert, G. W. (1989), 'Tests for unit roots: A Monte Carlo investigation', *Journal of Business and Economic Statistics*, 7, 147–160.

Wecker, W. E., and C. F. Ansely (1983), 'The signal extraction approach to non-linear regression and splint smoothing', *Journal of the American Statistical Association*, 78, 81–9.

10
Stochastic Linear Trends: Models and Estimators*

AGUSTÍN MARAVALL[†]

European University Institute

The paper considers stochastic linear trends in series with a higher than annual frequency of observation. Using an approach based on ARIMA models, some of the trend models (or the model interpretation of trend estimation filters) most often found in statistics and econometrics are analysed and compared. The properties of the trend optimal estimator are derived, and the analysis is extended to seasonally adjusted and/or detrended series. It is seen that, under fairly general conditions, the estimator of the unobserved component is noninvertible, and will not accept a convergent autoregressive representation. This has implications concerning unit root testing and VAR model fitting.

1 Introduction: the Concept of a Trend

The concept of a trend component (in short, a trend) in an economic time series is far from having a precise, universally accepted, definition. Trends have been modeled as deterministic functions of time (see, for example, Fellner 1956), as purely stochastic processes (in economics, a standard reference is Nelson and Plosser 1982), or as a mixture of the two (Pierce 1978). This paper centers on strictly stochastic trends and the stochastic process generating the trend will be assumed linear. (Nonlinear extensions, such as the one in Hamilton 1989, will not be considered.)

The trend is associated with the underlying smooth evolution of a series, free from transitory or cyclical (seasonal or not) effects. In the frequency domain, this long-term evolution is, in turn, associated with the low frequencies of the spectrum. Let the frequency be measured in radians; the zero frequency, with a cycle of infinite length, undoubtedly should be part of the trend. A frequency $\omega = (0.6)10^{-5}$ implies a period of 10^6 time units, and hence to all practical effects, indistinguishable from a trend. For $\omega = 0.006$, the associated period of

* Reprinted from *Journal of Econometrics*, Vol. 58, A. Maravall, "Stochastic Linear Trends. Models and Estimators", pp. 5–37, ©1993 with permission from Elsevier.

[†] Thanks are due to Fabio Canova, Grayham Mizon, Annalisa Fedelino, the Editor, and four referees for their helpful comments. Some referees showed interest in computational details. All calculations have been made with a program I have baptized SEATS, which stands for 'Signal Extraction in Arima Time Series'. The program originated from one developed by J. Peter Burman, for seasonal adjustment, at the Bank of England (1982 version); to him, thus, very special thanks are due. The program (jointly with the user manual) can be made available upon request.

Correspondence to: Agustín Maravall, Department of Economics, European University Institute, I-50016 S. Domenico di Fiesole (Fi), Italy.

1000 years should probably still be considered part of the trend. As ω increases and the associated period decreases, there will come a value which, clearly, should not be included in the trend. Since all economic series contain some degree of additive noise (with a flat spectrum), perhaps the most natural way to define a trend is, thus, by the spectral peak at the low frequencies; see Granger (1978) and Nerlove, Grether, and Carvalho (1976).

In so far as the trend represents mostly the variation in some frequency interval $(0, \omega_0)$, where ω_0 is small, it is possible to construct bandpass filters with a close to one gain in that interval, and close to zero gain for other frequencies. These types of filters are often used to estimate trends. Important examples are the Henderson filter used by the program X11 (see, for example, Gourieroux and Monfort 1990, pp. 102–103) and the Hodrick and Prescott (1980) filter. Both can be seen as the solution to a constrained least squares problem, where the constraints impose some degree of smoothness. Both provide linear moving average filters, similar to those obtained when the trend is estimated by approximating smooth functions with local polynomials in time (see Kendall 1976). These Moving Average (MA) filters have the advantage of computational and conceptual simplicity. They provide point estimates of the trend, but there is no underlying stochastic model for the component. As Prescott (1986) states, trend is thus 'defined by the computational procedure used to fit the smooth curve through the data'.

The price paid for conceptual and computational simplicity can be, however, large. The designed filter always requires fixing some arbitrary parameter, and this is done typically by judgement. The asymmetry of the filters implies a phase shift, which can be misleading, in particular for detecting and dating turning points. The fact that the filters are always the same, and do not depend on the stochastic properties of the series, simplifies matters, at the cost, though, of risking spurious detrending: in the limit, trends could be extracted from white-noise series. Moreover, since the estimate is, by definition, the trend, nothing in the procedure would detect those spurious trends or situations in which a given filter is not appropriate. Finally, the procedure does not allow for proper statistical inference; for example, one cannot obtain forecasts of the trend, let alone standard errors of the forecast.

Possibly fostered by the explosion in the use of ARIMA models (see Box and Jenkins 1970) for economic time series, the last ten years have experienced a growing interest in modeling trends. Since the work of Beveridge and Nelson (1981), Nelson and Plosser (1982), Watson (1986), and many others, stochastic models for the trend have become widespread in economics (see Stock and Watson 1988). In statistics, several modeling approaches have been suggested. Within the context of linear stochastic processes, we shall mostly focus on two general ones. First, the so-called ARIMA-Model-Based (AMB) approach, in which the model for the trend is derived from the ARIMA model identified for the observed series (see Box, Hillmer, and Tiao (1978) and Burman (1980)). The other approach starts by directly specifying a model for the trend; it has been denoted the Structural Time Series (STS) approach, and basic references are Harvey and Todd (1983) and Harvey (1985). Both approaches are closely related, and the models for the trend are also related, as we shall see, to those used by econometricians.

Since the trend component is never observed, one always works with estimators. In the context of ARIMA models for the trend and for the observed series, (optimal) Minimum Mean Squared Error (MMSE) estimators are easily obtained. These estimators are also moving averages, similar to the ones encountered in the design of filters; in fact, often these latter filters can be interpreted as optimal estimators for some particular models. Since the model-based approach offers a powerful tool for analysis, diagnosis, and inference, in the rest of the paper it will be used to analyse the models for the trends, and the properties of their MMSE estimators. First, Section 2 presents the basic framework and some notation. Then, in Sections 3, 4, and 5, some models often used for the trend component are analysed and discussed, and related to the stochastic structure of the observed series. Trends, of course, are never observed, and Section 6 looks at the properties of their estimators. Finally, Section 7 presents some implications for applied econometric work.

2 The General Statistical Framework

Let x_t be a time series which is the sum of a trend, p_t, and a nontrend component, n_t,

$$x_t = p_t + n_t, \tag{1}$$

where the two components are uncorrelated and each follows an ARIMA model, which we write in short as

$$\phi_p(B)p_t = \theta_p(B)b_t, \tag{2}$$

$$\phi_n(B)n_t = \theta_n(B)c_t, \tag{3}$$

where B denotes the lag operator, $\phi(B)$ and $\theta(B)$ are finite polynomials in B that may contain unit roots, and b_t and c_t are orthogonal white-noise variables, with variances V_b and V_c. (Throughout the paper, a white-noise variable denotes a variable that is normally, identically, and independently distributed.) It is assumed that the roots of the autoregressive (AR) polynomials $\phi_p(B)$ and $\phi_n(B)$ are different; since AR roots for the same frequency should belong to the same component, this is not a restrictive assumption. Of course, the two polynomials in (2) and in (3) are prime.

The paper is mostly aimed at quarterly or monthly data, in which case n_t can often be written as the sum of a seasonal component, s_t, and an irregular one, u_t, both the outcome of linear stochastic processes. Then (1) becomes

$$x_t = p_t + s_t + u_t, \tag{4}$$

where the seasonal component follows the model

$$\phi_s(B)s_t = \theta_s(B)e_t, \tag{5}$$

with $\phi_s(B)$ typically nonstationary, while u_t is assumed a stationary process, uncorrelated with b_t and e_t.

Combining (1), (2), and (3), it is obtained that

$$\phi_p(B)\phi_n(B)x_t = \phi_n(B)\theta_p(B)b_t + \phi_p(B)\theta_n(B)c_t,$$

and hence x_t also follows an ARIMA model of the type

$$\phi(B)x_t = \theta(B)a_t, \tag{6}$$

where $\phi(B) = \phi_p(B)\phi_n(B)$, and $\theta(B)a_t$ is the moving average (MA) process such that

$$\theta(B)a_t = \phi_n(B)\theta_p(B)b_t + \phi_p(B)\theta_n(B)c_t, \tag{7}$$

with a_t a white-noise variable with variance V_a (see Anderson (1971, p. 224)). Without loss of generality, V_a is set equal to one, so that the variances of the component innovations will be implicitly expressed as fractions of V_a, the variance of the one-period-ahead forecast error for the observed series. Since the sum of two uncorrelated MA processes (as in (7)) can only be noninvertible when the same unit root is shared by both MA polynomials, if we further assume that $\theta_p(B)$ and $\theta_n(B)$ have no common unit root, it follows that model (6) will be invertible. However, given that the concept of a trend or a seasonal component is intimately linked to nonstationary behavior, models (2) and (3) will typically be nonstationary (see Hillmer, Bell, and Tiao 1983). We shall still use the representation

$$\psi(B) = \theta(B)/\phi(B) \tag{8}$$

when the series is nonstationary, and similarly for $\psi_p(B)$. Further, letting ω denote frequency, the Fourier transform of $\psi(B)\psi(F)V_a$, where $F = B^{-1}$, will be referred to as the spectrum of x_t, $g_x(\omega)$ (for nonstationary series, it is often called the 'pseudospectrum'; see Hillmer and Tiao (1982) or Harvey (1990)). In a similar way, $g_p(\omega)$ will denote the spectrum of the trend.

Since observations are only available on x_t, the AMB approach starts with model (6), which can be identified and estimated directly from the data using Box–Jenkins techniques; then, looks at which models for the trend, that capture the spectral low frequency peak, are compatible with (6). From the set of all admissible models, some additional requirements permit the selection of a unique one. The STS approach proceeds in an inverse manner, by identifying *a priori* models (2) and (3) for the components. Ultimately, since (2) and (3) imply a model of the type (6), both approaches are closely linked. The models, however, are different, since the identification restrictions are not the same.

Given that the components are never observed, one can only use estimators. For known models (an assumption that will be made throughout the paper), both methods obtain the trend estimator as $E(p_t/X_T)$, where $X_T = (x_1, \ldots, x_T)$ represents the available sample. This conditional expectation can be efficiently computed with the Kalman or the Wiener–Kolmogorov (WK) filters. If the first one has the appeal of its programming easiness, the WK filter, as will become apparent, is particularly suited for statistical analysis. For the models we consider, the two filters provide MMSE estimators of the components; these estimators are considered in Section 6.

3 Some Models for the Trend Component

I shall consider some well-known ARIMA models, often encountered in practice when modeling monthly or quarterly economic time series. It will be seen what type of trend model is implicit in the overall ARIMA model, and the stochastic properties thereof. The trend model will be compared with several other statistical trend models, contained in well-known statistical packages. The comparison will also include the standard linear stochastic trend models used in econometrics.

Consider the general class of models for the observed series:

$$\nabla \nabla_s x_t = \theta(B)a_t, \tag{9}$$

where $\nabla = 1 - B$, $\nabla_s = 1 - B^s$, and s denotes the number of observations per year. Since ∇^2 causes a peak for $\omega = 0$ and S generates the peaks for the seasonal frequencies in $g_x(\omega)$, let us factorize the polynomial $\nabla \nabla_s$ into

$$\phi_p(B) - (1 - B)^2 = \nabla^2,$$
$$\phi_n(B) = 1 + B + B^2 + \cdots + B^{s-1} = S. \tag{10}$$

The decomposition (1) can be expressed as

$$\frac{\theta(B)}{\nabla \nabla_s} a_t = \frac{\theta_p(B)}{\nabla^2} b_t + \frac{\theta_n(B)}{S} c_t, \tag{11}$$

or, removing denominators,

$$\theta(B)a_t = S\theta_p(B)b_t + \nabla^2 \theta_n(B)c_t. \tag{12}$$

Let q_p and q_n denote the orders of the MA polynomials $\theta_p(B)$ and $\theta_n(B)$, respectively. Equation (12) implies that q, the order of $\theta(B)a_t$, will be equal to

$$q = \max(q_p + s - 1, q_n + 2).$$

From (12), $(q + 1)$ covariance equations can be derived; in the AMB approach $\theta(B)$ and V_a are assumed known, and the parameters of $\theta_p(B)$, $\theta_n(B)$, as well as the variances V_b and V_c, have to be derived from them. Since the number of unknowns is $(q_p + q_n + 2)$, it follows that, when

$$q_p + q_n + 1 > q,$$

there will be an infinite number of solutions to the system of covariance equations, and the decomposition (11) will be underidentified. It is straightforward to find that

$$q_p > 1 \quad \text{and} \quad q_n > s - 2$$

are necessary and sufficient conditions for the decomposition (11) to be underidentified. The AMB decomposition restricts the order of the AR and MA polynomials in model (2) for the trend to be of the same order. Therefore, $q_p = 2$, and the trend model becomes an IMA(2, 2), say

$$\nabla^2 p_t = (1 - \alpha_1 B - \alpha_2 B^2)b_t. \tag{13}$$

The decomposition (11) – or the models underlying it – is still underidentified, and a further condition is then imposed. Since the randomness of p_t in (13) is caused by the variable b_t, with variance V_b, of all the models of the type (13) that are compatible with the stochastic structure of the observed series (i.e., with model (9)), the one with smallest V_b is chosen. This yields the most stable trend, given the observed ARIMA model. As shown by Hillmer and Tiao (1982), minimizing V_b is equivalent to the requirement that it should not be possible to further decompose p_t into $p_t^* + u_t^*$, where u_t^* is white-noise, orthogonal to p_t^*. When a component satisfies this 'noise-free' requirement it is termed 'canonical'. The canonical trend is, therefore, uncontaminated by noise, and hence its spectrum should contain a zero, since otherwise, setting $\text{var}(u_t^*) = \min g_p(\omega)$, a further 'trend plus noise' decomposition could be achieved. The zero in the spectrum represents a unit root in the MA polynomial of the trend. Since the spectrum of the trend should be monotonically decreasing with ω, the zero should happen for $\omega = \Pi$, i.e., the unit root of the MA is $B = -1$. The model for the trend can then be rewritten

$$\nabla^2 p_t = (1 - \alpha B)(1 + B)b_t, \tag{14}$$

which contains two parameters, α and V_b. Now, the number of unknowns in the system of covariance equations is $(q_n + 3)$, and the number of equations $\geq q_n + 3$. The decomposition becomes, thus, identified, and there will be a unique model (14), which will represent the trend component contained in model (9).

The model for the trend in the basic Structural Model is a random walk with drift, with the drift generated also by a random walk. In particular,

$$\nabla p_t = \mu_t + u_t, \qquad \nabla \mu_t = v_t, \tag{15}$$

where u_t and v_t are mutually orthogonal white-noise variables. This trend model is also considered by Harrison and Stevens (1971) and, within a filter design approach, by Ng and Young (1990). It is immediately seen that the above model can be expressed as an IMA(2, 1) model

$$\nabla^2 p_t = (1 - \beta B)b_t, \tag{16}$$

where β and V_b depend on the variances of u_t and v_t. Model (16) represents an integrated of order 2, or I(2), model, with two parameters. Notice, however, that the trend given by (16) does not have the canonical property, so that orthogonal white-noise can still be extracted from it, and the trend can be expressed as p_t in (14) plus white-noise (Maravall 1985). This difference between the two models is a consequence of the different assumptions used to reach identification. While the AMB approach uses the canonical (noise-free) condition, the STS approach, by imposing $q_p = 1$, sets *a priori* some additional parameters equal to zero. If in simultaneous econometric models zero parameter constraints reflect, in principle, *a priori* information derived from economic theory, in the context of unobserved component models, no similar rationalization for the zero parameter constraint holds.

There is another difference between the STS trend and the canonical-model-based one which is worth mentioning. Writing (15) as

$$\nabla^2 p_t = v_t + \nabla u_t,$$

it follows that the lag 1 autocovariance of $\nabla^2 p_t$ in the STS case is always negative, so that β in (16) has to be positive. As a consequence, a model such as

$$\nabla^2 x_t = (1 + \theta B)a_t,$$

with $\theta > 0$, in the STS approach would not be a trend, nor would it be possible to extract a trend from it. (This would still be true if, more generally, u_t is allowed to be colored noise.) In the AMB approach, x_t above can be decomposed into orthogonal trend and noise, as in (1); for example, for $\theta = 0.2$, the trend is given by

$$\nabla^2 p_t = (1 - 0.092B)(1 + B)b_t, \quad V_b = 0.436,$$

and n_t is white-noise with $V_n = 0.040$. Therefore, the canonical trend in the AMB approach is less restrictive than that in the STS approach.

Moving on to other statistical procedures to estimate stochastic trends, consider first the well-known X11 procedure. Cleveland and Tiao (1976) showed how it could be interpreted (approximately) as a MMSE estimator in an AMB approach, where the model for the trend is given by

$$\nabla^2 p_t = (1 + 0.49B - 0.49B^2)b_t. \tag{17}$$

Therefore, the trend follows again an IMA(2, 2); moreover, for $B = -1$, the MA polynomial is close to zero, and hence the model is not far from a canonical trend, with a zero in the spectrum for $\omega = \Pi$. (For a discussion of Henderson's 13-term filter, see also Tiao and Hillmer (1978).) In a similar way, Tiao (1983) has shown how Akaike's BAYSEA seasonal adjustment method can also be roughly interpreted as an AMB method, with the model for the trend given now by

$$\nabla^2 p_t = b_t. \tag{18}$$

This is, in fact, the same trend model obtained by Gersch and Kitagawa (1983) using an alternative STS formulation, and the trend implied in the model-based interpretation of the Hodrick–Prescott filter (Hodrick and Prescott 1980). Model (18) does not satisfy the canonical property, but it can be expressed as the sum of a canonical trend, given by

$$\nabla^2 p_t^* = (1 - 0.172B)(1 + B)b_t^*,$$

with $\mathrm{var}(b_t^*) = 0.364V_b$, and an orthogonal white-noise variable, u_t, with variance $V_u = V_b/16$.

The four trend models, (14), (16), (17), and (18), can be seen as particular cases of the IMA(2, 2) model. These models and/or associated filters are routinely used on many hundreds of thousands of series (mostly for forecasting and seasonal adjustment); they all represent trends that are I(2) variables. This is apparently in sharp contrast with the standard linear stochastic model used to represent trends in econometrics, typically an I(1) process, most often the random walk plus drift model:

$$\nabla p_t = b_t + \mu, \tag{19}$$

where μ, the drift, is a constant (see, for example, Stock and Watson (1987) and the many references they contain). While the statistical models that have been mentioned are mostly aimed at monthly and quarterly (unadjusted) series, the attention of econometricians when modeling trends has been directed to annual or quarterly seasonally adjusted data. Be that as it may, in so far as neither time aggregation, nor seasonal adjustment, should change the order of integration (at the zero frequency), the differences in the type of data used do not explain the different order of integration typically used by statisticians and econometricians.

4 A Frequently Encountered Class of Models

It has been shown that a variety of statistical trend models can be expressed as (14) – perhaps with some added noise. The two parameters α and V_b will allow for some flexibility, and will depend, of course, on the overall model for the series. To get a closer look at that dependence, consider the particular case of (9), for which

$$\theta(B) = (1 - \theta_1 B)(1 - \theta_s B^s), \tag{20}$$

with $s = 12$. This is the so-called Airline Model, discussed in Box and Jenkins (1970), which has been found appropriate for many monthly macroeconomic series. The range for the parameters is given by $|\theta_1| < 1$ and $0 \leq \theta_{12} < 1$, in which case the model is invertible and accepts a decomposition as in (4), where the components have nonnegative spectra (Hillmer and Tiao 1982).

Table 1 presents the values of the trend parameters α and V_b as functions of the parameters of the overall ARIMA. Since V_a is set equal to one, V_b is expressed as a fraction of V_a.

A first striking result is the relative constancy of the MA trend root α. Its value is close to one, so that it nearly cancels out with one of the differences in model (14). It follows that the canonical trend implicit in the Airline Model is broadly similar to the model

$$\nabla p_t = (1 + B)b_t + \mu, \tag{21}$$

Table 1. Trend model parameters (monthly series)

	(a) Root α of the MA θ_{12}		(b) Variance V_b of the innovation θ_{12}	
	0.25	0.75	0.25	0.75
$\theta_1 = -0.75$	0.892	0.976	0.255	0.592
-0.25	0.892	0.976	0.130	0.302
0.25	0.892	0.976	0.047	0.109
0.75	0.899	0.976	0.006	0.012

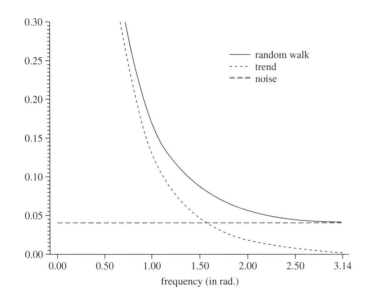

Fig. 1. Decomposition of a random walk.

the difference being that μ changes very slowly in time. The interpretation of (21) is straightforward. Let x_t be the random walk

$$\nabla x_t = a_t,$$

with $V_a = 1$. Then it is easily seen that x_t can be expressed as in (1), with p_t given by (21), with $\mu = 0$ and $V_b = 0.25$, and n_t orthogonal white-noise with $V_n = 0.25$ (see Fig. 1). Thus (21) represents the canonical trend in a random walk, in the sense that the latter is the former plus some orthogonal white-noise. (Notice that the random walk plus drift model has the same number of parameters as model (21).)

Therefore, for many series, the I(2) trend model (14) turns out to be surprisingly close to the I(1) model (21), closely related in turn to the random walk plus drift structure. It would be unlikely that sample information could distinguish between the roots $(1 - B)$ and $(1 - 0.95B)$. This indeed explains the fact that, when STS models, such as (15), are fitted, the estimator of the variance of v_t is quite frequently not significantly different from zero (see Harvey and Todd (1983) or Harvey and Peters (1990)). In this case, β of eq. (16) becomes one, and the STS trend model yields directly the random walk plus drift model. Therefore, the I(2) versus I(1) paradox can be reasonably explained in many cases.

Be that as it may, there still remains the question of which specification (I(1) versus I(2)) for the trend model should be used. The difference amounts to comparing the effect of adding a constant to the I(1) model versus imposing an additional difference and an MA factor with a root very close to one. If the trend is directly estimated, the I(1) model plus constant is likely to be obtained, since estimation would treat the two roots as overdifferencing. The specification (21) is simpler than (14), but if the overall ARIMA is efficiently estimated, derivation of the I(2) trend is straightforward, and the close-to-one trend MA root brings no special analytical or numerical problems. Conceptually, model (14) is slightly more flexible, since it allows for a slow adaptive behavior of μ, without increasing the number of parameters. Yet, ultimately, the pretension of finding a unique, universally accepted, solution to the problem of modeling a trend seems unrealistic and possibly unnecessary. What is important is that the particular model used in an application be well-specified, so that it can be properly understood and analysed, and that it agrees with the overall structure of the series.

An additional remark seems worth making: the paper is mostly concerned with monthly or quarterly data, and the models used are fundamentally short-term models (in fact, Box–Jenkins ARIMA models were meant for short-term analysis). While it is true that, in the short run, model (14) with $\alpha = 0.95$ and model (21) can be indistinguishable, in the very long run the differences can be large. The implication is that models built to capture the short-term behavior of a series will likely be unreliable tools for analysing the very long term (a similar point is made by Diebold and Rudebush 1991).

Back to the results of Table 1, since the value of α varies little for different values of the θ-parameters, differences in the trend model (14) will be due to differences in the variance in the trend innovation, V_b. Table 1 shows that V_b is in fact very sensitive to changes in the θ-parameters. Since b_t generates the stochastic variability in the trend, small values of V_b are associated with stable trends, while large values will produce unstable ones. Given that the spectrum of p_t will be proportional to V_b, a stable trend will denote a trend with a thin spectral peak, and hence a close to deterministic behavior. An unstable trend will display, on the contrary, a wide spectral peak, and hence more stochastic variability. It is seen in Table 1 that, as θ_1 moves from -1 to 1, V_b decreases and the trend becomes closer to being deterministic, as could be expected. Figure 2 presents the spectra of x_t for the two extreme cases considered in Table 1. For $\theta_1 = 0.75$, $\theta_{12} = 0.25$, the trend is very stable and the seasonal component is strongly stochastic, as can be seen from the width of the spectral peaks. For $\theta_1 = -0.75$, $\theta_{12} = 0.75$, the stochastic character of x_t is dominated by the trend variation, while seasonality becomes

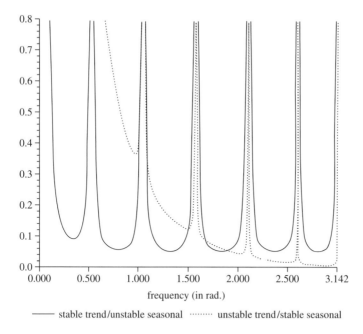

frequency (in rad.)

——— stable trend/unstable seasonal ········ unstable trend/stable seasonal

Fig. 2. Spectrum of the model: two extreme cases.

Table 2. Innovation variances: two extreme cases

	$\theta_1 = 0.75, \theta_{12} = 0.25$	$\theta_1 = -0.75, \theta_{12} = 0.75$
Variance of trend innovation	0.006	0.592
Variance of seasonal innovation	0.222	0.027
Variance of irregular	0.249	0.012

more stable. As for the white-noise irregular, the minimum of $g_x(\omega)$ is larger for the first model, and hence the irregular component will be more important in the first case. Table 2 evidences the behavior of the two models. The stable trend–unstable seasonal case presents a small trend innovation variance and a large variance of the seasonal component innovation. Also, the MA root $(1 + 0.75B)$ implies, in the unstable trend–stable seasonal case, a very small irregular component.

Figure 3 displays the trend spectra for the two extreme cases mentioned above. They have similar shapes and what varies considerably is the area under the curve. Comparison of Fig. 2 and Fig. 3 illustrates one of the reasons in favor of a flexible model-based approach: the model used for the trend, and the estimation filter this model implies, should depend on the particular series under consideration. It would clearly be inappropriate, for example, to use the filter implied by the stable trend model to capture the low frequency peak in the spectrum of the series with unstable trend; the trend would be grossly underestimated.

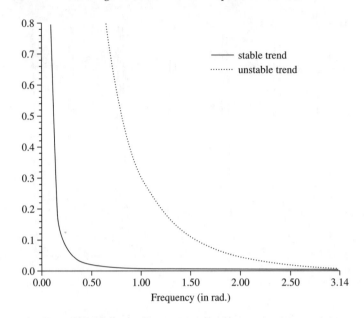

Fig. 3. Stable and unstable trend spectra.

Table 3. Trend model parameters (quarterly series)

	(a) Root α of the MA θ_4		(b) Variance V_b of the innovation θ_4	
	0.25	0.75	0.25	0.75
$\theta_1 = -0.75$	0.709	0.931	0.318	0.621
-0.25	0.710	0.931	0.163	0.317
0.25	0.712	0.931	0.106	0.203
0.75	0.718	0.931	0.062	0.114

5 Extensions and Examples

When dealing with quarterly observations, $s = 4$ in expression (9), the identification conditions remain the same, and the canonical trend is, again, given by (14).
When the MA polynomial of the overall model is of the type (20), computing the
trend parameters α and V_b, Table 1 is replaced by Table 3. Both tables roughly
tell the same story: the value of α is close to 1, and, if cancelled with one of the
differences, the trend component in a random walk (model (21)) is obtained. The
fact that the smallest seasonal frequency in monthly data ($\Pi/6$) is closer to zero
than the corresponding one for quarterly data ($\Pi/2$) constrains the trend spectrum
of the monthly series to be closer to the ordinate axis; this explains the larger values
of α obtained in the monthly case. The values of V_b in Table 3 are slightly larger
than those of Table 1, in accordance with the obvious fact that a quarterly series

allows for less seasonal variation than a monthly series, and hence the relative contribution of the trend increases.

As mentioned before, the model for the trend should depend on the overall model for the observed series, which can be directly identified from the data. If (9) is replaced by

$$\nabla_s x_t = \theta(B)a_t \tag{22}$$

or by

$$\nabla^2 \nabla_s x_t = \theta(B)a_t, \tag{23}$$

then similar derivations to that in Section 3 yield the canonical trend models

$$\nabla p_t = (1 + B)b_t, \tag{24}$$

$$\nabla^3 p_t - (1 - \alpha_1 B - \alpha_2 B^2)(1 + B)b_t, \tag{25}$$

respectively. Therefore, the trend in (22) is the same as the trend in a random walk, an I(1) process, while the trend in (23) is I(3), with an MA(3) polynomial. To see an example of the latter, the model

$$\nabla^2 \nabla_{12} x_t = (1 - 0.825B)(1 - 0.787B^{12})a_t \tag{26}$$

explained well the monthly series of the Spanish consumer price index net of the energy component (for the period 1978–1988). Deriving the implied model (25) for the trend, $V_b = 0.204$ and the MA polynomial $(1 - \alpha_1 B - \alpha_2 B^2)$ factorizes into $(1 - 0.98B)(1 - 0.825B)$. Both roots are close to one, and hence model (26) can be expressed as

$$\nabla p_t = (1 + B)b_t + \mu_0 + \mu_1 t,$$

where both μ_0 and μ_1 are parameters that change very slowly in time. Therefore, although the trend is theoretically I(3), again, it may be difficult to distinguish it from an I(1) model on the basis of sample information.

Figure 4 displays the spectra of the trend models for several examples; these are the following:

(a) The component of the consumer price index, i.e., the I(3) trend in model (26).
(b) The monthly series of Spanish tax revenues in the period 1979–1990, for which a model of the type (22) is appropriate. The I(1) trend is as in (24), with $V_b = 0.001$.
(c) The monthly series of the Spanish monetary aggregate for the period 1973–1985, discussed in Maravall (1988b). The overall model is of the type (9), with an I(2) trend given by

$$\nabla^2 p_t = (1 - 0.96B)(1 + B)b_t, \qquad V_b = 0.234.$$

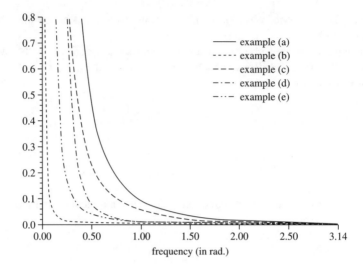

Fig. 4. Spectra for different trend models.

(d) The consumer durable series in Harvey and Peters (1990). For this example, the trend estimated by Harvey and Peters with a frequency domain method is equivalent to an IMA(2, 1) model of the type (16), with $\beta = 0.884$ and innovation variance 0.244. Removing the noise from this model yields a canonical trend with parameters $\alpha = 0.884$ and $V_b = 0.061$.

(e) The model-based approximation to the X11 trend of Cleveland and Tiao (model (17)). From their results, it is straightforward to find that $V_b = 0.020$.

Although the shapes are somewhat similar, they certainly represent different trends, whose stochastic nature is strongly linked to the variance of the trend innovation. These different models may capture, thus, different stochastic properties of the series having to do with different low frequency spectral peaks (as Fig. 2 clearly illustrated). It is worth noticing in Fig. 4 the relative proximity of the trend models in X11, in the canonical trend hidden in the STS example, and in the monetary aggregate series example. The three spectra, moreover, lie in between those of the more stable I(1) trend of example (b) and the more stochastic I(3) trend of example (a).

6 The MMSE Estimator of the Trend

In practice, the trend component is unobserved, and we are always forced to work with estimators. Once the models have been specified, for stationary series the MMSE estimator of p_t can be obtained with the Wiener–Kolmogorov (WK) filter (see Whittle 1963). The filter extends easily to nonstationary series (Bell 1984, or Maravall 1988a) and to finite realizations of the series by replacing unknown future and past observations with their forecasts and backcasts (Cleveland and Tiao 1976).

Numerical computation, moreover, can be greatly simplified by using the Wilson algorithm described in Burman (1980). The WK filter provides a method to obtain the conditional expectation of the trend given the available series, equivalent to the usual Kalman filter (Harvey 1989). Both are computationally efficient; the WK formulation will allow us to derive easily the theoretical properties of the MMSE estimator.

Using the notation of Section 3, and in particular the symbolic representation (8), the WK filter, for the case of a complete realization of the series (from $-\infty$ to ∞), is given by

$$\hat{p}_t = V_b \frac{\psi_p(B)\psi_p(F)}{\psi(B)\psi(F)} x_t, \tag{27}$$

where $F = B^{-1}$ is the forward operator. Replacing the ψ-polynomials by their rational expressions, after cancelling common factors, (27) becomes

$$\hat{p}_t = v(B, F)x_t = V_b \frac{\theta_p(B)\phi_n(B)}{\theta(B)} \frac{\theta_p(F)\phi_n(F)}{\theta(F)} x_t. \tag{28}$$

The filter $v(B, F)$ is seen to be centered at t, symmetric, and convergent (due to the invertibility of $\theta(B)$). In fact, (28) shows that the filter is equal to the autocovariance-generating function of the stationary process

$$\theta(B)z_t = \theta_p(B)\phi_n(B)b_t. \tag{29}$$

(For a long enough series, since $v(B, F)$ is convergent in B and in F, in practice, the results for the infinite realization will apply to the central years of the series.)

To illustrate what the filter (28) does, and how it adapts itself to the series, Fig. 5 plots the frequency domain representation of the trend filters $v(B, F)$ for the two extreme examples of Section 3 and Fig. 2. For $\omega = 0$ both present a gain of one, and for all seasonal frequencies they present a gain of zero, associated with the seasonal unit roots in the MA part of (29). For the stable trend–unstable seasonal model, the filter is very close to the ordinate axis, captures very low frequency variations and little else. For the unstable trend–stable seasonal model, since most of the stochastic variation in the series is accounted for by the trend, the filter does not have to remove much, besides the zeros at the seasonal frequencies.

If, in (28), x_t is replaced with (6), the MMSE estimator can be expressed as a linear filter in the series innovations (a_t):

$$\hat{p}_t = \xi(B, F)a_t = V_b \frac{\theta_p(B)}{\phi_p(B)} \frac{\theta_p(F)\phi_n(F)}{\theta(F)} a_t,$$

and hence the theoretical trend estimator follows the model

$$\phi_p(B)\hat{p}_t = \theta_p(B)\eta_p(F)a_t, \tag{30}$$

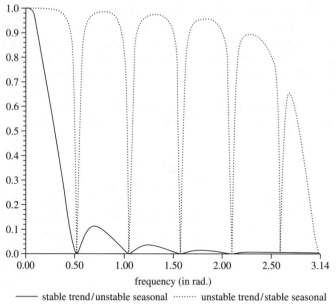

Fig. 5. Trend filters: two extreme cases.

where $\eta_p(F)$ is the forward filter:

$$\eta_p(F) = V_b \frac{\theta_p(F)\phi_n(F)}{\theta(F)}.$$

Comparing (30) with model (2) for the trend, it is seen that:

(1) As has been often pointed out, the model for the theoretical component and that for its theoretical MMSE estimator are not the same (even for an infinite realization of the series). The dynamic properties of the component and of its MMSE estimator are structurally different.

(2) From (30) or (29) it is seen that the trend estimator depends not only on the trend model, but also on the nontrend component. For example, due to the (nontrend) roots in $\eta(F)$, the trend estimator may display oscillatory behavior when the trend component model contains none.

(3) Both the component and its estimator share the same stationarity inducing transformation.

(4) The models for the component and for the estimator contain the same polynomials in B.

(5) The difference between the two models is due to the presence of the forward polynomial $\eta_p(F)$ in the model for the estimator. This polynomial expresses the dependence of $\hat{p}_t$ on future values of x, and will cause revisions in preliminary estimators as new observations (and hence new innovations $a_{t+k}, k > 0$) become available.

(6) When some of the nontrend AR roots of the overall model have unit modulus (i.e., when $\phi_n(B)$ contains some unit roots), then the filter (28) and the model (30) for the trend estimator will be noninvertible. This will be, for example, the case whenever the series presents nonstationary seasonality. Thus, in particular, the class of models (9), (22), and (23), as well as the basic STS model and the model version of X11, all contain the nonstationary seasonal AR polynomial S given by (10), so that the corresponding trend estimator will be noninvertible.

For example, for the class of models given by (9) with $s = 12$, the MMSE estimator (30) becomes

$$\nabla^2 \hat{p}_t = (1 - \alpha B)(1 + B)\eta_p(F)a_t,$$

$$\eta_p(F) = V_b \frac{(1 - \alpha F)(1 + F)(1 + F + \cdots + F^{11})}{\theta(F)}.$$

When $\theta(B)$ is given by (20), Figs 6 and 7 present the spectra of the models for the trend and its estimator, for the two extreme examples we have been considering. In the first case (stable trend–unstable seasonal), Fig. 6a shows that the spectrum of the trend estimator is similar to that of the component, with a slightly narrower band width for the low frequency peak. In the unstable trend–stable seasonal case in Fig. 7, the spectrum of the trend follows closely that of the theoretical component, except for noticeable dips at the seasonal frequencies (as shown in Fig. 6b, when Fig. 6a is amplified, similar dips are found).

The departures from the theoretical component model implied by MMSE estimation are easily interpreted in the frequency domain. From (27), the spectrum of the estimator, $g_{\hat{p}}(\omega)$, is given by

$$g_{\hat{p}}(\omega) = R^2(\omega)g_x(\omega), \tag{31}$$

where

$$R(\omega) = \frac{g_p(\omega)}{g_x(\omega)} = \frac{1}{1 + 1/r(\omega)}, \tag{32}$$

and $r(\omega) = g_p(\omega)/g_n(\omega)$. Since the trend is the signal of interest, $r(\omega)$ represents the signal-to-noise ratio. Therefore, when estimating the trend, what the MMSE method does is, for each ω, to look at the relative contribution of the theoretical trend to the spectrum of the series. If this relative contribution is high, then $r(\omega)$, and hence $R(\omega)$, will also be high, and the frequency will be mostly used for trend estimation. For example, for $\omega = 0$, $r(0)$ goes to ∞ and $R(0) = 1$. This implies that the zero frequency will only be used for estimation of the trend. If the nontrend component contains seasonal nonstationarity, then, for ω equal to the seasonal frequencies, $r(\omega)$ and $R(\omega)$ become both zero, and these frequencies are ignored when estimating the trend. Considering (31), these zeroes produce the dips in the spectra of Figs. 6 and 7.

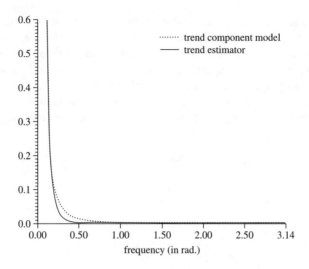

Fig. 6a. Stable trend spectrum: model and estimator.

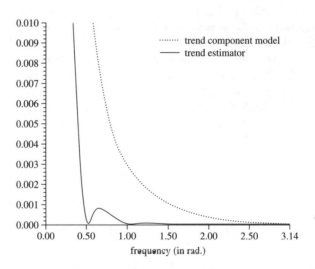

Fig. 6b. Stable trend spectrum: model and estimator.

From (31) and (32), the relationship between the spectrum of the theoretical trend component and that of its MMSE estimator is found to be

$$g_{\hat{p}}(\omega) = R(\omega)g_p(\omega) = \frac{1}{1 + 1/r(\omega)} g_p(\omega).$$

Since $r(\omega) \geq 0$, it follows that $0 \leq R(\omega) \leq 1$, and hence $g_{\hat{p}}(\omega) \leq g_p(\omega)$ for every frequency, so that the trend estimator will always underestimate the theoretical trend. This is clearly seen in Figs. 6 and 7, and in Table 4, which compares the

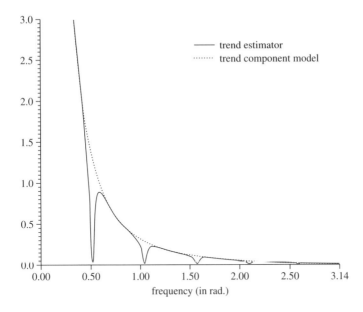

Fig. 7. Unstable trend spectrum: model and estimator.

Table 4. Variance of the stationary transformation: trend component and estimator

θ_{12}	0.25				0.75			
θ_1	−0.75	−0.25	0.25	0.75	−0.75	−0.25	0.25	0.75
Trend component	0.460	0.235	0.085	0.011	1.157	0.590	0.213	0.024
Estimator	0.212	0.078	0.014	<0.001	0.956	0.349	0.058	0.001

variance of the stationary transformation of the trend and of its estimator, for different values of the θ-parameters. The estimator always has a smaller variance, and the ratio of the two variances get further away from one as the trend becomes more stable. Therefore, the more stochastic the trend is, the less will its variance be underestimated (in relative terms). On the contrary, the variations of a very stable trend will be grossly underestimated. In summary, the estimator provides a more stable trend than the one implied by the theoretical model, and this effect will be particularly strong when the theoretical trend is already stable.

The difference between the dynamic properties of the theoretical component and its MMSE estimator can also be assessed in the time domain by comparing the correlations. In Section 4 it was seen how, for reasonable values of the parameter θ_1 and θ_{12}, the model for the trend derived from the Airline Model is an IMA(2, 2), with MA roots $B = -1$ and $B \doteq 1/0.9$, or approximately,

$$\nabla^2 p_t = (1 + 0.1B - 0.9B^2)b_t.$$

Table 5. Autocorrelations of the stationary transformation: trend component and estimator

Estimator $(\nabla^2 \hat{p}_t)$					
θ_{12}	θ_1	ρ_1	ρ_2	ρ_3	ρ_{12}
0.25	−0.75	0.04	−0.50	−0.01	−0.37
	−0.25	0.18	−0.52	−0.14	−0.37
	0.25	0.37	−0.37	−0.30	−0.37
	0.75	0.61	0.05	−0.11	−0.36
0.75	−0.75	0.03	−0.52	−0.01	−0.13
	−0.25	0.16	−0.54	−0.15	−0.13
	0.25	0.35	−0.41	−0.33	−0.13
	0.75	0.56	−0.07	−0.23	−0.14
Theoretical component $(\nabla^2 p_t)$		0.01	−0.49	—	—

The Autocorrelation Function (ACF) of $\nabla^2 p_t$, is, thus, $\rho_1 \doteq 0.01$, $\rho_2 \doteq -0.49$, and $\rho_k = 0$ for $k > 2$. Table 5 compares this ACF with that of the estimator for different values of the θ-parameters and for a few selected lags. The departures from the component ACF can be substantial, particularly for large values of θ_1 (associated with small values of V_b). Therefore, more stochastic trends (with large values of V_b) will have estimators more in agreement with the ACF of the component. It is worth noticing that, although for the theoretical trend $\rho_{12} = 0$, the MMSE always displays a negative value which can be quite substantial.

When Tables 4 and 5 are put together, the following result emerges: if the series is the sum of two components with varying degrees of stability, the distortion in the variance and ACF of the components induced by MMSE estimation is stronger for the more stable one. For example, when most of the stochastic variation in the series is attributable to the presence of a stochastic trend, the underestimation of the variance and the induced autocorrelations in the estimator will be relatively minor; when the stochastic trend accounts for little, the distortions can be remarkably large. This result is somewhat comforting: the distortions are large when the component matters little.

The underestimation of the component variance when using the MMSE estimator implies that, although the components are uncorrelated, their estimators will not be so, and cross-correlations between them will appear. Table 6 displays the contemporaneous cross-correlations between the trend estimator on the one hand, and the seasonal and irregular estimators on the other, for the case of the Airline Model with different values of the θ-parameters. Although none of the correlations is large, they are not negligible for relatively large values of θ_1.

One of the by-products of a model-based approach is that theoretical values of the estimator auto- and cross-correlations can be easily derived from the models. Comparison between these values and the ones obtained empirically in an application can provide a useful element for diagnosis (Maravall 1987).

Table 6. Cross-correlation between estimators of different components

	Trend and seasonal estimators θ_{12}		Trend and irregular estimators θ_{12}	
	0.25	0.75	0.25	0.75
$\theta_1 = -0.75$	−0.14	−0.08	0.17	0.17
−0.25	−0.15	−0.08	0.08	0.08
0.25	−0.17	−0.10	−0.10	−0.09
0.75	−0.22	−0.12	−0.31	−0.30

7 Some Implications for Econometric Modeling

The distinction between theoretical component and estimator, and the different dynamic properties they exhibit, has been on occasion a source of confusion in applied econometric work. Since the component is never observed, we can only use estimators; this has some important implications, which we proceed to discuss.

Consider the full decomposition into trend, seasonal, and irregular components given by (4). Denote by x_t^a the seasonally adjusted (SA) series, equal to

$$x_t^a = x_t - s_t = p_t + u_t.$$

If, in (1), p_t is replaced by x_t^a and n_t by s_t, most of the previous discussion remains valid. Since x_t^a is obtained by adding a stationary component to p_t, if

$$\phi_a(B)x_t^a = \theta_a(B)d_t$$

denotes the model for the SA series, it follows that $\phi_a(B)$ and $\phi_p(B)$ have the same unit roots, and this will also be true of $\phi_s(B)$ and $\phi_n(B)$. In fact, the models for p_t and x_t^a often are similar, although the addition of u_t will remove the canonical property from the SA series (it is indeed the case that x_t^a tends to be closer to the 'random walk plus drift' structure than p_t; see Maravall (1988b)).

The estimator of the SA series, $\hat{x}_t^a$, is obtained, in a manner similar to that described in Section 5 for estimation of the trend, with a centered, symmetric, and convergent filter. Expressing $\hat{x}_t^a$ in terms of the series innovations, results (1) to (6) in Section 6 remain basically unchanged. I shall continue to center the discussion on the trend estimator, bearing in mind that it is also valid for the estimator of the SA series.

Let $X_T = (x_1, \ldots, x_T)$ denote the observed series. Since the filter $v(B, F)$ in (28) is convergent in both directions, we may assume that it can be safely truncated at some point. Let the number of terms in the truncated filter be $(2k + 1)$. When $T - t < k$, the estimator of p_t (obtained by extending the series with forecasts) is not the estimator (30), but a preliminary one, which will be revised as new observations become available. As a consequence, the last k values of the series $(\hat{p}_1, \ldots, \hat{p}_T)$, computed with X_T, will be preliminary estimators; in a symmetric manner, the first k values require backcasts of the series, and will also differ from the estimator (28), with stochastic structure given by (30). The final estimator (28) will be denoted the 'historical' estimator.

The preliminary estimators $(\hat{p}_1, \ldots, \hat{p}_k, \hat{p}_{T-k}, \ldots, \hat{p}_T)$, have different stochastic structures (see, for example, Pierce (1980) and Burridge and Wallis 1984), different in turn from that of the historical estimator. Only the central values $(\hat{p}_{k+1}, \ldots, \hat{p}_{t-k})$ can properly be assumed to be homogeneous, being generated by the same process (30). The model-based approach permits us to compute the variance of any revision in the estimator of p_t, and hence the value of k after which the revision can be neglected. For the range of models considered in Section 3, it is found that, after three years of additional data, between 82% and 100% of the revision in the concurrent estimator of the trend has been completed; for X11 the revision variance decreases by 95%. (It can be seen that slower rates of convergence to the historical estimator (i.e., large values of k) are associated with smaller revisions; when the revision is large, the estimator tends to converge fast.) Although the trend estimator converges always faster, a similar result holds for the SA series: after three years of additional data, for the models of Section 3, between 80% and 100% of the revision variance has disappeared; for X11 the proportion is roughly 80%.

Therefore, when fitting models to unobserved components, care should be taken to use an homogeneous series of historical estimators. Although well-known, this is an often neglected correction. But, even if a homogeneous series of historical estimators is used, there remain problems in some standard econometric practices having to do with fitting models to series of unobserved component estimators. In order to analyse these problems, consider again the decomposition (4), with nonstationary trend and seasonal components, and a stationary irregular component. Thus, $\phi_p(B)$ will contain the factor ∇^d, with $d \geq 1$, and $\phi_s(B)$ will contain the factor S with seasonal unit roots, typically given by (10). Thus we can write

$$\nabla^d p_t = \lambda_p(B)b_t, \tag{33}$$

$$Ss_t = \lambda_s(B)e_t, \tag{34}$$

where $\lambda_p(B)b_t$ and $\lambda_s(B)e_t$ are stationary processes. Finally, let

$$u_t = \lambda_u(B)v_t \tag{35}$$

represent the stationary and invertible irregular component (in macroeconomics, often called the cyclical component). It is easily seen that (33), (34), and (35) imply that the overall model for the series can be expressed as

$$\nabla^d Sx_t = \lambda(B)a_t, \tag{36}$$

where $\lambda(B)a_t$ is also a stationary and invertible process. (Invertibility is guaranteed by the fact that the component u_t is invertible.)

Applying the WK filter and replacing x_t with (36), the model for the trend estimator can be finally expressed as

$$\nabla^d \hat{p}_t = \alpha_p(B, F)S(F)a_t, \qquad (37)$$

where $\alpha_p(B, F) = V_b \lambda_p(B)\lambda_p(F)/\lambda(F)$ is a convergent polynomial in F and in B.

Consider now the decomposition of the series:

$$x_t = x_t^a + s_t.$$

Since $x_t^a = p_t + u_t$ and u_t is stationary, the model for the SA series can be expressed as

$$\nabla^d x_t^a = \lambda_a(B)d_t, \qquad (38)$$

where $\lambda_a(B)d_t$ is a stationary and invertible process. Proceeding as in the case of the trend estimator, the MMSE estimator of x_t^a can be expressed as

$$\nabla^d \hat{x}_t^a = \alpha_a(B, F)S(F)a_t, \qquad (39)$$

where $\alpha_a(B, F) = V_d \lambda_a(B)\lambda_a(F)/\lambda(F)$ is also a polynomial convergent at both extremes.

Consider, finally, the estimator of u_t, the seasonally adjusted and detrended series (i.e., the irregular, or cyclical, component). From (35) and (36) it is obtained that the MMSE historical estimator $\hat{u}_t$, expressed as a function of the series innovations, can be written as

$$\hat{u}_t = \alpha_u(B, F)(1 - F)^d S(F)a_t, \qquad (40)$$

where $\alpha_u(B, F) = V_v \lambda_u(B)\lambda_u(F)/\lambda(F)$. Expressions (37), (39), and (40) imply that the historical estimators of the trend, of the SA series, and of the irregular component are all noninvertible series. The model for the three series contains the unit seasonal roots in the MA polynomial; for the series $\hat{u}_t$, the noninvertible factor $(1 - F)^d$ is also present.

More generally, it will be the case that the estimator of an unobserved component will be noninvertible whenever at least one of the other components present in the series is nonstationary: the unit AR roots of this other component will appear in the MA polynomial of the model for the estimator. This result is valid for AMB methods, independently of whether the components are canonical or not. It applies equally to unobserved components obtained with STS methods, and, in general, to the estimators obtained with any filter that can be given an MMSE-model-based interpretation (for symmetric filters, used for historical estimation, this requirement is relatively minor). As an example, for the model version of X11, Fig. 8 presents the spectrum of the SA series estimator, which contains the zeros at seasonal frequencies; Fig. 9 displays the nonconvergent weights of the (one-sided) AR representation of the SA series estimator.

In summary, whenever some nonstationarity is removed from the series in order to estimate a component, the estimator will be noninvertible. How restrictive

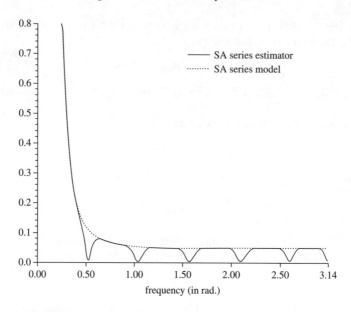

Fig. 8. X11 SA series spectrum: model and estimator.

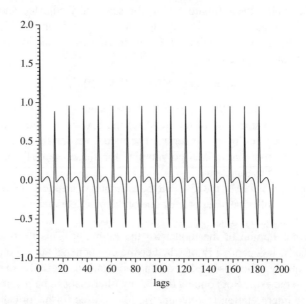

Fig. 9. X11 SA series estimator: one-sided AR weights.

can we expect this condition to be? Consider the estimators of p_t, x_t^a, and u_t. In order to obtain the three, the seasonal component has been removed. If seasonality is stochastic, the sum of the seasonal component over a year span (i.e., Ss_t) cannot be expected to be always exactly zero, since seasonality is moving. Still, the very concept of seasonality implies that its annual aggregate effect should not be too far from zero. This can be formally expressed as

$$Ss_t = w_t, \tag{41}$$

where w_t is a zero-mean, stationary process (with small variance). Expression (41) is equivalent to (34); unit AR roots are thus a sensible requirement for a stochastic seasonal component. In fact, expression (41), with different assumptions for the stationary process w_t, is overwhelmingly used as the specification of the seasonal component in model-based methods or model-based interpretation of filters (see Maravall 1989).

From the previous discussion, two important implications follow:

(A) Testing for unit roots in economic time series is often performed on seasonally adjusted data (examples can be found in Campbell and Mankiw (1987), Cochrane (1988), Perron and Phillips (1987), Schwert (1989), and Stock and Watson (1986)). Comparing (33) with (37) or (38) with (39), it is seen that the distributions of the (stationary transformation of the) component and of its estimator are different, and this will have an effect on unit root testing, as detected by Ghysels (1990) and Ghysels and Perron (1993) for the case of the seasonally adjusted series. The lag polynomials in the model for the estimator are more complex and of larger orders than those in the component model; their converging properties will be different, and so will be, for example, the spectral density at the zero frequency. In particular, for the important case in which nonstationary stochastic seasonality has been removed from the series (and that is what most moving average seasonal adjustment methods do), the estimator of the trend and SA series are noninvertible, and will not accept an AR representation. Therefore, unit root tests that rely on AR representations, such as the Augmented Dickey Fuller type (Dickey and Fuller 1979), should not be carried on SA series, nor on trends, nor, in general, on any unobserved component estimator when the series contains another component which is nonstationary.

As for the Phillips (1987) type test, it is worth noticing that, as reported by Phillips and Perron (1988) and by Schwert (1989), the test performs very poorly when the MA part of the series model contains a root close to -1. Since $B = -1$ is a root of $S(F)$, the noninvertible MA polynomial in the estimator model (37) or (39), one could expect a poor performance of the test when SA series or trends are used. For the first case, this is in fact what Ghysels and Perron (1992) find.

(B) In the same way that a noninvertible series does not accept a univariate AR representation, since the minimum of a VAR spectrum is strictly positive, no individual series in a VAR representation can be noninvertible. Again, thus, when the series contains nonstationary stochastic seasonal and trend components, expressions (37), (39), and (40) imply that VAR models would not be appropriate to model SA series, trends, or irregular (cyclical) components, not even as approximations. It follows, moreover, that these filtered series should not be used either in a Johansen-type test for cointegration. Fitting VAR models to SA series is, however, a standard practice, often aimed at reducing dimensionality of the VAR model.

Among many examples, some important ones are Blanchard and Quah (1989), Lütkepohl (1991), Hendry and Mizon (1990), Sims (1980), and Stock and Watson (1991).

Notice that, when the series is simply the sum of a stochastic trend and a stationary component, the same conclusion applies to the detrended series (obtained, for example, with the Hodrick and Prescott filter). Due to the presence of the MA factor $(1 - F)^d$, the detrended series will accept no convergent AR (or VAR) representation.

In the previous discussion, noninvertibility (i.e., the lack of a convergent AR representation or, equivalently, the presence of a zero in the spectral density) is a property of the theoretical model that generates the estimator of the unobserved component. Of course, a particular finite realization from that model will not exactly satisfy it. This does not invalidate, however, the result that AR and VAR models, when applied to series from which a nonstationary stochastic component has been filtered out, contain a specification error. This error is due to the finite truncation of a nonconvergent filter. The departure from noninvertibility due to sample variation, mixed with the fact that (often) the SA series used is not the homogeneous historical estimator, but contains preliminary estimators at both ends (as discussed at the beginning of Section 7), may well explain why, in practice, the specification error may easily pass undetected.

8 Summary and Conclusions

The paper deals with modeling and estimation of linear stochastic trends in economic time series, with a higher than annual frequency of observation (the series may, thus, contain seasonality). A model-based approach is followed, and Section 2 describes the general framework. The observed series is the sum of a trend and an orthogonal nontrend component, where the components (and hence the series) follow ARIMA models. The model for the trend is aimed at capturing the low frequency peak in the series spectrum; since different series will exhibit different peaks, the model for the trend should depend on the particular series being analysed, i.e., on the overall ARIMA model. (This point is illustrated throughout the paper.)

A fairly general class of models is considered: the one for which a transformation of the type $\nabla^d \nabla_s$ produces a stationary and invertible process ($d = 0, 1, 2$; s denotes the number of observations per year). The nonstationary part of the trend model is then ∇^{d+1}, and the stationary part depends on the rest of the overall model and on some additional assumptions needed to identify a unique decomposition. It is seen how different identification assumptions yield different models for the trend. Section 3 presents some of the trend models most frequently encountered in the statistics literature (or the model interpretation of some trend estimation filters), looks at their properties, and performs some comparisons. All the trend models considered can ultimately be expressed as the canonical trend obtained in an ARIMA-model-based method, plus some orthogonal white-noise.

An apparent paradox is that, while most statistical trend models (or filters) imply I(2) trends, I(1) trends are typically used in econometrics. Section 4 looks in more detail at a particular class of models for the observed series (with $\nabla\nabla_{12}$ as the stationary transformation), often reasonably appropriate for monthly macroeconomic series. The trend models obtained for different values of the parameters are compared; they are IMA(2, 2) models and present the common feature that the MA part always contains a root very close to 1. Thus, from an estimation point of view, the I(2) trend would be indistinguishable from an I(1) model with drift. Section 4 extends the analysis in several directions: first, to quarterly data and, second, to different values of d. It is concluded that the 'order of integration' paradox is more apparent than real. Finally, some of the advantages and disadvantages of using the 'I(1) plus drift' versus the I(2) specification are discussed.

In the model-based approach there is an important distinction between the theoretical (unobserved) component and its estimator. The MMSE estimator is obtained with the Wiener–Kolmogorov filter applied to the observed series, and its properties are discussed in Section 5. It is seen that the dynamic properties of the component and of its MMSE estimator are structurally different, and that the estimator will follow a model different from that of the theoretical component. The stationary transformation is preserved, but the spectrum and ACF will be different; for the estimator, they will depend on the structure of the nontrend component. The estimator always yields a more stable trend, and this effect is more pronounced when the theoretical trend is already stable.

It is further seen that, when the nontrend component contains some non-stationarity, the estimator of the trend and of the SA series is always noninvertible. Thus, for example, seasonal nonstationarity in the series implies that no convergent AR representation for the estimator of the trend, the SA series, or the irregular (or cyclical) component will exist. Heuristically, noninvertibility of these estimators will appear whenever the series has a stochastic seasonal component with the (most reasonable) property that the seasonal effect aggregated over a year is not far from zero. The result extends to estimators obtained with (noninvertible) 'ad hoc' filters, such as the ones most often used to detrend or seasonally adjust economic series.

Since, in practice, we are forced to always work with estimators, Section 7 presents two important implications for econometric work: first, due to the symmetry of the filters, care should be taken to use an homogeneous series of historical estimators. Perhaps more importantly, when the original series contains stochastic nonstationary trend and seasonal components, first contrary to common practice some popular unit root tests cannot be carried on SA series nor on trends, second, contrary to standard practice, too, VAR models are not appropriate for modeling SA series, nor trends, nor detrended series.

References

Akaike, H., 1980, Seasonal adjustment by a Bayesian modeling, *Journal of Time Series Analysis*, 1, 1–13.

Anderson, T.W., 1971, *The statistical analysis of time series* (Wiley, New York, NY).

Bell, W.R., 1984, Signal extraction for nonstationary time series, *Annals of Statistics*, 12, 646–664.

Beveridge, S. and C.R. Nelson, 1981, A new approach to decomposition of economic time series into permanent and transitory components with particular attention to measurement of the 'business cycle', *Journal of Monetary Economics*, 7, 151–174.

Blanchard, O.J. and D. Quah, 1989, The dynamic effects of aggregate demand and supply disturbances, *American Economic Review*, 79, 655–673.

Box, G.E.P. and G.M. Jenkins, 1976, *Time series analysis: Forecasting and control* (Holden-Day, San Francisco, CA).

Box, G.E.P., S.C. Hillmer, and G.C. Tiao, 1978, Analysis and modeling of seasonal time series, in: A. Zellner, ed., Seasonal analysis of economic time series (U.S. Department of Commerce, Bureau of the Census, Washington, DC) 309–334.

Burman, J.P., 1980, Seasonal adjustment by signal extraction, Journal of the Royal Statistical Society A 143, 321–337.

Burridge, P. and K.F. Wallis, 1984, Unobserved components models for seasonal adjustment filters, Journal of Business and Economic Statistics 2, 350–359.

Campbell, J.Y. and N.G. Mankiw, 1987, Permanent and transitory components in macro-economic fluctuations, American Economic Review Proceedings 1987, 111–117.

Cleveland, W.P. and G.C. Tiao, 1976, Decomposition of seasonal time series: A model for the X-11 program, Journal of the American Statistical Association 71, 581–587.

Cochrane, J.H., 1988, How big is the random walk in GNP?, Journal of Political Economy 96, 893–920.

Dickey, D.A. and W.A. Fuller, 1979, Distribution of the estimators for autoregressive time series with a unit root, Journal of the American Statistical Association 74, 427–431.

Diebold, F.X. and G.D. Rudebusch, 1991, Is consumption too smooth? Long memory and the Deaton paradox, Review of Economics and Statistics LXXIII, 1–9.

Fellner, W., 1956, Trends and cycles in economic activity (H. Holt, New York, NY).

Gersch, W. and G. Kitagawa, 1983, The prediction of time series with trends and seasonalities, Journal of Business and Economic Statistics 1, 253–264.

Ghysels, E., 1990, Unit root tests and the statistical pitfalls of seasonal adjustments: The case of U.S. post war real GNP, Journal of Business and Economic Statistics 8, 145–152.

Ghysels, E. and P. Perron, 1993, The effect of seasonal adjustment filters on tests for a unit root, Journal of Econometrics, 70, 69–97.

Granger, C.W.J., 1978, Seasonality: Causation, interpretation and implications, in: A. Zellner, ed., Seasonal analysis of economic time series (U.S. Department of Commerce, Bureau of the Census, Washington, DC) 33–46.

Gourieroux, C. and A. Monfort, 1990, Séries temporelles et modèles dynamiques (Economica, Paris).

Hamilton, J.D., 1989, A new approach to the economic analysis of nonstationary time series and the business cycle, Econometrica 57, 357–384.

Harrison, P.J. and C.F. Stevens, 1976, Bayesian forecasting, Journal of the Royal Statistical Society B 38, 205–247.

Harvey, A.C., 1985, Trends and cycles in macroeconomic time series, Journal of Business and Economic Statistics 3, 216–227.

Harvey, A.C., 1989, Forecasting, structural time series models and the Kalman filter (Cambridge University Press, Cambridge).

Harvey, A.C. and S. Peters, 1990, Estimation procedures for structural time series models, Journal of Forecasting 9, 89–108.

Harvey, A.C. and P.H.J. Todd, 1983, Forecasting economic time series with structural and Box–Jenkins models: A case study, Journal of Business and Economic Statistics 1, 299–306.

Hendry, D.F. and G.E. Mizon, 1990, Evaluating dynamic econometric models by encompassing the VAR, in: P.C.B. Phillips and V.B. Hall (eds.), Models, methods and applications of econometrics, Essays in honor of Rex Bergstrom (Basil Blackwell, Oxford).

Hillmer, S.C. and G.C. Tiao, 1982, An ARIMA-model based approach to seasonal adjustment, Journal of the American Statistical Association 77, 63–70.

Hillmer, S.C., W.R. Bell, and G.C. Tiao, 1983, Modeling considerations in the seasonal adjustment of economic time series, in: A. Zellner (ed.), Applied time series analysis of economic data (U.S. Department of Commerce, Bureau of the Census, Washington, DC).

Hodrick, R. and E. Prescott, 1980, Post-war U.S. business cycles: An empirical investigation, Manuscript (Carnegie Mellon University, Pittsburgh, PA).

Kendall, M., 1976, Time series (Griffin and Co., London).

Lütkepohl, H., 1991, Introduction to multiple time series analysis (Springer-Verlag, Berlin).

Maravall, A., 1985, On structural time series models and the characterization of components, Journal of Business and Economic Statistics 3, 350–355.

Maravall, A., 1987, On minimum mean squared error estimation of the noise in unobserved component models, Journal of Business and Economic Statistics 5, 115–120.

Maravall, A., 1988a, A note on minimum mean squared error estimation of signals with unit roots, Journal of Economic Dynamics and Control 12, 589–593.

Maravall, A., 1988b, The use of ARIMA models in unobserved components estimation, in: W. Barnett, E. Berndt, and H. White, eds., Dynamic econometric modeling (Cambridge University Press, Cambridge).

Maravall, A., 1989, On the dynamic structure of a seasonal component, Journal of Economic Dynamics and Control 13, 81–91.

Nelson, C.R. and G.J. Plosser, 1982, Trends and random walks in macroeconomic time series, Journal of Monetary Economics 10, 139–162.

Nerlove, M., D.M. Grether, and J.L. Carvalho, 1979, Analysis of economic time series: A synthesis (Academic Press, New York, NY).

Ng, C.N. and P.C. Young, 1990, Recursive estimation and forecasting of nonstationary time series, Journal of Forecasting 9, 173–204.

Perron, P. and P.C.B. Phillips, 1987, Does GNP have a unit root? A re-evaluation, Economics Letters 23, 139–145.

Phillips, P.C.B., 1987, Time series regression with a unit root, Econometrica 55, 277–301.

Phillips, P.C.B. and P. Perron, 1988, Testing for a unit root in time series regression, Biometrika 75, 335–346.

Pierce, D.A., 1978, Seasonal adjustment when both deterministic and stochastic seasonality are present, in: A. Zellner (ed.), Seasonal analysis of economic time series (U.S. Department of Commerce, Bureau of the Census, Washington, DC) 242–269.

Pierce, D.A., 1980, Data revisions in moving average seasonal adjustment procedures, Journal of Econometrics 14, 95–114.

Prescott, E.C., 1986, Theory ahead of business-cycle measurement, Carnegie–Rochester Conference Series on Public Policy 25, 11–44.

Schwert, G.W., 1989, Tests for unit roots: A Monte Carlo investigation, Journal of Business and Economic Statistics 7, 147–159.

Sims, C.A., 1987, Macroeconomics and reality, Econometrica 48, 1–48.

Stock, J.H. and M.W. Watson, 1986, Does GNP have a unit root?, Economics Letters 22, 147–151.

Stock, J.H. and M.W. Watson, 1988, Variable trends in economic time series, Journal of Economic Perspectives 2, 147–174.

Stock, J.H. and M.W. Watson, 1991, A probability model of the coincident economic indications, in: K. Lahiri and G.H. Moore, eds., Leading economic indicators: New approaches and forecasting records (Cambridge University Press, Cambridge) 63–85.

Tiao, G.C., 1983, Study notes on Akaike's seasonal adjustment procedures, in: A. Zellner, ed., Applied time series analysis of economic data (U.S. Department of Commerce, Bureau of the Census, Washington, DC) 44–45.

Tiao, G.C. and S.C. Hillmer, 1978, Some consideration of decomposition of a time series, Biometrika 65, 497–502.

Watson, M.W., 1986, Univariate detrending methods with stochastic trends, Journal of Monetary Economics 18, 49–75.

Whittle, P., 1963, Prediction and regulation by linear least-square methods (English Universities Press, London).

11

Estimation and Seasonal Adjustment of Population Means Using Data from Repeated Surveys*

DANNY PFEFFERMANN

Department of Statistics, Hebrew University

I consider estimation and seasonal adjustment of population means based on rotating panel surveys carried out at regular time intervals. The analysis uses a dynamic structural model that assumes a decomposition of the mean into a trend-level component and a seasonal component. The model accounts for the correlations between individual panel estimators and for possible rotation group effects. It can be applied to general rotation patterns using either the individual panel estimates or the aggregate sample estimates, depending on data availability. Empirical results illustrating the important features of the procedure are presented.

The problem considered in this article is the following: Suppose that data are available from repeated surveys carried out at regular time intervals on a given population. How can this data be combined to estimate population means and their components like trend levels and seasonal effects? As illustrated in subsequent sections, the answer to this question depends on three major factors:

1. The sampling design and, in particular, whether or not the samples are partially overlapping so that primary and/or ultimate sampling units are retained in the sample over more than one period.
2. The level of data availability: Sometimes all past and current individual data is available with appropriate identification labels, but in other applications, the only available data are the aggregate estimates based on the samples selected in the corresponding time periods. These estimates may or may not include estimates for the sampling errors.
3. The relationships between individual observations at different points of time and the long-term behavior of the population means and their components.

I adopt a time series approach by which the components of the population means are considered as random variates that evolve stochastically in time. The process underlying the evolution of the components is known up to a set of parameters that are estimated from the sample data. This approach is in contrast to the classical

* Reprinted from *The Journal of Business and Economic Statistics*, "Estimation and Seasonal Adjustment of Population Means Using Data from Repeated Surveys" by D. Pfeffermann, pp. 163–175, Vol. 9, No. 2, April 1991. Reproduced here by permission of the American Statistical Association.

sampling approach for the analysis of repeated surveys that considers the population means as fixed parameters and hence uses the past data for the estimation of current means only when the surveys are partially overlapping and the distinct panel estimates are known.

The model assumed for the population means is a special case of the model known in the time series literature as the *basic structural model*. A notable feature of this model is that it uses the traditional decomposition of the mean into a trend-level component and a seasonal effect. Such a decomposition has an immediate interpretation and is routinely used by government offices for the production of seasonally adjusted data. The model is extended to account for the correlations between the panel estimates, and it can be applied both in the case of a *primary analysis* for which the individual panel estimates are available and in the case of a *secondary analysis* in which only the published aggregate estimates are known. The immediate implication of this property is that the extended model permits the estimation of the trend levels and the seasonal effects, taking into account the correlations between individual data and employing the distinct panel estimates when available. Estimates for the mean squared error (MSE) of the estimated components are obtained as a by-product of the estimation process.

The plan of the article is as follows: In Section 1, I describe briefly the general form of state-space models and their associated computational method, the Kalman filter. Section 2 defines the basic structural model and discusses its application under various combinations of rotation patterns and data availability. The model is extended in Section 3 to account for rotation group effects, a phenomenon known to sometimes affect estimates obtained from repeated surveys. Section 4 describes the initialization of the Kalman filter and its use in the estimation of the unknown model parameters. Empirical results illustrating the main features of the model and comparing its performance to the performance of other procedures are presented in Section 5. The empirical study uses simulated data and two actual series collected as part of the Israel Labour Force Survey. Section 6 contains concluding remarks.

Some key references to the classical sampling approach for the analysis of repeated survey data are the articles by Jessen (1942), Patterson (1950), Rao and Graham (1964), Gurney and Daly (1965), and Cochran (1977, secs. 2.10–2.12). The time series approach was explored by Blight and Scott (1973), Scott and Smith (1974), Scott, Smith, and Jones (1977), Jones (1979, 1980), Hausman and Watson (1985), Tam (1987), Abraham and Vijayan (1988), and Binder and Dick (1989), Smith (1978) and Binder and Hidiroglou (1988) reviewed the preceding and other related articles, discussing in detail the pros and cons of the two approaches.

1 State-Space Models and the Kalman Filter

In this section, I review briefly the basic structure of state-space models and their accompanying Kalman-filter equations (Kalman 1960), focusing on aspects most germane to the analysis presented in subsequent sections.

State-space models consist in general of two sets of linear equations that define how observable and unobservable model components evolve stochastically in time.

Observation equation.

$$\mathbf{Y}_t = \mathbf{Z}_t \boldsymbol{\alpha}_t + \boldsymbol{\epsilon}_t, \tag{1.1}$$

where $\mathbf{Y}_t$ is the vector of observations (estimators) at time t, Z_t is a known design matrix, $\boldsymbol{\alpha}_t$ is a vector of unknown state components (e.g., components composing the population mean) that are allowed to vary in time, and $\boldsymbol{\epsilon}_t$ is a vector of disturbances (estimation errors) satisfying the requirements,

$$\mathrm{E}(\boldsymbol{\epsilon}_t) = \mathbf{0}; \qquad \mathrm{E}(\boldsymbol{\epsilon}_t \boldsymbol{\epsilon}_t') = V_t;$$
$$\mathrm{E}(\boldsymbol{\epsilon}_t \boldsymbol{\epsilon}_{t-k}') = \mathbf{0}, \quad k \geq 1 \tag{1.2}$$

System equation.

$$\boldsymbol{\alpha}_t = \mathbf{T}_t \boldsymbol{\alpha}_{t-1} + \boldsymbol{\eta}_t, \tag{1.3}$$

where $\mathbf{T}_t$ is a transition matrix and $\boldsymbol{\eta}_t$ is another vector of disturbances that is independent of the vectors $\{\boldsymbol{\epsilon}_{t-k}\}$ ($k = 0, 1, \ldots$) and satisfies the conditions

$$\mathrm{E}(\boldsymbol{\eta}_t) = \mathbf{0}; \qquad \mathrm{E}(\boldsymbol{\eta}_t \boldsymbol{\eta}_t') = \mathbf{Q}_t;$$
$$\mathrm{E}(\boldsymbol{\eta}_t \boldsymbol{\eta}_{t-k}') = \mathbf{0}, \quad k \geq 1. \tag{1.4}$$

Assuming that the variance–covariance (V–C) matrices $\mathbf{V}_t$ and $\mathbf{Q}_t$ are known, the state vectors $\boldsymbol{\alpha}_t$ can be estimated most conveniently by means of the Kalman filter. The filter consists of a set of recursive equations that can be used to update and smooth estimates of current and previous state vectors and to predict future vectors every time new data become available. A good reference to the theory of the Kalman filter is the book by Anderson and Moore (1979).

Let $\hat{\boldsymbol{\alpha}}_{t-1|t-1}$ be the best linear unbiased predictor (BLUP) of $\boldsymbol{\alpha}_{t-1}$ based on the data observed up to time $t - 1$. Since $\hat{\boldsymbol{\alpha}}_{t-1|t-1}$ is the BLUP for $\boldsymbol{\alpha}_{t-1}$, $\hat{\boldsymbol{\alpha}}_{t|t-1} = \mathbf{T}_t \hat{\boldsymbol{\alpha}}_{t-1|t-1}$ is the BLUP of $\boldsymbol{\alpha}_t$ based on all the information up to time $(t - 1)$. Furthermore, if $\mathbf{P}_{t-1|t-1} = \mathrm{E}(\hat{\boldsymbol{\alpha}}_{t-1|t-1} - \boldsymbol{\alpha}_{t-1})(\hat{\boldsymbol{\alpha}}_{t-1|t-1} - \boldsymbol{\alpha}_{t-1})'$ is the V–C matrix of the prediction errors at the time $t - 1$, then by Equations (1.3) and (1.4), $\mathbf{P}_{t|t-1} = \mathbf{T}_t \mathbf{P}_{t-1|t-1} \mathbf{T}_t' + \mathbf{Q}_t$ is the V–C matrix of the prediction errors $(\hat{\boldsymbol{\alpha}}_{t|t-1} - \boldsymbol{\alpha}_t)$.

When a new vector of observations $\mathbf{Y}_t$ becomes available, the predictor of $\boldsymbol{\alpha}_t$ and the V–C matrix of the prediction errors are updated according to the formulas

$$\hat{\boldsymbol{\alpha}}_{t|t} = \hat{\boldsymbol{\alpha}}_{t|t-1} + \mathbf{P}_{t|t-1} \mathbf{Z}_t' \mathbf{F}_t^{-1} (\mathbf{Y}_t - \hat{\mathbf{Y}}_{t|t-1}) \tag{1.5}$$

and

$$\mathbf{P}_{t|t} = \mathbf{P}_{t|t-1} - \mathbf{P}_{t|t-1} \mathbf{Z}_t' \mathbf{F}_t^{-1} \mathbf{Z}_t \mathbf{P}_{t|t-1}, \tag{1.6}$$

where $\mathbf{Y}_{t|t-1} = \mathbf{Z}_t \hat{\boldsymbol{\alpha}}_{t|t-1}$ is the BLUP of $\mathbf{Y}_t$ at time $(t-1)$ so that $(\mathbf{Y}_t - \hat{\mathbf{Y}}_{t|t-1})$ is the vector of innovations (prediction errors) with V–C matrix $\mathbf{F}_t = (\mathbf{Z}_t \mathbf{P}_{t|t-1} \mathbf{Z}_t' + \mathbf{V}_t)$.

An important use of the Kalman filter is the updating (smoothing) of past state estimates as new, more recent data become available—for example, smoothing the estimates of the seasonal effects for previous periods. Denoting by N the most recent period for which observations are available, the smoothing is carried out using the equation

$$\hat{\alpha}_{t|N} = \hat{\alpha}_{t|t} + \mathbf{P}_{t|t}\mathbf{T}'_{t+1}\mathbf{P}^{-1}_{t+1|t}(\hat{\alpha}_{t+1|N} - \mathbf{T}_{t-1}\hat{\alpha}_{t|t}), \quad t = 1, \ldots, N-1, \quad (1.7)$$

where $\mathbf{P}_{t|N} = \mathrm{E}(\hat{\alpha}_{t|N} - \alpha_t)(\hat{\alpha}_{t|N} - \alpha_t)'$ satisfies the equation

$$\mathbf{P}_{t|N} = \mathbf{P}_{t|t} + \mathbf{P}_{t|t}\mathbf{T}'_{t+1}\mathbf{P}^{-1}_{t+1|t}(\mathbf{P}_{t+1|N} - \mathbf{P}_{t+1|t})\mathbf{P}^{-1}_{t+1|t}\mathbf{T}_{t+1}\mathbf{P}_{t|t},$$

$$t = 1, \ldots, N-1. \tag{1.8}$$

The smoothing algorithm defined by (1.7) and (1.8) is known in the literature as the fixed interval smoother (Harvey 1984), and it is started with $\hat{\alpha}_{N/N}$ and $\hat{P}_{N/N}$.

The actual application of the Kalman filter requires the estimation of the V–C matrices V_t and Q_t, the initial state vector α_0, and the initial V–C matrix P_0. I address these issues in Section 4.

2 Basic Structural Models for Repeated Surveys

2.1 System equations for the components of the population mean
The model considered in this study consists of the following system equations describing the evolution of the population mean and its components over time. For convenience of presentation, I assume that the data are collected on a quarterly basis:

$$\theta_t = L_t + S_t$$

$$L_t = L_{t-1} + R_{t-1} + \eta_{Lt}; \qquad R_t = R_{t-1} + \eta_{Rt} \tag{2.1}$$

$$\sum_{j=0}^{3} S_{t-j} = \eta_{St},$$

where $\{\eta_{Lt}\}$, $\{\eta_{Rt}\}$, and $\{\eta_{St}\}$ are three independent white-noise processes with mean 0 and variances σ_L^2, σ_R^2, and σ_S^2, respectively. The first equation postulates an additive decomposition of the population mean θ_t into a trend-level component L_t and a seasonal effect S_t. Other components, like moving festivals and trading-days effects, can likewise be incorporated in the decomposition equation (e.g., see Dagum and Quenneville 1988; Morris and Pfeffermann 1984).

The second and third equations approximate a local linear trend (the case of a constant level is a special case by which $\sigma_L^2 = \sigma_R^2 = 0$ and $R_0 = 0$), whereas the last equation models the variation of the seasonal effects. The model permits changes in the seasonal pattern but imposes the condition that the expectation of the sum of the seasonal effects over a given span Δ (four quarters in our case) is 0. (Constant seasonality is obtained when $\sigma_S^2 = 0$.)

The traditional models employed for seasonal adjustment purposes contain also an irregular term in the decomposition equation. Notice, however, that these models are assumed for the observed survey estimators so that the added irregular terms contain in particular the survey errors. I extend the model defined by (2.1) to account for survey errors in Section 2.2. Although adding a separate white-noise irregular to the decomposition equation requires only minor modifications in the analysis, it could result in identifiability problems if the model holding for the survey errors contains a variance component that is approximately white noise. Thus, in situations in which most of the variation of the survey estimators around the trend and the seasonal components stems from the survey error (which can be expected in the case of large populations and small samples, see also the concluding remarks), assuming the reduced model (2.1) for the population mean and hence combining the decomposition error with the survey error might be preferable. [Binder and Dick (1989) analyzed unemployment series in the province of Nova Scotia employing autoregressive integrated moving average (ARIMA) models for the population means and the survey errors and found that the variance of the error terms in the models holding for the population means was of a much lower order than the variance of the survey errors.]

The model defined by (2.1) with the added white-noise term in the first equation is known in the statistical time series literature as the basic structural model. The theoretical properties of this model in relation to other models were discussed by Harrison and Stevens (1976), Harvey (1984), Harvey and Todd (1983), and Maravall (1985). Although this model is more restricted compared to the family of ARIMA models, it is flexible enough to approximate the behavior of many different time series as illustrated empirically by Dagum and Quenneville (1988), Harvey and Todd (1983), Morris and Pfeffermann (1984), and Quenneville and Dagum (1988). Important features of the model pertaining to the present problem are discussed in subsequent sections.

The model defined by the last three equations of (2.1) can be written alternatively as

$$\alpha_t^{(1)} = \mathbf{T}_{11}\alpha_{t-1}^{(1)} + \eta_t^{(1)}, \tag{2.1'}$$

where $\alpha_t^{(1)\prime} = (L_t, R_t, S_t, S_{t-1}, S_{t-2})$ is the state vector at time t,

$$\mathbf{T}_{11} = \begin{bmatrix} 1 & 1 & 0 & 0 & 0 \\ 0 & 1 & 0 & 0 & 0 \\ 0 & 0 & -1 & -1 & -1 \\ 0 & 0 & 1 & 0 & 0 \\ 0 & 0 & 0 & 1 & 0 \end{bmatrix}$$

is a time-invariant transition matrix and $\eta_t^{(1)}$ is the corresponding error vector with mean 0 and V–C matrix $\mathbf{Q}_{11} = \mathrm{diag}(\sigma_L^2, \sigma_R^2, \sigma_S^2, 0, 0)$. I use the representation (2.1') in subsequent sections.

2.2 Observation equations for the survey estimators

The model equations for the survey estimators depend on the sampling design, the rotation pattern, and the covariances between individual observations. In the present study, I follow Blight and Scott (1973) and assume that observations $\{Y_{ti}\}$ pertaining to the same unit i follow a first-order autoregressive (AR) model; that is,

$$Y_{ti} - \theta_t = \rho(Y_{(t-1),i} - \theta_{t-1}) + v_{ti}, \qquad (2.2)$$

where the errors $\{v_{ti}; t = 2, 3, \ldots\}$ are white noise with mean 0 and variance σ_v^2 and $|\rho| < 1$. This is a standard assumption made (sometimes implicitly) in most of the articles mentioned in the introduction. It implies that correlations between individual observations decay geometrically as time passes. (We are currently analyzing Canadian employment series allowing for higher order autoregressive relationships.) It is assumed also that the sampling design is ignorable (Sugden and Smith 1984) and that the errors $\varepsilon_{ti} = Y_{ti} - \theta_t$ pertaining to different individuals are independent. The model can be extended to the case of a two-stage sampling design by adding random components λ_{tk} to represent random cluster effects so that $Y_{tkj} = \theta_t + \lambda_{tk} + \varepsilon_{tkj}$. Assuming that the cluster effects λ_{tk} follow a separate autoregressive relationship, the model can be analyzed similarly to the present case. The model accounts then for contemporaneous and serial correlations between observations pertaining to different ultimate units belonging the same cluster (cf. Scott et al. 1977).

The other factor determining the observations equation for the survey estimators is the rotation pattern. Consider first the special case of a nonoverlapping survey. Assuming that the samples selected at different time periods can be considered as independent, the observation equation is

$$\bar{Y}_t = \theta_t + \bar{v}_t;$$

$$\mathrm{E}(\bar{v}_t) = 0, \qquad \mathrm{E}(\bar{v}_t \bar{v}_{t-k}) = \sigma_v^2/n_t, \quad k = 0$$

$$= 0, \qquad \text{otherwise}, \qquad (2.3)$$

where $\bar{Y}_t = (1/n_t) \sum_{i=1}^{n_t} Y_{ti}$ is the aggregate survey estimator at time t and v_t is the corresponding survey error. The model defined by (2.1′) and (2.3) specifies the basic structural model to be used in the case of a nonoverlapping survey.

Next I consider the case of overlapping surveys, and to illustrate the ideas, I focus for convenience on the Israel Labour Force Survey (ILFS), which provides the data used in the empirical study of Section 5. Other rotation patterns can be handled in a similar way. The ILFS is a quarterly survey of households carried out by the Central Bureau of Statistics (CBS) to provide information on employment and other important demographic and socioeconomic characteristics of the labour force in Israel. Every quarter the CBS surveys four panels, each composed of approximately 3,000 households, so that three panels have been included in some past surveys and one panel is new. Every new panel is included in the survey for two quarters, left out of the survey for the next two quarters, and then included again for two more quarters. This rotation pattern produces a 50% overlap between two successive quarters and a 50% overlap between quarters representing the same months in two successive years. For a brief description of the sampling design used for the ILFS, see Nathan and Eliav (1988). As discussed there, the four concurrent panels can be considered as independent simple random samples of households.

In what follows I define $\bar{Y}_t^{t-j} = 1/M \sum_{i=1}^{M} y_{ti}^{t-j}$ to be the mean observed at time t for the panel joining the survey for the first time at time $t - j$ ($j = 0, 1, 4, 5$). It is assumed for convenience that the panels are of fixed size M. The aggregate survey estimate at time t will be denoted as before by $\bar{Y}_t = \frac{1}{4}(\bar{Y}_t^t + \bar{Y}_t^{t-1} + \bar{Y}_t^{t-4} + \bar{Y}_t^{t-5})$. I distinguish between the case in which the panel estimates are known and the case in which the only available data at time t is the aggregate estimate $\bar{\mathbf{Y}}_t$. For the first case,

$$\bar{\mathbf{Y}}_t = \mathbf{1}_4 \theta_t + \bar{\boldsymbol{\epsilon}}_t, \tag{2.4}$$

where $\mathbf{1}_4$ is the unit vector of length 4, $\bar{\mathbf{Y}}_t' = (\bar{Y}_t^t, \bar{Y}_t^{t-1}, \bar{Y}_t^{t-4}, \bar{Y}_t^{t-5})$ is the row vector of panel estimators at time t, and $\bar{\boldsymbol{\epsilon}}_t' = (\bar{\epsilon}_t^t, \bar{\epsilon}_t^{t-1}, \bar{\epsilon}_t^{t-4}, \bar{\epsilon}_t^{t-5})$ is the corresponding vector of survey errors satisfying the transitive relationships

$$\boldsymbol{\alpha}_t^{(2)} = \begin{bmatrix} \bar{\epsilon}_t^t \\ \bar{\epsilon}_t^{t-1} \\ \bar{\epsilon}_t^{t-4} \\ \bar{\epsilon}_t^{t-5} \\ \bar{\epsilon}_{t-2}^{t-3} \\ \bar{\epsilon}_{t-1}^{t-2} \end{bmatrix} = \begin{bmatrix} 0 & 0 & 0 & 0 & 0 & 0 \\ \rho & 0 & 0 & 0 & 0 & 0 \\ 0 & 0 & 0 & 0 & \rho^3 & 0 \\ 0 & 0 & \rho & 0 & 0 & 0 \\ 0 & 0 & 0 & 0 & 0 & 1 \\ 0 & 1 & 0 & 0 & 0 & 0 \end{bmatrix} \begin{bmatrix} \bar{\epsilon}_{t-1}^{t-1} \\ \bar{\epsilon}_{t-1}^{t-2} \\ \bar{\epsilon}_{t-1}^{t-5} \\ \bar{\epsilon}_{t-1}^{t-6} \\ \bar{\epsilon}_{t-3}^{t-4} \\ \bar{\epsilon}_{t-2}^{t-3} \end{bmatrix} + \boldsymbol{\eta}_t^{(2)} = T_{22}\boldsymbol{\alpha}_{t-1}^{(2)} + \boldsymbol{\eta}_t^{(2)}, \tag{2.5}$$

where $\boldsymbol{\eta}_t^{(2)\prime} = (\bar{\epsilon}_t^t, \bar{v}_t^{t-1}, \rho^2 \bar{v}_{t-2}^{t-4} + \rho v_{t-1}^{t-4} + \bar{v}_t^{t-4}, \bar{v}_t^{t-5}, 0, 0)$ is a vector of independent disturbances that is uncorrelated with the vectors $\{\boldsymbol{\alpha}_{t-j}^{(2)}\}$ and $\{\boldsymbol{\eta}_{t-j}^{(2)}\}$ ($j \geq 1$) and has mean $\mathbf{0}$ and V–C matrix

$$V(\boldsymbol{\eta}_t^{(2)}) = ((1/M)\sigma_v^2) \operatorname{diag} [(1 - \rho^2)^{-1}, 1, (\rho^4 + \rho^2 + 1), 1, 0, 0] = \mathbf{Q}_{22}. \tag{2.6}$$

Equations (2.5) and (2.6) follow directly from the autoregressive assumption (2.2) so that $\bar{v}_{t-k}^{t-j} = (1/M) \sum_{i=1}^{M} v_{t-k,i}^{t-j}$ is the mean of the white-noise disturbances at time $(t - k)$ for the panel joining the sample for the first time at time $(t - j)$, $j \geq k$. I included the survey errors $\bar{\epsilon}_{t-1}^{t-2}$ and $\bar{\epsilon}_{t-1}^{t-6}$ in the vector $\boldsymbol{\alpha}_{t-1}^{(2)}$ and the errors $\bar{\epsilon}_t^t$ and $\bar{\epsilon}_{t-2}^{t-3}$ in the vector $\boldsymbol{\alpha}_t^{(2)}$ so that $\boldsymbol{\alpha}_{t-1}^{(2)}$ will contain the same components as $\boldsymbol{\alpha}_t^{(2)}$ with a time shift of 1. Since $\bar{\epsilon}_{t-2}^{t-3}$ had to be added to $\boldsymbol{\alpha}_t^{(2)}$, it was added also to $\boldsymbol{\alpha}_{t-1}^{(2)}$, ensuring that way that the error vector $\boldsymbol{\eta}_t^{(2)}$ will be independent of past state vectors. This in turn required that $\bar{\epsilon}_{t-1}^{t-2}$ be added to $\boldsymbol{\alpha}_t^{(2)}$. When the same components are included in both the vectors, the corresponding residual variance is set to 0. This strategy can be applied to general rotation patterns.

For the case of a secondary analysis, we have

$$\bar{Y}_t = \theta_t + \tfrac{1}{4}(\bar{\varepsilon}_t + \bar{\varepsilon}_t^{t-1} + \bar{\varepsilon}_t^{t-4} + \bar{\varepsilon}_t^{t-5})$$

$$= \theta_t + \tfrac{1}{4}\mathbf{1}'\bar{\boldsymbol{\epsilon}}_t \tag{2.7}$$

with (2.5) and (2.6) remaining unchanged.

Equations (2.4) and (2.7) define the observations equation for the case of overlapping surveys. Unlike the case of independent samples, however, the survey errors are now correlated. A simple way to overcome this problem in this case is by including the survey errors as part of the state vector and setting the residual variances of the observations equation to 0 (cf. Abraham and Vijayan 1988; Candy 1986). The resulting model is specified in Section 2.3.

2.3 A compact model representation

The model defined by (2.1′), (2.4), (2.5), and (2.6) corresponding to the case of a primary analysis can be written compactly as

$$\bar{Y}_t = [\mathbf{1}_4, \mathbf{0}_4, \mathbf{1}_4, \mathbf{0}_4, \mathbf{0}_4 | \mathbf{I}_4, \mathbf{0}_4, \mathbf{0}_4] \begin{bmatrix} \boldsymbol{\alpha}_t^{(1)} \\ \boldsymbol{\alpha}_t^{(2)} \end{bmatrix} = \mathbf{Z}\boldsymbol{\alpha}_t, \tag{2.8}$$

where $\mathbf{0}_4$ is a vector of zeros of length 4, $\mathbf{I}_4$ is the identity matrix of order 4 and $\boldsymbol{\alpha}_t' = (\boldsymbol{\alpha}_t^{(1)\prime}, \boldsymbol{\alpha}_t^{(2)\prime})$ is the augmented state vector satisfying the transition equation

$$\boldsymbol{\alpha}_t = \begin{bmatrix} \mathbf{T}_{11}, & {}_5\mathbf{0}_6 \\ {}_6\mathbf{0}_5, & \mathbf{T}_{22} \end{bmatrix} \boldsymbol{\alpha}_{t-1} + \begin{bmatrix} \boldsymbol{\eta}_t^{(1)} \\ \boldsymbol{\eta}_t^{(2)} \end{bmatrix} = \mathbf{T}\boldsymbol{\alpha}_{t-1} + \boldsymbol{\eta}_t. \tag{2.9}$$

In (2.9), $\mathbf{T}_{11}$ is the transition matrix of the state vector $\boldsymbol{\alpha}_t^{(1)}$ defining the evolution of the population mean components [Eq. (2.1′)], $\mathbf{T}_{22}$ is the transition matrix of the survey errors [Eq. (2.5)], and ${}_l\mathbf{0}_k$ defines a zero matrix of order $(l \times k)$. Notice that the random error terms in $\boldsymbol{\eta}_t$ are independent so that $\mathbf{Q} = V(\boldsymbol{\eta}_t)$ is diagonal with $\mathbf{Q}_{11} = V(\boldsymbol{\eta}_t^{(1)})$ and $\mathbf{Q}_{22} = V(\boldsymbol{\eta}_t^{(2)})$ composing the diagonal elements.

For the case of a secondary analysis [Eqs. (2.1′), (2.5), (2.6), and (2.7)], the matrix Z of Equation (2.8) is replaced by the row vector

$$\mathbf{z}' = (1, 0, 1, 0, 0, \tfrac{1}{4}, \tfrac{1}{4}, \tfrac{1}{4}, \tfrac{1}{4}, 0, 0) \tag{2.10}$$

so that $\bar{Y}_t = \mathbf{z}'\boldsymbol{\alpha}_t$ [compare with (2.7)]. The system equation (2.9) remains unchanged, however. Thus the model is based on the intrinsic relationships (2.5) among the separate panel estimators even though the only available data are the aggregate estimators $\{\bar{Y}_t\}$. An interesting consequence of this formulation is that one can actually predict the original panel estimates $\{\bar{Y}_t^{t-j}\}$ using the relationship $\bar{Y}_t^{t-j} = L_t + S_t + \bar{\varepsilon}_t^{t-j} = \mathbf{c}'\boldsymbol{\alpha}_t$, say. [Eq. (2.7) guarantees that the average of the four predictors equals the aggregate estimate $\bar{Y}_t$.] Such an analysis might be useful for model diagnostics—for example, by comparing the predictors one step ahead of the panel estimators as obtained under the secondary analysis with the corresponding predicted estimates (assuming that they are known); see Table 3 of Section 5.2.

2.4 Discussion

The common approach to the modeling of the behavior of the survey errors in the case of a secondary analysis is to postulate a moving average (MA) process for the errors $\bar{e}_t = \bar{Y}_t - \theta_t$ with the order of the process determined by the number of months (quarters) between the first and the last time that units are retained in the sample. Notice that by using a relationship of the form (2.2), the model holding for the survey errors includes only two unknown parameters compared to five parameters if a general MA process of order 5 is used. [For the model defined by (2.10) and (2.9), $\text{cov}(\bar{Y}_t, \bar{Y}_{t-j}) \neq 0$ for $j = 0, 1, 3, 4, 5$.] One could argue, on the other hand, that postulating a general MA process is more robust. In particular, the MA formulation does not require that the panel estimators corresponding to the same time period be independent. The use of MA models for the survey errors is less clear in the case of a primary analysis because of the different time gaps in which the panels are not observed.

The model defined by (2.8) [or (2.10)] and (2.9) conforms to the general state-space formulation presented in Section 1. Hence, once the unknown variances and the initial state components have been estimated, the Kalman filter equations can be applied to estimate the population means or changes in the means using the relationship $\theta_t = (L_t + S_t)$. Moreover, the use of the present model permits the extraction of the seasonal effects in a straightforward manner, taking into account the correlations between the survey errors and using the distinct panel estimates in the case of a primary analysis. Thus the approach outlined in this article enables us to decompose the means into a trend-level component and seasonal effects using more information than is commonly used by the traditional procedures for seasonal adjustments like, for example, X-11 ARIMA (Dagum 1980). These advantages are illustrated in the simulation study described in Section 5.1. The model also provides estimates of the MSE's of the estimated components by means of the Kalman-filter equations. [Quenneville and Dagum (1988) proposed estimating the variances of the X-11 ARIMA estimates by fitting basic structural models that approximate the behavior of the X-11 ARIMA components.] The price paid for this flexibility is that the analysis is more model dependent compared, for example, to the use of the X-11 ARIMA procedure.

The dependence on the model is of particular concern in the case of a secondary analysis because the time series of the aggregate survey estimators does not generally contain enough information to determine the separate models holding for the population means and the survey errors. Thus one has to rely in such cases on genuine prior knowledge and/or model diagnostics based on the observed prediction errors.

The situation is clearly different in the case of a primary analysis. As pointed out by William Bell in his discussion, the model holding for the survey errors can be identified in principle from the model holding for contrasts of the panel estimators.

Notice that any contrast in the panel estimators is a function of only the survey errors. For example, in the Israel LFS the panels joining the survey for the first time at time $(t-1)$ and at time $(t-5)$ are both observed at time $(t-1)$ and at time t and $(\bar{Y}_{t-k}^{t-1} - \bar{Y}_{t-k}^{t-5}) = (\bar{\varepsilon}_{t-k}^{t-1} - \bar{\varepsilon}_{t-k}^{t-5})$, $k = 0, 1$. For this particular survey, these are the only panels observed on the same two successive quarters. In addition, the panels joining the survey for the same time at time $(t-5)$ and at time $(t-4)$ are both observed at time $(t-4)$ and at time t. In the Canadian LFS, every new panel is retained in the survey for six successive months before being dropped so that two panels are observed for the same five successive months, three panels are observed for the same four successive months and so forth. This rotation pattern is therefore much more favorable for the identification and validation of the model holding for the survey errors.

The possibility of identifying and validating the model holding for the survey errors through constrasts of the panel estimators is another major advantage of the use of primary analysis (when possible) over the use of secondary analysis.

3 Accounting for Rotation Group Bias

The problem of rotation group bias (RGB) is that some of the panel estimators may be biased. In its classical use, RGB refers to a phenomenon by which respondents provide different information on different rounds of interview, depending on the length of time that they have been included in the sample. The phenomenon of RGB, or at least its magnitude, however, could be related to the method of data collection (e.g., home interview in some rounds and telephone interview in other rounds) or even result from differential non-response across the panels. Here and in Section 5.2 I refer to RGB in this broader context.

Bailar (1975) found clear evidence for rotation bias in some of the labor force data collected by the U.S. Current Population Survey. Kumar and Lee (1983) found similar evidence in the Canadian LFS. A review of these and other studies on rotation bias can be found in the article by Binder and Hidiroglou (1988).

Using previous notation, rotation bias implies that $E(\bar{Y}_t^{t-j} - \theta_t) = \beta_{jt} \neq 0$ for some j. Bailar (1975) and Kumar and Lee (1983) assumed that the bias factors are time invariant, which implies for the present case that $\bar{Y}_t^{t-j} = \theta_t + \bar{\varepsilon}_t^{t-j} + \beta_j$ or that

$$\bar{\mathbf{Y}}_t = \mathbf{1}_4(L_t + S_t) + \mathbf{I}_4\boldsymbol{\beta} + \bar{\boldsymbol{\epsilon}}_t, \tag{3.1}$$

where $\boldsymbol{\beta}' = (\beta_0, \beta_1, \beta_4, \beta_5)$ is a vector of constants. Equation (3.1), combined with (2.9), defines a model for incorporating constant RGB effects. The equations (3.1) and (2.9) alone, however, are not sufficient for estimating the group effects and securing unbiased predictors for the population means. This is so because of the confounding effects of the trend level and a fixed shift in the bias coefficients. Thus one needs to augment the model by a linear constraint of the form

$$\sum_j w_j \beta_j = w_0, \qquad \sum_j w_j \neq 0, \tag{3.2}$$

with known coefficients w_j, to secure the identifiability of all of the model components.

This problem is not unique to the present model. If all of the panel estimators are biased, one cannot hope for an unbiased estimator of the population mean without some information on the magnitude and relationship of the bias factors. Bailar (1975) assessed the bias by examining alternative data sources. Kumar and Lee (1983) assumed that the bias coefficients add to 0 in their analysis. I make a similar assumption in Section 5.2 based on preliminary analysis of the data. In the absence of external information, this is a reasonable condition, since it permits testing for the existence of group effects conditional on the assumption that the aggregate estimates are unbiased.

The model defined by (3.1) and (3.2) can be extended to the case of time-changing group effects by permitting the bias factors to vary stochastically over time similar to the other model components, taking into account the possible correlations between them. Such an extension is not considered in the present study.

4 Estimation and Initialization of the Kalman Filter

The actual application of the Kalman filter requires the estimation of the auto-correlation coefficient ρ and the unknown elements of the V–C matrix Q, as well as the initialization of the filter—that is, the estimation of the state vector α_0 and the V–C matrix P_0. In this section, I describe the estimation methods used in the present study.

Assuming that the disturbances $\eta_t' = (\eta_t^{(1)\prime}, \eta_t^{(2)\prime})$ are normally distributed, the log-likelihood function for the observations can be written as

$$L(\delta) = \text{constant} \left(-\frac{1}{2}\right) \sum_{t=1}^{T} (\log |\mathbf{F}_t| + \mathbf{e}_t' \mathbf{F}_t^{-1} \mathbf{e}_t), \tag{4.1}$$

where $\mathbf{e}_t = \mathbf{Y}_t - \hat{\mathbf{Y}}_{t|t-1}$ is the vector of innovations (prediction errors) and $\delta' = (\sigma_L^2, \sigma_R^2, \sigma_S^2, \sigma_V^2, \rho)$ is the vector of unknown model parameters.

Let $\delta_{(0)}$, $\hat{\alpha}_0$ and $\hat{P}_0$ define the initial estimates of δ, α_0, and P_0. A simple way to maximize the likelihood function (4.1) is by application of the method of scoring that consists of solving iteratively the equation

$$\delta_{(i)} = \delta_{(i-1)} + \lambda_i \{\mathbf{I}[\delta_{(i-1)}]\}^{-1} \mathbf{G}[\delta_{(i-1)}]. \tag{4.2}$$

In (4.2), $\delta_{(i-1)}$ is the estimator of δ as obtained in the $(i-1)$th iteration, $\mathbf{I}[\delta_{(i-1)}]$ is the information matrix evaluated at $\delta_{(i-1)}$, and $\mathbf{G}[\delta_{(i-1)}]$ is the gradient of the log-likelihood again evaluated at $\delta_{(i-1)}$. The coefficient λ_i is a variable step length determined by a grid search procedure. It is introduced to guarantee that $L[\delta_{(i)}] \geq L[\delta_{(i-1)}]$ on each iteration and hence that the algorithm will converge if the maximum lies in the interior of the parameter space. [I used the common strategy of first trying $\lambda_i = 1$ and then progressively reducing the value of λ_i until the likelihood function is increased. E.g., see Seber and Wild (1988, chap. 13) for further discussion.] The formulas for the kth element of the gradient vector and the klth element of the information matrix were given by Watson and Engle (1983). The model considered by these authors is very general and includes the model considered in the present article as a special case.

The iterative solution of (4.2) may converge to negative variance estimators or become unstable if an iteration produces negative estimates. A similar instability may occur if ρ is estimated by a value outside the unit circle. To avoid this possibility, I transformed the vector δ' to the vector $\delta^{*\prime} = [\sigma_L, \sigma_R, \sigma_S, \sigma_v, \psi]$, where $\rho = \psi/(1 + |\psi|)$ so that the likelihood function has been maximized with respect to the elements of δ^* rather than the elements of δ. I used two convergence criteria: $|\{L[\delta^*_{(i)}] - L[\delta^*_{(i-1)}]\}/L[\delta^*_{(i-1)}]| < 10^{-9}$ and $\max_j\{|\hat{\delta}^*_{(i)}(j) - \hat{\delta}^*_{(i-1)}(j)|/|\delta^*_{(i-1)}(j)|\} \leq .01$, where $\delta(j)$ stands for any one of the parameters. The algorithm has been satisfied when at least one of the criteria was satisfied (usually in less than 20 iterations). (The convergence of the algorithm requires that the maximum of the likelihood, expressed as a function of δ, lies in the interior of the parameter space for δ.)

Initialization of the Kalman filter was carried out following the approach proposed by Harvey and Peters (1984). By this approach, the nonstationary components of the state vector are initialized with very large error variances (which amounts to postulating a diffuse prior) so that the corresponding state estimates can conveniently be taken as zeros. The stationary components are initialized by the corresponding unconditional means and variances. For the model defined by (2.9), the stationary components are the six survey errors composing the subvector $\alpha_0^{(2)}$, having mean 0 and variance $(1/M)\sigma_v^2(1 - \rho^2)^{-1}$. In view of the use of large error variances for the nonstationary state components, the likelihood is estimated based on the last T-d observations, where d is the number of the nonstationary components.

The use of this procedure has the clear advantage of being computationally very simple. Other approaches to initializing the Kalman filter that could be applied to the models considered in the present article were discussed by Ansley and Kohn (1985) and DeJong (1988).

A computer program that implements the methods described in this section for the updating, smoothing, and predicting of the state vectors of the models proposed in Sections 2 and 3 has been written using the procedure PROC-IML of the SAS system. The program is a modification of the software DLM developed at Statistics Canada by Quenneville (1988).

I conclude this section with the following comment: The estimation methods described previously use only the time series of the macrodata (the panel estimators or the aggregate means), and they involve in particular the estimation of the variances and covariances of the survey errors. This is in contrast with much of the literature in which the survey parameters are estimated using survey microdata. Obviously, when microdata are available they should be used in the estimation process, but as practice dictates, this is often not the case. Computing the autocovariance function of the series $Z_t = (1 - B)(1 - B)^4 \bar{Y}_t$, where B is the lag operator, indicates that even in the case of a secondary analysis all of the model parameters, including the survey parameters, are identifiable. See Maravall (1985) for a similar analysis and also the simulation results of Section 5. Binder and Dick (1989) pointed out the need for a methodology of combining the survey microdata estimates with the model-dependent time series estimates. (The lack of access to the survey microdata emphasizes the importance of using a primary analysis when the panel estimators are known.)

5 Simulation and Empirical Results

In this section, I describe the results of an empirical study intended to illustrate some of the major features of the models presented in Section 2. The study consists of two parts. In the first part, discussed in Section 5.1, I use simulated series, enabling me to control the values of the model parameters. In the second part, I use two actual series collected as part of the Israel LFS. In this part, I extend the models of Section 2 by permitting for rotation group effects as described in Section 3. The results are discussed in Section 5.2.

5.1 Simulation results

I generated several data sets, each containing 15 independent series of panel estimates with four panels for every time period. The panel estimates were generated so that they obey the model and rotation pattern defined by (2.8) and (2.9). The difference between the various sets is in the values of the model parameters and in the length of the series.

Here I focus mainly on the results obtained for two groups of data, each consisting of two separate data sets. The first data set includes series of length $N = 100$, and the other set includes series of length $N = 36$. The latter is the length of the labour force series analyzed in Section 5.2. For the first group, I used very small values of σ_L^2, σ_R^2, and σ_S^2, implying an almost perfect linear trend with constant seasonality. I increased the values of the variances for the other group, that way imposing more rapid changes in the components of the population mean. I used a relatively high value of $\rho = .7$ for both series, thereby emphasizing the effect of the rotation pattern. (We are currently analyzing data from the Canadian LFS, and for many series $.6 \leq \rho \leq .8$. The month-to-month overlap in that survey is 83%. The value of ρ in the ILFS is about .4; see Table 3, Section 5.2.) The values of σ_v^2 are such that the survey errors account for about 20% of the MSE of the quarter-to-quarter difference in the aggregate means in the first group and for about 6% in the second group. In the following, I mention briefly the results obtained for other values of ρ and σ_v^2.

As benchmark comparisons with the model results, I have estimated the sampling variance of Patterson's (1950) estimator of the population mean for the case of "sampling on more than two occasions." The variance is specified in formula 12.84 of Cochran (1977). Notice that the variance of this estimator is minimized in the case of a 50% sample overlap between two successive surveys, which is the case in this study.

The results obtained for the two groups are exhibited in Tables 1 and 2 as averages over the 15 series considered in each case. I distinguish between the case where Q is known (denoted "Known Q") and the case where Q (and hence also the transition matrix T) is estimated, and between the results obtained for a primary analysis that uses the distinct panel estimates and the results obtained for a secondary analysis using only the aggregate estimates. Another distinction made is between the prediction one step ahead of the aggregate sample estimates (using either the correct model or the model that ignores the correlations between the survey errors) and the prediction of the distinct panel estimates (presented as averages over the four panels). In what follows, I define the rows of the tables:

1. Prediction bias:

    (a) Panels—$PB(p) = \frac{1}{4} \sum_{j=1}^{4} |\bar{e}_j|$, where $\bar{e}_j = 1/(N-d-1) \sum_{t=d+1}^{N-1} e_{t+1}^{(j)}$
    is the mean of the innovations when predicting the estimate $\bar{Y}_{t+1}^{(t+1-j)}$ at time t ($t = d+1, \ldots, N-1$; $j = 0, 1, 4, 5$).

    (b) Aggregate—$PB(a) = \frac{1}{4} \sum_{j=1}^{4} \bar{e}_j$.

2. Prediction MSE:

    (a) Panels—

    $$PM(p) = 1/(N - d - 1) \sum_{t=d+1}^{N-1} \left[\frac{1}{4} \sum_{j=1}^{4} (e_{t+1}^{(j)})^2 \right].$$

    (b) Aggregate—

    $$PM(a) = 1/(N - d - 1) \sum_{t=d+1}^{N-1} \left[\frac{1}{4} \sum_{j=1}^{4} e_{t+1}^{(j)} \right]^2.$$

    (c) $\rho = 0$—same as (b) but with the predictors computed under the assumption that the serial correlations between the panel survey errors are 0.

3. Estimation of survey error parameters:
    Bias $(\hat{\sigma}_e^2) = \frac{1}{15} \sum_{i=1}^{15} (\hat{\sigma}_{ei}^2 - \sigma_e^2)$, RMSE $(\hat{\sigma}_e^2) = [\frac{1}{15} \sum_{i=1}^{15} (\hat{\sigma}_{e,i}^2 - \sigma_e^2)^2]^{1/2}$, where $\hat{\sigma}_{e,i}^2$ is the estimator σ_e^2 obtained from the ith series ($i = 1, \ldots, 15$). The same is true for bias $(\hat{\rho})$ and RMSE $(\hat{\rho})$.

4. MSE of estimators of population means:

    (a) Model—$MSE(m) = 1/(N - d) \sum_{t=d+1}^{N} V(\hat{\theta}_t - \theta_t)$, where $V(\hat{\theta}_t - \theta_t)$ is the theoretical variance of the population mean predictor under the model.

    (b) Realized—$MSE(r) = 1/(N - d) \sum_{t=d+1}^{N} (\hat{\theta}_t - \theta_t)^2$.

    (c) Patterson—$MSE(P) = 1/(N - d) \sum_{t=d+1}^{N} S_t(P)$, where $S_t(P)$ is the sampling variance of Patterson's (1950) estimator at time t.

Table 1. Simulation results, data set 1

Measures of error			100 time points				36 time points			
			Primary		Secondary		Primary		Secondary	
			Known Q	Est. Q	Known Q	Est. Q	Known Q	Est. Q	Known Q	Est. Q
Prediction bias		Panels	.35	.65	.36	.38	.63	.67	.69	.60
		Aggregate	−.09	.25	−.16	−.14	−.05	.06	−.05	.09
Prediction MSE		Panels	26.00	26.20	32.70	32.90	25.80	25.40	32.40	32.60
		Aggregate	8.25	8.40	9.67	9.76	8.42	7.74	9.58	8.62
		$\rho = 0$[a]	10.75	—	10.75	—	11.32	—	11.32	—
Estimation of survey-error parameters	σ_e^2	Bias	—	−.24	—	−.66	—	−.72	—	−1.20
		RMSE	—	.56	—	3.20	—	1.44	—	6.20
	ρ	Bias	—	−.01	—	−.05	—	.00	—	−.27
		RMSE	—	.03	—	.10	—	.07	—	.26
MSE of estimator[b] of population means		Model	3.90	4.22	4.13	4.56	3.55	3.97	3.76	3.35
		Realized	4.10	4.45	4.35	4.85	3.65	4.20	3.84	5.53
		Patterson	6.50	6.50	—	—	6.60	6.60	—	—
MSE of estimator[c] of seasonal effects		Model	.003	.25	.003	.32	.001	.25	.001	.26
		Realized	.003	.21	.003	.38	.001	.47	.001	.88
		$\rho = 0$[d]	.003	—	.003	—	.001	—	.001	—

Note: Initial components: $L_0 = 100$, $R_0 = 5$, $S'_0 = (4, 1, −3, −2)$; residual state variances: $\sigma_L^2 = .1$, $\sigma_R^2 = \cdots$, $\sigma_S^2 = 10^{-4}$; survey error parameters: $\sigma_e^2 = 8$[d], $\rho = .7$.

[a] Results obtained when ignoring the serial correlations between the panel estimators.

[b] Estimators are based on past and current data.

[c] Estimators are "smoothed" using all of the data.

[d] $\sigma_e^2 = E(\bar{Y}_t − \theta_t)^2$ is the variance of the aggregate mean.

Table 2. Simulation results, data set 2

Measures of error		100 time points				36 time points			
		Primary		Secondary		Primary		Secondary	
		Known Q	Est. Q	Known Q	Est. Q	Known Q	Est. Q	Known Q	Est. Q
Prediction bias	Panels	.38	.38	.43	.39	.58	.58	.63	.59
	Aggregate	-.29	-.28	-.34	-.37	-.08	-.03	-.06	.00
Prediction MSE	Panels	20.85	20.45	25.30	24.70	20.80	19.34	25.40	22.97
	Aggregate	12.16	11.70	13.80	13.10	11.90	10.24	13.82	1.066
	$\rho = C^a$	14.20	—	14.20	—	14.20	—	14.20	—
Estimation of survey-error parameters	σ_e^2 Bias	—	-.12	—	-.72	—	-.06	—	.32
	RMSE	—	.36	—	2.80	—	.76	—	4.88
	ρ Bias	—	-.01	—	-.24	—	-.01	—	-.26
	RMSE	—	.03	—	.36	—	.08	—	.45
MSE of estimator[b] of population means	Model	2.90	2.87	3.31	2.40	2.81	2.84	3.20	1.95
	Realized	2.90	2.94	3.27	3.42	3.12	3.09	3.56	3.68
	Patterson	3.16	3.16	—	—	3.30	3.30	—	—
MSE of estimator[c] of seasonal effects	Model	.52	.51	.69	.68	.54	.45	.72	.55
	Realized	.53	.63	.61	.75	.51	.65	.67	.87
	$\rho = 0^a$	.70	—	.70	—	.71	—	.71	—

Note: Initial components: $L_0 = 100$, $R_0 = 5$, $S_0' = (4, 1, -3, -2)$; residual state variances: $\sigma_L^2 = .8$, $\sigma_R^2 = 1$, $\sigma_S^2 = .4$; survey error parameters: $\sigma_e^2 = 4^d$, $\rho = .7$. See footnotes to Table 1 for definitions of a–d.

5. MSE of estimators of seasonal effects:

   (a) Model—$\text{MSES}(m) = 1/(N-d) \sum_{t=d+1}^{N} V(\hat{S}_t - S_t)$, where $V(\hat{S}_t - S_t)$ is the theoretical variance of the (smoothed) predictor of the seasonal effect at time t.

   (b) Realized—$\text{MSES}(r) = 1/(N-d) \sum_{t=d+1}^{N} (\hat{S}_t - S_t)^2$.

   (c) $\rho = 0$—same as 5(b) but with the predictors computed under the assumption that the serial correlations between the panel survey errors are 0.

The main results emerging from the tables can be summarized as follows:

1. The use of primary analysis dominates the use of secondary analysis in almost every aspect studied (notice in particular the estimation of the survey-error parameters in the case of the short series). The better performance in the case of a primary analysis is seen to hold also in the estimation of the seasonal effects (see Table 2) despite the use of the smoothed estimators, an issue not investigated so far.

2. Estimating the unknown model parameters by the method of scoring yields satisfactory results in the case of a primary analysis. The results are less encouraging, however, in the case of a secondary analysis with respect to the estimation of the survey-error parameters. This outcome is explained by the fact that these parameters index the relationships between the panel estimators that are not observable in the case of a secondary analysis. As emphasized in Section 3, the survey parameters can be estimated consistently even in the case of a secondary analysis, which is illustrated very clearly by comparing the results obtained for the long and the short series.

Another notable result is the estimation of the seasonal effects in the case of the first group of data. The smoothed estimates of the seasonal effects using the correct Q matrix outperform in this case the smoothed empirical estimates obtained by using the estimated variances, a result that could be expected considering the very small value of σ_S^2. Still, the empirical estimates perform well, and so do the estimates of the MSE's of these estimators in the case of the long series. For the short series, the MSE's estimates underestimate the true MSE's (in both tables), a well-known phenomenon in other applications resulting from ignoring the contribution to the variance due to the estimation of the model variances. A similar phenomenon can be observed with the variances of the estimators of the population means. Ansley and Kohn (1986) proposed a correction factor of order $1/N$ to account for this extra variation in state-space modeling. See also Hamilton (1986) for a Monte Carlo procedure.

3. The use of the full model taking into account the intrinsic relationships between the survey errors decreases the prediction errors very significantly compared to the case in which these relationships are ignored. The same holds for the second group of data with respect to the estimation of the seasonal effects when using a primary analysis.

Although not shown in the table, I generated different data sets using smaller values of ρ but increasing each time the value of σ_v^2 so that the unconditional variance $\sigma_e^2 = E(\bar{Y}_t - \theta_t)^2$ remained fixed. Evidently, the smaller the value of ρ the larger are the prediction errors under both a primary and a secondary analysis (although the differences between the two analyzes are diminished) and the smaller is the impact of setting $\rho = 0$ in the analysis. Decreasing the value of ρ increases also the MSE's of the estimates of the seasonal effects under both a primary and a secondary analysis using either the correct Q or its sample estimate. The increase is again very evident. These results are quite intuitive considering the imposed autoregressive relationships between the survey errors. The smaller σ_v^2 is, the smaller are the prediction errors in predicting the survey errors and the better are the predictions of the survey estimators. The improvement in the prediction of the survey errors increases the precision of the estimators of the population-means components.

4. The use of the model yields more accurate estimates for the population means than the classical sampling approach. (For the first group, the model performs better even under a secondary analysis.) The major factor affecting the performance of the classical estimator is the variance of the survey errors, and since it is twice as large for the first group of data as for the second group, the variance of the estimator is likewise doubled. Under the model, the variance of the estimators depends also on the residual variances of the population mean components, and since they are much smaller for the first group than for the second, the overall increase in the variance of the estimators is only in the magnitude of about 30%. These results illuminate the possible advantages of modeling the evolution of the population means over time.

5.2 Empirical results using labour force data

I present the results obtained for two series—series 1: Number of hours worked in the week preceding the survey, and series 2: Number of weeks worked in the year preceding the survey. In order not to burden the computations, I restricted the analysis to households in the city of Tel-Aviv. The time period covered was 1979–1987 so that each series consists of 36×4 panel estimates. I did not include data for the years before 1979 because of changes in the sampling design and the questionnaire introduced in 1978. Data for 1988 was not available at the time of the analysis. Interested readers may obtain the data of the two series from me.

The trend levels of these two series are almost constant. The seasonal effects account for about 50% of the MSE of the quarter-to-quarter differences in the aggregate means in the case of the first series and for about 30% in the second series.

The results obtained when fitting the models of Sections 2 and 3 to the series are exhibited in Table 3. The column headed "Primrot" gives the results obtained when accounting for rotation group bias. I first analyzed the series without including the bias factors (other columns of the table) and found that for both series the predictor one step ahead of the first panel estimator is essentially unbiased. This result suggests that $\beta_1 \cong (\beta_2 + \beta_4 + \beta_5)/3$, but since there is no apparent reason for a bias associated with the first panel (see the following discussion), I presupposed also

Table 3. Empirical results, labour force survey, Israel, 1979–1987

Measures of error	Series 1			Series 2		
	Primary	Primrot[a]	Secondary	Primary	Primrot[a]	Secondary
Prediction bias						
Panel 1	.07	.16	.05	.02	.16	.02
Panel 2	.36	.08	.34	.27	−.02	.23
Panel 3	.27	.10	.26	.17	.07	.18
Panel 4	−.31	.11	−.21	−.20	.04	−.19
Aggregate	.10	.10	.11	.065	.06	.06
Prediction MSE						
Panels (average)	1.63	1.56	1.71	1.16	1.14	1.18
$\rho = 0$ (average)	2.44	2.38	2.60	1.51	1.49	1.48
Aggregate	.51	.50	.48	.21	.21	.24
$\rho = 0^b$	1.21	1.36	1.35	.51	.52	.50
$\hat{Y}_{tt-1} = Y_{t-1}$	1.47	1.47	1.47	41	41	.41
Estimated survey parameter						
σ_e^2	.42	.38	.69	.38	.36	.37
ρ	.39	.42	.07	.36	.38	.46
Var. estimated population means						
Model	.15	.14	.20	.10	.11	.10
Patterson	.39	.39	—	.31	.31	—

Note: Series 1: hours worked in the week preceding the survey; series 2: weeks worked in the year preceding the survey.
[a] Results obtained when accounting for rotation group effects.
[b] Results obtained when ignoring the serial correlations between the panel estimators.

that $\beta_1 = 0$, which combined with the other relationship implies that $\sum_j \beta_j = 0$. Nonetheless, when estimating the bias coefficients I only imposed the milder condition $\sum_j \beta_j = 0$. (Starting values for the coefficients were set to 0 with correspondingly large error variances.)

Comparing the panel prediction biases with and without the accounting for the group effects reveals relatively large biases for the other panels in the latter case. For the first series the smoothed estimators of the bias coefficients and the corresponding standard deviations in parentheses are $\hat{\beta}_1 = -.027(.17)$, $\hat{\beta}_2 = .26(.17)$, $\hat{\beta}_4 = .13(.17)$, and $\hat{\beta}_5 = -.37(.17)$. Thus $\hat{\beta}_5$ is significant at the .03 level and likewise with respect to the difference $(\hat{\beta}_5 - \hat{\beta}_2)$ (the standard deviation of the difference is .29). For the second series the corresponding values are $\hat{\beta}_1 = -.10(.16)$, $\hat{\beta}_2 = .20(.16)$, $\hat{\beta}_4 = .09(.16)$, and $\hat{\beta}_5 = -.19(.16)$, so none of the coefficients are significant even though they exhibit a similar pattern to that observed for the first series.

The fact that only one group effect is significant may result from the short length and the relatively large error variances of the two series. Notwithstanding, it is not clear that the observed prediction biases reflect real rotation group effects. It was suggested that the negative effect observed for the fourth panel could result from the fact that this is the only panel surveyed also on income. Another noteworthy feature of the LFS is that about half of the interviews of the second and third panels are carried out by telephone. Thus although the results of our analysis are inconclusive at this stage they suggest a more rigorous and comprehensive study using more series and if possible more detailed data.

Two other notable outcomes in Table 3 are: (a) The use of primary and secondary analysis gives consistent results. This is true in particular for the second series but holds also for the first series except for the estimation of the survey-error parameters and hence the estimation of the variance of the population-mean estimator. (b) The estimates of the variances of the model-dependent estimators of the population means are substantially smaller than the estimated variances of the sampling (Patterson) estimator. This outcome can be explained by the fact that these two series are characterized by an almost constant trend level and stable seasonal effects, which is ideal for the use of the model-based predictors. (See the discussion in point 4 of Section 5.1.)

One needs to be cautious, however, in comparing the variances obtained under the model with the design variances because the former are model dependent and employ estimates for the unknown model parameters. This point raises the question of the goodness of fit of the model. As implied by the discussion of Section 2.4, the appropriateness of the model can be tested in two ways: (1) by studying the correlation structure of contrasts in the panel estimators and (2) by analyzing the model-prediction errors.

The first alternative is very limited with the ILFS because only two panels are observed on the same two successive quarters and no panel is observed for more than two successive quarters. (This particular rotation pattern restricts the family of plausible parsimonious models for the survey errors in the first place.) Nonetheless, if we define $C_t^{i,j} = (\bar{Y}_t^{t-i} - \bar{Y}_t^{t-j})$, then under the autoregressive relationship (2.2), $r_1 = \text{corr}(c_t^{1,5}, c_{t-1}^{0,4}) \cong \rho$ and $r_4 = \text{corr}(c_t^{4,5}, c_{t-4}^{0,1}) \cong \rho^4$. For the first series $r_1 = .48$ and $r_4 = .10$, which is quite consistent with the model and the maximum likelihood estimator (MLE) $\hat{\rho} = .42$. (The second correlation was computed after deleting two outlier observations.) For the second series, $r_1 = .14$ and $r_4 = -.02$, which again is consistent with the model but with a lower coefficient than the MLE $\hat{\rho} = .38$. I have rerun the MLE procedure for this series with a starting value of $\hat{\rho}_{(0)} = .14$, but the algorithm converged to the same value. I also fitted the model with $\rho = .14$ and $\sigma_e^2 = [1/(12N)] \sum_{t=1}^{N} \sum_j (\bar{Y}_t^{t-j} - \bar{Y}_t)^2 = .33$ (very close to the MLE $\hat{\sigma}_e^2 = .36$). The prediction biases came out almost identical to the prediction biases obtained with the MLE but the prediction MSE's came out somewhat larger under both the primary and the secondary analyses.

The two correlations considered so far are not the only ones that could be computed. Thus under the model $r_3^{i,j} = \text{corr}(c_t^{i,4}, c_{t-3}^{j,1}) \cong \rho^3$ and $r_5^{i,j} = \text{corr}(c_t^{i,5}, c_{t-5}^{j,0}) \cong \rho^5$. As the notation indicates, however, there are actually nine combinations of contrasts that can be considered in each case. I computed the corresponding correlations and found that many of them are in a range that is consistent with the AR(1) assumption and that almost all of them have high p values indicating the large variability of the data.

The fact that not all the contrast correlations are consistent with what is implied by the AR(1) model could be expected considering in particular the short span of the two series. Notice that, while the MLE uses all of the data simultaneously, the correlations between the contrasts are each based on a single contrast.

The appropriateness of the model is further supported by the following results exhibited in Table 3: (a) The results obtained under the primary and secondary analyzes are generally very consistent. (b) The means of the prediction errors are all close to 0 after accounting for the rotation group effects. (c) The prediction MSE's are substantially smaller than the prediction MSE's obtained when ignoring the serial correlations between the survey errors.

Combining the results obtained for the two modes of model diagnostics suggests that the postulated autoregressive relationship with the unknown survey parameters estimated by MLE captures at least most of the time series variation of the survey errors.

6 Concluding Remarks

The results obtained in the empirical study illustrate the possible advantages of using a primary analysis as compared to the use of a secondary analysis. First, the use of a primary analysis enables one in principle to detect the model holding for the survey errors by considering contrasts of the panel estimators. Second, the use of a primary analysis yields more accurate estimates for the model parameters and in particular for the survey-error parameters. Third, it produces better predictors for the population means and the seasonal effects. Practitioners in the survey-sampling area often prefer the use of the aggregate estimators because of rotation group effects, but as I have illustrated, these effects can be incorporated in the model.

A natural question arising from this discussion is whether secondary analysis should be considered at all. My answer would be positive provided that the model is validated through the behavior of the prediction errors and that it can be shown to give a better fit than models that ignore the survey errors structure. The sensitiveness of the model-based predictors to possible model misspecifications and the ways by which to secure the robustness of the model predictors are important topics for future research.

I mention in this respect that where one is most likely to benefit from using the time series approach is in small-area estimation, where the small sample sizes often dictate the use of a model as the only alternative. The models considered in the present article can be extended to deal with small-area estimation by allowing for nonzero cross-sectional correlations between the residual terms of the models fitted to the trend and the seasonal effects. By introducing cross-sectional correlations, the estimators of any given area can "borrow information" from other neighboring areas. When applied to a small-area estimation problem, the robustness of the estimators can be partly secured by requiring that the model-dependent estimators of aggregates of the small-area means coincide with the corresponding survey estimators when the latter are based on sufficient data. See Pfefferman and Burck (1990) for the theory and application of such a modification.

The use of the model for seasonal-adjustment purposes is another important aspect that should be explored further. My study indicates the potential advantages of using a primary analysis, taking into account the correlations between the observed estimates. It is unfortunate that despite the increasing use of repeated surveys by statistical bureaus and the widely recognized need for producing accurate estimates for the seasonal effects, the special features of the data are generally ignored when producing these estimates. In this respect, the procedure proposed in the present article is a first attempt to use more data and take the design features into account when estimating the seasonal effects, which I hope will encourage further research.

Acknowledgements

Work on this article was completed while I was staying at Statistics Canada under its Research Fellowship Program. Particular thanks are due to D. Friedman for his assistance in an early version and to B. Quenneville for helping with the computations. I also thank William Bell, the associate editor, and a referee for very helpful comments.

References

Abraham, B., and Vijayan, K. (1988), "Repeated Surveys and Time Series Analysis," Technical Report STAT-88-04, University of Waterloo, Dept. of Statistics and Actuarial Science.

Anderson, B. D. O., and Moore, J. B. (1979), *Optimal Filtering*, Englewood Cliffs, NJ: Prentice-Hall.

Ansley, C. F., and Kohn, R. (1985), "Estimation, Filtering and Smoothing, in State Space Models With Incompletely Specified Initial Conditions," *The Annals of Statistics*, 13, 1286–1316.

—— (1986), "Prediction Mean Squared Error for State Space Models With Estimated Parameters," *Biometrika*, 73, 467–473.

Bailar, B. A. (1975). "The Effects of Rotation Group Bias on Estimates From Panel Surveys," *Journal of the American Statistical Association*, 70, 23–29.

Binder, D. A., and Dick, J. P. (1989), "Modelling and Estimation for Repeated Surveys," *Survey Methodology*, 15, 29–45.

Binder, D. A., and Hidiroglou, M. A. (1988), "Sampling in Time," in *Handbook of Statistics* (Vol. 6), P. R. Krishnaiah and C. R. Rao (eds.), Amsterdam: Elsevier Science, pp. 187–211.

Blight, B. J. N., and Scott, A. J. (1973), "A Stochastic Model for Repeated Surveys," *Journal of the Royal Statistical Society*, Ser. B, 35, 61–68.

Candy, J. (1986), *Signal Processing: The Model-Based Approach*, New York: McGraw-Hill.

Cochran, W. G. (1977), *Sampling Techniques* (3rd Ed.), New York: John Wiley.

Dagum, E. B. (1980). *The X-11 ARIMA Seasonal Adjustment Method* (Catalog No. 12-564E), Ottawa, Statistics Canada.

Dagum, E. B., and Quenneville, B. (1988), "Deterministic and Stochastic Models for the Estimation of Trading-Day Variations," Working Paper TSRAD-88-003E, Statistics Canada, Ottawa.

DeJong, P. (1988), "The Likelihood of a State-Space Model," *Biometrika*, 75, 165–169.

Gurney, M., and Daly, J. F. (1965), "A Multivariate Approach to Estimation in Periodic Sample Surveys," in *Proceedings of the Social Statistics Section, American Statistical Association*, pp. 242–257.

Hamilton, J. D. (1986), "A Standard Error for the Estimated State Vector of a State-Space Model," *Journal of Econometrics*, 33, 388–397.

Harrison, P. J., and Stevens, C. F. (1976), "Bayesian Forecasting" (with discussion), *Journal of the Royal Statistical Society*, Ser. B, 38, 205–247.

Harvey, A. C. (1984), "A Unified View of Statistical Forecasting Procedures," *Journal of Forecasting*, 3, 245–275.

Harvey, A. C., and Peters, S. (1984), "Estimation Procedures for Structural Time Series Models," Discussion Paper A.44. London School of Economics, Dememic Econometrics Programmes.

Harvey, A. C., and Todd, P. H. J. (1983), "Forecasting Economic Time Series with Structural and Box–Jenkins Models" (with discussion), *Journal of Business and Economic Statistics*, 1, 299–315.

Hausman, J. A., and Watson, M. W. (1985), "Errors in Variables and Seasonal Adjustment Procedures," *Journal of the American Statistical Association*, 80, 531–540.

Jessen, R. J. (1942), "Statistical Investigation of a Sample Survey for Obtaining Farm Facts," in *Iowa Agricultural Experimental Station, Research Bulletin 304*, pp. 54–59.

Jones, R. G. (1979), "The Efficiency of Time Series Estimators for Repeated Survey," *Australian Journal of Statistics*, 21, 1–12.

—— (1980), "Best Linear Unbiased Estimators for Repeated Survey," *Journal of the Royal Statistical Society*, Ser. B, 42, 221–226.

Kalman, R. E. (1960), "A New Approach to Linear Filtering and Prediction Problems," *Journal of Basic Engineering*, 82 D, 33–45.

Kumar, S., and Lee, H. (1983), "Evaluation of Composite Estimation for the Canadian Labour Force Survey," *Survey Methodology*, 9, 1–24.

Maravall, A. (1985), "On Structural Time Series Models and the Characterization of Components," *Journal of Business and Economic Statistics*, 3, 350–355.

Morris, N. D., and Pfeffermann, D. (1984), "A Kalman Filter Approach to the Forecasting of Monthly Time Series Affected by Moving Festivals," *Journal of Time Series*, 5, 255–268.

Nathan, G., and Elihav, T. (1988), "Comparison of Measurement Errors in Telephone Interviewing and Home Visits by Misclassification Models," *Journal of Official Statistics*, 4, 363–374.

Patterson, H. D. (1950), "Sampling on Successive Occasions With Partial Replacement of Units," *Journal of the Royal Statistical Society*, Ser. B, 12, 241–255.

Pfeffermann, D., and Burck, L. (1990), "Robust Small Area Estimation Combining Time Series and Cross-Sectional Data," *Survey Methodology*, 16, 217–338.

Quenneville, B. (1988), "DLM: Software for Dynamic Linear Models," Computer Software. Time Series Research and Analysis Division, Statistics Canada, Ottawa.

Quenneville, B., and Dagum, E. B. (1988), "Variance of X-11 ARIMA Estimates— A Structural Approach," Working Paper TSRAD-88-00, Statistics Canada, Ottawa.

Rao, J. N. K., and Graham, J. E. (1964), "Rotation Designs for Sampling on Repeated Occasions," *Journal of the American Statistical Association*, 50, 492–509.

Scott, A. J., and Smith. T. M. F. (1974), "Analysis of Repeated Surveys Using Time Series Models," *Journal of the American Statistical Association*, 69, 674–678.

Scott, A. J., Smith. T. M. F., and Jones, R. G. (1977), "The Application of Time Series Methods to the Analysis of Repeated Surveys," *International Statistical Review*, 45, 13–28.

Seber, G. A. F., and Wild, C. J. (1988), *Nonlinear Regression*, New York: John Wiley.

Smith, T. M. F. (1978), "Principles and Problems in the Analysis of Repeated Surveys," in *Survey Sampling and Measurement*, N. K. Nawboodivi (ed.), New York: Academic Press, pp. 201–216.

Sugden, R. A., and Smith, T. M. F. (1984), "Ignorable and Informative Designs in Survey Sampling Inference," *Biometrika*, 71, 495–506.

Tam, S. M. (1987), "Analysis of Repeated Surveys Using a Dynamic Linear Model," *International Statistical Review*, 55, 63–73.

Watson, M. W., and Engle, R. F. (1983), "Alternative Algorithms for the Estimation of Dynamic Factor, Mimic and Varying Coefficient Regression Models," *Journal of Econometrics*, 23, 385–400.

12

The Modeling and Seasonal Adjustment of Weekly Observations*

ANDREW HARVEY

Faculty of Economics and Politics, University of Cambridge

SIEM JAN KOOPMAN

Department of Statistics, London School of Economics

AND

MARCO RIANI

Dipartimento Statistico, Università di Firenze

Several important economic time series are recorded on a particular day every week. Seasonal adjustment of such series is difficult because the number of weeks varies between 52 and 53 and the position of the recording day changes from year to year. In addition certain festivals, most notably Easter, take place at different times according to the year. This article presents a solution to problems of this kind by setting up a structural time series model that allows the seasonal pattern to evolve over time and enables trend extraction and seasonal adjustment to be carried out by means of state-space filtering and smoothing algorithms. The method is illustrated with a Bank of England series on the money supply.

The weekly figures on the U.K. money supply are eagerly anticipated in the City of London because they are believed to be an important economic indicator. One of the key series is the value of the Bank of England notes and coins in circulation, plus cash deposits of commercial banks with the Bank of England. This basically corresponds to the measure known as M0, and we will refer to it in this way hereafter. These figures display considerable seasonal fluctuations and are particularly high just before Christmas. As a result there is a need for the Bank of England to produce a seasonally adjusted series for ease of interpretation.

Figure 1 shows a plot of the logarithms of the observations on M0 starting on May 28, 1969. Taking logarithms yields a series with a more stable seasonal pattern. The figures are recorded every Wednesday, except when the Wednesday falls on a public holiday, in which case the figure is recorded on the previous Tuesday (or Monday if Tuesday is also a holiday). The Christmas peak can be clearly seen

* Reprinted from *The Journal of Business and Economic Statistics*, "The modeling and seasonal adjustment of weekly observations" by A. C. Harvey, S. J. Koopman and M. Riani, pp. 364–68, Vol. 15, No. 3, July 1997. Reproduced here by permission of the American Statistical Association.

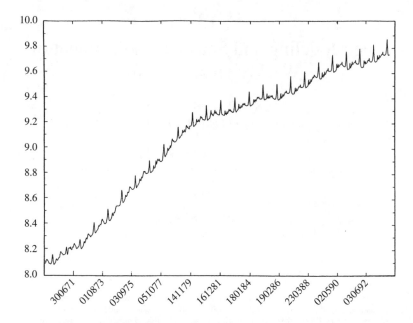

Fig. 1. Weekly observations on the U.K. money supply.

and, as with many economic time series, it is apparent that the seasonal pattern has evolved over time due to changing institutional and social factors. An excellent discussion of the changing nature of Christmas and its consequent economic impact is that of Scott (1995).

Modeling a changing seasonal component is relatively easy for quarterly and monthly observations, the seasonal component normally being combined with a stochastic trend and an irregular term. This is either done explicitly, as in the structural time series modeling approach, or implicitly, as in the autoregressive integrated moving average (ARIMA) approach. In the latter case, the seasonal component is specified by means of a "canonical decomposition" as shown by Hillmer and Tiao (1982). The seasonal component can be extracted by a state-space smoothing algorithm; see, for example, Kitagawa and Gersch (1984) or Harvey (1989). Carrying out such *model-based* seasonal adjustment, using either approach, has considerable attractions because the procedure adapts to the particular characteristics of the series involved. The relationship between the model-based procedures and the widely used Bureau of the Census X-11 program was discussed by Maravall (1985).

Seasonal adjustment of weekly data is not an easy task. The first problem is that, because the observations are normally recorded on a particular day of the week rather than on predetermined dates, the fact that there is not an integral number of weeks in the year means that the number of observations in the year varies between 52 and 53. Thus, even if the seasonal pattern were deterministic, it could not be modeled by a set of dummy variables. Furthermore, the position of the dates of the observation days changes with each year so that even with an integral number of weeks in the year the seasonal pattern would change from year to year. It makes a big difference, for example, if the money-supply figure is recorded on the day before Christmas or six days before Christmas. (The former case arises if Christmas is on a Thursday, the latter if it is on a Tuesday.) To make matters worse, these differing seasonal patterns do not even recur every seven years because of leap years.

The other major problem is that the position of Easter changes from year to year. Furthermore, its effect can be different depending on when it occurs. If it is late, its effects can overlap, and possibly interact with, those associated with the May Day public holiday. Of course, the position of Easter also affects models for monthly observations, but in this case it is more easily handled, and there is a considerable literature on its treatment; see Bell and Hillmer (1983).

The ARIMA-based procedure does not easily generalize to weekly data. One of the few published articles on weekly model-based seasonal adjustment, that by Pierce, Grupe, and Cleveland (1984), got around some of the problems by using regression to model some of the seasonal effects in a deterministic way and then grafting on stochastic effects using an ARIMA model. Our approach is to attack the problem using structural time series models. Such models can be interpreted as regressions on functions of time in which the parameters are time-varying. This makes them a natural vehicle for handling changing seasonality of a complex form. Once a suitable model has been fitted, the seasonal component can be extracted by a smoothing algorithm.

The plan of the article is as follows. Section 1 briefly reviews the basic structural model as it is typically used for quarterly and monthly data and explains why it cannot be directly applied to weekly data. Sections 2 and 3 describe the two seasonal components that we propose introducing into a structural model to allow it to cope with weekly data, and Section 4 explains how the model is handled statistically. The model is applied to the Bank of England money-supply data in Section 5. Section 6 presents the conclusions.

1 The Basic Structural Time Series Model

The basic structural model (BSM) is formulated in terms of trend, seasonal, and irregular components. All are assumed to be stochastic and driven by serially independent Gaussian disturbances that are mutually independent. If there are s seasons in the year, the model is

$$y_t = \mu_t + \gamma_t + \varepsilon_t, \quad \varepsilon_t \sim NID(0, \sigma_\varepsilon^2), \tag{1.1}$$

where the trend, seasonal, and irregular are denoted by μ_t, γ_t, and ε_t, respectively.

The trend is specified in the following way:

$$\mu_t = \mu_{t-1} + \beta_{t-1} + \eta_t, \quad \eta_t \sim NID(0, \sigma_\eta^2),$$
$$\beta_t = \beta_{t-1} + \zeta_t, \quad \zeta_t \sim NID(0, \sigma_\zeta^2), \tag{1.2}$$

where μ_t is the level and β_t is the slope. The disturbances η_t and ζ_t are assumed to be mutually independent. Setting $\sigma_\eta^2 = 0$ gives a trend that is relatively smooth.

The seasonal component is usually set up in terms of stochastic trigonometric functions at the $s/2$ seasonal frequencies, although dummy-variable formulations are also possible. The key point is that, although the seasonal component is non-stationary, it has the property that the expected value of the sum over the previous s time periods is 0. This ensures that seasonal effects are not confounded with the trend. It also means that the forecasts of the seasonal component will sum to 0 over any one-year period.

The statistical treatment of the model is based on the state-space form, with $s + 1$ elements in the state vector. Estimation, forecasting, and signal extraction are carried out by means of the Kalman filter and associated algorithms.

1.1 Trigonometric seasonality

The trigonometric form of stochastic seasonality used in models of the form (1.1) with s seasons in the year is

$$\gamma_t = \sum_{j=1}^{[s/2]} \gamma_{j,t}, \quad t = 1, \ldots, T, \tag{1.3}$$

where each $\gamma_{j,t}$ is generated by

$$\begin{bmatrix} \gamma_{j,t} \\ \gamma_{j,t}^* \end{bmatrix} = \begin{bmatrix} \cos \lambda_j & \sin \lambda_j \\ -\sin \lambda_j & \cos \lambda_j \end{bmatrix} \begin{bmatrix} \gamma_{j,t-1} \\ \gamma_{j,t-1}^* \end{bmatrix} + \begin{bmatrix} \omega_{j,t} \\ \omega_{j,t}^* \end{bmatrix}, \tag{1.4}$$

where $\lambda_j = 2\pi j/s$ is frequency, in radians, for $j = 1, \ldots, [s/2]$ and ω_t and ω_t^* are two mutually uncorrelated white-noise disturbances with zero means and common variance σ_ω^2. For s even, $[s/2] = s/2$, but for s odd, $[s/2] = (s - 1)/2$. Note that $\gamma_{j,t}^*$ is redundant for $j = s/2$.

The BSM consisting of the stochastic trend in (1.2) combined with trigonometric seasonality is easily put in state-space form by defining the $(s + 1) \times 1$ state vector $\alpha_t = (\mu_t, \beta_t, \gamma_{1t}, \gamma_{1t}^*, \gamma_{2t}, \gamma_{2t}^*, \ldots)'$. The measurement equation is then

$$y_t = (1, 0, \mathbf{z}_t')\alpha_t + \varepsilon_t, \tag{1.5}$$

where $\mathbf{z}_t' = (1, 0, 1, 0, \ldots)$. If the Kalman filter is initiated with a diffuse prior, as shown by De Jong (1991), an estimator of the state with a proper prior is effectively constructed from the first $s + 1$ observations.

1.2 Dummy-variable seasonality

The form of dummy-variable seasonality relevant to the development later in the article is one in which each element in an $s \times 1$ vector γ_t represents the effect of a particular month and these effects sum to 0; see Harvey (1989, pp. 40–41) for a discussion of different types of dummy-variable seasonality. The effects evolve over time according to a multivariate random walk

$$\gamma_t = \gamma_{t-1} + \chi_t, \tag{1.6}$$

where $\boldsymbol{\chi}_t$ is an $s \times 1$ vector of serially uncorrelated random disturbances with zero mean. The zero sum over the year constraint implies restrictions on the covariance matrix of disturbances. Specifically

$$\text{var}(\boldsymbol{\chi}_t) = \sigma_\chi^2(\mathbf{I} - (1/s)\mathbf{ii}'), \tag{1.7}$$

where σ_χ^2 is the variance parameter that governs the speed with which the seasonal pattern can change and $\mathbf{i}$ is an $s \times 1$ vector of ones. This covariance matrix enforces the constraint that $\mathbf{i}'\boldsymbol{\chi}_t = \mathbf{0}$ by making its variance 0. Thus, if $\mathbf{i}'\gamma_{t-1} = 0$, then $\mathbf{i}'\gamma_t = 0$.

One of the elements of γ_t can be dropped from Equation (1.6); it can always be recovered as minus the sum of the elements remaining. The state-space form of a BSM with this kind of seasonality is such that $s - 1$ elements of γ_t appear in the state vector and the measurement equation is as in (1.5) with $\mathbf{z}_t$ being an $(s - 1) \times 1$ vector that yields the effect of the current month. Thus if the sth element of γ_t has been dropped from the state vector, $\mathbf{z}_t$ has a 1 in position j for month $j, j = 1, \ldots, s - 1$, and zeros elsewhere, and all elements equal to -1 for month s.

1.3 Weekly data

The features of weekly data noted in the first section mean that the preceding approach cannot be applied directly. Our solution, like that of Pierce et al. (1984), is to model the seasonal pattern using two components. The first component is a function of the date in the year—that is, the number of days that have passed in the year. Thus, for example, it takes a particular value on day 358 (which happens to be Christmas Eve). The second component is a collection of effects associated with public holidays, such as Easter, that take place on different dates in different years but always fall on the same day of the week. Once these components have been specified as deterministic effects so that they could be handled by regression, it is straightforward to allow them to evolve stochastically over time by casting the whole model in state-space form. This is a considerable advantage over the approach adopted by Pierce et al. (1984) in which a stochastic ARIMA component is added to a regression component with no clear connection between the two.

In what follows, we will refer to the first seasonal effect, γ_t, as the *periodic* component and to the second, θ_t, as the *moving festival* component. It is possible to include an additional periodic component if there is a significant intramonthly effect.

Although our model is formulated on a daily basis, we could go further and set up the evolution of the parameters in continuous time. This is quite natural because the periodic component is a continuous function. Although continuous time is an elegant approach, it makes little or no difference to the form of the implied weekly models, however, and its use in the present context should be clear from the general discussion of Harvey (1989, chap. 9).

2 Periodic Effects

We wish to model the yearly pattern on a daily basis. For the moment, we will assume that there are no leap years, so each year has 365 days.

The periodic component will be modeled as a linear function of a set of parameters contained in a $g \times 1$ vector γ. If these parameters are fixed, the periodic pattern is fixed, and we may write the periodic effect for the dth day in the year as

$$\gamma_d = \mathbf{z}_d' \gamma, \quad d = 1, \ldots, 365, \tag{2.1}$$

where $\mathbf{z}_d$ is a $g \times 1$ vector of known values. The idea is to specify (2.1) so as to have g reasonably small—one hopes much less than 52. There are essentially two options. The first is to let γ_d be a mixture of trigonometric functions. The second is to model it by a periodic spline. In our application the second option seems to offer more scope for a parsimonious parameterization, mainly because of the need to capture the sharp peak at Christmas. The important point, however, is that both approaches can be generalized to allow the seasonal pattern to evolve over time by letting γ be stochastic. Stochastic trigonometric seasonals have long been a part of structural time series modeling methods. Stochastic, or time-varying, periodic splines were first used by Harvey and Koopman (1993) to model intraweekly patterns of hourly electricity demand.

Further scope for cutting down on the number of parameters may be afforded if there is an intramonthly pattern. Again either trigonometric terms or splines may be used.

2.1 Trigonometric seasonality

A fixed annual pattern may be represented by a trigonometric model as follows:

$$\gamma_d = \sum_{j=1}^{k} (\gamma_j \cos \lambda_j d + \gamma_j^* \sin \lambda_j d), \quad d = 1, \ldots, 365, \tag{2.2}$$

where $\lambda_j = 2\pi j / 365$. To include the full set of trigonometric terms, as is normally the case with a monthly or quarterly model, would mean setting $k = 182$. Pierce et al. (1984) found, however, that setting $k = 8$ is perfectly adequate when combined with intramonthly effects.

Now suppose that the periodic pattern changes over time on a daily basis, irrespective of whether there has been an observation. Each trigonometric component now evolves as in (1.3) and (1.4) with the λ_j's specified as in (2.2) and the subscript t denoting the seasonal effect on the tth day from the beginning of the sample. Thus the model is modified to

$$\gamma_t = \sum_{j=1}^{[s/z]} \gamma_{j,t}, \quad t = 1, 2, \ldots, T_d,$$

where T_d denotes the number of days covered by the sample period. When $\sigma_\omega^2 = 0$, the deterministic model is obtained.

2.2 Periodic time-varying splines

To set up a spline we need to choose h knots in the range $[0, 365]$. Then

$$\gamma_d = \mathbf{w}_d' \gamma^\dagger, \quad d = 1, \ldots, 365, \tag{2.3}$$

where $\mathbf{w}_d$ is an $h \times 1$ vector that depends on the position of the knots and is defined in such a way as to ensure continuity of the spline from one year to the next—that is, make it periodic; see the Appendix and Poirier (1976, pp. 43–47). To have the periodic seasonal effects summing to 0 over the year, one of the elements in $\gamma^\dagger$, say the last one, is dropped. Then, in terms of the formulation in (2.1), γ consists of the first $g = h - 1$ elements of $\gamma^\dagger$, and the ith element in $\mathbf{z}_d$ is given by

$$z_{di} = w_{di} - w_{dh} w_{*i} / w_{*h}, \quad i = 1, \ldots, g, \quad d = 1, \ldots, 365, \tag{2.4}$$

where ω_{*i} is the ith element of the vector

$$\mathbf{w}_* = \sum_{d=1}^{365} \mathbf{w}_d. \tag{2.5}$$

Note that it is the effects summed over all the days in the year that come to 0 rather than the effects summed over the particular days when there are observations. (If we want to regard d as continuous, then $\mathbf{w}_*$ is an integral; this can be evaluated in practice by summing over many points or by using the formula at the end of Appendix A.)

The splines can be allowed to evolve over time by letting the parameters follow random walks. If we assume that the parameters change every day, irrespective of whether or not there is an observation, we may write

$$\gamma_t^\dagger = \gamma_{t-1}^\dagger + \chi_t, \quad t = 1, 2, \ldots, T_d, \tag{2.6}$$

where χ_t is an $h \times 1$ vector of serially uncorrelated random disturbances with zero mean and covariance matrix

$$\text{var}(\chi_t) = \sigma_\chi^2 (\mathbf{I} - (1/\mathbf{w}_*' \mathbf{w}_*) \mathbf{w}_* \mathbf{w}_*'), \tag{2.7}$$

where σ_χ^2 is the variance parameter that governs the speed with which the spline can change. This covariance matrix enforces the constraint that $\mathbf{w}_*' \chi_t = \mathbf{0}$. Note that, if there is a knot for each day, the seasonal dummy model of (1.6) is obtained with $h = s$ and $\mathbf{w}_* = \mathbf{i}$.

As before, one of the elements of $\gamma_t^\dagger$ can be dropped to give a $g \times 1$ vector γ_t. The effect in the tth day from the beginning of the sample is then

$$\gamma_t = \mathbf{z}_{t(d)}' \gamma_t, \quad t = 1, \ldots, T_d,$$

where the notation $t(d)$ for the subscript of $\mathbf{z}$ stresses dependence on the day of the year.

In some circumstances, a part of the periodic pattern may change more rapidly than the rest of the pattern. For money demand, this seems to be the case with the Christmas effect. This phenomenon can be modeled by letting the parameters at the knots close to the points at which rapid changes take place be subject to relatively larger disturbances. Thus, suppose that the first m elements in $\gamma_t^\dagger$ have associated with them a variance of σ_m^2, and the second $n = h - m$ have a larger variance, σ_n^2. The covariance matrix of χ_t then becomes

$$\mathrm{var}(\chi_t) = \begin{bmatrix} \sigma_m^2 \mathbf{I}_m & \mathbf{0} \\ \mathbf{0} & \sigma_n^2 \mathbf{I}_n \end{bmatrix} - \frac{1}{\mathbf{w}_*' \mathbf{w}_*} \begin{bmatrix} \sigma_m^2 \mathbf{w}_m \mathbf{w}_m' & \frac{1}{2}(\sigma_m^2 + \sigma_n^2)\mathbf{w}_m \mathbf{w}_n' \\ \frac{1}{2}(\sigma_m^2 + \sigma_n^2)\mathbf{w}_n \mathbf{w}_m' & \sigma_n^2 \mathbf{w}_n \mathbf{w}_n' \end{bmatrix},$$

(2.8)

where $\mathbf{w}_m$ consists of the first m elements of $\mathbf{w}_*$ and $\mathbf{w}_n$ contains the last n; that is, $\mathbf{w}_* = (\mathbf{w}_m', \mathbf{w}_n')'$. This additional flexibility is an attractive feature of the spline formulation. Again, $\mathbf{w}_*' \chi_t = \mathbf{0}$.

2.3 Intramonthly effects
Pierce et al. (1984) observed significant intramonthly effects in U.S. monetary aggregates, primarily due to the higher money supply toward the end of the month when wages are paid. Such effects were captured by the inclusion of trigonometric terms as in (2.2) but with d denoting the day of the month and 365 replaced by the number of days in the month. An intramonthly pattern of this form can be made time-varying exactly as in Subsection 2.1. An additional hyperparameter is needed to fulfil the role of σ_ω^2.

It is only worth using intramonthly effects if most of the months display a similar pattern. This may well be a reasonable assumption for monetary aggregates, although December may be different if people tend to be paid before the Christmas break.

Intramonthly effects can also be modeled by a time-varying periodic spline. A trigonometric intramonthly component can be used together with an intrayearly spline and vice versa.

2.4 Leap years
There are two ways to handle leap years. The first is to set the periodic effect for February 29 the same as for February 28—that is, to regard day 59 as occurring twice. By proceeding in this way we ensure that Christmas falls at exactly the same point every year—that is, day 359. Note that day 59 must be counted twice in the summation in (2.5).

A slightly different approach is to let the leap-year effect be spread throughout the whole year. For the trigonometric model, this is easily accomplished by replacing 365 by 366 in the λ_j's. For the spline, we modify $\mathbf{w}_d$, and hence $\mathbf{z}_{t(d)}$, by multiplying the knot positions by 366/365.

3 Moving Festivals: Variable-Dummy Effects

The effect of each public holiday may be modeled by a set of dummy variables that are assigned to the surrounding weeks. The day of the year on which the holiday falls, and hence the days on which the surrounding observations fall, depends on the calendar.

Suppose that m dummy variables are used to pick up public-holiday effects. Each effect takes up seven days. Thus the number of days remaining is, averaging over four years,

$$k_{m+1} = 365.25 - 7m. \tag{3.1}$$

These days must be allocated an effect to counterbalance the effect of the public holidays, thereby making the component sum to 0. Averaging over four years avoids a slight end-of-year discontinuity associated with leap years. Thus, if $\theta_1, \ldots, \theta_m$ denote the holiday effects, the nonholiday factor must be

$$\theta_{m+1} = -(\theta_1 + \cdots + \theta_m)7/k_{m+1}. \tag{3.2}$$

To allow the dummy-variable effects to evolve over time, we let them follow constrained random walks as in Subsection 2.4. There is no need to include θ_{m+1} because it may be inferred from (3.2). Thus, following the treatment of the daily-effects model as set out by Harvey (1989, pp. 43–44),

$$\theta_{jt} = \theta_{j,t-1} + v_{jt}, \qquad j = 1, \ldots, m, \quad t = 1, \ldots, T_d, \tag{3.3}$$

where v_{jt} is a zero mean, serially uncorrelated disturbance with variance

$$\operatorname{var}(v_j) = \sigma_v^2(1 - 49/K), \quad j = 1, \ldots, m, \tag{3.4}$$

where $K = 49m + k_{m+1}^2$. The covariances between disturbances are given by

$$\operatorname{cov}(v_j v_l) = -\sigma_v^2 49/K, \quad j, l = 1, \ldots, m. \tag{3.5}$$

The model may be generalized to allow some effects to change more rapidly by giving them a larger variance.

4 Statistical Treatment of the Model

The full daily model is

$$y_t = \mu_t + \gamma_t + \theta_t + \varepsilon_t, \quad t = 1, 2, \ldots, T_d, \tag{4.1}$$

with the trend defined as in (1.2) and γ_t and θ_t denoting the periodic and moving-festival effects. The irregular term, ε_t, is assumed to be white noise, and the disturbances in the different components are uncorrelated with each other. The model is easily put into state-space form by letting the state vector be

$\alpha_t = (\mu_t, \beta_t, \gamma_t', \theta_t')'$. The transition equation is made up of (1.2), (2.6), and (3.3), and the measurement equation is

$$y_t = (1, 0, z_{t(d)}', x_{t(c)}')\alpha_t + \varepsilon_t, \quad t = 1, \ldots, T_d, \tag{4.2}$$

where $z_{t(d)}$ depends on the number of days that have passed in the year and $x_{t(c)}$ depends on the calendar. The role of $x_{t(c)}$ is to pick out from the variable dummy vector, θ_t, the appropriate element or elements if there is no direct holiday effect and (3.2) is relevant.

The preceding formulation is independent of the observations. These can be weekly, which is the focus of attention here, or they can arrive on various days with no particular pattern. When there is no observation on a particular day, the Kalman filter simply treats it as a missing observation: There is no difficulty in carrying out prediction, smoothing, and estimation. The hyperparameters—that is, the variances of the disturbances—can be estimated by maximizing the (exact) log-likelihood function computed via the Kalman filter using the prediction error decomposition; see Appendix B. The use of "square root" filter is recommended because it appears to be much more stable for weekly data. Numerical optimization needs to be carried out with respect to the hyperparameters relative to the variance of the irregular, which can be concentrated out of the likelihood function.

With weekly data, the observations are, for the most part, equally spaced. It is therefore more efficient to convert the model to a weekly basis. If y_τ denotes the observation in week τ of the sample, we can write $y_\tau = \mu_\tau + \gamma_\tau + \theta_\tau + \varepsilon_\tau$, $\tau = 1, 2, \ldots, T$, and the transition equation is modified appropriately. For parameters evolving according to random walks, as in (2.6) and (3.3), all that needs to be done is to observe that the variance for a weekly model will be seven times the variance for a daily model. For the local linear trend, the modification to the covariance matrix of the trend disturbances, η_t and ζ_t in (1.2), was given by Harvey (1989, p. 312). In the case of the trigonometric formulation, the frequencies must be multiplied by 7, and if there is an intramonthly effect, it is necessary to take account of the fact that different months may have different numbers of days. There are occasions in which a figure is not recorded on the usual day of the week due to a holiday. In such cases it is straightforward to modify the state-space formulation to make allowance for the different time intervals involved. This generally involves multiplying disturbance variances (and frequencies, if relevant) by a factor of $p/7$, where p is the number of days since the last observation.

Estimates of the various components in the model using all the observations can be computed by smoothing. The algorithm devised by Koopman (1993) allows smoothing to be carried out with computational efficiency without excessive storage requirements; see Appendix B. Smoothing forms the basis for seasonal adjustment because all that needs to be done is to remove the periodic and moving-festival smoothed seasonal components. Note that the best estimate of the seasonal effect at the end of the series is given by filtering, so a seasonally adjusted figure can be provided as each new observation becomes available. This figure can subsequently be revised as further observations become available.

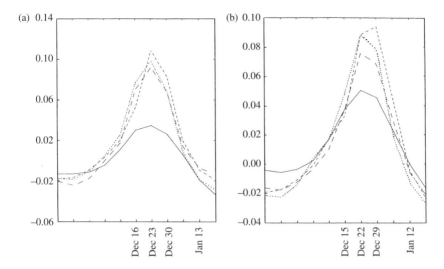

Fig. 2. Detrended series over the Christmas period for (a) observations on December 16, 23, and 30 and January 6 for 1970, - -; 1981, – –; 1987, . . .; and 1992, ——; (b) observations on December 15, 22, and 29 and January 5 for 1971, - -; 1976, – –; 1982, . . .; and 1993, ——.

5 U.K. Money Supply

To get some idea of the seasonal pattern in the M0 series shown in Fig. 1, it was subject to simple detrending using the Hodrick–Prescott filter. This filter can be obtained very easily as the smoother for a local linear-trend model—that is, (1.1) and (1.2) without the seasonal—in which $\sigma_\eta^2 = 0$ and $\sigma_\zeta^2/\sigma_\varepsilon^2 = .000625$. A plot of the observations in each year shows clear and permanent changes in the seasonal pattern. This is particularly marked at Christmas. Figure 2 shows the pattern of detrended observations over the Christmas period when Christmas falls on a Friday and on a Saturday. At the beginning of the sample, the peak is about 5% above the trend, whereas at the end it is about 10%. The same features appear when Christmas falls on other days of the week.

The periodic component was modeled using a time-varying spline. A good deal of experimentation was carried out in positioning the knots and dummy variables. To capture the peaks at times such as Christmas, a relatively large number of knots are needed in a short period. At other times, the seasonal pattern changes quite slowly and only a few knots are needed. Similar considerations applied in modeling the intradaily electricity demand of Harvey and Koopman (1993). Here the situation is more complicated because the interaction between the positioning of the dummy variables needed to capture the moving festivals and the knots used to pick up the rest of the seasonal pattern. The final specification had 19 knots and was decided by factors such as the "t ratios" of the knot coordinates and dummies, diagnostics and residual plots, goodness-of-fit statistics, and forecasting performance. Increasing the number of knots gives a better fit and reduces the residual serial correlation at lags 1 and 2 and at the annual lag of 52 (and 53). The less smooth the pattern is and the more knots are included, however, the less easy it is to distinguish the periodic pattern from the moving-festival pattern.

All moving public holidays fall on Mondays, except for Good Friday, and the moving-festival dummy variables were specified as follows:

1. Easter—the two weeks before and the week after
2. May Day—the week before and the week after (from 1978)
3. Spring Bank Holiday—two weeks before and the week after
4. August Bank Holiday—two weeks before and the week after

No restrictions were put on these holiday effects, although this is easily done. For example, the same state variable could be used for the Spring and August Bank Holidays. Thus, there are 11 stochastic dummy variables in the state vector. An additional dummy was included in June 1977 to allow for the special holiday for the Queen's Silver Jubilee.

No evidence was found for a significant intramonthly effect. A smooth trend— that is, σ_η^2 set to 0—was preferred because it was not much affected by the seasonal pattern.

The residuals exhibit considerable variability around Christmas. Because of the importance of Christmas and the speed with which the pattern can change, we found that a better model could be obtained by increasing the variance of the disturbances driving the movements in the knots around Christmas; see (2.8). When we doubled the variance of the Christmas knots, we found that the residuals close to Christmas were much more akin to residuals in other parts of the year. Furthermore, the unstandardized prediction errors were also smaller around Christmas; see Fig. 3. (It could be argued that one of the reasons the Christmas effect changes so rapidly is because it is different for Christmas falling on different days of the week. We were unable to capture such an effect by additional dummies; indeed, given that each day occurs only three or four times in our sample, this may be impossible to do. An examination of Fig. 2 and the plots for other days, however, indicates that the evolution over time far outweighs any possible day-of-the-week effect.)

Table 1 shows the estimated hyperparameters for the specification with and without the doubling of the periodic variance at Christmas. The q's denote hyperparameters relative to the variance of the irregular. Because of the sharp change in the trend in the late 1970s, it turned out to be more satisfactory to drop the first 400 observations in estimating the hyperparameters. They were retained for all other purposes, however. For the reasons given in the previous paragraph and confirmed in the following discussion, the doubled variance model is our preferred specification. Table 2 shows the estimates of the state for this model at the end of the sample, together with their t ratios—that is, the estimates divided by the corresponding root mean squared errors. In assessing the relative importance of the various estimates from their t ratios, it must be remembered that they are liable to change over time. Thus, although some knots are not significant at the end of the sample, they may have been in the past.

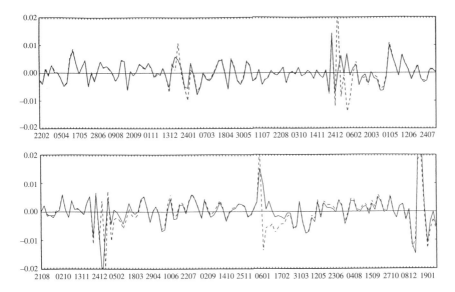

Fig. 3. Prediction errors over the last five years (broken line is when periodic variance not doubled at Christmas).

Table 1. Estimates of hyperparameters

Model	q_ζ	q_ν	q_χ	σ_ε^2
Constant periodic variance	.0149	.0052	.0483	947×10^{-8}
Doubled at Christmas	.0109	.0063	.0401	794×10^{-8}

Figure 4 graphs the smoothed trend. Its relatively slow changes seem to be quite suitable for this series. Figure 5 shows the smoothed pattern of the periodic component over the last four years, and Fig. 6 shows the moving-festival component. Note that there are very few knots in periods when there are public holidays—for example, in April and May. Small changes in both periodic and moving-festival patterns are apparent even over a short period of time. Figure 7 illustrates the much more dramatic changes that can take place over a longer period. It shows the evolution of the dummies in the weeks before and after Easter over the full sample. As with the Christmas effect, there is a doubling effect, with a movement from around 1.5% of the underlying level to over 3%.

The equation standard error, s, which is the square root of the one-step-ahead prediction-error variance, is normally used as a measure of goodness of fit, but here there is a problem because the nature of the model means that it changes over time and never goes to a steady state. A rough idea of the size of s can be gauged from Fig. 3.

Table 2. Final state vector

Description	State	Estimate	t ratio
Level slope	μ_T	9.7814	2.521
	β_T	.0012	1.50
Moving-festival dummies	$\theta_{1,T}$	.0122	4.84
	$\theta_{2,T}$	.0249	9.80
	$\theta_{3,T}$	.0058	2.31
	$\theta_{4,T}$	.0120	5.04
	$\theta_{5,T}$	.0224	9.22
	$\theta_{6,T}$	.0034	1.39
	$\theta_{7,T}$	.0188	7.45
	$\theta_{8,T}$	.0079	3.09
	$\theta_{9,T}$	.0360	13.9
	$\theta_{10,T}$	.0368	14.1
	$\theta_{11,T}$	.0043	1.66
Coefficients of knots	$\gamma_{1,T}$	.0574	13.3
	$\gamma_{2,T}$	.0131	3.48
	$\gamma_{3,T}$	−.0200	−7.33
	$\gamma_{4,T}$	−.0336	−9.82
	$\gamma_{5,T}$	−.0281	−6.50
	$\gamma_{6,T}$	−.0189	−4.45
	$\gamma_{7,T}$	−.0025	−.68
	$\gamma_{8,T}$	.0054	1.36
	$\gamma_{9,T}$	.0177	4.90
	$\gamma_{10,T}$	.0034	.92
	$\gamma_{11,T}$	−.0013	−.34
	$\gamma_{12,T}$	−.0068	−1.78
	$\gamma_{13,T}$	−.0051	−1.38
	$\gamma_{14,T}$	.0007	.20
	$\gamma_{15,T}$	.0298	7.71
	$\gamma_{16,T}$	.0540	13.8
	$\gamma_{17,T}$	.1040	25.1
	$\gamma_{18,T}$	.1058	13.7
Silver Jubilee	ϕ_T	.0122	7.57

Residual serial correlation can be assessed by the autocorrelations at lag τ, denoted $r(\tau)$, and the Box–Ljung statistics, $Q(P)$, based on the first P auto-correlation. Tables 3 and 4 report these statistics for the last five years. It seems to be difficult to eliminate serial correlation completely unless many knots are used, and our preference is to keep the number of knots reasonably small. The model with constant periodic variance shows quite strong serial correlation at lag 52, and the plot of the residual correlogram in Fig. 8(a) confirms the impression of some residual seasonal effects. Figure 8(b) indicates that this feature is eliminated in the model with the periodic variance doubled around Christmas. There is now more serial correlation, however, at lags 1 and 2. If this were felt to be of any

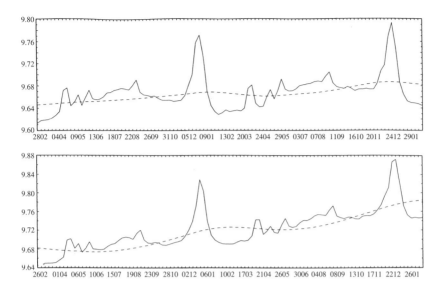

Fig. 4. Smoothed estimate of trend.

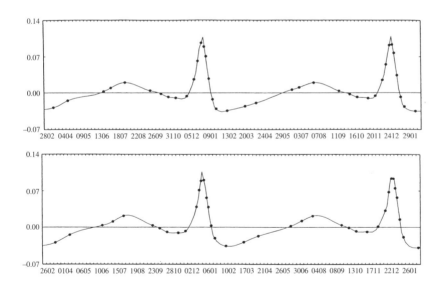

Fig. 5. Smoothed periodic component over the last four years, starting in February 1990, with position of knots (•).

practical importance, it could be removed by letting the disturbance follow a low-order autoregressive moving average process.

Table 5 reports the skewness and kurtosis moment test statistics and the Bowman–Shenton normality test statistic. When the model is correctly specified

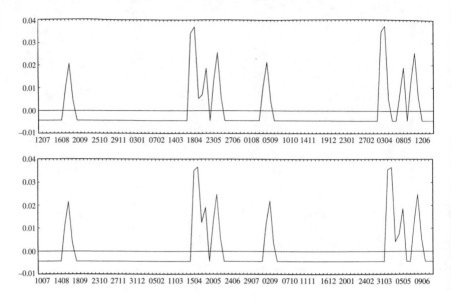

Fig. 6. Smoothed moving-festival component over the last four years, starting in July 1989.

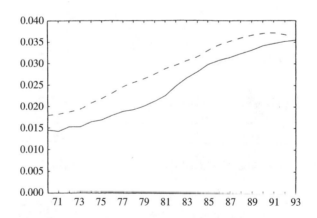

Fig. 7. Smoothed estimates of the effect of Easter: Wednesday before (solid line);
Wednesday after (dashed line).

Table 3. Diagnostics: residual autocorrelations

Model	r_1	r_2	r_3	r_{52}	r_{53}
Constant periodic variance	.06	.08	−.13	.31	.01
Doubled at Christmas	.23	−.16	−.02	.09	−.02

Table 4. Diagnostics: Box–Ljung statistics

Model	$Q(6)$	$Q(26)$	$Q(53)$	$Q(125)$
Constant periodic variance	16.78	40.88	130.8	271.0
Doubled at Christmas	27.29	55.40	111.2	231.4

Note: $Q(P)$ is based on first P residual autocorrelations.

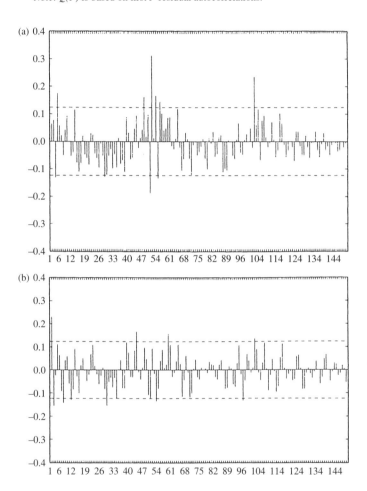

Fig. 8. Residual correlogram: (a) constant periodic variance; (b) variance doubled around Christmas.

with Gaussian disturbances, the skewness and kurtosis statistics are asymptotically distributed as chi squares with 1 df, whereas Bowman–Shenton has a chi-squared distribution with 2 df; see Harvey (1989, chap. 5). The extremely high kurtosis is due to the Christmas effect, but it is reduced to a reasonable level when the periodic variance is doubled around Christmas.

Table 5. Diagnostics: normality test statistics

Model	Skewness	Kurtosis	Bowman–Shenton
Constant periodic variance	10.82	93.11	103.9
Doubled at Christmas	1.00	7.94	9.94

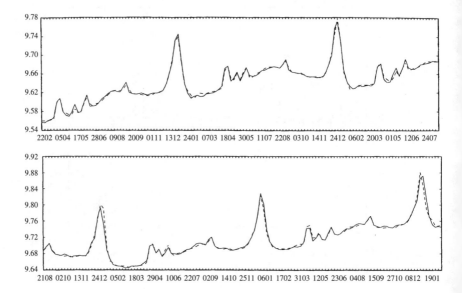

Fig. 9. One-step-ahead predictions (- -) and actual values (———).

The fact that the model is successful comes out in the predictions over the last few years. Figure 9 shows the one-step-ahead predictions obtained by filtering. This effectively gives the same information as the prediction-error plot in Fig. 3, but it brings home more clearly how accurate the predictions are, being less than .5% of the level most of the time. Even more impressive is Fig. 10, which shows the multistep predictions made from September 9, 1992. Overall the model is successful in providing a relatively parsimonious representation of the data.

6 Conclusions

This article has set out a method of building a time series model for weekly observations. The key feature of the model is the setting up of the seasonal component in terms of a periodic component and a movable dummy component. The former is parsimoniously modeled with a periodic spline, though a trigonometric formulation could also be adopted and might be preferable in different circumstances.

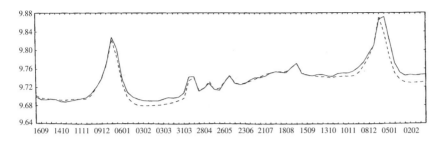

Fig. 10. Multistep predictions from September 9, 1992.

In our application the moving-festival component was primarily needed to deal with observations about Easter. Note, however, that, in countries where carnival is celebrated, the position of Easter may have important effects in February or early March. In other countries, other moving festivals, such as Chinese New Year, may be more relevant.

The structural time series approach has the advantage that once a regression formulation has been found it can be extended to allow the effects to evolve over time. In other words, a deterministic component can be generalized so that it becomes stochastic. Furthermore, it is possible to build in constraints that ensure that the forecasts of the seasonal component sum to 0 over a year, thereby ensuring that there is no confounding of trend and seasonal effects. Once such a model has been formulated, statistical handling via the state-space form is relatively straightforward. When the parameters have been estimated, seasonal adjustment can be carried out by subtracting the smoothed periodic and moving-festival components. This seasonally adjusted series can be continuously updated as new observations arrive.

The preceding approach is fairly general and should be applicable, with minor modifications, to other weekly series and indeed to other types of series in which data arrive at regular or irregular intervals throughout the year.

Acknowledgements

We thank John Thorp and Andrew Derry at the Bank of England, for supplying the data and related information, and two referees and Andrew Scott for helpful comments. We are grateful to the Economic and Social Research Council for financial support as part of our project on Interrelationships in Economic Time Series, grant R000 23 5330.

Appendix A: Periodic Cubic Splines

This appendix presents the derivation of a cubic spline function $g(x)$ that approximates an unknown function $f(x)$. Periodic cubic splines are subjected to special end-conditions. The cubic spline is defined as a set of polynomial functions differentiable up to order 3 with the first two derivatives continuous. The set of coordinates $(x_i^\dagger, y_i^\dagger)$ with $i = 0, 1, \ldots, k$, will be referred to as the set of knot points associated with the mesh $(x_0^\dagger, \ldots, x_k^\dagger)$. In this appendix, the knot coordinates are treated as fixed and known. Section 2.2 describes how the $y_i^\dagger$'s are estimated when they are allowed to change over time. It will be shown that the cubic spline function is derived as a set of linear equations; see also Poirier (1976).

Let us assume that the mesh is in ascending order,

$$x_0^\dagger < x_1^\dagger < \cdots < x_k^\dagger. \tag{A.1}$$

Let $h_j = x_j^\dagger - x_{j-1}^\dagger$, $j = 1, \ldots, k$, and let $d_j(x)$ and $d_j^2(x)$ denote the first and second derivatives, respectively, of the spline function $g(x)$ calculated in the interval $[x_{j-1}^\dagger, x_j^\dagger]$. The cubic spline function is a mixture of polynomials of order 3, so its second derivative within $[x_{j-1}^\dagger, x_j^\dagger]$ will be linear; that is,

$$d_j^2(x) = \frac{x_j^\dagger - x}{h_j} a_{j-1} + \frac{x - x_{j-1}^\dagger}{h_j} a_j, \quad j = 1, \ldots, k. \tag{A.2}$$

The scalar a_j is the second derivative of the spline function at the knot point $x_j^\dagger$; that is, $a_j = d_j^2(x_j^\dagger)$. Starting from (A.2), the cubic spline and the periodic spline are easily derived by the following steps:

1. Expressions for the first derivative function and the cubic spline function $g(x)$ are obtained via standard rules of integration. The spline function is forced to cross the knots; that is, $g_j(x_j^\dagger) = y_j^\dagger$ and $g_j(x_{j-1}^\dagger) = y_{j-1}^\dagger$. This leads to

$$g_j(x) = (x_j^\dagger - x)\frac{[(x_j^\dagger - x)^2 - h_j^2]}{6h_j}a_{j-1} + \frac{x_j^\dagger - x}{h_j}y_{j-1}^\dagger$$
$$+ (x - x_{j-1}^\dagger)\frac{[(x - x_{j-1}^\dagger)^2 - h_j^2]}{6h_j}a_j + \frac{x - x_{j-1}^\dagger}{h_j}y_j^\dagger \tag{A.3}$$

and

$$d_j(x) = -\left[\frac{1}{2}\frac{(x_j^\dagger - x)^2}{h_j} - \frac{h_j}{6}\right]a_{j-1} + \left[\frac{1}{2}\frac{(x - x_{j-1}^\dagger)^2}{h_j} - \frac{h_j}{6}\right]a_j \tag{A.4}$$

with $x_{j-1}^\dagger \leq x \leq x_j^\dagger$, $j = 1, 2, \ldots, k$.

2. The spline function (A.3) can be expressed in vector notation via

$$g_j(x) = \mathbf{r}'_j \mathbf{y}^\dagger + \mathbf{s}'_j \mathbf{a}, \tag{A.5}$$

where $\mathbf{a} = (a_0, \ldots, a_k)'$, $\mathbf{y}^\dagger = (y_0^\dagger, \ldots, y_k^\dagger)'$, and the vectors $\mathbf{r}_j$ and $\mathbf{s}_j$ are equal to 0 except for their jth and $(j+1)$th elements, which correspond to the appropriate weights of (A.3).

3. The continuity restriction also applies to the first derivative (A.4), $d_j(x_j^\dagger) = d_{j+1}(x_j^\dagger)$. After some minor manipulations, we obtain a set of $k - 1$ linear restrictions

$$\frac{h_j}{h_j + h_{j+1}} a_{j-1} + 2a_j + \frac{h_{j+1}}{h_j + h_{j+1}} a_{j+1} = \frac{6y_{j-1}^\dagger}{h_j(h_j + h_{j+1})} - \frac{6y_j^\dagger}{h_j h_{j+1}}$$

$$+ \frac{6y_{j+1}^\dagger}{h_{j+1}(h_j + h_{j+1})}, \quad j = 1, 2, \ldots, k - 1. \tag{A.6}$$

4. A system of $k - 1$ linear equations with $k + 1$ unknowns a_j cannot be solved unless two linear restrictions are added. Poirier (1976) suggested setting $a_0 = a_k = 0$, which he defined as a *natural* condition for a spline. With these two additional constraints the system of equations (A.6) can be represented in matrix notation as

$$\mathbf{Pa} = \mathbf{Qy}^\dagger, \tag{A.7}$$

where

$$\mathbf{P} = \begin{pmatrix} 2 & 0 & 0 & \cdots & 0 & 0 \\ \dfrac{h_1}{h_1 + h_2} & 2 & \dfrac{h_2}{h_1 + h_2} & \cdots & 0 & 0 \\ 0 & \dfrac{h_2}{h_2 + h_3} & 2 & \cdots & 0 & 0 \\ 0 & 0 & \dfrac{h_3}{h_3 + h_4} & \cdots & 0 & 0 \\ 0 & 0 & 0 & \cdots & 0 & 0 \\ \vdots & \vdots & \vdots & \ddots & \vdots & \vdots \\ 0 & 0 & 0 & \cdots & 2 & \dfrac{h_k}{h_{k-1} + h_k} \\ 0 & 0 & 0 & \cdots & 0 & 2 \end{pmatrix} \tag{A.8}$$

and

$$
Q = \begin{pmatrix}
0 & 0 & 0 & \cdots & 0 & 0 \\
\dfrac{6}{h_1(h_1+h_2)} & -\dfrac{6}{h_1 h_2} & \dfrac{6}{h_2(h_1+h_2)} & \cdots & 0 & 0 \\
0 & \dfrac{6}{h_2(h_2+h_3)} & -\dfrac{6}{h_2 h_3} & \cdots & 0 & 0 \\
0 & 0 & \dfrac{6}{h_3(h_3+h_4)} & \cdots & 0 & 0 \\
0 & 0 & 0 & \cdots & 0 & 0 \\
\vdots & \vdots & \vdots & \ddots & \vdots & \vdots \\
0 & 0 & 0 & \cdots & -\dfrac{6}{h_{k-1}h_k} & \dfrac{6}{h_k(h_{k-1}+h_k)} \\
0 & 0 & 0 & \cdots & 0 & 0
\end{pmatrix}.
$$

$$(A.9)$$

5. The matrices $\mathbf{P}$ and $\mathbf{Q}$ have dimension $(k+1) \times (k+1)$. Note that the first and the last rows of $\mathbf{P}$ and $\mathbf{Q}$ represent the *natural* constraints $a_0 = a_k = 0$. The solution for $\mathbf{a}$ is

$$\mathbf{a} = \mathbf{P}^{-1}\mathbf{Q}\mathbf{y}^{\dagger} \tag{A.10}$$

so that (A.5) becomes

$$g_j(x) = \mathbf{w}_j' \mathbf{y}^{\dagger} \tag{A.11}$$

with

$$\mathbf{w}_i' = \mathbf{r}_j' + \mathbf{s}_j' \mathbf{P}^{-1}\mathbf{Q}. \tag{A.12}$$

This shows that, given a set of k knots with a particular vector $\mathbf{y}^{\dagger}$, the *natural* spline $g(x)$ can be calculated for any $x_0^{\dagger} \le x \le x_k^{\dagger}$. Note that if x equals $x_j^{\dagger}, 0 \le j \le k$, vector $\mathbf{w}_j$ is $\mathbf{0}$ except for its jth element, which equals unity and hence $g(x_j^{\dagger}) = y_j^{\dagger}$.

6. The cubic spline becomes periodic when the first and the last knots are restricted to be the same. The continuity is enforced by letting the corresponding first and second derivatives to be the same as well; that is,

$$y_0^{\dagger} = y_k^{\dagger}, \qquad d_1(x_0^{\dagger}) = d_k(x_k^{\dagger}), \qquad d_1^2(x_0^{\dagger}) = d_k^2(x_k^{\dagger}). \tag{A.13}$$

The second restriction of (A.13) implies

$$\frac{h_k}{h_1+h_k}a_{k-1} + 2a_k + \frac{h_1}{h_1+h_k}a_1 = \frac{6y_{k-1}^{\dagger}}{h_k(h_1+h_k)} - \frac{6y_k^{\dagger}}{h_1 h_k} + \frac{6y_1^{\dagger}}{h_1(h_1+h_k)}, \tag{A.14}$$

which can be added to the set of linear restrictions (A.6). The last restriction of (A.13) sets $a_0 = a_k$. Therefore, the *natural* constraints are no longer required because we now have a system of k linear restrictions and k unknowns. The $(k \times k)$ matrices $\mathbf{P}_p$ and $\mathbf{Q}_p$ for a periodic spline become

$$\mathbf{P}_p = \begin{pmatrix} 2 & \dfrac{h_2}{h_1+h_2} & 0 & \cdots & 0 & \dfrac{h_1}{h_1+h_2} \\[2mm] \dfrac{h_2}{h_2+h_3} & 2 & \dfrac{h_3}{h_2+h_3} & \cdots & 0 & 0 \\[2mm] 0 & \dfrac{h_3}{h_3+h_4} & 2 & \cdots & 0 & 0 \\[2mm] 0 & 0 & \dfrac{h_4}{h_4+h_5} & \cdots & 0 & 0 \\[2mm] 0 & 0 & 0 & \cdots & 0 & 0 \\[1mm] \vdots & \vdots & \vdots & \vdots & \vdots & \vdots \\[1mm] 0 & 0 & 0 & \cdots & 2 & \dfrac{h_k}{h_{k-1}+h_k} \\[2mm] \dfrac{h_1}{h_1+h_k} & 0 & 0 & \cdots & \dfrac{h_k}{h_1+h_k} & 2 \end{pmatrix} \tag{A.15}$$

and

$$\mathbf{Q}_p = \begin{pmatrix} -\dfrac{6}{h_1 h_2} & \dfrac{6}{h_2(h_1+h_2)} & 0 & \cdots & 0 & \dfrac{6}{h_1(h_1+h_2)} \\[2mm] \dfrac{6}{h_2(h_2+h_3)} & -\dfrac{6}{h_2 h_3} & \dfrac{6}{h_3(h_2+h_3)} & \cdots & 0 & 0 \\[2mm] 0 & \dfrac{6}{h_3(h_3+h_4)} & -\dfrac{6}{h_3 h_4} & \cdots & 0 & 0 \\[2mm] 0 & 0 & \dfrac{6}{h_4(h_4+h_5)} & \cdots & 0 & 0 \\[2mm] 0 & 0 & 0 & \cdots & 0 & 0 \\[1mm] \vdots & \vdots & \vdots & \ddots & \vdots & \vdots \\[1mm] 0 & 0 & 0 & \cdots & -\dfrac{6}{h_{k-1}h_k} & \dfrac{6}{h_k(h_{k-1}+h_k)} \\[2mm] \dfrac{6}{h_1(h_1+h_k)} & 0 & 0 & \cdots & \dfrac{6}{h_k(h_1+h_k)} & -\dfrac{6}{h_1 h_k} \end{pmatrix}.$$

$$\tag{A.16}$$

Furthermore, the $(k \times 1)$ vectors $\mathbf{a}, \mathbf{y}, \mathbf{r}_j$, and $\mathbf{s}_j$, $j = 1, \ldots, k$, are adjusted appropriately, also with respect to the first restriction of (A.13).

In the main body of the article vector $\mathbf{w}_*$ is defined in (2.5) as

$$\mathbf{w}_* = \sum_{j=1}^{k} \mathbf{w}_j, \tag{A.17}$$

where $\mathbf{w}_j$, $j = 1, \ldots, k$, must be computed even if the evaluation of the spline at position j is not required. Therefore, when k is large, the calculation of $\mathbf{w}_*$ may become a computational burden. An alternative expression for $\mathbf{w}_*$ is

$$\mathbf{w}'_* = \mathbf{r}'_* + \mathbf{s}'_* \mathbf{P}_p^{-1} \mathbf{Q}_p, \tag{A.18}$$

where $\mathbf{r}_* = \sum_{j=1}^{k} \mathbf{r}_j$ and $\mathbf{s}_* = \sum_{j=1}^{k} \mathbf{s}_j$ can be analytically derived as

$$\mathbf{r}_* = \left(\frac{x_2^\dagger - x_0^\dagger}{2}, \ldots, \frac{x_k^\dagger - x_{k-2}^\dagger}{2}, \frac{x_1^\dagger - x_0^\dagger + x_k^\dagger - x_{k-1}^\dagger}{2} \right)' \tag{A.19}$$

and

$$\mathbf{s}_* = \left(\frac{x_2^\dagger - x_0^\dagger - h_2^3 - h_1^3}{24}, \ldots, \frac{x_k^\dagger - x_{k-2}^\dagger - h_k^3 - h_{k-1}^3}{24}, \right.$$

$$\left. \frac{h_1(1 - h_1^2) + h_k(1 - h_k^2)}{24} \right)'. \tag{A.20}$$

Appendix B: State-Space Methods and Seasonal Adjustment

The full model (4.1) can be put in state-space form; that is,

$$y_t = \mathbf{Z}_t \boldsymbol{\alpha}_t + \mathbf{G}_t \mathbf{u}_t, \quad \mathbf{u}_t \sim NID(\mathbf{0}, \mathbf{I}),$$

$$\boldsymbol{\alpha}_{t+1} = \mathbf{T}_t \boldsymbol{\alpha}_t + \mathbf{H}_t \mathbf{u}_t, \quad t = 1, \ldots, T, \tag{B.1}$$

where $\mathbf{Z}_t$ is given in (4.2) and the matrices $\mathbf{T}_t$, $\mathbf{G}_t$, and $\mathbf{H}_t$ are constructed straightforwardly. Note that the matrices $\mathbf{G}_t$ and $\mathbf{T}_t$ are time-invariant, but matrix $\mathbf{H}_t$ is time-varying because the variances of the periodic effect are forced to increase around the Christmas period. The disturbance vector $\mathbf{u}_t$ is the stack of all disturbances associated with the unobserved components of the model including the irregular ε_t. The initial state $\boldsymbol{\alpha}_1$ is treated as a random vector generated from a diffuse distribution.

The Kalman filter, or its more stable counterpart the "square root" Kalman filter, is used for the evaluation of the likelihood and for the calculation of one-step-ahead prediction errors. The Kalman filter is given by

$$v_t = y_t - \mathbf{Z}_t \mathbf{a}_{t|t-1},$$

$$f_t = \mathbf{Z}_t \mathbf{P}_{t|t-1} \mathbf{Z}'_t + \mathbf{G}_t \mathbf{G}'_t,$$

$$\mathbf{K}_t = \mathbf{T}_t \mathbf{P}_{t|t-1} \mathbf{Z}'_t f_t^{-1},$$

$$\mathbf{a}_{t+1|t} = \mathbf{T}_t \mathbf{a}_{t|t-1} + \mathbf{K}_t v_t,$$

$$\mathbf{P}_{t+1|t} = \mathbf{T}_t \mathbf{P}_{t|t-1} \mathbf{T}'_t - f_t \mathbf{K}_t \mathbf{K}'_t + \mathbf{H}_t \mathbf{H}'_t, \tag{B.2}$$

with the initializations $\mathbf{a}_{1|0} = \mathbf{0}$ and $\mathbf{P}_{1|0} = \kappa \mathbf{I}$, where κ is a suitably chosen large number. The vector $\mathbf{a}_{t|t-1}$ is the one-step-ahead prediction of the state $\boldsymbol{\alpha}_t$ with

Table	B.1. Computational		performance
		of smoothing	

Algorithm	Multiplications	Storage	Seconds
De Jong (1989)	1,024	594	14.7
Koopman (1993)	62	34	1.8

its mean squared error matrix $\mathbf{P}_{t|t-1}$. The one-step-ahead prediction error and its variance are given by v_t and f_t, respectively. The vector $\mathbf{K}_t$ is referred to as the Kalman gain. Usually, the Kalman filter is computationally not very demanding but model (4.1) requires a large state vector that leads to a computational effort with respect to $\mathbf{P}_{t|t-1}$. Of course, the computations take longer as the number of observations increases.

A state smoothing algorithm is designed to compute full-sample estimates of the state vector. The estimated trend and periodic components can be extracted from the smoothed state vector, and they can be graphically reproduced as part of a validation procedure of the estimated model. Seasonal adjustment procedures remove seasonal and periodic variation from the observed series and, therefore, in the context of state-space models, they require a state smoother. Smoothing algorithms are computationally expensive, especially when the state vector is large, and they require much storage space because a selection of Kalman filter quantities needs to be stored for $t = 1, \ldots, T$.

We consider two different state smoothers, proposed by De Jong (1989) and Koopman (1993). Table B.1 reports the number of multiplications for each time index t, the number of values to be stored for each time index t, and total computer time required for smoothing a series of 1,500 observations on a Pentium processor with clock speed 90 MHz. The model considered is (4.1) with 20 knots for the periodic spline and 10 stochastic dummy variables for the moving-festival effects. The results show dramatically that the smoothing algorithm of Koopman (1993) outperforms the algorithm of De Jong (1989) with respect to all indicators. Koopman's algorithm does not give the mean squared errors of the smoothed estimators of the state vector, but for many applications this is not necessary. Koopman's smoothing algorithm is a two-step approach. First, a backward disturbance smoother is applied; that is, $e_t = v_t/f_t - \mathbf{K}_t'\mathbf{r}_t$, $\mathbf{r}_{t-1} = \mathbf{Z}_t'e_t + \mathbf{T}_t'\mathbf{r}_t$, $t = T, \ldots, 1$, with initialization $\mathbf{r}_T = \mathbf{0}$. The Kalman filter only needs to store the scalar v_t/f_t and the vector $\mathbf{K}_t$, $t = 1, \ldots, T$. The storage space can be overwritten to store the vector $\mathbf{n}_t = \mathbf{H}_t\mathbf{H}_t'\mathbf{r}_t$. Second, the forward recursion $\mathbf{a}_{t+1|T} = \mathbf{T}_t\mathbf{a}_{t|T} + \mathbf{n}_t$, $t = 1, \ldots, T - 1$, must be used with initialization $\mathbf{a}_{1|T} = \mathbf{a}_{1|0} + \mathbf{P}_{1|0}\mathbf{r}_0$. The storage space can be overwritten by the smoothed state vector $\mathbf{a}_{t|T}$.

References

Bell, W. R., and Hillmer, S. C. (1983), "Modeling Time Series With Calendar Variation," *Journal of the American Statistical Association*, 78, 526–534.

De Jong, P. (1989), "Smoothing and Interpolation With the State Space Model," *Journal of the American Statistical Association*, 84, 1085–1088.

——(1991), "The Diffuse Kalman Filter," *The Annals of Statistics*, 19, 1073–1083.

Harvey, A. C. (1989), *Forecasting, Structural Time Series Models and the Kalman Filter*, Cambridge, U.K.: Cambridge University Press.

Harvey, A. C., and Koopman, S. J. (1993), "Forecasting Hourly Electricity Demand Using Time-Varying Splines," *Journal of the American Statistical Association*, 88, 1228–1236.

Hillmer, S. C., and Tiao, G. C. (1982), "An ARIMA-Model-Based Approach to Seasonal Adjustment," *Journal of the American Statistical Association*, 77, 63–70.

Kitagawa, G., and Gersch, W. (1984), "A Smoothness Priors-State Space Modeling of Time Series With Trend and Seasonality," *Journal of the American Statistical Association*, 79, 378–389.

Koopman, S. J. (1993), "Disturbance Smoother for State Space Models," *Biometrika*, 80, 117–126.

Maravall, A. (1985), "On Structural Time Series Models and the Characterization of Components," *Journal of Business & Economic Statistics*, 3, 350–355.

Pierce, D. A., Grupe, M. R., and Cleveland, W. P. (1984), "Seasonal Adjustment of the Weekly Monetary Aggregates: A Model-Based Approach," *Journal of Business & Economic Statistics*, 2, 260–270.

Poirier, D. (1976), *The Econometrics of Structural Change: With Special Emphasis on Spline Functions*, Amsterdam: North-Holland.

Scott, A. (1995), "Why Is Consumption so Seasonal?" CEP discussion paper, London School of Economics.

Part III

Testing in Unobserved Components Models

13

Introduction

This part of the book considers the issues involved in testing in unobserved components models. The most important, and most interesting, tests are those concerned with whether or not certain variances are zero. In other words is a particular component actually present? The non-stationary nature of many components means that the asymptotic distributions of the test statistics are non-standard. However, it turns out that using the Lagrange multiplier principle to construct tests often leads to statistics that have asymptotic distributions belonging to the class of under of Cramér-von Mises distributions. The same ideas can be used in tests of unit roots, leading to a nice unification of the statistical theory. However, the emphasis here is on tests for the presence of unobserved components. Particular attention is paid to stationarity tests and seasonality tests. There is also some discussion of how structural breaks may be handled and what hypotheses may be tested in multivariate models.

1 Stationarity and Unit Roots Tests

The issues which arise in testing in unobserved components models can be introduced by considering a simple AR(1) plus noise model for a set of T observations, y_t,

$$ y_t = \alpha + \mu_t + \varepsilon_t, \qquad \mu_t = \phi\mu_{t-1} + \eta_t, \quad t = 1, \ldots, T, \tag{13.1} $$

where the $\eta_t's$ and $\varepsilon_t's$ are mutually and serially independent Gaussian disturbances with variances σ_η^2 and σ_ε^2 respectively and $\mu_0 = 0$. If $\sigma_\varepsilon^2 = 0$, the model reduces to a pure AR(1). A test of the hypothesis that $\phi = 0$, against the alternative that $\phi \neq 0$ is straightforwardly carried out. It can be based either on the t-statistic of the coefficient of y_{t-1} in a regression of y_t on y_{t-1} and a constant or on the first-order autocorrelation. In both cases the test statistic is asymptotically standard normal, though a small sample test is available in the form of the von Neumann ratio. A test of the null hypothesis that $\phi = 1$ against the alternative that $\phi < 1$ can also be tested using the t-statistic of the coefficient of y_{t-1}, but this time the dependent variable is Δy_t. Thus the null hypothesis is that the series is a random walk (plus drift if α is non-zero) while the alternative is that the series is stationary. Under the null hypothesis this statistic has a non-standard limiting distribution that depends on functions of Brownian motion. It is known as the Dickey-Fuller test and is the leading example of a unit root test; see Maddala and Kim (2000). The augmented

Dickey-Fuller test is a generalisation in which lagged difference are included in the regression to account for serial correlation; the asymptotic distribution of the *t-statistic* is not affected.

Setting $\phi = 1$ in (13.1) yields the random walk plus noise model, introduced earlier in (7.3). This is the simplest example of a structural time series model, often referred to as the local level model. If $\sigma_\eta^2 = 0$, the random walk becomes a constant level. A test of the null hypothesis that $\sigma_\eta^2 = 0$, against the alternative that $\sigma_\eta^2 > 0$, is therefore fundamental. Nyblom and Mäkeläinen (1983) showed that the locally best invariant test (LBI) test can be formulated as

$$\eta = T^{-2} \sum_{i=1}^{T} \left[\sum_{t=1}^{i} e_t \right]^2 \bigg/ s^2 > c, \qquad (13.2)$$

where $e_t = y_t - \bar{y}$, $s^2 = T^{-1} \sum_{t=1}^{T} (y_t - \bar{y})^2$ and c is a critical value. The test can also be interpreted as a one-sided Lagrange multiplier (LM) test. This is in contrast to the Dickey-Fuller test, which is a Wald test. It is the simplest example of a stationarity test. While a unit root test takes the null hypothesis to be one of non-stationarity, with the alternative a stationary process, a stationarity test operates in the opposite direction.

The asymptotic distribution of the η statistic under the null hypothesis is the (first level) Cramér-von Mises distribution, denoted CvM_1; see Harvey (2001). The normality assumption is not necessary. It is sufficient for the observations to be martingale differences (with finite variance) to yield this asymptotic distribution; see, for example, Stock (1994, p. 2745). The result follows because the partial sum of deviations from the mean converges weakly to a standard Brownian bridge, that is

$$\sigma^{-1} T^{-1/2} \sum_{s=1}^{[Tr]} e_s \Rightarrow B(r), \quad r \in [0, 1], \qquad (13.3)$$

where $[Tr]$ is the largest integer less than or equal to Tr, while $s^2 \xrightarrow{P} \sigma^2$. If a linear time trend is included in (13.1) the resulting test statistic, η_2, has a (second level) Cramér-von Mises distribution, CvM_2, under the null hypothesis. The paper by Nyblom (1986, Chapter 14) deals with this case. Nyblom (1989) tabulates critical values using an analytic expression for the distribution function. Tanaka (1996, pp 405–16) describes a slightly different approach based on Fredholm determinants. Reference should also be made to MacNeill (1978). An analysis of the local asymptotic power of the above tests can be found in Stock and Watson (1998).

Now suppose that the model is extended so that ε_t is any indeterministic stationary process. In this case the asymptotic distribution of the η test statistic remains the same if s^2 is replaced by a consistent estimator of the long-run variance (the spectrum at frequency zero). Kwiatkowski et al (1992) – often referred to as

KPSS – construct such an estimator nonparametrically as

$$s_L^2(\ell) = T^{-1} \sum_{t=1}^{T} e_t^2 + 2T^{-1} \sum_{\tau=1}^{\ell} w(\tau, \ell) \sum_{t=\tau+1}^{T} e_t e_{t-\tau}$$

$$= \hat{\gamma}(0) + 2 \sum_{\tau=1}^{\ell} w(\tau, \ell)\hat{\gamma}(\tau), \tag{13.4}$$

where $w(\tau, \ell)$ is a weighting function, such as $w(\tau, \ell) = 1 - \tau/(\ell + 1)$, $\tau = 1, \ldots, \ell$ and ℓ is the lag length. Other weighting functions may be used; see Andrews (1993).

Leybourne and McCabe (1994) attack the problem of serial correlation by introducing lagged dependent variables into the model. The test statistic obtained after removing the effect of the lagged dependent variables is then of the same form as (13.2). The practical implication, as demonstrated in their Monte Carlo results, is a gain in power. However, more calculation is involved since the coefficients of the lagged dependent variables are estimated under the alternative hypothesis and this requires numerical optimization. Since we are testing for the presence of an unobserved component it seems natural to work with structural time series models. If the process generating the stationary part of the model were known, the LBI test for the presence of a random walk component could be constructed. Harvey and Streibel (1997) derive such a test and show how it is formed from a set of 'smoothing errors'. As shown in Harvey and Koopman (1992, Chapter 5), the smoothing errors are, in general, serially correlated but the form of this serial correlation may be deduced from the specification of the model. Hence a (parametric) estimator of the long-run variance may be constructed and used to form a statistic which has a Cramér-von Mises distribution, asymptotically, under the null hypothesis. An alternative possibility is to use the standardized one-step ahead prediction errors (innovations), calculated assuming that μ_0 is fixed[1]. No correction is then needed and, although the test is not strictly LBI, its asymptotic distribution is the same and the evidence presented in Harvey and Streibel (1997) suggests that, in small samples, it is more reliable in terms of size. As in the Leybourne-McCabe test, the nuisance parameters need to be estimated and this is best done under the alternative hypothesis. The test statistic is then calculated from the innovations or the smoothing errors with σ_η^2 set to zero.

Kuo (1999) presents the asymptotic theory for the local (marginal) ML estimator of the signal-noise ratio $q = \sigma_\eta^2/\sigma_\varepsilon^2$ in the local level model. He gives tables for the LR test of the null hypothesis that $q = 0$, with critical values established empirically for $T = 50$ and $T = 100$ and theoretically for $T = \infty$. These tests may have higher power than the LM test of (13.2), but this needs to be demonstrated. There is also the question as to whether the same tables can be used when the model contains other components, such as trends and cycles.

Unit root tests can also be set up using the Lagrange multiplier principle and this has the attraction that asymptotic distributions belonging to the class of Cramér-von

Mises distributions are obtained under the null hypothesis. Further details can be found in Harvey (2004).

Before leaving model (13.1) we consider how to test the hypothesis that $\sigma_\varepsilon^2 = 0$. This is actually a more standard problem than testing whether $\sigma_\eta^2 = 0$, since the presence or otherwise of ε_t does not affect whether the model is stationary in levels or differences. However, the fact that the parameter is on a boundary under the null means that the likelihood ratio test statistic has an asymptotic distribution under the null that is an equal mixture of χ_1^2 and χ_0^2 variables. On the other hand the Lagrange multiplier test can be based on $\sqrt{T}r(1)$, where $r(1)$ is the first-order residual autocorrelation in the differenced series. The test is one-sided, rejecting for negative values smaller than the critical value obtained from the standard normal distribution. More generally, though, constructing an LM test for the presence of an irregular component is not straightforward; see Tanaka (2002).

2 Seasonality

Stationarity tests may be generalised to test whether other components are deterministic or nonstationary. With quarterly or monthly time series, structural time series models typically include a nonstationary seasonal component. The extent to which the seasonal pattern evolves depends on the variance of disturbances driving the process. If this is zero the seasonal pattern is fixed and so can be captured by dummy variables.

Consider a Gaussian model with a trigonometric seasonal component:

$$y_t = \mu + \gamma_t + \varepsilon_t, \quad t = 1, \ldots, T, \tag{13.5}$$

where μ is a constant and

$$\gamma_t = \sum_{j=1}^{[s/2]} \gamma_{j,t}, \tag{13.6}$$

where s is the number of seasons and each $\gamma_{j,t}$ is generated by

$$\begin{bmatrix} \gamma_{j,t} \\ \gamma_{j,t}^* \end{bmatrix} = \begin{bmatrix} \cos\lambda_j & \sin\lambda_j \\ -\sin\lambda_j & \cos\lambda_j \end{bmatrix} \begin{bmatrix} \gamma_{j,t-1} \\ \gamma_{j,t-1}^* \end{bmatrix} + \begin{bmatrix} \omega_{j,t} \\ \omega_{j,t}^* \end{bmatrix}, \quad \begin{matrix} j = 1, \ldots, [s/2], \\ t-1, \ldots, T, \end{matrix} \tag{13.7}$$

where $\lambda_j = 2\pi j/s$ is frequency, in radians, and $\omega_{j,t}$ and $\omega_{j,t}^*$ are two mutually uncorrelated white noise disturbances with zero means and common variance σ_j^2. For s even $[s/2] = s/2$, while for s odd, $[s/2] = (s-1)/2$. For s even, the component at $j = s/2$ collapses to

$$\gamma_{j,t} = \gamma_{j,t-1}\cos\lambda_j + \omega_{j,t} = \gamma_{j,t-1}(-1)^t + \omega_{j,t}, \quad j = s/2. \tag{13.8}$$

This is the standard formulation of a non-stationary seasonal component in the structural time series modelling framework. The presence of the disturbances allows the seasonal pattern to evolve over time; if they are not present, the seasonal pattern is fixed. The paper by Canova and Hansen (1995), the second reading in this part, sets up a test against the presence of a stochastic trigonometric component at any one of the seasonal frequencies, λ_j. If ε_t is white noise, the LBI test for the null hypothesis that σ_j^2 is zero is, for $j = 1, \ldots, [(s-1)/2]$,

$$\omega_j = 2T^{-2}s^{-2} \sum_{i=1}^{T} \left[\left(\sum_{t=1}^{i} e_t \cos \lambda_j t \right)^2 + \left(\sum_{t=1}^{i} e_t \sin \lambda_j t \right)^2 \right], \qquad (13.9)$$

where s^2 is the sample variance of the OLS residuals from a regression on sines and cosines. Canova and Hansen show that the asymptotic distribution of this statistic is Cramér-von Mises with two degrees of freedom[2], that is $CvM_1(2)$. The component at π gives rise to a test statistic

$$\omega_{s/2} = T^{-2}s^{-2} \sum_{i=1}^{T} \left(\sum_{t=1}^{i} e_t \cos \lambda_{s/2} t \right)^2, \qquad (13.10)$$

which has a Cramér-von Mises asymptotic with only one degree of freedom. A joint test against the presence of stochastic trigonometric components at all seasonal frequencies is based on a statistic, ω, obtained by summing the individual test statistics. Busetti and Harvey (2003) show that this is the LM test if $\sigma_j^2 = \sigma_\omega^2$ for all j except $j = s/2$ when $\sigma_{s/2}^2 = \sigma_\omega^2/2$. The statistic has an asymptotic distribution which is $CvM_1(s-1)$. If desired it can be combined with a test against a random walk to give a test statistic which is $CvM_1(s)$ when both level and seasonal are deterministic.

Canova and Hansen show how the above tests can be generalized to handle serial correlation and heteroscedasticity by making a correction similar to that in KPSS. If the model contains a stochastic trend, then the test must be carried out on differenced observations. A parametric test may be carried out by fitting an unobserved components model. If there is a trend it may be a deterministic trend, a random walk, with or without drift, or a trend with a stochastic slope. Busetti and Harvey (2003) compare the two types of test.

Busetti and Harvey (2003) propose a test for any kind of seasonality, deterministic or stochastic. No seasonal dummies are fitted and the asymptotic distribution of the test statistic is $CvM_0(s-1)$. If seasonal slopes are included, as in Smith and Taylor (1998), the test statistic is $CvM_2(s-1)$.

3 Multivariate Stationarity and Unit Root Tests

If y_t is a vector containing N time series the Gaussian multivariate local level model is

$$\begin{aligned} y_t &= \mu_t + \varepsilon_t, & \varepsilon_t &\sim NID(0, \Sigma_\varepsilon), \\ \mu_t &= \mu_{t-1} + \eta_t, & \eta_t &\sim NID(0, \Sigma_\eta), \quad t = 1, \ldots, T, \end{aligned} \qquad (13.11)$$

where Σ_ε is an $N \times N$ positive definite (p.d.) matrix. Nyblom and Harvey (2000) show that an LBI test of the null hypothesis that $\Sigma_\eta = 0$ can be constructed against the homogeneous alternative $\Sigma_\eta = q\Sigma_\varepsilon$. The test has the rejection region

$$\eta(N) = \text{tr}[S^{-1}C] > c, \qquad (13.12)$$

where

$$C = T^{-2} \sum_{i=1}^{T} \left[\sum_{t=1}^{i} e_t \right] \left[\sum_{t=1}^{i} e_t \right]' \quad \text{and} \quad S = T^{-1} \sum_{t=1}^{T} e_t e_t', \qquad (13.13)$$

where $e_t = y_t - \bar{y}$. Under the null hypothesis, the limiting distribution of (13.12) is Cramér-von Mises with N degrees of freedom, $CvM(N)$. The distribution is $CvM_2(N)$ if the model contains a vector of time trends. Although the test maximizes the power against homogeneous alternatives, it is consistent against all nonnull $\Sigma_\eta's$ since $T^{-1}\eta(N)$ has a nondegenerate limiting distribution. This limiting distribution depends only on the rank of Σ_η.

The $\eta(N)$ test can be generalized along the lines of the KPSS test quite straightforwardly. Parametric adjustments can also be made by the procedure outlined for univariate models. This requires estimation under the alternative hypothesis, but is likely to lead to an increase in power. If there are no constraints across parameters, it may be more convenient to construct the test statistic, (13.12), using the innovations from fitted univariate models. Kuo and Mikkola (2001) use the lagged dependent variable method of Leybourne and McCabe (1994) in their study of purchasing power parity. They conclude that dealing with serial correlation in this way leads to tests with higher power than those formed using the nonparametric correction.

4 Common Trends and Co-integration

If the rank of Σ_η in (13.11) is K, the model has K common trends. Suppose we wish to test the null hypothesis that model (13.11) has a specific number of common trends against the alternative that it has more. Formally the test is of

$$H_0 : \text{rank}(\Sigma_\eta) = K \qquad \text{against} \qquad H_1 : \text{rank}(\Sigma_\eta) > K, \quad K = 1, \ldots, N-1.$$
$$(13.14)$$

Let $\lambda_1 \geq \cdots \geq \lambda_N$ be the ordered eigenvalues of $S^{-1}C$. The $\eta(N)$ test statistic is the sum of these eigenvalues, but when the rank of Σ_η is $K^\dagger$, the limiting distribution of $T^{-1}\eta(N)$ is the limiting distribution of T^{-1} times the sum of the $K^\dagger$ largest eigenvalues. This suggests basing a test of the hypothesis that $\text{rank}(\Sigma_\eta) = K$ on the sum of the $N - K$ smallest eigenvalues, that is

$$\eta(K, N) = \lambda_{K+1} + \cdots + \lambda_N, \quad K = 1, \ldots, N-1. \qquad (13.15)$$

Then if $K^\dagger > K$ the relatively large values taken by the first $K^\dagger - K$ of these eigenvalues will tend to lead to the null hypothesis being rejected. This is the *common trends* test.

The distribution of the common trends test statistic under the null hypothesis is not of the Cramér-von Mises form but it does depend on functions of Brownian motion. The significance points for $\eta(K, N)$ depend on both K and N and are tabulated in Nyblom and Harvey (2000). A different set of critical values are used if the model has been extended to include time trends. Parametric and nonparametric adjustment for serial correlation may be made in the common trends test in much the same way as was suggested for the $\eta(N)$ test.

It is instructive to compare the common trends test with the co-integration test of Johansen (1988). In its simplest form this is based on the first-order vector autoregression, $y_t = \phi y_{t-1} + \varepsilon_t$, and the aim is determining the number of co-integrating vectors by testing the rank of $\Phi - I$. The number of co-integrating vectors is N minus the number of common trends. There is a parallel with unit roots and stationarity tests in that the hypotheses for the co-integration and common trends tests are in the opposite direction.

5 Structural Breaks

Busetti and Harvey (2001) show how the stationarity tests are affected by the inclusion of dummy variables designed to pick up structural breaks. Although the form of the test statistics is unchanged, their asymptotic distributions are altered. However, the additive properties of the Cramér-von Mises distribution suggest a simplified test that is much easier to implement. The effect on LM type unit root tests is then examined. These remain the same unless there are breaks in the slope in which case a modification along the lines proposed for stationarity tests leads to simplified statistics with Cramér-von Mises distributions under the null hypothesis. Similar results hold for seasonality tests when breaks in the seasonal pattern are modelled by dummy variables; see Busetti and Harvey (2003).

Busetti (2002) extends the multivariate tests to deal with situations where there are breaks in some or all of a set of N time series. He shows that a simplified version of the test against a multivariate random walk can be constructed by allowing for a break in all the series at the same point in time. This statistic has the $CvM(2N)$ asymptotic distribution. The modification of multivariate unit root tests follows along similar lines.

Notes

1. Note that backward smoothing recursions may be avoided simply by reversing the order of the observations and calculating the innovations starting from the filtered estimator of the final state.
2. Actually, Canova and Hansen derive the above statistic from a slightly different form of the stochastic cycle model in which the coefficients of a sine-cosine wave are taken to be random walks. However, it is not difficult to show that the model as defined above leads to the same test statistic.

14

Testing for Deterministic Linear Trend in Time Series*

JUKKA NYBLOM[†]

Department of Economics and Statistics, University of Joensuu, Finland

Most powerful tests are derived for the hypothesis that deterministic linear trend occurs in time series against the alternative that trend consists of random walk subject to drift. Comparisons of these tests and of the tests suggested by LaMotte and McWhorter (1978) are made in terms of exact powers and Pitman asymptotic relative efficiencies.

1 Introduction

In this article the simple time-varying parameter model

$$y_t = \mu_t + \varepsilon_t, \tag{1.1}$$

$$\mu_t = \mu_{t-1} + \beta + \delta_t, \quad t = 1, \ldots, T, \tag{1.2}$$

is considered. The disturbances $\varepsilon_1, \ldots, \varepsilon_T, \delta_1, \ldots, \delta_T$ are independent random variables with $\varepsilon_t \sim N(0, \sigma^2)$ and $\delta_t \sim N(0, \tau^2)$. Despite its simplicity, the model (1.1)–(1.2) may be useful in modeling macroeconomic time series. From (1.2) we see that the (unobserved) systematic part μ_t is a random walk with drift. The initial value μ_0 and the drift parameter β are taken fixed (but unknown). This model is a particular case of those studied by Garbade (1977), Harvey (1981, chap. 7), and LaMotte and McWhorter (1978). Permitting $\tau^2 = 0$, we obtain the global linear trend model. On the other hand, if $\tau^2 > 0$ we may think of the slopes $\mu_t - \mu_{t-1}$ as random variables independently drawn from the same distribution $N(\beta, \tau^2)$. From the prediction point of view (1.1)–(1.2) is one representative of those models that lead to exponentially smoothed forecasts. The Box–Jenkins approach provides another viewpoint. It is easily seen that (1.1)–(1.2) belongs to the subfamily of the integrated moving average (IMA)(1, 1) processes (see Box and Jenkins 1976, pp. 119–120).

* Reprinted from *Journal of the American Statistical Association*, "Testing for Deterministic Linear Trends in Time Series" by J. Nyblom, 545–549, Vol. 81, No. 394, June 1996. Reproduced here with the permission of the American Statistical Association.

[†] Jukka Nyblom is Lecturer in Statistics, Department of Economics and Statistics, University of Joensuu, P.O. Box 111, SF-80101 Joensuu, Finland. This research was made when the author was a Junior Research Fellow in the Academy of Finland. It is a part of his Ph.D. thesis, made under the supervision of T. Mäikelänen, to whom the author is deeply indebted. The author also thanks the referees and the associate editor for their helpful comments.

Because of the simplicity of the global linear-trend model, it may be argued that a diagnostic check for its adequacy is desirable before employing the more complex model (1.1)–(1.2). Therefore we wish to develop tests for the hypothesis $\rho = \tau^2/\sigma^2 = 0$ against $\rho > 0$—that is, for the presence of random walk coefficients in a particular linear regression model. Different test criteria are available, those suggested by LaMotte and McWhorter (1978) and the most powerful (invariant) tests put forward by Nyblom and Mäkeläinen (1983) (NM for short). Under the simple model obtained from (1.1)–(1.2) by imposing $\beta = 0$, the latter writers made detailed comparisons between the LaMotte–McWhorter tests and the locally most powerful test (the test having the steepest increase in power at the null hypothesis). In a recent article, Franzini and Harvey (1983) have developed most powerful tests for deterministic trend and seasonal components under a model containing (1.1)–(1.2) as a special case.

The main theme of this article is to make comparisons between the LaMotte–McWhorter tests and the most powerful tests. Thus requisite tables for the null distributions are given, and some exact powers and Pitman asymptotic relative efficiencies are calculated. Although the Pitman efficiency in the present case depends on the chosen significance level and on the asymptotic power, it is by no means useless. In fact, it offers a sound method for finding the most powerful test that promises to have good finite sample power properties over a wide range of alternatives. The success of the method is borne out by exact numerical calculations in Section 2.

Finally, any testing procedure involving the maximum likelihood estimator of ρ results in much more formidable distributional difficulties than those met in the following sections.

2 Test Statistics

Let us consider the model (1.1)–(1.2). We want to test the hypothesis $H_0 : \rho = \tau^2/\sigma^2 = 0$ against the alternative $H_A : \rho > 0$. Since the covariance matrix for the observations $(y_1, \ldots, y_T)' = \mathbf{y}$ is $\sigma^2(\mathbf{I} + \rho\mathbf{W})$ with $\mathbf{W} = [\min(s, t)]$, we are, in fact, testing the hypothesis of a scalar covariance matrix against an alternative involving one additional parameter—a problem that has been treated in some generality by King (1980). The most powerful invariant test against the alternative ρ_1 has the rejection region

$$M(\rho_1) = \tilde{\mathbf{e}}'(\mathbf{I} + \rho_1\mathbf{W})^{-1}\tilde{\mathbf{e}}/\hat{\mathbf{e}}'\hat{\mathbf{e}} < c, \tag{2.1}$$

where $\hat{\mathbf{e}}$ contains the ordinary least squares residuals and $\tilde{\mathbf{e}}$ contains the generalized least squares residuals with respect to the covariance matrix of the alternative hypothesis. The formula (2.1) involves an inversion of a large $T \times T$ matrix. In actual computation of $M(\rho_1)$, however, this inversion can be avoided by using the one-step prediction errors obtained recursively from the Kalman filter updating formula (Schweppe 1965; see also Garbade 1977; Harvey 1981, p. 205; and Franzini and Harvey 1983). The first two observations are used as starting values. Since (2.1) depends explicitly on ρ_1, no uniformly most powerful test exists. Therefore the locally most powerful test with the rejection region

$$L = \hat{\mathbf{e}}'\mathbf{W}\hat{\mathbf{e}}/\hat{\mathbf{e}}'\hat{\mathbf{e}} > c, \qquad (2.2)$$

is worth considering.

Let a $T \times (T-2)$ matrix be denoted by $\mathbf{Z}$ such that $E(\mathbf{Z}'\mathbf{y}) \equiv \mathbf{0}$ and $\mathbf{Z}'\mathbf{Z} = \mathbf{I}$. From King (1980) we find that

$$\tilde{\mathbf{e}}'(\mathbf{I} + \rho_1\mathbf{W})^{-1}\tilde{\mathbf{e}} = \mathbf{y}'\mathbf{Z}(\mathbf{I} + \rho_1\mathbf{Z}'\mathbf{W}\mathbf{Z})^{-1}\mathbf{Z}'\mathbf{y}.$$

Using the distribution of $\mathbf{Z}'\mathbf{y}$ and the identity $\hat{\mathbf{e}}'\hat{\mathbf{e}} = \mathbf{y}'\mathbf{Z}\mathbf{Z}'\mathbf{y}$, after an appropriate linear transformation we obtain

$$M(\rho_1) = \sum_{k=1}^{T-2}(1 + \rho_1\lambda_{k,T-2})^{-1}u_{k,T-2}^2 \left/ \sum_{k=1}^{T-2}u_{k,T-2}^2 \right. \qquad (2.3)$$

and

$$L = \sum_{k=1}^{T-2}\lambda_{k,T-2}u_{k,T-2}^2 \left/ \sum_{k=1}^{T-2}u_{k,T-2}^2, \right. \qquad (2.4)$$

where $\lambda_{1,T-2} > \lambda_{2,T-2} > \cdots > \lambda_{T-2,T-2} > 0$ are the eigenvalues of the matrix $\mathbf{Z}'\mathbf{W}\mathbf{Z}$ and $\mu_{k,T-2} \sim N[0, \sigma^2(1 + \rho\lambda_{k,T-2})]$, these variables being independent, $k = 1, 2, \ldots, T-2$. The eigenvalues $\lambda_{k,T-2}$ are given in Section 3.

LaMotte and McWhorter (1978) have proposed, in a more general situation, tests of the form

$$F_g = \left[\sum_{k=1}^{g}u_{k,T-2}^2 \left/ g \right.\right] \left/ \left[\sum_{k=g+1}^{T-2}u_{k,T-2}^2 \left/ (T-g-2) \right.\right] \right. > c. \qquad (2.5)$$

In contrast to (2.3)–(2.4), the null distribution of (2.5) is the standard $F(g, T-g-2)$.

Both the null distribution and the powers of our tests (2.1)–(2.2) and (2.5) can be calculated by the method of Imhof (1961). Numerical results are given in Tables 1–3. Apart from round-off errors, the given figures should be correct.

The tabulated M test needs some comment. The alternative ρ_1 occurring in (2.1) and (2.3) is taken to depend on the number of observations. The rationale of the choice $\rho_1 = 375.1/(T-2)^2$ used in Tables 2 and 3 is based on the asymptotic efficiency considerations explained in Section 4. The statistic actually tabulated is $(T-2)[1 - M(375.1/(T-2)^2)]/375.1$, which has a nondegenerate limiting distribution.

Franzini and Harvey (1983) have proposed another method for choosing the alternative ρ_1 in (2.1) and (2.3). The proportion of total variance due to variation

Table 1. Critical points of $L/(T-2)$

$T-2$	α			
	.10	.05	.025	.01
10	.152	.179	.203	.231
20	.136	.164	.192	.227
30	.131	.159	.187	.224
40	.128	.156	.185	.223
50	.126	.155	.183	.222
60	.125	.154	.182	.221
80	.124	.152	.181	.220
100	.123	.151	.181	.220
∞	.119	.149	.178	.218

Table 2. Critical points of $(T-2)[1 - M(375.1/(T-2)^2)]/375.1$

$T-2$	α			
	.10	.05	.025	.01
10	.0199	.0206	.0212	.0218
20	.0263	.0280	.0295	.0313
30	.0285	.0308	.0328	.0353
40	.0294	.0320	.0344	.0374
50	.0299	.0327	.0354	.0386
60	.0302	.0332	.0360	.0394
80	.0306	.0337	.0367	.0404
100	.0307	.0340	.0371	.0410
∞	.0312	.0350	.0385	.0431

Note: This test is the most efficient in the Pitman sense when the limiting power is $\gamma = .80$ at the significance level $\alpha = .05$. The transformed statistic tabulated here has significant large values.

of the random walk is

$$\eta = \rho_1 \, \text{tr} \, \mathbf{Z}'\mathbf{WZ}/(\text{tr} \, \mathbf{Z}'\mathbf{Z} + \rho_1 \, \text{tr} \, \mathbf{Z}'\mathbf{WZ}). \tag{2.6}$$

Franzini and Harvey suggested the value ρ_1 obtained from (2.6) with $\eta = \frac{1}{2}$. Their justification for this choice is based on numerical power comparisons.

Table 3 gives some powers of the tests under study. The relative performance of the F_g and L tests is much the same as that of the corresponding tests in the setting of NM. The new tests (the M test proposed here and the Franzini–Harvey test) are superior, however, to all of the other tests over a wide range of most interesting alternatives; furthermore, there is no great difference between

Table 3. Power functions for some tests at the .05 level

ρ	F_2	F_4	F_6	F_8	L	M[a]	FH[b]
			$T-2=20$[a]				
.1	.165	.146	.126	.109	.173	.164	.168
.2	.261	.241	.208	.176	.267	.269	.275
.3	.332	.321	.282	.240	.337	.354	.359
.4	.386	.385	.346	.298	.390	.422	.426
.5	.429	.438	.401	.350	.431	.476	.479
.6	.461	.481	.447	.395	.465	.521	.523
.8	.510	.547	.520	.469	.515	.588	.588
1.0	.545	.594	.575	.527	.551	.637	.636
2.0	.630	.712	.716	.685	.643	.759	.754
3.0	.664	.759	.774	.753	.681	.808	.801
5.0	.694	.800	.823	.813	.716	.850	.842
			$T-2=50$[b]				
.01	.127	.116	.106	.098	.134	.123	.116
.02	.205	.192	.174	.158	.215	.204	.192
.03	.273	.264	.242	.221	.284	.281	.266
.04	.331	.330	.307	.283	.344	.350	.335
.05	.380	.387	.366	.340	.394	.412	.396
.10	.539	.586	.580	.560	.564	.625	.614
.15	.624	.694	.702	.691	.660	.740	.737
.20	.677	.760	.777	.773	.720	.811	.810
.25	.713	.804	.825	.826	.762	.856	.858
.30	.739	.834	.859	.863	.793	.887	.890
.35	.759	.856	.883	.889	.816	.909	.912

[a] The most powerful test from Table 2.

[b] The most powerful test suggested by Franzini and Harvey (1983).

these two. The discussion in Section 4, nevertheless, reveals that as a general rule the Franzini–Harvey criterion is not recommendable.

3 Eigenvalues of $\mathbf{Z'WZ}$

In deriving the exact eigenvalues of $\mathbf{Z'WZ}$, we proceed by generalizing the argument of NM. Let $\mathbf{A}$ be a matrix that transforms $\mathbf{y}$ to the successive second differences. From the covariance structure of $\mathbf{Ay}$ we obtain

$$\mathbf{AWA'} = \mathbf{V}_1 = \begin{bmatrix} 2 & -1 & 0 & \cdots & 0 & 0 \\ -1 & 2 & -1 & \cdots & 0 & 0 \\ \cdot & \cdot & \cdot & \cdots & \cdot & \cdot \\ 0 & 0 & 0 & \cdots & 2 & -1 \\ 0 & 0 & 0 & \cdots & -1 & 2 \end{bmatrix} \tag{3.1}$$

and

$$\mathbf{AA'} = \mathbf{V}_2 = \begin{bmatrix} 6 & -4 & 1 & 0 & \cdots & 0 & 0 & 0 \\ -4 & 6 & -4 & 1 & \cdots & 0 & 0 & 0 \\ 1 & -4 & 6 & -4 & \cdots & 0 & 0 & 0 \\ \cdot & \cdot & \cdot & & \cdots & & \cdot & \cdot \\ 0 & 0 & 0 & 0 & \cdots & 6 & -4 & 1 \\ 0 & 0 & 0 & 0 & \cdots & -4 & 6 & -4 \\ 0 & 0 & 0 & 0 & \cdots & 1 & -4 & 6 \end{bmatrix}. \qquad (3.2)$$

If $\mathbf{B}$ is a nonsingular $(T-2) \times (T-2)$ matrix such that $\mathbf{B'B} = \mathbf{V}_2$, then one choice of $\mathbf{Z}$ is $\mathbf{Z} = \mathbf{A'B}^{-1}$.

With this $\mathbf{Z}$ we have $\mathbf{Z'WZ} = (\mathbf{B'})^{-1}\mathbf{V}_1\mathbf{B}^{-1}$. Thus the eigenvalues are found by solving

$$\mathbf{V}_1\mathbf{x} = \lambda\mathbf{V}_2\mathbf{x} \qquad (3.3)$$

for nonnull vectors $\mathbf{x}$. From (3.1)–(3.3) we see that Equation (3.3) is equivalent to the difference equation

$$-\Delta^2 x_{t-1} = \lambda \Delta^4 x_{t-2} \qquad (3.4)$$

with the boundary conditions

$$x_{-1} = x_0 = x_{T-1} = x_T = 0. \qquad (3.5)$$

The standard technique for solving the boundary value problems of the type (3.4)–(3.5) (e.g., see Anderson 1971, sec. 6.5) yields the eigenvalues

$$\lambda_{2j-1,T-2} = [2(1 - \cos(2j\pi/T))]^{-1}, \quad j = 1, \ldots, [\tfrac{1}{2}(T-1)],$$
$$\lambda_{2j,T-2} = [2(1 - \cos\xi_{j,T-2})]^{-1}, \quad j = 1, \ldots, [\tfrac{1}{2}(T-2)],$$

where $\xi_{j,T-2} \in (2j\pi/T, (2j+1)\pi/T)$ satisfies $T\tan\xi/2 = \tan T\xi/2$. Furthermore, a lengthy but straightforward calculation shows that

$$T^{-2}\lambda_{2j-1,T-2} = (2j\pi)^{-2} + O(T^{-2}),$$
$$\text{uniformly for } j = 1, \ldots, [\tfrac{1}{2}(T-1)], \qquad (3.6)$$

and

$$T^{-2}\lambda_{2j,T-1} = \zeta_j^{-2} + O(T^{-2}),$$
$$\text{uniformly for } j = 1, \ldots, [\tfrac{1}{2}(T-2)], \qquad (3.7)$$

where $\zeta_j \in (2j\pi, (2j+1)\pi)$ satisfies $\tan\zeta/2 = \zeta/2$.

4 Asymptotic Distributions and Efficiency

When the drift is absent [i.e., $\beta = 0$ in (1.2)], several asymptotic comparisons of the tests (2.4)–(2.5) were made in NM using the Pitman and Bahadur efficiency measures and a new efficiency measure due to Gregory (1980). It turned out, however, that only the Pitman efficiencies agreed reasonably well with the finite sample powers. Therefore comparisons are made here in terms of the Pitman efficiency only. A short discussion of this efficiency measure admitting different limiting distributions for competing test statistics can be found in appendix A.1 of NM.

On the basis of the expansions (3.6)–(3.7), we obtain various limiting distributions of the statistics (2.3)–(2.5). The detailed proofs are omitted, since the method used for theorem 1 of NM is also applicable to the present situation. In the sequel it is written $\lim T^{-2}\lambda_{k,T-2} = \lambda_k$. Thus under H_0, (2.4)–(2.5) give

$$T^{-1}L \xrightarrow{d} \sum_{k=1}^{\infty} \lambda_k u_k^2 \tag{4.1}$$

and

$$gF_g \xrightarrow{d} \chi^2(g), \tag{4.2}$$

where $u_1, u_2, \ldots$ are iid $N(0, 1)$ variables. For the Pitman approach we must find a sequence of alternatives $\rho_T \to 0$ as $T \to \infty$, such that the limiting power of the test under consideration stays below one at the fixed significance level. In fact, it is easily seen from (2.4)–(2.5) that under the sequence of alternatives $\rho_T = \delta/T^2 + o(T^{-2})$, we have

$$T^{-1}L \xrightarrow{d} \sum_{k=1}^{\infty} \lambda_k (1 + \delta\lambda_k) u_k^2 \tag{4.3}$$

and

$$gF_g \xrightarrow{d} \sum_{k=1}^{g} (1 + \delta\lambda_k) u_k^2. \tag{4.4}$$

Thus it is clear that the sequences of interest are of the form $\rho_T = \delta/T^2 + o(T^{-2})$.

From the expressions (4.1)–(4.4), we can determine those values δ that give the limiting power γ at the significance level α. Let these values be $\delta_L(\alpha, \gamma)$ for the L test and $\delta_g(\alpha, \gamma)$ for the F_g test. Then the asymptotic relative efficiency of the L test with respect to the F_g test is $[\delta_g(\alpha, \gamma)/\delta_L(\alpha, \gamma)]^{1/2}$. Other comparisons are made similarly. Some numerical values are given in Table 4. The values $\delta_g(\alpha, \gamma)$ have been found by the Imhof technique. Unfortunately, the same technique is inapplicable as such to the infinite quadratic forms (4.1) and (4.3). To overcome

Table 4. Asymptotic relative efficiencies, with
respect to the most efficient test

Test	$\alpha = .05$		$\alpha = .01$	
	$\gamma = .06$	$\gamma = .08$	$\gamma = .06$	$\gamma = .08$
F_2	.860	.735	.835	.704
F_4	.946	.910	.939	.896
F_5	.949	.934	.949	.925
F_6	.947	.944	.950	.940
F_7	.940	.947	.946	.946
F_8	.932	.946	.941	.948
F_9	.923	.943	.933	.946
F_{10}	.914	.938	.926	.943
L	.924	.867	.883	.818
M	.994	1.000	.999	.995
FH	.000	.000	.000	.000

this difficulty, an approximation of the type

$$P\left(\sum_{k=1}^{\infty} \lambda'_k u_k^2 \leq x\right) \simeq P\left(\sum_{k=1}^{n} \lambda'_k u_k^2 \leq x - \sum_{k=n+1}^{\infty} \lambda'_k\right) \qquad (4.5)$$

is used; that is, the tail of the random series is replaced by its expectation.
The accuracy of this kind of an approximation can be checked in the particular
case $\lambda'_k = (\pi k)^{-2}$ in which the exact values have been tabulated in Anderson
and Darling (1952). Numerical calculations show that in this particular case
with $n = 10$, the error is of order $\pm.0001$ if the true probability is $\geq .10$. In the
lower tail the error is larger, perhaps of order $\pm.001$. During the preparation of
Tables 1, 2, and 4, the value $n = 30$ was used, but the efficiencies of the L test
were computed with $n = 20$.

The preceding discussion of the Pitman efficiencies of the L and F_g tests
suggests considering the sequence $M(\delta/T^2)$ of M tests. It is plain that this
sequence is one of the most efficient tests against $\delta/T^2 + o(T^{-2})$. From (2.3)
we obtain that under H_0,

$$\frac{T}{\delta}[1 - M(\delta/T^2)] \xrightarrow{d} \sum_{k=1}^{\infty} \frac{\lambda_k}{1 + \delta\lambda_k} u_k^2, \qquad (4.6)$$

and under $\delta'/T^2 + o(T^{-2})$,

$$\frac{T}{\delta}[1 - M(\delta/T^2)] \xrightarrow{d} \sum_{k=1}^{\infty} \lambda_k \frac{1 + \delta'\lambda_k}{1 + \delta\lambda_k} u_k^2. \qquad (4.7)$$

In the important special case $\delta' = \delta$, the limiting distribution of (4.7) reduces to
that of (4.1). Next it is shown how one may choose the value δ in order to pick out

the most efficient test $M(\delta/T^2)$ having the limiting power γ at the significance level α. First, according to (4.7) with $\delta' = \delta$, we solve

$$P\left(\sum_{k=1}^{\infty} \lambda_k u_k^2 \geq c\right) = \gamma \qquad (4.8)$$

for c, and then, using this $c = c(\gamma)$ and (4.6), we obtain the desired δ as the solution of

$$P\left(\sum_{k=1}^{\infty} \frac{\lambda_k}{1 + \delta\lambda_k} u_k^2 \geq c(\gamma)\right) = \alpha. \qquad (4.9)$$

Table 4 gives some numerical information about the asymptotic behavior of the tests. We see that the Pitman efficiencies are rather insensitive to the choice of α and γ. This is especially true for the particular M test that is the most efficient test having the limiting power $\gamma = .80$ at the significance level $\alpha = .05$. With these α and γ, (4.8)–(4.9) give $\delta = 375.1$. Note, however, that instead of $M(375.1/T^2)$, the asymptotically equivalent statistic $M(375.1/(T-2)^2)$ appears in Tables 2–4. We see that this M test is clearly superior to all of the other tests in the Pitman sense. Notwithstanding the fact that the LaMotte–McWhorter tests are supported by no optimality criterion, some of them, especially F_6 and F_7, are highly efficient. On the contrary, the efficiencies of the L test are comparatively low.

Finally, it is shown that the method of Franzini and Harvey (1983) described in Section 2 produces an inefficient test sequence in the Pitman sense. From (2.6) and (3.6)–(3.7), it is obtained that for any fixed η,

$$\rho_1 = \left[\eta \bigg/ (1 - \eta) \sum_{k=1}^{\infty} \lambda_k\right] T^{-1} + O(T^{-3}).$$

Thus the Franzini–Harvey method gives the most powerful test against an alternative of the type δ_T/T, $\delta_T \to \delta > 0$.

After some calculations, the numerator of the Franzini–Harvey test statistic is seen to satisfy the Lindeberg condition for asymptotic normality. Furthermore, the test statistic has the same limiting normal distribution under both the null hypothesis and the alternatives $\delta'/T^2 + o(T^{-2})$. Consequently, it is unable to detect the alternatives of order $O(T^{-2})$, although it performs well in the finite sample situations reported in Table 3.

5 Asymptotic Moment-Generating Functions

An approximation of the type (4.5) requires the computation of a remainder of the series $\sum_1^{\infty} \lambda_k = E(\sum_1^{\infty} \lambda_k u_k^2)$. If this expectation were known, only a partial sum would be needed; finding this boils down to computing a finite number of the values ζ_j in (3.7). In finding out these expectations, our main tool is the asymptotic moment-generating function for the null distribution of $T^{-1}L$. From (4.1) and (3.6)–(3.7), we obtain

$$G(\theta) = \lim_{T \to \infty} E(e^{\theta T^{-1}L}) = \prod_{k=1}^{\infty} [1 - 2\theta\lambda_k]^{-1/2}$$

$$= \prod_{j=1}^{\infty} [1 - 2\theta/(2j\pi)^2]^{-1/2} [1 - 2\theta/\zeta_j^2]^{-1/2}$$

$$\text{if } \theta < (2\lambda_1)^{-1} = 2\pi^2. \tag{5.1}$$

By comparing these product expansions to those of the sine function and of the Bessel function $J_{3/2}(x) = (2/\pi)^{1/2} x^{-3/2}(\sin x - x \cos x)$ (e.g., see Abramowitz and Stegun 1972, pp. 75 and 370), we obtain

$$G(\theta) = \left[\frac{\sin\sqrt{\theta/2}}{\sqrt{\theta/2}} \right]^{-1/2} \left[\frac{3(\sin\sqrt{\theta/2} - \sqrt{\theta/2}\cos\sqrt{\theta/2})}{(\theta/2)\sqrt{\theta/2}} \right]^{-1/2}. \tag{5.2}$$

By expanding the logarithm of (5.2) in a Taylor series at origin, we obtain the cumulants; in particular, the expectation and variance are

$$E\left[\sum_{k=1}^{\infty} \lambda_k u_k^2 \right] = \sum_{k=1}^{\infty} \lambda_k = \frac{1}{15} \tag{5.3}$$

and

$$\text{var}\left[\sum_{k=1}^{\infty} \lambda_k u_k^2 \right] = 2\sum_{k=1}^{\infty} \lambda_k^2 = \frac{11}{6,300}. \tag{5.4}$$

The calculation of higher cumulants is straightforward (but rather tedious).

The random series in (4.6) has the moment-generating function

$$G(\theta; \delta) = \prod_{k=1}^{\infty} \left[1 - \frac{2\theta\lambda_k}{1 + \delta\lambda_k} \right]^{-1/2} = \frac{G(\theta - \delta/2)}{G(-\delta/2)}.$$

Thus the cumulants are obtained by differentiating G logarithmically at $-\delta/2$. The expectation is

$$\mu(\delta) = E\left[\sum_{k=1}^{\infty} \frac{\lambda_k u_k^2}{1 + \delta\lambda_k} \right] = \frac{G'(-\delta/2)}{G(-\delta/2)}. \tag{5.5}$$

The moment-generating functions of the random series (4.3) and (4.7) can also be written by means of G, but the expressions are rather involved and perhaps not very useful. The expectations are easily found, however. From (5.3)–(5.4) we get for (4.3) that

$$E\left[\sum_{k=1}^{\infty} \lambda_k (1 + \delta\lambda_k) u_k^2\right] = \frac{1}{15} + \delta \frac{11}{12,600}.$$

Finally, (5.3) and (5.5) imply for (4.6) that

$$E\left[\sum_{k=1}^{\infty} \lambda_k \frac{1 + \delta'\lambda_k}{1 + \delta\lambda_k} u_k^2\right] = \left(1 - \frac{\delta'}{\delta}\right) \mu(\delta) + \frac{\delta'}{15\delta}.$$

6 Conclusions and Extensions

The comparisons based on exact powers and on asymptotic relative efficiencies show that the Pitman approach provides a suitable criterion for choosing the value ρ_1 in the most powerful test (2.1). The competitive method of choice suggested by Franzini and Harvey (1983) suffers from being inefficient asymptotically. The finite sample power calculations, however, imply that the Franzini–Harvey method is practical if the number of observations does not greatly exceed 50.

The method employed in this article is applicable also to cases in which we have, instead of the single parameter ρ, several relative variances $\rho = (\rho_1, \ldots, \rho_p)$. An example (with $p = 2$) occurs when the slope β in (1.2) is not constant but rather obeys a random walk as in Franzini and Harvey (1983). The class of most efficient tests is determined, with general p, analogously to the single-parameter case. First, the sequences of alternatives ρ_T and the corresponding most powerful tests are found such that their powers stay below one and above the significance level, as $T \to \infty$ and $\rho_T \to 0$. Second, the particular sequence that gives the desired limiting power γ at the significance level α is chosen (e.g., one may take $\gamma = .8$ and $\alpha = .05$ as in this article). Unfortunately, there may be an infinite number of sequences for given α and γ, depending on the direction of the convergence $\rho_T \to 0$. In these problems some extra considerations, specific for each case, are called for.

References

Abramowitz, M., and Stegun, I. A. (1972), *Handbook of Mathematical Functions*, New York: Dover Publications.

Anderson, T. W. (1971), *The Statistical Analysis of Time Series*, New York: John Wiley.

Anderson, T. W., and Darling, D. A. (1952), "Asymptotic Theory of Certain 'Goodness of Fit' Criteria Based on Stochastic Processes," *Annals of Mathematical Statistics*, 23, 193–212.

Box, G. E. P., and Jenkins, G. M. (1976), *Time Series Analysis, Forecasting and Control*, San Francisco: Holden-Day.

Franzini, L., and Harvey, A. C. (1983), "Testing for Deterministic Trend and Seasonal Components in Time Series Models," *Biometrika*, 70, 673–682.

Garbade, K. (1977), "Two Methods of Examining the Stability of Regression Coefficients," *Journal of the American Statistical Association*, 72, 54–63.

Gregory, G. G. (1980), "On Efficiency and Optimality of Quadratic Tests," *The Annals of Statistics*, 8, 116–131.

Harvey, A. C. (1981), *Time Series Models*, Deddington, U.K.: Philip Allan.

Imhof, J. P. (1961), "Computing the Distribution of Quadratic Forms in Normal Variables," *Biometrika*, 48, 419–426.

King, M. L. (1980), "Robust Tests for Spherical Symmetry and Their Applications to Least Squares Regression," *The Annals of Statistics*, 8, 1265–1271.

Lamotte, L. R., and McWhorter, A. (1978), "An Exact Test for the Presence of Random Walk Coefficients in a Linear Regression Model," *Journal of the American Statistical Association*, 73, 816–820.

Nyblom, J., and Mäkeläinen, T. (1983), "Comparisons of Tests for the Presence of Random Walk Coefficients in a Simple Linear Model," *Journal of the American Statistical Association*, 78, 856–864.

Schweppe, F. C. (1965), "Evaluation of Likelihood Functions for Gaussian Signals," *IEEE Transactions on Information Theory*, 11, 61–70.

15

Are Seasonal Patterns Constant Over Time?
A Test for Seasonal Stability*

FABIO CANOVA

Department of Economics, Universitat Pompeu Fabra and Department of Economics, University of Catania

AND

BRUCE E. HANSEN

Department of Economics, Boston College and Department of Economics, University of Rochester

This article introduces Lagrange multiplier tests of the null hypothesis of no unit roots at seasonal frequencies against the alternative of a unit root at either a single seasonal frequency or a set of seasonal frequencies. The tests complement those of Dickey, Hasza, and Fuller and Hylleberg, Engle, Granger, and Yoo that examine the null of seasonal unit roots. We derive an asymptotic distribution theory for the tests, and investigate their size and power with a Monte Carlo exercise. Application of the tests to three sets of seasonal variables shows that in most cases seasonality is nonstationary.

The study of seasonal fluctuations has a long history in the analysis of economic time series. Traditionally, seasonal fluctuations have been considered a nuisance that obscures, the more important components of the series (presumably the growth and cyclical components; e.g., see Burns and Mitchell 1946), and seasonal adjustment procedures have been devised and implemented to eliminate seasonality (Shiskin, Young, and Musgrave 1967). This view dominated applied time series econometrics until quite recently. In the past few years a new viewpoint has emerged. Seasonal fluctuations are not necessarily a nuisance, but they are an integral part of economic data and should not be ignored or obscured in the analysis of economic models. Contributors to this view include Ghysels (1988), Barsky and Miron (1989), Braun and Evans (1990), Chattarjee and Ravikumar (1992), and Hansen and Sargent (1993).

Many reasonable time series models of seasonality are conceivable. One approach is to model seasonality as deterministic, as did Barsky and Miron (1989), or as periodic with unchanged periodicity, as done by Hansen and Sargent (1993). A second approach is to model seasonality as the sum of a deterministic process and a stationary stochastic process (Canova 1992). A third approach is to model

* Reprinted from *The Journal of Business and Economic Statistics*, "Are Seasonal Patterns Stable over Time? A Test for Seasonal Stability" by F. Canova and B. E. Hansen, pp. 237–252, Vol. 13, No. 3, July 1995. Reproduced here by permission of the American Statistical Association.

seasonal patterns as nonstationary by allowing for (or imposing) seasonal unit roots (Box and Jenkins 1976).

It is hard to know a priori which approach yields the best statistical description of the data. The assumption of stable seasonal patterns seems reasonable when one considers that Christmas has been in December for as many years as we can remember and that this period is historically the major retail season. On the other hand, selected series have shown monumental changes in the seasonal patterns, in which even the location of seasonal peaks and troughs has changed. Examples include the energy consumption series examined by Engle, Granger, and Hallman (1989), the Japanese consumption and income series examined by Engle, Granger, Hylleberg, and Lee (1993), the industrial production series examined by Canova (1993), and some of the gross domestic product series analyzed by Hylleberg, Jorgensen, and Sorensen (1993). Although there certainly are examples of such large changes in seasonal patterns, one might conjecture that they are relatively rare events and isolated to just a few of the many aggregate macroeconomic series.

It is unsatisfactory to rely on hunches, intuition, stylized facts, and/or ad hoc statistical techniques to determine which statistical model makes the best fit. We need simple statistical techniques that can discriminate between various forms of seasonality. One such testing framework was introduced by Dickey, Hasza, and Fuller (DHF) (1984) and Hylleberg, Engle, Granger, and Yoo (HEGY) (1990), who generalized the unit-root testing methodology of Dickey and Fuller (1979) to the seasonal case. They took the null hypothesis of a unit root at one or more seasonal frequencies and tested for evidence of stationarity. Rejection of their null hypothesis implies the strong result that the series has a stationary seasonal pattern. Due to the low power of the tests in moderate sample sizes, however, nonrejection of the null hypothesis unfortunately cannot be interpreted as evidence "for" the presence of a seasonal unit root.

A useful complement to the preceding testing methodology would be tests that take the null hypothesis to be *stationary* seasonality and the alternative to be *nonstationary* seasonality. In this context, rejection of the null hypothesis would imply the strong result that the data are indeed nonstationary, a conclusion that the DHF or HEGY tests cannot yield. Viewed jointly with these tests, such a procedure would allow researchers a more thorough analysis of their data. A family of such tests is introduced and studied in this article. Even though our null is stationary seasonality, we will for simplicity refer to our tests as seasonal unit-root tests.

The idea is perfectly analogous to that of testing the null of stationarity against the alternative of a unit root at the zero frequency. A Lagrange multiplier (LM) statistic for this null and alternative was recently proposed by Kwiatkowski, Phillips, Schmidt, and Shin (KPSS) (1992). The KPSS test is analogous to the tests of Tanaka (1990) and Saikkonen and Luukkonen (1993), who examined the null hypothesis of a moving average (MA) unit root. In the same sense that HEGY generalized the Dickey–Fuller framework from the zero frequency to the seasonal frequencies, we generalize the KPSS framework from the zero frequency to the seasonal frequencies.

Another set of tests, which may appeal to applied macro-economists, is to examine whether or not seasonal patterns can be accurately represented with a set of deterministic functions of time. Within our framework, we can also introduce tests of the proposition that the seasonal intercepts are constant over time. Under the null hypothesis of stationarity, seasonal intercepts represent the deterministic component of seasonality and are assumed to remain constant over the sample. In this case our tests apply the methodology of Nyblom (1989) and Hansen (1990), who designed LM tests for parameter instability. Interestingly, the LM test for joint instability of the seasonal intercepts is numerically identical to the LM test for unit roots at all seasonal frequencies. Thus the test we describe can be viewed as either a test for seasonal unit roots or for instability in the seasonal pattern, and both views are equally correct.

Our test statistics are precisely LM tests in models with iid Gaussian errors. Because this is not a reasonable assumption for time series applications, we show how to modify the test statistics (by using robust covariance matrix estimates) so that the tests can be applied to a wide class of data, including heteroscedastic and serially correlated processes. We only require relatively weak mixing conditions on the data. It is important to note that we exclude from the regression any trending regressors, such as a unit-root process or a deterministic trend. This is not simply for technical reasons because it is possible to show that the asymptotic distribution is not invariant to such variables. We also require that our dependent variable be free of trends. Thus, we are presuming that the data have already been appropriately transformed to eliminate unit roots at the zero frequency.

The test statistics are derived from the LM principle, which requires only estimation of the model under the null, so least squares techniques are all that is needed. The statistics are fairly simple functions of the residuals. The large-sample distributions are nonstandard but are free from nuisance parameters and only depend on one "degrees-of-freedom" parameter.

To study both the power and the size of the proposed tests, we conducted a Monte Carlo exercise, and we compared their performance with two other standard types of tests, a test for the presence of stochastic (stationary) seasonality and the HEGY tests for unit roots at seasonal frequencies. We show that our tests have reasonable size and power properties.

We apply the tests to the data set originally examined by Barsky and Miron (1989). We are interested in establishing if their maintained hypothesis that quarterly seasonal fluctuations in U.S. macrovariables are well approximated by deterministic patterns is appropriate or not. The second data set used is the set of quarterly industrial production indexes for eight industrialized countries used by Canova (1993). The third is a data set on stock returns on value-weighted indexes for seven industrialized countries. This last data set deserves special attention because "January effects" and other abnormal periodic patterns in stock returns have been repeatedly documented and known for a long time (see Thaler 1987 for a survey of these anomalies). It is therefore of interest to examine whether the knowledge of these patterns had changed their properties or, in other words, if information about the existence of periodic patterns has led to structural changes due to profit-taking activities. We show that for 20 of the 25 series examined by Barsky and Miron the assumption of unchanged seasonality is problematic and that, in some cases, the economic significance of these changes is substantial. Similarly the seasonal patterns of the European industrial production indexes display important instabilities. On the other hand, we find that the seasonal pattern of stock returns has substantially changed only in Japan and in the United Kingdom.

The rest of the article is organized as follows. Section 1 describes the regression model. Two methods to model the deterministic component of seasonality are discussed. Section 2 derives LM tests for unit roots at seasonal frequencies and develops an asymptotic theory of inference for the tests. Section 3 presents LM tests for instability in the seasonal intercepts. Section 4 presents a Monte Carlo exercise. Three applications to economic data appear in Section 5. Conclusions are summarized in Section 6.

1 Regression Models with Stationary Seasonality

1.1 Regression equation
We start from a linear time series model with stationary seasonality:

$$y_i = \mu + x_i'\beta + S_i + e_i, \quad i = 1, 2, \ldots, n. \tag{1}$$

In (1), y_i is real valued, x_t is a $k \times 1$ vector of explanatory variables, S_i is a real-valued deterministic seasonal component of period s, where s is a positive even integer, to be discussed in Subsection 1.2, and $e_i \sim (0, \sigma^2)$ is an error uncorrelated with x_i and S_i. The number of observations is n. If there are exactly T years of data, then $n = Ts$.

To distinguish between nonstationarity at a seasonal frequency and at the zero frequency, we must require that the dependent variable y_i, not have a unit root at the zero frequency (or any other form of nonstationarity in the overall mean). This does not restrict the set of possible applications of the tests because it is widely believed that most macro-economic time series are stationary at the zero frequency after suitable transformations, such as taking the first-difference of the natural logarithm. For some series, such as the price level, double-differencing may be necessary to eliminate the zero frequency unit root. In either case, the deterministic seasonal component S_i of the differenced series y_t can be related to the seasonal component of the original undifferenced series through a result of Pierce (1978, theorem 1).

The regressors x_i may be any nontrending variables that satisfy standard weak dependence conditions. To identify the regression parameters β, we exclude from x_i any variables that are collinear with S_i. In many cases, no x_i will be included. One suggestion we discuss in Section 1.3 is to use the first lag of the dependent variable, $x_i = y_{i-1}$.

When there are no regressors x_i, the error e_t represents the deviation y_i from its seasonal mean. Thus, e_i includes all of the random variation in the dependent variable, will be serially correlated, and may include fluctuations that are seasonal in nature. Because we have no desire to exclude a priori stationary stochastic seasonal patterns under the null hypothesis, our distributional theory is derived under mild mixing-type conditions for the error term e_i that allow for general forms of stochastic behavior, including stationary (and mildly heteroscedastic) stochastic seasonality.

1.2 Modeling deterministic seasonal patterns

A common specification for the deterministic seasonal component in (1) is

$$S_i = d_i'\alpha, \tag{2}$$

where d_i is an $s \times 1$ vector of seasonal dummy indicators and α is an $s \times 1$ parameter vector (e.g., $s = 4$ for quarterly data and $s = 12$ for monthly data). Combined with (1), we obtain the regression model

$$y_i = x_i'\beta + d_i'\alpha + e_i, \quad i = 1, 2, \ldots, n, \tag{3}$$

where we have dropped the intercept μ from the model to achieve identification. The advantage of this formulation is that the coefficients α represent *seasonal effects*. Plotting recursive estimates of the subcoefficients α_s against time is often used to reveal the structure of seasonal patterns (Franses 1994).

A mathematically equivalent formulation is obtained using the trigonometric representation

$$S_i = \sum_{j=1}^{q} f_{ji}' \gamma_j, \tag{4}$$

where $q = s/2$, and for $j < q$, $f_{ji}' = (\cos((j/q)\pi i), \sin((j/q)\pi i))$, while for $j = q$, $f_{qi} = \cos(\pi i) = (-1)^t$, where the latter holds because $\sin(\pi i)$ is identically 0 for all integer i. Stacking the q elements of (4) in a vector, we have $S_i = f_i'\gamma$, where

$$\gamma = \begin{pmatrix} \gamma_1 \\ \cdot \\ \cdot \\ \gamma_q \end{pmatrix}, \qquad f_i = \begin{pmatrix} f_{1i} \\ \cdot \\ \cdot \\ f_{qi} \end{pmatrix}. \tag{5}$$

Note that both γ and f_i have $s - 1$ elements. Inserting in (1), we have the regression equation

$$y_i = \mu + x_t'\beta + f_i'\gamma + e_t, \quad i = 1, 2, \ldots, n. \tag{6}$$

Note that f_i is a mean zero process because for any n that is an integer power of s, $\sum_{i=1}^{n} f_i = 0$. It is also a full-rank process (by the properties of trigonometric series) so that if we define the $s \times (s - 1)$ matrix

$$R_1 = \begin{pmatrix} f_1' \\ \cdot \\ \cdot \\ f_s' \end{pmatrix},$$

then $f_i = R_1' d_i$. Because $1 = \iota' d_i$, where ι is an $(s \times 1)$ vector of ones, we have $(f_i' 1)' = R' d_i$, where $R = [R_1 \ \iota]$. Thus, (3) and (6) are equivalent, and $(\gamma' \mu)' = R^{-1}\alpha$.

The formulation (6) is useful because it allows seasonality to be interpreted as *cyclical.* By construction, the elements of f_i are cyclical processes at the seasonal frequencies: $(j/q)\pi$, $j = 1, \ldots, q$, and the coefficients γ_j represent the contribution of each cycle to the seasonal process S_i. The dummy formulation (2) is primarily employed in applied macroeconomics (Barsky and Miron 1989), but the trigonometric representation (4) is common in the time series literature (e.g., see Granger and Newbold 1986, p. 36; Hannan 1970, p. 174; Harvey 1990, p. 42).

1.3 Lagged dependent variables

The distribution theory we present in Sections 2 and 3 will not be affected if the regressors x_i include lagged dependent variables. But if lagged variables capture one or more seasonal unit roots, the tests we present may have no power. Essentially, what must be excluded are lags of the dependent variable that capture seasonal unit roots. This may be easier to see if we take (1), where the x_t are exclusively lags of the dependent variable:

$$y_i = \mu + \beta(\ell)y_{i-1} + S_i + e_i, \tag{7}$$

with $\beta(\ell) = \beta_1 + \cdots + \beta_\zeta \ell^{\zeta-1}$. When $\zeta = 1$ and $\beta_1 \neq -1$, the autoregressive polynomial $\beta(\ell)$ will not be able to extract a seasonal pattern from y_i. But if $\zeta \geq 2$, $\beta(\ell)$ may absorb some of the seasonal roots. Thus, testing for a seasonal unit root in S_i will be useless.

This discussion should not be interpreted as suggesting that all lagged dependent variables should be excluded from x_i. Indeed, exclusion of lagged dependent variables means that the error e_i will be serially correlated in most applications. Because the inclusion of a single lag of the dependent variable in x_i will reduce this serial correlation (we can think of this as a form of pre-whitening), yet not pose a danger of extracting a seasonal root, we recommend that x_i contain y_{i-1}. The fact that the e_i may be serially correlated will be accounted for at the stage of inference.

1.4 Estimation and covariance matrices

Both (3) and (6) are valid regression equations and can be consistently estimated (under standard regularity conditions) by ordinary least squares (OLS). Let the estimates from (3) be denoted $(\hat{\beta}, \hat{\alpha})$ and the estimates from (6) be denoted $(\hat{\mu}, \hat{\beta}, \hat{\gamma})$. Due to the equivalence in parameterization, the estimates of β and the regression residuals $\hat{e}_t$ in the two equations are identical.

Our tests will require a consistent estimate of Ω, the long-run covariance matrix of $d_i e_i$:

$$\Omega = \lim_{n\to\infty} \frac{1}{n} E(D_n D_n'), \qquad D_n = \sum_{i=1}^{n} d_i e_i,$$

where Ω depends on the stochastic structure of the error. When e_i is serially uncorrelated and seasonally homoscedastic, then

$$\Omega = \frac{1}{n} \sum_{i=1}^{n} d_i d_i' E(e_i^2) = \frac{\sigma^2}{s} I_s$$

(since $(1/n)\sum_{i=1}^{n} d_i d_i' = I_s/s$), which can be estimated by $\hat{\Omega} = (\hat{\sigma}^2/s)I_s$. When e_i is uncorrelated but possibly seasonally heteroscedastic, then $\Omega = \text{diag}\{\sigma_1^2/s, \ldots, \sigma_s^2/s\}$, where σ_j^2 is the variance of e_i for the jth season. In many cases of interest, however, e_i is likely to be serially correlated so that we need an estimate of Ω that is robust to serial correlation as well. Following Newey and West (1987), we suggest a kernel estimate of the form

$$\hat{\Omega} = \sum_{k=-m}^{m} w\left(\frac{k}{m}\right)\frac{1}{n}\sum_{t} d_{i+k}\hat{e}_{i+k}d_i'\hat{e}_i, \tag{8}$$

where $w(\cdot)$ is any kernel function that produces positive semidefinite covariance matrix estimates, such as the Bartlett, Parzen, or quadratic spectral. It is desirable to select the bandwidth number m sufficiently large to be able to capture the serial correlation properties of the data. Andrews (1991) proposed methods for minimum mean squared error estimation of such variances, and Hansen (1992a) gave sufficient conditions for consistent estimation. Here we assume that $m \to \infty$ as $n \to \infty$ such that $m^5/n = O(1)$ as recommended by Andrews (1991) for the efficient Parzen and quadratic spectral kernels.

We will also require an estimate of the long-run covariance matrix of $f_i e_i$:

$$\Omega^f = \lim_{n\to\infty}\frac{1}{n}E(F_n F_n'), \qquad F_n = \sum_{i=1}^{n} f_i e_i.$$

Since $f_i = R_1' d_i$, we see that $F_n = R_1' D_n$, and thus $\Omega^f = R_1'\Omega R_1$. Hence a consistent estimate is given by

$$\hat{\Omega}^f = R_1'\hat{\Omega}R_1 = \sum_{k=-m}^{m} w\left(\frac{k}{m}\right)\frac{1}{n}\sum_{i} f_{i+k}\hat{e}_{i+k}f_i'\hat{e}_i. \tag{9}$$

2 Testing for Seasonal Unit Roots

2.1 The testing problem

Our goal here is to develop tests of the hypothesis that (6) is valid against the alternative that there is a seasonal unit root in S_i. To do so rigorously, we have to write down a specific alternative hypothesis. Hannan (1970, p. 174) suggested that one reasonable model for changing seasonal patterns can be obtained by allowing the coefficients γ to vary over time as a random walk, in which case (6) is

$$y_i = \mu + x_i'\beta + f_i'\gamma_i + e_i, \tag{10}$$

with

$$\gamma_i = \gamma_{i-1} + u_i, \tag{11}$$

γ_0 fixed, and u_i iid. If the covariance matrix of u_i is full ranked, then Models (10)–(11) imply that y_i has unit roots at each seasonal frequency. His model reduces to the stationary seasonal model (6) when the covariance matrix of u_i is identically 0.

We would like to generalize Hannan's model to allow for unit roots potentially at only a subset of the seasonal frequencies. This is equivalent to allowing only a subset of the vector γ_i to be time varying. We can do so by defining a full-rank $(s-1) \times a$ matrix A that selects the a elements of γ_i that we wish to test for nonstationarity. For example, to test whether the entire vector γ is stable, set $A = I_{s-1}$, and to test for a unit root only at frequency $j/q\pi$, set $A = (\tilde{0}\ I_2\ \tilde{0})'$ (commensurate with γ_i) and for frequency π, set $A = (\tilde{0}\ 1)'$. Then modify (11) as

$$A'\gamma_i = A'\gamma_{i-1} + u_i. \tag{12}$$

We assume that, for some increasing sequence of sigma fields $\mathcal{F}_i$, $\{u_i, \mathcal{F}_i\}$ is an $a \times 1$ martingale difference sequence (MDS) with covariance matrix $E(u_i u_i') = \tau^2 G$, where $G = (A'\Omega^f A)^{-1}$ is a full-rank $a \times a$ matrix and $\tau^2 \geq 0$ is real valued. When $\tau^2 = 0$, the parameter $\gamma_i = \gamma_0$ and the model has no seasonal unit roots. When $\tau^2 > 0$, y_i has a unit root at the seasonal frequencies determined by A.

Our model specification is closely related to the trigonmetric seasonal model of Harvey (1990, eq. (2.3.49)). For quarterly data $(s = 4)$ Harvey specified $S_i = S_{1i} + S_{2i}$, where $(1 + \ell^2)S_{1i} = \xi_{1i}$, $(1 + \ell)S_{2i} = \xi_{2i}$, and ξ_{1i} and ξ_{2i} are mutually independent. Hence his model also produced unit roots at the seasonal frequencies but imposed a somewhat different set of correlations across seasonal fluctuations. Bell (1993) showed that the models of Hannan and Harvey generate equivalent structures for the seasonal components.

2.2 The hypothesis test

When $\tau^2 = 0$, S_i is purely deterministic and stationary in the models (10)–(12). This suggests considering the hypothesis test of $H_0 : \tau^2 = 0$ against $H_1 : \tau^2 > 0$. Nyblom (1989) showed that this testing problem is particularly easy to implement in a correctly specified probability model using maximum likelihood estimation. Hansen (1990) extended Nyblom's analysis to general econometric estimators, and Hansen (1992b) developed their specific form for linear regression models. Because (6) is linear, these techniques are directly applicable.

Following these articles, a good test for H_0 versus H_1 takes the form of rejecting H_0 for large values of

$$\begin{aligned} L &= \frac{1}{n^2} \sum_{i=1}^{n} \hat{F}_i' A (A'\hat{\Omega}^f A)^{-1} A' \hat{F}_i \\ &= \frac{1}{n^2} \text{tr}\left((A'\hat{\Omega}^f A)^{-1} A' \sum_{i=1}^{n} \hat{F}_i \hat{F}_i' A \right), \end{aligned} \tag{13}$$

where $\hat{F}_i = \sum_{t=1}^{i} f_t \hat{e}_t$, $\hat{e}_t$ are the OLS residuals from (6), $\hat{\Omega}^f$ is defined in (9), and $\text{tr}(Q)$ stands for the trace of Q. When e_i are iid normal and the x_i are strictly exogenous, L is the LM test for H_0 against H_1. When these assumptions are relaxed, L can be interpreted as an "LM-like" test derived from the generalized least squares criterion function or as an asymptotic equivalent of the true LM test. In addition, when e_i is directly observed (rather than a residual), L is an asymptotic approximation to the locally most powerful test for H_0 versus H_1, suggesting that L should have good power for local departures from the null of no seasonal unit roots.

To be precise, (13) is the LM statistic for H_0 against H_1 under the assumption that $G = (A'\Omega^f A)^{-1}$ [recall that $E(u_i u_i') = \tau^2 G$, where u_i is the error in (12)]. This choice for G may seem arbitrary, but it is guided by the fact that only this choice produces an asymptotic distribution for L that is free of nuisance parameters and hence allows the tabulation of critical values for use in applications. This technique is not without precedent. Indeed, the same criterion is used to construct the standard Wald test. It may be helpful to digress briefly on this point. The general form of the Wald test for the hypothesis $\gamma = 0$ against $\gamma \neq 0$ is $W = \hat{\gamma}'G\hat{\gamma}$. The matrix G determines the direction of the hypothesis test. Indeed, for any G the power of the Wald test W against an alternative γ is determined by the noncentrality parameter $\gamma'G\gamma$, and thus the power is maximized against alternatives γ, which are proportional to the eigenvector of G corresponding to its largest eigenvalue. Hence G could (in principle) be selected to maximize power against particular directions of interest. This is never done in practice. Instead, we set $G = \hat{V}^{-1}$, where $\hat{V}$ is a consistent estimate of the asymptotic covariance matrix of $\hat{\gamma}$. This is not because the eigenvector of $\hat{V}^{-1}$ corresponding to its largest eigenvalue is a particularly interesting direction for the alternative γ but because it is the unique choice, which yields an asymptotic distribution for W free of nuisance parameters. The same reasoning applies to our L tests. Although better power against particular alternatives could in principle be obtained by selecting an appropriate matrix G, this would result in a test with unknown asymptotic size and would hence be useless in practice.

The large-sample distribution of L was studied by Nyblom (1989) and Hansen (1990, 1992b). To simplify the presentation, we introduce the following notation. Let $\rightarrow_d$ denote convergence in distribution, W_p denote a vector standard Brownian bridge of dimension p, and let VM(p) denote a random variable obtained by the transformation

$$\text{VM}(p) = \int_0^1 W_p(r)'W_p(r)dr. \tag{14}$$

When $p = 1$, the distribution of VM(p) simplifies to that known as the *Von Mises goodness-of-fit distribution* widely used in the statistical literature (e.g., see Anderson and Darling 1952), so we will refer to VM(p) as the *generalized Von Mises distribution with p degrees of freedom*. Critical values are given in Table 1.

Theorem 1 Under H_0, $L \rightarrow_d$ VM(a).

Proof The proof is omitted and available on request from the authors.

Table 1. Critical values for VM(p)

p	Significance level					
	1%	2.5%	5%	7.5%	10%	20%
1	.748	.593	.470	.398	.353	.243
2	1.070	.898	.749	.670	.610	.469
3	1.350	1.160	1.010	.913	.846	.679
4	1.600	1.390	1.240	1.140	1.070	.883
5	1.880	1.630	1.470	1.360	1.280	1.080
6	2.120	1.890	1.680	1.580	1.490	1.280
7	2.350	2.100	1.900	1.780	1.690	1.460
8	2.590	2.330	2.110	1.990	1.890	1.660
9	2.820	2.550	2.320	2.190	2.100	1.850
10	3.050	2.760	2.540	2.400	2.290	2.030
11	3.270	2.990	2.750	2.600	2.490	2.220
12	3.510	3.180	2.960	2.810	2.690	2.410

Source: Hansen (1990), Table 1.

Theorem 1 shows that the large-sample distribution of the L statistic does not depend on any nuisance parameters other than a (the rank of A), which refers to the number of elements of γ that are being tested for constancy.

2.3 Joint test for unit roots at all seasonal frequencies

If the alternative of interest is seasonal nonstationarity, then we should simultaneously test for unit roots at all seasonal frequencies. This can be accomplished by using Statistic (13) with $A = I_{s-1}$. This yields the statistic

$$L_f = \frac{1}{n^2} \sum_{i=1}^{n} \hat{F}_i' (\hat{\Omega}^f)^{-1} \hat{F}_i$$

$$= \frac{1}{n^2} \text{tr} \left((\hat{\Omega}^f)^{-1} \sum_{i=1}^{n} \hat{F}_i \hat{F}_i' \right). \tag{15}$$

The subscript f on L indicates that the test is for nonstationarity at *all* seasonal frequencies.

We would like to emphasize that, although the form of the statistic L_f is nonstandard, it is quite simple to calculate. It only requires estimation under the null hypothesis of stationary seasonality, and it is calculated directly from the OLS residuals and the trigonometric coefficients f_i.

The large-sample distribution of L_f follows directly from Theorem 1.

Theorem 2 Under H_0, $L_f \to_d$ VM($s - 1$).

Theorem 2 indicates that the large-sample distribution of the test for unit roots at all seasonal frequencies is given by the generalized Von Mises distribution with $s - 1$ df. This result shows that not only is the test statistic L_f easy to calculate but that its large-sample distribution theory takes a simple form. For quarterly data, the appropriate critical values are found in Table 1 using the row corresponding to $p = s - 1 = 3$. For monthly data, the appropriate critical values are found using the row corresponding to $p = s - 1 = 11$.

2.4 Tests for unit roots at specific seasonal frequencies

Writing (6) to emphasize the seasonal components at individual seasonal frequencies, we have

$$y_i = \mu + x_i'\beta + \sum_{j=1}^{q} f_{ji}'\gamma_j + e_i, \quad i = 1, 2, \ldots, n. \tag{16}$$

Recall that the jth coefficient γ_j corresponds to the seasonal cycle for the frequency $(j/q)\pi$. Testing for a seasonal unit root at frequency $(j/q)\pi$ therefore reduces to testing for a unit root in γ_j. This corresponds to the hypothesis test H_0 versus H_1, where the A matrix has the block diagonal form $A = (\tilde{0}\ I_2\ \tilde{0})'$ for $j < q$ and $A = (\tilde{0}\ 1)'$ for $j = q$, where the 1s correspond to the subvector γ_j. Letting $\hat{\Omega}_{jj}^f$ denote the jth block diagonal element of $\hat{\Omega}^f$ (commensurate with γ), we find that the test statistic L reduces to

$$L_{(\pi j/q)} = \frac{1}{n^2} \sum_{i=1}^{n} \hat{F}_{ii}'(\hat{\Omega}_{jj}^f)^{-1}\hat{F}_{ji}, \tag{17}$$

for $j = 1, \ldots, q$, where $\hat{F}_{ji} = \sum_{t=1}^{i} f_{jt}\hat{e}_t$ is the subvector of $\hat{F}_i$ partitioned conformally with γ.

Again, we would like to emphasize the convenience of the statistics $L_{(\pi j/q)}$. They can be computed as by-products of the calculation of the joint test L_f because $L_{(\pi j/q)}$ only make use of subcomponents of the vector $\hat{F}_i$ and of the matrix $\hat{\Omega}^f$. Their asymptotic distributions are readily obtained:

Theorem 3 Under H_0,

1. For $j < q$, $L_{\pi j/q} \rightarrow_d$ VM(2).
2. $L_\pi \rightarrow_d$ VM(1).

Theorem 3 states that the large-sample distributions of the tests for seasonal unit roots are given by the generalized Von Mises distribution with 2 df for frequencies different than π and with 1 df for frequency π. This stems from the dimensionality of the subvectors γ_j in the two cases. For quarterly data, the two seasonal frequencies are at $\pi/2$ (annual) and π (biannual).

The $L_{(\pi j/q)}$ tests are useful complements to the joint test L_f. If the joint test rejects, it could be due to unit roots at any of the seasonal frequencies. The $L_{(\pi j/q)}$ tests are specifically designed to detect at which particular seasonal frequency nonstationarity emerges.

3 Testing for Nonconstant Seasonal Patterns

3.1 The testing problem

The tests for seasonal unit roots proposed in Section 2 were derived from the trigonometric seasonal model (6). To study whether the seasonal intercepts α have changed over time, we return to the more conventional seasonal dummy model (3), which we modify as

$$y_i = x_i'\beta + d_i'\alpha_i + e_i, \quad i = 1, 2, \ldots, n. \tag{18}$$

There are many forms of potential nonstationarity for α_i that could be considered. Here we consider stochastic variation of a martingale form:

$$A'\alpha_i = A'\alpha_{i-1} + u_i, \tag{19}$$

where α_0 is fixed and $\{u_i, \mathcal{F}_i\}$ is an MDS with covariance matrix $E(u_i u_i') = \tau^2 G$. The $s \times a$ matrix A selects the elements of α that we allow to stochastically vary under the alternative hypothesis. Note that when $\tau = 0$ the coefficient vector is fixed at α_0 for the entire sample.

This specification of coefficient variation is quite general. One special case is the Gaussian random walk, under which the seasonal intercepts α_i slowly (but continuously) evolve over time. Another interesting case discussed by Nyblom (1989) is when the martingale differences u_t come from an "infrequent innovation" process. Let $u_i = \delta_i v_i$, where v_i is iid $\mathcal{N}(0, I_a)$ and δ_i is a discrete random variable equaling 1 with probability ψ and 0 with probability $1 - \psi$ (and v_i and δ_i are independent). For ψ sufficiently small, the martingale α_i will be constant for most observations but will exhibit infrequent and unpredictable "structural breaks." If desired, (19) can be generalized to a random array α_{ni}, which can have exactly one "structural break" of unknown timing (in all or a subset of the seasonal intercepts α_{ni}) in a given sample.

As in Section 2.2, the LM test for $H_0 : \tau = 0$ against $H_1 : \tau \neq 0$ is given by the statistic [setting $G = (A'\hat{\Omega}A)^{-1}$]

$$\begin{aligned} L &= \frac{1}{n^2} \sum_{t=1}^{n} \hat{D}_t' A(A'\hat{\Omega}A)^{-1}A'\hat{D}_t \\ &= \frac{1}{n^2} \text{tr}\left[(A'\hat{\Omega}A)^{-1}A' \sum_{t=1}^{n} \hat{D}_t \hat{D}_t' A \right], \end{aligned} \tag{20}$$

where $\hat{D}_t = \sum_{i=1}^{t} d_i \hat{e}_i$, $\text{tr}(Q)$ is the trace of Q, and $\hat{\Omega}$ is defined in (8).

3.2 Testing for instability in an individual season

Testing the stability of the ath seasonal intercept (where $1 \leq a \leq s$) can be achieved by choosing A to be the unit vector with a 1 in the ath element and zeros elsewhere. This produces the test statistic

$$L_a = \frac{1}{\hat{\Omega}_{aa} n^2} \sum_{t=1}^{n} \hat{D}_{at}^2, \qquad (21)$$

where $\hat{D}_{at}$ is the ath element of $\hat{D}_t$, and $\hat{\Omega}_{aa}$ is the ath diagonal element of $\hat{\Omega}$.

Theorem 4 Under H_0, $L_a \to_d$ VM(1) for each $a = 1, \ldots, s$.

Theorem 4 shows that the asymptotic distribution of the test for instability in an individual seasonal intercept is given by the generalized Von Mises distribution with 1 df, for which critical values are given in the first row of Table 1.

To calculate these test statistics, note that, because the ath dummy variable is 0 for all but one out of every s observations, the cumulative sum $\hat{D}_{at}$ is only a function of the residuals from the ath season. Thus the test statistic L_a can be calculated using only the residuals from the ath season. To see this, let $j = 1, \ldots, T_1$ denote the annual observations for the ath season, and let $\tilde{e}_j, j = 1, \ldots, T_1$, denote the OLS residuals for this season. Then

$$L_a = \frac{1}{T_1^2 \tilde{\sigma}_1^2} \sum_{j=1}^{T_1} \left(\sum_{t=1}^{j} \tilde{e}_t \right)^2, \qquad (22)$$

where $\tilde{\sigma}_1^2 = \sum_{k=-m}^{m} w(k/m) 1/T_1 \sum_i \tilde{e}_{i+k} \tilde{e}_i$.

Hence the statistics L_a are essentially the KPSS statistic applied to the seasonal subseries (only the observations from the ath season are used). Thus, the KPSS test is for instability in the average level of the series, but the L_a tests are for instability in the seasonal subseries.

3.3 Joint test for instability in the seasonal intercepts
Just as we computed a joint test for unit roots at all the seasonal frequencies, we can construct joint tests for instability in all the seasonal intercepts. One straightforward test statistic can be obtained by taking (20) with $A = I$, yielding

$$L_J = \frac{1}{n^2} \sum_{t=1}^{n} \hat{D}_t' \hat{\Omega}^{-1} \hat{D}_t. \qquad (23)$$

Standard analysis shows that, under H_0, $L_J \to_d$ VM(s). Note that L_J is a test for instability in any of the seasonal intercepts so that it will have power against zero-frequency movements in y_t. In other words L_J is a joint test for instability at the zero frequency as well as at the seasonal frequencies. This is an undesirable feature because rejections of H_0 could be a consequence of long-run instability at the zero frequency. This objection could also be raised with individual test statistics L_a, but the problem appears more acute with the joint test L_J.

To cope with this problem one could test for variation in the joint seasonal intercept process that keeps the overall mean constant. Specifically, decompose the seasonal intercepts α in (3) into an overall mean and deviations from the mean. We can write this as

$$\alpha = \iota_s \mu + H\eta, \tag{24}$$

where ι_s is an s vector of ones, $\mu = \iota'_s \alpha / s$ is the overall mean, η is the $(s-1) \times 1$ vector of deviations from μ for the first $s - 1$ seasons (the deviation for the sth season is redundant), and H is the $s \times (s-1)$ matrix

$$H = \begin{pmatrix} I_{s-1} \\ -\iota'_{s-1} \end{pmatrix},$$

where ι_{s-1} is an $(s-1)$ vector of ones. This is simply a reparameterization of the model (3), which can now be written as

$$y_i = \mu + x'_i \beta + d_i^{*\prime} \eta + e_i, \tag{25}$$

where $d_i^* = H' d_i$ is a full-rank, $(s-1)$-dimensional, mean-zero deterministic seasonal process. We can test for stability of the seasonal intercepts, holding constant the overall mean μ, by testing for the stability of the coefficients η via the specification

$$y_i = \mu + x'_i \beta + d_i^{*\prime} \eta_i + e_i \tag{26}$$

and

$$\eta_i = \eta_{i-1} + u_i, \tag{27}$$

where $u_i \sim (0, \tau^2 G)$, using the methods outlined in the previous sections. Rejection of the null hypothesis implies that some seasonal intercepts have changed. Note that Models (26)–(27) allow for time variation in the seasonal pattern, but the seasonal intercepts are constrained to sum to the constant μ. As the associate editor has pointed out, this unusual specification embeds as special cases the periodic models of seasonality studied by Osborn and Smith (1989) and Hansen and Sargent (1993).

The fact that (26)–(27) are unusual is not crucial, however, once one considers the algebraic structure of the models and test statistics. Because f_i and d_i^* are linear combinations of one another, in the sense that, for some invertible matrix B, $d_i^* = B' f_i$, (6) can be written as

$$y_i = \mu + x'_i \beta + f'_i \gamma + e_i, \tag{28}$$

where $\gamma = B^{-1} \eta$. By uniqueness of the representation, this γ is the same as the coefficients in (6). By linearity, testing the joint stability of η in (25) using the alternative (26)–(27) is algebraically equivalent to testing the joint stability of γ in (28) against (10)–(11). It follows that the joint test for seasonal instability obtained from (26)–(27) is exactly L_f.

To put the finding in another way, we have found that either construction—testing for instability as viewed through the lens of seasonal intercepts or from the angle of seasonal unit roots—gives exactly the same joint test. There is no need to choose one approach or the other because both yield the same answer. Thus the appearance of the alternative model given by (26)–(27) as overly restrictive is an artifact of the analysis of the seasonal dummy model and not a substantive restriction.

4 A Monte Carlo Experiment

To examine the performance of our proposed test statistics, we conducted a small Monte Carlo exercise. We consider two quarterly models, one roughly consistent with our specification and the other consistent with the setup of HEGY. The first model is

$$y_t = b y_{t-1} + \sum_{j=1}^{2} f'_{jt} \gamma_{jt} + \epsilon_t, \quad \epsilon_t \sim \mathcal{N}(0, 1), \tag{29}$$

and

$$\gamma_t = \gamma_{t-1} + u_t, \quad u_t \sim \mathcal{N}(0, \tau^2 G), \tag{30}$$

where $\gamma_0 = [0, 0, 0]$. The second model is

$$(1 - bL)(1 + g_2 L)(1 + g_3 L^2)[y_t - 10 + 4.0 d_1 - 4.0 d_2 + 6.0 d_3] = \epsilon_t, \tag{31}$$

where $\epsilon_t \sim \mathcal{N}(0, 1)$ and d's are seasonal dummies. For the first model [(29)–(30)] we use three data-generating processes (DGP) under the alternative:

$$\text{DGP1} : G = \begin{bmatrix} 0 & 0 & 0 \\ 0 & 0 & 0 \\ 0 & 0 & 1 \end{bmatrix}, \tag{32}$$

$$\text{DGP2} : G = \begin{bmatrix} 1 & 0 & 0 \\ 0 & 1 & 0 \\ 0 & 0 & 0 \end{bmatrix}, \tag{33}$$

and

$$\text{DGP3} : G = \begin{bmatrix} 1 & 0 & 0 \\ 0 & 1 & 0 \\ 0 & 0 & 1 \end{bmatrix}. \tag{34}$$

The model implied by DGP1 is exactly that for which the test L_π is designed: When $\tau = 0$, there are no unit roots, but when $\tau \neq 0$, there is a unit root at frequency π. DGP2 is designed for the $L_{\pi/2}$ test, in that $\tau = 0$ implies no unit roots and $\tau \neq 0$ implies a pair of complex conjugate roots at frequency $\pi/2$. DGP3 has no unit roots when $\tau = 0$ but has unit roots at both seasonal frequencies when $\tau \neq 0$.

For the second model (31) we consider several specifications—a case in which seasonality is deterministic ($g_2 = g_3 = 0$), another in which there is a deterministic and a stochastic component to seasonality ($0 < g_2$ and $g_3 < 1$), a third in which there is a unit root at π ($g_2 = 1$ and $g_3 < 1$), a fourth in which there are a pair of unit roots at $\pi/2$ ($g_2 < 1$ and $g_3 = 1$), and finally one with unit roots at both π and $\pi/2$ ($g_2 = g_3 = 1$).

For both seasonal models we vary the first-order autoregressive parameter among $b = [.5, .95, 1.0]$, and the sample size among $T = [50, 150]$. For model (29)–(30) we select the strength of the seasonal unit-root component among $\tau = [.00, .10, .20]$. For model (31) we select the strength of the stochastic seasonal component among $g_2, g_3 = [.0, .5, .95, 1.0]$. The choices for the first-order autoregressive parameter and sample size were selected to correspond to typical macroeconomic time series (and our applications).

For each parameter configuration, we created 1,000 independent samples for each DGP and calculated the tests for unit roots at the seasonal frequencies π and $\pi/2$, the joint test at both frequencies, and the tests for instability in the four seasonal dummies. Because the alternative here is a seasonal unit root, the tests for instability in the four individual seasons had similar performances, so we only report the results for the first seasonal dummy, D1. We ran the tests on the level of simulated data, but we also experimented, for the case in which $b = 1$, running the test on the first difference of the simulated data. Furthermore, we follow the suggestion of Section 1.3 and include one lag of the dependent variable. Thus the model for OLS estimation is

$$y_t = \mu + \beta y_{t-1} + f_t'\gamma + e_t. \tag{35}$$

To implement the tests, we need to select estimates of the long-run covariance matrix $\hat{\Omega}$, which reduces to the choice of kernel and lag truncation number m. In the simulations reported here, we use the Bartlett kernel and, following Andrews (1991, Table 1), select $m = 3$ if $T = 50$ and $m = 5$ if $T = 150$. The effect of selecting other values is discussed later.

The performance of our LM tests is compared with two alternative testing methodologies. The first is a simple t test for the existence of stochastic seasonality, which is obtained from testing $\delta_2 = 0$ in the model

$$(1 - \delta_1 \ell)(1 - \delta_2 \ell^4)\left(y_t - \sum_{j=1}^{4} \alpha_j d_{jt}\right) = e_t. \tag{36}$$

Within our Monte Carlo design, the null hypothesis for this test is the same as for our LM tests (although this would not be true in more general models because our tests take the null to include *stationary* stochastic fluctuations) and thus provides a valid basis for comparison.

The second alternative testing procedure is that developed by HEGY. The approach is based on testing the nullity of the coefficients ρ_j in the auxiliary regression

$$A(\ell)w_{1t} = \rho_1 w_{2t-1} + \rho_2 w_{3t-1} + \rho_3 w_{4t-1} + \rho_4 w_{4t-2} + \sum_{j=1}^{4} \alpha_j d_{jt} + e_t, \quad (37)$$

where $w_{1t} = (1 - \ell^4)y_t$, $w_{2t} = (1 + \ell + \ell^2 + \ell^3)y_t$, $w_{3t} = -(1 - \ell + \ell^2 - \ell^3)y_t$, and $w_{4t} = -(1 - \ell^2)y_t$. We examine augmented Dickey–Fuller t statistics for the hypothesis $\rho_2 = 0$ (unit root at frequency π) and the HEGY F statistic for the hypothesis $\rho_3 = \rho_4 = 0$ (a pair of conjugate complex unit roots at frequency $\pi/2$). For each experiment we use six-lag augmentation; that is, $A(\ell) = 1 - a_1\ell - a_2\ell^2 - a_3\ell^3 - a_4\ell^4 - a_5\ell^5 - a_6\ell^6$. As an anonymous referee and an associate editor have pointed out, model (29)–(30) generates moving average (MA) components in y_t so that the lag augmentation should be sufficiently long for the HEGY test to be reasonably powerful. Our LM tests and the HEGY tests take the opposite null and alternative hypotheses and are thus not directly comparable.

Other Monte Carlo experiments to evaluate tests for unit roots at seasonal frequencies have been conducted by Hylleberg (1992) and Ghysels, Lee, and Noh (GLN) (1992). Hylleberg also contrasted the HEGY tests with our tests for structural stability in the dummies but used a simple AR process for the DGP of the data. GLN examined the relative performance of the HEGY and DHF tests.

The results of the experiments are contained in Tables 2–4 for Models (29)–(30) and Tables 5–6 for Model (31). Each table reports the percentage rate of rejection of the relevant null hypothesis at the asymptotic 5% significance level.

4.1 First seasonal model

4.1.1 Size of the test. Table 2 reports the results for Models (29)–(30) when $\tau = 0$, which corresponds to the hypothesis of no seasonal unit roots.

All of our LM tests have good size, especially for $T = 150$. In nearly every case, the rejection frequency is close to or slightly above the nominal level of 5%. The size of the tests does not appear to be very sensitive to the magnitude of b.

The test for stochastic seasonality also takes the null $\tau = 0$; thus, the rejection frequencies in Table 2 are also the finite sample sizes of the test. The results are somewhat mixed. The test tends to underreject, regardless of the sample size, when $b < 1$, but it overrejects when $b = 1$.

The HEGY tests take the null of unit roots at the seasonal frequencies, so the parameter configurations of Table 2 lie in the alternative hypothesis for these tests. Thus, we should expect the statistics to reject frequently. Indeed, the tests for frequency π and $\pi/2$ reject in nearly every trial when $T = 150$, but the power of the tests is substantially reduced when $T = 50$.

4.1.2 Power under the alternative. Tables 3 and 4 report the rejection frequency of the tests under the hypothesis of seasonal unit roots. In Table 3 we set $\tau = .1$, and in Table 4 $\tau = .2$.

Table 2. First seasonal model, size and power of asymptotic 5% tests,
Monte Carlo comparison, 1,000 replications: $\tau = 0$

Sample size	b	HEGY		Stationary	Dummy D1	Seasonals		
		π	$\pi/2$			π	$\pi/2$	Joint
150	.50	97.6	100.0	2.2	4.8	4.6	5.6	5.8
150	.95	98.8	100.0	3.4	6.6	6.4	4.0	5.2
150	1.00	98.4	100.0	7.4	3.6	6.4	5.4	5.6
50	.50	29.6	19.2	2.3	6.4	4.6	8.6	6.0
50	.95	38.8	26.4	2.2	5.4	4.8	5.6	4.6
50	1.00	29.6	37.2	8.4	4.2	7.6	7.4	8.2

Note: "HEGY" is the Hylleberg, Engle, Granger, and Yoo (1990) test for unit roots at seasonal frequencies, "Stationary" is a test for the presence of stochastic seasonality "Dummy" is the test for the instability of the first seasonal dummy proposed in Section 3, and "Seasonals" are the tests for unit roots at seasonal frequencies proposed in Section 2. The HEGY test is run with a six-lag augmentation.

Table 3. First seasonal model, size and power of asymptotic 5% tests,
Monte Carlo comparison, 1,000 replications: $\tau = .1$

Sample size	b	DGP	HEGY		Stationary	Dummy D1	Seasonals		
			π	$\pi/2$			π	$\pi/2$	Joint
150	.5	DGP1	40.0	100.0	38.6	39.8	73.4	3.6	61.4
		DGP2	98.8	87.2	25.2	30.8	3.4	64.8	59.6
		DGP3	77.2	96.2	22.4	28.2	43.2	44.8	65.2
150	.95	DGP1	42.4	100.0	49.6	42.4	77.8	2.0	70.4
		DGP2	98.6	93.6	29.8	28.6	4.4	64.6	61.8
		DGP3	77.8	99.0	29.4	31.0	45.6	46.2	65.8
150	1.00	DGP1	42.0	100.0	21.8	44.8	74.2	3.2	67.2
		DGP2	97.6	95.2	25.0	28.2	3.0	65.4	61.6
		DGP3	75.8	98.8	20.0	31.8	45.2	41.8	64.0
50	.50	DGP1	19.4	18.2	5.6	11.4	30.0	6.8	21.4
		DGP2	24.4	15.4	3.0	7.4	4.0	18.8	14.2
		DGP3	24.0	15.6	4.2	6.4	11.6	3.0	14.6
50	.95	DGP1	21.8	31.0	8.8	13.2	30.0	4.4	20.6
		DGP2	34.0	24.4	5.4	7.2	6.6	14.6	13.6
		DGP3	31.6	26.2	4.6	9.2	10.8	10.8	13.0
50	1.00	DGP1	18.4	34.2	12.4	9.4	31.4	5.6	21.8
		DGP2	28.8	28.8	9.8	5.0	5.6	18.4	13.8
		DGP3	26.2	28.4	10.6	4.8	14.6	10.4	15.6

Note: See note to Table 2.

Our proposed LM tests perform remarkably well. First, examine the test for non-constancy in the first seasonal dummy (D1). Because all three alternative models induce seasonal unit roots into the model, this will appear as an unstable seasonal intercept, and we should expect this test to reject the null of stationarity. Indeed,

Table 4. First seasonal model, size and power of asymptotic 5% tests, Monte Carlo comparison, 1,000 replications: $\tau = .2$

Sample size	b	DGP	HEGY		Stationary	Dummy D1	Seasonals		
			π	$\pi/2$			π	$\pi/2$	Joint
150	.5	DGP1	13.0	100.0	78.6	59.6	90.0	.6	82.4
		DGP2	98.4	39.0	77.0	57.8	.2	91.8	90.0
		DGP3	40.4	65.2	77.8	54.8	67.8	73.2	92.0
150	.95	DGP1	14.2	100.0	89.0	69.6	93.0	1.0	88.0
		DGP2	96.2	49.0	81.4	58.4	1.6	92.6	91.6
		DGP3	38.0	71.6	86.4	58.2	69.6	77.8	94.0
150	1.00	DGP1	15.2	100.0	39.6	72.4	94.4	1.0	87.8
		DGP2	96.0	55.4	64.8	54.2	1.6	91.2	88.4
		DGP3	38.6	79.2	56.4	57.0	75.2	73.8	95.2
50	.50	DGP1	12.2	21.4	18.6	21.0	55.8	2.4	40.4
		DGP2	37.0	10.0	10.0	17.0	2.8	47.2	38.6
		DGP3	20.6	13.0	10.0	17.4	27.2	24.8	36.6
50	.95	DGP1	14.6	28.0	27.0	26.8	60.0	2.8	46.6
		DGP2	33.8	12.2	15.4	16.8	2.8	40.6	34.2
		DGP3	24.8	16.6	13.8	19.0	31.0	23.8	39.0
50	1.00	DGP1	11.8	39.0	19.0	21.4	59.8	2.2	47.8
		DGP2	28.8	17.4	15.2	16.0	2.2	45.4	37.6
		DGP3	15.6	23.2	14.2	15.2	27.0	26.0	36.6

Note: See note to Table 2.

for $T = 150$, the statistic rejects in 28%–44% of the trials when $\tau = .1$, and in 54%–72% of the trials when $\tau = .2$. As expected, the power is less for $T = 50$.

Second, examine the test for a unit root at frequency π. For illustration, take $T = 150$ and $\tau = .1$. Under DGP1 (a unit root at the frequency π), the test rejects in 73%–77% of the trials. When both seasonal unit roots are present (DGP3), the test rejects in only 43%–45% of the trials, indicating an adverse effect of the presence of a contaminating unit root. A remarkable result is that under DGP2, when there is a unit root at the frequency $\pi/2$ (the wrong seasonal frequency), the test rejects in only 3%–4% of the trials. This is good news, for it implies that the statistic has no tendency to "spuriously reject" due to the presence of another seasonal unit root.

The results are similar for the test at frequency $\pi/2$. Again taking $T = 150$ and $\tau = .1$, we note that in the presence of a unit root at $\pi/2$ (DGP2) the rejection frequency is 64%–65%, and in the presence of both seasonal unit roots (DGP3) the rejection frequency is 41%–46%. In the presence of the wrong unit root (DGP1), the rejection rate is an excellent 2%–3%.

The joint test also performed quite well, having power against a unit root at frequency π or $\pi/2$ close to that found by the L_π or $L_{\pi/2}$ test. When unit roots are present at both frequencies, then typically the joint test has greater power than either individual test.

Summarizing, the power performance of the LM tests, with the first seasonal design, is essentially independent of the parameter b and increases with τ and T, and the tests reject against the correct alternatives.

The rejection frequency of the test for stationary stochastic seasonality is similar to that of the LM test for a nonstationary dummy variable, and both are lower than the power of the LM test for seasonal unit roots when $\tau = .1$. The power dramatically improves when $\tau = .2$. It also drops when $b = 1$ regardless of the size of the other parameters. Because the test misbehaved when $b = 1$ under the null hypothesis as well, however, this result may be an artifact of size distortion.

The HEGY tests have trouble dealing with this design. First consider the test for a unit root at frequency π. Since $\tau > 0$, DGP1 and DGP3 lie in the test's null hypothesis (because there is a unit root at π), while DGP2 lies in the alternative hypothesis. Yet for $T = 150$, the rejection rate against DGP1 when $\tau = .1$ is 40%–42%, and when $\tau = .2$ it is reduced to 13%–15%. Against DGP3, the rejection rate when $\tau = .1$ is 75%–77% and is 38%–40% when $\tau = .2$. These are rejections under the null, and hence this indicates massive size distortion.

Second, consider the test for a pair of complex conjugate unit roots at the frequency $\pi/2$, for which DGP2 and DGP3 are included under the null hypothesis and DGP1 is the alternative. Under the local alternative $\tau = .1$, the test rejects in nearly every trial under the null (87%–100% when $T = 150$), indicating that the statistic cannot discriminate between the null and the alternative. In this case also, this massive distortion diminishes when we increase τ to .2, even though it is still very sizable (39%–79% rejection rates when $T = 150$). Apparently, HEGY tests find it hard to deal with designs in which unit roots appear as large masses as opposed to sharp peaks in the spectrum.

4.1.3 Some robustness experiments. The simulation results for the LM test reported previously used a consistent kernel-based estimate of the long-run covariance matrix. It is fairly straightforward to see that, under the alternative hypothesis of a seasonal unit root, the value of the L statistic will be *decreasing* (at least in large samples) as a function of m. Thus, selecting too large a value will have adverse effects on power. Selecting a too-small value, however risks size distortion if there is unaccounted-for serial correlation in the errors. This is the same problem as arises in the LM test for a unit root at the zero frequency and was discussed by Kwiatkowski, Phillips, Schmidt, and Shin (1992).

To investigate the robustness of the results to alternative estimates of the covariance matrix, we have experimented with two other values for m. As an extreme choice, we set $m = \sqrt{n}$ [as done, for example, by Hylleberg (1992)]. The decreased the power of our LM tests by approximately 50%. We consider this an upper bound on the power loss. At the opposite extreme we used a naive OLS estimator, which can be viewed as setting the lag window $m = 0$ in the general expression, and it is optimal within our design. For this last choice, we found the gain of power of our test to be approximately 5%–10%. We conclude that a conservative choice of m along the lines of Andrews (1991) is important to retain significant finite-sample power.

We also experimented with the larger sample size $T = 300$ and for the case in which no lagged y_t was included in (35). As expected, all of the tests performed much better in terms of both size and power when T was larger, but no significant size or power distortion occurred when no lagged dependent variable was included in the estimated model.

We also examined the size and the power of our tests when a preliminary first-order differencing transformation was used on the simulated data when $b = 1$. None of the results are changed by this modification. We believe that the inclusion of one lag of the dependent variable in the regressions effectively soaks up the unit root at the zero frequency without the need for any preliminary transformation.

4.2 Second seasonal model

4.2.1 Size of the tests. Table 5 reports the results for Model (31) when $0 \le g_2$, $g_3 < 1$, which corresponds to the null hypothesis of deterministic or deterministic-plus-stochastic stationary seasonality. In this case we should expect our tests to reject in 5% of the trials and the HEGY tests to reject often (because the design lies in the alternative).

The performance of all tests is reasonable when only deterministic seasonality is present ($g_2 = g_3 = 0$). When there are also stationary stochastic seasonal components (e.g., $g_2 = g_3 = .5$) our seasonal tests overreject in many cases, in particular the test for a unit root at $\pi/2$. As g_2 and g_3 approach unity (so that stochastic

Table 5. Second seasonal model, size and power of asymptotic 5% tests, Monte Carlo comparison, 1,000 replications

Sample size	b	g_2	g_3	HEGY		Stationary	Dummy D1	Seasonals		
				π	$\pi/2$			π	$\pi/2$	Joint
150	.5	.0	.0	98.6	100.0	1.9	5.2	3.6	4.9	3.8
150	.95	.0	.0	98.6	100.0	1.5	3.5	3.8	3.6	3.5
150	1.0	.0	.0	97.7	99.7	1.8	5.7	3.1	3.8	3.8
150	.5	.5	.5	95.8	95.9	64.4	8.7	4.0	15.6	12.6
150	.95	.5	.5	96.9	98.6	96.1	17.6	5.0	15.8	12.9
150	1.00	.5	.5	97.7	98.4	98.2	20.2	6.2	16.8	15.2
150	.5	.95	.95	16.7	10.0	100.0	68.6	42.5	94.2	96.9
150	.95	.95	.95	17.1	7.7	100.0	65.3	51.1	92.5	96.6
150	1.00	.95	.95	17.8	9.7	100.0	68.3	55.9	90.8	95.4
50	.5	.0	.0	32.6	20.6	1.5	5.5	4.4	4.4	4.0
50	.95	.0	.0	35.0	25.0	1.8	6.4	4.2	5.6	4.7
50	1.0	.0	.0	36.3	28.8	.8	4.3	4.0	3.8	3.3
50	.5	.5	.5	23.5	9.0	14.9	12.7	4.0	21.1	16.9
50	.95	.5	.5	33.0	12.2	36.7	16.0	4.1	17.1	15.6
50	1.00	.5	.5	28.7	13.3	42.7	17.5	5.4	17.7	15.9
50	.5	.95	.95	11.1	4.6	98.4	55.1	48.0	83.4	90.5
50	.95	.95	.95	11.4	3.6	99.4	55.2	51.0	82.3	89.5
50	1.00	.95	.95	10.9	4.2	99.6	57.0	52.2	81.4	90.0

Note: See note to Table 2.

seasonality approaches the nonstationary region), both the seasonal unit root and the dummy tests exhibit size distortion and cannot distinguish a unit-root from a non-unit-root process. Again the size of the test is independent of T and, to a certain extent, b.

The performance of the stationary test is very similar to the one for dummies, even though the distortions become very large as b approaches 1.

The HEGY tests are reasonable regardless of b when g_2 and g_3 are small. As g_2 and g_3 increase, although remaining less than 1, the power of the tests decreases substantially. Reducing the sample size from 150 to 50 greatly affects the perform-ance of the HEGY test but has practically no influence on our LM tests or on the stochastic seasonality test.

4.2.2 Power under the alternative. Table 6 reports the rejection frequency of the tests under the hypothesis of at least one seasonal unit root. (There is a unit root at frequency π when $g_2 = 1$ and a pair of conjugate unit roots at $\pi/2$ when $g_3 = 1$.) Therefore we should expect our tests and the stochastic stationarity test to reject frequently and the HEGY tests to reject in about 5% of the trials.

With this simple AR DGP, the performance of our dummy test is in general good, rejecting in about 80% of the trials when $T = 150$. The power is independent of b and lower when $T = 50$.

Our LM test performs reasonably well with this DGP even though the tests at π reject less frequently than expected when a unit root appears. Moreover, when g_2 and g_3 are close to unity, the test overrejects the null of stationarity. This is particularly evident when $g_2 = 1$ and $g_3 = .95$. The performance of the test is slightly worse when the sample size is small and is independent of b.

The power of the stochastic stationarity test is good with this design, and the test rejects whenever unit roots are present regardless of the size of the parameters b and T.

Finally, the HEGY tests perform well when $T = 150$, even though some power losses appear when there are near unit roots at the other seasonal frequency. As previously noted, the performance of the HEGY tests strongly depend on the sample size, but it is practically independent of b.

Overall, these results suggest that neither our new tests nor the HEGY tests are "superior" in either Monte Carlo design. For Models (29)–(30) our new LM tests perform as expected, just as the HEGY tests work somewhat well with the DGP (31). At this stage we see the two testing procedures as complementary to each other, and making meaningful comparisons between these testing frameworks will be an interesting subject for future research (see also Hylleberg 1992; Hylleberg and Pagan 1994).

5 Applications

5.1 U.S. post World War II macroeconomic series

The first data set we examine is that originally examined by Barsky and Miron (1989) in their study of the relationship between seasonal and cyclical fluctu-ations. The data set includes 25 variables that cover practically all of the major

Table 6. Second seasonal model, size and power of asymptotic 5% tests, Monte Carlo comparison, 1,000 replications

Sample size	b	g_2	g_3	HEGY		Stationary	Dummy D1	Seasonals		
				π	$\pi/2$			π	$\pi/2$	Joint
150	.5	.5	1.0	97.3	3.9	100.0	84.3	.0	98.4	96.3
150	.5	1.0	.5	3.8	97.6	98.1	82.9	87.9	2.1	78.3
150	.95	.5	1.0	98.6	4.6	100.0	83.0	3.0	98.8	96.7
150	.95	1.0	.5	5.1	98.8	100.0	78.1	87.8	1.0	74.5
150	1.00	.5	1.0	98.9	4.8	100.0	85.0	.0	98.7	97.0
150	1.00	1.0	.5	6.1	98.9	100.0	83.4	87.2	1.0	72.5
150	.5	.95	1.0	17.3	4.8	100.0	84.5	41.4	98.5	99.1
150	.5	1.0	.95	6.0	9.9	100.0	76.0	83.1	89.8	98.5
150	.95	.95	1.00	18.1	4.0	100.0	81.1	43.7	97.8	99.2
150	.95	1.00	.95	5.4	7.2	100.0	75.4	81.3	89.0	98.7
150	1.00	.95	1.00	17.9	4.0	100.0	80.3	49.1	98.0	99.2
150	1.00	1.00	.95	6.5	10.3	100.0	81.2	84.7	85.8	97.9
150	.5	1.00	1.00	4.4	4.6	100.0	85.5	79.2	98.2	99.7
150	.95	1.00	1.00	6.7	4.6	100.0	79.2	78.6	97.7	99.8
150	1.00	1.00	1.00	5.0	4.1	100.0	82.8	81.8	96.5	99.7
50	.5	.5	1.0	32.6	3.4	98.4	65.4	3.2	40.6	86.6
50	.5	1.0	.5	8.8	12.7	94.6	56.9	67.5	15.4	64.5
50	.95	.5	1.0	36.0	2.8	99.2	62.5	2.7	89.9	86.5
50	.95	1.0	.5	8.0	13.7	91.1	54.0	66.3	11.7	62.1
50	1.00	.5	1.0	33.3	3.9	99.0	62.1	3.8	88.6	85.2
50	1.00	1.0	.5	8.9	13.3	94.9	61.2	68.3	11.7	64.6
50	.5	.95	1.0	12.1	3.4	99.3	63.9	48.4	90.0	93.9
50	.5	1.00	.95	8.7	4.7	99.3	60.9	67.8	82.7	94.1
50	.95	.95	1.0	11.8	3.0	99.7	61.8	50.1	88.7	94.3
50	.95	1.00	.95	9.3	3.5	99.7	63.0	67.8	81.3	93.1
50	1.00	.95	1.0	11.2	4.5	99.7	63.8	51.2	89.4	94.0
50	1.00	1.00	.95	9.6	4.2	99.6	64.7	63.4	81.2	92.7
50	.5	1.00	1.00	8.8	4.0	99.0	64.8	63.4	90.2	95.5
50	.95	1.00	1.00	4.2	3.5	99.6	63.9	66.1	86.8	95.7
50	1.00	1.00	1.00	9.0	3.0	99.8	64.0	65.3	86.4	95.4

Note: See note to Table 2.

nonseasonally adjusted U.S. macroeconomic variables (total fixed investment, fixed residential investments, fixed nonresidential investments, fixed nonresidential structures, fixed nonresidential producer durables, total consumption, consumption of durables, consumption of nondurables, consumption of services, federal government expenditure, imports and exports, final business sales, changes in business inventories, Consumer Price Index (CPI), one-month treasury bill (T-bill) rates, M1, unemployment, labor force, employment, monetary base, money multiplier, and hours and wage rates). The original sources are described in the appendix of Barsky and Miron. The sample covers data from 1946,1 to 1985,4 except for M1 (starting date 1947,1), for unemployment and labor force (starting date 1948,1), employment (starting date 1951,1), the monetary base and the money multiplier (starting date 1959,1), and hours and wage (starting date 1964,1).

In constructing an estimate of the covariance matrix $\hat{\Omega}$, we use the Newey and West (1987) procedure using Bartlett windows with lag truncation $m = 5$ for all series but hours and wage, for which we choose $m = 4$. For all variables we run the tests on the log differences to maintain comparability with previous analyses, and one lag of the dependent variable is included among the regressors. Table 7 reports significate dummies, the value of the L_t statistic for testing the stability of each separate dummy coefficient ($i = 1, 2, 3, 4$), the values of the L_π and $L_{\pi/2}$ statistics for nonstationarity at the seasonal frequencies, and the joint test statistic L_f. For four variables that display unstable seasonal patterns (fixed investment, consumption, government expenditure, and unemployment rate), Fig. 1 plots recursive least squares estimates of the dummy coefficients in the spirit of Franses (1994). Under the assumption of unchanged seasonal patterns, the plot should depict four almost parallel lines. If lines intersect (e.g., spring becomes summer) unit-root behavior at seasonal frequencies is likely to occur. If changes in seasonal patterns changed primarily in the intensity of the fluctuations, the lines should tend to converge or diverge.

The results indicate that 24 out of the 25 variables display statistically significant seasonal patterns (the one-month T-bill rate is the only exception) and that for 20 of these the seasonal pattern has changed over the sample (according to the joint L_f test). The four variables that possess stable seasonal patterns are consumption of durables, imports, exports, and CPI. We also find that changes occur almost equally in all seasons but the third, that for 18 variables the null of constant seasonality is rejected at the annual frequencies, and that at the biannual frequency the test rejects the null in 11 cases. These results indicate that the comparison of deterministic seasonal and stochastic cyclical patterns as done by Barsky and Miron (1989) may not be appropriate because there are important time variations neglected in the analysis. They may also be viewed as consistent with results recently obtained by Ghysels (1991) that show that the seasonal pattern displayed by this set of macroeconomic variables tends to change with business-cycle conditions.

It is encouraging to observe that the individual dummy stability tests give similar conclusions to "eyeball" tests on the recursive estimates displayed in Fig. 1. The first-quarter fixed-investment dummy trends toward 0, and the test rejects its constancy. The test also rejects the constancy of all government-expenditure dummies, except for the third-quarter dummy, a result that conforms with the plot of the recursive estimate. For the consumption series, the first and the fourth quarter dummies are the largest in absolute value, they trend toward 0 over time, and the test rejects their stability at the 1% level. A similar picture arises for the unemployment rate, except that it is the first- and the second-quarter dummies that are "large" in absolute value. In general, for all four variables considered in Fig. 1 there is a tendency for the overall mean to be constant, for seasonals to become milder, and for the intensity of the fluctuations to be reduced with some dummy coefficients turning insignificant in the last two decades. In addition, for the consumption and

Table 7. Test for structural stability in the seasonal pattern of U.S. macroeconomic variables. Sample 46,1–85,4

Series	Quarter 1	Quarter 2	Quarter 3	Quarter 4	π	$\pi/2$	Joint
Investments	× .78*	× .29	.89*	.46	.10	2.16*	2.29*
Residential investments	× .66*	× .09	.93*	× .04	.09	1.35*	1.52*
Nonresidential investments	× .33	× .28	× .26	× .35	.17	1.13*	1.37*
Nonresidential structures	× .43	× .38	× .43	× .55*	.99*	.38	1.36*
Nonresidential producer durables	.41	× .47*	× .19	× .30	.33	.94*	1.38*
Consumption	× 2.16*	× 1.00*	× .63*	× 1.66*	2.11*	2.73*	4.98*
Consumption durables	× .22	× .12	× .36	× .31	.39	.57	.96
Consumption nondurables	× 1.26*	× 1.60*	× 1.10*	× 1.74*	1.70*	2.22*	3.92*
Consumption services	× 1.36*	× .70*	× 1.21*	× .98*	1.49*	1.24*	2.74*
Gross national product	× 1.05*	× 1.14*	× .57*	× .88*	.46	2.88*	3.44*
Government expenditure	× 1.15*	× .70*	× .07	× .67*	.99*	.80*	1.79*
Imports	.15	× .44	× .08	.29	.30	.54	.85
Exports	.19	× .17	× .38	× .22	.25	.33	.60
Final sales	× 2.03*	× .26	× .17	× 1.47*	2.09*	2.97*	5.01*
CPI	.39	× .67*	× .29	.29	.26	.61	.87
T-bill rate	.35	.20	.09	.07	.32	.34	.66
Business inventories	× .24	1.53*	.34	.60*	.47*	1.08*	1.56*
M1	× .07	2.10*	× .13	× .18	1.79*	1.77*	3.67*
Unemployment rate	× 1.11*	× 1.23*	.44	× .12	.88*	2.20*	3.10*
Labor force	× 1.33*	× .31	× .09	.45	1.05*	1.21*	2.29*
Employment	× .36	× .31	× .09	.57*	.32	.84*	1.16*
Monetary base	× .58*	× .33	× .20	× .23	.12	.93*	1.08*
Monetary multiplier	.57*	.81*	.30	× .72*	.31	1.59*	1.98*
Hours	× .07	× .81*	× .30	× .72*	.08	1.35*	1.44*
Wage	× .29	× .43	× .16	× .36	.83*	.30	1.14*

Note: An "×" indicates a dummy that is significant at the 5% level. The numbers reported in the columns for Quarters 1–4 are the values of the L statistics for each quarter. The next two columns report the values of the L_π and $L_{\pi/2}$ statistics, and the last column reports the joint test for instability at both frequencies. An asterisk indicates significance at the 5% level.

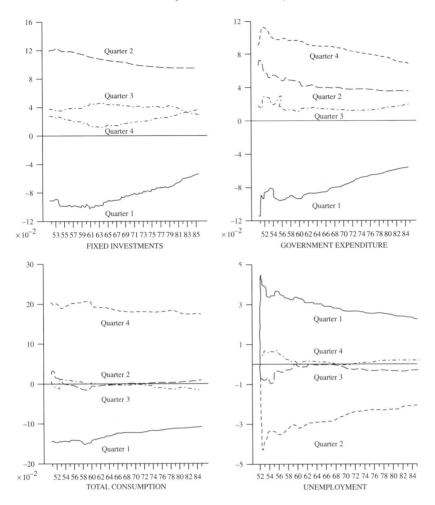

Fig. 1. Recursive estimates of seasonal dummies.

unemployment series, the coefficients of the dummies of two quarters change sign throughout the sample even though their value is always close to 0. Despite these large changes, none of the variables examined display a significant change in the location of seasonal peaks and troughs over time. Because these patterns are very typical of those we found among all the variables in the sample, one conclusion that emerges is that the intensity of seasonal fluctuations has substantially subsided in the past two decades, but no major seasonal inversion has occurred.

5.2 European industrial production

The second data set includes quarterly nonseasonally adjusted industrial production (IP) indexes for eight European countries (the United Kingdom, Germany, France, Italy, Spain, Austria, Belgium, and the Netherlands) for the

Table 8. Test for structural stability in the seasonal pattern of quarterly industrial production indexes, sample 60,1–89,2

Series	Quarter 1	Quarter 2	Quarter 3	Quarter 4	π	$\pi/2$	Joint
France	.13	× .57*	× .25	× .43	.57*	.39	.99
Germany	× .33	× 1.15*	.35	× .14	.47*	1.59*	2.06*
U.K.	× .19	1.16*	× .76*	× .12	1.09*	1.11*	2.20*
Italy	× .39	× .40	× 1.42*	× .78*	.85*	2.42*	3.20*
Austria	× .18	× .46	× .69*	× .15	.10	1.30*	1.45*
Belgium	1.19*	× .53*	× .81*	× .24	.36	1.59*	2.01*
Netherlands	.64*	× 1.15*	1.58*	× .92*	.21	2.72*	2.89*
Spain	.22	× 0.45	× 1.15*	× .56*	.87*	1.16*	2.11*

Note: An "×" indicates a dummy that is significant at the 5% level. The numbers reported in columns for Quarters 1–4 are the values of the L statistics for each quarter. The next two columns report the value of the L statistics at each of the two seasonal frequencies. The last column reports the joint test for instability at both seasonal frequencies. An asterisk indicates significance at the 5% level.

sample 1960,3 to 1989,2. Canova (1993) described the original sources of the data. In this case, we also selected $m = 5$ and estimated the model in log differences with a lag of the dependent variable. The results of testing for seasonal instability appear in Table 8.

The joint test indicates that all series, except possibly France, clearly display statistically significant changes in their seasonal patterns. The evidence of instability is stronger at the annual frequency, where the tests reject the null of no instability for all variables but the French IP index. At the biannual frequency, the test rejects the null for the IP index of the five largest countries. When we examine the stability of individual dummy coefficients, we find that, over the cross-section, all quarters appear to be subject to structural change but that the highest concentration of rejections of the null hypothesis of constancy emerges in the third quarter. This does not come as a surprise because the third quarter has been traditionally the vacation time in European countries, and in the last decade rescheduling programs have reduced the closing time of factories and offices to 10–14 days only, down from the 21 days which was the average in the 70s. Finally, the estimated coefficients of the dummies over three different decades and the recursive least squares plots (not presented for reasons of space) indicate changes in intensity, pattern and, in some cases location of seasonal peaks and troughs over time.

5.3 Monthly stock returns

The third data we examine are a set of monthly stock returns on value-weighted indexes for seven industrialized countries (the United States, Japan, Germany, France, the United Kingdom, Italy, and Canada). This data set was obtained from the Citibase Tape and covers the period 1950,3 to 1989,9. As with the previous data sets, we set $m = 5$ and add one lagged dependent variable in the regression. The results of testing for the instability of the seasonal patterns in these variables are presented in Table 9.

Table 9. Test for structural stability in the seasonal pattern of monthly stock returns: sample 50,1–89,9

	U.S.	Japan	Germany	France	UK	Italy	Canada
Significant dummies	1	1, 2, 11	7		1, 4, 7	7	1, 8	1
January	.07	.57*	.34	.05	.44	.61*	.08
February	.06	.39	.12	.40	.33	.10	.15
March	.14	.14	.18	.05	.28	.13	.19
April	.32	.11	.16	.28	.21	.14	.14
May	.33	.08	.25	.07	.24	.11	.16
June	.11	.30	.15	.11	.10	.12	.11
July	.06	.26	.22	.17	.08	.05	.05
August	.05	.12	.12	.09	.41	.26	.26
September	.30	.18	.28	.06	.11	.07	.06
October	.11	.52*	.12	.15	.12	.16	.11
November	.09	.33	.22	.07	.42	.15	.10
December	.17	.19	.14	.12	.41	.22	.08
Joint	1.74	3.02*	2.17	1.43	2.88*	1.84	1.25
$\pi/6$	.56	1.78*	.65	.70	1.44*	.70	.31

Note: The first 12 rows after the space report the values of the L statistic for each month. The next row reports the value of the L statistic for the joint test of instability at all seasonal frequencies. The last row reports the test for seasonal instability at frequency $\pi/6$. An asterisk indicates significance at the 5% level.

All stock returns display some form of seasonality. The most significant seasonal dummies are for January returns (except for Germany and the United Kingdom). July and August returns have significant coefficients in four European countries. When we test for the structural stability of individual dummy coefficients, we find that significant time variations have emerged only for returns on a value-weighted index in Japan, the United Kingdom, and Italy. The joint test only rejects for Japan and the United Kingdom, where the rejection is due to a unit root at the annual frequency. It appears, therefore, that knowledge of predictable returns in four of the seven countries did not result in changes in these patterns, possibly indicating an inefficient propagation of information across these markets.

6 Conclusions

This article proposes a set of tests to examine the structural stability of seasonal patterns over time. The tests are built on the null hypothesis of unchanged seasonality and can be tailored to test for unit roots at seasonal frequencies or for time variation in seasonal dummy variables. We derive the asymptotic distribution of the statistics under general conditions that accommodate weakly dependent processes. A small Monte Carlo exercise demonstrates that the asymptotic distribution is a good approximation to the finite-sample distribution, and the test has good power against reasonable alternatives.

We apply the test to the three data sets. We find that in most cases deterministic dummies poorly capture the essence of seasonal variation in U.S. macroeconomic variables and that significant time variations are present in the seasonal patterns of the IP indexes of eight major industrialized countries and in the stock return indexes of some G-7 countries. The presence of seasonal time variations in quarterly U.S. macroeconomic variables partially invalidates some of the conclusions obtained by Barsky and Miron (1989), confirms recent findings of Ghysels (1991), and suggests the need for a more thorough and comprehensive examination of the statistical properties of macroeconomic variables.

The extension of our testing procedures to a vector of time series is straightforward. In that framework one can examine, for example, whether at least one of the seasonal intercepts of the system has changed. This extension would be analogous to that which Choi and Ahn (1993) made to the KPSS tests.

Acknowledgements

Canova thanks the European Community for an EUI research grant, and Hansen thanks the National Science Foundation for a research grant. Part of this research was undertaken while Canova was associated with the European University Institute, Florence. The comments and the suggestions of John Geweke, Eric Ghysels, Sven Hylleberg, Adrian Pagan, two anonymous referees, the participants at seminars at the European University Institute, Institute of Advanced Studies, and the 1992 Winter Meetings of the Econometric Society are gratefully acknowledged. We are particularly grateful to an associate editor for extensive comments, in particular for his suggestion to use the trigonometric seasonal models of Hannan and Harvey to simplify our original presentation.

References

Anderson, T. W., and Darling, D. A. (1952), "Asymptotic Theory of Certain 'Goodness of Fit' Criteria on Stochastic Processes," *The Annals of Mathematical Statistics*, 23, 193–212.

Andrews, D. (1991), "Heteroskedasticity and Autocorrelation Consistent Covariance Matrix Estimation," *Econometrica*, 59, 817–858.

Barsky, R., and Miron, J. (1989), "The Seasonal and the Business Cycle," *Journal of Political Economy*, 97, 503–534.

Bell, W. R. (1993), "Empirical Comparison of Seasonal ARIMA and ARIMA Components (Structural) Time Series Models," unpublished paper presented at the 1993 Joint Statistical Meetings, San Francisco, August 8–12.

Braun, T., and Evans, C. (1990), "Seasonality and Equilibrium Business Cycle Theories," discussion paper 217, University of Virginia, Dept. of Economics.

Box, G, and Jenkins, G. (1976), *Time Series Analysis: Forecasting and Control*, San Francisco, Holden-Day.

Burns, A. F., and Mitchell, W. C. (1946), *Measuring Business Cycles*, New York: Columbia University Press (for the National Bureau of Economic Research).

Canova, F. (1992), "An Alternative Approach to Modeling and Forecasting Seasonal Time Series," *Journal of Business & Economic Statistics*, 10, 97–108.

—— (1993), "Forecasting Time Series With Common Seasonal Patterns," *Journal of Econometrics*, 55, 173–200.

Chattarjee, S., and Ravikumar, B. (1992), "A Neoclassical Growth Model With Seasonal Fluctuations," *Journal of Monetary Economics*, 29, 59–86.

Choi, I., and Ahn, B. C. (1993), "Testing the Null of Stationarity for Multiple Time Series," unpublished manuscript, Ohio State University, Dept. of Economics.

Dickey, D., and Fuller, W. (1979), "Distribution of the Estimators for Autoregressive Time Series With a Unit Root," *Journal of the American Statistical Association*, 79, 355–367.

Dickey, D., Hasza, D., and Fuller, W. (1984), "Testing Seasonal Unit Roots in Seasonal Time Series," *Journal of the American Statistical Association*, 79, 355–367.

Engle, R., Granger, C., and Hallman, J. (1989), "Merging Short and Long Run Forecasts: An Application of Seasonal Cointegration to Monthly Electricity Sales Forecasts," *Journal of Econometrics*, 40, 45–62.

Engle, R., Granger, C., Hylleberg, S., and Lee, H. (1993), "Seasonal Cointegration: The Japanese Consumption Function," *Journal of Econometrics*, 55, 275–298.

Franses, P. H. (1994), "A Multivariate Approach to Modeling Univariate Seasonal Time Series," *Journal of Econometrics*, 63, 133–151.

Ghysels, E. (1988), "A Study Toward a Dynamic Theory of Seasonality for Economic Time Series," *Journal of the American Statistical Association*, 83, 168–172.

—— (1991), "On the Seasonal Asymmetries and Their Implications for Stochastic and Deterministic Models of Seasonality," unpublished manuscript, University of Montreal, Dept. of Economics.

Ghysels, E., Lee, H., and Noh, J. (1992), "Testing for Unit Roots in Seasonal Time Series: Some Theoretical Extension and a Monte Carlo Investigation," unpublished manuscript, University of Montreal, Dept. of Economics.

Granger, C. W. J., and Newbold, P. (1986), *Forecasting Economic Time Series* (2nd ed), New York: Academic Press.

Hannan, E. J. (1970), *Multiple Time Series*, New York: John Wiley.

Hansen, B. E. (1990), "Lagrange Multiplier Tests for Parameter Instability in Non-linear Models," unpublished manuscript, University of Rochester, Dept. of Economics.

—— (1992a), "Consistent Covariance Matrix Estimation for Dependent Heterogeneous Processes," *Econometrica*, 60, 967–972.

—— (1992b), "Testing for Parameter Instability in Linear Models," *Journal of Policy Modeling*, 14, 517–533.

Hansen, L., and Sargent, T. (1993), "Seasonality and Approximation Errors in Rational Expectations Models," *Journal of Econometrics*, 55, 21–55.

Harvey, A. C. (1990), *Forecasting, Structural Time Series Models and the Kalman Filter*, Cambridge, U K.: Cambridge University Press.

Hylleberg, S. (1992), "Tests for Seasonal Unit Roots: A Comparative Study," unpublished manuscript, submitted to *Journal of Econometrics*.

Hylleberg, S., Engle, R., Granger, C., and Yoo, S. (1990), "Seasonal Integration and Cointegration," *Journal of Econometrics*, 44, 215–238.

Hylleberg, S., Jorgensen, C., and Sorensen, N. K. (1993), "Seasonality in Macroeconomic Time Series," *Empirical Economics*, 18, 321–335.

Hylleberg, S., and Pagan, A. (1994), "Seasonal Integration and the Evolving Seasonal Model," unpublished manuscript, Australian National University.

Kwiatkowski, D., Phillips, P. C. B., Schmidt, P., and Shin, Y. (1992),"Testing the Null Hypothesis of Stationarity Against the Alternative of a Unit Root. How Sure Are We That Economic Time Series Have a Unit Root?" *Journal of Econometrics*, 44, 159–178.

Newey, W. K., and West, K. D. (1987), "A Simple, Positive Semidefinite, Heteroskedastic and Autocorrelation Consistent Covariance Matrix," *Econometrica*, 55, 703–708.

Nyblom, J. (1989), "Testing for the Constancy of Parameters Over Time," *Journal of the American Statistical Association*, 84, 223–230.

Osborn, D., and Smith, J. (1989), "The Performance of Periodic Autoregressive Models in Forecasting Seasonal U.K. Consumption," *Journal of Business & Economic Statistics*, 7, 117–127.

Pierce, D. (1978), "Seasonal Adjustment When Both Deterministic and Stochastic Seasonality Are Present," in *Seasonal Analysis of Economic Time Series* A. Zellner (ed.), Washington, DC: U.S. Department of Commerce, Bureau of the Census, pp. 242–269.

Saikkonen, P., and Luukkonen, R. (1993), "Testing for a Moving Average Unit Root in Autoregressive Integrated Moving Average Models," *Journal of the American Statistical Association*, 88, 596–601.

Shiskin, J., Young, A., and Musgrave, J. (1967), "The X-11 Variant of the Census Method II Seasonal Adjustment Program," Technical Paper 15, Washington, DC, Government Printing Office.

Tanaka, K. (1990), "Testing for a Moving Average Unit Root," *Econometric Theory*, 6, 433–444.

Thaler, R. (1987), "Anomalies: The January Effect." *Journal of Economic Perspectives*, 1, 197–201.

Part IV

Non-Linear and Non-Gaussian Models

16

Introduction

The general framework for handling non-linear and non-Gaussian state space models is such that the measurement equation is replaced by the observation conditional density,

$$p(y_1, \ldots, y_T | \alpha_1, \ldots, \alpha_T; \psi) = \prod_{t=1}^{T} p(y_t | \alpha_t; \psi), \qquad (16.1)$$

specifying that α_t is sufficient for y_t, whereas the transition equation is replaced by the Markovian transition density,

$$p(\alpha_1, \ldots, \alpha_T | \psi) = p(\alpha_1 | \psi) \prod_{t=1}^{T} p(\alpha_{t+1} | \alpha_t; \psi). \qquad (16.2)$$

Here, ψ denotes a vector of hyperparameters that uniquely characterise the measurement and the transition density within a given family.

The seven papers selected for this collection of readings provide only a small sample of a literature that has has been growing very rapidly during the last decade, paralleling the advances in computational inference using stochastic simulation techniques. In order to highlight the potentials of the general analytic framework, we point out the kind of applications that have been considered in the literature.

i. Models for time series observations originating from the exponential family, such as count data with Poisson, binomial, negative binomial and multinomial distributions, and continuous data with skewed distributions such as the exponential and gamma (see Chapters 17, 20 and 21).

ii. Stochastic variance models, allowing the variability of the series or its components to change over time (Chapters 20 and 21). The basic univariate specification aims at capturing the empirical regularities found in financial time series, such as leptokurtosis and volatility clustering. Comprehensive reviews are Shephard (1996) and Harvey, Ghysels and Renault (1996).

iii. Robust signal extraction. In the linear state space model, the disturbances of the measurement and the transition equations can be replaced by heavy-tailed densities, such as Student's t (Chapter 21), or scale mixtures of normals (Chapter 18). As pointed out and illustrated by Kitagawa (1987), heavy tailed densities have the flexibility of accommodating outliers and both smooth and abrupt changes in the evolution of the unobserved components. This extension is thus tailor made for robust signal extraction.

    iv. Regime switching. Dynamic models with Markov switching (see Chapter 18), introduced by Harrison and Stevens (1976), postulate that the system matrices vary according to the states of a latent first order Markov chain, s_t. They fit in to the general state space representation set up above ((16.1)–(16.2)) if s_t is added to the state vector. These models are the subject of a recent monograph by Kim and Nelson (1999).

    v. Nonlinear models. A typical specification is such the measurements are non-linearly related to the states, which evolve according to a nonlinear first order vector autoregression: $y_t = Z_t(\alpha_t) + G_t \varepsilon_t, \alpha_{t+1} = T_t(\alpha_t) + H_t \varepsilon_t$, where $Z_t(\cdot)$, $T_t(\cdot)$ are known functions, and $\varepsilon_t \sim \text{IID}(0, I_g)$. See Kitagawa and Gersch (1996) for examples, and Shephard (1994) for an application to a multiplicative model for seasonal adjustment. The methods proposed in Chapter 21 can be extended to nonlinear models (see Durbin and Koopman, 2001).

For the general state space model, the recursive formulae for the one-step-ahead predictive densities of the states and the observations, and the filtering density are respectively:

$$p(\alpha_{t+1}|Y_t; \psi) = \int p(\alpha_{t+1}|\alpha_t; \psi) p(\alpha_t|Y_t; \psi) d\alpha_t$$
$$p(y_{t+1}|Y_t; \psi) = \int p(y_{t+1}|\alpha_{t+1}; \psi) p(\alpha_{t+1}|Y_t; \psi) d\alpha_{t+1} \qquad (16.3)$$
$$p(\alpha_{t+1}|Y_{t+1}; \psi) = p(\alpha_{t+1}|Y_t; \psi) p(y_{t+1}|\alpha_{t+1}; \psi) / p(y_{t+1}|Y_t; \psi)$$

The smoothing density is:

$$p(\alpha_t|Y_T; \psi) = p(\alpha_t|Y_t; \psi) \int \frac{p(\alpha_{t+1}|Y_T; \psi) p(\alpha_{t+1}|\alpha_t; \psi)}{p(\alpha_{t+1}|Y_t; \psi)} d\alpha_{t+1} \qquad (16.4)$$

A stream of the literature, reviewed in the next section, has investigated the possibility of deriving exact finite dimensional filters for the densities in (16.3); unfortunately this approach has limited applicability as analytic filters are available only under very special circumstances, and with severe limitations, as the smoothing and multi-step predictive densities are not available.

Direct numerical integration methods have also been considered (see Kitagawa, 1987, and West and Harrison, 1997, section 13.4), but they are prone to the *curse of dimensionality* problem, that is, they become more computationally cumbersome and inaccurate as the dimension of the state vector increases.

The various approximate modes of inference that have been proposed, such as the extended Kalman filter (Anderson and Moore, 1979), the Gaussian mixture approximations with collapsing (see West and Harrison, 1997, ch. 12, Kitagawa and Gersch, 1996, sec. 6.4, and the references therein), the approximate conjugate analysis of dynamic generalised linear models (West, Harrison and Migon, 1985), to quote a few, prove neither satisfactory nor easily generalisable (e.g. they cannot accommodate smoothing and multistep forecasting).

Stochastic simulation methods based on *Markov chain Monte Carlo* or Monte Carlo integration via *importance sampling* provide the kind of generality that is required to produce inferences for nonlinear and non-Gaussian models; moreover, the accuracy of the estimates is under the control of the investigator and can be assessed by diagnostics. The methods exploit the conditional independence structure of the general state space model and integrate fast and reliable algorithms such as the Kalman filter and smoother to generate samples from the required densities.

1 Analytic Filters for Non-Gaussian Models

Analytic filters completely determine the conditional distributions (16.3). Outside the linear-Gaussian framework, where this role is played by the Kalman filter, exact filters are admissible only under rather special circumstances. Fundamentally, it is necessary (Bather, 1965, Ferrante and Runggaldier, 1990) that the measurement, filtering and predictive densities belong to the exponential family, and that the latter is conjugate with the measurement density, so that $p(y_{t+1}|Y_t)$ is also fully determined[1].

Models for exponential family measurements were developed as a generalisation of the linear-Gaussian local level model, for which the updated estimate of the level and the one-step-ahead prediction are an exponentially weighted moving average (EWMA) of current and past observations. A peculiar trait is that model specification is not completed through the transition density (1.2) for the latent variable, but via the formulation of a transition scheme from $p(\alpha_t|Y_t)$ to $p(\alpha_{t+1}|Y_t)$, and the requirement that the latter is conjugate to the $p(y_t|\alpha_t)$.

Smith (1979) introduced the *power steady model*, such that $p(\alpha_{t+1}|Y_t) \propto p(\alpha_t|Y_t)^\omega$, where ω is a discount factor between zero and one. This formulation implies that the predictive density will have the same mode, but larger dispersion with respect to $p(\alpha_t|Y_t)$. He motivates the approach in a Bayesian decision theory framework and by analogy with the Gaussian local level model. The conditions under which the power steady model leads to EWMA forecasts have been rigorously established by Grunwald, Guttorp and Raftery (1993).

The paper by Harvey and Fernandes (HF), reproduced in Chapter 17, builds on work by Smith and Miller (1979) to derive exact analytic recursions for several models for count data within the classical framework, using the fundamental idea that, for a given measurement density, the state predictive distribution is conjugate to it and such that $\mathsf{E}(\alpha_{t+1}|Y_t) = \mathsf{E}(\alpha_t|Y_t)$ and $\mathsf{Var}(\alpha_{t+1}|Y_t) > \mathsf{Var}(\alpha_t|Y_t)$. They show that the predictions constitute an EWMA of the available information and that the parameter regulating the discounting can be estimated by maximum likelihood.

As stated above, the transition density of the latent process is only implicitly defined. However, for Poisson observations with mean α_t, the HF filter can be shown to be exact for the Gamma multiplicative transition density $\alpha_t = \omega^{-1}\alpha_{t-1}\eta_t$, with $\eta_t \sim \text{Beta}(\omega a_{t-1}, (1 - \omega)a_{t-1})$, and initial density $\alpha_1 \sim \text{Gamma}(a_1, b_1)$. This is equivalent to a random walk transition model for the canonical parameter $\theta_t = \ln \alpha_t$, $\theta_{t+1} = \theta_t + \eta_t^*$, with "centered" log-beta disturbances $\eta_t^* = \ln \eta_t - \ln \omega$ (note that the mode of η_t^* is zero, but $\mathsf{E}(\eta_t^*) < 0$).

Shephard (1994b) proposed the *local scale model* for stochastic volatility using a slightly modified Gamma transition kernel for the time-varying precision parameter, according to which the measurement density is specified as $y_t|\alpha_t \sim \text{NID}(0, \alpha_t^{-1})$, and $\alpha_{t+1} = e^{r_t}\alpha_t\eta_t$, where η_t and α_1 are as above, and $r_t = -\text{E}(\ln \eta_t)$. This modifications ensures that the random walk followed by the log-precision is driven by zero mean disturbances.

The local scale model has been extended to Bayesian vector autoregressive models with stochastic volatility by Uhlig (1997). Another application of the analytical filtering approach concerns time series of compositional data (Grunwald, Raftery and Guttorp, 1993). Vidoni (1999) derived analytic filters for two new classes of exponential family state space models using a constructive procedure which chooses the initial density of the latent process to be conjugate to (16.1) and defines a suitable conditional transition kernel $p(\alpha_{t+1}|\alpha_t, Y_t)$ that preserves conjugacy of the state predictive density. His approach gives rise to prediction rules that differ from the steady forecasting model.

The most serious limitation of the analytic approach is that it can only entertain very specialised models with a unique latent component, usually evolving in a random walk fashion, although other components can be introduced as regression effects via the appropriate link function, see Chapter 17, Section 6. Also, the formulation is such that the location and the dispersion of the predictive and filtering densities are tied together, as their evolution depends on a single parameter, and this again limits the range of models considered; this point is discussed in Grunwald, Hamza and Hyndman (1997). Finally, only the mean of the multistep predictive distribution is available via the law of iterated expectations and no exact recursion can be derived for the smoothing density (16.4).

2 Stochastic Simulation Methods

Let $y = (y_1', \ldots, y_T')'$, $\alpha = (\alpha_1', \ldots, \alpha_T')'$, and $\psi = (\psi_1, \ldots, \psi_K)$. Interest lies in aspects of the posterior marginal densities $p(\alpha|y)$ and $p(\psi|y)$, for instance $\bar{x}(\alpha) = \int x(\alpha)p(\alpha|y)d\alpha$ for some function $h(\cdot)$. Were it possible to generate independent samples from these posterior densities, or equivalently from the joint posterior, $p(\alpha, \psi|y)$, we could use Monte Carlo integration methods to estimate any feature of interest. Standard techniques are composition, importance sampling and accept/reject methods, see e.g. Ripley (1987) and Tanner (1997, ch. 3). Unfortunately, drawing directly from these densities can be infeasible since they are of complicated mathematical form and/or highly dimensional.

Markov chain Monte Carlo (MCMC) methods produce correlated random draws from the density $p(\alpha, \psi|y)$ by repeatedly sampling an ergodic Markov chain whose invariant distribution is the target density. Fundamental results are the data augmentation algorithm (Tanner and Wong, 1987, see Frühwirth-Schnatter, 1994 for application to the Bayesian analysis of linear state space models), the Metropolis-Hastings algorithm, and the Gibbs sampler, which can be derived as a special case of the previous two; see Casella and George (1992) and Chib and Greenberg (1995) for introductory treatments, and Gilks, Richardson and Spiegelhalter

(1996), Gamerman (1997), Robert and Casella (2001) for extensive discussion and references.

If we let z denote a random vector and consider the problem of sampling from $p(z|y)$. Suppose that we propose a new value for z^* according to a proposal transition density $q(z, z^*|y)$, which is available for sampling. A draw from the proposal is accepted with probability

$$\gamma(z, z^*) = \min\left\{1, \frac{p(z^*|y)q(z^*, z|y)}{p(z|y)q(z, z^*|y)}\right\}.$$

This scheme (Metropolis-Hastings) defines a reversible Markov chain that has $p(z|y)$ as invariant distribution, under mild regularity conditions.

Writing $z = (\alpha, \psi)$, suppose that we are unable to define a suitable $q(z, z^*|y)$, but that we can update the components one at a time by subsequently drawing α^* from the conditional proposal density $p(\alpha|\psi, y)$ and $\psi^* \sim p(\psi|\alpha, y)$ where the conditioning variables are set equal to their most recent value. To be precise, we iterate according to the following scheme:

1. draw $\alpha^{(i)} \sim p(\alpha|\psi^{(i-1)}, y)$
2. draw $\psi^{(i)} \sim p(\psi^{(i)}|\alpha^{(i)}, y)$

Then, each move is accepted with probability one, as the test ratio is identically one. This "one at a time" scheme accomplished with respect to the two blocks, α, ψ, is known as *Gibbs sampling* (GS), and defines a homogeneous MC such that the transition kernel is formed by the full conditional distributions and the invariant distribution is the unavailable target density.

The same argument can be iterated to divide the blocks into smaller components, whose full conditional distribution is available for sampling. For instance we can go down to a GS scheme where the blocks are the single states α_t and hyperparameters ψ_i. The speed of convergence of the GS crucially depends on the issue of blocking.

In the following sections we shall concentrate on the problem of sampling the states given the hyperparameters, the observations and any other quantity such as the indicator of a mixture, s_t. For simplicity we shall drop these conditioning variables from the notation. This will also allow us to discuss the samplers in a non Bayesian framework, where ψ is considered as fixed.

3 Single Move State Samplers

Carlin, Polson and Stoffer (CSP, 1992) introduced Bayesian analysis of specialised nonlinear and non-Gaussian state space models via Gibbs sampling with blocks represented by α_t and ψ_i, that are sampled in a fixed updating order. The states are sampled one at a time from the full conditional distribution $p(\alpha_t|\alpha_{\backslash t}, y)$ where $\alpha_{\backslash t}$ denotes the set α excluding α_t. Given the conditional independence structure of the state space model and applying Bayes' theorem,

$$p(\alpha_t|\alpha_{\backslash t}, y) = p(\alpha_t|\alpha_{t-1}, \alpha_{t+1}, y_t) \propto p(\alpha_t|\alpha_{t-1}, \alpha_{t+1})p(y_t|\alpha_t)$$
$$= p(\alpha_t|\alpha_{t-1})p(\alpha_{t+1}|\alpha_t)p(y_t|\alpha_t).$$

Sampling from the full conditional distribution can be achieved by standard methods if the three densities in the last expressions are Gaussian (CSP, 1992, Lemma p. 495). For stochastic volatility models $p(\alpha_t|\alpha_{\setminus t}, y)$ cannot be sampled directly; Kim, Shephard and Chib (KSC, 1998, sec. 2.2) illustrate the use of the classical acceptance-rejection sampling method, showing how to determine a strictly dominating Gaussian density from which candidate draws can be generated; Shephard and Pitt (SP, 1997, chapter 20, sec. 2.2) develop a pseudo-dominating acceptance-rejection algorithm using a second-order approximation of $p(y_t|\alpha_t)$.

The evidence in Chapters 18 (Section 3) 19 (Section 2) indicates that single move samplers may result extremely inefficient. This is due to the high correlation between the state parameters, which occurs when the state components are slowly evolving over time.

Gamerman (1998), in the context of Bayesian analysis of dynamic generalised linear models, proposes to alleviate this problem by a reparameterisation: he provides a single-move sampler, simulating from the full conditional distribution of the transition equation disturbances $\eta_t = H_t \epsilon_t$, based on:

$$p(\eta_t|\eta_{\setminus t}, y) \propto p(\eta_t)p(y|\eta) = p(\eta_t) \prod_{j=1}^{T} p(y_j|\eta_1, \ldots, \eta_{j-1}).$$

4 Multimove State Samplers

Another strategy is *blocking* highly correlated parameters into a higher dimensional component; in particular, samples of the states (or the disturbances) are generated in one move. This proves very effective in certain situations, such as sampling from $\alpha|y$ within a Gibbs sampling scheme in conditionally Gaussian models and for importance sampling via a Gaussian importance density (Section 16.6).

A multimove state sampler hinges upon the factorisation:

$$p(\alpha|y) = p(\alpha_T|y) \prod_{t=1}^{T-1} p(\alpha_t|\alpha_{t+1}, Y_t).$$

When the single conditional densities on the right hand side are Gaussian, the sampling scheme would amount to:

1. run the KF and store $\tilde{\alpha}_{t|t}, P_{t|t}$;
2. sample $\alpha_T^{(i)} \sim N(\tilde{\alpha}_{T|T}, P_{T|T})$;
3. for $t = T - 1, \ldots, 1$, sample

$$\alpha_t^{(i)} \sim N\big(\tilde{\alpha}_{t|t} + P_{t|t}T_t'P_{t+1|t}^{-1}(\alpha_{t+1}^{(i)} - T_t\tilde{\alpha}_{t|t}),$$

$$P_{t|t} - P_{t|t}T_t'(T_t P_{t|t}T_t' + H_t H_t')^{-1}T_t P_{t|t}\big).$$

This version of the multimove sampler was independently developed by Frühwirth-Schnatter (1994) and Carter and Kohn (1994), reproduced in Chapter 18.

Both, however, develop more efficient algorithms: Frühwirth-Schnatter deals with the case in which $H_t H_t'$ is singular but T_t is full rank and considers a linear transformation that separates out the random component from the deterministic ones. Situations in which the state distribution is singular arise when the transition equation contains identities or the same disturbance drives several components.

Carter and Kohn (Chapter 18, appendix 1) propose an algorithm that avoids the inversion of an $m \times m$ matrix: they compute the mean and the variance of $\alpha_t | \alpha_{t+1}, Y_t$ by a filtering approach that can be extended to deal with nonsingular state vectors in the following manner. In a time invariant model, let us assume that HH' is singular and is rewritten as RQR' where Q is $q \times q$ diagonal and $R'R = I$; transforming both sides of the transition equation we obtain

$$\alpha_{t+1}^* = T^* \alpha_t + \eta_t, \qquad \alpha_{t+1}^* = R' \alpha_{t+1}, \quad T^* = R'T, \quad \eta_t \sim N(0, Q).$$

Consider now the following pseudo-model:

$$y_i^* = Z_i \alpha_i + \eta_i,$$
$$\alpha_{i+1} = \alpha_i, \quad \alpha_1 \sim N(\tilde{\alpha}_{t|t}, P_{t|t}),$$

where the pseudo observations y_i^* are represented by the i-th element of the vector $R' \alpha_{t+1}$, for which a draw is available from the previous iteration, whilst Z_i and η_i are respectively the i-th row of the matrix T^*, and the i-th element of η_t. The Kalman filter can be run for $i = 1, 2, \ldots, q$ on the pseudo-model and will provide $\tilde{\alpha}_{q+1|q}$ and $P_{q+1|q}$, that are respectively the mean and the variance of the conditional distribution $\alpha_t | \alpha_{t+1}, Y_t$.

5 The Simulation Smoother

A more efficient multimove sampler can be constructed by focussing on the disturbances, rather than the states. This is the idea underlying the simulation smoother proposed by De Jong and Shephard (1996, Chapter 19 of this volume).

Consider the linear-Gaussian state space model of section 1.1 with initial conditions $\alpha_1 = a_1 + H_0 \varepsilon_0$, where a_1 and H_0 are known and finite, and $\varepsilon_0 \sim N(0, I_g)$. Assuming, without loss of generality, that the matrix $[G_t', H_t']'$ is full column rank, the structure of the model is such that the states are a (possibly singular) linear transformation of the disturbances and that $G_t \varepsilon_t$ can be recovered from $H_t \varepsilon_t$ via the measurement equation, which implies that the distribution of $\varepsilon | y$ is singular. Thus, to achieve efficiency and to avoid degeneracies we need to focus on a suitably selected subset of the disturbances.

Let $\eta_t = \Gamma_t^* \varepsilon_t$ denote this subset, where Γ^* is chosen by selecting a basis for the row space of H_t: if H_t is written as $H_t^* \Gamma_t^*$ (which is always possible via a singular value decomposition) such that Γ_t^* is full row rank and $H_t^{*'} H_t^* = I$, then a draw from $H_t \epsilon_t | Y_T$ is constructed from that of $\eta_t | Y_T$, and α is in turn obtained from $\eta = (\eta_0, \ldots, \eta_T)$ using the transition equation.

The simulation smoother hinges on the decomposition:

$$p(\eta_0, \ldots, \eta_T | y) = g(\eta_T | y) \prod_{t=0}^{T-1} p(\eta_t | \eta_{t+1}, \ldots, \eta_T, y).$$

Conditional random vectors are generated recursively. In the forward step we run the KF and the innovations, their covariance matrix and the Kalman gain are stored. In the backwards sampling step conditional random vectors are generated recursively from $\eta_t | \eta_{t+1}, \ldots, \eta_T, y$; the algorithm keeps track of all the changes in the mean and the covariance matrix of these conditional densities.

A more efficient simulation smoother has been recently developed by Durbin and Koopman (2002). Its derivation uses the support of the *disturbance smoother*; it should be recalled from Section 1.6.1 and Chapter 5 that this is a backwards smoothing algorithm that evaluates $\tilde{\varepsilon}_{t|T} = \mathsf{E}(\varepsilon_t | Y_T)$ as a linear combination of the Kalman filter innovations, along with its covariance matrix.

Their argument proceeds from the decomposition $\varepsilon = \tilde{\varepsilon} + \varepsilon^*$, where $\tilde{\varepsilon} = \{\tilde{\varepsilon}_{t|T}\}$ is evaluated by the disturbance smoother, and $\varepsilon^* = \varepsilon - \tilde{\varepsilon}$ is the disturbance smoothing error. The authors show that it is relatively straightforward to simulate from $\varepsilon - \tilde{\varepsilon} | y$: we first draw the disturbances from their unconditional Gaussian distribution $\varepsilon_t^+ \sim \mathsf{NID}(0, I_g), t = 0, 1, \ldots, T$, and generate "pseudo-innovations", v_t^+, from the following filter:

$$v_t^+ = Z_t x_t^+ + G_t \varepsilon_t^+, \qquad x_{t+1}^+ = L_t x_t^+ + (H_t - K_t G_t)\varepsilon_t^+,$$

with starting value $x_1^+ = H_0 \varepsilon_0^+$. One could alternatively think of generating from the draws ε^+ simulated observations, y^+, recursively from the model 1.1 and 1.2, and then running the KF to obtain the innovations, but this is achieved more efficiently in one step by working directly with the prediction error representation of the model.

The disturbance smoother applied to v^+ computes $\tilde{\varepsilon}^+ = \mathsf{E}(\varepsilon | v^+) = \mathsf{E}(\varepsilon | y^+)$. It should be noticed that $\varepsilon^+ - \tilde{\varepsilon}^+$ is then a draw from $\varepsilon - \tilde{\varepsilon} | y \sim \mathsf{N}(0, V)$, where V is the MSE matrix that does not depend on the observations, and thus does not vary across the simulations; hence, adding back the smoothed disturbance we get the desired draw from the distribution $\varepsilon | y$. It is clear that the gain in efficiency over the algorithm presented in Chapter 19 stems from the fact that only the first moments of the conditional distributions need to be evaluated.

Multimove samplers are a very effective strategy for the class of "partial non-Gaussian" models, considered in Carter and Kohn (1994, Ch. 18) and Shephard (1994). These arise when, conditional on a Markov latent process s_t, such that $p(s) = p(s_1) \prod_{t=1} p(s_{t+1} | s_t)$, the system is linear and Gaussian. Then α is drawn by multimove sampler; see KSC, section 3, for an application to stochastic volatility models. Carter and Kohn also propose a multimove sampler for a latent discrete Markov chain s.

When the state space model is intrinsically non-Gaussian the multimove sampler can be based on a Gaussian approximation to the true density. Acceptance rejection schemes can be adopted but the rejections are usually high. An intermediate strategy, based on sampling blocks of disturbances, is considered in Chapter 20, Section 3.

6 Importance Sampling

Stochastic simulation methods for non-Gaussian state space models using importance sampling were introduced by Shephard and Pitt (Chapter 20) and Durbin and Koopman (1997) and later extended to Bayesian inference and non-linear models by Durbin and Koopman (DK, 2000, reproduced as Chapter 21, and 2001). Unlike MCMC methods, importance sampling generates independent samples, unless correlation is purposively induced by the use of antithetic and control variables.

Let us consider the problem of estimating the expectation of a function of the states (e.g. a percentile, or a moment) with respect to their smoothing density:

$$\bar{x} = \mathsf{E}[x(\alpha)|y] = \int x(\alpha)p(\alpha|y)d\alpha$$

Since direct simulation from $p(\alpha|y)$ is not feasible, a Gaussian importance density, $g(\alpha|y, \psi)$, is introduced, which is available for sampling and is designed to be as close as possible to the target density. Then, writing

$$\bar{x} = \frac{g(y)}{p(y)} \int x(\alpha) \frac{p(\alpha, y)}{g(\alpha, y)} g(\alpha|y)d\alpha = \frac{\mathsf{E}_g[x(\alpha)w(\alpha, y)]}{\mathsf{E}_g[w(\alpha, y)]}$$

where $w(\alpha, y) = p(\alpha, y)/g(\alpha, y)$, and E_g denotes the expectation with respect to the Gaussian importance density.

In the basic implementation of importance sampling, N independent samples, $\alpha^{(i)}, i = 1, \ldots, N$, are drawn from $g(\alpha|y)$ using the simulation smoother. The draws are used to form the MC estimate:

$$\hat{x} = \frac{\sum_i x_i w_i}{\sum_i w_i}, \qquad x_i = x(\alpha^{(i)}), \qquad w_i = \frac{p(\alpha^{(i)}, y)}{g(\alpha^{(i)}, y)}.$$

The estimator is unbiased and, under weak assumptions (Geweke, 1989), converges almost surely to $\bar{x}$. Importance sampling gives more weight to samples for which the density ratio is large and downweights samples for which it is small. The adequacy of the approximation can be assessed by examining the distribution of the weights.

The choice of the importance density is essential to the efficiency of the method; to achieve high efficiency we need to sample $g(\alpha|y)$ in regions where $|x(\alpha)|p(\alpha|y)$ is large. The tails of the importance density should not decay faster than the tails of the target density.

DK obtain the importance density by linearisation techniques imposing the condition that the mode of the approximating linear Gaussian model is coincident with that of the target density. This amounts to constructing pseudo-observations and choosing the system matrices so that $g(\alpha|y)$ and $p(\alpha|y)$ have the same mode.

The mode estimating equations for the Gaussian approximating equations are solved by a suitable number of iterations of the Kalman filter and smoother.

Chapter 21 discusses classical maximum likelihood estimation, Bayesian inference, and several computational issues, such as reparameterisation in terms of the disturbances, the use of variance reduction techniques to improve the efficiency of the Monte Carlo estimates.

The importance sampling approach is powerful and computationally attractive, as the illustrations suggest, but it has less general applicability than MCMC methods; for instance, it cannot deal with those situations in which multimodality arises in the posterior distribution of the states or the observational density.

7 Sequential Monte Carlo Methods

MCMC and the importance sampling approach are essentially static, or *batch*, modes of inference. They are not suitable for recursive estimation, since as a new observation is obtained the importance weights need to be recomputed or the Gibbs sampling be reiterated. Sequential Monte Carlo methods provide algorithms, known as *particle filters*, for recursive, or *on-line*, estimation of the predictive and filtering densities in (16.3). Simulation from these densities is also relevant for the construction of diagnostics (see Kim, Shephard and Chib, 1998). A comprehensive reference is Doucet, de Freitas and Gordon (2001).

Assume that an IID sample of size N from the filtering density at time t, $p(\alpha_t|Y_t)$, is available; each draw represents a "particle" and will be denoted $\alpha_t^{(i)}$, $i = 1, \ldots, N$; the true density is then approximated by the empirical density function:

$$\hat{p}(\alpha_t \in A|Y_t) = \frac{1}{N} \sum_{i=1}^{N} I(\alpha_t^{(i)} \in A), \tag{16.5}$$

where $I(\cdot)$ is the indicator function.

The method of composition (mixtures) is applied to generate a Monte Carlo approximation to the state and measurement predictive densities; in particular, replacing the empirical density for $p(\alpha_t|Y_t)$ in the analytical expressions for $p(\alpha_{t+1}|Y_t)$ and $p(y_{t+1}|Y_t)$, we generate $\alpha_{t+1|t}^{(i)} \sim p(\alpha_{t+1}|\alpha_t^{(i)})$, $i = 1, \ldots, N$ and $y_{t+1|t}^{(i)} \sim p(y_{t+1}|\alpha_t^{(i)})$, $i = 1, \ldots, N$.

The characterisation of the filtering density is achieved by an *importance sampling step*: the importance weights $w_i = p(y_{t+1}|\alpha_{t+1|t}^{(i)})/\sum_{j=1}^{N} p(y_{t+1}|\alpha_{t+1|t}^{(j)})$ are evaluated and any aspect of interest, $\bar{x}(\alpha_{t+1}) = \int x(\alpha_{t+1})p(\alpha_{t+1}|Y_{t+1})d\alpha_{t+1}$, is estimated by $\hat{\bar{x}}(\alpha_{t+1}) = \sum_i w_i x(\alpha_{t+1|t}^{(i)})$.

To iterate the process it is necessary to generate new particles from $p(\alpha_{t+1}|Y_{t+1})$ with probability mass equal to $1/N$, so that the approximation to the filtering density will have the same form as (16.5), and the sequential simulation process can progress. This is achieved via Sampling/Importance Resampling (SIR, Rubin, 1987), according to which N particles $\alpha_{t+1}^{(i)}$ are sampled from $\alpha_{t+1|t}^{(i)}$

with probabilities proportional to the importance weights, w_i; the *resampling step* eliminates particles with low importance weights and propagates those with high w_i's.

This basic particle filter is known as the bootstrap (or SIR) filter; see Gordon, Salmond and Smith (1993) and Kitagawa (1996). Notice that the particles, $\alpha_{t+1|t}^{(i)}$, originate from the prior density and are "blind" to the information carried by y_{t+1}; this may cause problems when the prior is at conflict with the likelihood, $p(y_{t+1}|\alpha_{t+1|t}^{(i)})$, resulting in a highly uneven distribution of the weights w_i. A variety of sampling schemes have been proposed to overcome this conflict, see Pitt and Shephard (1999) and Doucet, de Freitas and Gordon (2001).

Doucet, Godsill and Andrieu (2000, reproduced in Chapter 22) present the general framework of sequential importance sampling/resampling MC filters, which includes the basic particle filter presented above as a special case. They also discuss how sequential MC algorithms can be extended to deal with multi-step prediction, smoothing and likelihood evaluation and illustrate two strategies for deriving the importance distribution (local linearisation) and improving the efficiency of the methods (Rao-Blackwellisation).

Note

1. In this section we suppress dependence on ψ to simplify the notation.

17
Time Series Models for Count or Qualitative Observations*

A. C. HARVEY AND C. FERNANDES
Department of Statistical and Mathematical Sciences,
London School of Economics

Time series sometimes consist of count data in which the number of events occurring in a given time interval is recorded. Such data are necessarily nonnegative integers, and an assumption of a Poisson or negative binomial distribution is often appropriate. This article sets up a model in which the level of the process generating the observations changes over time. A recursion analogous to the Kalman filter is used to construct the likelihood function and to make predictions of future observations. Qualitative variables, based on a binomial or multinomial distribution, may be handled in a similar way. The model for count data may be extended to include explanatory variables. This enables nonstochastic slope and seasonal components to be included in the model, as well as permitting intervention analysis. The techniques are illustrated with a number of applications, and an attempt is made to develop a model-selection strategy along the lines of that used for Gaussian structural time series models. The applications include an analysis of the results of international football matches played between England and Scotland and an assessment of the effect of the British seat-belt law on the drivers of light-goods vehicles.

1 Introduction

It is not unusual to find time series consisting of *count data*. Such series record the number of events occurring in a given interval and are necessarily nonnegative integers. An example would be the number of accidents occurring in a given period. The number of goals scored by England against Scotland in international football matches also has the characteristics of count data. Count data models are usually based on distributions such as the Poisson or negative binomial. If the means of these distributions are constant or can be modeled in terms of observable variables, then estimation is relatively easy; see, for example, the book on generalized linear models (GLIM) by McCullagh and Nelder (1983). The essence of time series models, however, is that the mean of a series cannot be modeled in terms of observable variables but depends on some stochastic mechanism.

The nature of count data makes autoregressive integrated moving average (ARIMA) models inappropriate unless the values of the observations are large enough to justify the assumption of normally distributed disturbances as a reasonable approximation. The structural time series models used, for example,

* Reprinted from *The Journal of Business and Economic Statistics*, "Time series models for count or qualitative observations", by A. C. Harvey and C. Fernandes, pp. 407–422, Vol. 7, No. 4, 1989. Reproduced here by permission of the American Statistical Association.

by Harvey and Durbin (1986) or Kitagawa and Gersch (1984) offer a way out of these difficulties because they are set up in terms of permanent and transitory components, which are driven by separate disturbance terms. The simplest structural model, the local level plus noise, takes the form

$$y_t = \mu_t + \varepsilon_t, \quad t = 1, \ldots, T, \tag{1.1}$$

and

$$\mu_t = \mu_{t-1} + \eta_t, \tag{1.2}$$

where μ_t is a permanent or level component that can move up or down because of the disturbance term η_t and ε_t is a transitory disturbance term. If both η_t and ε_t are normally distributed, with zero means and variances σ_η^2 and σ_ε^2, respectively, then the model is equivalent to an ARIMA(0, 1, 1) process but is inappropriate for count data. The structural framework, however, allows one to specify ε_t in such a way that the distribution of y_t conditional on μ_t is Poisson or negative binomial. The stochastic process governing the evolution of μ_t should then be such that it is always positive.

The structural framework can also be adapted to handle qualitative variables. The simplest such case is binary data, in which the two possible outcomes are dependent on a binomial distribution. The setup may be generalized to several outcomes, dependent on a multinomial distribution.

The essence of the problem is to formulate a model that allows the distribution of y_t, given past observations, to be obtained. If this can be done, the likelihood function can be formed and used as the basis for estimating unknown parameters in the model. Predictions of future observations may then be made. The solution to the problem rests on the use of natural-conjugate distributions of the type used in Bayesian statistics. Our approach, however, is still essentially a classical one, and we attempt to develop a model-fitting procedure based on the kind of methodology used by Harvey and Durbin (1986).

We focus our attention on formulating models for count and qualitative data that are analogous to (1.1) and (1.2) in that they allow the underlying mean of the process to change over time. By introducing a hyperparameter, ω, into these local-level models, past observations are discounted in making forecasts of future observations. Indeed it transpires that in all cases the predictions can be constructed by an *exponentially weighted moving average* (EWMA) procedure. This is exactly what happens in (1.1) and (1.2) under the normality assumption (see Muth 1960).

Explanatory variables can be introduced into our local-level models via the kind of link functions that appear in GLIM models. Time trends and seasonal effects can be introduced as special cases. The framework does not extend to allowing these effects to be stochastic, as is typically the case in linear structural models. We believe that this is not a serious restriction. Even with data on continuous variables, it is not unusual to find that the slope and seasonal effects are close to being deterministic (e.g., see Harvey and Durbin 1986; Harvey and Todd 1983). With count and qualitative data, it seems even less likely that the observations will provide enough information to pick up changes in the slope and seasonal effects over time.

The use of natural-conjugate distributions to formulate local-level models for count and qualitative observations was suggested by Smith (1979, 1981). He observed that such procedures gave rise to EWMA predictions. His models were set up within a Bayesian framework, however, and he did not advocate the estimation of the hyperparameter, ω, by maximum likelihood (ML). The same is true of the work of West, Harrison, and Migon (1985) and West and Harrison (1986), in which various approximations are used to tackle a more general problem in which components other than the level are allowed to change over time. The approach adopted in this article is more like that employed by Smith and Miller (1986) in their study on predicting records in athletics. Their article is not concerned with count or qualitative observations, however, but with observations that, when transformed, are exponentially distributed.

The plan of the article is as follows. Section 2 sets out the basis of our approach and applies it to modeling Poisson data. Section 3 deals with data from a binomial distribution, and Section 4 makes the extension to the multinomial distributions. The negative binomial is examined in Section 5. Explanatory variables are introduced into the models in Section 6, and Section 7 deals with model selection and applications.

2 Observations from a Poisson Distribution

Suppose that the observation at time t is drawn from a Poisson distribution,

$$p(y_t|\mu_t) = \mu_t^{y_t} e^{-\mu_t} / y_t!. \tag{2.1}$$

This corresponds to the measurement equation of (1.1).

The conjugate prior for a Poisson distribution is the gamma distribution. Let $p(\mu_{t-1}|Y_{t-1})$ denote the pdf of μ_{t-1} conditional on the information at time $t-1$. Suppose that this distribution is gamma; that is, it is given by

$$p(\mu; a, b) = \frac{e^{-b\mu} \mu^{a-1}}{\Gamma(a) b^{-a}}, \quad a, b > 0, \tag{2.2}$$

with $\mu = \mu_{t-1}$, $a = a_{t-1}$, and $b = b_{t-1}$, where a_{t-1} and b_{t-1} are computed from the first $t-1$ observations, Y_{t-1}. In models (1.1) and (1.2) with normally distributed observations, $\mu_{t-1} \sim N(m_{t-1}, p_{t-1})$ at time $t-1$ implies that $\mu_t \sim N(m_{t-1}, p_{t-1} + \sigma_\eta^2)$ at time $t-1$. In other words, the mean of $\mu_t|Y_{t-1}$ is the same as that of $\mu_{t-1}|Y_{t-1}$, but the variance increases. The same effect can be induced in the gamma distribution by multiplying a and b by a factor less than 1. We therefore suppose that $p(\mu_t|Y_{t-1})$ follows a gamma distribution with parameters $a_{t|t-1}$ and $b_{t|t-1}$ such that

$$a_{t|t-1} = \omega a_{t-1}, \tag{2.3}$$

$$b_{t|t-1} = \omega b_{t-1}, \tag{2.4}$$

and $0 < \omega \leqslant 1$. Then

$$E(\mu_t|Y_{t-1}) = a_{t|t-1}/b_{t|t-1} = a_{t-1}/b_{t-1} = E(\mu_{t-1}|Y_{t-1}),$$

whereas

$$\text{var}(\mu_t|Y_{t-1}) = a_{t|t-1}/b_{t|t-1}^2$$

$$= \omega^{-1}\text{var}(\mu_{t-1}|Y_{t-1}).$$

The stochastic mechanism governing the transition of μ_{t-1} to μ_t is, therefore, defined implicitly rather than explicitly. It is possible, however, to show that it is formally equivalent to a multiplicative transition equation of the form $\mu_t = \omega^{-1}\mu_{t-1}\eta_t$, where η_t has a beta distribution, of the form (3.2), with parameters ωa_{t-1} and $(1 - \omega)a_{t-1}$ (see Smith and Miller 1986).

Once the observation y_t becomes available, the posterior distribution, $p(\mu_t|Y_t)$, is given by a gamma distribution with parameters

$$a_t = a_{t|t-1} + y_t \tag{2.5}$$

and

$$b_t = b_{t|t-1} + 1. \tag{2.6}$$

The initial prior gamma distribution—that is, the distribution of μ_t at time $t = 0$—tends to become diffuse, or noninformative, as $a, b \to 0$, although it is actually degenerate at $a = b = 0$ with $\Pr(\mu = 0) = 1$. None of this prevents the recursions [(2.3)–(2.6)] being initialized at $t = 0$ with $a_0 = b_0 = 0$, however. A proper distribution for μ_t is then obtained at time $t = \tau$, where τ is the index of the first nonzero observation. It follows that, conditional on Y_τ, the joint density of the observations $y_{\tau+1}, \ldots, y_T$ is

$$p(y_{\tau+1}, \ldots, y_T; \omega) = \prod_{t=\tau+1}^{T} p(y_t|Y_{t-1}). \tag{2.7}$$

The predictive pdf's are given by

$$p(y_t|Y_{t-1}) = \int_0^\infty p(y_t|\mu_t)p(\mu_t|Y_{t-1}) \, d\mu_t, \tag{2.8}$$

and, for Poisson observations and a gamma prior, this operation yields a negative binomial distribution

$$p(y_t|Y_{t-1}) = \binom{a + y_t - 1}{y_t} b^a (1 + b)^{-(a+y_t)}, \tag{2.9}$$

where $a = a_{t|t-1}$ and $b = b_{t|t-1}$ and

$$\binom{a + y_t - 1}{y_t} = \frac{\Gamma(a + y)}{\Gamma(y + 1)\Gamma(a)},$$

although, since y is an integer, $\Gamma(y+1) = y!$ Hence the log-likelihood function for the unknown hyperparameter ω is

$$\log L(\omega) = \sum_{t=\tau+1}^{T} \{\log \Gamma(a_{t|t-1} + y_t) - \log y_t! - \log \Gamma(a_{t|t-1})$$
$$+ a_{t|t-1} \log b_{t|t-1} - (a_{t|t-1} + y_t) \log(1 + b_{t|t-1})\}. \qquad (2.10)$$

It follows from the properties of the negative binomial that the mean and variance of the predictive distribution of y_{T+1}, given Y_T, are, respectively,

$$\tilde{y}_{T+1|T} = E(y_{T+1}|Y_T)$$
$$= a_{T+1|T}/b_{T+1|T} = a_T/b_T \qquad (2.11)$$

and

$$\text{var}(y_{T+1} + Y_T) = a_{T+1|T}(1 + b_{T+1|T}) \mid b_{T+1|T}^2$$
$$= \omega^{-1}\text{var}(\mu_T|Y_T) + E(\mu_T|Y_T). \qquad (2.12)$$

Repeated substitution from (2.3)–(2.6) shows that the forecast function is

$$\tilde{y}_{T+1|T} = a_T/b_T = \sum_{j=0}^{T-1} \omega^j y_{T-j} \Big/ \sum_{j=0}^{T-1} \omega^j. \qquad (2.13)$$

This is a weighted mean in which the weights decline exponentially. It has exactly the same form as the discounted least squares estimate of a mean. In large samples, the denominator of (2.13) is approximately equal to $1/(1 - \omega)$ when $\omega < 1$ and the forecasts can be obtained recursively by the EWMA scheme

$$\tilde{y}_{t+1|t} = (1 - \lambda)\tilde{y}_{t|t-1} + \lambda y_t, \quad t = 1, \ldots, T, \qquad (2.14)$$

where $y_{1|0} = 0$ and $\lambda = 1 - \omega$ is the smoothing constant. When $\omega = 1$, the right side of (2.13) is equal to the sample mean. Regarding this as an estimate of μ, the choice of zeros as initial values for a and b in the filter is seen to be justifed insofar as it yields the classical solution. It is also worth noting that, unlike the Gaussian case, no approximations are involved in the use of a diffuse prior in this model.

Now consider multistep prediction. The l-step-ahead predictive distribution at time T is given by

$$p(y_{T+l}|Y_T) = \int_0^\infty p(y_{T+l}|\mu_{T+l})p(\mu_{T+l}|Y_T) \, d\mu_{T+l}. \qquad (2.15)$$

It could be argued that the assumption embodied in (2.3) and (2.4) suggests that $p(\mu_{T+l}|Y_T)$ has a gamma distribution with parameters

$$a_{T+l|T} = \omega^l a_T \qquad (2.16)$$

and

$$b_{T+l|T} = \omega^l b_T. \tag{2.17}$$

This would mean that the predictive distribution for y_{T+l} was negative bino-
mial (2.9), with a and b given by $a_{T+l|T}$ and $b_{T+l|T}$ in (2.16) and (2.17).
Unfortunately, the evolution that this implies for μ_t is not consistent with that
which would occur if observations were made at times $T+1, T+2, \ldots, T+l-1$.
In the latter case, the distribution of y_{T+l} at time T is

$$p(y_{T+l}|Y_T) = \sum_{y_{T+l-1}} \cdots \sum_{y_{T+1}} \prod_{j=1}^{l} p(y_{T+j}|Y_{T+j-1}). \tag{2.18}$$

It is difficult to derive a close-form expression for $p(y_{T+l|T})$ from (2.18) for
$l > 1$, but it can, in principle, be evaluated numerically.

Although finding a closed-form expression for $p(y_{T+l}|Y_T)$ is difficult, it is
possible to show that

$$E(y_{T+l}|Y_T) = a_T/b_T \tag{2.19}$$

for all lead times. To see this result, first note that taking the conditional expectation
of y_{T+l} at time $T+l-1$ gives, from (2.11),

$$\underset{T+l-1}{E}(y_{T+l}) = a_{T+l-1}/b_{T+l-1}.$$

Using (2.3)–(2.6) and taking conditional expectations at time $T+l-2$ gives

$$\underset{T+l-2}{E}\underset{T+l-1}{E}(y_{T+l}) = \underset{T+l-2}{E}\left[\frac{\omega a_{T+l-2} + y_{T+l-1}}{\omega b_{T+l-2} + 1}\right]$$

$$= \frac{a_{T+l-2}}{b_{T+l-2}}, \quad l \geqslant 2.$$

Repeating this procedure by taking conditional expectations at time $T+l-3$ and
so on gives (2.19).

3 Binomial Distribution

If the observations at time t are generated from a binomial distribution then

$$p(y_t|\pi_t) = \binom{n_t}{y_t} \pi_t^{y_t} (1-\pi_t)^{n_t-y_t}, \quad y_t = 0, \ldots, n_t, \tag{3.1}$$

where π is the probability that y_t is unity when n_t is 1. The value of n_t is assumed
to be fixed and known. Thus observations from the binomial can be regarded as a
special case of count data in which there is a fixed number of opportunities for the
event in question to occur. When n_t is 1, the data are *binary* or *dichotomous*.

The conjugate prior for the binomial distribution is the beta distribution

$$p(\pi; a, b) = [B(a, b)]^{-1}\pi^{a-1}(1 - \pi)^{b-1}, \tag{3.2}$$

where the beta function is

$$B(a, b) = \Gamma(a)\Gamma(b)/\Gamma(a + b).$$

Let $p(\pi_{t-1}|Y_{t-1})$ have a beta distribution with parameters a_{t-1} and b_{t-1}. Assume that $p(\pi_t|Y_{t-1})$ is also beta with parameters given by equations exactly the same as those in (2.3) and (2.4). This again ensures that the mean of $\pi_t|Y_{t-1}$ is the same as that of $\pi_{t-1}|Y_{t-1}$, but the variance increases. Specifically

$$E(\pi_t|Y_{t-1}) = a_{t|t-1}/(a_{t|t-1} + b_{t|t-1})$$
$$= a_{t-1}/(a_{t-1} + b_{t-1})$$

and

$$\text{var}(\pi_t|Y_{t-1}) = \frac{a_{t|t-1}b_{t|t-1}}{(a_{t|t-1} + b_{t|t-1})^2(a_{t|t-1} + b_{t|t-1} + 1)}$$
$$= \frac{a_{t-1}b_{t-1}}{(a_{t-1} + b_{t-1})^2(\omega a_{t-1} + \omega b_{t-1} + 1)}.$$

Once the tth observation becomes available, the distribution of $\pi_t|Y_t$ is beta with parameters

$$a_t = a_{t|t-1} + y_t \tag{3.3}$$

and

$$b_t = b_{t|t-1} + n_t - y_t. \tag{3.4}$$

The predictive distribution, $p(y_t|Y_{t-1})$, is beta-binomial

$$p(y_t|Y_{t-1}) = \frac{1}{n_t + 1}\frac{B(a + y_t, b + n_t - y_t)}{B(y_t + 1, n_t - y_t + 1)B(a, b)}, \tag{3.5}$$

where $a = a_{t|t-1}$ and $b = b_{t|t-1}$. The likelihood function is again (2.7) with τ defined as the first time period for which

$$0 < \sum_{t=1}^{\tau} y_t < \sum_{t=1}^{\tau} n_t.$$

This condition ensures that a_τ and b_τ are strictly positive, although again there is nothing to prevent us starting the recursions (2.3)–(2.4) and (3.3)–(3.4) at $t = 1$ with $a_0 = b_0 = 0$ (see Lehmann 1983, p. 243). [This does not correspond to the use of a uniform prior. Since the range of a beta distribution is between 0 and 1, a uniform prior is a proper prior and the summation in the likelihood runs from $t = 1$ to T. A uniform distribution is obtained by setting the beta parameters, a and b, equal to unity; alternatively, Jeffreys (1961) argued that it is more appropriate to have $a = b = 1/2$, corresponding to $\arcsin(\pi 1/2)$ having a uniform distribution.]

From the properties of the beta-binomial distribution, the mean and variance of y_{T+1} conditional on the information at time T are

$$\tilde{y}_{T+1|T} = E(y_{T+1}|Y_T) = n_{T+1}a_T/(a_T + b_T) \tag{3.6}$$

and

$$\text{var}(y_{T+1}|Y_T) = \frac{n_{T+1}a_T b_T (a_T + b_T + \omega^{-1}n_{T+1})}{(a_t + b_T)^2(a_T + b_T + \omega^{-1})}. \tag{3.7}$$

By substituting repeatedly from the recursive equations (3.3) and (3.4), it can be seen that, for n_t constant, $\tilde{y}_{T+1|T}$ is effectively an EWMA.

For binary data, $n_t = 1$, the beta-binomial distribution in (3.5) reduces to a binomial distribution with

$$\Pr(y_t = 1|Y_{t-1}) = a_{t|t-1}/(a_{t|t-1} + b_{t|t-1}).$$

As regards forecasts, it can be shown, by evaluating (2.18), that the distribution of $y_{T+l}|Y_T$ is binomial with expected value $a_T/(a_T + b_T)$ for all $l = 1, 2, 3, \ldots$. Hence its variance does not increase with the lead time.

The model for binary data can easily be extended to handle Markov chains in which there are two parameters evolving over time, but the one which pertains at time t depends on the observation at $t - 1$. Thus if y_{t-1}, then $\Pr(y_t = 1) = \pi_{t|t-1}$, whereas if $y_{t-1} = 0$, then $\Pr(y_t = 1) = \pi^*_{t|t-1}$. When $y_{t-1} = 1$, the parameters $a_{t|t-1}$ and $b_{t|t-1}$, associated with $\pi_{t|t-1}$, are used to form the predictive distribution for y_t and are updated via (3.3) and (3.4) when y_t becomes available. From the point of view of π_t^*, y_t is treated as though it were missing. When $y_{t-1} = 0$, the situation is reversed.

4 Multinomial Distribution

When there are more than two categories, the observations are said to be *polytomous* and the multinomial distribution is appropriate. Let there be $m + 1$ possible categories, and suppose that the probability that at time t an object belongs to the ith category is π_{it}. If there are n_t trials and the number of objects in the ith category is y_{it}, then

$$p(y_{ot}, \ldots, y_{mt}) = \binom{n_t}{y_{1t}, \ldots, y_{mt}} \prod_{i=0}^{m} \pi_{it}^{y_{it}}, \tag{4.1}$$

with $\sum_{i=0}^{m} y_{it} = n_t$ and $\sum_{i=0}^{m} \pi_{it} = 1$.

The conjugate prior for the multinomial distribution is the multivariate beta or *Dirichlet* distribution

$$p(\pi_0, \ldots, \pi_m; a_0, \ldots, a_m) = \frac{\Gamma(\sum a_i)}{\Pi \Gamma(a_i)} \prod_{i=0}^{m} \pi_i^{a_i-1}, \tag{4.2}$$

where the summations are from $i = 0$ to m. (When $m = 1$, this collapses to the beta distribution with $a_0 = a$ and $a_1 = b$.) Proceeding as in the previous section, it is not difficult to show that the recursive equations corresponding to (2.3) and (3.3) become

$$a_{i,t|t-1} = \omega a_{i,t-1} \tag{4.3}$$

and

$$a_{i,t} = a_{i,t|t-1} + y_{it}, \quad i = 0, \ldots, m. \tag{4.4}$$

The likelihood for ω is as in (2.7), with τ the first value of t, which yields $a_{i,t} > 0$ for all $i = 0, \ldots, m$. The predictive distribution in this case is known as the Dirichlet multinomial. The forecasts can again be expressed in terms of EWMA's.

5 Negative Binomial

The negative binomial distribution is

$$p(y_t|\pi_t) = \binom{v + y_t - 1}{y_t} \pi_t^v (1 - \pi_t)^{y_t}, \quad y_t = 0, 1, 2, \ldots, \tag{5.1}$$

where $0 < \pi_t < 1$ and $v > 0$. This is known as the Pascal distribution if v is an integer and $v = 1$ corresponds to the geometric distribution. The mean and variance are

$$E(y_t|\pi_t) = v(1 - \pi)/\pi \tag{5.2}$$

and

$$\text{var}(y_t|\pi_t) = E(y_t|\pi_t)[1 + v^{-1} E(y_t|\pi_t)]. \tag{5.3}$$

The distribution, therefore, exhibits overdispersion compared with the Poisson distribution; that is, the variance exceeds the mean. If the mean is kept constant, however, the negative binomial tends toward the Poisson distribution as $v \to \infty$.

The conjugate prior distribution for the negative binomial is the beta distribution, (3.2). At first sight, it might appear that the recursions in (2.3) and (2.4) are again appropriate. In view of (5.2), however, it is the expected value of $(1 - \pi)/\pi$, rather than π, that needs to be kept constant while the variance increases. For a beta distribution (3.2),

$$E((1-\pi)/\pi) = \int_0^1 \pi^{a-2}(1-\pi)^b \, d\pi$$

$$= \frac{B(a-1, b+1)}{B(a,b)} = \frac{b}{a-1}, \tag{5.4}$$

provided that $a > 1$. Hence we require that

$$\frac{b_{t|t-1}}{a_{t|t-1} - 1} = \frac{b_{t-1}}{a_{t-1} - 1}. \tag{5.5}$$

This can be achieved by multiplying the numerator and denominator in the expression on the right side of (5.5) by ω. The prediction equation, (2.3), is, therefore, modified to

$$a_{t|t-1} = \omega a_{t-1} + (1-\omega), \quad 0 < \omega \leqslant 1, \tag{5.6}$$

but (2.4) remains unchanged. The updating equations have the more standard form

$$a_t = a_{t|t-1} + v \tag{5.7}$$

and

$$b_t = b_{t|t-1} + y_t. \tag{5.8}$$

The predictive distribution is the beta-Pascal

$$p(y_t|Y_{t-1}) = \frac{1}{v+y_t} \frac{B(v+a_{t|t-1}, y_t+b_{t|-1})}{B(v, y_t+1)B(a_{t|t-1}, b_{t|t-1})}, \tag{5.9}$$

and the likelihood function is as in (2.7) with τ the first value of t for which y_t is nonzero.

The expected value of the one-step-ahead predictive distribution at time T is

$$\tilde{y}_{T+1|T} = E(y_{T+1}|Y_T)$$

$$= \int_0^1 E(y_{T+1}|\pi_{T+1})p(\pi_{T+1}|Y_T) \, d\pi_{T+1}$$

$$\frac{vb_{T+1|T}}{a_{T+1|T} - 1} = \frac{vb_T}{a_T - 1} \tag{5.10}$$

in view of (5.4) and the way in which prediction operates via (5.5). As in the previous models, b_T can be written as an exponentially weighted average of past weights, and repeatedly substituting from (5.6) and (5.7) gives

$$a_T = v \sum_{j=0}^{T-1} \omega^j + (1-\omega) \sum_{j=0}^{T-1} \omega^j. \tag{5.11}$$

As $T \to \infty$, $(a_T - 1) \to v/(1 - \omega)$, so $\tilde{y}_{T+1|T}$ again has the EWMA form of (2.13). Furthermore, using an argument similar to that employed to show (2.19), it is possible to verify that the forecasts l steps ahead are also given by (5.10).

The parameter v can be estimated by ML along with ω. Alternatively, it may be preset (see Cameron and Trivedi 1986).

6 Explanatory Variables

Explanatory variables may be brought into the random-walk-plus-noise model [(1.1)–(1.2)] with normal disturbances by extending (1.1), so it becomes

$$y_t = \mu_t + x_t'\delta + \varepsilon_t, \tag{6.1}$$

where x_t is a $k \times 1$ vector of exogenous explanatory variables and δ is a $k \times 1$ vector of parameters. If δ were known, the optimal prediction of y_t given Y_{t-1} would be $E(\mu_t|Y_{t-1}) + x_t'\delta$, and the updating of the estimate of the state would be carried out in the same way as for (1.1) and (1.2) but with y_t replaced by $y_t - x_t'\delta$ in the Kalman filter. When δ is unknown, the linearity of the model may be exploited to concentrate δ out of the likelihood function. Thus nonlinear optimization only needs to be carried out with respect to the signal–noise ratio, $q = \sigma_\eta^2/\sigma_\varepsilon^2$.

In a model with Poisson, binomial, or negative binomial observations but no dynamic structure, explanatory variables are introduced via a *link* function; see the discussion of the GLIM framework by McCullagh and Nelder (1983). For a Poisson model, the exponential link function

$$\mu_t = \exp(x_t'\delta) \tag{6.2}$$

ensures that μ_t remains positive. For a binomial model, the logit link function

$$\pi_t = \exp(x_t'\delta)/\{1 + \exp(x_t'\delta)\}$$

ensures that π_t remains between 0 and 1. Recent applications of GLIM models to count data include those of Hausman, Hall, and Griliches (1984), who studied the number of patents applied for by firms, and Cameron and Trivedi (1986), who studied the number of consultations with a doctor. Note that it may be unsatisfactory to include a lagged dependent variable as an explanatory variable when the observations are small and discrete.

Explanatory variables can be introduced into models for count data as follows. Consider the Poisson model of Section 2. As in (6.1), the level μ_t may be thought of as a component that has a separate effect from that of the explanatory variables in x_t, none of which is a constant. Suppose that $\mu_{t-1} \sim \Gamma(a_{t-1}, b_{t-1})$ and that, conditional on Y_{t-1}, $\mu_t \sim \Gamma(\omega a_{t-1}, \omega b_{t-1})$. This level component may be combined multiplicatively with an exponential link function for the explanatory variables so that the distribution of y_t conditional on μ_t is Poisson with mean

$$\mu_t^\dagger = \mu_t \exp(x_t'\delta). \tag{6.3}$$

It follows from the properties of the gamma distribution that, conditional on Y_{t-1}, $\mu_t^\dagger \sim \Gamma(a_{t|t-1}^\dagger, b_{t|t-1}^\dagger)$, where

$$a_{t|t-1}^\dagger = \omega a_{t-1}$$

and

$$b_{t|t-1}^\dagger = \omega b_{t-1} \exp(-x_t'\delta), \tag{6.4}$$

respectively. The log-likelihood of the observations is, therefore, as in (2.10) with $a_{t|t-1}$ and $b_{t|t-1}$ replaced by $a_{t|t-1}^\dagger$ and $b_{t|t-1}^\dagger$. This must be maximized with respect to ω and δ.

As regards updating, $\mu_t^\dagger \sim \Gamma(a_t^\dagger, b_t^\dagger)$, where $a_t^\dagger$ and $b_t^\dagger$ are obtained from $a_{t|t-1}^\dagger$ and $b_{t|t-1}^\dagger$ via updating equations of the form (2.5)–(2.6). Therefore, the posterior distribution of μ_t is $\Gamma(a_t, b_t)$, where a_t and b_t are given by

$$a_t = \omega a_{t-1} + y_t \tag{6.5}$$

and

$$b_t = \omega b_{t-1} + \exp(x_t'\delta), \quad t = \tau + 1, \ldots, T. \tag{6.6}$$

Thus the only amendment as compared with the recursions in Section 2 is the replacement of unity by $\exp(x_t'\delta)$ in the equation for b_t.

For a given value of δ, we can proceed as in (2.19) to show that the mean of the predictive distribution of y_{T+l} is

$$\underset{T}{E}(y_{T+l}) = \exp(x_{T+l}'\delta) \sum \omega^j y_{T-j} \Big/ \sum \omega^j \exp(x_{T-j}'\delta)$$

$$= \exp(x_{T+l}'\delta)\text{EWMA}(y)/\text{EWMA}[\exp(x'\delta)], \tag{6.7}$$

where EWMA(y) is given by (2.13) and EWMA$[\exp(x'\delta)]$ is defined similarly.

It is interesting to compare (6.7) with the result obtained from the Gaussian model (6.1) for a given discount factor, ω. Since the level and explanatory variables are combined multiplicatively in (6.3), it seems sensible to make the comparison with a Gaussian model in which logarithms have been taken. The optimal estimator of μ_t is obtained by applying the EWMA operation to $\log y_t - x_t'\delta$. The optimal estimate of $\log y_{T+l}$ can then be expressed as

$$\underset{T}{E}(\log y_{T+l}) = x_{T+l}'\delta + \text{EWMA}(\log y) - \text{EWMA}(x'\delta). \tag{6.8}$$

The other point of comparison with the Gaussian model is in the maximization of the respective likelihood functions. In the Gaussian case, the computational burden is eased considerably by the fact that δ may be concentrated out of the likelihood function by estimating it by generalized least squares (see Kohn and Ansley 1985). This suggests that it may be possible to use estimates from the Gaussian model as starting values; the difficulty lies in how to handle zero observations when logarithms are being taken.

Explanatory variables can also be introduced into a Gaussian model via the level. Thus (6.1) and (1.2) become

$$y_t = \mu_t^* + \varepsilon_t \tag{6.9}$$

and

$$\mu_t^* = \mu_{t-1}^* + (\Delta x_t)'\delta + \eta_t. \tag{6.10}$$

This is equivalent to (6.1) and (1.2), the only difference being that μ_t^* includes the effect of the exogenous variables, whereas μ_t does not; in fact, $\mu_t^* = \mu_t + x_t'\delta$. Following Smith and Miller (1986), explanatory variables can be brought into a Poisson model in an analogous way. If $\mu_{t-1}^* \sim \Gamma(a_{t-1}^*, b_{t-1}^*)$, then, conditional on Y_{t-1}, μ_t^* is gamma with

$$a_{t|t-1}^* = \omega a_{t-1}^*, \qquad b_{t|t-1}^* = \omega b_{t-1}^* \exp(-\Delta x_t'\delta). \tag{6.11}$$

The posterior distribution of μ_t^* is then $\Gamma(a_t^*, b_t^*)$, where a_t^* and b_t^* are obtained from $a_{t|t-1}^*$ and $b_{t|t-1}^*$ via equations of the form (2.5)–(2.6). Repeated substitutions show that

$$b_T^* = 1 + \sum_{j=1}^{T-1} \omega^j \exp(-\Delta_j x_T'\delta),$$

where $\Delta_j = 1 - L^j$, and further rearrangement yields a forecast function that is exactly the same as (6.7).

The appropriate way of proceeding with the negative binomial is to introduce the explanatory variables directly into the distribution of $y_t|\pi_t$ via an exponential link function. This may be done by replacing v with $v_t = v \exp(x_t'\delta)$. Such a negative binomial distribution has, for a constant, π, a constant variance–mean ratio (see Cameron and Trivedi 1986, p. 33). Proceeding in this way leads to the updating equations (5.7) being modified to

$$a_t = a_{t|t-1} + v \exp(x_t'\delta), \tag{6.12}$$

but (5.8) remains unchanged. Combining the prediction and updating equation for a_t gives

$$a_t = \omega a_{t-1} + (1 - \omega) + v \exp(x_t'\delta).$$

The mean of the predictive distribution is

$$\underset{T}{E}(y_{T+l}) = v_{T+l} b_{T+l|T} / (a_{T+l|T} - 1)$$

$$= v \exp(x_{T+l}'\delta) b_T / (a_T - 1),$$

and it is not difficult to deduce that it can be expressed in terms of an equation identical to (6.7).

It was noted earlier that bringing stochastic slope and seasonals components into count-data models is not easy. They can, however, enter in a deterministic fashion, and this is done by treating them as explanatory variables. A slope is introduced by setting one of the elements of x_t equal to time, t. The seasonals are modeled by $s - 1$ explanatory variables constructed so that the seasonal effects sum to 0 over a period of one year. The form of (6.3) means that the trend and seasonals combine multiplicatively, just as in a logarithmic Gaussian model. As in such a model, the coefficient of the slope is to be interpreted as a growth rate, whereas the seasonal coefficients are multiplicative seasonal factors.

The extension of count-data models to include explanatory variables opens up the possibility of carrying out *intervention analysis*. The explanatory variables x_t are replaced or augmented by a variable w_t that is designed to pick up the effect of some event or policy change.

7 Model Selection and Applications for Count Data

Many of the issues that arise in the selection of GLIM models are also relevant here. There is the additional problem of testing for serial correlation; however, this is currently under investigation.

The standardized (Pearson) residuals are defined by

$$v_t = \frac{y_t - E(y_t|Y_{t-1})}{SD(y_t|Y_{t-1})}. \tag{7.1}$$

If the parameters in the model are known, it follows from the decomposition of the likelihood in (2.7) that these residuals are independently distributed with mean 0 and unit variance. They are not, however, in general, identically distributed.

The following diagnostic checks are suggested:

1. An examination of the plot of the residuals against time and against an estimate of the level.
2. An examination of a plot of the cumulative sum (CUSUM) of the residuals against time. A test for systematic underprediction or overprediction may be effected by comparing the mean of the residuals with a standard normal distribution. This test is analogous to the recursive t test suggested for Gaussian regression models by Harvey and Collier (1977).
3. A check on whether the sample variance of the residuals is close to 1. A value greater than 1 indicates overdispersion relative to the model that is being fitted. (Note that since the mean of the residuals is not necessarily 0, the sample variance and raw second moment will not usually be the same.)
4. As in the standard GLIM models, a goodness-of-fit test may be carried out by comparing the sum of the squared residuals with a χ^2 distribution in which the number of degrees of freedom is equal to $T - \tau$ minus the number of fitted parameters. Whether or not such a distribution is a reasonable approximation under the null hypothesis that the model is correctly specified is,

however, a matter for investigation. The same would apply to the goodness-of-fit statistic referred to in the GLIM literature as the deviance. This statistic is computed by subtracting the likelihood from the likelihood obtained by fitting the observation model exactly by using T parameters and then multiplying by 2. In the case of a Poisson observation equation, the likelihood given by fitting each observation exactly is

$$\log L^* = \sum_{t=1}^{T}(y_t \log y_t - y_t - \log y_t!).$$

An alternative measure of deviance for dynamic models would be to construct an L^* based on the predictive distribution with ω set equal to the ML estimate obtained for the actual model. The degrees of freedom would then be $T - \tau - k$. In a univariate Poisson model, the test statistic would then be as in expression (7.2) with the summation running from $t = \tau + 1$ to T.

5. An examination of the CUSUM-of-squares plot.

Post-sample predictive testing may also be carried out. For the model with Poisson observations, the post-sample predictive test statistic is

$$\xi(l) = 2 \sum_{t=T+1}^{T+l} a_{t|t-1} \log(a_{t|t-1}/y_t b_{t|t-1})$$

$$- 2 \sum_{t=T+1}^{T+l} (a_{t|t-1} + y_t) \log(y_t + a_{t|t-1}/(1 + b_{t|t-1})y_t), \qquad (7.2)$$

where $a_{t|t-1}$ and $b_{t|t-1}$ are computed from the recursions (2.5)–(2.6). In the special case in which y_t is 0, the term in $\xi(l)$ at time t is

$$-2a_{t|t-1} \log((1 + b_{t|t-1})/b_{t|t-1}).$$

Under the null hypothesis that the model is correctly specified, $\xi(l)$ is asymptotically χ^2 with l df. The test is analogous to the test developed by Chow (1960) for a Gaussian regression model. The derivation in the Appendix is based on the introduction of a dummy variable into the model for each of the observations in the post-sample period.

7.1 Goals scored by England against Scotland

Figure 1 shows the number of goals scored by England in international football matches played against Scotland at Hampden Park in Glasgow. Except during the war years, these matches were played in Glasgow every other year. (The year 1985 is also an exception; the match should have been played at Wembley, but Margaret Thatcher decreed that it be played in Scotland to save Londoners from the ravages of marauding Scottish football supporters.) With the observations treated as though they were evenly spaced, estimation of the Poisson–gamma model gave $\tilde{\omega} = .844$.

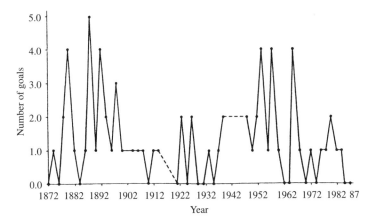

Fig. 1. Goals scored by England against Scotland at Hampden Park, Glasgow.

Table 1. Predictive probability distribution of goals
in next match

0 goal	1 goal	2 goals	3 goals	4 goals	>4 goals
.471	.326	.138	.046	.013	.005

The variance of the standardized residuals is 1.269, and a plot of them shows no indication of misspecification. A post-sample predictive test carried out over the last five observations gave no hint of model breakdown with $\xi(5) = 4.54$.

The forecasted value for the mean of future observations is .82. This corresponds to the forecast that would have been obtained from the Gaussian random-walk-plus-noise model (1.1)–(1.2) by setting $q = .029$. The general formula is

$$q = (1 + \omega^2 - 2\omega)/\omega. \tag{7.3}$$

The full one-step-ahead predictive distribution is shown in Table 1. The smooth line in Fig. 2 shows the estimate of the level of the process obtained by applying the fixed-interval smoothing algorithm to a random-walk-plus-noise model with $q = .029$. Since there is no firm theoretical foundation for constructing a smoother in this way, we will refer to it as the *quasi smoother*.

Fitting the negative binomial-beta model using a crude grid search for v yields an estimate of $v = 5$ with the corresponding estimate of ω being .916. Thus the introduction of an adjustable scale parameter has resulted in less movement in the level. The variance of the standardized residuals is 1.077 and the prediction is 1.187. The likelihood function is relatively insensitive with respect to changes in v. Furthermore, its value at the maximum is only marginally greater than the maximized likelihood for the Poisson–gamma model. If an allowance is made for the extra parameter via the Akaike information criterion, the Poisson–gamma model gives a better fit.

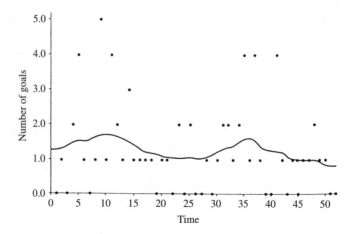

Fig. 2. Goals scored by England against Scotland at Hampden Park, with underlying trend.

We now consider the full set of results of England–Scotland matches, by including the matches played at Wembley in England. Playing at home tends to confer
an advantage, so we extend the model by introducing a dummy explanatory variable, W_E, that takes a value of unity when England is at home, and is 0 when the
team is away. The ML estimates of the parameters are $\tilde{\omega} = .903$ and $\tilde{\delta} = .498$.
As expected, the estimate of δ is positive. The likelihood-ratio test statistic is
10.57; this statistic is asymptotically χ_1^2 under the null hypothesis that δ is 0 and
so is clearly highly significant. Since exp(.498) is equal to 1.64, the results can be
interpreted as saying that the expected number of goals scored by England rises
by 64% when they are playing at home.

7.2 Purse snatching in Chicago

In their textbook, McCleary and Hay (1980) listed a time series of reported
purse snatchings in the Hyde Park neighborhood of Chicago. The observations
are 28 days apart, starting in January 1968. McCleary and Hay decided that the
series was stationary, and on the basis of the correlogram and the sample partial
auto-correlation function they fitted an (autoregressive) AR(2) model.

The assumption of stationarity for this series implies that the level of purse
snatchings remained constant throughout the period in question and that the
variations observed were simply fluctuations around this constant level. This in
turn implies that purse snatching is in some kind of equilibrium. Although this
may be true, a more plausible working hypothesis is that the level of this crime
is gradually changing over time. This suggests a random-walk-plus-noise model
[(1.1)–(1.2)]. Estimating such a model under the normality assumption gives a
signal–noise ratio of $q = .208$. The residuals give no indication of serial correlation. For example, $Q(8)$ is equal to 7.88, and this should be tested against
a chi-square distribution with 7 df. The prediction-error variance is estimated to

be 38.94, and this is only slightly above the figure reported by McCleary and Hay for their AR(2) model, which, of course, contains one more parameter. The practical implications for forecasting become apparent when it is noted that the forecasted level of future observations is 7.39 but the mean of the series is 13.92.

In summary, basic a priori considerations give rise to a structural time series model which not only has a clearer interpretation than the ARIMA model fitted by McCleary and Hay but is more parsimonious as well. The model is not, however, strictly speaking, data admissible. The forecast function is horizontal and cannot be negative, but a prediction interval of one root mean squared error on either side rapidly strays into the region of negative values of *y*. A logarithmic formulation, on the other hand, is not satisfactory because it fails the Bowman–Shenton normality test. A much better model is obtained by carrying out a square-root transformation before fitting the model. This yields an estimated signal–noise ratio of $q = .132$ while squaring the forecasted values gives predictions of 7.432 and a much narrower prediction interval.

Of course, the purse snatchings are an example of count data, but since the numbers are not too small, fitting various Gaussian models is a useful preliminary exercise. (For example, extending the model to include a stochastic slope indicates that such a component is unnecessary.) In particular it should be noted that the square-root transformation is the variance-stabilizing transformation for a Poisson distribution (see McCullagh and Nelder 1983, pp. 129–130).

When the data are treated explicitly as count data, a negative binomial-beta model with $v = 20$ seems to give the best fit. The estimate of ω is $\tilde{\omega} = .697$. The predicted level is 7.573, corresponding to predictions from the Gaussian model with $q = .131$. A plot of the residuals shows no evidence of heteroscedasticity, and the sample variance of the standardized residuals is 1.008.

7.3 Effect of the seat-belt law on van drivers in Great Britain

The effect of the seat-belt law of January 1983 on various classes of road users in Great Britain was analyzed by Harvey and Durbin (1986). For certain categories, the numbers involved were relatively small, with the result that a Gaussian model could not be regarded as a reasonable approximation. One such series is the monthly totals of drivers of light-goods vehicles killed. Here the numbers, from January 1969 to December 1984, range from 2 to 17.

Since the series contains no zero observations, a Gaussian model can be fitted to the logarithms of the observations. This gives preliminary estimates for the seasonal and intervention effects that can be used as starting values in the iterative procedure used to calculate the ML estimators in a count-data model. It is clear from doing this, however, that a Gaussian model is not at all satisfactory in these circumstances, and the results are very different for different specifications. In particular, fitting a model with fixed seasonals and no slope gives an estimate of the intervention effect that implies a 45% fall in fatalities as a result of the seat-belt law. This is quite out of line with estimates obtained for other series and indeed with the results obtained when a slope is included.

Table 2. Estimated seasonal factors for LGV drivers killed

Jan.	Feb.	March	April	May	June	July	Aug.	Sept.	Oct.	Nov.	Dec.
1.16	.79	.94	.89	.91	1.06	.97	.92	.92	1.16	1.19	1.19

For the Poisson model, it is reassuring to note that the conclusions regarding the effect of the seat-belt law are affected very little by the inclusion or otherwise of a slope term. In fact, the preferred specification does not have a slope. The explanatory variables are, therefore, an intervention and seasonals, and fitting the model gives the estimates of ω and the intervention effect as $\tilde{\omega} = .934$ and $\tilde{\lambda} = -.276$. The estimate of λ implies a 24.1% reduction in fatalities, which is quite close to the figures reported earlier for car drivers by Harvey and Durbin (1986). The likelihood-ratio test statistic for the inclusion of the intervention variable is 25.96, and this is clearly significant when set against a χ_1^2 distribution. Finally, the estimated seasonal factors, given by exponentiating the estimated seasonal coefficients, are very reasonable and not dissimilar to the seasonal factors reported by Harvey and Durbin (1986) for car drivers killed and seriously injured. See Table 2.

Acknowledgements

An earlier version of this article was presented at the European Meeting of the Econometric Society, Bologna, September 1988, at the Economic and Social Research Council (ESRC) Econometric Study Group Meeting in Bristol in June 1988, and at the National Bureau of Economic Research Time Series Conference in Chicago in October 1988. We thank Jim Durbin and Richard L. Smith for helpful comments. The research was supported by the ESRC Grant B00-23-2155 (Harvey) and the Conselho Nacional de Desenvolvimento Scientifico e Technologico (Fernandes).

Appendix: The Post-Sample Predictive Test for the Poisson Model

The post-sample predictive test statistic for the Poisson observation model is obtained by introducing l dummy variables into the model at times $T + 1$ to $T + l$. The statistic $\xi(l)$ is obtained by subtracting the likelihood obtained without these variables from the likelihood with these variables and multiplying by a factor of two.

To find the likelihood function for the model with dummy variables in the post-sample period, first consider the case of $l = 1$. The likelihood function is of the form (2.10) with T replaced by $T + 1$. The dummy variable parameter δ, however, only enters the likelihood via $b_{t/t-1}^\dagger$, which from (6.4) is

$$b_{T+1|T}^\dagger = \omega b_T e^{-\delta}. \tag{A.1}$$

Thus the log-likelihood can be written as

$$\log L_{T+1} = \log L^*_{T+1} + a_{T+1|T} \log b^\dagger_{T+1|T}$$

$$- (a_{T+1|T} + y_{T+1}) \log(1 + b^\dagger_{T+1|T}), \qquad \text{(A.2)}$$

where L^*_{T+1} does not depend on δ. Differentiating (A.2) with respect to δ yields

$$\exp(-\tilde{\delta}) = a_{T+1|T}/y_{T+1}b^\dagger_{T+1|T}$$

$$= a_T/y_{T+1}b_T \qquad \text{(A.3)}$$

and so, from (A.1),

$$\tilde{b}_{T+1|T} = a_{T+1|T}/y_{T+1}. \qquad \text{(A.4)}$$

Substituting into (A.2) gives the likelihood concentrated with respect to δ. Note that, in the special case when $y_{T+1} = 0$, the last two terms on the right side of (A.2) are 0 when taken together, so $\log L_{T+1} = L^*_{T+1}$.

Now consider $l > 1$. The log-likelihood function with l dummy variables, $\delta_1, \ldots, \delta_l$, in the post-sample period is

$$\log L_{T+l} = \log L^*_{T+l} + \sum_{t=T+1}^{T+l} a_{t|t-1} \log b^\dagger_{t|t-1}$$

$$- \sum_{t=T+1}^{T+l} (a_{t|t-1} + y_t) \log(1 + b^\dagger_{t|t-1}), \qquad \text{(A.5)}$$

where $b^\dagger_{t|t-1}$ obeys the recursion (6.4) and (6.6). This implies that $b^\dagger_{T+j|T+j-1}$ depends on $\delta_1, \ldots, \delta_{j-1}$ for $j = 2, \ldots, l$, thereby making differentiation of $\log L_{T+l}$ with respect to $\delta_1, \ldots, \delta_l$ rather tedious. If we differentiate with respect to δ_l first, however, we obtain a result analogous to (A.4), namely,

$$\tilde{b}_{T+l|T+l-1} = a_{T+l|T+l-1}/y_{T+l}. \qquad \text{(A.6)}$$

This is independent of previous values of $b^\dagger_{t|t-1}$ and hence of $\delta_1, \ldots, \delta_{l-1}$.

Concentrating the likelihood with respect to δ_l and proceeding to treat $\delta_1, \ldots, \delta_{l-1}$ in the same way gives the following concentrated log-likelihood function:

$$\log L_{T+l} = \log L^*_{T+l} + \sum_{t=T+1}^{T+l} a_{t|t-1} \log(a_{t|t-1}/y_t)$$

$$- \sum_{t=T+1}^{T+l} (a_{t|t-1} + y_t) \log(1 + a_{t|t-1}/y_t). \qquad \text{(A.7)}$$

The likelihood function under the null hypothesis—that is without dummy variables—is

$$\log L_{T+l} = \log L^*_{T+l|T} + \sum_{t=T+1}^{T+l} a_{t|t-1} \log b_{t|t-1}$$

$$- \sum_{t=T+1}^{T+l} (a_{t|t-1} + y_t) \log(1 + b_{t|t-1}), \qquad (A.8)$$

where $b_{t|t-1}$ is computed via the recursion in (2.4) and (2.6). Subtracting (A.8) from (A.7) and multiplying by 2 gives the likelihood ratio test statistic (7.2).

References

Cameron, C. C., and Trivedi, P. K. (1986), "Econometric Models Based on Count Data: Comparisons and Applications of Some Estimators and Tests," *Journal of Applied Econometrics*, 1, 29–53.

Chow, G. C. (1960), "Tests of Equality Between Sets of Coefficients on Two Linear Regressions," *Econometrica*, 28, 591–605.

Harvey, A. C., and Collier, P. (1977), "Testing for Functional Mis-specification in Regression Analysis," *Journal of Econometrics*, 6, 103–119.

Harvey, A. C., and Durbin, J. (1986), "The Effects of Seat Belt Legislation on British Road Casualties: A Case Study in Structural Time Series Modelling," *Journal of the Royal Statistical Society*, Ser. A, 149, 187–227.

Harvey, A. C., and Todd, P. H. J. (1983), "Forecasting Economic Time Series With Structural and Box–Jenkins Models" (with discussion), *Journal of Business and Economic Statistics*, 1, 229–315.

Hausman, J. A., Hall, B. H., and Griliches, Z. (1984), "Econometric Models for Count Data With an Application to the Patents–R & D Relationship," *Econometrica*, 52, 909–938.

Jeffreys, H. (1961), *The Theory of Probability*, Oxford, U.K.: Oxford University Press.

Key, P., and Godolphin, E. J. (1981), "On the Bayesian Steady Forecasting Model," *Journal of the Royal Statistical Society*, Ser. B, 43, 92–96.

Kitagawa, G., and Gersch, W. (1984), "A Smoothness Priors–State Space Modeling of Time Series With Trend and Seasonality," *Journal of the American Statistical Association*, 79, 378–389.

Kohn, R., and Ansley, C. F. (1985), "Efficient Estimation and Prediction in Time Series Regression Models," *Biometrika*, 72, 694–697.

Lehmann, E. L. (1983), *Theory of Point Estimation*, New York: John Wiley.

McCleary, R., and Hay, R. A., Jr. (1980), *Applied Time Series Analysis for the Social Sciences*, Beverly Hills, CA: Sage Publications.

McCullagh, P., and Nelder, J. A. (1983), *Generalised Linear Models*, London: Chapman & Hall.

Muth, J. F. (1960), "Optimal Properties of Exponentially Weighted Forecasts," *Journal of the American Statistical Association*, 55, 299–305.

Smith, J. Q. (1979), "A Generalization of the Bayesian Steady Forecasting Model," *Journal of the Royal Statistical Society*, Ser. B, 41, 375–387.

—— (1981), "The Multiparameter Steady Model," *Journal of the Royal Statistical Society*, Ser. B, 43, 256–260.

Smith, R. L., and Miller, J. E. (1986), "A Non-Gaussian State Space Model and Application to Prediction of Records," *Journal of the Royal Statistical Society*, Ser. B, 48, 79–88.

West, M., and Harrison, P. J. (1986), "Monitoring and Adaptation in Bayesian Forecasting Models," *Journal of the American Statistical Association*, 81, 741–750.

West, M., Harrison, P. J., and Migon, H. S. (1985), "Dynamic Generalized Linear Models and Bayesian Forecasting" (with discussion), *Journal of the American Statistical Association*, 80, 73–97.

18

On Gibbs Sampling for State Space Models*

C. K. CARTER AND R. KOHN

Australian Graduate School of Management, University of New South Wales

SUMMARY

We show how to use the Gibbs sampler to carry out Bayesian inference on a linear state space model with errors that are a mixture of normals and coefficients that can switch over time. Our approach simultaneously generates the whole of the state vector given the mixture and coefficient indicator variables and simultaneously generates all the indicator variables conditional on the state vectors. The states are generated efficiently using the Kalman filter. We illustrate our approach by several examples and empirically compare its performance to another Gibbs sampler where the states are generated one at a time. The empirical results suggest that our approach is both practical to implement and dominates the Gibbs sampler that generates the states one at a time.

1 Introduction

Consider the linear state space model

$$y(t) = h(t)'x(t) + e(t), \tag{1.1}$$

$$x(t+1) = F(t+1)x(t) + u(t+1), \tag{1.2}$$

where $y(t)$ is a scalar observation and $x(t)$ is an $m \times 1$ state vector. We assume that the error sequences $\{e(t), t \geqslant 1\}$ and $\{u(t), t \geqslant 1\}$ are mixtures of normals. Let θ be a parameter vector whose value determines $h(t)$ and $F(t)$ and also the distributions of $e(t)$ and $u(t)$. Further details of the structure of the model are given in Section 2.1. Equation (1.1) is called the observation equation and (1.2) the state transition equation. When $e(t)$ and $u(t)$ are independent Gaussian sequences unknown parameters are usually estimated by maximum likelihood following Schweppe (1965). The Kalman filter and state space smoothing algorithms are used to carry out the computations.

There are a number of applications in the literature where it is necessary to go beyond the Gaussian linear state space model: e.g. Harrison & Stevens (1976), Gordon & Smith (1990), Hamilton (1989) and Shumway & Stoffer (1991). Meinhold & Singpurwalla (1989) robustify the Kalman filter by taking both $e(t)$ and $u(t)$ to be t distributed. A general approach to estimating non-Gaussian and

* This work was previously published as C. K. Carter and R. Kohn, "On Gibbs Sampling for State Space Models", *Biometrika*, 1994, Vol. 81, 541–553. Reproduced by permission of Biometrika Trustees.

nonlinear state space models is given by Kitagawa (1987). Except when the dimension of the state vector is very small, Kitagawa's approach appears computationally intractable at this stage. Various approximate filtering and smoothing algorithms for nonlinear and non-Gaussian state space models have been given in the literature. See, for example, Anderson & Moore (1979, ch. 8) and West & Harrison (1989).

Using the Gibbs sampler, Carlin, Polson & Stoffer (1992) provide a general approach to Bayesian statistical inference in state space models allowing the errors $e(t)$ and $u(t)$ to be non-Gaussian and the dependence on $x(t)$ in (1.1) and (1.2) to be nonlinear. They generate the states one at a time utilizing the Markov properties of the state space model to condition on neighbouring states. In this paper we take a different Gibbs sampling approach, generating all the states at once by taking advantage of the time ordering of the state space model. We show how to carry out all the necessary computations using standard Gaussian filtering and smoothing algorithms. Although our approach is less general than that of Carlin et al. (1992), for the class of models considered in this paper our approach will be more efficient than theirs, in the sense that convergence to the posterior distribution will be faster and estimates of the posterior moments will have smaller variances. To quantify the difference between our approach and that of Carlin et al. (1992), we study empirically the performance of both algorithms for two simple and commonly-used trend and seasonal models. For both examples generating the states simultaneously produces Gibbs iterates which converge rapidly to the posterior distribution from arbitrary starting points. In contrast, when the states are generated one at a time there was slow convergence to the posterior distribution for one of the examples and the estimates of the posterior means were far less efficient than the corresponding estimates when generating the states simultaneously. In the second example there is no convergence to the posterior distribution when the states were generated one at a time because the resulting Markov chain is reducible. Our approach is supported theoretically by the results of Liu, Wong & Kong (1994) who show that when measured in some norm generating variables simultaneously produces faster convergence than generating them one at a time.

Section 2 discusses Gibbs sampling and how to generate the states and the indicator variables. Section 3 illustrates the general theory with four examples and empirically compares the performance of our algorithm with that of generating the states one at a time. Appendix 1 shows how to generate the state vector using a state space filtering algorithm and Appendix 2 shows how to generate the indicator variables.

2 The Gibbs Sampler

2.1 General

Let $Y^n = \{y(1), \ldots, y(n)\}'$ be the vector of observations and $X = \{x(1)', \ldots, x(n)'\}'$ the total state vector. Let $K(t)$ be a vector of indicator variables showing which members of the mixture each of $e(t)$ and $u(t)$ belong to and which values $h(t)$ and $F(t)$ take, and let $K = \{K(1), \ldots, K(n)\}'$. We write the parameter vector $\theta = \{\theta_1, \ldots, \theta_p\}$. We assume that, conditional on K and θ, $e(t)$

and $u(t)$ are independent Gaussian sequences which are also independent of each other. To illustrate our notation we consider the following simple example. Let

$$y(t) = x(t) + e(t), \qquad x(t) = x(t-1) + u(t),$$

with $x(t)$ univariate. The errors $e(t)$ are a mixture of two normals with $e(t) \sim N(0, \sigma^2)$ with probability p_1 and $e(t) \sim N(0, C\sigma^2)$ with probability $1 - p_1$, where $C > 1$ and p_1 are assumed known. The disturbance $u(t) \sim N(0, \tau^2)$. Then $\theta = (\sigma^2, \tau^2)$ is the unknown parameter vector. We define the indicator variable $K(t)$ as $K(t) = 0$ if $\text{var}\{e(t)\} = \sigma^2$ and $K(t) = 1$ if $\text{var}\{e(t)\} = C\sigma^2$.

Let $p(X, K, \theta | Y^n)$ be the joint posterior density of X, K and θ. The Gibbs sampler (Gelfand & Smith, 1990) is an iterative Monte Carlo technique that, in our case, successively generates X, K and θ from the conditional densities $p(X | Y^n, K, \theta)$, $p(K | Y^n, X, \theta)$ and $p(\theta_i | Y^n, X, K, \theta_{j \neq i})$ for $i = 1, \ldots, p$ until eventually (X, K, θ) is generated from the joint posterior distribution $p(X, K, \theta | Y^n)$. Tierney (1994) proves the convergence of the Gibbs sampler under appropriate regularity conditions. For any given example it is usually straightforward to check whether these conditions hold.

We will assume that θ_i can be generated from $p(\theta_i | Y^n, X, K, \theta_{j \neq i})$ for $i = 1, \ldots, p$. Efficient ways of doing so will be determined on a case by case basis. Sections 2.2 and 2.3 show how to generate from $p(X | Y^n, K, \theta)$ and $p(K | Y^n, X, \theta)$.

2.2 Generating the state vector

We assume that $x(1)$ has a proper distribution and that conditional on K and the parameter vector $\theta, h(t)$ and $F(t)$ are known, and $e(t)$ and $u(t)$ are Gaussian with known means and variances. For notational convenience we usually omit dependence on K and θ in this section. For $t = 1, \ldots, n$ let Y^t consist of all $y(j)$ ($j \leqslant t$). The following lemma shows how to generate the whole of X given Y^n, K and θ. Its proof is straightforward and is omitted.

Lemma 2.1 *We have*

$$p(X | Y^n) = p\{x(n) | Y^n\} \prod_{t=1}^{n-1} p\{x(t) | Y^t, x(t+1)\}.$$

Thus to generate X from $p(X | Y^n)$ we first generate $x(n)$ from $p\{x(n) | Y^n\}$ and then for $t = n - 1, \ldots, 1$ we generate $x(t)$ from $p\{x(t) | Y^t, x(t+1)\}$. Because $p\{x(n) | Y^n\}$ and $p\{x(t) | Y^t, x(t+1)\}$ are Gaussian densities, in order to generate all the $x(t)$ we need to compute $E\{x(n) | Y^n\}$ and $\text{var}\{x(n) | Y^n\}$ and

$$E\{x(t) | Y^t, x(t+1)\}, \qquad \text{var}\{x(t) | Y^t, x(t+1)\} \quad (t = n-1, \ldots, 1).$$

Let $x(t|j) = E\{x(t) | Y^j\}$ and $S(t|j) = \text{var}\{x(t) | Y^j\}$. We obtain $x(t|t)$ and $S(t|t)$ for $t = 1, \ldots, n$ using the Kalman filter (Anderson & Moore 1979, p. 105). To obtain $E\{x(t) | Y^t, x(t+1)\}$ and $\text{var}\{x(t) | Y^t, x(t+1)\}$ we treat the equation

$$x(t+1) = F(t+1)x(t) + u(t+1)$$

as m additional observations on the state vector $x(t)$ and apply the Kalman filter to them. Details are given in Appendix 1.

In many applications the distribution of the initial state vector $x(1)$ is partly unknown and this part is usually taken as a constant to be estimated or equivalently to have a diffuse distribution making $x(1)$ partially diffuse. By this we mean that $x(1) \sim N(0, S_0^{[0]} + k S_0^{[1]})$ with $k \to \infty$. The generation algorithm can be applied as outlined above and in Appendix 1, except that now we use the modified filtering and smoothing algorithms of Ansley & Kohn (1990).

Remark In specific models it may be possible to use a faster filtering algorithm than the Kalman filter to obtain $x(t|t)$ and $S(t|t)$. See, for example, the fast filtering algorithms of Anderson & Moore (1979, Ch. 6) when $e(t)$ and $u(t)$ are Gaussian and $F(t)$ and $h(t)$ are constant. A referee has suggested the use of a Metropolis step within the Gibbs sampler to speed up the generation of the states (Tierney 1994). To do so it is necessary to find a candidate density $q(X|K, \theta)$ for generating X which is faster to generate from than $p(X|Y, K, \theta)$ and yet is close enough to it so the rejection rate in the Metropolis step is not too high. We tried using the prior for X as $q(X|K, \theta)$, but this resulted in huge rejection rates and was therefore not practical.

2.3 Generating the indicator variables

Recall that $K(t)$ $(t = 1, \ldots, n)$ is a vector of indicator variables showing which members of the mixture each of $e(t)$ and $u(t)$ belong to and which values $h(t)$ and $F(t)$ take. Let $K^t = \{K(1), \ldots, K(t)\}$ and $X^t = \{x(1), \ldots, x(t)\}$. For notational convenience we omit dependence on θ. Conditionally on K and θ, $e(t)$ and $u(t)$ are independent for $t = 1, \ldots, n$ in (1.1) and (1.2). This implies that

$$p\{y(t)|Y^{t-1}, X^t, K^t\} = p\{y(t)|x(t), K(t)\},$$

$$p\{x(t)|X^{t-1}, K^t\} = p\{x(t)|x(t-1), K(t)\}.$$

We assume that the prior distribution of K is Markov. The next lemma shows how to generate the whole of K given Y^n, X and θ. We omit its proof as it is straightforward.

Lemma 2.2 *We have*

$$p(K|Y^n, X) = p\{K(n)|Y^n, X\} \prod_{t=1}^{n-1} p\{K(t)|Y^t, X^t, K(t+1)\}.$$

Thus to generate K from $p(K|Y^n, X)$ we first generate $K(n)$ from $p\{K(n)|Y^n, X\}$ and then for $t = n-1, \ldots, 1$ we generate $K(t)$ from $p\{K(t)|Y^t, X^t, K(t+1)\}$. Because $p\{K(n)|Y^n, X\}$ and $p\{K(t)|Y^t, X^t, K(t+1)\}$ are discrete valued we can generate from them easily, once we have calculated them. To calculate $p\{K(n)|Y^n, X\}$ and $p\{K(t)|Y^t, X^t, K(t+1)\}$ we use recursive filtering equations (Anderson & Moore 1979, Ch. 8) in a similar way to our use of the Kalman filter in Section 2.2. Details are in Appendix 2. Because $K(t)$ is discrete valued, the filtering equations can be evaluated efficiently.

3 Examples

3.1 General

We illustrate the results in Section 2 and Appendices 1 and 2 by applying them to four examples. The first is a stochastic trend model giving a cubic spline smoothing estimate of the signal. The second example is a trend plus seasonal model. In the third example the errors $e(t)$ are a discrete mixture of normals with Markov dependence. The fourth example discusses switching regression. The first two examples compare empirically the performance of the approach that generates all the states simultaneously with the approach that generates the states one at a time.

3.2 Example 1: Cubic smoothing spline

Our first example is a continuous time stochastic trend model for which the signal estimate is a cubic smoothing spline. We implement the Gibbs sampler using the first element of the state vector and make the important point that in many applications only a subset of the elements of the state vector is needed.

Suppose we have observations on the signal plus noise model

$$y(i) = g(t_i) + e(i) \quad (i = 1, \dots, n), \tag{3.1}$$

with the $e(i)$ independent $N(0, \sigma^2)$ with the signal $g(t)$ generated by the stochastic differential equation

$$d^2 g(t)/dt^2 = \tau dW(t)/dt; \tag{3.2}$$

$W(t)$ is a Wiener process with $W(0) = 0$ and $\text{var}\{W(t)\} = 1$ and τ is a scale parameter. We assume that the initial conditions on $g(t)$ and $dg(t)/dt$ are diffuse; that is, with $k \to \infty$,

$$\{g(t_1), dg(t_1)/dt\}' \sim N(0, kI_2). \tag{3.3}$$

We take $0 \leqslant t_1 < t_2 < \cdots < t_n$. Following Kohn & Ansley (1987) we can write (3.1) and (3.2) in state space form as

$$y(i) = h'x(t_i) + e(i), \qquad x(t_i) = F(\delta_i)x(t_{i-1}) + u(i),$$

where the state vector $x(t) = \{g(t), dg(t)/dt\}'$, the increments $\delta_i = t_i - t_{i-1}$ ($t_0 = 0$), and the $u(i)$ are independent $N\{0, \tau^2 U(\delta_i)\}$. The vector $h = (1, 0)'$ and the 2×2 matrices $F(\delta)$ and $U(\delta)$ are given by

$$F(\delta) = \begin{pmatrix} 1 & \delta \\ 0 & 1 \end{pmatrix}, \qquad U(\delta) = \begin{pmatrix} \delta^3/3 & \delta^2/2 \\ \delta^2/2 & \delta \end{pmatrix}.$$

The vector of unknown parameters is $\theta = (\sigma^2, \tau^2)'$ and from (3.3) the initial state vector $x(t_1)$ has a diffuse distribution. For a further discussion of this model and its connection with spline smoothing see Wahba (1983) and Kohn & Ansley (1987).

To complete the Bayesian specification of the model we impose the improper priors $p(\sigma^2) \propto 1/\sigma^2 \exp(-\beta_\sigma/\sigma^2)$, with β_σ small, and $p(\tau^2) \propto 1$. As we only use the first element of $x(t)$ in the Gibbs sampler let $G = \{g(t_1), \ldots, g(t_n)\}$. The vectors G and θ are generated as follows. For given θ, X is generated as explained in Section 2.2 and Appendix 1. We then extract G. To generate σ^2, we can show that

$$p(\sigma^2|Y^n, G, \tau^2) \propto (\sigma^2)^{-n/2-1} \times \exp\left[-\frac{1}{\sigma^2}\left\{\frac{1}{2}\sum_{i=1}^{n} e(i)^2 + \beta_\sigma\right\}\right],$$

where $e(i) = y(i) - h'x(t_i)$. Hence σ^2 is generated from an inverse gamma distribution with parameters $n/2$ and $\frac{1}{2}\sum e(i)^2 + \beta_\sigma$. To generate τ^2, note that for given $k > 0$

$$p(\tau^2|Y^n, G, \sigma^2; k) = p(\tau^2|G; k) \propto p(G|\tau^2; k)p(\tau^2) \propto p(G|\tau^2; k).$$

It follows from Ansley & Kohn (1985) that

$$\lim_{k\to\infty} p(\tau^2|G; k) \propto (\tau^2)^{-n/2+1} \times \exp\left\{-\frac{1}{2\tau^2}\sum_{i=3}^{n} \varepsilon(i)^2/R(i)\right\},$$

where $\varepsilon(i)$ and $R(i)$ are the innovations and innovation variances respectively obtained from running the modified Kalman filter on the state space model

$$g(t_i) = h'x(t_i), \qquad x(t_i) = F(\delta_i)x(t_{i-1}) + u(i).$$

Hence τ^2 is generated from an inverse gamma distribution with parameters $n/2-2$ and $\frac{1}{2}\sum \varepsilon(i)^2/R(i)$.

For this model we now describe the Gibbs sampler approach of Carlin et al. (1992). The state vector $x(t)$ is generated from $p\{x(t)|y(t), x(t-1), x(t+1), \sigma^2, \tau^2\}$. The error variance σ^2 is generated as above by noting that $p(\sigma^2|Y^n, X, \tau^2) = p(\sigma^2|Y^n, G, \tau^2)$. To generate τ^2 note that for given $k > 0$

$$p(\tau^2|Y^n, X, \sigma^2; k) = p(\tau^2|X; k) \propto p(X|\tau^2; k)p(\tau^2) \propto p(X|\tau^2; k).$$

It follows from Ansley & Kohn (1985) that

$$\lim_{k\to\infty} p(\tau^2|X; k) \propto (\tau^2)^{-n+1} \times \exp\left\{-\frac{1}{2\tau^2}\sum_{i=2}^{n} u(i)'U(\delta_i)^{-1}u(i)\right\},$$

where $u(i) = x(t_i) - F(\delta_i)x(t_{i-1})$. Hence we generate τ^2 given Y^n, X and σ^2 from an inverse gamma distribution with parameters $n - 2$ and $\frac{1}{2}\sum u(i)'U(\delta_i)^{-1}u(i)$.

We now compare empirically the approach generating all the states at once to the approach that generates the states one at a time. The data are generated by (3.1) with the function

$$g(t) = \tfrac{1}{3}\beta_{10,5}(t) + \tfrac{1}{3}\beta_{\tau,\tau}(t) + \tfrac{1}{3}\beta_{5,10}(t),$$

where $\beta_{p,q}$ is a beta density with parameters p and q, and $0 \leqslant t \leqslant 1$. This function was used by Wahba (1983) in her simulations. The error standard deviation is $\sigma = 0.2$, the sample size is $n = 50$ and the design is equally spaced with $t_i = i/50$ ($i = 1, \ldots, 50$). For both algorithms we first ran the Gibbs sampler with the starting values

$$(\sigma^2)^{[0]} = 1, \qquad x(t)^{[0]} = E\{x(t)|\sigma^2 = 1, \tau^2 = 1\}.$$

The value of τ^2 was generated by the Gibbs sampler. Figure 1(a) is a plot of the iterates of σ^2 and Fig. 1(b) a plot of the iterates of τ^2 when the states are generated one at a time. The horizontal axis is the iterate number. It appears that for this approach the Gibbs sampler takes about 15000 iterations to converge. Figures 1(c) and (d) are plots of the first 2000 iterates of the Gibbs sampler of σ^2 and τ^2 respectively when the states are generated simultaneously. The same starting values are used for both approaches. The Gibbs sampler appears to converge after 100 iterations. Similar results are obtained for other arbitrary starting values.

To study the relative efficiencies of the two algorithms once the Gibbs sampler has converged we use the marginal likelihood estimates of σ^2 and τ^2 as starting

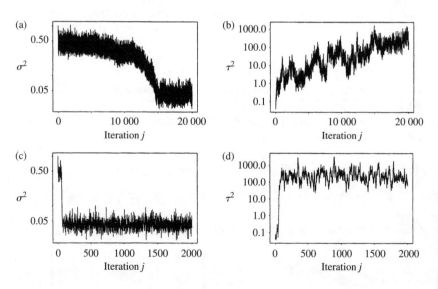

Fig. 1. Example 1: generated values of σ^2 and τ^2 with starting values $\sigma^2 = 1$ and $X = E(X|\sigma^2 = 1, \tau^2 = 1)$. In (a) and (b) the states are generated one at a time and in (c) and (d) they are generated simultaneously.

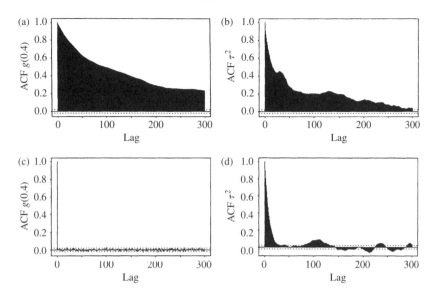

Fig. 2. Example 1: sample autocorrelation function (ACF) for $g(0.25)$ and τ^2. In (a) and (b) the states are generated one at a time and in (c) and (d) they are generated simultaneously.

values. For a definition and discussion of the marginal likelihood estimates see Kohn & Ansley (1987). For both algorithms we ran the Gibbs sampler for a warm-up period of 1000 iterations followed by a sampling run of 10000 iterations. Using the final 10000 iterates we computed the first 300 autocorrelations of the signal estimate at the abscissa $t = 0.4$, which we call $g(0.4)$, and also for τ^2. Figures 2(a) and (b) are plots of the autocorrelations of the iterates of $g(0.25)$ and τ^2 respectively when the states are generated one at a time and Fig. 2(c) and (d) are the corresponding plots for the algorithm when the states are generated simultaneously. Clearly the autocorrelations for the first algorithm are much higher than for the second.

Using the sampling run of 10000 iterates we now present the relative efficiencies of the two algorithms in estimating the posterior mean $E\{g(t)|Y\}$ of the signal. There are two ways to estimate the posterior mean. The first is to use the sample moments of the Gibbs iterates to form what is called a histogram estimate. The second way is to form a mixture estimate. When generating all the states simultaneously the histogram and mixture estimates of the posterior mean of $g(t)$ are respectively

$$\frac{1}{N}\sum_{j=1}^{N}g(t)^{[j]}, \qquad \frac{1}{N}\sum_{j=1}^{N}E\{g(t)|Y,\theta^{[j]}\}, \qquad (3.4)$$

where $N = 10000$ and $g^{[j]}(t)$ is the jth Gibbs iterate of $g(t)$ during the sampling period. The smoothed values $E\{g(t)|Y,\theta^{[j]}\}$ in (3.4) are obtained using the smoothing algorithm of Ansley and Kohn (1990). For the algorithm generating the states one at a time the histogram estimates are as in (3.4) while the mixture estimates are computed as in Section 2 of Carlin et al. (1992). The results of Gelfand and Smith (1990) and Liu et al. (1994) suggest that mixture estimates will usually have smaller variance than histogram estimates. We first consider the efficiency of the histogram estimates of the signal by estimating the posterior mean of the signal at the abscissae $t = 0.02, 0.25$ and 0.5 and calling $\hat{g}(t)$ the estimate at t. We assume that in the sampling period the Gibbs sampler has converged so the $g(t)^{[j]}$ form a stationary sequence for each t. For a given t let $\gamma_{it} = \text{cov}\{g(t)^{[j]}, g(t)^{[j+i]}\}$ be the ith autocovariance of $g(t)^{[j]}$ with corresponding sample autocovariance $\hat{\gamma}_{it}$. We estimate $N\text{var}\{\hat{g}(t)\}$ by

$$\sum_{|i| \leqslant 1000} (1 - |i|/N)\hat{\gamma}_{it}$$

using the first 1000 sample autocovariances. For a discussion of variance estimation from simulation experiments see Moran (1975).

Table 1 presents the results for the histogram estimates. The first column gives the abscissa t, the second column the sample variance estimate $\hat{\gamma}_{0t}$, and the third column the variance estimate of $N\text{var}\{\hat{g}(t)\}$ when the states are generated simultaneously. The fourth and fifth columns have the same interpretation as the second and third columns except that now the states are generated one at a time. The sixth column is the ratio of the fifth and third columns and is an estimate of the factor by which the number of Gibbs iterates for the approach which generates one state at a time would have to increase in order to have the same accuracy as the approach which generates all the states at once. We take it to be the measure of the efficiency of the two algorithms. Table 1 shows that the efficiencies range from 91 to 358 so that the number of iterates of the algorithm that generates the states one at a time would need to increase by a factor of about 350 to achieve the same accuracy as that which generates the states simultaneously. We also note from the table that the sample variances $\hat{\gamma}_{0t}$ are approximately the same for both algorithms suggesting that we are generating from the correct distribution for the algorithm that generates the states one at a time.

Table 2 has the same interpretation as Table 1 but we now deal with the iterates generated by the mixture estimates. The efficiencies now range from 498 to 178 000.

Table 1. Histogram estimates of $E\{g(t)|Y^n\}$

	Simultaneous		One at a time		
t	$\tilde{\gamma}_{0,t}$	$N\text{var}\{\hat{g}(t)\}$	$\hat{\gamma}_{0,t}$	$N\text{var}\{\hat{g}(t)\}$	Ratio
0.02	2.3×10^{-2}	4.4×10^{-2}	2.2×10^{-2}	4	91
0.25	6.8×10^{-3}	7.7×10^{-2}	7.6×10^{-3}	2.5	318
0.5	7.0×10^{-3}	7.0×10^{-3}	9.3×10^{-3}	2.5	358

Table 2. Mixture estimates of $E\{g(t)|Y^n\}$

	Simultaneous		One at a time		
t	$\tilde{\gamma}_{0,t}$	$N\operatorname{var}\{\hat{g}(t)\}$	$\hat{\gamma}_{0,t}$	$N\operatorname{var}\{\hat{g}(t)\}$	Ratio
0.02	2.9×10^{-3}	7.8×10^{-3}	2.1×10^{-2}	3.9	498
0.25	5.8×10^{-6}	1.4×10^{-5}	7.5×10^{-3}	2.5	178 731
0.5	1.1×10^{-4}	1.4×10^{-4}	9.2×10^{-3}	2.5	17 455

We repeated this study with different functions $g(t)$, different sample sizes and different values of error standard deviation and obtained similar results to those reported above. We conclude that for this simple model the approach that generates the states one at a time is far slower to converge and is far less efficient than the approach that generates all the states simultaneously.

3.3 Example 2: Trend plus seasonal components time series model

A popular model for quarterly economic time series is

$$y(t) = g(t) + T(t) + e(t) \quad (t = 1, \ldots, n), \tag{3.5}$$

with the errors $e(t)$ independent $N(0, \sigma^2)$ and with the seasonal $g(t)$ and trend $T(t)$ generated by the stochastic difference equations

$$\sum_{j=0}^{3} g(t - j) = v(t), \tag{3.6}$$

$$T(t) - 2T(t - 1) + T(t - 2) = w(t), \tag{3.7}$$

where the $v(t)$ are independent $N(0, \tau^2)$ and the $w(t)$ are independent $N(0, \omega^2)$. This model is proposed by Kitagawa and Gersch (1984) who regard (3.6) and (3.7) as priors for the seasonal and trend and who express (3.5)–(3.7) in state space form with the state vector

$$x(t) = \{g(t), g(t - 1), g(t - 2), T(t), T(t - 1)\}'.$$

For the approach generating the states simultaneously estimation of the model using the Gibbs sampler can be done as in Section 3.2. For the approach generating the states one at a time the state vector $x(t)$ is known, for $1 < t < n$, if we condition on $x(t - 1)$ and $x(t + 1)$ and so new variation is only introduced when generating $x(1)$ and $x(n)$. Thus the resulting Gibbs sampler does not converge to the posterior distribution.

To study empirically the approach that generates the states simultaneously we consider for simplicity the pure seasonal model

$$y(t) = g(t) + e(t).$$

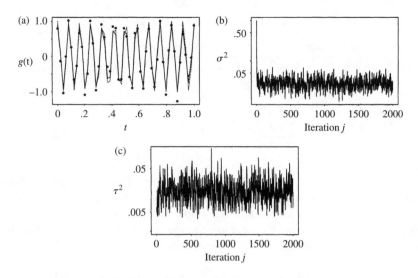

Fig. 3. Example 2: (a) shows the data (dots) together with the function $g(t)$ (dashes) and the mixture estimates of $g(t)$ (solid); (b) and (c) show the generated values of σ^2 and τ^2. The states are generated simultaneously.

We generated 50 observations using $g(t) = \sin(2\pi t/4.1)$ and $\sigma = 0.2$. The priors for σ^2 and τ^2 are the same as in Section 3.2. Figure 3 shows the output from the Gibbs sampler with the starting values $(\sigma^2)^{[0]} = 1$ and $x(t)^{[0]} = E\{x(t)|\,\sigma^2 = 1, \tau^2 = 1\}$. Figure 3(a) shows the data together with the function $g(t)$ and the mixture estimates of $g(t)$. Figures 3(b) and (c) show the generated values of σ^2 and τ^2 respectively. The warm-up period was 1000 iterations and the sampling period was 1000 iterations. From Fig. 3 the algorithm to generate the states simultaneously appears to converge within a hundred iterations. Similar results were obtained for other abitrary starting values.

To understand the difference in performance of the two algorithms we view the state transition equation (1.2) as a prior for the state vector. If this prior is tight then generating the states one at a time will produce Gibbs iterates of the states which are highly dependent and so will tend to move very little in successive iterations. An extreme case is the seasonal plus trend model (3.5)–(3.7).

3.4 Normal mixture errors with Markov dependence
We illustrate our algorithm to generate the indicator variables by considering the case where $e(t)$ and $u(t)$ are normal mixtures. It is sufficient to discuss the case where $e(t)$ is a mixture of two normals and $u(t)$ is normal as the general case can be handled similarly. We assume that we have a linear state space model as given in (1.1) and (1.2), and that $e(t)$ has mean zero and variance equal to either σ^2 or $\kappa^2\sigma^2$. Such a normal mixture model for $e(t)$ with $\kappa > 1$ has been used by

Box and Tiao (1968) to handle outliers. Let $K(t) = 1$ if $e(t)$ has variance σ^2, and let $K(t) = 2$ otherwise, and let $K = \{K(1), \ldots, K(n)\}'$.

We note that, conditionally on K, the $e(t)$ and $u(t)$ are Gaussian so that the results in Sections 2 and 3.2 apply to the generation of X and θ. Thus we will only consider the generation of K. We first assume that a priori the $K(t)$ come from a Markov chain with

$$p\{K(t+1) = 2 | K(t) = i\} = p_i \quad (i = 1, 2).$$

For simplicity we take the probabilities p_1 and p_2 as fixed, for example we could take $p_1 = 0.05$ and $p_2 = 0.5$ for detecting outliers that cause a temporary increase in variance. Alternatively we could place a prior on p_1 and p_2, for example a beta prior. To simplify notation we omit dependence on θ. From Lemma 2.2 the distribution of K given Y^n and X is

$$p(K | Y^n, X) = p\{K(n) | Y^n, X\} \prod_{t=1}^{n-1} p\{K(t) | Y^t, X^t, K(t+1)\}.$$

We show how to calculate each term in Appendix 2.

We now consider the simpler case where a priori the $K(t)$ are independent. In this case Lemma 2.2 becomes

$$p(K | Y^n, X) = \prod_{t=1}^{n} p\{K(t) | y(t), x(t)\} \propto \prod_{t=1}^{n} p\{y(t) | x(t), K(t)\} p\{K(t)\},$$

so that the $K(t)$ are independent and binomial and it is straightforward to generate them.

Our approach can also handle errors that are general normal scale mixtures, for example t distributed errors. Some further details and examples are given by Carlin et al. (1992).

3.5 Switching regression model

In the switching regression model the coefficients $\{h(t), F(t), t = 1, \ldots, n\}$ take on a small number of different values determined by some probabilistic distribution. Shumway and Stoffer (1991) use a switching regression model to identify targets when a large number of targets with unknown identities is observed. To show how our results apply it is sufficient to discuss the simplest case in which $F(t)$ is constant for all t and $h(t)$ takes on just two values, h_1 and h_2 say. Let $K(t) = 1$ if $h(t) = h_1$, and let $K(t) = 2$ otherwise. As in Section 3.4 we assume that a priori the $K(t)$ come from a Markov chain with parameters p_1 and p_2. If p_1 and p_2 are unknown we would place a beta prior on them. Given $K = \{K(1), \ldots, K(n)\}$ we generate X as in Section 2.1. Generating K given Y^n, X and θ is very similar to the way we generated it in Section 3.4 and we omit details.

Acknowledgement

We would like to thank the Division of Mathematics and Statistics, CSIRO, and the Australian Research Council for partial support. We would also like to thank David Wong for help with the computations.

Appendix 1

Algorithm to generate state vector

We show how to generate X conditional on Y^n, K and θ. We omit dependence on K and θ, and, as in Section 2.2, let

$$x(t|j) = E\{x(t)|Y^j\}, \qquad S(t|j) = \mathrm{var}\{x(t)|Y^j\}.$$

For $t = 1, \ldots, n$ the conditional mean $x(t|t)$ and the conditional variance $S(t|t)$ are obtained using the Kalman filter (Anderson and Moore, 1979, p. 105).

Using Lemma 2.1 we show how to generate $x(n), \ldots, x(1)$ in that order conditioning on Y^n. First, $p\{x(n)|Y^n\}$ is normal with mean $x(n|n)$ and variance $S(n|n)$. To generate $x(t)$ conditional on Y^t and $x(t+1)$ we note that we can regard the equation

$$x(t+1) = F(t+1)x(t) + u(t+1)$$

as m additional observations on $x(t)$. If $U(t+1)$ is diagonal then the $u_i(t+1)$ $(i = 1, \ldots, m)$ are independent and we can apply the observation update step of the Kalman filter m times as shown below to obtain

$$E\{x(t)|Y^t, x(t+1)\}, \qquad \mathrm{var}\{x(t)|Y^t, x(t+1)\}.$$

More generally we can factorize $U(t+1) = L(t+1)\Delta(t+1)L(t+1)'$ using the Cholesky decomposition with $L(t+1)$ a lower triangular matrix with ones on the diagonal and $\Delta(t+1)$ a diagonal matrix. Let

$$\tilde{x}(t+1) = L(t+1)^{-1}x(t+1), \qquad \tilde{F}(t+1) = L(t+1)^{-1}F(t+1),$$

$$\tilde{u}(t+1) = L(t+1)^{-1}u(t+1).$$

We can then write

$$\tilde{x}(t+1) = \tilde{F}(t+1)x(t) + \tilde{u}(t+1)$$

so that, for $i = 1, \ldots, m$,

$$\tilde{x}_i(t+1) = \tilde{F}_i(t+1)'x(t) + \tilde{u}_i(t+1), \qquad (A1.1)$$

where $\tilde{F}_i(t+1)'$ is the ith row of $\tilde{F}(t+1)$ and $\tilde{x}_i(t+1)$ and $\tilde{u}_i(t+1)$ are the ith elements of $\tilde{x}(t+1)$ and $\tilde{u}(t+1)$. The elements $\tilde{u}_i(t+1)$ are independent

$N\{0, \Delta_i(t+1)\}$, where $\Delta_i(t+1)$ is the ith diagonal element of $\Delta(t+1)$. For $i = 1, \ldots, m$ let

$$x(t|t, i) = E\{x(t)|Y^t, x_1(t+1), \ldots, x_i(t+1)\},$$
$$S(t|t, i) = \text{var}\{x(t)|Y^t, x_1(t+1), \ldots, x_i(t+1)\},$$

and define $x(t|t, 0) = x(t|t)$ and $S(t|t, 0) = S(t|t)$. We now apply the observation update step of the Kalman filter m times to (A1.1) as follows.

For $i = 1, \ldots, m$ let

$$\varepsilon(t, i) = \tilde{x}_i(t+1) - \tilde{F}_i(t+1)'x(t|t, i-1),$$
$$R(t, i) = \tilde{F}_i(t+1)'S(t|t, i-1)\tilde{F}_i(t+1) + \Delta_i(t+1).$$

Then

$$x(t|t, i) = x(t|t, i-1) + S(t|t, i-1)\tilde{F}_i(t+1)\varepsilon(t, i)/R(t, i),$$
$$S(t|t, i) = S(t|t, i-1) - S(t|t, i-1)\tilde{F}_i(t+1)\tilde{F}_i(t+1)'S(t|t, i-1)/R(t, i).$$

We therefore obtain

$$x(t|t, m) = E\{x(t)|Y^t, x(t+1)\}, \qquad S(t|t, m) = \text{var}\{x(t)|Y^t, x(t+1)\}.$$

It is now straightforward to generate $x(t)$ conditionally on Y^t and $x(t+1)$, as it is normally distributed with mean $x(t|t, m)$ and variance $S(t|t, m)$.

Appendix 2

Algorithm to generate indicator variables

We show how to generate K conditional on Y^n, X and θ. We omit dependence on θ. Let $k_1, \ldots, k_m$ be the possible values assumed by $K(t)$ $(t = 1, \ldots, n)$ and suppose that the transition matrices specifying $p\{K(t)|K(t-1)\}$ $(t = 2, \ldots, n)$ are known. We note that if $y(t)$ is observed then

$$p\{K(t)|Y^t, X^t\} \propto p\{y(t)|x(t), K(t)\}p\{x(t)|x(t-1), K(t)\}p\{K(t)|Y^{t-1}, X^{t-1}\},$$

and if $y(t)$ is not observed then

$$p\{K(t)|Y^t, X^t\} \propto p\{x(t)|x(t-1), K(t)\}p\{K(t)|Y^{t-1}, X^{t-1}\}.$$

The following algorithm uses recursive filtering equations following Anderson and Moore (1979, Ch. 8) to calculate $p\{K(t)|Y^t, X^t\}$.

Discrete filter: For $t = 1, \ldots, n$.

Step 1. Performed for $t > 1$,

$$p\{K(t)|Y^{t-1}, X^{t-1}\} = \sum_{j=1}^{m} p\{K(t)|K(t-1) = k_j\}$$
$$\times p\{K(t-1) = k_j|Y^{t-1}, X^{t-1}\}.$$

Step 2a. If $y(t)$ is observed set

$$p^*\{K(t)|Y^t, X^t\} = p\{y(t)|x(t), K(t)\}p\{x(t)|x(t-1), K(t)\}$$
$$\times p\{K(t)|Y^{t-1}, X^{t-1}\}.$$

Step 2b. If $y(t)$ is not observed set

$$p^*\{K(t)|Y^t, X^t\} = p\{x(t)|x(t-1), K(t)\}p\{K(t)|Y^{t-1}, X^{t-1}\}.$$

Step 3. Obtain $p\{K(t)|Y^t, X^t\}$ using

$$p\{K(t)|Y^t, X^t\} = p^*\{K(t)|Y^t, X^t\} \left/ \sum_{j=1}^{m} p^*\{K(t) = k_j|Y^t, X^t\} \right. .$$

We note that $p\{y(t)|x(t), K(t)\}$ and $p\{x(t)|x(t-1), K(t)\}$ for $t = 1, \ldots, n$ are known from the specification of the state space model.

Using Lemma 2.2 we show how to generate $K(n), \ldots, K(1)$ in that order conditioning only on Y^n and X. First, we calculate $p\{K(t)|Y^t, X^t\}$ for $t = 1, \ldots, n$ using the discrete filter shown above. To generate $K(t)$ conditional on Y^t, X^t and $K(t+1)$ we use the following result for $t = n - 1, \ldots, 1$:

$$p\{K(t)|Y^t, X^t, K(t+1)\} = \frac{p\{K(t+1)|K(t)\}p\{K(t)|Y^t, X^t\}}{p\{K(t+1)|Y^t, X^t\}}.$$

References

Anderson, B. D. O. & Moore, J. B. (1979). *Optimal Filtering*. Englewood Cliffs, New Jersey: Prentice Hall.

Ansley, C. F. & Kohn, R. (1985). Estimation filtering and smoothing in state space models with partially diffuse initial conditions. *Ann. Statist.*, 13, 1286–316.

Ansley, C. F. & Kohn, R. (1990). Filtering and smoothing in state space models with partially diffuse initial conditions. *J. Time Ser. Anal.*, 11, 277–93.

Box, G. E. P. & Tiao, G. C. (1968). A Bayesian approach to some outlier problems. *Biometrika*, 55, 119–29.

Carlin, B. P., Polson, N. G. & Stoffer, D. S. (1992). A Monte Carlo approach to nonnormal and nonlinear state space modeling. *J. Am. Statist. Assoc.*, 87, 493–500.

Gelfand, A. E. & Smith, A. F. M. (1990). Sampling-based approaches to calculating marginal densities. *J. Am. Statist. Assoc.*, 85, 398–409.

Gordon, K. & Smith, A. F. M. (1990). Monitoring and modeling biomedical time series. *J. Am. Statist. Assoc.*, 85, 328–37.

Hamilton, J. D. (1989). A new approach to the economic analysis of nonstationary time series and the business cycle. *Econometrica*, 57, 357–84.

Harrison, P. J. & Stevens, C. F. (1976). Bayesian forecasting (with discussion). *J. R. Statist. Soc.* B 38, 205–47.

Kitagawa, G. (1987). Non-Gaussian state space modeling of nonstationary time-series (with discussion). *J. Am. Statist. Assoc.*, 82, 1032–63.

Kitagawa, G. & Gersch, W. (1984). A smoothness priors-state space approach to time series with trend and seasonalities. *J. Am. Statist. Assoc.*, 79, 378–89.

Kohn, R. & Ansley, C. F. (1987). A new algorithm for spline smoothing based on smoothing a stochastic process. *SIAM J. Sci. Statist. Comput.*, 8, 33–48.

Liu, J., Wong, W. H. & Kong, A. (1994). Covariance structure of the Gibbs sampler with applications to the comparison of estimators and augmentation schemes. *Biometrika*, 81, 27–40.

Meinhold, R. J. & Singpurwalla, N. D. (1989). Robustification of Kalman filter models. *J. Am. Statist. Assoc.*, 84, 479–86.

Moran, P. A. P. (1975). The estimation of standard errors in Monte Carlo simulation experiments. *Biometrika*, 62, 1–4.

Schweppe, C. F. (1965). Evaluation of likelihood functions for Gaussian signals. *IEEE Trans. Info. Theory*, 11, 61–70.

Shumway, R. H. & Stoffer, D. S. (1991). Dynamic linear models with switching. *J. Am. Statist. Assoc.*, 86, 763–9.

Tierney, L. (1994). Markov chains for exploring posterior distributions. *Ann. Statist.*, 22, 1701–86.

Wahba, G. (1983). Bayesian 'confidence intervals' for the cross-validated smoothing spline. *J. R. Statist. Soc.* B 45, 133–50.

West, M. & Harrison, J. (1989). *Bayesian Forecasting and Dynamic Models*, Springer Series in Statistics. New York: Springer-Verlag.

19

The Simulation Smoother for Time Series Models*

PIET DE JONG

*Faculty of Commerce and Business Administration,
University of British Columbia*

AND

NEIL SHEPHARD

Nuffield College

SUMMARY

Recently suggested procedures for simulating from the posterior density of states given a Gaussian state space time series are refined and extended. We introduce and study the simulation smoother, which draws from the multivariate posterior distribution of the disturbances of the model, so avoiding the degeneracies inherent in state samplers. The technique is important in Gibbs sampling with non-Gaussian time series models, and for performing Bayesian analysis of Gaussian time series.

1 Introduction

This paper introduces a simple and efficient method, the simulation smoother, for sampling from the smoothing density associated with time series models. The simulation smoother exploits the common structure which most time series models possess.

Simulation smoothing comes up in a number of papers, e.g. Frühwirth-Schnatter (1994, 1995), Carter and Kohn (1994), Shephard (1994), Chib and Greenberg (1994), and may be of importance in future time series work. One area of application is the Markov chain Monte Carlo method or Gibbs sampling, described by Smith and Roberts (1993) and Ripley (1987, pp. 113–6). General time series papers using these methods are by Carlin, Polson and Stoffer (1992), Carter and Kohn (1994) and Shephard (1994). Papers tackling specific cases of models using this framework include Chib (1993), Jacquier, Polson and Rossi (1994), Albert and Chib (1993), Shumway and Stoffer (1991) and Frühwirth-Schnatter (1994). Its application to robust nonparametric regression, which exploits the state space form for computational convenience, has been suggested by Carter and Kohn (1994).

The objective of Gibbs sampling (Tierney 1994; Tanner 1991, pp. 89–106) is to produce draws from the 'smoothing' density $p(\alpha, \omega | y)$, where y is the vector of

---

* This work was previously published as P. de Jong and N. Shephard, "The Simulation Smoother", *Biometrika*, 1995, Vol. 82, 339–50. Reproduced by permission of the Biometrika Trustees.

observed data. The vectors α and ω contain quantities of interest or facilitate the estimation of the same. They are viewed as unobserved 'latent' data. There is flexibility in choosing α and ω, depending on the structure of the model, objectives of the analysis and estimation method. With Gibbs sampling, draws from $p(\alpha, \omega|y)$, are produced by cycling over the steps $\alpha \sim p(\alpha|y, \omega)$ and $\omega \sim p(\omega|y, \alpha)$, where each draw serves to redefine the conditioning variable on the next draw.

In time series applications α is usually defined as the stack of state vectors with respect to a state space form and $p(\alpha|y, \omega)$ is typically Gaussian. Carlin et al. (1992) propose that the draw from $p(\alpha|y, \omega)$ be replaced by the 'single-state' Gibbs sampler which samples from $p(\alpha_t|y, \alpha^t, \omega)$, where α^t is α excluding α_t and cycling over t and likewise for the individual elements of ω. With the single-state sampler each draw serves to redefine a single state α_t in contrast to the 'multi-state' Gibbs sampler where the entire α is drawn at once from $p(\alpha|y, \omega)$.

Recently there has been a series of papers which suggest that the single-state Gibbs sampler may be extremely inefficient for a class of time series models which includes many of the most interesting non-Gaussian and nonlinear models. In response, Carter and Kohn (1994) and Frühwirth-Schnatter (1994) have independently suggested a direct implementation of multi-state sampling for time series models. The implementation is based on the identity:

$$p(\alpha|y, \omega) = p(\alpha_n|y, \omega)p(\alpha_{n-1}|y, \alpha_n, \omega) \cdots p(\alpha_0|y, \alpha_1, \ldots, \alpha_n, \omega). \qquad (1)$$

A draw from $p(\alpha|y, \omega)$ can thus be constructed recursively provided the subdraws from the densities in the right of (1) are practical. Carter and Kohn (1994) and Frühwirth-Schnatter (1994) show how to implement these subdraws if $p(\alpha|y, \omega)$ is Gaussian.

The multi-state sampler is simpler to implement than the single-state sampler and more efficient in that there is less correlation between successive α or ω draws and so it converges more quickly: see Liu, Kong and Wong (1994), who show that generating variables from reduced conditionals produces faster convergence. Shortcomings of the multi-state sampler as implemented by Carter and Kohn (1994) and Frühwirth-Schnatter (1994) flow from the fact that a draw from $p(\alpha|y, \omega)$ is constructed recursively in terms of α_t. Typically α is of very high dimension with many identities linking the state variables. The identities are a consequence of forcing the model into state space form. These identities must be kept track of in the direct recursive construction of the draw, necessitating mechanisms for dealing with degeneracies and imposing a large computational overhead.

In this paper we develop an alternative multi-state Gibbs sampler for time series models, in which it is disturbances rather than states which are drawn. Drawing disturbances is not subject to automatic identities, and is typically simpler. All random variables in the state space model are linear combinations of the disturbances, and hence can be constructed from simulated disturbances as required.

Section 2 illustrates the advantages of multi-state over single-state sampling. The multi-state sampler is constructed in terms of the disturbance draws. Section 3 gives the general algorithm for the disturbance sampler. Section 4 discusses some examples, and Section 5 deals with regression effects. An appendix proves the correctness of the algorithm.

2 Single Versus Multi-State Sampling

2.1 Illustration

To illustrate the importance of multi-state sampling, consider the stochastic volatility model:

$$y_t = \varepsilon_t \exp(\tfrac{1}{2}\alpha_t), \qquad \alpha_{t+1} = \phi\alpha_t + \eta_t,$$

where ε_t and η_t are mutually and serially independent Gaussian random variables with zero means and variances 1 and σ^2 respectively. This non-Gaussian state space model has been used to generalise the Black–Scholes option pricing equation to allow the variance to change over time (Hull and White 1987; Chesney and Scott 1989; Melino and Turnbull 1990).

The single-state sampler involves drawing α_t, ideally from its conditional distribution

$$p(\alpha_t|\alpha^t, y) = p(\alpha_t|\alpha_{t-1}, \alpha_{t+1}, y_t) = cp(y_t|\alpha_t)p(\alpha_{t+1}|\alpha_t)p(\alpha_t|\alpha_{t-1}),$$

where c, the constant of proportionality, is unknown. A good approach to overcoming the problem is suggested by Jacquier et al. (1994), building on the accept/reject Metropolis work of Carlin et al. (1992). However, we are going to avoid using this by noting that $\log\{p(\alpha_t|\alpha^t, y)\}$ is concave in α_t. This means we can directly sample from $p(\alpha_t|\alpha_{t-1}, \alpha_{t+1}, y_t)$ using the routine of Wild and Gilks (1993), and so use the single-state Gibbs sampler.

This Gibbs sampler will converge to drawings from $p(\alpha|y)$ so long as $\sigma^2 > 0$. However, the speed of convergence may be slow, in the sense of taking a large number of draws. To illustrate these features, Fig. 1 reports some results using two sets of parameter values: $\phi = 0.9, \sigma^2 = 0.05$ and $\phi = 0.99, \sigma^2 = 0.01$. These lines report the average over 1000 replications of α_t for $t = 0, 1, \ldots, 100$ after k iterations, all initialised at zero. The experiment shows how long the initial conditions last in the single-state sampler and so reflect the memory or correlation in the sampler. Figure 2 shows the results from running a single sampler for 100000 iterations, discarding the first 10000. The resulting correlogram of that series, recording the draw for α_{50}, compactly presents the correlation in the sampler in equilibrium.

The results of Fig. 1 show that as ϕ increases, and similarly as $\sigma^2 \to 0$, the sampler slows up, reflecting the increased correlation amongst the states drawn. This unfortunate characteristic of the single-state Gibbs sampler is common in state space models. If a component, such as α_t, changes slowly and persistently, the single-state sampler will be slow.

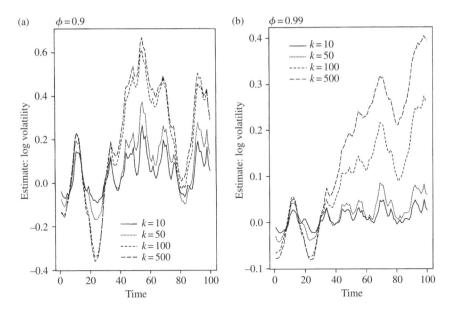

Fig. 1. Signal extraction of stochastic volatility model using single-move Gibbs, indicating rate of convergence.

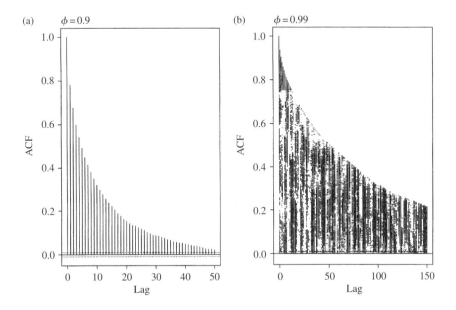

Fig. 2. Correlograms from Fig. 1.

2.2 Multi-state sampling

To use the simulation smoother in this context we transform the Stochastic
Volatility model (Harvey, Ruiz and Shephard 1994; Shephard 1994):

$$\log(y_t^2) = \alpha_t + \log(\varepsilon_t^2).$$

Carter and Kohn (1993) and Shephard (1994) have suggested using the multi-state
samplers on this model by approximating the distribution of $\log(\varepsilon_t^2)$ by a mixture of
normals, so that $p\{\log(\varepsilon_t^2)|\omega_t\}$ is Gaussian with mean $\mu(\omega_t)$ and variance $\sigma^2(\omega_t)$,
where the ω_t are assumed independent and identically distributed integer random
variables. The advantage of this representation of the model is that, conditionally
on the ω_t, the state space model is Gaussian. It is possible to directly draw from
$p(\alpha|y, \omega)$ using the simulation smoother developed in this paper. The smoother,
specialised to the current model, is based on running forwards, for $t = 1, 2, \ldots, n$,
the Kalman filter

$$e_t = \log(y_t^2) - \mu(\omega_t) - a_t, \qquad d_t = p_t + \frac{\sigma^2(\omega_t)}{\sigma^2}, \qquad k_t = \frac{p_t}{\phi d_t},$$

$$a_{t+1} = \phi a_t + k_t e_t, \qquad p_{t+1} = 1 + \phi p_t(1 - k_t),$$

with starting conditions $a_1 = 0$, $p_1 = 1/(1 - \phi^2)$. On the forward pass, only the
scalars e_t, d_t and k_t are stored. These are respectively the innovation, innovation
variance, and Kalman gain. Then setting $r_n = 0$, $w_n = 0$, we compute, for
$t = n, n - 1, \ldots, 1$,

$$c_t = 1 - w_t, \qquad \eta_t \sim N(r_t, \sigma^2 c_t), \qquad v_t = w_t(\phi - k_t),$$

$$r_{t-1} = \frac{e_t}{d_t} + (\phi - k_t)r_t - \frac{v_t(\eta_t - r_t)}{c_t}, \qquad w_{t-1} = \frac{1}{d_t} + (\phi - k_t)^2 w_t + \frac{v_t^2}{c_t},$$

where $\eta_t \sim N(r_t, \sigma^2 c_t)$ indicates that η_t is drawn from a Gaussian density with
mean r_t and variance $\sigma^2 c_t$. The final η_0 is drawn from $N\{p_1 r_0, \sigma^2 p_1(1 - p_1 w_0)\}$.
The simulated α vector is then constructed via the recursion $\alpha_{t+1} = \phi \alpha_t + \eta_t$
$(t = 0, 1, \ldots, n - 1)$ starting with $\alpha_0 = 0$.

The simulation smoother is based on simulating from the posterior distribution
of the disturbances of the model, η_t, which then allow us, as required, to form
the simulation from the states α_t. Simulation smoothing is the analogue of the
recent analytic disturbance smoothers, introduced partially by de Jong (1988) and
elaborated by Koopman (1993). In fact, putting $v_t = 0$ for all t gives the Koopman
algorithm to compute $E(\eta_t|y, \omega)$ and $\text{cov}(\eta_t|y, \omega)$.

Likewise, it is easy to draw from $p(\omega|y, \alpha)$ using uniform random numbers.
This means it is possible to use a multi-state sampler on this model. Figures 3 and 4
repeat the experiments of Figs 1 and 2, but now using the multi-state sampler.

It is possible to argue that, although there are substantial differences between
Figs 1 and 3, and particularly Figs 2 and 4, it is not worth the trouble of blocking
and using the multi-state sampler. This is a dangerous view. The inclusion of any
really slowly moving component will retard the single-state sampler unacceptably.

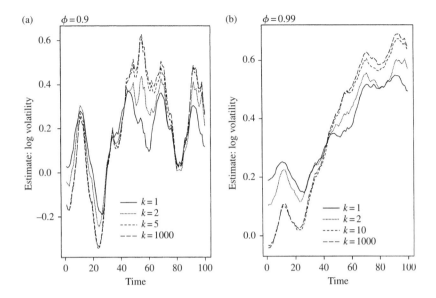

Fig. 3. Signal extraction of stochastic volatility model using multi-move Gibbs, indicating rate of convergence.

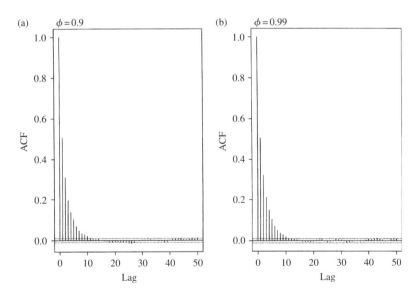

Fig. 4. Correlograms from Fig. 3.

3 The Simulation Smoother

We shall use lower case letters to denote column vectors, and upper case letters for matrices. Dimensions may vary with time. If A and B have the same number of columns, then $(A; B) = (A', B')'$ denotes the matrix formed by placing A above B.

We work with the following general model. Conditional on $\omega = (\omega_0; \omega_1; \ldots; \omega_n)$, it is supposed that y_t is generated by the state space model (de Jong, 1991):

$$y_t = X_t\beta + Z_t\alpha_t + G_t u_t \quad (t = 1, 2, \ldots, n),$$
$$\alpha_{t+1} = W_t\beta + T_t\alpha_t + H_t u_t \quad (t = 0, 1, \ldots, n),$$

where $\alpha_0 = 0$. The coefficients matrices may depend, implicitly, on ω_t. The u_t are independent $N(0, \sigma^2 I)$ variables.

Initially we suppose β is known: the case of unknown β is discussed in Section 5. Our simulation smoother draws $\eta \sim p(\eta|y, \omega)$, where $\eta = (\eta_0; \eta_1; \ldots; \eta_n)$ with $\eta_t = F_t u_t$ and the F_t are arbitrary matrices whose choice is discussed below. Initially we run, for $t = 1, 2, \ldots, n$, the Kalman filter

$$e_t = y_t - X_t\beta - Z_t a_t, \qquad D_t = Z_t P_t Z_t' + G_t G_t',$$
$$K_t = (T_t P_t Z_t' + H_t G_t')D_t^{-1}, \qquad a_{t+1} = W_t\beta + T_t a_t + K_t e_t, \qquad (2)$$
$$P_{t+1} = T_t P_t L_t' + H_t J_t',$$

where $a_1 = W_0\beta$, $P_1 = H_0 H_0'$, $L_t = T_t - K_t Z_t$ and $J_t = H_t - K_t G_t$. On this Kalman filter pass, the quantities e_t, D_t and K_t are stored. Then setting $r_n = 0$ and $U_n = 0$, we run, for $t = n, n - 1, \ldots, 1$,

$$C_t = F_t(I - G_t'D_t^{-1}G_t - J_t'U_t J_t)F_t', \qquad \varepsilon_t \sim N(0, \sigma^2 C_t),$$
$$V_t = F_t(G_t'D_t^{-1}Z_t + J_t'U_t L_t), \qquad r_{t-1} = Z_t'D_t^{-1}e_t + L_t'r_t - V_t'C_t^{-1}\varepsilon_t, \qquad (3)$$
$$U_{t-1} = Z_t'D_t^{-1}Z_t + L_t'U_t L_t + V_t'C_t^{-1}V_t,$$

and store $\eta_t = F_t(G_t'D_t^{-1}e_t + J_t'r_t) + \varepsilon_t$, where we take $G_0 = 0$. The vector $\eta = (\eta_0; \eta_1; \ldots; \eta_n)$ is a draw from $p(\eta|y, \omega)$. The proof is given in the Appendix.

If $F_t = I$ then η_t is drawn from $p(u_t|y, \omega)$. This choice is typically not optimal since, as shown in the next section, it implies that C_t is singular for some t.

If $F_t = G_t$ or $F_t = H_t$ then the sampled η_t correspond to the measurement noise $G_t u_t$ or state noise $H_t u_t$ respectively. The filters (2) and (3) are conceptually easier in this case provided measurement and state noise are uncorrelated, $G_t H_t' = 0$. For example if $F_t = H_t$, a sensible choice for most models, then, putting $\Omega_t = H_t H_t'$, (3) reduces to

$$C_t = \Omega_t - \Omega_t U_t \Omega_t, \qquad \varepsilon_t \sim N(0, \sigma^2 C_t), \qquad V_t = \Omega_t U_t L_t,$$
$$r_{t-1} = Z_t'D_t^{-1}e_t + L_t'r_t - V_t'C_t^{-1}\varepsilon_t, \qquad (4)$$
$$U_{t-1} = Z_t'D_t^{-1}Z_t + L_t'U_t L_t + V_t'C_t^{-1}V_t,$$

and $\eta_t = \Omega_t r_t + \varepsilon_t$ is a draw from $p(H_t u_t | y, \omega)$. Similarly if $F_t = G_t$ then, putting $\Gamma_t = G_t G_t'$, $n_t = D_t^{-1} e_t - K_t' r_t$ and $N_t = D_t^{-1} + K_t' U_t K_t$, (3) becomes

$$C_t = \Gamma_t - \Gamma_t N_t \Gamma_t, \qquad \varepsilon_t \sim N(0, \sigma^2 C_t), \qquad V_t = \Gamma_t (N_t Z_t - K_t' U_t T_t),$$

$$r_{t-1} = Z_t' D_t^{-1} e_t + L_t' r_t - V_t' C_t^{-1} \varepsilon_t, \tag{5}$$

$$U_{t-1} = Z_t' D_t^{-1} Z_t + L_t' U_t L_t + V_t' C_t^{-1} V_t,$$

and $\eta_t = \Gamma_t n_t + \varepsilon_t$ is a draw from $p(G_t u_t | y, \omega)$, or, equivalently, $y_t - \eta_t$ is a draw from the conditional 'signal' distribution, $p(X_t \beta + Z_t \alpha_t | y, \omega)$.

The recursion (3) generalises analytic smoothing in the sense that, if V_t and ε_t are set to zero for each t, then (3) reduces to the smoothing recursions given by de Jong (1988, 1989), Kohn and Ansley (1989) and Koopman (1993), and the computed η_t equal $E(F_t u_t | y, \omega)$ while $\sigma^2 C_t = \text{cov}(F_t u_t | y, \omega)$. More particularly if V_t and ε_t are set to zero in (4) or (5) then we obtain the analytic smoothed disturbances of Koopman (1993) and de Jong (1988); that is η_t equals $E(H_t u_t | y, \omega)$ or $E(G_t u_t | y, \omega)$, with associated mean squared error matrix $\sigma^2 C_t$.

The stored Kalman filter quantities e_t, D_t and K_t are, respectively, the innovation vector, scaled innovation covariance matrix and Kalman gain matrix. On the simulation smoothing pass (3), η_t is a draw from $p(F_t u_t | y, \eta_{t+1}, \ldots, \eta_n, \omega)$ since $F_t(G_t' D_t^{-1} e_t + J_t' r_t)$ and $\sigma^2 C_t$ are the conditional mean and covariance matrix of this Gaussian density. Thus the η draw is built up using the decomposition (1), written in terms of η rather than α.

The advantages of the simulation smoother over the state sampler are as follows. First, the storage requirements are typically much less than that required for the state sampler, which stores the one-step-ahead state vector estimates a_t and associated scaled covariance matrices P_t. Secondly, the recursion operates in minimal dimension and does not require inversion of the matrix P_t, which is typically of large dimension and/or singular. Thirdly, the recursion can be operated in square root form, enhancing numerical stability. Fourthly, provided the F_t are of full row rank, there are no automatic degeneracies in $p(\eta | \omega)$. In turn, degeneracies in $p(\eta | y, \omega)$ can always be avoided through a transparent choice of the F_t, as discussed in Section 4. Finally, it is often easier to draw from $p(\omega | y, \eta)$ as opposed to $p(\omega | y, \alpha)$.

4 Examples

Example 4.1 MA (q) *model*. This model can be written in state space form with $G_t \equiv 1$ and $H_t \equiv (h_1, \ldots, h_q)'$, where $(h_1, \ldots, h_q)$ is the vector of moving average coefficients with $h_q \neq 0$. If $F_t = I = 1$ then the ε_t and C_t are scalar. However the only nonzero C_t are $C_n, C_{n-1}, \ldots, C_{n-q+1}$ since, given y and $u_n, u_{n-1}, \ldots, u_{n-q+1}$, the remaining u_t are determined recursively from

$$u_t = (y_{t+q} - u_{t+q} - h_1 u_{t+q-1} - \cdots - h_{q-1} u_{t+1})/h_q.$$

Hence a draw from $p(u|y)$ amounts to drawing q random variables $u_n, u_{n-1}, \ldots, u_{n-q+1}$, which go on to determine the remaining disturbances.

Example 4.2 *Stochastic volatility model.* Consider the stochastic volatility model transformed into the partial Gaussian state space form discussed in Section 2, written as

$$\log(y_t^2) = \mu(\omega_t) + \alpha_t + g(\omega_t)u_{1t}, \qquad \alpha_{t+1} = \phi\alpha_t + u_{2t},$$

where $g(\omega_t) = \sigma(\omega_t)/\sigma$ and the $u_t = (u_{1t}; u_{2t})$ are independent $N(0, \sigma^2 I)$ vectors. Thus $\log(y_{t+1}^2) - \log(y_t^2)$ is, apart from the mean,

$$\alpha_{t+1} - \alpha_t + g(\omega_{t+1})u_{1,t+1} - g(\omega_t)u_{1t} = u_{2t} + g(\omega_{t+1})u_{1,t+1} - g(\omega_t)u_{1t}.$$

Hence, for $t = n-1, \ldots, 1$, $g(\omega_t)u_{1t}$ is determined from subsequent u_t and data y. Hence if $F_t = ((g(\omega_t), 0); (0, 1))$, then C_n is nonsingular but $C_{n-1}, \ldots, C_1$ are of rank 1. Further $C_0 = 0$ since

$$H_0 u_0 = \alpha_1 = \log(y_1^2) - \mu(\omega_1) - g(\omega_1)u_{11}.$$

Thus drawing from the $2n + 1$ dimensional density $p(\eta|y, \omega)$ amounts to drawing $n + 1$ Gaussian random variables.

An issue that arises in running (3) is the occurrence of singularities in one or more of the C_t. These singularities will always occur if, for each t, the rows of F_t span the row space of $(G_t; H_t)$. For then, without loss of generality we may assume that $(G_t; H_t)$ is of full column rank, which implies u_t can be determined from $F_t u_t$, and hence we may assume $F_t = I$ implying $\eta = u = (u_0; u_1; \ldots; u_n)$. The vector u satisfies $y = X\beta + Gu$ for some matrices X and G. Thus $Gu = y - X\beta$ and hence $p(u|y, \omega)$ is degenerate. Thus the sampled vector η in (3) is subject to linear constraints. These constraints reflect themselves in the C_t, since

$$p(\eta|y, \omega) = p(\eta_n|y, \omega)p(\eta_{n-1}|y, \eta_n, \omega) \ldots p(\eta_0|y, \eta_1, \ldots, \eta_n, \omega),$$

and $\sigma^2 C_t$ is the covariance matrix associated with the conditional density on the right corresponding to η_t. Thus, if for each t, the rows of F_t span the row space of $(G_t; H_t)$ then C_t will be singular for at least some t.

It is possible to deal with singular C_t in (3) via generalised inversion. However it is more sensible to choose F_t to have rows making up a basis for the row space of H_t, as this often avoids singularities in the C_t. The next two examples provide illustrations.

Example 4.2 *Stochastic volatility model (cont.).* For this model put $F_t = H_t = (0, 1)$. Then $G_t = (g(\omega_t), 0)$ is not in the row space of F_t. In this case all the C_t in (2) are scalar of rank 1. Drawing from $p(\eta|y, \omega)$ reduces to drawing $n + 1$ Gaussian random variables. Now C_t is scalar and nonzero for all t. The sampler given in Section 2 for the stochastic volatility model is (2) and (3) specialised to this case.

Example 4.3 *Seasonal model.* Consider the stochastic volatility model given above with the addition of a seasonal term

$$s_{t+1} = -\sum_{j=1}^{p-1} s_{t+1-j} + hu_{3t}.$$

In this case $G_t = (g(\omega_t), 0, 0)$, while H_t is $(p+1) \times 3$ with p the number of seasons. The first two rows of H_t are $(0, 1, 0)$ and $(0, 0, h)$ while the rest are zero, reflecting the identities amongst state elements. Form F_t from the first two rows of H. All the C_t are nonsingular, and the drawn ε_t in (2) are nondegenerate random vectors of length 2. The state vector for this model is of length $p + 1$, and state sampling, if p is say 12, is highly inefficient compared to disturbance sampling.

In general if, for each t, the rows of F_t form a basis for the row space of H_t then $H_t u_t$ can be determined from η_t. In turn the α_t and $G_t u_t$ can be determined from the $H_t u_t$ via the equations

$$\alpha_{t+1} = W_t \beta + T_t \alpha_t + H_t u_t, \qquad G_t u_t = y_t - X_t \beta - Z_t \alpha_t,$$

which can be conveniently computed alongside the next Kalman filter pass. The advantage of this choice for F_t is that if there is measurement noise, that is if for each t the rows of G_t are not in the row space of H_t, then C_t will be nonsingular.

Example 4.4 *Multiplicative model.* Consider the model

$$y_t = \omega_t \alpha_t + gu_{1t}, \qquad \alpha_{t+1} = \alpha_t + hu_{2t}, \qquad \omega_{t+1} = \rho \omega_t + v_t,$$

where v_t is Gaussian noise with variance σ^2, uncorrelated with the u_t. Conditional on ω this is a Gaussian state space model and hence the scalar $\eta_t = hu_{2t}$ can be drawn as described above. In turn the simulated α_t can be built up in a forward pass from the equation $\alpha_{t+1} = \alpha_t + \eta_t$. Conditional on η and hence the α, the first and third equation define a Gaussian state space model and the above shows how to draw v_t, which in turn can be used to build up the draw of ω_t conditional on y and α.

5 Regression Effects

Situations with unknown regression vector β can be handled by supposing $p(\beta|\omega)$ is Gaussian with $E(\beta|\omega) = b$ and $\text{cov}(\beta|\omega) = \sigma^2 BB'$, which may be singular. In this case the draw $\eta \sim p(\eta|y, \omega)$ is built up using the decomposition

$$p(\beta, \eta|y, \omega) = p(\beta|y, \omega)p(\eta|\beta, y, \omega).$$

Drawing from $p(\eta|\beta, y, \omega)$ was, in effect, considered in Sections 2 and 3. Drawing from $p(\beta|y, \omega)$ is achieved by replacing the equations for e_t and a_{t+1} in (2) by

$$E_t = (0, y_t) - X_t(B, b) - Z_t A_t, \qquad A_{t+1} = W_t(B, b) + T_t A_t + K_t E_t$$

and adding the recursion $Q_{t+1} = Q_t + E_t' D_t^{-1} E_t$, where $A_1 = W_0(B, b)$ and $Q_1 = 0$. Thus the Kalman filter (2) is modified in two of its equations, yielding the so-called diffuse Kalman filter. It is shown by de Jong (1991) that $p(\beta|y, \omega)$ is Gaussian with mean and covariance matrix given by

$$E(\beta|y, \omega) = b + B(S + I)^{-1}s, \qquad \text{cov}(\beta|y, \omega) = \sigma^2 B(S + I)^{-1} B',$$

where S and s are defined such that the matrix $(S, -s)$ equals the matrix formed from the k top rows of the $k + 1$ order matrix Q_{n+1}.

Thus a draw from $p(\beta, \eta|y, \omega)$ is made as follows. First the Kalman filter (4) is run, modified as described above. This is followed by the draw

$$\delta \sim N\{(S + I)^{-1}s, \sigma^2(S + I)^{-1}\}.$$

Given δ draw η is made with the simulation smoothing pass (3), where $e_t = E_t(\delta; 1)$.

The above steps assume $p(\beta|\omega)$ is a proper prior for β. In some cases it is reasonable to suppose a vague or improper prior for β: a Gaussian density with $\text{cov}(\beta|\omega) = \sigma^2 \kappa BB'$, where $\kappa \to \infty$. In this case, δ is drawn from $N(S^{-1}s, \sigma^2 S^{-1})$ and the draw from $p(\eta|\beta, y, \omega)$ proceeds as above. A similar treatment can be given for the case where α_1 has a vague prior.

Example 5.1 *Stochastic volatility model.* We continue with the stochastic volatility model transformed into the partial Gaussian state space form discussed in Sections 2 and 4. Suppose $\mu(\omega_t)$ as specified in Section 2.2 is of the form $x'(\omega_t)\beta$, where β is unknown and $x(\omega_t)$ a vector of zeros except in one position where it contains a one, indicating the state of ω_t. If β is completely unknown we put $b = 0$ and $B = I$ and, at the completion of the modified Kalman filter pass (2), draw β from the Gaussian density $N(S^{-1}s, \sigma^2 S^{-1})$. The simulation smoother (3) is then applied with $e_t = E_t(\beta; 1)$. The resulting vector $(\beta; \eta)$ is a draw from $p(\beta, \eta|y, \omega)$ and a sequence of such draws, cycling over draws from $p(\beta, \eta|y, \omega)$ and $p(\omega|y, \beta, \eta)$, behaves like draws from the posterior $p(\beta, \eta|y)$.

Acknowledgement

The comments of the referees are gratefully acknowledged. The authors would like to thank NSERC and ESRC for financial support.

Appendix

Proof of correctness
Conditioning on ω will be implicit. Put

$$\eta_t = F_t u_t \quad (t = 0, 1, \dots, n), \qquad \varepsilon_n = \eta_n - E(\eta_n|y).$$

Then, since $\sigma^2 D_n = \text{cov}(e_n)$ and $\text{cov}(u_n, e_n) = \sigma^2 G'_n$,

$$E(\eta_n|y) = E(\eta_n|e) = E(\eta_n|e_n) = \sigma^{-2}\text{cov}(\eta_n, e_n)D_n^{-1}e_n = F_n G'_n D_n^{-1}e_n,$$

$$\text{cov}(\eta_n|y) = \text{cov}(\varepsilon_n) = \text{cov}(\eta_n, \eta_n - F_n G'_n D_n^{-1}e_n)$$

$$= \sigma^2 F_n(I - G'_n D_n^{-1}G_n)F_n = \sigma^2 C_n,$$

and hence the assertions of Section 3 hold for $t = n$. For $t < n$ put $\varepsilon_t = \eta_t - E(\eta_t|y, \eta_{t+1}, \ldots, \eta_n)$ and suppose the assertions hold for $s > t$. Then

$$E(\eta_t|y, \eta_{t+1}, \ldots, \eta_n)$$

$$= E(\eta_t|e_t, e_{t+1}, \ldots, e_n, \eta_{t+1}, \ldots, \eta_n)$$

$$= \sum_{s=t}^{n} E(\eta_t|e_s) + \sum_{s=t+1}^{n} E\{\eta_t|\eta_s - E(\eta_s|e_t, \ldots, e_n, \eta_{s+1}, \ldots, \eta_n)\}$$

$$= E(\eta_t|e_t) + \sum_{s=t+1}^{n} \{E(\eta_t|e_s) + E(\eta_t|\varepsilon_s)\}$$

$$= F_t\left[G'_t D_t^{-1}e_t + \sigma^{-2}\sum_{s=t+1}^{n}\{\text{cov}(u_t, e_s)D_s^{-1}e_s + \text{cov}(u_t, \varepsilon_s)C_s^{-1}\varepsilon_s\}\right].$$

The first equality follows on orthogonalising y, since $\eta_t = F_t u_t$ is uncorrelated with $e_1, e_2, \ldots, e_{t-1}$. The second follows from orthogonalising $e_t, e_{t+1}, \ldots, e_n, \eta_{t+1}, \ldots, \eta_n$. It is shown below that, for $s > t$,

$$\text{cov}(e_s, u_t) = \sigma^2 Z_s(L_{s-1} \ldots L_{t+1})J_t, \tag{A1}$$

$$\text{cov}(\varepsilon_s, u_t) = -\sigma^2 V_s(L_{s-1} \ldots L_{t+1})J_t. \tag{A2}$$

Substituting into the above expression yields $E(\eta_t|y, \eta_{t+1}, \ldots, \eta_n)$ as given in Section 3. Next note that

$$\text{cov}(\eta_t|y, \eta_{t+1}, \ldots, \eta_n) = \text{cov}(\varepsilon_t) = \text{cov}\{\eta_t, \eta_t - E(\eta_t|y, \eta_{t+1}, \ldots, \eta_n)\}$$

$$= \sigma^2 F_t\{I - \text{cov}(u_t, G'_t D_t^{-1}e_t + J'_t r_t)\}F'_t$$

$$= \sigma^2 F_t\{I - \text{cov}(u_t, e_t)D_t^{-1}G_t - \text{cov}(u_t, r_t)J_t\}F'_t,$$

which expands to $\sigma^2 C_t$.

It remains to prove the relations in (A1) and (A2). For $s > t$,

$$e_s = Z_s(\alpha_s - a_s) + G_s u_s = Z_s\{L_{s-1}(\alpha_{s-1} - a_{s-1}) + J_{s-1}u_{s-1}\} + G_s u_s$$

$$= Z_s(L_{s-1} \ldots L_{t+1})\{(\alpha_t - a_t) + J_t u_t\} + (\text{terms linear in } u_{t+1}, \ldots, u_s).$$

Thus

$$\text{cov}(e_s, u_t) = Z_s(L_{s-1} \ldots L_{t+1})\text{cov}(J_t u_t, u_t) = \sigma^2 Z_s(L_{s-1} \ldots L_{t+1})J_t,$$

which establishes (A1). Next note that

$$\operatorname{cov}(\varepsilon_n, u_t) = \operatorname{cov}(u_n - G'_n D_n^{-1} e_n, u_t) = -\sigma^2 G'_n D_n^{-1} Z_n (L_{n-1} \dots L_{t+1}) J_t,$$

which proves (A2) for $s = n$. For $t < s < n$, using the inductive hypothesis.

$$\operatorname{cov}(\varepsilon_s, u_t) = \operatorname{cov}(u_s - G'_s D_s^{-1} e_s - J'_s r_s, u_t)$$

$$= -G'_s D_s^{-1} \operatorname{cov}(e_s, u_t) - J'_s \operatorname{cov}(r_s, u_t)$$

$$= -\sigma^2 G'_s D_s^{-1} Z_s (L_{s-1} \dots L_{t+1}) J_t - J'_s \sum_{j=s+1}^{n} (L'_{s+1} \dots L'_{j-1})$$

$$\times \{ Z'_j D_j^{-1} \operatorname{cov}(e_j, u_t) - V'_j C_j^{-1} \operatorname{cov}(\varepsilon_j, u_t) \}.$$

Assuming the truth of the expression for $\operatorname{cov}(\varepsilon_j, u_t)$ for $j > s$ yields

$$\operatorname{cov}(\varepsilon_s, u_t) = -\sigma^2 (G'_s D_s^{-1} Z_s + J'_s U_s L_s)(L_{s-1} \dots L_{t+1}) J_t$$

$$= -\sigma^2 V_s (L_{s-1} \dots L_{t+1}) J_t,$$

which completes the proof.

References

Albert, J. H. & Chib, S. (1993). Bayesian inference via Gibbs sampling of autoregressive time series subject to Markov mean and variance shifts. *J. Econ. Bus. Statist.*, 11, 1–15.

Carlin, B. P., Polson, N. G. & Stoffer, D. (1992). A Monte Carlo approach to nonnormal and nonlinear state-space modelling *J. Am. Statist. Assoc.*, 87, 493–500.

Carter, C. K. & Kohn, R. (1993). On the applications of Markov Chain Monte Carlo methods to linear state space models. In *Proc. Bus. Econ. Statist. Sect.*, pp. 131–6. Washington, D.C.: Am. Statist. Assoc.

Carter, C. K. & Kohn, R. (1994). On Gibbs sampling for state space models. *Biometrika*, 81, 541–53.

Cheeney, M. & Scott, L. O. (1989). Pricing European options: a comparison of the modified Black–Scholes model and a random variance model. *J. Financ. Qualitat. Anal.*, 24, 267–84.

Chib, S. (1993). Bayes regression with autoregression errors: A Gibbs sampling approach. *J. Economet.*, 58, 275–94.

Chib, S. & Greenberg, E. (1994). Bayes inference in regression models with arma (p, q) errors. *J. Economet.*, 64, 183–206.

de Jong, P. (1988). A cross validation filter for time series models. *Biometrika*, 75, 594–600.

de Jong, P. (1989). Smoothing and interpolation with the state space model. *J. Am. Statist. Assoc.*, 84, 1085–8.

de Jong, P. (1991). The diffuse Kalman filter. *Ann. Statist.*, 2, 1073–83.

Frühwirth-Schnatter, S. (1994). Data augmentation and dynamic linear models. *J. Time Ser. Anal.*, 15, 183–202.

Frühwirth-Schnatter, S. (1995). Bayesian model discrimination and Bayes factors for linear Gaussian state space models. *J. R. Statist. Soc.* B 57, 237–46.

Harvey, A. C., Ruiz, E. & Shephard, N. (1994). Multivariate stochastic variance models. *Rev. Econ. Studies*, 61, 247–64.

Hull, J. & White, A. (1987). Hedging the risk for writing foreign currency options. *J. Int. Money Finance*, 6, 131–52.

Jacquier, E., Polson, N. G. & Rossi, P. E. (1994). Bayesian analysis of stochastic volatility. *J. Bus. Econ. Statist.*, 12, 371–417.

Kohn, R. & Ansley, C. F. (1989). A fast algorithm for signal extraction, influence and cross validation in state-space models. *Biometrika*, 76, 65–79.

Koopman, S. J. (1993). Disturbance smoother for state space models. *Biometrika*, 80, 117–26.

Liu, J., Wong, W. H. & Kong, A. (1994). Correlation structure and convergence rate of the Gibbs sampler (I): applications to the comparison of estimators and augmentation schemes. *Biometrika*, 81, 27–40.

Melino, A. & Turnbull, S. M. (1990). Pricing foreign currency options with stochastic volatility. *J. Economet.*, 45, 239–65.

Ripley, B. D. (1987). *Stochastic Simulation*. New York: Wiley.

Shephard, N. (1994). Partial non-Gaussian state space. *Biometrika*, 81, 115–31.

Shumway, R. H. & Stoffer, D. S. (1991). Dynamic linear models with switching. *J. Am. Statist. Assoc.*, 86, 763–9.

Smith, A. F. M. & Roberts, G. (1993). Bayesian computations via the Gibbs sampler and related Markov Chain Monte Carlo Methods. *J. R. Statist. Soc.*, B 55, 3–23.

Tanner, M. A. (1991). *Tools for Statistical Inference, Observed Data and Data Augmentation Methods*. New York: Springer-Verlag.

Tierney, L. (1994). Markov chain for exploring posterior distributions. *Ann. Statist.*, 22, 1701–86.

Wild, P. & Gilks, W. R. (1993). AS 287: Adaptive rejection sampling from log-concave density functions. *Appl. Statist.*, 42, 701–9.

20

Likelihood Analysis of Non-Gaussian Measurement Time Series*

NEIL SHEPHARD

Nuffield College

AND

MICHAEL K. PITT

Department of Statistics, University of Oxford

SUMMARY

In this paper we provide methods for estimating non-Gaussian time series models. These techniques rely on Markov chain Monte Carlo to carry out simulation smoothing and Bayesian posterior analysis of parameters, and on importance sampling to estimate the likelihood function for classical inference. The time series structure of the models is used to ensure that our simulation algorithms are efficient.

1 Introduction

In this paper we provide a likelihood analysis of an extension of the usual Gaussian state space form (Harvey 1989, ch. 3). The Kalman filter and simulation smoother are used to perform efficient signal extraction and parameter estimation.

The univariate observations y_t are assumed to be distributed, conditionally on a univariate θ_t, according to $f(y_t|\theta_t)(t = 1, \dots, n)$. Throughout $\log f$ is assumed to be twice continuously differentiable with respect to θ_t. An example of this is the exponential family, written as

$$\log f(y_t|\theta_t) = y_t\theta_t - b(\theta_t) + c(y_t), \tag{1.1}$$

where b and c are flexible but known functions. Here θ_t is the stochastic process

$$h(\theta_t) = d_t = z_t\alpha_t + x_t\beta$$

$$\alpha_{t+1} = W_t\beta + T_t\alpha_t + H_tu_t, \quad u_t \sim \text{NID}(0, I), \tag{1.2}$$

$$\alpha_1 \sim N(a_{1|0}, p_{1|0}).$$

Further $h(.)$ is a known function which is continuously twice differentiable, while the α_t are called states and NID denotes normal and independently distributed.

* This work was previously published as N. Shephard and M. K. Pitt, "Likelihood Analysis of Non-Gaussian Measurement Time Series", *Biometrika*, 1997, Vol. 84, 653–667. Reproduced by permission of the Biometrika Trustees.

Typically T_t, z_t and H_t are selection matrices indexed by a small number of unknown parameters denoted by ψ, while x_t and W_t are sparse regressors.

Only a small number of simple non-Gaussian models possess conjugate filtering recursions. They are studied in Smith (1979, 1981), Smith and Miller (1986), Harvey and Fernandes (1989) and Shephard (1994a). West, Harrison and Migon (1985) propose a dynamic generalised linear class of processes, which is made up of equations (1.1) and (1.2). Fahrmeir (1992), Singh and Roberts (1992) and Durbin and Koopman (1997) develop algorithms which find the exact mode of the smoothing density, $f(\alpha|y)$, and perform approximate likelihood inference on ψ. Here $y = (y_1, \ldots, y_n)'$ and $\alpha = (\alpha_1', \ldots, \alpha_n')'$.

General state space models are discussed by Kitagawa (1987) who used numerical integration rules to approximate the required filtering and smoothing recursions. Unfortunately the integrals are of the dimension of α_t and so for many problems these methods are inaccurate and quite slow, although there has been work to overcome these problems (Fruhwirth-Schnatter 1992). More recently importance sampling has been used to approximate the likelihood by Danielsson and Richard (1993), while Markov chain Monte Carlo methods have been used to perform smoothing and parameter estimation (Carlin, Polson and Stoffer 1992; Jacquier, Polson and Rossi 1994; Chan and Ledolter 1995).

The merging of the Kalman filter with Markov chain simulation methods has been successful, exploiting the time series structure of the model to improve the efficiency of the simulations, where it has been possible to condition on some latent indicator functions or other component to make y_t into a Gaussian state space. Leading references include Carter and Kohn (1994, 1996) and Shephard (1994b). Unfortunately, it has so far been unclear how to adapt these methods to deal with fundamentally non-Gaussian models. We tackle this problem here by presenting a new methodology which is based on the estimation by simulation of particular features of the model. This has the advantage that the estimates can be made as accurate as needed and their degree of accuracy can be assessed statistically. These simulation methods replace, in the Gaussian case, the role of the Kalman filter and smoother which usually estimate the states α from the observations y. In a simple example, if it were possible to simulate from $\alpha|y, \psi$, then any interesting function of α can be straightforwardly estimated from the draws. Likewise, if a Bayesian paradigm is adopted for ψ, then ψ can be estimated by recording appropriate summaries of the simulations from $(\alpha', \psi')'|y$. If a classical view is taken, then an approximate Gaussian simulation smoother can be used as an input into an importance sample estimator of the likelihood.

It is possible to simulate from $\alpha|y, \psi$, which is a highly multivariate non-Gaussian random variable, by employing Markov chain methods (Gilks, Richardson and Spiegelhalter 1996). We use the independence chain Metropolis algorithm to simulate from the joint distribution of $x_1, x_2, \ldots, x_m$, denoted by f, where x_i stands for a group of states or parameters in the model, given the data. Proposals z are made possibly to replace the current x_i, keeping constant $x_{\backslash i}$ which denotes all the other elements of the x vector. The proposal density is proportional to $q(z, x_{\backslash i})$ while the true density is $f(x_i|x_{\backslash i})$. Both of these densities are assumed to be everywhere positive (Tierney 1994). If $x^{(k)}$ is the current state of the sampler then the proposal is accepted with probability

$$\min\left\{ \frac{f(z|x_{\backslash i}^{(k)})q(x_i^{(k)}, x_{\backslash i}^{(k)})}{f(x_i^{(k)}|x_{\backslash i}^{(k)})q(z, x_{\backslash i}^{(k)})}, 1 \right\}.$$

In our work we would like to select q to be $f(z|x_{\backslash i})$, but this density is generally difficult to sample directly. Instead we approximate f by $ch(z)$ and then we can sample from a density proportional to $\min\{f(z|x_{\backslash i}), ch(z)\}$ by the scheme: (1) generate a candidate value z from $h(.)$ and a value u from a standard uniform; (2) if $u \leqslant f(z|x_{\backslash i})/ch(z)$ return z, otherwise return to (1). Tierney (1994) calls this type of method a pseudo-dominating rejection algorithm. It is discussed in more detail in Chib and Greenberg (1995).

This scheme suggests taking x_i to stand for individual states or parameters (Carlin et al. 1992). Then the Markov chain simulation algorithm updates a single variable at a time which has the advantage that the conditional densities are usually simple. The main disadvantage is the correlation between variables over successive sweeps of the Metropolis sample, a particularly severe problem in time series models (Carter and Kohn 1994; Shephard 1994b).

Multi-move, or block, samplers work by updating several variables at the same time. When carried out sensibly, block samplers tend to be very effective. Liu, Wong and Kong (1994) produce results which show that 'grouping random components in a Gibbs sampler with two or more components usually results in more efficient sampling schemes'.

Block samplers raise a number of issues. How should the blocks be constructed so that they are easy to sample? Should the blocks be the same for each sweep, a deterministically updated Markov chain Monte Carlo, or should they be randomly selected, a random block algorithm?

The simulations from $f(\alpha|y)$ are correlated. We can estimate $Eg(\alpha)$ by $M^{-1} \sum g(\alpha^k)$, where α^k is the kth simulated value after reaching equilibrium, while the variance of this estimator is computed using a Parzen window $K()$; see Priestley (1981, p. 443). Let $\hat{J}_M$ denote the estimation of the $\sqrt{M}$ scaled variance of the sample mean. Then

$$\hat{J}_M = \hat{\Gamma}(0) + \frac{2M}{M-1} \sum_{i=1}^{B_M} K\left(\frac{i}{B_M}\right) \hat{\Gamma}(i),$$

where

$$\hat{\Gamma}(i) = \frac{1}{M} \sum_{k=i+1}^{M} (\alpha^k - \bar{\alpha})(\alpha^{k-i} - \bar{\alpha}),$$

and B_M, the bandwidth, is stated in all our calculations.

The structure of the paper is as follows. In Section 2 we look at a simple example of the model and investigate the properties of simple single move Markov chain simulator for this problem. The core of our contribution comes in Section 3, which discusses the design of our methods to maximise efficiency for these models. Section 4 looks at importance sampling. Section 5 concludes, while an Appendix details some key algorithms.

2 Example: Stochastic Volatility

2.1 The model

The stochastic volatility model has attracted much recent attention as a way of generalising the Black–Scholes option pricing formula to allow volatility clustering in asset returns (Hull and White 1987; Harvey, Ruiz and Shephard 1994; Jacquier et al. 1994). The basic stochastic volatility model has

$$y_t = \varepsilon_t \beta \exp(\alpha_t/2), \qquad \alpha_{t+1} = \phi \alpha_t + \eta_t, \tag{2.1}$$

where ε_t and η_t are independent Gaussian processes with variances of 1 and σ_η^2 respectively. Markov chain Monte Carlo methods have been used on this model by, for instance, Jacquier et al. (1994).

In this paper we analyse the daily returns, i.e. the difference of the log of the series, on the pound sterling/US dollar exchange rate from 1 October 1981 to 28 June 1985. The dataset has been previously analysed using quasi-likelihood methods in Harvey et al. (1994).

2.2 Pseudo-dominating Metropolis sampler

We exploit a second-order expansion of the log-density as the basis of our pseudo-dominating Metropolis sampler. The expansion is, writing $\alpha_t | \alpha_{t-1}, \alpha_{t+1} \sim N(\mu_t, \sigma_t^2)$, suppressing dependence on ψ, of the form

$$\log f(\alpha_t | y_t, \alpha_{\backslash t}) = \log f(\alpha_t | \alpha_{t-1}, \alpha_{t+1}) + \log f(y_t | \alpha_t)$$

$$= -\frac{(\alpha_t - \mu_t)^2}{2\sigma_t^2} - \frac{\alpha_t}{2} - \frac{y_t^2}{2\beta^2} \exp(-\alpha_t)$$

$$\doteq -\frac{(\alpha_t - \mu_t)^2}{2\sigma_t^2} - \frac{\alpha_t}{2} - \frac{y_t^2}{2\beta^2}$$

$$\times \exp(-\mu_t)\{1 - (\alpha_t - \mu_t) + \tfrac{1}{2}(\alpha_t - \mu_t)^2\}$$

$$= \log g.$$

A similar quadratic expansion appears in Green and Han (1990) in their analysis of Poisson images with a Gaussian prior. The quadratic term in $\log g$ means that it does not bound $\log f$. This delivers a pseudo-dominating suggestion, with suggested draws z for $\alpha_t | y_t, \alpha_{\backslash t}$ being made from

$$N\left[\frac{\sigma_t^{*2}}{\sigma_t^2}\mu_t + \frac{\sigma_t^{*2}}{2}\left\{\frac{y_t^2}{\beta^2}\exp(-\mu_t)(1 + \mu_t) - 1\right\}, \sigma_t^{*2}\right],$$

where

$$\sigma_t^{*-2} = \sigma_t^{-2} + \frac{y_t^2}{2\beta^2 \exp(\mu_t)}.$$

Notice that, if $y_t = 0$, then $\sigma_t^{*2} = \sigma_t^2$ and f is truly normally distributed and equals g. The precision of σ_t^{*-2} increases with y_t^2.

In the accept/reject part of the algorithm, these suggestions are made until acceptance with probability $\min(f/g, 1)$, while the Metropolis probability of accepting the resulting z is

$$\min\left[\frac{f(z|y_t, \alpha_{\backslash t}^{(k)}) \min\{f(\alpha_t^{(k)}|y_t, \alpha_{\backslash t}^{(k)}), g(\alpha_t^{(k)})\}}{f(\alpha_t^{(k)}|y_t, \alpha_{\backslash t}^{(k)}) \min\{f(z|y_t, \alpha_{\backslash t}^{(k)}), g(z)\}}, 1 \right].$$

A slightly less direct way of thinking about this analysis is that we are using a Gaussian approximation to the log-likelihood, $\log f(y_t|\alpha_t)$, which is then added to the then-conjugate Gaussian prior to deliver a Gaussian posterior. Notice that as y_t goes to zero this likelihood becomes uninformative, although the posterior is perfectly well-behaved. This way of thinking about this problem is easily extended to updating more than a single state at a time.

Here we pursue a Bayesian analysis of the parameters in the model. Given the states, sampling from the parameters is straightforward for β and σ_η^2. First assuming a flat prior for $\log \beta$ we achieve the posterior $\beta^2|y, \alpha \sim \chi_n^{-2} \sum y_t \exp(-\alpha_t)$, while assuming a prior of $\chi_p^{-2} S_0$ for $\sigma_\eta^2|\phi$ we have

$$\sigma_\eta^2|\phi, \alpha \sim \chi_{n+p}^{-2} \left\{ \sum_{t=2}^n (\alpha_t - \phi\alpha_{t-1})^2 + \alpha_1^2(1 - \phi^2) + S_0 \right\}.$$

In this work we assume that for daily data $p = 10$ and $S_0 = p \times 0.01$, while for weekly data S_0 is taken to be $p \times 0.05$. Our prior on the persistence parameter ϕ is designed to ensure that the log volatility process is stationary. To carry this out we employ a beta prior on $(\phi + 1)/2$, with $E(\phi) = \{2\delta/(\gamma + \delta)\} - 1$. In the analysis we use below, we set $\delta = 20$ and $\gamma = 1.5$ so the prior mean is 0.86 and standard deviation is 0.11. As a result of our prior choice, the posterior is nonconjugate and we sample from $\phi|\sigma_\eta^2, \alpha$ using an accept/reject algorithm.

2.3 Empirical effectiveness

Our Markov chain sampler is initialised by setting all the log-volatilities to zero and $\phi = 0.95$, $\sigma_\eta^2 = 0.02$ and $\beta = 1$. We iterated the sampler on the states for 1000 iterations and then on the parameters and states for 50000 more iterations before recording any answers. The next 1000000 iterations are graphed in Fig. 1 and summarised in Table 1.

The correlogram shows significant autocorrelations for ϕ at 10000 lags, for β at 25000 lags and for σ_η at 5000 lags.

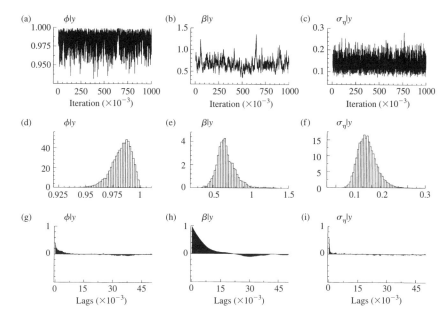

Fig. 1. Returns for pound sterling/US dollar: (a)–(c), simulations against iteration; (d)–(f), histograms of marginal distribution; (g)–(i), corresponding correlograms for simulation.

Table 1. Returns for the pound sterling/US dollar: summaries of Fig. 1. The standard error of simulation computed using $B_M = 100\,000$; correlations are in italics; computer time: 233 303 seconds on a P5/133

	Mean	Monte Carlo SE	Covariance and *Correlation* of posterior		
$\phi\|y$	0.9821	0.000277	8.434×10^{-5}	*−0.629*	*0.217*
$\sigma_\eta\|y$	0.1382	0.000562	−0.0001479	0.0006631	*−0.156*
$\beta\|y$	0.6594	0.0121	0.0002089	−0.0004228	0.01209

3 Designing Blocks

3.1 Background

Liu et al. (1994) suggest blocking to improve the speed of convergence for simulators. This idea has motivated a considerable time series statistics literature on this topic in models built out of Gaussianity, but with some nonnormality mixed in (Carter and Kohn 1994; Shephard 1994b). However, the non-Gaussian measurement state space models are not of this form: they are fundamentally non-Gaussian. Hence there is a substantial need for a new strategy.

Before we discuss our suggestion, a comment on our notation is in order. The states α in (1.2) usually have many identities linking the state variables over time, and consequently when we simulate from $\alpha|y$ we simulate from a possibly highly degenerate density. To avoid this complication we can focus on the fundamental disturbances in the model u_t, ensuring that $u|y$ is nondegenerate. To simplify the exposition we remove the regressors, W_t and x_t, from the analysis in the remainder of this section.

Sampling directly from $u|y$ may be too ambitious as this is highly multivariate and so if n is very large it is likely that we will run into very large rejection frequencies, counteracting the effectiveness of the blocking. Hence we employ an intermediate strategy. Our sampling method is based around sampling blocks of disturbances, say $u_{t,k} = (u_{t-1}, \ldots, u_{t+k-1})'$, given beginning and end conditions α_{t-1} and α_{t+k+1}, and the observations. We call these end conditions 'stochastic knots'. At the beginning and end of the dataset, there is no need to use two-sided knots. In these cases only single knots are required, simulating, for example, from $u_{1,k}|\alpha_{t+k+1}, y_1, \ldots, y_{t+k}$.

3.2 Proposal density

The only viable way of carrying out sampling from $u_{t,k}|\alpha_{t-1}, \alpha_{t+k+1}, y_t, \ldots, y_{t+k}$ seems to be to place it within a Metropolis algorithm, employing multivariate Gaussian proposals. We use a Taylor-type expansion of

$$\log f = \log f(u_{t-1}, \ldots, u_{t+k-1}|\alpha_{t-1}, \alpha_{t+k+1}, y_t, \ldots, y_{t+k})$$

around some preliminary estimate of $u_{t,k}$ made using the conditioning arguments α_{t-1}, α_{t+k+1} and $y_t, \ldots, y_{t+k}$. These estimates, and the corresponding $\alpha_t, \ldots, \alpha_{t+k}$ and $\theta_t, \ldots, \theta_{t+k}$, are denoted by hats. How they are formed will be discussed in a moment. We write $l(\theta_t)$ to denote $\log f(y_t|\theta_t)$ and write the derivative of this log-density with respect to d_t as l' and l'' respectively. The expansion is then

$$\log f = -\frac{1}{2}u'_{t,k}u_{t,k} + \sum_{s=t}^{t+k} l(\theta_s), \qquad \alpha_{s+1} = T_s\alpha_s + H_s u_s,$$

$$\log f \simeq -\frac{1}{2}u'_{t,k}u_{t,k} + \sum_{s=t}^{t+k} l(\hat{\theta}_s) + z_s(\alpha_s - \hat{\alpha}_s)l'(\hat{\theta}_s) + \frac{1}{2}\{z_s(\alpha_s - \hat{\alpha}_s)\}^2 D_s(\hat{\theta}_s)$$

$$= \log g.$$

We require the assumption that the as yet unspecified $D_s(\theta)$ is everywhere strictly negative as a function of θ. Typically we take $D_s(\hat{\theta}_s) = l''(\hat{\theta}_s)$ so that the approximation is a second-order Taylor expansion. This is convenient, for in the vast majority of cases l'' is everywhere strictly negative. However, it is useful in covering unusual cases to have the possibility of not setting D_s equal to the second derivative. Of course, for those cases, we have to provide sensible rules for the selection of D_s.

A crucial and attractive feature of this expansion is that the error in the approximation involves only the difference between $l(\theta_s)$ and $l(\hat{\theta}_s) + z_s(\alpha_s - \hat{\alpha}_s)l'(\hat{\theta}_s) + \frac{1}{2}\{z_s(\alpha_s - \hat{\alpha}_s)\}^2 D_s(\hat{\theta}_s)$, not the transition equation $u'_{t,k}u_{t,k}$. The implication is that the algorithm should not become significantly less effective as the dimension of u_t increases. This can be contrasted with the numerical integration routines used in Kitagawa (1987), which usually deteriorate in effectiveness as the dimension of α_t increases.

Some interesting relations can be found for the crucial l' function. First, in general,

$$l'(\hat{\theta}_s) = \frac{\partial \theta_t}{\partial d_t}\bigg|_{\theta_t = \hat{\theta}_s} \times \frac{\partial l(\theta_t)}{\partial \theta_t}\bigg|_{\theta_t = \hat{\theta}_s},$$

which for the exponential family becomes

$$l'(\hat{\theta}_s) = \frac{\partial \theta_t}{\partial d_t}\bigg|_{\theta_t = \hat{\theta}_s} \times \{y_t - \dot{b}(\hat{\theta}_s)\}.$$

Similar manipulations are possible for $l''(\hat{\theta}_t)$. The most interesting case of this is the canonical link, where $l''(\hat{\theta}_t) = -\ddot{b}(\hat{\theta}_t)$.

The density of g is highly multivariate Gaussian. It is not a dominating density for $\log f$, but it is usually a good approximation. If we write $v_s^{-1} = -D_s(\hat{\theta}_s)$, then the joint density can be calculated by defining the artificial variables

$$\hat{y}_s = z_s \hat{\alpha}_s + v_s l'(\hat{\theta}_s) \quad (s = t, \ldots, t+k)$$

and then modelling them as

$$\hat{y}_s = z_s \alpha_s + \varepsilon_s, \quad \varepsilon_s \sim N(0, v_s), \quad \alpha_{s+1} = T_s \alpha_s + H_s u_s, \quad u_s \sim \text{NID}(0, I).$$

$$(3.1)$$

Consequently, it is possible to simulate from the approximating posterior density of $u_{t,k}$, given knots, using the de Jong and Shephard (1995) simulation smoother on the artificial $\hat{y}_t, \ldots, \hat{y}_{t+k}$. As g does not bound f these draws from the simulation smoother provide suggestions for the pseudo-dominating Metropolis algorithm discussed in Section 1.

A similar expansion to (3.1), but without the knots, is used in Fahrmeir (1992), Singh and Roberts (1992) and Durbin and Koopman (1997). These authors use a moment smoother (A.4) to provide an estimate of $u|y$ using this Taylor-expanded approximation. By iterating around the latest smoothed values, this algorithm converges to the mode of the density of $u|y$ in cases where $\partial^2 \log l/\partial \alpha_t \partial \alpha_t'$ is negative semidefinite; the same condition is needed for generalised linear regression models to have a unique maximum (McCullagh and Nelder 1989, p. 117). It is typically stated as a requirement that the link function be log-concave. In the case being addressed here, the iterations are an efficient way of carrying out a Newton–Raphson hill climbing algorithm using analytic first and second derivatives on a concave objective function. Thus the approximations suggested by previous authors can be interpreted as Laplace approximations to a very high

dimensional density function. Our algorithm, by contrast, converges to a sequence
of simulations from $u|y$.

It is informative to look at some special cases of the set-up given in (3.1), to see
the effect of non-Gaussianity on the approximating model.

Example 1 *Canonical link.* If a canonical link is assumed, that is $\theta_t = d_t$ and
$\log f = y_t\theta_t - b(\theta_t) + c(y_t)$, then

$$v_s^{-1} = \ddot{b}(\hat{\theta}_s), \qquad \hat{y}_s = \hat{d}_s + v_s\{y_s - \dot{b}(\hat{\theta}_s)\}.$$

A special case of this is the Poisson model, where $b(\theta_s) = \exp(\theta_s)$ and so

$$v_s^{-1} = \exp(\hat{d}_s), \qquad \hat{y}_s = \hat{d}_s + \exp(-\hat{d}_s)\{y_s - \exp(\hat{d}_s)\}.$$

Another important example is the binomial, where $b(\theta_s) = n\log\{1 + \exp(\theta_t)\}$.
For this model

$$v_s^{-1} = np_t(1 - p_t), \qquad \hat{y}_s = \hat{d}_s + (y_s - np_s)/\{np_t(1 - p_t)\},$$

where $p_t = \exp(\hat{d}_t)/\{1 + \exp(\hat{d}_t)\}$.

Example 2 *Stochastic volatility model.* This model has

$$\log f(y_t|\alpha_t) = -\alpha_t/2 - y_t^2\exp(-\alpha_t)/2\beta^2.$$

Thus

$$v_s^{-1} = \frac{y_s^2}{2\beta^2}\exp(-\hat{d}_s), \qquad \hat{y}_s = \hat{d}_s + \frac{v_s}{2}\{y_s^2\exp(-\hat{d}_s)/\beta^2 - 1\}.$$

This case is particularly interesting as v_s depends on y_s, unlike with canonical
links. As $y_s \to 0$ so $v_s^{-1} \to 0$ and $\hat{y}_s \to \infty$, suggesting that the draws from the
simulation smoother might always be rejected. However, this observation ignores
the fact that $v_s \to \infty$, which effectively treats such observations as missing.
Of course there is a numerical overflow problem here, but that can be dealt with
in a number of ways without resulting in any approximation.

Example 3 *Heavy-tailed stochastic volatility model.* This argument extends to
allow ε_t in (2.1) to follow a scaled t-distribution, $\varepsilon_t = t_t/\{(v - 2)/v\}^{1/2}$, where
$t_t \sim t_v$. Then

$$\log f(y_t|\alpha_t) = -\frac{\alpha_t}{2} - (v + 1)\Big/2\log\left\{1 + \frac{y_t^2\exp(-\alpha_t)}{\beta^2(v - 2)}\right\},$$

so

$$l'(\alpha_t) = \frac{1}{2}\left[\frac{(v + 1)\{2\beta^2(v - 2)\}^{-1}y_t^2\exp(-\alpha_t)}{1 + y_t^2\exp(-\alpha_t)\{\beta^2(v - 2)\}^{-1}} - 1\right],$$

$$l''(\alpha_t) = -\left(\frac{v + 1}{4}\right)\left(\frac{y_t^2\exp(-\alpha_t)/\beta^2(v - 2)}{[1 + y_t^2\exp(-\alpha_t)\{\beta^2(v - 2)\}^{-1}]^2}\right).$$

The resulting v_s^{-1} and $\hat{y}_s$ are easy to compute. This approach has some advantages over the generic outlier approaches for Gaussian models suggested in Shephard (1994b) and Carter and Kohn (1994), which explicitly use the mixture representation of a t-distribution.

It is important to select sensible values for the sequence $\hat{\theta}_t, \ldots, \hat{\theta}_{t+k}$. The most straightforward choice would be to take them as the mode of

$$f(\theta_t, \ldots, \theta_{t+k} | \alpha_{t-1}, \alpha_{t+k+1}, y_t, \ldots, y_{t+k}),$$

the points at which the quadratic expansion is carried out. Although we have just noted that iterating the smoothing algorithm on (3.1) achieves this mode, this will slow our simulation algorithm if we have to iterate this procedure until full convergence, although rapid convergence is typical for these procedures. Instead we suggest using the pseudo-dominating Markov chain Monte Carlo method and only a fixed number of iterations of the smoothing algorithm to get a reasonably good sequence $\hat{\theta}_t, \ldots, \hat{\theta}_{t+k}$ instead of an 'optimal' one. Typically we use two to five iterations.

3.3 Stochastic knots
The stochastic knots play a crucial role. They ensure that as the sample size increases our algorithm does not fail due to excessive numbers of rejections. In our discussion so far the knots are regarded as being fixed, but in practice there are advantages in selecting them randomly, allowing the points of conditioning to change over the iterations. Our proposal is to work with a collection of stochastic knots, at times $k = (k_1, \ldots, k_K)'$ and corresponding values $\alpha = (\alpha'_{k_1}, \ldots, \alpha'_{k_K})'$, which appropriately cover the time span of the sample.

The selection of the knots is carried out randomly and independently of the outcome of the Markov chain simulation process, with U_i being independent uniforms and

$$k_i = \text{int}[n \times \{(i + U_i)/(K + 2)\}] \quad (i = 1, \ldots, K). \tag{3.2}$$

Thus the selection of knots is indexed by a single parameter K which we control. Notice that, in the way we have set this up, it is not possible to select K to recover the single-move algorithm as a special case.

In practice K is a tuning parameter, allowing the lengths of blocks to be selected. If K is too large the sampler will be slow because of rejections; if K is too small it will be correlated because of the structure of the model.

In our experience it is helpful to increase K for a few iterations at regular intervals to ensure that the method does not get firmly stuck due to excessive rejection.

3.4 Illustration on stochastic volatility model
To illustrate the effect of blocking we work with the stochastic volatility model, analysing the Markov chain Monte Carlo algorithms on simulated and real data. Our simulated data allow two sets of parameters, designed to reflect

Table 2. Relative efficiency of block to single-move Markov chain Monte Carlo sampler; K denotes number of stochastic knots. Reported are the ratio of the computed variances, which reflect efficiency gains. The variances are computed using $B_M = 10000$ and 100000 iterations in all cases except for the single-move sampler on daily parameters cases. For that problem $B_M = 100000$ and 1000000 iterations were used. The burn-in period is B_M

Weekly parameters	(a) *Weekly parameter case*								
	$K=0$	$K=1$	$K=3$	$K=5$	$K=10$	$K=20$	$K=50$	$K=100$	$K=200$
States| parameters	1.7	4.1	7.8	17	45	14	12	4.3	3.0
States	20	22	32	28	39	12	12	21	1.98
σ_η	1.3	1.3	1.1	1.7	2.2	1.7	1.5	1.7	1.5
ϕ	1.5	1.4	1.1	1.6	2.6	1.7	1.5	2.0	1.5
β	16	14	32	14	23	6	9	10	1

Daily parameters	(b) *Daily parameter case*								
	$K=0$	$K=1$	$K=3$	$K=5$	$K=10$	$K=20$	$K=50$	$K=100$	$K=200$
States| parameters	66	98	98	85	103	69	25	8.5	2.5
States	91	40	30	60	47	80	14	27	18
σ_η	2.7	3.1	2.9	2.8	3.4	3.8	2.6	3.6	1.8
ϕ	16	13	18	18	16	18	6.8	11	5.7
β	93	51	51	76	65	106	23	27	26

typical problems for weekly and daily financial datasets. In the weekly case, $\beta = 1, \sigma_\eta^2 = 0.1$ and $\phi = 0.9$, while in the daily case $\beta = 1, \sigma_\eta^2 = 0.01$ and $\phi = 0.99$.

Table 2 reports some results from a simulation using $n = 1000$: it is in two parts. Table 2(a) is concerned with estimating the states given the parameters, a pure signal extraction problem. It is clearly difficult to summarise the results for all 1000 time periods and so we focus on the middle state, α_{500}, in all our calculations. Extensive simulations suggest that our results reported here are representative of these general results.

The last four rows in (a) and (b) of Table 2 look at the estimation of the states at the same time as estimating the parameters of the model. Hence for that simulation the problem is a four-fold one: estimate the states and three parameters.

Table 2 reports the ratio of the resulting variance of the single-move sampler to the multi-move sampler. Numbers bigger than one reflect gains from using a multi-move sampler. One interpretation of the table is that if the ratio is x then the single-move sampler has to be iterated x times more than the multi-move sampler to achieve the same degree of precision in the estimates of interest. So, if a sample is 10 times more efficient, it produces the same degree of accuracy from 1000 iterations as from 10000 iterations from the inferior simulator.

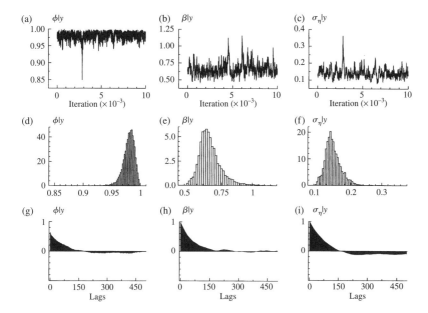

Fig. 2. Returns for pound sterling/US dollar: (a)–(c), simulations against iteration; (d)–(f), histograms of marginal distribution; (g)–(i), corresponding correlograms for simulation.

Table 2 shows that, when the number of knots is extremely small, say 0, there is a possibility in low persistence cases that the sampler actually performs worse than a single-move algorithm. This is because of large rejection rates. However, this result is very specialised. In the vast majority of cases the gains are quite significant and, most importantly, they are largest in cases where the single-move algorithms do badly. This suggests that the use of block samplers does increase the reliability of Markov chain simulation techniques for state space models.

To illustrate the effectiveness of this method we return to the application considered in Section 2. We use 10 stochastic knots in our block sampler. The results are displayed in Fig. 2. This was generated by using 200 iterations using the initial parameter, 300 iterations updating the parameters and states and finally we record 10000 iterations from the equilibrium path of the sampler. Figure 2 shares the features of Fig. 1, with the same distribution for the parameters. However, the correlations amongst the simulations are now quite manageable.

The precision of the results from the simulation is calculated using the Parzen window with $B_M = 1000$. The results given in Table 3 are consistent with those given in Table 1 for the single-move algorithm. However, the precision achieved with the 1000000 iterations is broadly comparable with that achieved by 10000 iterations from the multi-move sampler.

One of the most powerful aspects of the approach we are advocating is that the block size controls the efficiency of the methods. It is important to note, however, that the methods work whatever the block size.

Table 3. Returns for the pound sterling/US dollar: summaries of Fig. 2. The standard error of simulation computed using $B_M = 1000$; correlations are in italics; computer time: 322 seconds on a P5/133

	Mean	Monte Carlo SE	Covariance and *Correlation* of posterior		
$\phi\|y$	0.9802	0.000734	0.000105	−0.689	*0.294*
$\sigma_\eta\|y$	0.1431	0.00254	−0.000198	0.000787	−0.178
$\beta\|y$	0.6589	0.0100	0.000273	−0.000452	0.00823

It would be convenient if we had a method which would automatically find the 'optimal' value for K, but it seems likely that this size will be different for different aspects of the problem and, in any case, our results suggest extensive robustness of the efficiency gains, with large efficiency gains for blocks between 50 and 500.

4 Classical Estimation

4.1 An importance sampler

So far this paper has focused on Bayesian estimation of the parameters which index the models. We now turn our attention to classical inference. Our suggestion is to construct the likelihood via the use of importance sampling (Ripley 1987, pp. 122–3) drawing samples from the Gaussian approximation to the smoothing density we developed in Section 3. There is no use of stochastic knots, nor of acceptance/rejection sampling. We write this density as $f(u|y; \psi)^\sim$, using the disturbances rather than the states, and then use the manipulation

$$f(y; \psi) = \int \frac{f(y|u; \psi)f(u; \psi)}{f(u|y; \psi)^\sim} f(u|y; \psi)^\sim \, du.$$

The estimator of this integral takes on the form

$$\hat{f}(y; \psi)_M = \frac{1}{M} \sum_{j=1}^{M} \frac{f(y|u^j; \psi)f(u^j; \psi)}{f(u^j|y; \psi)^\sim}, \tag{4.1}$$

where $u^j \sim f(u|y; \psi)^\sim$. Crucially, this estimator is differentiable in ψ thanks to the Gaussianity of the smoothing density. If $f(u|y; \psi)^\sim = f(u|y; \psi)$ then this estimate is exact even if $M = 1$. Further, it is straightforward to exploit antithetic variables (Ripley 1987, pp. 129–32) for this problem by simply switching the signs on the κ_t in the simulation smoother (A.1).

4.2 Technical issues

The estimate (4.1) involves simulating from $f(u|y; \psi)^\sim$ and evaluating $f(u^j|y; \psi)^\sim$, $f(u^j; \psi)$ and $f(y|u^j; \psi)$. The simulation is straightforward using the simulation smoother, while $f(u^j; \psi)$ and $f(y|u^j; \psi)$ are trivial to evaluate. The term $f(u^j|y; \psi)^\sim$ can be found using the smoothing density (de Jong and Shephard 1995).

Proposition 1 *Define* $X_j = f(u^j|y; \psi)/f(u^j|y; \psi)^\sim$, *where* $u^j \sim f(u^j|y; \psi)^\sim$. *Then* X_j *is, conditional on* y, *independent and identically distributed with the moments*

$$E(X_j|y) = 1, \qquad \text{var}(X_j|y; \psi) = \int \left\{ \frac{f(u|y; \psi)}{f(u|y; \psi)^\sim} - 1 \right\}^2 f(u|y; \psi)^\sim \, du$$

$$= \sigma^2(y; \psi).$$

We define $f(y; \psi)^j = f(y|u^j; \psi) f(u^j; \psi)/f(u^j|y; \psi)^\sim$, *so that*

$$f(y; \psi)^j = f(y; \psi) \frac{f(u^j|y; \psi)}{f(u^j|y; \psi)^\sim} = f(y; \psi) X_j.$$

Consequently the estimator $\hat{f}(y; \psi)_M$ *is unbiased with variance* $\sigma^2(y; \psi)/M$.

For classical inference it is the log-likelihood which is the focus of attention. Our estimator of this log $\hat{f}(y; \psi)_M$ has the property

$$\log \hat{f}(y; \psi)_M = \log f(y; \psi) + \log \frac{1}{M} \sum_{j=1}^{M} X_j.$$

The implication of this is that

$$E\left[\log \left\{ 1 + \frac{1}{M} \sum_{j=1}^{M} (X_j - 1) \right\} \right] = -\frac{\sigma^2(y; \psi)}{2M} + O(M^{-2}),$$

and so the estimator of log $f(y; \psi)_M$ is biased to $O(M^{-1})$. As the $\sigma^2(y; \psi)$ depends on the parameters of the model, this causes an $O(M^{-1})$ bias in the estimators of the parameters of the model. The magnitude of this bias will depend on the merit of the importance sampling device. However, importantly, it is likely that $\sigma^2(y; \psi) = O(n)$. This means that, as the sample size increases, the importance sampling bias will become larger unless M increases at a rate larger than n. This is unfortunate.

The bias is proportional to $\sigma^2(y; \psi)$, which can be unbiasedly estimated by

$$\frac{1}{M-1} \sum_{j=1}^{M} \{f(y; \psi)^j - \hat{f}(y; \psi)_M\}^2,$$

and hence

$$\log \hat{f}(y; \psi)_M + \frac{1}{2M} \frac{1}{M-1} \sum_{j=1}^{M} \{f(y; \psi)^j - \hat{f}(y; \psi)_M\}^2,$$

gives an unbiased estimator to $O(M^{-2})$. Of course this does not mean that the resulting estimator of ψ is superior, for the addition of this term may sufficiently increase the variance of the estimator of the log-likelihood so as to compensate for the reduction in bias.

5 Conclusions

This paper uses simulation to provide a likelihood basis for non-Gaussian extensions of state space models. We argue that the development of Taylor expansion-based multi-move simulation smoothing algorithms can deliver reliable methods.

The methods have five basic advantages. (i) They integrate the role of the Kalman filter and simulation smoother into the analysis of non-Gaussian models, thereby exploiting the structure of the model to improve the speed of the methods. (ii) They exploit the Taylor expansion which has been previously used in various approximate methods suggested in the literature. (iii) They approximate only $\log f(y_t|\theta_t)$ and so, as the dimension of the state increases, the computational efficiency of the method should not diminish significantly. (iv) They extend to many multivariate cases by using a multivariate Taylor expansion of $\log f$ to deliver a multivariate approximating version of the model (3.1). (v) They allow the transition equation (1.2) to become non-Gaussian by Taylor expanding the transition density $\log f(\alpha_{t+1}|\alpha_t)$. Then the Metropolis rejection rate will additionally depend on the accuracy of the approximation to transition density.

Although there have been very significant recent advances in signal extraction of non-Gaussian processes, there is much work to be carried out in this area. We have not provided any model checking devices for our fitted models. In principle this is straightforward if based on one-step-ahead prediction densities. Some progress has recently been made in finding methods for computing these densities (Gordon, Salmond and Smith 1993; Muller 1991; West 1993).

Acknowledgement

We would like to thank the Economic and Social Research Council for their financial support. All the computations reported in this paper were generated using C++ code dynamically linked to the Ox Matrix Programming Language (Doornik 1996). We thank Jurgen Doornik for helpful computational advice and Aurora Manrique, the referee and the Associate Editor for making some useful suggestions.

Appendix

Some algorithms

This appendix details Gaussian filtering and smoothing. The Gaussian state space puts

$$y_t = x_t\beta + Z_t\alpha_t + G_t u_t, \quad u_t \sim \text{NID}(0, I),$$
$$\alpha_{t+1} = W_t\beta + T_t\alpha_t + H_t u_t, \quad \alpha_1|Y_0 \sim N(a_{1|0}, P_{1|0}).$$

We assume that $G_t'H_t = 0$ and write the nonzero rows of H_t as M_t. The Kalman filter (de Jong 1989) computes $a_{t|t-1} = E(\alpha_t|Y_{t-1}, \beta)$ and $P_{t|t-1}$, containing the mean squared errors of $\alpha_t | Y_{t-1}, \beta$,

$$\alpha_{t+1|t} = W_t\beta + T_t a_{t|t-1} + K_t v_t, \qquad P_{t+1|t} = T_t P_{t|t-1} L_t' + H_t H_t',$$
$$v_t = y_t - Z_t a_{t|t-1} - x_t\beta, \qquad F_t = Z_t P_{t|t-1} Z_t' + G_t G_t',$$
$$K_t = T_t P_{t|t-1} Z_t' F_t^{-1}, \qquad L_t = T_t - K_t Z_t.$$

The filter yields forecast errors v_t, their mean squared errors F_t and the Gaussian log-likelihood

$$\log f(y_1, \ldots, y_n) = \text{const} - \frac{1}{2}\sum_t \log|F_t| - \frac{1}{2}\sum_t v_t' F_t^{-1} v_t.$$

The simulation smoother (de Jong and Shephard 1995) samples from $\alpha | Y_n, \beta$. Setting $r_n = 0$ and $N_n = 0$, for $t = n, \ldots, 1$, we have

$$C_t = M_t M_t' \quad M_t H_t' N_t H_t M_t', \qquad \kappa_t \sim N(0, C_t),$$
$$r_{t-1} = Z_t' F_t^{-1} v_t + L_t' r_t - L_t' N_t H_t M_t' C_t^{-1} \kappa_t, \qquad \text{(A.1)}$$
$$N_{t-1} = Z_t' F_t^{-1} Z_t + L_t' N_t L_t + L_t' N_t H_t M_t' C_t^{-1} M_t H_t' N_t L_t.$$

Then we can add $M_t H_t' r_t + \kappa_t$ to the corresponding zero rows so that we simulate from the whole $H_t u_t$ vector, written $\hat{\eta}_t$. The end condition $\hat{\eta}_0$ is calculated by

$$C_0 = P_{1|0} - P_{1|0} N_0 P_{1|0}, \qquad \kappa_0 \sim N(0, C_0), \qquad \eta_0 = P_{1|0} r_0 + \kappa_0. \quad \text{(A.2)}$$

The α vector is simulated via the forward recursion, starting with $\alpha_0 = 0$,

$$\alpha_{t+1} = W_t\beta + T_t\alpha_t + \hat{\eta}_t \quad (t = 0, \ldots, n-1). \qquad \text{(A.3)}$$

The moment smoother (de Jong 1989; Koopman 1993) computes $a_{t|n} = E(\alpha_t | Y_n, \beta)$. With $r_n = 0$ it runs backwards:

$$r_{t-1} = Z_t' F_t^{-1} v_t + L_t' r_t \quad (t = n, \ldots, 1). \qquad \text{(A.4)}$$

The $M_t H_t' r_t$ completes, as above, $\hat{\eta}_t$ allowing a recursion of the form (A.3) for the conditional expectations.

References

Carlin, B. P., Polson, N. G. & Stoffer, D. (1992). A Monte Carlo approach to nonnormal and nonlinear state-space modelling. *J. Am. Statist. Assoc.*, 87, 493–500.

Carter, C. K. & Kohn, R. (1994). On Gibbs sampling for state space models. *Biometrika*, 81, 541–53.

Carter, C. K. & Kohn, R. (1996). Markov chain Monte Carlo in conditionally Gaussian state space models. *Biometrika*, 83, 589–601.

Chan, K. S. & Ledolter, J. (1995). Monte Carlo EM estimates for time series models involving counts. *J. Am. Statist. Assoc.*, 89, 242–52.

Chib, S. & Greenberg, E. (1995). Understanding the Metropolis–Hastings algorithm. *Am. Statistician*, 49, 327–35.

Danielsson, J. & Richard, J. F. (1993). Accelerated Gaussian importance sampler with application to dynamic latent variable models. *J. Appl. Economet.*, 8, S153–74.

de Jong, P. (1989). Smoothing and interpolation with the state space model. *J. Am. Statist. Assoc.*, 84, 1085–8.

de Jong, P. & Shephard, N. (1995). The simulation smoother for time series models. *Biometrika*, 82, 339–50.

Doornik, J. A. (1996). *Ox: Object Oriented Matrix Programming, 1.10*. London: Chapman and Hall.

Durbin, J. & Koopman, S. J. (1997). Monte Carlo maximum likelihood estimation for non-Gaussian state space models. *Biometrika*, 84, 669–84.

Fahrmeir, L. (1992). Posterior mode estimation by extended Kalman filtering for multivariate dynamic generalised linear models. *J. Am. Statist. Assoc.*, 87, 501–9.

Fruhwirth-Schnatter, S. (1992). Approximate predictive integrals for dynamic generalized linear models. In *Advances in GLIM and Statistical Modelling, Proceedings of the GLIM92 Conference and the 7th International Workshop on Statistical Modelling, Munich, 13–17 July 1992*, L. Fahrmeir, B. Francis, R. Gilchrist and G. Tutz (eds.), pp. 101–6. New York: Springer-Verlag.

Gilks, W. K., Richardson, S. & Spiegelhalter, D. J. (1996). *Markov Chain Monte Carlo in Practice*. London: Chapman and Hall.

Gordon, N. J., Salmond, D. J. & Smith, A. F. M. (1993). A novel approach to non-linear and non-Gaussian Bayesian state estimation. *IEE Proc. F* 140, 107–33.

Green, P. J. & Han, X. L. (1992). Metropolis, Gaussian proposals and antithetic variables. In *Stochastic Models, Statistical Methods and Algorithms in Image Analysis*, 47, Ed. P. Barone, A. Frigessi and M. Piccioni (eds.), pp. 142–64. Berlin: Springer-Verlag.

Harvey, A. C. (1989). *Forecasting, Structural Time Series Models and the Kalman Filter*. Cambridge. Cambridge University Press.

Harvey, A. C. & Fernandes, C. (1989). Time series models for count data or qualitative observations. *J. Bus. Econ. Statist.*, 7, 407–17.

Harvey, A. C., Ruiz, E. & Shephard, N. (1994). Multivariate stochastic variance models. *Rev. Econ. Studies*, 61, 247–64.

Hull, J. & White, A. (1987). The pricing of options on assets with stochastic volatilities. *J. Finance*, 42, 281–300.

Jacquier, R., Polson, N. G. & Rossi, P. E. (1994). Bayesian analysis of stochastic volatility models (with Discussion). *J. Bus. Econ. Statist.*, 12, 371–417.

Kitagawa, G. (1987). Non-Gaussian state space modelling of non-stationary time series. *J. Am. Statist. Assoc.*, 82, 503–14.

Koopman, S. J. (1993). Disturbance smoother for state space models. *Biometrika*, 80, 117–26.

Liu, J., Wong, W. H. & Kong, A. (1994). Covariance structure of the Gibbs sampler with applications to the comparison of estimators and augmentation schemes. *Biometrika*, 81, 27–40.

McCullagh, P. & Nelder, J. A. (1989). *Generalized Linear Models*, 2nd ed. London: Chapman and Hall.

Muller, P. (1991). Numerical integration in general dynamic models. *Contemp. Math.*, 115, 145–63.

Priestley, M. B. (1981). *Spectral Analysis and Time Series*. London: Academic Press.

Ripley, B. D. (1987). *Stochastic Simulation*. New York: Wiley.

Shephard, N. (1994a). Local scale model: state space alternative to integrated GARCH processes. *J. Economet.*, 60, 181–202.

Shephard, N. (1994b). Partial non-Gaussian state space. *Biometrika*, 81, 115–31.

Singh, Λ. C. & Roberts, G. R. (1992). State space modelling cross-classified time series and counts. *Int. Statist. Rev.*, 60, 321–35.

Smith, J. Q. (1979). A generalization of the Bayesian steady forecasting model. *J. R. Statist. Soc.*, B 41, 375–87.

Smith, J. Q. (1981). The multiparameter steady model. *J. R. Statist. Soc.*, B 43, 256–60.

Smith, R. L. & Miller, J. E. (1986). A non-Gaussian state space model and application to prediction records. *J. R. Statist. Soc.*, B 48, 79–88.

Tierney, L. (1994). Markov Chains for exploring posterior distributions (with Discussion). *Ann. Statist.*, 21, 1701–62.

West, M. (1993). Approximating posterior distributions by mixtures. *J. R. Statist. Soc.*, B 55, 409–42.

West, M., Harrison, P. J. & Migon, H. S. (1985). Dynamic generalised models and Bayesian forecasting (with Discussion). *J. Am. Statist. Assoc.*, 80, 73–97.

21

Time Series Analysis of Non-Gaussian Observations Based on State Space Models from Both Classical and Bayesian Perspectives*

J. DURBIN

London School of Economics and Political Science

AND

S. J. KOOPMAN

Tilburg University

SUMMARY

The analysis of non-Gaussian time series using state space models is considered from both classical and Bayesian perspectives. The treatment in both cases is based on simulation using importance sampling and antithetic variables; Markov chain Monte Carlo methods are not employed. Non-Gaussian disturbances for the state equation as well as for the observation equation are considered. Methods for estimating conditional and posterior means of functions of the state vector given the observations, and the mean-square errors of their estimates, are developed. These methods are extended to cover the estimation of conditional and posterior densities and distribution functions. Choice of importance sampling densities and antithetic variables is discussed. The techniques work well in practice and are computationally efficient. Their use is illustrated by applying them to a univariate discrete time series, a series with outliers and a volatility series.

1 Introduction

This paper discusses the analysis of non-Gaussian time series using state space models from both classical and Bayesian points of view. A major advantage of the state space approach is that we can model the behaviour of different components of the series separately and then put the submodels together to form an overall model for the series. State space models are very general and can handle a remarkably wide range of applications ranging from autoregressive integrated moving average models and unobserved components time series models to smoothing models with roughness penalties.

An example of the application of state space methods to a problem in applied time series analysis was the assessment for the Department of Transport of the effects of seat-belt legislation on road traffic accidents in the UK described by

* This work was previously published as J. Durbin and S.J. Koopman, "Time Series Analysis of Non-Gaussian Observations based on State Space Models from both Classical and Bayesian Perspectives", *Journal of the Royal Statistical Society*, 2000, Vol. 62, no. 1, pp. 3–29. Reproduced here by kind permission of Blackwell Publishing.

Harvey and Durbin (1986). Although the observations were count data and hence non-Gaussian, the analysis was based on linear Gaussian methods since these were the only appropriate state space methods that were available at the time. The realization that no exact treatment of count data existed at the time led to the work in this paper.

State space models contain two classes of variables: the unobserved state variables which describe the development over time of the underlying system and the observations. We consider departures from normality both for the state variables and for the conditional distributions of the observations given the state. For the state, our primary interest is in heavy-tailed densities which enable us to model structural shifts. For the conditional densities of the observations, we consider general classes of distributions which include both exponential family distributions and heavy-tailed densities. The exponential family densities allow us to model count data such as Poisson, binomial and multinomial observations as well as to model skewed data by, for example, gamma densities. The heavy-tailed densities allow us to model outliers. For a classical analysis we calculate maximum likelihood estimates of model parameters and then estimate conditional means of functions of the state given the observations, together with the mean-square errors of the estimates. We also show how to estimate conditional distribution functions and conditional densities. For the Bayesian analysis we estimate posterior means and variances, posterior distribution functions and densities and show how to draw random samples from the estimated posterior distributions of functions of the state. The methods are simple and computationally efficient. For the most part we present a general theory for multivariate observations.

The techniques used are based on the Kalman filter and smoother and on Monte Carlo simulation using Gaussian importance sampling and antithetic variables. Using these techniques we develop methods that are new, elegant and efficient for problems in time series analysis, and we provide estimates that are as accurate as is desired. Our simulation techniques are based on independent samples and not on Markov chains, thus enabling us to avoid convergence problems and also to obtain simple and accurate estimates of sampling variances due to simulation.

Some early work on state space modelling with non-Gaussian data is reviewed in chapter 8 of Anderson and Moore (1979). A further review of early work is given by Kitagawa (1987) and in the accompanying published discussion, particularly in the extensive comments of Martin and Raftery (1987). Gaussian mixtures were used by Harrison and Stevens (1971, 1976) under the name multiprocess models for problems involving non-Gaussian data. Most of this work deals only with filtering. However, a comprehensive treatment of both filtering and smoothing was given by Kitagawa (1989, 1990) based on approximating non-Gaussian densities by Gaussian mixtures. At each update he collapsed the conditional density into a smaller number of components to prevent the number of components in the mixtures from becoming unmanageable, so the method is essentially approximative.

State space models for exponential family observations with Gaussian state were introduced by West et al. (1985). They used a Bayesian approach using conjugate priors and at each update the posterior density was approximated to retain the conjugate structure. Further developments were given by West and Harrison (1997) within a more general treatment of dynamic models. The exponential family model was also considered by Fahrmeir (1992) who estimated the state variables by approximating their conditional modes given the observations. Singh and Roberts (1992) obtained iterative estimates of the conditional modes by methods that are different from those used in this paper. West (1993) has considered approximating models for a Bayesian analysis based on mixtures. Frühwirth-Schnatter (1994) developed an approximate Bayesian technique by approximating the prior of the state density at each step of the filtering process by a Gaussian density and then performing the update using the new observation by means of a numerical integration of dimensionality equal to the dimensionality of the observation vector.

The disadvantage of all these methods is that they involve approximation errors of unknown magnitude whereas, with our techniques, errors are due only to simulation and their extent can be measured and made as small as desired. Smith (1979, 1981) and Harvey and Fernandes (1989) gave an exact solution for a special case: they based their methods on conjugate distributions and they developed them for specific count data models for which the state equation is a univariate random walk. However, this approach does not lend itself to generalization.

Using full Bayesian inference models, simulation techniques based on Markov chain Monte Carlo (MCMC) sampling for non-Gaussian state space models have been developed by Carlin et al. (1992), Carter and Kohn (1994, 1996, 1997), Shephard (1994), Shephard and Pitt (1997) and Cargnoni et al. (1997). A review of simulation techniques in a broader context has been given by Geweke (1996). General accounts of Bayesian methodology and computation are given by Gelman et al. (1995) and Bernardo and Smith (1994). New developments in this paper are based on earlier work of Durbin and Koopman (1992, 1997). In Durbin and Koopman (1992) we considered conditional mode estimation based on Kalman filtering and smoothing methods for exponential family models; in Durbin and Koopman (1997) we considered the special case where the observations given the state are non-Gaussian whereas the state is Gaussian and the objective was to calculate maximum likelihood estimates of model parameters by simulation. The simulation methods were highly efficient computationally in the sense that accurate results were obtained using small simulation sample sizes in the low hundreds. Shephard and Pitt (1997) also considered maximum likelihood estimation of parameters of non-Gaussian state space models by simulation. Geyer and Thompson (1992) have developed simulation methods of estimation for specific autologistic models and other exponential family models without dynamic structures.

The structure of the paper is as follows. In Section 2 we present the state space models that we shall consider. Section 3 develops some basic formulae that underlie the simulation techniques that we shall describe in detail later. In Section 4 we obtain a linear Gaussian model that approximates the non-Gaussian model in the neighbourhood of the conditional mode of the stacked state vector given the observations; this is used to provide the Gaussian densities that we use for importance sampling. Section 5 develops the computational techniques that are required for practical applications. These are based on importance sampling using two types of antithetic variables: one for location and one for scale. We obtain computationally efficient estimates of the means and variances of arbitrary functions of the stacked state vector given the observations; these enable us to estimate conditional distribution and density functions and to draw random samples from conditional distributions. We also obtain simple estimates of the variances of errors due to simulation. The results are extended in a straightforward manner to analogous problems in Bayesian inference.

Section 6 applies the techniques to three real data sets. The first is a series of numbers of deaths in road accidents, the second is a series of UK gas consumption and the third is an exchange rate volatility series. The examples demonstrate the feasibility of the techniques for different models and show the differences between results based on the classical methods and results from using a Bayesian approach. Section 7 provides some final comments.

2 Models

2.1 The linear Gaussian model

In this section we present the state space models that will be considered in the paper. We begin with the linear Gaussian model. Although our main concern is with non-Gaussian models, the linear Gaussian model provides the basis from which all our methods will be developed. The model can be formulated in a variety of ways; we shall take the form

$$y_t = Z_t\alpha_t + \epsilon_t, \quad \epsilon_t \sim N(0, H_t), \tag{1}$$

$$\alpha_t = T_t\alpha_{t-1} + R_t\eta_t, \quad \eta_t \sim N(0, Q_t). \tag{2}$$

for $t = 1, \ldots, n$. Here, y_t is a $p \times 1$ vector of observations, α_t is an unobserved $m \times 1$ state vector, R_t is a selection matrix composed of r columns of the identity matrix I_m, which need not be adjacent, and the variance matrices H_t and Q_t are non-singular. The disturbance vectors ϵ_t and η_t are serially independent and independent of each other. Matrices H_t, Q_t, Z_t and T_t are assumed known apart from a possible dependence on a parameter vector ψ which in classical inference is assumed fixed and unknown, and in Bayesian inference is treated as random. Equations (1) and (2) are called respectively the observation equation and the state equation of the state space model. It is worth noting that model (1) can be regarded as a multiple-regression model whose coefficient vector α_t is determined by the first-order vector autoregression (2). The state space model (1) and (2) is essentially equivalent to model (16) and (17) of the seminal Kalman (1960) paper.

2.2 Non-Gaussian models

We shall use the generic notation $p(\cdot)$, $p(\cdot, \cdot)$ and $p(\cdot|\cdot)$ for marginal, joint and conditional densities. The general non-Gaussian model that we shall consider has a state space structure that is similar to model (1) and (2) in the sense that observations are determined by a relationship of the form

$$p(y_t|\alpha_1, \ldots, \alpha_t, y_1, \ldots, y_{t-1}) = p(y_t|Z_t\alpha_t), \tag{3}$$

while the state vectors are determined independently of previous observations by the relationship

$$\alpha_t = T_t \alpha_{t-1} + R_t \eta_t, \quad \eta_t \sim p(\eta_t), \tag{4}$$

for $t = 1, \ldots, n$, where the η_t are serially independent. Here, either $p(y_t | Z_t \alpha_t)$ or $p(\eta_t)$ or both can be non-Gaussian. We denote $Z_t \alpha_t$ by θ_t and refer to it as the signal. Although we begin by considering a general form for $p(y_t | \theta_t)$, we shall pay particular attention to two special cases:

(a) observations which come from exponential family distributions with densities of the form

$$p(y_t | \theta_t) = \exp\{y_t' \theta_t - b_t(\theta_t) + c_t(y_t)\}, \tag{5}$$

where $b_t(\theta_t)$ is twice differentiable and $c_t(y_t)$ is a function of y_t only;

(b) observations generated by the relationship

$$y_t = \theta_t + \epsilon_t, \quad \epsilon_t \sim p(\epsilon_t), \tag{6}$$

where the ϵ_t are non-Gaussian and serially independent.

In the next section we shall develop estimation formulae which provide the basis for our simulation methodology. We shall do this for both classical and Bayesian inference. In the terminology of Bayesian analysis, all the models in this section are hierarchical models, in which the elements of $\alpha_1, \ldots, \alpha_n$ are the parameters and the elements of ψ are the hyperparameters; see, for example, Bernardo and Smith (1994), page 371.

3 Basic Simulation Formulae

3.1 Introduction

In this section we develop the basic formulae underlying our simulation methods; details for practical calculation will be given in Section 5. Denote the stacked vectors $(\alpha_1', \ldots, \alpha_n')'$ and $(y_1', \ldots, y_n')'$ by α and y. Most of the problems considered in this paper are essentially the estimation of the conditional mean

$$\bar{x} = E[x(\alpha) | y] \tag{7}$$

of an arbitrary function $x(\alpha)$ of α given the observation vector y. This formulation includes estimates of quantities of interest such as the mean $E[\alpha_t | y]$ of the state vector α_t given y and its conditional variance matrix $\mathrm{var}(\alpha_t | y)$; it also includes estimates of the conditional density and distribution function of $x(\alpha)$ given y in the classical case and the posterior density and distribution function of $x(\alpha)$ in the Bayesian case. We shall estimate $\bar{x}$ by simulation methods that are similar to those used in Shephard and Pitt (1997) and Durbin and Koopman (1997) for estimating the likelihood in non-Gaussian state space models. The methods are based on standard ideas in simulation methodology, namely importance sampling and antithetic variables, as described, for example, in Ripley (1987), pages 122–123; in particular, we make no use of MCMC methods. Nevertheless, our methods are computationally very efficient as we shall demonstrate. The techniques that we shall describe will be based on Gaussian importance densities. We shall use the generic notation $g(\cdot)$, $g(\cdot, \cdot)$ and $g(\cdot|\cdot)$ for Gaussian marginal, joint and conditional densities.

3.2 Formulae for classical inference

Let us first consider the classical inference case where the parameter vector ψ is assumed to be fixed and unknown and is estimated by its maximum likelihood estimate $\hat{\psi}$ obtained by numerically maximizing the Monte Carlo likelihood function as discussed in Section 5.4. For given ψ, let $g(\alpha|y)$ be a Gaussian importance density which is chosen to resemble $p(\alpha|y)$ as closely as is reasonably possible; we have from equation (7)

$$\bar{x} = \int x(\alpha) p(\alpha|y)\, d\alpha = \int x(\alpha) \frac{p(\alpha|y)}{g(\alpha|y)} g(\alpha|y)\, d\alpha = E_g\left[x(\alpha) \frac{p(\alpha|y)}{g(\alpha|y)}\right], \quad (8)$$

where E_g denotes expectation with respect to the importance density $g(\alpha|y)$. For the models of Section 2, $p(\alpha|y)$ and $g(\alpha|y)$ are complicated algebraically, whereas the corresponding joint densities $p(\alpha, y)$ and $g(\alpha, y)$ are straightforward. We therefore put

$$p(\alpha|y) = p(\alpha, y)/p(y)$$

and

$$g(\alpha|y) = g(\alpha, y)/g(y)$$

in equation (8), giving

$$\bar{x} = \frac{g(y)}{p(y)} E_g\left[x(\alpha) \frac{p(\alpha, y)}{g(\alpha, y)}\right]. \quad (9)$$

Putting $x(\alpha) = 1$ in equations (7) and (9) we have

$$1 = \frac{g(y)}{p(y)} E_g\left[\frac{p(\alpha, y)}{g(\alpha, y)}\right]. \quad (10)$$

Taking the ratios of these gives

$$\bar{x} = \frac{E_g[x(\alpha) w(\alpha, y)]}{E_g[w(\alpha, y)]}, \quad \text{where } w(\alpha, y) = \frac{p(\alpha, y)}{g(\alpha, y)}. \quad (11)$$

This formula provides the basis for the bulk of the work in this paper. For example, it can be used to estimate conditional variances of quantities of interest as well as conditional densities and distribution functions. We could in principle obtain a

Monte Carlo estimate $\hat{x}$ of $\bar{x}$ in the following way. Choose a series of independent draws $\alpha^{(1)}, \ldots, \alpha^{(N)}$ from the distribution with density $g(\alpha|y)$ and take

$$\hat{x} = \sum_{i=1}^{N} x_i w_i \Big/ \sum_{i=1}^{N} w_i, \quad \text{where } x_i = x(\alpha^{(i)}) \text{ and } w_i = w(\alpha^{(i)}, y). \tag{12}$$

Since the draws are independent, and under assumptions which are satisfied in practical cases. $\hat{x}$ converges to $\bar{x}$ probabilistically as $N \to \infty$. However, this simple estimate is numerically inefficient and we shall refine it considerably in Section 5.

An important special case is where the observations are non-Gaussian but the state vector is generated by the linear Gaussian model (2). We then have $p(\alpha) = g(\alpha)$ so

$$\frac{p(\alpha, y)}{g(\alpha, y)} = \frac{p(\alpha)p(y|\alpha)}{g(\alpha)g(y|\alpha)} = \frac{p(y|\alpha)}{g(y|\alpha)} = \frac{p(y|\theta)}{p(y|\theta)}.$$

Thus equation (11) becomes the simpler formula

$$\bar{x} = \frac{E_g[x(\alpha)w^*(\theta, y)]}{E_g[w^*(\theta, y)]}, \quad \text{where } w^*(\theta, y) = \frac{p(y|\theta)}{g(y|\theta)}; \tag{13}$$

its estimate $\hat{x}$ is given by an obvious analogue of equation (12).

3.3 Formulae for Bayesian inference
Now let us consider the problem from a Bayesian point of view. The parameter vector ψ is regarded as random with prior density $p(\psi)$ which to begin with we take as a proper prior. As before, suppose that we wish to calculate $\bar{x} = E[x(\alpha)|y]$. This now takes the form

$$\bar{x} = \int x(\alpha)p(\psi, \alpha|y) \, d\psi \, d\alpha.$$

We have

$$p(\psi, \alpha|y) = p(\psi|y)p(\alpha|\psi, y),$$

where by Bayes's theorem

$$p(\psi|y) = Kp(\psi)p(y|\psi)$$

in which K is a normalizing constant. Thus

$$\bar{x} = K \int x(\alpha)p(\psi)p(y|\psi)p(\alpha|\psi, y) \, d\psi \, d\alpha. \tag{14}$$

Consider the approximation of the posterior density $p(\psi|y)$ by its large sample normal approximation

$$g(\psi|y) = N(\hat{\psi}, \hat{V}),$$

where $\hat{\psi}$ is the solution of the equation

$$\frac{\partial[\log\{p(\psi|y)\}]}{\partial\psi} = \frac{\partial[\log\{p(\psi)\}]}{\partial\psi} + \frac{\partial[\log\{p(y|\psi)\}]}{\partial\psi} = 0, \qquad (15)$$

and

$$\hat{V}^{-1} = -\frac{\partial^2[\log\{p(\psi)\}]}{\partial\psi\partial\psi'} - \frac{\partial^2[\log\{p(y|\psi)\}]}{\partial\psi\partial\psi'}\Bigg|_{\psi=\hat{\psi}}. \qquad (16)$$

The value $\hat{\psi}$ is computed iteratively by an obvious extension of the techniques of Durbin and Koopman (1997) using a linearization at a trial value $\tilde{\psi}$ of ψ, whereas the second derivatives can be calculated numerically. For a discussion of large sample approximations to $p(\psi|y)$ see Gelman et al. (1995), chapter 4, and Bernardo and Smith (1994), section 5.3.

We shall use $g(\psi|y)$ as an importance density for $p(\psi|y)$. Let $g(\alpha|\psi, y)$ be an appropriate Gaussian importance density for $p(\alpha|\psi, y)$ analogous to $g(\alpha|y)$ in equation (8). We can then rewrite equation (14) as

$$
\begin{aligned}
\bar{x} &= K\int x(\alpha)\frac{p(\psi)p(y|\psi)}{g(\psi|y)}\frac{p(\alpha|\psi, y)}{g(\alpha|\psi, y)}g(\psi|y)g(\alpha|\psi, y)\,\mathrm{d}\psi\,\mathrm{d}\alpha \\
&= K\int x(\alpha)\frac{p(\psi)g(y|\psi)}{g(\psi|y)}\frac{p(\alpha, y|\psi)}{g(\alpha, y|\psi)}g(\psi, \alpha|y)\,\mathrm{d}\psi\,\mathrm{d}\alpha \\
&= KE_g\left[x(\alpha)\frac{p(\psi)g(y|\psi)}{g(\psi|y)}\frac{p(\alpha, y|\psi)}{g(\alpha, y|\psi)}\right], \qquad (17)
\end{aligned}
$$

where E_g now denotes expectation with respect to the importance joint density

$$g(\psi, \alpha|y) = g(\psi|y)g(\alpha|\psi, y).$$

It is very fortunate that the quantity $p(y|\psi)$, which is difficult to compute, conveniently drops out of this expression. Taking the ratio of this expression for $\bar{x}$ to the same expression with $x(\alpha)$ equal to 1, the term K disappears, giving, analogously to equation (11),

$$\bar{x} = \frac{E_g[x(\alpha)z(\psi, \alpha, y)]}{E_g[z(\psi, \alpha, y)]}, \quad \text{where } z(\psi, \alpha, y) = \frac{p(\psi)g(y|\psi)}{g(\psi|y)}\frac{p(\alpha, y|\psi)}{g(\alpha, y|\psi)}. \qquad (18)$$

This formula provides the basis for our results in the Bayesian case. It can be used to obtain estimates of posterior means, variances, densities and distribution functions. In principle we could compute a Monte Carlo point estimate $\hat{x}$ of $\bar{x}$ as follows. Let $\psi^{(i)}$ be a random draw from $g(\psi|y)$ and let $\alpha^{(i)}$ be a random draw from $g(\alpha|\psi^{(i)}, y)$ for $i = 1, \ldots, N$; we assume here that we only draw one $\alpha^{(i)}$ for each $\psi^{(i)}$ though, of course, more could be drawn if desired. Then take

$$\hat{x} = \sum_{i=1}^{N} x_i z_i \bigg/ \sum_{i=1}^{N} z_i, \quad \text{where } x_i = x(\alpha^{(i)}) \text{ and } z_i = z(\psi^{(i)}, \alpha^{(i)}, y). \qquad (19)$$

We see that the only difference between equations (19) and (12) is the replacement of w_i by z_i which allows for the effect of drawing values of ψ from $g(\psi|y)$. This simple form of the simulation will be improved later. The term $g(y|\psi^{(i)})$ in z_i is easily calculated by the Kalman filter.

For cases where a proper prior is not available we may wish to use a non-informative prior in which we assume that the prior density is proportional to a specified function $p(\psi)$ in a domain of ψ of interest even though the integral $\int p(\psi)\,d\psi$ does not exist. For a discussion of non-informative priors see, for example, chapters 2 and 3 of Gelman et al. (1995). Where it exists, the posterior density is

$$p(\psi|y) = Kp(\psi)p(y|\psi)$$

as in the proper prior case so all the previous formulae apply without change. This is why we use the same symbol $p(\psi)$ for both cases even though in the non-informative case $p(\psi)$ is not a density. An important special case is the diffuse prior for which $p(\psi) = 1$ for all ψ.

3.4 Bayesian analysis for the linear Gaussian model

Although this paper is directed at non-Gaussian models, let us digress briefly to consider the application of the above Bayesian treatment to the linear Gaussian model (1) and (2), since this model is important in practical applications and our methodology is new. Let

$$\bar{x}(\psi) = E[x(\alpha)|\psi, y] = \int x(\alpha)p(\alpha|\psi, y)\,d\alpha,$$

and assume that, for given ψ, $\bar{x}(\psi)$ is obtainable by a routine Kalman filtering and smoothing operation; for example, $x(\psi)$ could be an estimate of the trend at time t or it could be a forecast of y_t at time $t > n$. Then

$$\bar{x} = \int \bar{x}(\psi)p(\psi|y)\,d\psi = K \int \bar{x}(\psi)p(\psi)p(y|\psi)\,d\psi$$

$$= K \int \bar{x}(\psi)z^g(\psi, y)g(\psi|y)\,d\psi = K E_g[\bar{x}(\psi)z^g(\psi, y)],$$

where $z^g(\psi, y) = p(\psi)g(y|\psi)/g(\psi|y)$

and E_g is the expectation with respect to the importance density $g(\psi|y)$; note that we write $g(y|\psi)$ in place of $p(y|\psi)$ since $p(y|\psi)$ is Gaussian. Analogously to equation (18) we therefore have

$$\bar{x} = \frac{E_g[\bar{x}(\alpha)z^g(\psi, y)]}{E_g[z^g(\psi, y)]}, \tag{20}$$

whereas for practical calculation there is an obvious analogue of equation (19). In equation (20), $z^g(\psi, y)$ depends on the likelihood $g(y|\psi)$ which can be computed by routine Kalman filtering for the linear Gaussian model.

4 Approximating Linear Gaussian Models

4.1 Introduction

In this section we obtain the Gaussian importance densities that we need for simulation by constructing linear Gaussian models which approximate the non-Gaussian model in the neighbourhood of the conditional mode of α given y. Let $g(\alpha|y)$ and $g(\alpha, y)$ be the conditional and joint densities generated by model (1) and (2) and let $p(\alpha|y)$ and $p(\alpha, y)$ be the corresponding densities generated by model (3) and (4). We shall determine the approximating model by choosing H_t and Q_t so that densities $g(\alpha|y)$ and $p(\alpha|y)$ have the same mode $\hat{\alpha}$. The possibility that $p(\alpha, y)$ might be multimodal will be considered in Section 4.6. Taking the Gaussian model first, $\hat{\alpha}$ is the solution of the vector equation

$$\partial[\log\{g(\alpha|y)\}]/\partial\alpha = 0.$$

Now $\log\{g(\alpha|y)\} = \log\{g(\alpha, y)\} - \log\{g(y)\}$. Thus, the mode is also the solution of the vector equation

$$\partial[\log\{g(\alpha, y)\}]/\partial\alpha = 0.$$

This version of the equation is easier to manage since $g(\alpha, y)$ has a simple form whereas $g(\alpha|y)$ does not. Since R_t consists of columns of I_m, $\eta_t = R_t'(\alpha_t - T_t\alpha_{t-1})$. We therefore have

$$\log\{g(\alpha, y)\} = \text{constant} - \frac{1}{2}\sum_{t=1}^{n}(\alpha_t - T_t\alpha_{t-1})'R_t Q_t^{-1} R_t'(\alpha_t - T_t\alpha_{t-1})$$

$$- \frac{1}{2}\sum_{t=1}^{n}(y_t - Z_t\alpha_t)'H_t^{-1}(y_t - Z_t\alpha_t).$$

Differentiating with respect to α_t and equating to 0 gives the equations

$$- R_t Q_t^{-1} R_t'(\alpha_t - T_t\alpha_{t-1}) + d_t T_{t+1}' R_{t+1} Q_{t+1}^{-1} R_{t+1}'(\alpha_{t+1} - T_{t+1}\alpha_t)$$
$$+ Z_t' H_t^{-1}(y_t - Z_t\alpha_t) = 0, \tag{21}$$

for $t = 1, \ldots, n$, where $d_t = 1$ for $t < n$ and $d_n = 0$. The solution to these equations is the conditional mode $\hat{\alpha}$. Since $g(\alpha|y)$ is Gaussian the mode is equal to the mean so $\hat{\alpha}$ can be routinely calculated by the Kalman filter and smoother (KFS); for details of the KFS see Harvey (1989), chapter 3. It follows that linear equations of the form (21) can be solved by the KFS which is known to be very efficient computationally.

Assuming that the non-Gaussian model (3) and (4) is sufficiently well behaved, the mode $\hat{\alpha}$ of $p(\alpha|y)$ is the solution of the vector equation

$$\partial[\log\{p(\alpha|y)\}]/\partial\alpha = 0$$

and hence of the equation

$$\partial[\log\{p(\alpha, y)\}]/\partial\alpha = 0.$$

Let $q_t(\eta_t) = -\log\{p(\eta_t)\}$ and let $h_t(y_t|\theta_t) = -\log\{p(y_t|\theta_t)\}$. Then,

$$\log\{p(\alpha, y)\} = \text{constant} - \sum_{t=1}^{n}\{q_t(\eta_t) + h_t(y_t|\theta_t)\}. \tag{22}$$

with $\eta_t = R_t'(\alpha_t - T_t\alpha_{t-1})$, so $\hat{\alpha}$ is a solution of the equations

$$\frac{\partial[\log\{p(\alpha, y)\}]}{\partial\alpha_t} = -R_t\frac{\partial q_t(\eta_t)}{\partial\eta_t} + d_t T_{t+1}' R_{t+1}\frac{\partial q_{t+1}(\eta_{t+1})}{\partial\eta_{t+1}} - Z_t'\frac{\partial h_t(y_t|\theta_t)}{\partial\theta_t}$$

$$= 0, \tag{23}$$

for $t = 1, \ldots, n$, where, as before, $d_t = 1$ for $t = 1, \ldots, n - 1$ and $d_n = 0$. We solve these equations by iteration, where at each step we linearize, put the result in the form (21) and solve by the KFS. Convergence is fast and normally only around 10 iterations or fewer are needed. A different method of solving these equations was given by Fahrmeir and Kaufmann (1991) but it is more cumbersome than our method.

4.2 Linearization for non-Gaussian observation densities: method 1

We shall consider two methods of linearizing the observation component of equation (23). The first method enables exponential family observations, such as Poisson-distributed observations, to be handled; the second method is given in Section 4.4 and deals with observations having the form (6) when $p(\epsilon_t)$ is a function of ϵ_t^2; this is suitable for distributions with heavy tails such as the t-distribution.

Suppose that $\tilde{\alpha} = (\tilde{\alpha}_1', \ldots, \tilde{\alpha}_n')'$ is a trial value of α, let $\tilde{\theta}_t = Z_t\tilde{\alpha}_t$ and define

$$\dot{h}_t = \frac{\partial h_t(y_t|\theta_t)}{\partial\theta_t}\bigg|_{\theta_t=\tilde{\theta}_t},$$

$$\ddot{h}_t = \frac{\partial^2 h_t(y_t|\theta_t)}{\partial\theta_t\partial\theta_t'}\bigg|_{\theta_t=\tilde{\theta}_t}. \tag{24}$$

Expanding about $\tilde{\theta}_t$ gives approximately

$$\partial h_t(y_t|\theta_t)/\partial\theta_t = \dot{h}_t + \ddot{h}_t(\theta_t - \tilde{\theta}_t). \tag{25}$$

Substituting in the final term of equation (23) gives the linearized form

$$-Z_t'(\dot{h}_t + \ddot{h}_t\theta_t - \ddot{h}_t\tilde{\theta}_t). \tag{26}$$

To put this in the same format as the final term of equation (21) put

$$\tilde{H}_t = \ddot{h}_t^{-1},$$
$$\tilde{y}_t = \tilde{\theta}_t - \ddot{h}_t^{-1}\dot{h}_t. \tag{27}$$

Then the final term becomes $Z_t'\tilde{H}_t^{-1}(\tilde{y}_t - \theta_t)$ as required.

Consider, for example, the important special case in which the state equation retains the original linear Gaussian form (2). Equations (23) then have the linearized form

$$- R_t Q_t^{-1} R_t'(\alpha_t - T_t\alpha_{t-1}) + d_t T_{t+1}' R_{t+1} Q_{t+1}^{-1} R_{t+1}'(\alpha_{t+1} - T_{t+1}\alpha_t)$$
$$+ Z_t'\tilde{H}_t^{-1}(\tilde{y}_t - Z_t\alpha_t) = 0, \tag{28}$$

analogous to equation (21), which can be solved for α by the KFS to give a new trial value and the process is repeated until convergence. The values of α and θ after convergence to the mode are denoted by $\ddot{\alpha}$ and $\hat{\theta}$ respectively.

It is evident from equations (27) that method 1 only works when $\ddot{h}_t$ is positive definite. When $\ddot{h}_t$ is negative definite or semidefinite, method 2 should normally be used. Finally, it is important to note that the second derivative of the observation component of the log-Gaussian-density of y_t given θ_t is the same as the second derivative of $-h_t(y_t|\theta_t)$ at the mode $\theta = \hat{\theta}$, for $t = 1, \ldots, n$, since $\tilde{H}_t = \ddot{h}_t^{-1}$ in equations (27). This means that not only does the approximating linear Gaussian model have the same conditional mode as model (3) and (2) but it also has the same curvature at the mode.

4.3 Exponential family observations

The most important application of these results is to time series of observations from exponential family distributions, such as Poisson, binomial and multinomial observations. The model with observational density (5) together with linear Gaussian state equation (2) was introduced by West et al. (1985). They called it the dynamic generalized linear model and they fitted it by an approximate Bayesian technique based on conjugate priors.

For density (5),

$$h_t(y_t|\theta_t) = -\log\{p(y_t|\theta_t)\} = -\{y_t'\theta_t - b_t(\theta_t) + c_t(y_t)\}. \tag{29}$$

Define

$$\dot{b}_t = \left.\frac{\partial b_t(\theta_t)}{\partial \theta_t}\right|_{\theta_t=\tilde{\theta}_t},$$
$$\ddot{b}_t = \left.\frac{\partial^2 b_t(\theta_t)}{\partial \theta_t \partial \theta_t'}\right|_{\theta_t=\tilde{\theta}_t}.$$

Then $\dot{h}_t = \dot{b}_t - y_t$ and $\ddot{h}_t = \ddot{b}_t$ so using equations (27) we take $\tilde{H}_t = \ddot{b}_t^{-1}$ and $\tilde{y}_t = \tilde{\theta}_t - \ddot{b}_t^{-1}(\dot{b}_t - y_t)$. These values can be substituted in equation (28) to obtain a solution for the case where the state equation is linear and Gaussian. Since, as is well known, $\ddot{b}_t = \text{var}(y_t | \theta_t)$, it is positive definite in non-degenerate cases, so, for the exponential family, method 1 can always be used.

4.4 Linearization for non-Gaussian observation densities: method 2

We now consider the case where the observations are generated by model (6). We shall assume that y_t is univariate and that $p(\epsilon_t)$ is a function of ϵ_t^2; this case is important for heavy-tailed densities such as the t-distribution, and for Gaussian mixtures with zero means.

Let $\log\{p(\epsilon_t)\} = -\frac{1}{2} h_t^*(\epsilon_t^2)$. Then the contribution of the observation component to the equation $\partial[\log\{p(\alpha, y)\}]/\partial\alpha$ is

$$-\frac{1}{2}\frac{\partial h_t^*(\epsilon_t^2)}{\partial\epsilon_t^2}\frac{\partial\epsilon_t^2}{\partial\alpha_t} = Z_t'\frac{\partial h_t^*(\epsilon_t^2)}{\partial\epsilon_t^2}(y_t - \theta_t). \tag{30}$$

Let

$$\dot{h}_t^* = \left.\frac{\partial h_t^*(\epsilon_t^2)}{\partial\epsilon_t^2}\right|_{\epsilon_t = y_t - \tilde{\theta}_t}. \tag{31}$$

Then take $Z_t'\dot{h}_t^*(y_t - \theta_t)$ as the linearized form of equation (30). By taking $\tilde{H}_t^{-1} = \dot{h}_t^*$ we have the observation component in the correct form (21) so we can use the KFS at each step of the solution of the equation $\partial[\log\{p(\alpha, y)\}]/\partial\alpha = 0$. We emphasize that now only the first derivative of the logarithm of the implied Gaussian density of ϵ_t is equal to that of $p(\epsilon_t)$, compared with method 1 which equalized the first and second derivatives.

For this method to work it is of course necessary that $\dot{h}_t^*$ is positive with probability 1; however, this condition is satisfied for the applications that we consider below. Strictly it is not essential that $p(\epsilon_t)$ is a function of ϵ_t^2. In other cases we could define

$$\dot{h}_t^* = -\frac{1}{\epsilon_t}\left.\frac{\partial[\log\{p(\epsilon_t)\}]}{\partial\epsilon_t}\right|_{\epsilon_t = y_t - \tilde{\theta}_t} \tag{32}$$

and proceed in the same way. Again, the method only works when $\dot{h}_t^*$ is positive with probability 1.

4.5 Linearization when the state errors are non-Gaussian

We now consider the linearization of the state component in equations (23) when the state errors η_t are non-Gaussian. Suppose that $\tilde{\eta} = (\tilde{\eta}_1', \ldots, \tilde{\eta}_n')'$ is a trial value of $\eta = (\eta_1', \ldots, \eta_n')'$ where $\tilde{\eta}_t = R_t'(\tilde{\alpha}_t - T_t\tilde{\alpha}_{t-1})$. In this paper we shall confine ourselves to the situation where the elements η_{it} of η_t are mutually independent and where the density $p(\eta_{it})$ of η_{it} is a function of η_{it}^2. These assumptions are not very restrictive since they enable us to deal relatively easily with two cases of particular interest in practice, namely heavy-tailed errors and models with structural shifts using method 2 of Section 4.4.

Let $q_{it}^*(\eta_{it}^2) = -2\log\{p(\eta_{it})\}$ and denote the ith column of R_t by R_{it}. Then the state contribution to the conditional mode equations (23) is

$$-\frac{1}{2}\sum_{i=1}^{r}\left\{R_{it}\frac{\partial q_{it}^*(\eta_{it}^2)}{\partial \eta_{it}} - d_t T_{t+1}' R_{i,t+1}\frac{\partial q_{i,t+1}^*(\eta_{i,t+1}^2)}{\partial \eta_{i,t+1}}\right\}, \quad t = 1,\ldots,n. \quad (33)$$

The linearized form of expression (33) is

$$-\sum_{i=1}^{r}(R_{it}\dot{q}_{it}^*\eta_{it} - d_t T_{t+1}' R_{i,t+1}\dot{q}_{i,t+1}^*\eta_{i,t+1}), \quad (34)$$

where

$$\dot{q}_{it}^* = \frac{\partial q_{it}^*(\eta_{it}^2)}{\partial \eta_{it}^2}\bigg|_{\eta_t=\tilde{\eta}_t}. \quad (35)$$

Putting $\tilde{Q}_t^{-1} = \mathrm{diag}(\dot{q}_{1t}^*,\ldots,\dot{q}_{rt}^*)$, $\eta_t = R_t'(\alpha_t - T_t\alpha_{t-1})$, and similarly for $\tilde{Q}_{t+1}$ and η_{t+1}, we see that expression (34) has the same form as the state component of equation (21). Consequently, in the iterative estimation of $\hat{\alpha}$ the KFS can be used to update the trial value $\tilde{\alpha}$.

4.6 Discussion

So far in this section we have emphasized the use of the mode $\hat{\alpha}$ of $p(\alpha|y)$ to obtain a linear approximating model which we use to calculate the Gaussian densities for simulation by using the techniques of the next section. If, however, the sole object of the investigation was to estimate α and if economy in computation was desired, then $\hat{\alpha}$ could be used for the purpose; indeed, this was the estimator used by Durbin and Koopman (1992) and an approximation to it was used by Fahrmeir (1992). Our experience has been that in the examples that we have examined there is very little difference between the mode and the mean $E[\alpha|y]$. A disadvantage of this use of the mode, however, is that there is no accompanying estimate of its error variance matrix.

We have assumed above that there is a single mode and the question arises whether multimodality will create complications. We emphasize that for the estimation of $\bar{x}$ we only use the mode to obtain an importance density. Given any importance density, our estimates converge probabilistically to the true values and, as we shall show in Section 5, we have accurate estimates of their sampling variances due to simulation, whether the importance density is close to optimality or not. Thus use of a poor mode does not invalidate our estimate; at worst it increases the simulation sampling variance to an extent that is routinely calculated. Secondly, if multimodality is suspected it can be investigated by using different starting-points and checking whether iterations from them converge to the same mode. In none of the cases that we have examined has multimodality of $p(\alpha|y)$ caused any difficulties. For this reason we do not believe that this will give rise to problems in routine time series analysis. If, however, it is believed that in a

particular case the simulation variance is unacceptably high owing to the use of a
poor mode, then a linear Gaussian approximating model of the form

$$y_t = \theta_t + d_t + \epsilon_t, \quad \epsilon_t \sim N(0, H_t),$$

can be fitted to the data by a short simulated iterative exercise, where d_t and H_t are
chosen so that $E(\theta_t|y) \simeq E_g(\theta_t|y)$ and $\text{var}(\theta_t|y) \simeq \text{var}_g(\theta_t|y)$ to a rough degree
of accuracy, in which E and var refer to the original model and E_g and var_g refer
to the approximating model. The approximating model is then used to generate a
Gaussian importance density as in the model case. Since this approximating model
is based on means and variances, which are unique, doubts analogous to those due
to multimodality do not arise. Further details will be given in a later publication.

5 Computational Methods

5.1 Introduction
In this section we discuss suitable computational methods for estimating $\bar{x}$ given
by equation (11) when classical inference is used and $\bar{x}$ given by equation (18)
when Bayesian inference is used. We begin with equation (11). The starting-point
for classical analysis is that we take $\psi = \hat{\psi}$ where $\hat{\psi}$ is the maximum likelihood
estimate of ψ determined as described in Section 5.4. During the simulations it is
important to work with variables in their simplest forms. Thus for the observation
equation (3) we work with the signal $\theta_t = Z_t\alpha_t$ and for the state equation (4) we
work with the state disturbance η_t. Substituting for α in terms of η in equation (11)
gives

$$\bar{x} = \frac{E_g[x(\eta)w(\eta, y)]}{E_g[w(\eta, y)]} \quad \text{where } w(\eta, y) = \frac{p(\eta, y)}{g(\eta, y)} \qquad (36)$$

and α is obtained from η by using the relationships $\alpha_t = T_t\alpha_{t-1} + R_t\eta_t$ for
$t = 1, \ldots, n$. We take the symbols $x(\eta)$ and $w(\eta, y)$ as denoting here the functions of η that we obtain by substituting for α in terms of η in $x(\alpha)$ and $w(\alpha, y)$
in equation (11). Also we take E_g as denoting expectation with respect to the
importance density $g(\eta|y)$.

5.2 Simulation smoother and antithetic variables
The simulations are based on random draws of η from the importance density
$g(\eta|y)$ by using the simulation smoother of de Jong and Shephard (1995); this
computes efficiently a draw of η as a linear function of rn independent standard
normal deviates where r is the dimension of vector η_t and n is the number of
observations. The efficiency is increased by the use of antithetic variables. We shall
employ two types of antithetic variable. The first is the standard type given by
$\check{\eta} = 2\hat{\eta} - \eta$ where $\hat{\eta} = E_g(\eta)$ can be obtained via the disturbance smoother; for
details of the disturbance smoother see Koopman (1993). Since $\check{\eta} - \hat{\eta} = -(\eta - \hat{\eta})$
and η is normal, the two vectors η and $\check{\eta}$ are equiprobable. Thus we obtain two
simulation samples from each draw of the simulation smoother; moreover, values

of the conditional mean calculated from the two samples are negatively correlated, giving further efficiency gains.

The second antithetic variable was developed by Durbin and Koopman (1997). Let u be the vector of $rn\ N(0, 1)$ variables that is used in the simulation smoother to generate η and let $c = u'u$; then $c \sim \chi^2_{rn}$. For a given value of c let $q = \Pr(\chi^2_{rn} < c) = F(c)$ and let $\acute{c} = F^{-1}(1 - q)$. Then, as c varies, c and $\acute{c}$ have the same distribution. Now take $\acute{\eta} = \hat{\eta} + \sqrt{(\acute{c}/c)}(\eta - \hat{\eta})$. Then $\acute{\eta}$ has the same distribution as η. This follows because c and $(\eta - \hat{\eta})/\sqrt{c}$ are independently distributed. Finally, take $\acute{\eta} = \hat{\eta} + \sqrt{(\acute{c}/c)}(\check{\eta} - \hat{\eta})$. Thus we obtain a balanced set of four equiprobable values of η for each run of the simulation smoother.

The number of antithetic variables can be increased without difficulty. For example, take c and q as above. Then q is uniform on $(0,1)$ and we write $q \sim U(0, 1)$. Let $q_1 = q + 0.5$ modulo 1; then $q_1 \sim U(0, 1)$ and we have a balanced set of four $U(0, 1)$ variables: $q, q_1, 1 - q$ and $1 - q_1$. Take $\acute{c} = F^{-1}(1 - q)$ as before and similarly $c_1 = F^{-1}(q_1)$ and $\acute{c}_1 = F^{-1}(1 - q_1)$. Then each of c_1 and $\acute{c}_1$ can be combined with η and $\check{\eta}$ as was $\acute{c}$ previously and we emerge with a balanced set of eight equiprobable values of η for each simulation. In principle this process could be extended indefinitely by taking $q_1 = q$ and $q_{j+1} = q_j + 2^{-k}$ modulo 1, for $j = 1, \ldots, 2^{k-1}$ and $k = 2, 3, \ldots$; however, four values of q are probably enough in practice. By using the standard normal distribution function applied to elements of u, the same idea could be used to obtain a new balanced value η_1 from η so by taking $\check{\eta}_1 = 2\hat{\eta} - \eta_1$ we would have four values of η to combine with the four values of c. In the following we shall assume that we have generated N draws of η by using the simulation smoother and the antithetic variables; in practice, we shall work with the two basic antithetic variables so N will be a multiple of 4.

In theory, importance sampling could give an inaccurate result on a particular occasion if in the basic formula (36) very high values of $w(\eta, y)$ are associated with very small values of the importance density $g(\eta|y)$ in such a way that together they make a significant contribution to $\bar{x}$, and if also, on this particular occasion, these values happen to be over-represented or under-represented; for a further discussion of this point see Gelman et al. (1995), page 307. In practice we have not experienced difficulties from this source in any of the examples that we have considered. Nevertheless we recognize that difficulties could occur if the tail densities of $p(\eta|y)$ were substantially thicker than those of $g(\eta|y)$. We therefore devised a way of transforming Gaussian elements of η given y coming from the simulation smoother into values from the t-distribution with low degrees of freedom, thus giving an importance density with thicker tails. However, since the technique has not been needed in any of the applications that we have considered, the details of this approach are omitted.

5.3 Estimating means, variances, densities and distribution functions

We first consider the estimation of conditional means and error variances of our estimates. Let

$$w(\eta) = p(\eta, y)/g(\eta, y),$$

taking the dependence of $w(\eta)$ on y as implicit since y is constant from now on. Then equation (36) gives

$$\bar{x} = \frac{E_g[x(\eta)w(\eta)]}{E_g[w(\eta)]}, \qquad (37)$$

which is estimated by

$$\hat{x} = \sum_{i=1}^{N} x_i w_i \Big/ \sum_{i=1}^{N} w_i, \quad \text{where } x_i = x(\eta^{(i)}), \ w_i = w(\eta^{(i)}) = p(\eta^{(i)}, y)/g(\eta^{(i)}, y), \qquad (38)$$

and $\eta^{(i)}$ is the ith draw from the importance density $g(\eta|y)$ for $i = 1, \ldots, N$. For the case where $x(\eta)$ is a vector we could at this point present formulae for estimating the matrix $\mathrm{var}\{x(\eta)|y\}$ and also the variance matrix due to simulation of $\hat{x} - \bar{x}$. However, from a practical point of view the covariance terms are of little interest so it seems sensible to focus on variance terms by taking $x(\eta)$ as a scalar; an extension to include covariance terms is straightforward. We estimate $\mathrm{var}\{x(\eta)|y\}$ by

$$\widehat{\mathrm{var}}\{x(\eta)|y\} = \sum_{i=1}^{N} x_i^2 w_i \Big/ \sum_{i=1}^{N} w_i - \hat{x}^2. \qquad (39)$$

The estimation error from the simulation is

$$\hat{x} - \bar{x} = \sum_{i=1}^{N} w_i(x_i - \bar{x}) \Big/ \sum_{i=1}^{N} w_i.$$

Denote the sum of the four values of $w_i(x_i - \bar{x})$ that come from the jth run of the simulation smoother by v_j and the sum of the corresponding values of $w_i(x_i - \hat{x})$ by $\hat{v}_j$. For N sufficiently large, since the draws from the simulation smoother are independent, the variance due to simulation is, to a good approximation,

$$\mathrm{var}_s(\hat{x}) = \frac{N}{4} \mathrm{var}(v_j) \Big/ \left(\sum_{i=1}^{N} w_i \right)^2, \qquad (40)$$

which we estimate by

$$\widehat{\mathrm{var}}_s(\hat{x}) \sum_{j=1}^{N/4} \hat{v}_j^2 \Big/ \left(\sum_{i=1}^{N} w_i \right)^2. \qquad (41)$$

The fact that we can estimate simulation variances so easily is one of the advantages of our methods over MCMC methods.

When $x(\eta)$ is a scalar the above technique can be used to estimate the conditional distribution function and the conditional density function of x. Let $G(x|y) = \Pr\{x(\eta) \leqslant x|y\}$ and let $I_x(\eta)$ be an indicator which is 1 if $x(\eta) \leqslant x$ and is 0 if $x(\eta) > x$. Then $G(x|y) = E[I_x(\eta)|y]$. Since $I_x(\eta)$ is a function of η we can treat it in the same way as $x(\eta)$. Let S_x be the sum of the values of w_i for which $x_i \leqslant x$, for $i = 1, \ldots, N$. Then estimate $G(x|y)$ by

$$\hat{G}(x|y) = S_x \bigg/ \sum_{i=1}^{N} w_i. \tag{42}$$

This can be used to estimate quantiles. Similarly, if δ is the interval $(x - \frac{1}{2}d, x + \frac{1}{2}d)$ where d is suitably small and positive, let S^δ be the sum of the values of w_i for which $x(\eta) \in \delta$. Then the estimator of the conditional density $p(x|y)$ of x given y is

$$\hat{p}(x|y) = d^{-1} S^\delta \bigg/ \sum_{i=1}^{N} w_i. \tag{43}$$

This estimator can be used to construct a histogram.

We now show how to generate a sample of M independent values from the estimated conditional distribution of $x(\eta)$ by using importance resampling; for further details of the method see Gelfand and Smith (1999) and Gelman et al. (1995). Take $x^{[k]} = x_j$ with probability $w_j / \sum_{i=1}^{N} w_i$ for $j = 1, \ldots, N$. Then

$$\Pr(x^{[k]} \leqslant x) = \sum_{x_j \leqslant x} w_j \bigg/ \sum_{i=1}^{N} w_i = \hat{G}(x|y).$$

Thus $x^{[k]}$ is a random draw from the distribution function given by equation (42). Doing this M times with replacement gives a sample of $M \leqslant N$ independent draws. The sampling can also be done without replacement but the values are not then independent.

A weakness of the classical approach is that it does not automatically allow for the effect on estimates of variance of estimation errors in $\hat{\psi}$. For the present problem the effect is usually $O(n^{-1})$ relative to the variance being estimated so the investigator could decide just to ignore it. If an allowance for the effect is desired, we suggest that an easy way to achieve it is to perform a Bayesian analysis as described in Section 5.5 with a diffuse prior for ψ. Estimates of posterior variances in this analysis automatically contain an allowance for the effect and can be used in a classical analysis to provide estimates of conditional variance that are unbiased to $O(n^{-1})$.

5.4 Maximum likelihood estimation of parameter vector

Estimation of the parameter vector ψ by maximum likelihood using importance sampling was considered by Shephard and Pitt (1997) and in more detail by

Durbin and Koopman (1997) for the case where α_t is generated by the linear Gaussian model (2). We now extend the treatment to models with non-Gaussian state errors under the assumptions made in Section 2 about the density of η. Denote the likelihood for model (3) and (4) by $L(\psi)$ and the likelihood for the linear Gaussian approximating model by $L_g(\psi)$. In terms of the notation of Section 2, $L(\psi) = p(y)$ and $L_g(\psi) = g(y)$, so it follows from equation (10) that

$$L(\psi) = L_g(\psi)E_g[w(\eta)],$$

where E_g and $w(\eta)$ are defined in Sections 5.1 and 5.3. We estimate this by

$$\hat{L}(\psi) = L_g(\psi)\bar{w}, \tag{44}$$

where $\bar{w} = (1/N)\sum_{i=1}^{N} w_i$. We note that $\hat{L}(\psi)$ is obtained as an adjustment to $L_g(\psi)$; thus the closer the underlying model is to a linear Gaussian model the smaller is the value of N needed to attain preassigned accuracy. In practice we work with $\log\{\hat{L}(\psi)\}$ which has a bias of $O(N^{-1})$; if desired, a correction can be made as in Durbin and Koopman (1997), equation (16), but for most cases in practice the bias will be sufficiently small to be neglected.

To estimate ψ, $\log\{\hat{L}(\psi)\}$ is maximized by any convenient and effective numerical technique. To ensure stability in the iterative process, it is important to use the same random numbers from the simulation smoother for each value of ψ. Initial parameter values for ψ are obtained by maximizing the approximate log-likelihood

$$\log\{L(\psi)\} \simeq \log\{L_g(\psi)\} + \log\{w(\hat{\eta})\}; \tag{45}$$

this does not require simulation. Alternatively, the more accurate non-simulated approximation given in expression (21) of Durbin and Koopman (1997) may be used.

Denote the resulting maximum likelihood estimate of ψ by $\hat{\psi}$, and denote the 'true' estimate that would be obtained by maximizing $\log\{L(\psi)\}$, if this could be done exactly, by $\tilde{\psi}$. We estimate the mean-square error matrix of errors due to simulation,

$$\mathrm{MSE}_g(\hat{\psi}) = E_g[(\hat{\psi} - \tilde{\psi})(\hat{\psi} - \tilde{\psi})'],$$

as in Durbin and Koopman (1997) by

$$\widehat{\mathrm{MSE}}_g(\tilde{\psi}) = \hat{V}\left\{\frac{1}{N^2\bar{w}^2}\sum_{i=1}^{N}(q^{(i)} - \bar{q})(q^{(i)} - \bar{q})'\right\}\hat{V}, \tag{46}$$

where $q^{(i)} = \partial w_i/\partial\psi$, $\bar{q} = (1/N)\sum_{i=1}^{N} q^{(i)}$ and

$$\hat{V} = \left(-\frac{\partial^2[\log\{L(\psi)\}]}{\partial\psi\,\partial\psi'}\right)^{-1}\Bigg|_{\psi=\hat{\psi}} \tag{47}$$

is the large sample estimate of the variance matrix of $\hat{\psi}$. The derivatives $q^{(i)}$ and $-\hat{V}^{-1}$ are calculated numerically from neighbouring values of ψ in the neighbourhood of $\hat{\psi}$. Square roots of diagonal elements of equation (46) can be compared with square roots of diagonal elements of equation (47) to give relative standard errors due to simulation. These methods are very efficient computationally. For the examples considered in Durbin and Koopman (1997) it was shown that simulation sample sizes of N equal to around 800 based on 200 draws from the simulation smoother were sufficient for accurate estimation of ψ.

5.5 Bayesian inference

To perform a Bayesian analysis we begin by implementing formula (18) by simulation. When the prior density of ψ is diffuse the approximate density of ψ given y is $g(\psi|y) = N(\hat{\psi}, \hat{V})$ where $\hat{\psi}$ and $\hat{V}$ are obtained as described in the previous section. When the prior is not diffuse there is a straightforward modification based on equations (15) and (16). Usually, $\hat{V}$ is $O(n^{-1})$ whereas $\text{var}\{x(\alpha)|\psi, y\}$ is $O(1)$ so it is reasonable to expect that the coefficients of variation of elements of ψ given y will be significantly smaller than those $x(\alpha)$ given ψ and y. Let us therefore assume to begin with that antithetic variables are not needed in simulation from density $g(\psi|y)$ whereas they are definitely needed in simulation from density $g(\eta|\psi, y)$. Substitute for α in terms of η in equation (18) giving, analogously to equation (36),

$$\bar{x} = \frac{E_g[(x(\eta)z(\psi, \eta, y)]}{E_g[z(\psi, \eta, y)]} \quad \text{where } z(\psi, \eta, y) = \frac{p(\psi)g(y|\psi)}{g(\psi|y)} \frac{p(\eta, y|\psi)}{g(\eta, y|\psi)} \quad (48)$$

and where E_g denotes expectation with respect to density $g(\psi, \eta|y)$. Let $\psi^{(i)}$ be a random draw from $g(\psi|y)$, which is obtainable in a routine way from a sample of independent $N(0, 1)$ variables, and let $\eta^{(i)}$ be a random draw from density $g(\eta|\psi^{(i)}, y)$ for $i = 1, \ldots, N$. To do this we need an approximation to the mode $\hat{\eta}^{(i)}$ of density $g(\eta|\psi^{(i)}, y)$ but this is rapidly obtained in a few iterations starting from the mode of $g(\eta|\hat{\psi}, y)$. Let

$$z_i = \frac{p(\psi^{(i)})g(y|\psi^{(i)})}{g(\psi^{(i)}|y)} \frac{p(\eta^{(i)}, y|\psi^{(i)})}{g(n^{(i)}, y|\psi^{(i)})} = \frac{p(\psi^{(i)})g(y|\psi^{(i)})}{g(\psi^{(i)}|y)} w_i, \quad (49)$$

and estimate $\bar{x}$ in equation (18) by

$$\hat{x} = \sum_{i=1}^{N} x_i z_i \Big/ \sum_{i=1}^{N} z_i. \quad (50)$$

Estimates of the posterior distribution function and density of $x(\eta)$ can be obtained in the same way as for the conditional distribution function and density in Section 5.2. Similarly, the posterior variance and simulation variance are obtained from formulae that are analogous to equations (39) and (41) except that w_i are replaced by z_i. Formula (50) for $\hat{x}$ has been written on the assumption that no antithetic variables are used for the draws from density $g(\psi|y)$; however, the formula is easily extended to the case where antithetic variables are used. We could, for example, employ the standard antithetic variable $\check{\psi} = 2\hat{\psi} - \psi$ as in Section 5.2.

We now consider the estimation of the posterior density of a single element of ψ, which we can take to be ψ_1, the first element of ψ. Denote the vector of the remaining elements of ψ by ψ_2, giving $\psi = (\psi_1, \psi_2')'$. Let $g(\psi_2|\psi_1, y)$ be the approximate conditional density of ψ_2 given ψ_1 and y, which is easily obtained by applying standard regression theory to $g(\psi|y)$. We shall use $g(\psi_2|\psi_1, y)$ as an importance density in place of $g(\psi|y)$. Then

$$p(\psi_1|y) = \int p(\psi|y)\,d\psi_2 = \int \frac{p(\psi|y)}{g(\psi_2|\psi_1, y)} g(\psi_2|\psi_1, y)\,d\psi_2. \quad (51)$$

By the methods of Sections 3.2, 3.3, 5.4 and 5.5 we have

$$p(\psi|y) = Kp(\psi)p(y|\psi) = Kp(\psi)g(y|\psi)\int \frac{p(\eta, y|\psi)}{g(\eta, y|\psi)} g(\eta|\psi, y)\,d\eta. \quad (52)$$

Putting equations (51) and (52) together gives

$$p(\psi_1|y) = KE_g\left[\frac{p(\psi)g(y|\psi)}{g(\psi_2|\psi_1, y)}\frac{p(\eta, y|\psi)}{g(\eta, y|\psi)}\right], \quad (53)$$

where E_g denotes the expectation with respect to the joint importance density $g(\psi_2, \eta|\psi_1, y)$. Let $\psi_2^{(i)}$ be a draw from density $g(\psi_2|\psi_1, y)$, take $\psi^{(i)} = (\psi_1, \psi_2^{(i)'})'$, let $\eta^{(i)}$ be a draw from $g(\eta|\psi^{(i)}, y)$ and let

$$z_i^* = \frac{p(\psi^{(i)})g(y|\psi^{(i)})}{g(\psi_2^{(i)}|\psi_1, y)}\frac{p(\eta^{(i)}, y|\psi^{(i)})}{g(\eta^{(i)}, y|\psi^{(i)})}, \quad i = 1, \ldots, N. \quad (54)$$

Noting that the form of z_i^* differs from the form of z_i in equation (49) only in the substitution of $g(\psi_2^{(i)}|\psi_1, y)$ for $g(\psi^{(i)}|y)$ and that $K^{-1} = E_g[z(\psi, \eta, y)]$ as is easily shown, the required estimate of $p(\psi_1|y)$ has the simple and elegant form

$$\hat{p}(\psi_1|y) = \sum_{i=1}^N z_i^* \bigg/ \sum_{i=1}^N z_i. \quad (55)$$

In the implementation of equation (55) it is important that the draw of $\psi_2^{(i)}$ from $g(\psi_2|\psi_1, y)$ is obtained directly from the draw of $\psi^{(i)}$ from $g(\psi|y)$ in equation (49). Details can easily be worked out from elementary regression theory but there is not the space to include them here. A simpler alternative is to denote by $S(\psi_1, d)$ the sum of values of z_i that fall in the interval $(\psi_1 - \frac{1}{2}d, \psi_1 + \frac{1}{2}d), d > 0$, and then to estimate the posterior density of ψ_1 by

$$d^{-1}S(\psi_1, d)\bigg/ \sum_{i=1}^N z_i$$

for d sufficiently small. A further possibility is to calculate the posterior density of ψ_1 while ψ_2 is held fixed at its maximum likelihood estimate.

6 Real Data Illustrations

In this section we discuss the use of the methodology by applying it to three real data sets. The calculations are carried out using the object-oriented matrix programming language Ox 2.0 of Doornik (1998) together with the library of state space functions SsfPack 2.2 by Koopman et al. (1999). The data and programs are freely available on the Internet at `http://center.kub.nl/stamp/ssfpack.htm`. We shall refer to specific Ox programs and SsfPack functions in the discussion below where appropriate. Documentation on the functions used here and a discussion of computational matters can be found of the Internet work page of SsfPack. We do not present a complete analysis of each of the three examples because of limitations on space; instead, we focus on items of particular interest in each of the three cases in such a way that we cover collectively the main features of the output that can be obtained by using our approach.

6.1 Van drivers killed in UK: a Poisson application

The data are monthly numbers of light goods vehicle (van) drivers killed in road accidents from 1969 to 1984 in Great Britain. These data led directly to the work presented in this paper. They were part of the data set that Durbin and Harvey (1985) analysed on behalf of the Department of Transport to provide an independent assessment of the effects of the British seat-belt law on road casualties. Durbin and Harvey analysed all the data except these van data by an approximating linear Gaussian state space model. However, they used an *ad hoc* method to analyse the van data because they thought that the numbers of deaths were too small to justify the use of the linear Gaussian model. The Ox program `dkrss_van.ox` is used for calculating all the reported results below.

We model the data by the Poisson density with mean $\exp(\theta_t)$,

$$p(y_t|\theta_t) = \exp\{\theta_t' y_t - \exp(\theta_t) - \log(y_t!)\}, \quad t = 1, \ldots, n, \quad (56)$$

with signal θ_t generated by

$$\theta_t = \mu_t + \gamma_t + \lambda x_t,$$

where the trend μ_t is the random walk

$$\mu_t = \mu_{t-1} + \eta_t, \quad (57)$$

λ is the intervention parameter which measures the effects of the seat-belt law, x_t is an indicator variable for the post-legislation period and the monthly seasonal component γ_t is generated by

$$\sum_{j=0}^{11} \gamma_{t-j} = \omega_t. \quad (58)$$

The disturbances η_t and ω_t are mutually independent Gaussian white noise terms with variances $\sigma_\eta^2 = \exp(2\psi_\eta)$ and $\sigma_\omega^2 = \exp(2\psi_\omega)$ respectively. The parameter

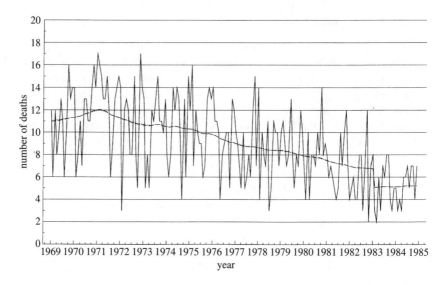

Fig. 1. Numbers of van drivers killed and estimated level including intervention:
———, drivers killed; ...., conditional level;- - - -, posterior level.

estimates are reported by Durbin and Koopman (1997) as $\hat{\sigma}_\eta = \exp(\hat{\psi}_\eta) = \exp(-3.708) = 0.0245$ and $\hat{\sigma}_\omega = 0$. The fact that $\hat{\sigma}_\omega = 0$ implies that the seasonal component is constant over time.

It follows that $b_t(\theta_t) = \exp(\theta_t)$ in equation (29), so $\dot{b}_t = \ddot{b}_t = \exp(\tilde{\theta}_t)$ and, from Section 4.3, $\tilde{H}_t = \exp(-\tilde{\theta}_t)$ and $\tilde{y}_t = \tilde{\theta}_t + \tilde{H}_t y_t - 1$ where $\tilde{\theta}_t$ is some trial value for θ_t ($t = 1, \ldots, n$). The iterative process of determining the approximating model as described in Section 4.2 converges quickly; usually, between three and five iterations are needed. The conditional mean of $\mu_t + \lambda x_t$ for ψ_η fixed at $\hat{\psi}_\eta$ is computed from a classical perspective and exponentiated values of this mean are plotted together with the raw data in Fig. 1. The posterior mean from a Bayesian perspective with ψ_η diffuse was also calculated and its exponen-tiated values are also plotted in Fig. 1. The difference between the graphs is almost imperceptible. Conditional and posterior standard deviations of $\mu_t + \lambda x_t$ are plotted in Fig. 2. The posterior standard deviations are about 12% larger than the conditional standard deviations; this is because in the Bayesian analysis ψ_η is random. The ratios of simulation standard deviations to standard deviations proper never exceeded the 9% level before the break and never exceeded the 7% level after the break. The ratios for a Bayesian analysis increase slightly, obtaining 10% and 8% respectively.

In a real analysis, the main objective is the estimation of the effect of the seat-belt law on the number of deaths. Here, this is measured by λ which in the Bayesian analysis has a posterior mean of -0.280; this corresponds to a reduction in the number of deaths of 24.4%. The posterior standard deviation is 0.126 and the

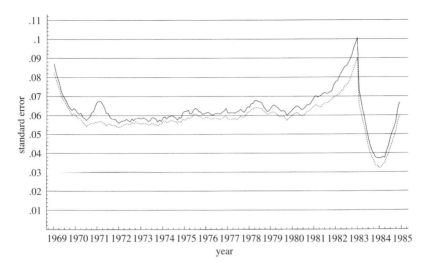

Fig. 2. Standard errors for level including intervention: ...., conditional standard error; ———, posterior standard error.

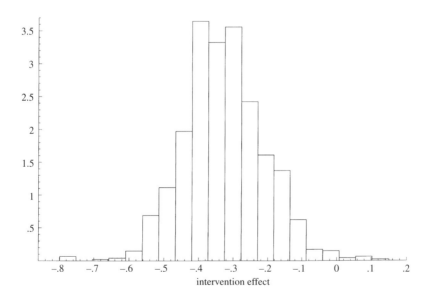

Fig. 3. Posterior distribution of the intervention effect.

standard error due to simulation is 0.0040. The corresponding values for the classical analysis are −0.278, 0.114 and 0.0036, which are not very different. It is clear that the value of λ is significant as is obvious visually from Fig. 1. The posterior distribution of λ is presented in Fig. 3 in the form of a histogram. This is based on the estimate of the posterior distribution function calculated as indicated in Section 5.5. There is a strange dip near the maximum which remains for different simulation sample sizes so we infer that it must be determined by the observations and not by the simulation. All the above calculations were based on a sample of 250 draws from the simulation smoother with four antithetic variables per draw. The results reported show that this relatively small number of samples is adequate for this particular example.

What we learn from this exercise so far as the underlying real investigation is concerned is that up to the point where the law was introduced there was a slow regular decline in the number of deaths coupled with a constant multiplicative seasonal pattern, whereas at that point there was an abrupt drop in the trend of around 25%; afterwards, the trend appeared to flatten out, with the seasonal pattern remaining the same. From a methodological point of view we learn that our simulation and estimation procedures work straightforwardly and efficiently. We find that the results of the conditional analysis from a classical perspective and the posterior analysis from a Bayesian perspective are very similar apart from the posterior densities of the parameters. So far as computing time is concerned, we cannot present a comprehensive study in this paper because of the pressure of space, but, to illustrate with one example, the calculation of trend and variance of trend for $t = 1, \ldots, n$ took 78 s on a Pentium II computer for the classical analysis and 216 s for the Bayesian analysis. While the Bayesian analysis time is greater, the time required is not large by normal standards.

6.2 Gas consumption in UK: a heavy-tailed application

In this example we analyse the logged quarterly demand for gas in the UK from 1960 to 1986. We use a structural time series model of the basic form

$$y_t = \mu_t + \gamma_t + \epsilon_t, \tag{59}$$

where μ_t is the local linear trend, y_t is the dummy seasonal component and ϵ_t is the observation disturbance. Further details of the model are discussed by Harvey (1989), page 172. The purpose of the real investigation underlying the analysis is to study the seasonal pattern in the data with a view to seasonally adjusting the series. It is known that for most of the series the seasonal component changes smoothly over time, but it is also known that there was a disruption in the gas supply in the third and fourth quarters of 1970 which has led to a distortion in the seasonal pattern when a standard analysis based on a Gaussian density for ϵ_t is employed. The question under investigation is whether the use of a heavy-tailed density for ϵ_t would improve the estimation of the seasonal component in 1970.

To model ϵ_t we use the t-distribution with log-density

$$\log\{p(\epsilon_t)\} = \text{constant} + \log\{a(v)\} + \frac{1}{2}\log(k) - \frac{v+1}{2}\log(1 + k\epsilon_t^2), \tag{60}$$

where

$$a(v) = \Gamma\left(\frac{v}{2} + \frac{1}{2}\right)\Big/\Gamma\left(\frac{v}{2}\right), \qquad k^{-1} = (v-2)\sigma_\epsilon^2, \quad v > 2, \quad t = 1, \ldots, n.$$

The mean of ϵ_t is 0 and the variance is σ_ϵ^2, for any ν degrees of freedom which need not be an integer. The approximating model is easily obtained by method 2 of Section 4.4 with

$$h_t^*(\epsilon_t^2) = \cdots + (\nu + 1)\log(1 + k_t\epsilon_t^2),$$

$$\dot{h}_t^{*-1} = H_t = \frac{1}{\nu+1}\tilde{\epsilon}_t^2 + \frac{\nu-2}{\nu+1}\sigma_\epsilon^2.$$

The iterative scheme is started with $H_t = \sigma_\epsilon^2$, for $t = 1, \ldots, n$. The number of iterations required for a reasonable level of convergence using the t-distribution is usually higher than for densities from the exponential family; for this example we required around 10 iterations. In the classical analysis, the parameters of the model, including the degrees of freedom ν, were estimated by Monte Carlo maximum likelihood as reported in Durbin and Koopman (1997); the estimated value for ν was 12.8.

The most interesting feature of this analysis is to compare the estimated seasonal and irregular components based on the Gaussian model and the model with a t-distribution for ϵ_t. Figures 4 and 5 give the graphs of the estimated seasonal and irregular components for the Gaussian model and the t-model. The most striking feature of these graphs is the greater effectiveness with which the t-model picks and corrects for the outlier relative to the Gaussian model. We observe that in the graph of the seasonal component the difference between the classical and Bayesian analyses is imperceptible. Differences are visible in the graphs of the residuals, but they are not large since the residuals themselves are small. The t-model estimates

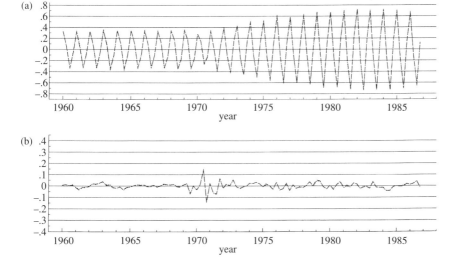

Fig. 4. Analysis of the gas data based on the Gaussian model (.........., conditional; - - - -, posterior): (a) seasonal component; (b) irregular component.

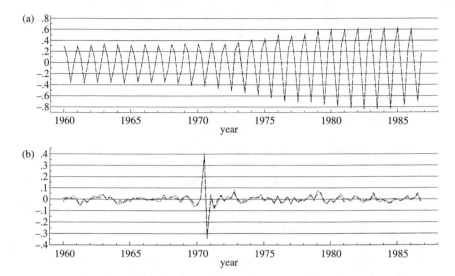

Fig. 5. Analysis of the gas data based on the *t*-model (........., conditional;
- - - -, posterior): (a) seasonal component; (b) irregular component.

are based on 250 simulation samples from the simulation smoother with four
antithetic variables for each sample. The number of simulation samples is sufficient
because the ratio of the variance due to simulation to the variance never exceeds
2% for all estimated components in the state vector except at the beginning and
end of the series, where it never exceeds 4%. The Ox program dkrss_gas.ox
was used for calculating these results.

We learn from the analysis that the change over time of the seasonal pattern in
the data is smooth. We also learn that, if model (59) is to be used to estimate the
seasonal component for this or similar cases with outliers in the observations, then
a Gaussian model for ϵ_t is inappropriate and a heavy-tailed model should be used.

6.3 Pound–dollar daily exchange rates: a volatility application

The data are the pound–dollar daily exchange rates from October 1st, 1981, to June
28th, 1985, which have been used by Harvey et al. (1994). Denoting the exchange
rate by x_t, the series of interest is given by $y_t = \Delta \log(x_t)$, for $t = 1, \dots, n$.
A stochastic volatility (SV) model of the form

$$y_t = \sigma \exp(\tfrac{1}{2}\theta_t)u_t, \qquad u_t \sim N(0, 1), \quad t = 1, \dots, n, \qquad (61)$$

$$\theta_t = \phi\theta_{t-1} + \eta_t, \qquad \eta_t \sim N(0, \sigma_\eta^2), \quad 0 < \phi < 1,$$

was used for analysing these data by Harvey et al. (1994); for a review of related
work and developments of the SV model see Shephard (1996) and Ghysels et al.
(1996). Exact treatments of the SV model based on MCMC or different importance
sampling methods have been developed; see, for example, Jacquier et al. (1994),

Danielsson (1994) and Shephard and Pitt (1997). The purpose of the investigations for which this type of analysis is carried out is to study the structure of the volatility of price ratios in the market, which is of considerable interest to financial analysts. The level of θ_t determines the amount of volatility and the value of ϕ measures the autocorrelation in the logged squared data.

To illustrate our approach to SV models we consider the Gaussian log-density of model (61),

$$\log\{p(y_t|\theta_t)\} = -\frac{1}{2}\log(2\pi\sigma^2) - \frac{1}{2}\theta_t - \frac{y_t^2}{2\sigma^2}\exp(-\theta_t). \qquad (62)$$

The linear approximating model can be obtained by method 1 of Section 4.2 with

$$\tilde{H}_t = 2\sigma^2\frac{\exp(\tilde{\theta}_t)}{y_t^2},$$

$$\tilde{y}_t = \tilde{\theta}_t - \tfrac{1}{2}\tilde{H}_t + 1,$$

for which $\tilde{H}_t$ is always positive. The iterative process can be started with $\hat{H}_t = 2$ and $\tilde{y}_t = \log(y_t^2/\sigma^2)$, for $t = 1, \ldots, n$, since it follows from equation (61) that $y_t^2/\sigma^2 \approx \exp(\theta_t)$. When y_t is 0 or very close to 0, it should be replaced by a small constant value to avoid numerical problems; this device is only needed to obtain the approximating model so we do not depart from our exact treatment. The number of iterations required is usually fewer than 10.

The interest here is usually focused on the estimates of the parameters or their posterior distributions. For the classical analysis we obtain by the maximum likelihood methods of Section 5.4 the estimates

$$\hat{\sigma} = 0.6338, \qquad \hat{\psi}_1 = \log(\hat{\sigma}) = -0.4561, \qquad \mathrm{SE}(\hat{\psi}_1) = 0.1033,$$

$$\hat{\sigma}_\eta = 0.1726, \qquad \hat{\psi}_2 = \log(\hat{\sigma}_\eta) = -1.7569, \qquad \mathrm{SE}(\hat{\psi}_2) = 0.2170,$$

$$\hat{\phi} = 0.9731, \qquad \hat{\psi}_3 = \log\left(\frac{\hat{\phi}}{1 - \hat{\phi}}\right) = 3.5876, \qquad \mathrm{SE}(\hat{\psi}_3) = 0.5007.$$

We present the results in this form since we estimate the log-transformed parameters, so the standard errors that we calculate apply to them and not to the original parameters of interest. For the Bayesian analysis we present in Fig. 6 the posterior densities of each transformed parameter given the other two parameters held fixed at their maximum likelihood values. These results confirm that SV models can be handled by our methods from both classical and Bayesian perspectives. The computations are carried out by the Ox program `dkrss_sv.ox`.

7 Discussion

We regard this paper as much more a paper on time series analysis than on simulation. Methodology is developed that can be used by applied researchers for

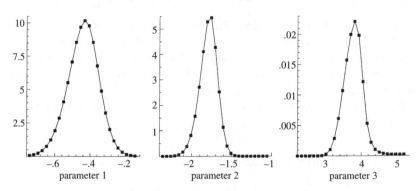

Fig. 6. Posterior densities of the transformed parameters.

dealing with real non-Gaussian time series data without their having to be time series specialists or enthusiasts for simulation methodology. Easy-to-use software is freely available on the Internet from

```
http://center.kub.nl/stamp/ssfpack.htm
```

in a relatively straightforward format including documentation.

Methods are presented for classical and Bayesian inference side by side using common simulation methodology. This widens the choices that are available for applications. The illustrations provided show the differences that are found when both approaches are applied to real data. Generally, the differences are small except for the variances of estimates for which the differences are obviously due to the fact that in classical inference the parameters are regarded as fixed whereas in Bayesian inference the parameters are regarded as random variables.

Almost all previous work on non-Gaussian time series analysis by simulation has been done by using MCMC methodology. In contrast, our approach is based entirely on importance sampling and antithetic variables which have been available for many years but which we have shown to be very efficient for our problem. Because our approach is based on independent samples it has the following advantages relative to MCMC methods: first, we avoid completely the convergence problems that are associated with MCMC algorithms; second, we can easily compute error variances due to simulation as a routine part of the analysis; thus the investigator can attain any predetermined level of simulation accuracy by increasing the simulation sample size, where necessary, by a specific amount.

We and our collaborators have applied our techniques to well over 50 series and have not so far encountered problems due to such features as multimodality and heavy-tailed densities. We have developed analogous techniques for dealing with non-linear state space models but these have been omitted for brevity.

Acknowledgement

S. J. Koopman is a Research Fellow of the Royal Netherlands Academy of Arts and Sciences and its financial support is gratefully acknowledged.

References

Anderson, B. D. O. and Moore, J. B. (1979), *Optimal Filtering*, Englewood Cliffs: Prentice Hall.

Bernardo, J. M. and Smith, A. F. M. (1994), *Bayesian Theory*, Chichester: Wiley.

Cargnoni, C., Müller, P. and West, M. (1997), "Bayesian forecasting of multinomial time series through conditionally Gaussian dynamic models," *J. Am. Statist. Ass.*, 92, 640–647.

Carlin, B. P., Polson, N. G. and Stoffer, D. S. (1992), "A Monte Carlo approach to nonnormal and nonlinear state-space modeling," *J. Am. Statist. Ass.*, 87, 493–500.

Carter, C. K. and Kohn, R. (1994), "On Gibbs sampling for state space models," *Biometrika*, 81, 541–553.

—— (1996), "Markov chain Monte Carlo in conditionally Gaussian state space models," *Biometrika*, 83, 589–601.

—— (1997), "Semiparametric Bayesian inference for time series with mixed spectra," *J. R. Statist. Soc.* B, 59, 255–268.

Danielsson, J. (1994), "Stochastic volatility in asset prices: estimation with simulated maximum likelihood," *J. Econometr.*, 61, 375–400.

Doornik, J. A. (1998), *Object-oriented Matrix Programming using Ox 2.0.*, London: Timberlake.

Durbin, J. and Harvey, A. C. (1985), *The Effect of Seat Belt Legislation on Road Casualties*, London: Her Majesty's Stationery Office.

Durbin, J. and Koopman, S. J. (1992), "Filtering, smoothing and estimation for time series models when the observations come from exponential family distributions," London School of Economics and Political Science, London. Unpublished.

—— (1997), "Monte Carlo maximum likelihood estimation for non-Gaussian state space models," *Biometrika*, 84, 669–684.

Fahrmeir, L. (1992), "Conditional mode estimation by extended Kalman filtering for multivariate dynamic generalised linear models," *J. Am. Statist. Ass.*, 87, 501–509.

Fahrmeir, L. and Kaufmann, H. (1991), "On Kalman filtering, conditional mode estimation and Fisher scoring in dynamic exponential family regression," *Metrika*, 38, 37–60.

Frühwirth-Schnatter, S. (1994), "Applied state space modelling of non-Gaussian time series using integration-based Kalman filtering," *Statist. Comput.*, 4, 259–269.

Gelfand, A. E. and Smith A. F. M. (eds.) (1999), *Bayesian Computation*, Chichester: John Wiley and Sons.

Gelman, A., Carlin, J. B., Stern, H. S. and Rubin, D. B. (1995), *Bayesian Data Analysis*, London: Chapman and Hall.

Geweke J. (1996), "Monte Carlo simulation and numerical integration," In *Handbook of Computational Economics*, H. Amman, D. Kendrick and J. Rust, (eds.). Amsterdam: North-Holland.

Geyer, C. J. and Thompson, E. A. (1992), "Constrained Monte Carlo maximum likelihood for dependent data (with discussion)," *J. R. Statist. Soc.* B, 54, 657–699.

Ghysels, E., Harvey, A. C. and Renault, E. (1996), "Stochastic volatility," In *Statistical Methods in Finance*, C. R. Rao and G. S. Maddala (eds.). Amsterdam: North-Holland.

Harrison, P. J. and Stevens, C. F. (1971), "A Bayesian approach to short-term forecasting," *Oper. Res. Q.*, 22, 341–362.

—— (1976), "Bayesian forecasting (with discussion)," *J. R. Statist. Soc.* B, 38, 205–247.

Harvey, A. C. (1989), *Forecasting, Structural Time Series Models and the Kalman Filter*, Cambridge: Cambridge University Press.

Harvey, A. C. and Durbin, J. (1986), "The effects of seat belt legislation on British road casualties: a case study in structural time series modelling (with discussion)," *J. R. Statist. Soc.* A, 149, 187–227.

Harvey, A. C. and Fernandes, C. (1989), "Time series models for count or qualitative observations (with discussion)," *J. Bus. Econ. Statist.*, 7, 407–422.

Harvey, A. C., Ruiz, E. and Shephard, N. (1994), "Multivariate stochastic variance models," *Rev. Econ. Stud.*, 61, 247–264.

Jacquier, E., Polson, N. G. and Rossi, P. E. (1994), "Bayesian analysis of stochastic volatility models (with discussion)," *J. Bus. Econ. Statist.*, 12, 371–417.

de Jong, P. and Shephard, N. (1995), "The simulation smoother for time series models," *Biometrika*, 82, 339–350.

Kalman, R. E. (1960), "A new approach to linear prediction and filtering problems," *ASME Trans.* D, 82, 35–45.

Kitagawa, G. (1987), "Non-Gaussian state-space modelling of nonstationary time series (with discussion)," *J. Am. Statist. Ass.*, 82, 1032–1063.

—— (1989), Non-Gaussian seasonal adjustment," *Comput. Math. Applic.*, 18, 503–514.

—— (1990), "The two-filter formula for smoothing and an implementation of the Gaussian-sum smoother," *Technical Report*. Institute of Statistical Mathematics, Tokyo.

Koopman, S. J. (1993), "Disturbance smoother for state space models," *Biometrika*, 80, 117–126.

Koopman, S. J., Shephard, N. and Doornik, J. A. (1999), "Statistical algorithms for models in state space using SsfPack 2.2," *Econometr. J.*, to be published.

Martin, R. D. and Raftery, A. E. (1987), "Discussion on 'Non-Gaussian state-space modelling of nonstationary time series' (by G. Kitagawa)," *J. Am. Statist. Ass.*, 82, 1032–1063.

Ripley, B. D. (1987), *Stochastic Simulation*, New York: Wiley.

Shephard, N. (1994), "Partial non-Gaussian state space," *Biometrika*, 81, 115–131.

—— (1996), "Statistical aspects of ARCH and stochastic volatility," In *Time Series Models in Econometrics, Finance and Other Fields*, D. R. Cox, D. V. Hinkley and O. E. Barndorff-Nielsen (eds.). London: Chapman and Hall.

Shephard, N. and Pitt, M. K. (1997), "Likelihood analysis of non-Gaussian measurement time series," *Biometrika*, 84, 653–667.

Singh, A. C. and Roberts, G. R. (1992), "State space modelling cross-classified time series and counts," *Int. Statist. Rev.*, 60. 321–335.

Smith. J. Q. (1979), "A generalization of the Bayesian steady forecasting model," *J. R. Statist. Soc.* B, 41, 375–387.

—— (1981), "The multiparameter steady model. *J. R. Statist. Soc.* B," 43, 256–260.

West, M. (1993), "Approximating posterior distributions by mixtures," *J. R. Statist. Soc.* B, 55, 409–422.

West, M. and Harrison, P. J. (1997), *Bayesian Forecasting and Dynamic Models*, 2nd edn. New York: Springer.

West, M., Harrison, P. J. and Migon, H. S. (1985), "Dynamic generalized linear models and Bayesian forecasting (with discussion)," *J. Am. Statist. Ass.*, 80, 73–97.

22

On Sequential Monte Carlo Sampling Methods for Bayesian Filtering*

ARNAUD DOUCET, SIMON GODSILL AND
CHRISTOPHE ANDRIEU

*Signal Processing Group, Department of Engineering, University of Cambridge,
Trumpington Street, CB2 1PZ Cambridge, UK*

In this article, we present an overview of methods for sequential simulation from posterior distributions. These methods are of particular interest in Bayesian filtering for discrete time dynamic models that are typically nonlinear and non-Gaussian. A general importance sampling framework is developed that unifies many of the methods which have been proposed over the last few decades in several different scientific disciplines. Novel extensions to the existing methods are also proposed. We show in particular how to incorporate local linearisation methods similar to those which have previously been employed in the deterministic filtering literature; these lead to very effective importance distributions. Furthermore we describe a method which uses Rao-Blackwellisation in order to take advantage of the analytic structure present in some important classes of state-space models. In a final section we develop algorithms for prediction, smoothing and evaluation of the likelihood in dynamic models.

1 Introduction

Many problems in applied statistics, statistical signal processing, time series analysis and econometrics can be stated in a state space form as follows. A transition equation describes the prior distribution of a hidden Markov process $\{\mathbf{x}_k; k \in \mathbb{N}\}$, the so-called hidden state process, and an observation equation describes the likelihood of the observations $\{\mathbf{y}_k; k \in \mathbb{N}\}$, k being a discrete time index. Within a Bayesian framework, all relevant information about $\{\mathbf{x}_0, \mathbf{x}_1, \ldots, \mathbf{x}_k\}$ given observations up to and including time k can be obtained from the posterior distribution $p(\mathbf{x}_0, \mathbf{x}_1, \ldots, \mathbf{x}_k | \mathbf{y}_0, \mathbf{y}_1, \ldots, \mathbf{y}_k)$. In many applications we are interested in *estimating recursively in time* this distribution, and particularly one of its marginals, the so-called filtering distribution $p(\mathbf{x}_k | \mathbf{y}_0, \mathbf{y}_1, \ldots, \mathbf{y}_k)$. Given the filtering distribution one can then routinely proceed to filtered point estimates such as the posterior mode or mean of the state. This problem is known as the Bayesian filtering problem or the optimal filtering problem. Practical applications include target tracking (Gordon, Salmond and Smith 1993), blind deconvolution of digital communications channels (Clapp and Godsill 1999, Liu and Chen 1995), estimation of

* This work was previously published as A. Doucet, S. J. Godsill, and C. Andrieu, "On Sequential Monte Carlo Sampling Methods for Bayesian Filtering", *Statistical and Computing*, 1997, Vol. 10, pp. 197–208. Reproduced here by kind permission of Kluwer Academic/Plenum Publishers.

stochastic volatility (Pitt and Shephard 1999) and digital enhancement of speech and audio signals (Godsill and Rayner 1998).

Except in a few special cases, including linear Gaussian state space models (Kalman filter) and hidden finite-state space Markov chains, it is impossible to evaluate these distributions analytically. From the mid 1960's, a great deal of attention has been devoted to approximating these filtering distributions, see for example Jazwinski (1970). The most popular algorithms, the extended Kalman filter and the Gaussian sum filter, rely on analytical approximations (Anderson and Moore 1979). Interesting work in the automatic control field was carried out during the 1960's and 70's using sequential Monte Carlo (MC) integration methods, see Akashi and Kumamoto (1975), Handschin and Mayne (1969), Handschin (1970), and Zaritskii, Svetnik and Shimelevich (1975). Possibly owing to the severe computational limitations of the time, these Monte Carlo algorithms have been largely neglected until recent years. In the late 80's, massive increases in computational power allowed the rebirth of numerical integration methods for Bayesian filtering (Kitagawa 1987). Current research has now focused on MC integration methods, which have the great advantage of not being subject to the assumption of linearity or Gaussianity in the model, and relevant work includes Müller (1992), West (1993), Gordon, Salmond and Smith (1993), Kong, Liu and Wong (1994) and Liu and Chen (1998).

The main objective of this article is to include in a unified framework many old and more recent algorithms proposed independently in a number of applied science areas. Both Liu and Chen (1998) and Doucet (1997, 1998) underline the central rôle of sequential importance sampling in Bayesian filtering. However, contrary to Liu and Chen (1998) which emphasizes the use of hybrid schemes combining elements of importance sampling with Markov Chain Monte Carlo (MCMC), we focus here on computationally cheaper alternatives. We describe also how it is possible to improve current existing methods via Rao-Blackwellisation for a useful class of dynamic models. Finally, we show how to extend these methods to compute the prediction and fixed-interval smoothing distributions as well as the likelihood.

The paper is organised as follows. In Section 2, we briefly review the Bayesian filtering problem and classical Bayesian importance sampling is proposed for its solution. We then present a sequential version of this method which allows us to obtain a general recursive MC filter: the sequential importance sampling (SIS) filter. Under a criterion of minimum conditional variance of the importance weights, we obtain the optimal importance function for this method. Unfortunately, for most models of applied interest the optimal importance function leads to non-analytic importance weights, and hence we propose several suboptimal distributions and show how to obtain as special cases many of the algorithms presented in the literature. Firstly we consider local linearisation methods of either the state space model or the optimal importance function, giving some important examples. These linearisation methods seem to be a very promising way to proceed in problems of this type. Secondly we consider some simple importance functions which lead to algorithms currently known in the literature. In Section 3, a resampling scheme is used to limit practically the degeneracy of the algorithm. In Section 4, we apply the Rao-Blackwellisation method to SIS and obtain efficient hybrid analytical/MC filters. In Section 5, we show how to use the MC filter to compute the prediction and fixed-interval smoothing distributions as well as the likelihood. Finally, simulations are presented in Section 6.

2 Filtering via Sequential Importance Sampling

2.1 Preliminaries: Filtering for the state space model

The state sequence $\{x_k; k \in \mathbb{N}\}$, $x_k \in \mathbb{R}^{n_x}$, is assumed to be an unobserved (hidden) Markov process with initial distribution $p(x_0)$ (which we subsequently denote as $p(x_0|x_{-1})$ for notational convenience) and transition distribution $p(x_k|x_{k-1})$, where n_x is the dimension of the state vector. The observations $\{y_k; k \in \mathbb{N}\}$, $y_k \in \mathbb{R}^{n_y}$, are conditionally independent given the process $\{x_k; k \in \mathbb{N}\}$ with distribution $p(y_k|x_k)$ and n_y is the dimension of the observation vector. To sum up, the model is a hidden Markov (or state space) model (HMM) described by

$$p(x_k|x_{k-1}) \quad \text{for } k \geq 0 \tag{1}$$

$$p(y_k|x_k) \quad \text{for } k \geq 0 \tag{2}$$

We denote by $x_{0:n} \triangleq \{x_0, \dots, x_n\}$ and $y_{0:n} \triangleq \{y_0, \dots, y_n\}$, respectively, the state sequence and the observations up to time n. Our aim is to estimate recursively in time the distribution $p(x_{0:n}|y_{0:n})$ and its associate features including $p(x_n|y_{0:n})$ and expectations of the form

$$I(f_n) = \int f_n(x_{0:n}) p(x_{0:n}|y_{0:n}) dx_{0:n} \tag{3}$$

for any $p(x_{0:n}|y_{0:n})$-integrable $f_n: \mathbb{R}^{(n+1) \times n_x} \rightarrow \mathbb{R}$. A recursive formula for $p(x_{0:n}|y_{0:n})$ is given by:

$$p(x_{0:n+1}|y_{0:n+1}) = p(x_{0:n}|y_{0:n}) \frac{p(y_{n+1}|x_{n+1}) p(x_{n+1}|x_n)}{p(y_{n+1}|y_{0:n})} \tag{4}$$

The denominator of this expression cannot typically be computed analytically, thus rendering an analytic approach infeasible except in the special cases mentioned above. It will later be assumed that samples can easily be drawn from $p(x_k|x_{k-1})$ and that we can evaluate $p(x_k|x_{k-1})$ and $p(y_k|x_k)$ pointwise.

2.2 Bayesian Sequential Importance Sampling (SIS)

Since it is generally impossible to sample from the state posterior $p(x_{0:n}|y_{0:n})$ directly, we adopt an importance sampling (IS) approach. Suppose that samples $\{x_{0:n}^{(i)}; i = 1, \dots, N\}$ are drawn independently from a normalised importance function $\pi(x_{0:n}|y_{0:n})$ which has a support including that of the state posterior. Then an estimate $\tilde{I}_N(f_n)$ of the posterior expectation $I(f_n)$ is obtained using Bayesian IS

(Geweke 1989):

$$\widehat{I_N}(f_n) = \sum_{i=1}^{N} f_n\left(\mathbf{x}_{0:n}^{(i)}\right) \tilde{w}_n^{(i)}, \quad \tilde{w}_n^{(i)} = \frac{w_n^{*(i)}}{\sum_{j=1}^{N} w_n^{*(j)}} \tag{5}$$

where $w_n^{*(i)} = p(\mathbf{y}_{0:n}|\mathbf{x}_{0:n})p(\mathbf{x}_{0:n})/\pi(\mathbf{x}_{0:n}|\mathbf{y}_{0:n})$ is the unnormalised importance weight. Under weak assumptions $\widehat{I_N}(f_n)$ converges to $I(f_n)$, see for example Geweke (1989). However, this method is not recursive. We now show how to obtain a sequential MC filter using Bayesian IS.

Suppose one chooses an importance function of the form

$$\pi(\mathbf{x}_{0:n}|\mathbf{y}_{0:n}) = \pi(\mathbf{x}_0|\mathbf{y}_0) \prod_{k=1}^{n} \pi(\mathbf{x}_k|\mathbf{x}_{0:k-1}, \mathbf{y}_{0:k}) \tag{6}$$

Such an importance function allows recursive evaluation in time of the importance weights as successive observations $\mathbf{y}_k$ become available. We obtain directly the sequential importance sampling filter.

Sequential Importance Sampling (SIS)

For times $k = 0, 1, 2, \ldots$

- For $i = 1, \ldots, N$, sample $\mathbf{x}_k^{(i)} \sim \pi(\mathbf{x}_k|\mathbf{x}_{0:k-1}^{(i)}, \mathbf{y}_{0:k})$ and set $\mathbf{x}_{0:k}^{(i)} \triangleq (\mathbf{x}_{0:k-1}^{(i)}, \mathbf{x}_k^{(i)})$.

- For $i = 1, \ldots, N$, evaluate the importance weights up to a normalising constant:

$$w_k^{*(i)} = w_{k-1}^{*(i)} \frac{p\left(\mathbf{y}_k|\mathbf{x}_k^{(i)}\right) p\left(\mathbf{x}_k^{(i)}|\mathbf{x}_{k-1}^{(i)}\right)}{\pi\left(\mathbf{x}_k^{(i)}|\mathbf{x}_{0:k-1}^{(i)}, \mathbf{y}_{0:k}\right)} \tag{7}$$

- For $i = 1, \ldots, N$, normalise the importance weights:

$$\tilde{w}_k^{(i)} = \frac{w_k^{*(i)}}{\sum_{j=1}^{N} w_k^{*(j)}} \tag{8}$$

A special case of this algorithm was introduced in 1969 by Handschin and Mayne (1969) and Handschin (1970). Many of the other algorithms proposed in the literature are later shown also to be special cases of this general (and simple) algorithm. Choice of importance function is of course crucial and one obtains poor performance when the importance function is not well chosen. This issue forms the topic of the following subsection.

2.3 Degeneracy of the algorithm

If Bayesian IS is interpreted as a Monte Carlo sampling method rather than as a Monte Carlo integration method, the best possible choice of importance function is of course the posterior distribution itself, $p(\mathbf{x}_{0:k}|\mathbf{y}_{0:k})$. We would ideally like to be close to this case. However, for importance functions of the form (6), the variance of the importance weights can only increase (stochastically) over time.

Proposition 1 The unconditional variance of the importance weights, i.e. with the observations $\mathbf{y}_{0:k}$ being interpreted as random variables, increases over time.

The proof of this proposition is a straightforward extension of a Kong-Liu-Wong theorem (Kong, Liu and Wong 1994) to the case of an importance function of the form (6). Thus, it is impossible to avoid a degeneracy phenomenon. In practice, after a few iterations of the algorithm, all but one of the normalised importance weights are very close to zero and a large computational effort is devoted to updating trajectories whose contribution to the final estimate is almost zero.

2.4 Selection of the importance function

To limit degeneracy of the algorithm, a natural strategy consists of selecting the importance function which minimises the variance of the importance weights conditional upon the simulated trajectory $\mathbf{x}_{0:k-1}^{(i)}$ and the observations $\mathbf{y}_{0:k}$.

Proposition 2 $\pi(\mathbf{x}_k|\mathbf{x}_{0:k-1}^{(i)}, \mathbf{y}_{0:k}) = p(\mathbf{x}_k|\mathbf{x}_{k-1}^{(i)}, \mathbf{y}_k)$ is the importance function which minimises the variance of the importance weight $w_k^{*(i)}$ conditional upon $\mathbf{x}_{0:k-1}^{(i)}$ and $\mathbf{y}_{0:k}$.

Proof Straightforward calculations yield

$$
var_{\pi(\mathbf{x}_k|\mathbf{x}_{0:k-1}^{(i)}, \mathbf{y}_{0:k})}\left[w_k^{*(i)}\right]
$$

$$
= \left(w_{k-1}^{*(i)}\right)^2 \left[\int \frac{\left(p(\mathbf{y}_k|\mathbf{x}_k)p\left(\mathbf{x}_k|\mathbf{x}_{k-1}^{(i)}\right)\right)^2}{\pi\left(\mathbf{x}_k|\mathbf{x}_{0:k-1}^{(i)}, \mathbf{y}_{0:k}\right)}d\mathbf{x}_k - p^2\left(\mathbf{y}_k|\mathbf{x}_{k-1}^{(i)}\right)\right]
$$

This variance is zero for $\pi(\mathbf{x}_k|\mathbf{x}_{0:k-1}^{(i)}, \mathbf{y}_{0:k}) = p(\mathbf{x}_k|\mathbf{x}_{k-1}^{(i)}, \mathbf{y}_k)$. ∎

2.4.1 Optimal importance function The optimal importance function $p(\mathbf{x}_k|\mathbf{x}_{k-1}^{(i)}, \mathbf{y}_k)$ was introduced by Zaritskii, Svetnik and Shimelevich (1975) then by Akashi and Kumamoto (1977) for a particular case. More recently, this importance function has been used in Chen and Liu (1996), Kong, Liu and Wong (1994) and Liu and Chen (1995). For this distribution, we obtain from (7) the importance weight $w_k^{*(i)} = w_{k-1}^{*(i)} p(\mathbf{y}_k|\mathbf{x}_{k-1}^{(i)})$. The optimal importance function suffers from two major drawbacks. It requires the ability to sample from $p(\mathbf{x}_k|\mathbf{x}_{k-1}^{(i)}, \mathbf{y}_k)$ and to evaluate $p(\mathbf{y}_k|\mathbf{x}_{k-1}^{(i)}) = \int p(\mathbf{y}_k|\mathbf{x}_k)p(\mathbf{x}_k|\mathbf{x}_{k-1}^{(i)})d\mathbf{x}_k$. This integral will have no analytic form in the general case. Nevertheless, analytic evaluation is possible for the important class of models presented below, the Gaussian state space model with non-linear transition equation.

Example 3 Nonlinear Gaussian State Space Models. Let us consider the following model:

$$\mathbf{x}_k = f(\mathbf{x}_{k-1}) + \mathbf{v}_k, \quad \mathbf{v}_k \sim \mathcal{N}\left(\mathbf{0}_{n_v \times 1}, \boldsymbol{\Sigma}_\mathbf{v}\right) \tag{9}$$

$$\mathbf{y}_k = \mathbf{C}\mathbf{x}_k + \mathbf{w}_k, \quad \mathbf{w}_k \sim \mathcal{N}\left(\mathbf{0}_{n_w \times 1}, \boldsymbol{\Sigma}_\mathbf{w}\right) \tag{10}$$

where $f : \mathbb{R}^{n_x} \rightarrow \mathbb{R}^{n_x}$ is a real-valued non-linear function, $\mathbf{C} \in \mathbb{R}^{n_y \times n_x}$ is an observation matrix, and $\mathbf{v}_k$ and $\mathbf{w}_k$ are mutually independent i.i.d. Gaussian sequences with $\boldsymbol{\Sigma}_\mathbf{v} > 0$ and $\boldsymbol{\Sigma}_\mathbf{w} > 0$; $\mathbf{C}$, $\boldsymbol{\Sigma}_\mathbf{v}$ and $\boldsymbol{\Sigma}_\mathbf{w}$ are assumed known. Defining

$$\boldsymbol{\Sigma}^{-1} = \boldsymbol{\Sigma}_\mathbf{v}^{-1} + \mathbf{C}'\boldsymbol{\Sigma}_\mathbf{w}^{-1}\mathbf{C} \tag{11}$$

$$\mathbf{m}_k = \boldsymbol{\Sigma}\left(\boldsymbol{\Sigma}_\mathbf{v}^{-1}f(\mathbf{x}_{k-1}) + \mathbf{C}'\boldsymbol{\Sigma}_\mathbf{w}^{-1}\mathbf{y}_k\right) \tag{12}$$

one obtains

$$\mathbf{x}_k|(\mathbf{x}_{k-1}, \mathbf{y}_k) \sim \mathcal{N}(\mathbf{m}_k, \boldsymbol{\Sigma}) \tag{13}$$

and

$$p(\mathbf{y}_\mathbf{y}|\mathbf{x}_{k-1}) \propto \exp\left(-\frac{1}{2}(\mathbf{y}_k - \mathbf{C}f(\mathbf{x}_{k-1}))'(\boldsymbol{\Sigma}_\mathbf{v} + \mathbf{C}\boldsymbol{\Sigma}_\mathbf{w}\mathbf{C}')^{-1}\right.$$

$$\left. \times (\mathbf{y}_k - \mathbf{C}f(\mathbf{x}_{k-1}))\right) \tag{14}$$

For many other models, such evaluations are impossible. We now present sub-optimal methods which allow approximation of the optimal importance function. Several Monte Carlo methods have been proposed to approximate the importance function and the associated importance weight based on importance sampling (Doucet 1997, 1998) and Markov chain Monte Carlo (Berzuini et al. 1998, Liu and Chen 1998). These iterative algorithms are computationally intensive and there is a lack of theoretical convergence results. However, they may be useful when non-iterative schemes fail. In fact, the general framework of SIS allows us to consider other importance functions built so as to approximate analytically the optimal importance function. The advantages of this alternative approach are that it is computationally less expensive than Monte Carlo methods and that the standard convergence results for Bayesian importance sampling are still valid. There is no general method to build sub-optimal importance functions and it is necessary to build these on a case by case basis, dependent on the model studied. To this end, it is possible to base these developments on previous work in suboptimal filtering (Anderson and Moore 1979, West and Harrison 1997), and this is considered in the next subsection.

2.4.2 Importance distribution obtained by local linearisation A simple choice selects as the importance function $\pi(\mathbf{x}_k | \mathbf{x}_{k-1}, \mathbf{y}_k)$ a parametric distribution $\pi(\mathbf{x}_k | \theta(\mathbf{x}_{k-1}, \mathbf{y}_k))$, with finite-dimensional parameter $\theta(\theta \in \Theta \subset \mathbb{R}^{n_\theta})$ determined by $\mathbf{x}_{k-1}$ and $\mathbf{y}_k, \theta \colon \mathbb{R}^{n_x} \times \mathbb{R}^{n_y} \rightarrow \Theta$ being a deterministic mapping. Many strategies are possible based upon this idea. To illustrate such methods, we present here two novel schemes that result in a Gaussian importance function whose parameters are evaluated using local linearisations, *i.e.* which are dependent on the simulated trajectory $i = 1, \dots, N$. Such an approach seems to be a very promising way of proceeding with many models, where linearisations are readily and cheaply available. In the auxiliary variables framework of Pitt and Shephard (1999), related 'suboptimal' importance distributions are proposed to sample efficiently from a finite mixture distribution approximating the filtering distribution. We follow here a different approach in which the filtering distribution is approximated directly without resort to auxiliary indicator variables.

Local linearisation of the state space model

We propose to linearise the model locally in a similar way to the Extended Kalman Filter. However, in our case, this linearisation is performed with the aim of obtaining an importance function and the algorithm obtained still converges asymptotically towards the required filtering distribution under the usual assumptions for importance functions.

Example 4 Let us consider the following model

$$\mathbf{x}_k = f(\mathbf{x}_{k-1}) + \mathbf{v}_k, \quad \mathbf{v}_k \sim \mathcal{N}\left(0_{n_v \times 1}, \Sigma_{\mathbf{v}}\right) \tag{15}$$

$$\mathbf{y}_k = g(\mathbf{x}_k) + \mathbf{w}_k, \quad \mathbf{w}_k \sim \mathcal{N}\left(0_{n_w \times 1}, \Sigma_{\mathbf{w}}\right) \tag{16}$$

where $f \colon \mathbb{R}^{n_x} \rightarrow \mathbb{R}^{n_x}, g \colon \mathbb{R}^{n_y} \rightarrow \mathbb{R}^{n_y}$ are differentiable, $\mathbf{v}_k$ and $\mathbf{w}_k$ are two mutually independent i.i.d. sequences with $\Sigma_{\mathbf{v}} > 0$ and $\Sigma_{\mathbf{w}} > 0$. Performing an approximation up to first order of the observation equation (Anderson and Moore 1979), we get

$$\mathbf{y}_k = g(\mathbf{x}_k) + \mathbf{w}_k$$

$$\simeq g(f(\mathbf{x}_{k-1})) + \left.\frac{\partial g(\mathbf{x}_k)}{\partial \mathbf{x}_k}\right|_{\mathbf{x}_k = f(\mathbf{x}_{k-1})} (\mathbf{x}_k - f(\mathbf{x}_{k-1})) + \mathbf{w}_k \tag{17}$$

We have now defined a new model with a similar evolution equation to (15) but with a linear Gaussian observation equation (17), obtained by linearising $g(\mathbf{x}_k)$ in $f(\mathbf{x}_{k-1})$. This model is not Markovian as (17) depends on $\mathbf{x}_{k-1}$. However, it is of the form (9)–(10) and one can perform similar calculations to obtain a Gaussian importance function $\pi(\mathbf{x}_k | \mathbf{x}_{k-1}, \mathbf{y}_k) \sim \mathcal{N}(\mathbf{m}_k, \Sigma_k)$ with mean $\mathbf{m}_k$ and covariance

Σ_k evaluated for each trajectory $i = 1, \ldots, N$ using the following formula:

$$\Sigma_k^{-1} = \Sigma_v^{-1} + \left[\frac{\partial g(\mathbf{x}_k)}{\partial \mathbf{x}_k} \bigg|_{\mathbf{x}_k = f(\mathbf{x}_{k-1})} \right]^t \Sigma_w^{-1} \frac{\partial g(\mathbf{x}_k)}{\partial \mathbf{x}_k} \bigg|_{\mathbf{x}_k = f(\mathbf{x}_{k-1})} \tag{18}$$

$$\mathbf{m}_k = \Sigma_k \left(\Sigma_v^{-1} f(\mathbf{x}_{k-1}) + \left[\frac{\partial g(\mathbf{x}_k)}{\partial \mathbf{x}_k} \bigg|_{\mathbf{x}_k = f(\mathbf{x}_{k-1})} \right]^t \Sigma_w^{-1} \right. \tag{19}$$

$$\left. \times \left(\mathbf{y}_k - g(f(\mathbf{x}_{k-1})) + \frac{\partial g(\mathbf{x}_k)}{\partial \mathbf{x}_k} \bigg|_{\mathbf{x}_k = f(\mathbf{x}_{k-1})} f(\mathbf{x}_{k-1}) \right) \right) \tag{20}$$

The associated importance weight is evaluated using (7).

Local linearisation of the optimal importance function
We assume here that $l(\mathbf{x}_k) \triangleq \log p(\mathbf{x}_k | \mathbf{x}_{k-1}, \mathbf{y}_k)$ is twice differentiable wrt $\mathbf{x}_k$ on $\mathbb{R}^{n_x}$. We define:

$$l'(\mathbf{x}) \triangleq \frac{\partial l(\mathbf{x}_k)}{\partial \mathbf{x}_k} \bigg|_{\mathbf{x}_k = \mathbf{x}} \tag{21}$$

$$l''(\mathbf{x}) \triangleq \frac{\partial^2 l(\mathbf{x}_k)}{\partial \mathbf{x}_k \partial \mathbf{x}_k^t} \bigg|_{\mathbf{x}_k = \mathbf{x}} \tag{22}$$

Using a second order Taylor expansion in $\mathbf{x}$, we get:

$$l(\mathbf{x}_k) \simeq l(\mathbf{x}) + [l'(\mathbf{x})]^t (\mathbf{x}_k - \mathbf{x}) + \frac{1}{2} (\mathbf{x}_k - \mathbf{x})^t l''(\mathbf{x}) (\mathbf{x}_k - \mathbf{x}) \tag{23}$$

The point $\mathbf{x}$ about which we perform the expansion is arbitrary (but given by a deterministic mapping of $\mathbf{x}_{k-1}$ and $\mathbf{y}_k$). Under the additional assumption that $l''(\mathbf{x})$ is negative definite, which is true if $l(\mathbf{x}_k)$ is concave, then setting

$$\Sigma(\mathbf{x}) = -l''(\mathbf{x})^{-1} \tag{24}$$

$$\mathbf{m}(\mathbf{x}) = \Sigma(\mathbf{x}) l'(\mathbf{x}) \tag{25}$$

yields

$$[l'(\mathbf{x})]^t (\mathbf{x}_k - \mathbf{x}) + \frac{1}{2} (\mathbf{x}_k - \mathbf{x})^t l''(\mathbf{x}) (\mathbf{x}_k - \mathbf{x})$$

$$= const - \frac{1}{2} (\mathbf{x}_k - \mathbf{x} - \mathbf{m}(\mathbf{x}))^t \Sigma^{-1}(\mathbf{x}) (\mathbf{x}_k - \mathbf{x} - \mathbf{m}(\mathbf{x})) \tag{26}$$

This suggests adoption of the following importance function:

$$\pi(\mathbf{x}_k | \mathbf{x}_{k-1}, \mathbf{y}_k) = \mathcal{N}(\mathbf{m}(\mathbf{x}) + \mathbf{x}, \Sigma(\mathbf{x})) \tag{27}$$

If $p(\mathbf{x}_k | \mathbf{x}_{k-1}, \mathbf{y}_k)$ is unimodal, it is judicious to adopt $\mathbf{x}$ as the mode of $p(\mathbf{x}_k | \mathbf{x}_{k-1}, \mathbf{y}_k)$, thus $\mathbf{m}(\mathbf{x}) = \mathbf{0}_{n_x \times 1}$. The associated importance weight is evaluated using (7).

Example 5 Linear Gaussian Dynamic/Observations according to a distribution from the exponential family. We assume that the evolution equation satisfies:

$$\mathbf{x}_k = \mathbf{A}\mathbf{x}_{k-1} + \mathbf{v}_k \quad \text{where } \mathbf{v}_k \sim \mathcal{N}\left(\mathbf{0}_{n_v \times 1}, \mathbf{\Sigma}_v\right) \tag{28}$$

where $\mathbf{\Sigma}_v > 0$ and the observations are distributed according to a distribution from the exponential family, i.e.

$$p(\mathbf{y}_k | \mathbf{x}_k) = \exp\left(\mathbf{y}_k^t \mathbf{C}\mathbf{x}_k - b(\mathbf{C}\mathbf{x}_k) + c(\mathbf{y}_k)\right) \tag{29}$$

where $\mathbf{C}$ is a real $n_y \times n_x$ matrix, $b\colon \mathbb{R}^{n_y} \to \mathbb{R}$ and $c\colon \mathbb{R}^{n_y} \to \mathbb{R}$. These models have numerous applications and allow consideration of Poisson or binomial observations, see for example West and Harrison (1997). We have

$$l(\mathbf{x}_k) = const + \mathbf{y}_k^t \mathbf{C}\mathbf{x}_k - b(\mathbf{C}\mathbf{x}_k) - \frac{1}{2}(\mathbf{x}_k - \mathbf{A}\mathbf{x}_{k-1})^t \mathbf{\Sigma}_v^{-1}(\mathbf{x}_k - \mathbf{A}\mathbf{x}_{k-1}) \tag{30}$$

This yields

$$l''(\mathbf{x}) = -\left.\frac{\partial^2 b(\mathbf{C}\mathbf{x}_k)}{\partial \mathbf{x}_k \partial \mathbf{x}_k^t}\right|_{\mathbf{x}_k = \mathbf{x}} - \mathbf{\Sigma}_v^{-1} = -b''(\mathbf{x}) - \mathbf{\Sigma}_v^{-1} \tag{31}$$

but $b''(\mathbf{x})$ is the covariance matrix of $\mathbf{y}_k$ for $\mathbf{x}_k = \mathbf{x}$, thus $l''(\mathbf{x})$ is definite negative. One can determine the mode $\mathbf{x} = \mathbf{x}^*$ of this distribution by applying an iterative Newton-Raphson method initialised with $\mathbf{x}_{(0)} = \mathbf{x}_{k-1}$, which satisfies at iteration j:

$$\mathbf{x}_{(j+1)} = \mathbf{x}_{(j)} - [l''(\mathbf{x}_{(j)})]^{-1} l'(\mathbf{x}_{(j)}) \tag{32}$$

We now present two simpler importance functions, leading to algorithms which previously appeared in the literature.

2.4.3 Prior importance function A simple choice uses the prior distribution of the hidden Markov model as importance function. This is the choice made by Handschin and Mayne (1969) and Handschin (1970) in their seminal work. This is one of the methods recently proposed in Tanizaki and Mariano (1998). In this case, we have $\pi(\mathbf{x}_k | \mathbf{x}_{0:k-1}, \mathbf{y}_{0:k}) = p(\mathbf{x}_k | x_{k-1})$ and $w_k^{*(i)} = w_{k-1}^{*(i)} p(\mathbf{y}_k | \mathbf{x}_k^{(i)})$. The method is often inefficient in simulations as the state space is explored without any knowledge of the observations. It is especially sensitive to outliers. However, it does have the advantage that the importance weights are easily evaluated. Use of the prior importance function is closely related to the Bootstrap filter method of Gordon, Salmond and Smith (1993), see Section III.

2.4.4 Fixed importance function An even simpler choice fixes an importance function independently of the simulated trajectories and of the observations. In this case, we have $\pi(\mathbf{x}_k | \mathbf{x}_{0:k-1}, \mathbf{y}_{0:k}) = \pi(\mathbf{x}_k)$ and

$$w_k^{*(i)} = w_{k-1}^{*(i)} \frac{p(\mathbf{y}_k | \mathbf{x}_k^{(i)}) p(\mathbf{x}_k^{(i)} | \mathbf{x}_{k-1}^{(i)})}{\pi(\mathbf{x}_k^{(i)})} \tag{33}$$

This is the importance function adopted by Tanizaki (1993, 1994) who present this method as a stochastic alternative to the numerical integration method of Kitagawa (1987). The results obtained can be rather poor as neither the dynamic of the model nor the observations are taken into account and lead in most cases to unbounded (unnormalised) importance weights (Geweke 1989).

3 Resampling

As has previously been illustrated, the degeneracy of the SIS algorithm is unavoidable. The basic idea of resampling methods is to eliminate trajectories which have small normalised importance weights and to concentrate upon trajectories with large weights. A suitable measure of degeneracy of the algorithm is the effective sample size N_{eff} introduced in Kong, Liu and Wong (1994) and Liu (1996) and defined as:

$$
N_{eff} = \frac{N}{1 + var_{\pi(\cdot|y_{0:k})}(w^*(\mathbf{x}_{0:k}))}
$$

$$
= \frac{N}{\mathbb{E}_{\pi(\cdot|y_{0:k})}[(w^*(\mathbf{x}_{0:k}))^2]} \leq N \tag{34}
$$

One cannot evaluate N_{eff} exactly but, an estimate $\widehat{N_{eff}}$ of N_{eff} is given by:

$$
\widehat{N_{eff}} = \frac{1}{\sum_{i=1}^{N} \left(\tilde{w}_k^{(i)} \right)^2} \tag{35}
$$

When $\widehat{N_{eff}}$ is below a fixed threshold N_{thres}, the SIR resampling procedure is used (Rubin 1988). Note that it is possible to implement the SIR procedure exactly in $O(N)$ operations by using a classical algorithm (Ripley 1987, p. 96) and Carpenter, Clifford and Fearnhead (1997), Doucet (1997, 1998) and Pitt and Shephard (1999). Other resampling procedures which reduce the MC variation, such as stratified sampling (Carpenter, Clifford and Fearnhead 1997, Kitagawa and Gersch 1996) and residual resampling (Higuchi 1997, Liu and Chen 1998), may be applied as an alternative to SIR.

An appropriate algorithm based on the SIR scheme proceeds as follows at time k.

SIS/Resampling Monte Carlo filter

1. Importance sampling
   - For $i = 1, \ldots, N$ sample $\tilde{\mathbf{x}}_k^{(i)} \sim \pi(\mathbf{x}_k|\mathbf{x}_{0:k-1}^{(i)}, \mathbf{y}_{0:k})$ and set $\tilde{\mathbf{x}}_{0:k}^{(i)} \triangleq (\mathbf{x}_{0:k-1}^{(i)}, \tilde{\mathbf{x}}_k^{(i)})$.

- For $i = 1, \ldots, N$, evaluate the importance weights up to a normalising constant:

$$w_k^{*(i)} = w_{k-1}^{*(i)} \frac{p\left(\mathbf{y}_k | \tilde{\mathbf{x}}_k^{(i)}\right) p\left(\tilde{\mathbf{x}}_k^{(i)} | \tilde{\mathbf{x}}_{k-1}^{(i)}\right)}{\pi\left(\tilde{\mathbf{x}}_k^{(i)} | \tilde{\mathbf{x}}_{0:k-1}^{(i)}, \mathbf{y}_{0:k}\right)} \tag{36}$$

- For $i = 1, \ldots, N$, normalise the importance weights:

$$\tilde{w}_k^{(i)} = \frac{w_k^{*(i)}}{\sum_{j=1}^{N} w_k^{*(j)}} \tag{37}$$

- Evaluate $\widehat{N_{eff}}$ using (35).
2. Resampling
   If $\widehat{N_{eff}} \geq N_{thres}$
   - $\mathbf{x}_{0:k}^{(i)} = \tilde{\mathbf{x}}_{0:k}^{(i)}$ for $i = 1, \ldots, N$; otherwise
   - For $i = 1, \ldots, N$, sample an index $j(i)$ distributed according to the discrete distribution with N elements satisfying $\Pr\{j(i) = l\} = \tilde{w}_k^{(l)}$ for $l = 1, \ldots, N$.
   - For $i = 1, \ldots, N$, $\mathbf{x}_{0:k}^{(i)} = \tilde{\mathbf{x}}_{0:k}^{j(i)}$ and $w_k^{(i)} = \frac{1}{N}$.

If $\widehat{N_{eff}} \geq N_{thres}$, the algorithm presented in Subsection II-B is thus not modified and if $\widehat{N_{eff}} < N_{thres}$ the SIR algorithm is applied. One obtains at time k:

$$\hat{P}(d\mathbf{x}_{0:k} | \mathbf{y}_{0:k}) = \frac{1}{N} \sum_{i=1}^{N} \delta_{\mathbf{x}_{0:k}^{(i)}}(d\mathbf{x}_{0:k}) \tag{38}$$

Resampling procedures decrease algorithmically the degeneracy problem but introduce practical and theoretical problems. From a theoretical point of view, after one resampling step, the simulated trajectories are no longer statistically independent and so we lose the simple convergence results given previously. Recently, Berzuini et al. (1998) have however established a central limit theorem for the estimate of $I(f_k)$ obtained when the SIR procedure is applied at each iteration. From a practical point of view, the resampling scheme limits the opportunity to parallelise since all the particles must be combined, although the IS steps can still be realized in parallel. Moreover the trajectories $\{\tilde{\mathbf{x}}_{0:k}^{(i)}, i = 1, \ldots, N\}$ which have high importance weights $\tilde{w}_k^{(i)}$ are statistically selected many times. In (38), numerous trajectories $\mathbf{x}_{0:k}^{(i_1)}$ and $\mathbf{x}_{0:k}^{(i_2)}$ are in fact equal for $i_1 \neq i_2 \in [1, \ldots, N]$. There is thus a loss of "diversity". Various heuristic methods have been proposed to solve this problem (Gordon, Salmond and Smith 1993, Higuchi 1997).

4 Rao-Blackwellisation for Sequential Importance Sampling

In this section we describe variance reduction methods which are designed to make the most of any structure within the model studied. Numerous methods have been developed for reducing the variance of MC estimates including antithetic sampling (Handschin and Mayne 1969, Handschin 1970) and control variates (Akashi and Kumamoto 1975, Handschin 1970). We apply here the Rao-Blackwellisation method, see Casella and Robert (1996) for a general reference on the topic. In a sequential framework, MacEachern, Clyde and Liu (1999) have applied similar ideas for Dirichlet process models and Kong, Liu and Wong (1994) and Liu and Chen (1998) have used Rao-Blackwellisation for fixed parameter estimation. We focus on its application to dynamic models. We show how it is possible to successfully apply this method to an important class of state space models and obtain hybrid filters where a part of the calculations is realised analytically and the other part using MC methods.

The following method is useful for cases when one can partition the state $\mathbf{x}_k$ as $(\mathbf{x}_k^1, \mathbf{x}_k^2)$ and analytically marginalize one component of the partition, say $\mathbf{x}_k^2$. For instance, as demonstrated in Example 6, if one component of the partition is a conditionally linear Gaussian state-space model then all the integrations can be performed analytically on-line using the Kalman filter. Let us define $\mathbf{x}_{0:n}^j \triangleq (\mathbf{x}_0^j, \ldots, \mathbf{x}_n^j)$. We can rewrite the posterior expectation $I(f_n)$ in terms of marginal quantities:

$$
\begin{aligned}
I(f_n) &= \frac{\int g\left(\mathbf{x}_{0:n}^1\right) p\left(\mathbf{x}_{0:n}^1\right) d\mathbf{x}_{0:n}^1}{\int \left[p\left(\mathbf{y}_{0:n}|\mathbf{x}_{0:n}^1, \mathbf{x}_{0:n}^2\right) p\left(\mathbf{x}_{0:n}^2|\mathbf{x}_{0:n}^1\right) d\mathbf{x}_{0:n}^2\right] p\left(\mathbf{x}_{0:n}^1\right) d\mathbf{x}_{0:n}^1} \\
&= \frac{\int g\left(\mathbf{x}_{0:n}^1\right) p\left(\mathbf{x}_{0:n}^1\right) d\mathbf{x}_{0:n}^1}{\int p\left(\mathbf{y}_{0:n}|\mathbf{x}_{0:n}^1\right) p\left(\mathbf{x}_{0:n}^1\right) d\mathbf{x}_{0:n}^1}
\end{aligned}
$$

where

$$
g\left(\mathbf{x}_{0:n}^1\right) \triangleq \int f_n\left(\mathbf{x}_{0:n}^1, \mathbf{x}_{0:n}^2\right) p\left(\mathbf{y}_{0:n}|\mathbf{x}_{0:n}^1, \mathbf{x}_{0:n}^2\right) p\left(\mathbf{x}_{0:n}^2|\mathbf{x}_{0:n}^1\right) d\mathbf{x}_{0:n}^2 \tag{39}
$$

Under the assumption that, conditional upon a realisation of $\mathbf{x}_{0:n}^1$, $g(\mathbf{x}_{0:n}^1)$ and $p(\mathbf{y}_{0:n}|\mathbf{x}_{0:n}^1)$ can be evaluated analytically, two estimates of $I(f_n)$ based on IS are possible. The first "classical" one is obtained using as importance distribution $\pi(\mathbf{x}_{0:n}^1, \mathbf{x}_{0:n}^2|\mathbf{y}_{0:n})$:

$$
\widehat{I_N}(f_n) = \frac{\sum_{i=1}^N f_n\left(\mathbf{x}_{0:n}^{1,(i)}, \mathbf{x}_{0:n}^{2,(i)}\right) w^*\left(\mathbf{x}_{0:n}^{1,(i)}, \mathbf{x}_{0:n}^{2,(i)}\right)}{\sum_{i=1}^N w^*\left(\mathbf{x}_{0:n}^{1,(i)}, \mathbf{x}_{0:n}^{2,(i)}\right)} \tag{40}
$$

where $w^*(\mathbf{x}_{0:n}^{1,(i)}, \mathbf{x}_{0:n}^{2,(i)}) \propto p(\mathbf{x}_{0:n}^{1,(i)}, \mathbf{x}_{0:n}^{2,(i)}|\mathbf{y}_{0:n})/\pi(\mathbf{x}_{0:n}^{1,(i)}, \mathbf{x}_{0:n}^{2,(i)}|\mathbf{y}_{0:n})$. The second "Rao-Blackwellised" estimate is obtained by analytically integrating out $\mathbf{x}_{0:n}^2$, and using as importance distribution $\pi(\mathbf{x}_{0:n}^1|\mathbf{y}_{0:n}) = \int \pi(\mathbf{x}_{0:n}^1, \mathbf{x}_{0:n}^2|\mathbf{y}_{0:n})d\mathbf{x}_{0:n}^2$. The new estimate is given by:

$$\widehat{I_N}(f_\mathrm{n}) = \frac{\sum_{i=1}^N g\left(\mathbf{x}_{0:n}^{1,(i)}\right) w^*\left(\mathbf{x}_{0:n}^{1,(i)}\right)}{\sum_{i=1}^N w^*\left(\mathbf{x}_{0:n}^{1,(i)}\right)} \tag{41}$$

where $w^*(\mathbf{x}_{0:n}^{1,(i)}) \propto p(\mathbf{x}_{0:n}^{1,(i)}|\mathbf{y}_{0:n})/\pi(\mathbf{x}_{0:n}^{1,(i)}|\mathbf{y}_{0:n})$. Using the decomposition of the variance, it is straightforward to show that the variances of the importance weights obtained by Rao-Blackwellisation are smaller than those obtained using the direct Monte Carlo method (40), see for example Doucet (1997, 1998) and MacEachern, Clyde and Liu (1999). We can use this method to estimate $I(f_\mathrm{n})$ and marginal quantities such as $p(\mathbf{x}_{0:n}^1|\mathbf{y}_{0:n})$.

One has to be cautious when applying the MC methods developed in the previous sections to the marginal state space $\mathbf{x}_k^1$. Indeed, even if the observations $\mathbf{y}_{0:n}$ are independent conditional upon $(\mathbf{x}_{0:n}^1, \mathbf{x}_{0:n}^2)$, they are generally no longer independent conditional upon the single process $\mathbf{x}_{0:n}^1$. The required modifications are, however, straightforward. For example, $p(\mathbf{x}_k^1|\mathbf{y}_{0:k}, \mathbf{x}_{0:k-1}^1)$ is the optimal importance function and $p(\mathbf{y}_k|\mathbf{y}_{0:k-1}, x_{0:k-1}^1)$ the associated importance weight. We now present two important applications of this general method.

Example 6 (Conditionally linear Gaussian state space model). Let us consider the following model

$$p\left(\mathbf{x}_k^1|\mathbf{x}_{k-1}^1\right) \tag{42}$$

$$\mathbf{x}_k^2 = \mathbf{A}_k\left(\mathbf{x}_k^1\right)\mathbf{x}_{k-1}^2 + \mathbf{B}_k\left(\mathbf{x}_k^1\right)\mathbf{v}_k \tag{43}$$

$$\mathbf{y}_k = \mathbf{C}_k\left(\mathbf{x}_k^1\right)\mathbf{x}_k^2 + \mathbf{D}_k\left(\mathbf{x}_k^1\right)\mathbf{w}_k \tag{44}$$

where $\mathbf{x}_k^1$ is a Markov process, $\mathbf{v}_k \sim \mathcal{N}(\mathbf{0}_{n_v \times 1}, \mathbf{I}_{n_v})$ and $\mathbf{w}_k \sim \mathcal{N}(\mathbf{0}_{n_w \times 1}, \mathbf{I}_{n_w})$. One wants to estimate $p(\mathbf{x}_{0:n}^1|\mathbf{y}_{0:n})$, $\mathbb{E}(f(\mathbf{x}_n^1)|\mathbf{y}_{0:n})$, $\mathbb{E}(\mathbf{x}_n^2|\mathbf{y}_{0:n})$ and $\mathbb{E}(\mathbf{x}_n^2(\mathbf{x}_n^2)^t|\mathbf{y}_{0:n})$. It is possible to use a MC filter based on Rao-Blackwellisation. Indeed, conditional upon $\mathbf{x}_{0:n}^1$, $\mathbf{x}_{0:n}^2$ is a linear Gaussian state space model and the integrations required by the Rao-Blackwellisation method can be realized using the Kalman filter.

Akashi and Kumamoto (Akashi and Kumamoto 1977, Tugnait 1982) introduced this algorithm under the name of RSA (Random Sampling Algorithm) in the particular case where $\mathbf{x}_k^1$ is a homogeneous scalar finite state-space Markov chain. In this case, they adopted the optimal importance function $p(\mathbf{x}_k^1|\mathbf{y}_{0:k}, \mathbf{x}_{0:k-1}^1)$. Indeed, it is possible to sample from this discrete distribution and to evaluate the importance weight $p(\mathbf{y}_k|\mathbf{y}_{0:k}, \mathbf{x}_{0:k-1}^1)$ using the Kalman filter (Akashi and

Kumamoto 1977). Similar developments for this special case have also been proposed by Svetnik (1986), Billio and Monfort (1998) and Liu and Chen (1998). The algorithm for blind deconvolution proposed by Liu and Chen (1995) is also a particular case of this method where $\mathbf{x}_k^2 = \mathbf{h}$ is a time-invariant channel having Gaussian prior distribution. Using the Rao-Blackwellisation method in this framework is particularly attractive as, while $\mathbf{x}_k$ has some continuous components, we restrict ourselves to the exploration of a discrete state space.

Example 7 (Finite State-Space HMM). Let us consider the following model

$$p\left(\mathbf{x}_k^1 | \mathbf{x}_{k-1}^1\right) \tag{45}$$

$$p\left(\mathbf{x}_k^2 | \mathbf{x}_k^1, \mathbf{x}_{k-1}^2\right) \tag{46}$$

$$p\left(\mathbf{y}_k | \mathbf{x}_k^1, \mathbf{x}_k^2\right) \tag{47}$$

where $\mathbf{x}_k^1$ is a Markov process and $\mathbf{x}_k^2$ is a finite state-space Markov chain whose parameters at time k depend on $\mathbf{x}_k^1$. We want to estimate $p(\mathbf{x}_{0:n}^1 | \mathbf{y}_{0:n})$, $\mathbb{E}(f(\mathbf{x}_n^1) | \mathbf{y}_{0:n})$ and $\mathbb{E}(f(\mathbf{x}_n^2) | \mathbf{y}_{0:n})$. It is possible to use a "Rao-Blackwellised" MC filter. Indeed, conditional upon $\mathbf{x}_{0:n}^1$, $\mathbf{x}_{0:n}^2$ is a finite state-space Markov chain of known parameters and thus the integrations required by the Rao-Blackwellisation method can be done analytically (Anderson and Moore 1979).

5 Prediction, smoothing and likelihood

The estimate of the joint distribution $p(\mathbf{x}_{0:k} | \mathbf{y}_{0:k})$ based on SIS, in practice coupled with a resampling procedure to limit the degeneracy, is at any time k of the following form.

$$\hat{P}(d\mathbf{x}_{0:k} | \mathbf{y}_{0:k}) = \sum_{i=1}^{N} \tilde{w}_k^{(i)} \delta_{\mathbf{x}_{0:k}^{(i)}}(d\mathbf{x}_{0:k}) \tag{48}$$

We show here how it is possible to obtain, based on this distribution, some approximations of the prediction and smoothing distributions as well as the likelihood.

5.1 Prediction
Based on the approximation of the filtering distribution $\hat{P}(d\mathbf{x}_k | \mathbf{y}_{0:k})$, we want to estimate the p step-ahead prediction distribution, $p \geq 2 \in \mathbb{N}^*$, given by:

$$p(\mathbf{x}_{k+p} | \mathbf{y}_{0:k}) = \int p(\mathbf{x}_k | \mathbf{y}_{0:k}) \left[\prod_{j=k+1}^{k+p} p(\mathbf{x}_j | \mathbf{x}_{j-1}) \right] d\mathbf{x}_{k:k+p-1} \tag{49}$$

where $\mathbf{x}_{i:j} \stackrel{\triangle}{=} \{\mathbf{x}_i, \mathbf{x}_{i+1}, \ldots, \mathbf{x}_j\}$. Replacing $p(\mathbf{x}_k|\mathbf{y}_{0:k})$ in (49) by its approximation obtained from (48), we obtain:

$$\sum_{i=1}^{N} \tilde{w}_k^{(i)} \int p\left(\mathbf{x}_{k+1}|\mathbf{x}_k^{(i)}\right) \prod_{j=k+2}^{k+p} p(\mathbf{x}_j|\mathbf{x}_{j-1}) d\mathbf{x}_{k+1:k+p-1} \qquad (50)$$

To evaluate these integrals, it is sufficient to extend the trajectories $\mathbf{x}_{0:k}^{(i)}$ using the evolution equation.

---

p step-ahead prediction

- For $j = 1$ to p
- For $i = 1, \ldots, N$, sample $\mathbf{x}_{k+j}^{(i)} \sim p(\mathbf{x}_{k+j}|\mathbf{x}_{k+j-1}^{(i)})$ and

  $\mathbf{x}_{0:k+j}^{(i)} \stackrel{\triangle}{=} (\mathbf{x}_{0:k+j-1}^{(i)}, \mathbf{x}_{k+j}^{(i)})$.

We obtain random samples $\{\mathbf{x}_{0:k+p}^{(i)}; i = 1, \ldots, N\}$. An estimate of $\hat{P}(d\mathbf{x}_{0:k+p}|\mathbf{y}_{0:k})$ is given by

$$\hat{P}(d\mathbf{x}_{0:k+p}|\mathbf{y}_{0:k}) = \sum_{i=1}^{N} \tilde{w}_k^{(i)} \delta_{\mathbf{x}_{0:k+p}^{(i)}}(d\mathbf{x}_{0:k+p})$$

Thus

$$\hat{P}(d\mathbf{x}_{k+p}|\mathbf{y}_{0:k}) \sum_{i=1}^{N} \tilde{w}_k^{(i)} \delta_{\mathbf{x}_{k+p}^{(i)}}(d\mathbf{x}_{k+p}) \qquad (51)$$

5.2 Fixed-lag smoothing

We want to estimate the fixed-lag smoothing distribution $p(\mathbf{x}_k|\mathbf{y}_{0:k+p})$, $p \in \mathbb{N}^*$ being the length of the lag. At time $k + p$, the MC filter yields the following approximation of $p(\mathbf{x}_{0:k+p}|\mathbf{y}_{0:k+p})$:

$$\hat{P}(d\mathbf{x}_{0:k+p}|\mathbf{y}_{0:k+p}) \sum_{i=1}^{N} \tilde{w}_{k+p}^{(i)} \delta_{\mathbf{x}_{0:k+p}^{(i)}}(d\mathbf{x}_{0:k+p}) \qquad (52)$$

By marginalising, we obtain an estimate of the fixed-lag smoothing distribution:

$$\hat{P}(d\mathbf{x}_k|\mathbf{y}_{0:k+p}) \sum_{i=1}^{N} \tilde{w}_{k+p}^{(i)} \delta_{\mathbf{x}_k^{(i)}}(d\mathbf{x}_k) \qquad (53)$$

When p is high, such an approximation will generally perform poorly.

5.3 Fixed-interval smoothing

Given $\mathbf{y}_{0:n}$, we want to estimate $p(\mathbf{x}_k|\mathbf{y}_{0:n})$ for any $k = 0, \ldots, n$. At time n, the filtering algorithm yields the following approximation of $p(\mathbf{x}_{0:n}|\mathbf{y}_{0:n})$:

$$\hat{P}(d\mathbf{x}_{0:n}|\mathbf{y}_{0:n}) = \sum_{i=1}^{N} \tilde{w}_n^{(i)} \delta_{\mathbf{x}_{0:n}^{(i)}}(d\mathbf{x}_{0:n}) \tag{54}$$

Thus one can theoretically obtain $p(\mathbf{x}_k|\mathbf{y}_{0:n})$ for any k by marginalising this distribution. Practically, this method cannot be used as soon as $(n - k)$ is significant as the degeneracy problem requires use of a resampling algorithm. At time n, the simulated trajectories $\{\mathbf{x}_{0:n}^{(i)}; i = 1, \ldots, N\}$ have been usually resampled many times: there are thus only a few distinct trajectories at times k for $k \ll n$ and the above approximation of $p(\mathbf{x}_k|\mathbf{y}_{0:n})$ is poor. This problem is even more severe for the bootstrap filter where one resamples at each time instant.

It is necessary to develop an alternative algorithm. We propose an original algorithm to solve this problem. This algorithm is based on the following formula (Kitagawa 1987):

$$p(\mathbf{x}_k|\mathbf{y}_{0:n}) = p(\mathbf{x}_k|\mathbf{y}_{0:k}) \int \frac{p(\mathbf{x}_{k+1}|\mathbf{y}_{0:n})p(\mathbf{x}_{k+1}|\mathbf{x}_k)}{p(\mathbf{x}_{k+1}|\mathbf{y}_{0:k})} d\mathbf{x}_{k+1} \tag{55}$$

We seek here an approximation of the fixed-interval smoothing distribution with the following form:

$$\hat{P}(d\mathbf{x}_k|\mathbf{y}_{0:n}) \triangleq \sum_{i=1}^{N} \tilde{w}_{k|n}^{(i)} \delta_{\mathbf{x}_k^{(i)}}(d\mathbf{x}_k) \tag{56}$$

i.e. $\hat{P}(d\mathbf{x}_k|\mathbf{y}_{0:n})$ has the same support $\{\mathbf{x}_k^{(i)}; i = 1, \ldots, N\}$ as the filtering distribution $\hat{P}(d\mathbf{x}_k|\mathbf{y}_{0:k})$ but the weights are different. An algorithm to obtain these weights $\{\tilde{w}_{k|n}^{(i)}; i - 1, \ldots, N\}$ is the following.

Fixed-interval smoothing

1. Initialisation at time $k = n$.

   - For $i = 1, \ldots, N$, $\tilde{w}_{n|n}^{(i)} = \tilde{w}_n^{(i)}$.

2. For $k = n - 1, \ldots, 0$.

   - For $i = 1, \ldots, N$, evaluate the importance weight

$$\tilde{w}_{k|n}^{(i)} = \sum_{j=1}^{N} \tilde{w}_{k+1|n}^{(j)} \frac{\tilde{w}_k^{(i)} p\left(\mathbf{x}_{k+1}^{(j)}|\mathbf{x}_k^{(i)}\right)}{\left[\sum_{l=1}^{N} \tilde{w}_k^{(l)} p\left(\mathbf{x}_{k+1}^{(j)}|\mathbf{x}_k^{(l)}\right)\right]} \tag{57}$$

This algorithm is obtained by the following argument. Replacing $p(\mathbf{x}_{k+1}|\mathbf{y}_{0:n})$ by its approximation (56) yields

$$\int \frac{p(\mathbf{x}_{k+1}|\mathbf{y}_{0:n})p(\mathbf{x}_{k+1}|\mathbf{x}_k)}{p(\mathbf{x}_{k+1}|\mathbf{y}_{0:k})}d\mathbf{x}_{k+1} \simeq \sum_{i=1}^{N} \tilde{w}_{k+1|n}^{(i)} \frac{p\left(\mathbf{x}_{k+1}^{(i)}|\mathbf{x}_k\right)}{p\left(\mathbf{x}_{k+1}^{(i)}|\mathbf{y}_{0:k}\right)} \qquad (58)$$

where, owing to (48), $p(\mathbf{x}_{k+1}^{(i)}|\mathbf{y}_{0:k})$ can be approximated by

$$p\left(\mathbf{x}_{k+1}^{(i)}|\mathbf{y}_{0:k}\right) = \int p\left(\mathbf{x}_{k+1}^{(i)}|\mathbf{x}_k\right) p(\mathbf{x}_k|\mathbf{y}_{0:k})d\mathbf{x}_k$$

$$\simeq \sum_{j=1}^{N} \tilde{w}_k^{(i)} p\left(\mathbf{x}_{k+1}^{(i)}|\mathbf{x}_k^{(j)}\right) \qquad (59)$$

An approximation $\hat{P}(d\mathbf{x}_k|\mathbf{y}_{0:n})$ of $p(\mathbf{x}_k|\mathbf{y}_{0:n})$ is thus $\hat{P}(d\mathbf{x}_k|\mathbf{y}_{0:n})$

$$= \left[\sum_{i=1}^{N} \tilde{w}_k^{(i)}\delta_{\mathbf{x}_k^{(i)}}(d\mathbf{x}_k)\right] \sum_{j=1}^{N} \tilde{w}_{k+1|n}^{(j)} \frac{p\left(\mathbf{x}_{k+1}^{(j)}|\mathbf{x}_k\right)}{\left[\sum_{l=1}^{N} \tilde{w}_k^{(l)} p\left(\mathbf{x}_{k+1}^{(j)}|\mathbf{x}_k^{(l)}\right)\right]}$$

$$= \sum_{i=1}^{N} \tilde{w}_k^{(i)} \left[\sum_{j=1}^{N} \tilde{w}_{k+1|n}^{(j)} \frac{p\left(\mathbf{x}_{k+1}^{(j)}|\mathbf{x}_k^{(i)}\right)}{\left[\sum_{l=1}^{N} \tilde{w}_k^{(l)} p\left(\mathbf{x}_{k+1}^{(j)}|\mathbf{x}_k^{(l)}\right)\right]}\right] \delta_{\mathbf{x}_k^{(i)}}(d\mathbf{x}_k)$$

$$\stackrel{\triangle}{=} \sum_{i=1}^{N} \tilde{w}_{k|n}^{(i)}\delta_{\mathbf{x}_k^{(i)}}(d\mathbf{x}_k) \qquad (60)$$

The algorithm follows.

This algorithm requires storage of the marginal distributions $\hat{P}(d\mathbf{x}_k|\mathbf{y}_{0:k})$ (weights and supports) for all $k \in \{0, \ldots, n\}$. The memory requirement is $O(nN)$. Its complexity is $O(nN^2)$, which is quite important as $N \gg 1$. However this complexity is a little lower than that of Kitagawa and Gersch (1996) and Tanizaki and Mariano (1998) as it does not require any new simulation step.

5.4 Likelihood
In some applications, in particular for model choice (Kitagawa 1987, Kitagawa and Gersch 1996), we may wish to estimate the likelihood of the data

$$p(\mathbf{y}_{0:n}) = \int w_n^* \pi(\mathbf{x}_{0:n}|\mathbf{y}_{0:n})d\mathbf{x}_{0:n}$$

A simple estimate of the likelihood is thus given by

$$\hat{P}(\mathbf{y}_{0:n}) = \frac{1}{N} \sum_{j=1}^{N} w_n^{*(j)} \qquad (61)$$

In practice, the introduction of resampling steps once again makes this approach impractical. We will use an alternative decomposition of the likelihood:

$$p(\mathbf{y}_{0:n}) = p(\mathbf{y}_0) \prod_{k=1}^{n} p(\mathbf{y}_k|\mathbf{y}_{0:k-1}) \tag{62}$$

where:

$$p(\mathbf{y}_k|\mathbf{y}_{0:k-1}) = \int p(\mathbf{y}_k|\mathbf{x}_k)p(\mathbf{x}_k|\mathbf{y}_{0:k-1})d\mathbf{x}_k \tag{63}$$

$$= \int p(\mathbf{y}_k|\mathbf{x}_{k-1})p(\mathbf{x}_{k-1}|\mathbf{y}_{0:k-1})d\mathbf{x}_{k-1} \tag{64}$$

Using (63), an estimate of this quantity is given by

$$\hat{P}(\mathbf{y}_k|\mathbf{y}_{0:k-1}) = \sum_{i=1}^{N} p\left(\mathbf{y}_k|\tilde{\mathbf{x}}_k^{(i)}\right) \tilde{w}_{k-1}^{(i)} \tag{65}$$

where the samples $\{\tilde{\mathbf{x}}_k^{(i)}; i = 1, \ldots, N\}$ are obtained using a one-step ahead prediction based on the approximation $\hat{P}(d\mathbf{x}_{k-1}|\mathbf{y}_{0:k-1})$ of $p(\mathbf{x}_{k-1}|\mathbf{y}_{0:k-1})$. Using expression (64), it is possible to avoid one of the MC integrations if we know analytically $p(\mathbf{y}_k|\mathbf{x}_{k-1}^{(i)})$:

$$\hat{P}(\mathbf{y}_k|\mathbf{y}_{0:k-1}) = \sum_{i=1}^{N} p\left(\mathbf{y}_k|\mathbf{x}_{k-1}^{(i)}\right) \tilde{w}_{k-1}^{(i)} \tag{66}$$

6 Simulations

In this section, we apply the methods developed previously to a linear Gaussian state space model and to a classical nonlinear model. We perform, for these two models, $M = 100$ simulations of length $n = 500$ and we evaluate the empirical standard deviation for the filtering estimates $\mathbf{x}_{k|k} = \mathbb{E}[\mathbf{x}_k|\mathbf{y}_{0:k}]$ obtained by the MC methods:

$$\sqrt{VAR}(\mathbf{x}_{k|l}) = \frac{1}{n} \sum_{k=1}^{n} \left(\frac{1}{M} \sum_{j=1}^{M} \left(x_{k|l}^j - x_k^j\right)^2 \right)^{1/2}$$

where:

- $\mathbf{x}_k^j$ is the true simulated state for the jth simulation, $j = 1, \ldots, M$.
- $x_{k|l}^j \stackrel{\triangle}{=} \sum_{i=1}^{N} \tilde{w}_{k|l}^{(i)} x_k^{j,(i)}$ is the MC estimate of $\mathbb{E}[\mathbf{x}_y|\mathbf{y}_{0:l}]$ for the jth test signal and $\mathbf{x}_k^{j,(i)}$ is the ith simulated trajectory, $i = 1, \ldots, N$, associated with the signal j. (We define $\tilde{w}_{k|k}^{(i)} \stackrel{\triangle}{=} \tilde{w}_k^{(i)}$).

These calculations have been realised for $N = 100, 250, 500, 1000, 2500$ and 5000. The implemented filtering algorithms are the bootstrap filter, the SIS with the prior importance function and the SIS with the optimal or a suboptimal importance function. The fixed-interval smoothers associated with these SIS filters are then computed.

For the SIS-based algorithms, the SIR procedure has been used when $\widehat{N_{eff}} < N_{thres} = N/3$. We state the percentage of iterations where the SIR step is used for each importance function.

6.1 Linear Gaussian model

Let us consider the following model

$$x_k = x_{k-1} + v_k \tag{67}$$

$$y_k = x_k + w_k \tag{68}$$

where $x_0 \sim \mathcal{N}(0, 1)$, v_k and w_k are white Gaussian noise and mutually independent, $v_k \sim \mathcal{N}(0, \sigma_v^2)$ and $w_k \sim \mathcal{N}(0, \sigma_w^2)$ with $\sigma_v^2 = \sigma_w^2 = 1$. For this model, the optimal filter is the Kalman filter (Anderson and Moore 1979).

6.1.1 Optimal importance function The optimal importance function is

$$x_k \,|(x_{k-1}, y_k) \sim \mathcal{N}(m_k, \sigma_k^2) \tag{69}$$

where

$$\sigma_k^{-2} = \sigma_w^{-2} + \sigma_v^{-2} \tag{70}$$

$$m_k = \sigma_k^2 \left(\frac{x_{k-1}}{\sigma_v^2} + \frac{y_k}{\sigma_w^2} \right) \tag{71}$$

and the associated importance weight is proportional to:

$$p(y_k|x_{k-1}) \propto \exp\left(-\frac{1}{2} \frac{(y_k - x_{k-1})^2}{(\sigma_v^2 + \sigma_\omega^2)} \right) \tag{72}$$

6.1.2 Results For the Kalman filter, we obtain $\sqrt{VAR}(\mathbf{x}_{k|k}) = 0.79$. For the different MC filters, the results are presented in Tables 1 and 2.

With $N = 500$ trajectories, the estimates obtained using MC methods are similar to those obtained by Kalman. The SIS algorithms have similar performances to the bootstrap filter for a smaller computational cost. The most interesting algorithm

Table 1. MC filters: linear Gaussian model

$\sqrt{VAR}(\mathbf{x}_{k|k})$	Bootstrap	Prior dist.	Optimal dist.
$N = 100$	0.80	0.86	0.83
$N = 250$	0.81	0.81	0.80
$N = 500$	0.79	0.80	0.79
$N = 1000$	0.79	0.79	0.79
$N = 2500$	0.79	0.79	0.79
$N = 5000$	0.79	0.79	0.79

Table 2. Percentage of SIR steps: linear Gaussian model

Percentage SIR	Prior dist.	Optimal dist.
$N = 100$	40	16
$N = 250$	23	10
$N = 500$	20	8
$N = 1000$	15	6
$N = 2500$	13	5
$N = 5000$	11	4

is based on the optimal importance function which limits seriously the number of resampling steps.

6.2 Nonlinear series
We consider here the following nonlinear reference model (Gordon, Salmond and Smith 1993, Kitagawa 1987, Tanizaki and Mariano 1998):

$$x_k = f(x_{k-1}) + v_k \tag{73}$$

$$= \frac{1}{2}x_{k-1} + 25\frac{x_{k-1}}{1 + (x_{k-1})^2} + 8\cos(1.2k) + v_k$$

$$y_k = g(x_k) + w_k \tag{74}$$

$$= \frac{(x_k)^2}{20} + w_k$$

where $x_0 \sim \mathcal{N}(0, 5)$, v_k and w_k are mutually independent white Gaussian noise, $v_k \sim \mathcal{N}(0, \sigma_v^2)$ and $w_k \sim \mathcal{N}(0, \sigma_w^2)$ with $\sigma_v^2 = 10$ and $\sigma_w^2 = 1$. In this case, it is not possible to evaluate analytically $p(y_k|x_{k-1})$ or to sample simply from $p(x_k|x_{k-1}, y_k)$. We propose to apply the method described in Subsection II-2 which consists of local linearisation of the observation equation.

6.2.1 Importance function obtained by local linearisation We get

$$y_k \simeq g(f(x_{k-1})) + \frac{\partial g(x_k)}{\partial x_k}\bigg|_{x_k = f(x_{k-1})} (x_k - f(x_{k-1})) + w_k$$

$$= -\frac{f^2(x_{k-1})}{20} + \frac{f(x_{k-1})}{10} x_k + w_k \tag{75}$$

Then we obtain the linearised importance function $\pi(x_k | x_{k-1}, y_k) = \mathcal{N}(x_k; m_k, (\sigma_k)^2)$ where

$$(\sigma_k)^{-2} = \sigma_v^{-2} + \sigma_w^{-2} \frac{f^2(x_{k-1})}{100} \tag{76}$$

and

$$m_k = (\sigma_k)^2 \left[\sigma_v^{-2} f(x_{k-1}) + \sigma_w^{-2} \frac{f(x_{k-1})}{10} \left(y_k + \frac{f^2(x_{k-1})}{20} \right) \right] \tag{77}$$

6.2.2 Results In this case, it is not possible to estimate the optimal filter. For the MC filters, the results are displayed in Table 3. The average percentages of SIR steps are presented in Table 4.

This model requires simulation of more samples than the preceding one. In fact, the variance of the dynamic noise is more important and more trajectories are

Table 3. MC filters: nonlinear time series

$\sqrt{VAR}(\mathbf{x}_{k|k})$	Bootstrap	Prior dist.	Linearised dist.
$N = 100$	5.67	6.01	5.54
$N = 250$	5.32	5.65	5.46
$N = 500$	5.27	5.59	5.23
$N = 1000$	5.11	5.36	5.05
$N = 2500$	5.09	5.14	5.02
$N = 5000$	5.04	5.07	5.01

Table 4. Percentage of SIR steps: nonlinear time series

Percentage SIR	Prior dist.	Linearised dist.
$N = 100$	22.4	8.9
$N = 250$	19.6	7.5
$N = 500$	17.7	6.5
$N = 1000$	15.6	5.9
$N = 2500$	13.9	5.2
$N = 5000$	12.3	5.3

necessary to explore the space. The most interesting algorithm is the SIS with a sub-optimal importance function which greatly limits the number of resampling steps over the prior importance function while avoiding a MC integration step needed to evaluate the optimal importance function. This can be roughly explained by the fact that the observation noise is rather small so that y_k is highly informative and allows a limitation of the regions explored.

7 Conclusion

We have presented an overview of sequential simulation-based methods for Bayesian filtering of general state-space models. We include, within the general framework of SIS, numerous approaches proposed independently in the literature over the last 30 years. Several original extensions have also been described, including the use of local linearisation techniques to yield more effective importance distributions. We have shown also how the use of Rao-Blackwellisation allows us to make the most of any analytic structure present in some important dynamic models and have described procedures for prediction, fixed-lag smoothing and likelihood evaluation.

These methods are efficient but still suffer from several drawbacks. The first is the depletion of samples which inevitably occurs in all of the methods described as time proceeds. Sample regeneration methods based upon MCMC steps are likely to improve the situation here (MacEachern, Clyde and Liu 1999). A second problem is that of simulating fixed hyperparameters such as the covariance matrices and noise variances which were assumed known in our examples. The methods described here do not allow for any regeneration of new values for these non-dynamic parameters, and hence we can expect a very rapid impoverishment of the sample set. Again, a combination of the present techniques with MCMC steps could be useful here, as could Rao-Blackwellisation methods ((Liu and Chen 1998) give some insight into how this might be approached).

The technical challenges still posed by this problem, together with the wide range of important applications and the rapidly increasing computational power, should stimulate new and exciting developments in this field in coming years.

References

Akashi H. and Kumamoto H. 1975. Construction of discrete-time nonlinear filter by Monte Carlo methods with variance-reducing techniques. *Systems and Control*, 19, 211–221 (in Japanese).

Akashi H. and Kumamoto H. 1977. Random sampling approach to state estimation in switching environments. *Automatica*, 13, 429–434.

Anderson B.D.O. and Moore J.B. 1979. *Optimal Filtering*. Englewood Cliffs.

Berzuini C., Best N., Gilks W., and Larizza C. 1997. Dynamic conditional independence models and markov chain Monte Carlo methods. *Journal of the American Statistical Association*, 92, 1403–1412.

Billio M. and Monfort A. 1998. Switching state-space models: Likelihood function, filtering and smoothing. *Journal of Statistical Planning and Inference*, 68, 65–103.

Carpenter J., Clifford P., and Fearnhead P. 1997. An improved particle filter for nonlinear problems. *Technical Report*. University of Oxford, Dept. of Statistics.

Casella G. and Robert C.P. 1996. Rao-Blackwellisation of sampling schemes. *Biometrika*, 83, 81–94.

Chen R. and Liu J.S. 1996. Predictive updating methods with application to Bayesian classification. *Journal of the Royal Statistical Society* B, 58, 397–415.

Clapp T.C. and Godsill S.J. 1999. Fixed-lag smoothing using sequential importance sampling. In: Bernardo J.M., Berger J.O., Dawid A.P., and Smith A.F.M. (eds.), *Bayesian Statistics, 6*, Oxford University Press, pp. 743–752.

Doucet A. 1997. Monte Carlo methods for Bayesian estimation of hidden Markov models. Application to radiation signals. *Ph.D. Thesis*, University Paris-Sud Orsay (in French).

Doucet A. 1998. On sequential simulation-based methods for Bayesian filtering. *Technical Report*. University of Cambridge, Dept. of Engineering, CUED-F-ENG-TR310. Available on the MCMC preprint service at http://www.stats.bris.ac.uk/MCMC/.

Geweke J. 1989. Bayesian inference in Econometrics models using Monte Carlo integration. *Econometrica*, 57, 1317–1339.

Godsill S.J. and Rayner P.J.W. 1998. *Digital audio restoration—A statistical model-based approach*. Berlin: Springer-Verlag.

Gordon N.J. 1997. A hybrid bootstrap filter for target tracking in clutter. *IEEE Transactions on Aerospace and Electronic Systems*, 33, 353–358.

Gordon N.J., Salmond D.J., and Smith A.F.M. 1993. Novel approach to nonlinear/non-Gaussian Bayesian state estimation. *IEE-Proceedings-F*, 140, 107–113.

Handschin J.E. 1970. Monte Carlo techniques for prediction and filtering of nonlinear stochastic processes. *Automatica*, 6, 555–563.

Handschin J.E. and Mayne D.Q. 1969. Monte Carlo techniques to estimate the conditional expectation in multi-stage non-linear filtering. *International Journal of Control*, 9, 547–559.

Higuchi T. 1997. Monte Carlo filtering using the genetic algorithm operators. *Journal of Statistical Computation and Simulation*, 59, 1–23.

Jazwinski A.H. 1970. *Stochastic Processes and Filtering Theory*. Academic Press.

Kitagawa G. 1987. Non-Gaussian state-space modeling of nonstationary time series. *Journal of the American Statistical Association*, 82, 1032–1063.

Kitagawa G. and Gersch G. 1996. Smoothness Priors Analysis of Time Series. Springer. *Lecture Notes in Statistics*, Vol. 116.

Kong A., Liu J.S., and Wong W.H. 1994. Sequential imputations and Bayesian missing data problems. *Journal of the American Statistical Association*, 89, 278–288.

Liu J.S. 1996. Metropolized independent sampling with comparison to rejection sampling and importance sampling. *Statistics and Computing*, 6, 113–119.

Liu J.S. and Chen R. 1995. Blind deconvolution via sequential imputation. *Journal of the American Statistical Association*, 90, 567–576.

Liu J.S. and Chen R. 1998. Sequential Monte Carlo methods for dynamic systems. *Journal of the American Statistical Association*, 93, 1032–1044.

MacEachern S.N., Clyde M., and Liu J.S. 1999. Sequential importance sampling for nonparametric Bayes models: The next generation. *Canadian Journal of Statistics*, 27, 251–267.

Müller P. 1991. Monte Carlo integration in general dynamic models. *Contemporary Mathematics*, 115, 145–163.

Müller P. 1992. Posterior integration in dynamic models. *Computing Science and Statistics*, 24, 318–324.

Pitt M.K. and Shephard N. 1999. Filtering via simulation: Auxiliary particle filters. *Journal of the American Statistical Association*, 94, 590–599.

Ripley B.D. 1987. *Stochastic Simulation*. New York, Wiley.

Rubin D.B. 1988. Using the SIR algorithm to simulate posterior distributions. In: Bernardo J.M., DeGroot M.H., Lindley D.V., and Smith A.F.M. (eds.), *Bayesian Statistics, 3*, Oxford University Press, 395–402.

Smith A.F.M. and Gelfand A.E. 1992. Bayesian statistics without tears: A sampling-resampling perspective. *The American Statistician*, 46, 84–88.

Svetnik V.B. 1986. Applying the Monte Carlo method for optimum estimation in systems with random disturbances. *Automation and Remote Control*, 47, 818–825.

Tanizaki H. 1993. Nonlinear Filters: Estimation and Applications. Springer. Berlin, *Lecture Notes in Economics and Mathematical Systems*, Vol. 400.

Tanizaki H. and Mariano R.S. 1994. Prediction, filtering and smoothing in nonlinear and non-normal cases using Monte Carlo integration. *Journal of Applied Econometrics*, 9, 163–179.

Tanizaki H. and Mariano R.S. 1998. Nonlinear and non-Gaussian state-space modeling with Monte-Carlo simulations. *Journal of Econometrics*, 83, 263–290.

Tugnait J.K. 1982. Detection and Estimation for abruptly changing systems. *Automatica*, 18, 607–615.

West M. 1993. Mixtures models, Monte Carlo, Bayesian updating and dynamic models. *Computer Science and Statistics*, 24, 325–333.

West M. and Harrison J.F. 1997. *Bayesian forecasting and dynamic models*, 2nd edn. Springer Verlag Series in Statistics.

Zaritskii V.S., Svetnik V.B., and Shimelevich L.I. 1975. Monte Carlo technique in problems of optimal data processing. *Automation and Remote Control*, 12, 95–103.

References

Anderson, T.W. (1971). *The Statistical Analysis of Time Series*. Wiley, New York.

Anderson, B.D.O., and Moore, J.B. (1979). *Optimal Filtering*. Prentice-Hall, Englewood Cliffs.

Andrews, D.W.K. (1991). Heteroscedasticity and autocorrelation consistent covariance matrix estimation. *Econometrica*, 59, 817–58.

Ansley, C.F., and Kohn, R. (1985). Estimation, filtering and smoothing in state space models with incompletely specified initial conditions. *The Annals of Statistics*, 13, 1286–316.

Ansley, C.F., and Kohn, R. (1990). Filtering and smoothing in state space models with partially diffuse initial conditions. *Journal of Time Series Analysis*, 11, 275–93.

Bather, J.A. (1965). Invariant conditional distributions. *Annals of Mathematical Statistics*, 36, 829–46.

Beveridge, S., and Nelson, C.R. (1981). A new approach to decomposition of economic time series into permanent and transitory components with particular attention to measurement of the 'Business cycle'. *Journal of Monetary Economics*, 7, 151–74.

Burridge, P., and Wallis, K.F. (1988). Prediction theory for autoregressive-moving average processes. *Econometric Reviews*, 7, 65–9. Reproduced in Chapter 2 of this volume.

Busetti, F. (2002). Testing for (common) nonstationary components in multivariate time series with breaking trends. *Journal of Forecasting*, 21, 81–105.

Busetti, F., and Harvey, A.C. (2001). Testing for the presence of a random walk in series with structural breaks. *Journal of Time Series Analysis*, 22, 127–50.

Busetti, F., and Harvey, A.C. (2003). Seasonality tests. *Journal of Business and Economic Statistics* (to appear).

Canova, F., and Hansen, B.E. (1995). Are seasonal patterns constant over time? A test for seasonal stability. *Journal of Business and Economic Statistics*, 13, 237–52. Reprinted in Chapter 15 of this volume.

Carlin, B.P., Polson, N.G., and Stoffer, D.S. (1992). A Monte Carlo approach to nonnormal and nonlinear state space modeling. *Journal of the American Statistical Association*, 87, 493–500.

Carter, C.K., and Kohn, R. (1994). On Gibbs sampling for state space models. *Biometrika*, 81, 541–53. Reprinted in Chapter 18 of this volume.

Casella, G., and George, E. (1992). Explaining the Gibbs sampler. *The American Statistician*, 46, 167–74.

Chib, S., and Greenberg, E. (1995). Understanding the Metropolis-Hastings algorithm. *American Statistician*, 49, 327–335.

de Jong, P. (1988a). The likelihood for a state space model. *Biometrika*, 75, 165–9.

de Jong, P. (1988b). A cross-validation filter for time series models. *Biometrika*, 75, 594–600.

de Jong, P. (1989). Smoothing and interpolation with the state space model. *Journal of the American Statistical Association*, 84, 1085–8. Reproduced in Chapter 4 of this volume.

de Jong, P. (1991). The diffuse Kalman filter. *Annals of Statistics*, 19, 1073–83.

de Jong, P., and Chu-Chun-Lin, S. (1994). Fast likelihood evaluation and prediction for nonstationary state space models. *Biometrika*, 81, 133–42.

de Jong, P., and Shephard, N. (1996). The simulation smoother. *Biometrika*, 2, 339–50. Reprinted in Chapter 19 of this volume.

de Jong, P., and Chu-Chun-Lin, S. (2003). Smoothing with an unknown initial condition. *Journal of Time Series Analysis*, 81, 133–42.

Doornik, J.A. (2001). *Ox. An Object-Oriented Matrix Programming Language*. Timberlake Consultants Press, London.

Doran, E. (1992). Constraining Kalman filter and smoothing estimates to satisfy time-varying restrictions. *Review of Economics and Statistics*, 74, 568–72.

Doucet, A., Godsill, S.J., and Andrieu, C. (2000). On sequential Monte Carlo sampling methods for Bayesian filtering. *Statistics and Computing*, 10, 197–208. Reprinted in Chapter 22 of this volume.

Doucet, A., de Freitas, J.F.G., and Gordon, N.J. (2001). *Sequential Monte Carlo Methods in Practice*. Springer-Verlag, New York.

Duncan, D.B., and Horn, S.D. (1972). Linear dynamic recursive estimation from the viewpoint of regression analysis. *Journal of the American Statistical Association*, 67, 815–21.

Durbin, J., and Koopman, S.J. (1997). Monte Carlo maximum likelihood estimation for non-Gaussian state space models. *Biometrika*, 84, 669–84.

Durbin, J., and Koopman, S.J. (2000). Time series analysis of non-Gaussian observations based on state-space models from both classical and Bayesian perspectives (with discussion). *Journal of Royal Statistical Society, Series B*, 62, 3–56. Reprinted in chapter 21 of this volume.

Durbin, J., and Koopman, S.J. (2001). *Time Series Analysis by State Space Methods*. Oxford University Press, Oxford.

Durbin, J., and Koopman, S.J. (2002). A simple and efficient simulation smoother for state space time series analysis. *Biometrika*, 89, 603–15.

Fan, J., and Gijbels, I. (1996). *Local Polynomial Modelling and Its Applications*. Monographs on Statistics and Applied Probability, 66. Chapman & Hall, London.

Ferrante, M., and Runggaldier, W.J. (1990). On necessary conditions for the existence of finite-dimensional filters in discrete time. *Systems and Control Letters*, 14, 63–9.

Frühwirth-Schnatter, S. (1994). Data augmentation and dynamic linear models. *Journal of Time Series Analysis*, 15, 183–202.

Gamerman, D. (1997). *Markov Chain Monte Carlo Methods. Stochastic Simulation for Bayesian Inference*. Chapman & Hall, London.

Gamerman, D. (1998). Markov chain Monte Carlo for dynamic generalised linear models. *Biometrika*, 85, 215–27.

Geweke, J. (1989). Bayesian inference in econometric models using Monte Carlo integration. *Econometrica*, 57, 1317–39.

Ghysels, E., Harvey, A.C., and Renault, E. (1996). Stochastic Volatility, In C.R. Rao and G.S. Maddala (eds.), *Statistical Methods in Finance*, pp. 119–91. North-Holland, Amsterdam.

Gilks, W.K., Richardson, S., and Spiegelhalter, D.J. (1996). *Markov Chain Monte Carlo in Practice*. Chapman & Hall, London.

Godolphin, E.J. (1976). Discussion on the paper by P.J. Harrison and C.F. Stevens "Bayesian Forecasting". *Journal of the Royal Statistical Society, Series B*, 38, 238–9.

Gómez, V. (2001). The use of butterworth filters for trend and cycle estimation in economic time series. *Journal of Business and Economic Statistics*, Vol. 19, No. 3, 365–73.

Gordon, N.J., Salmond, D.J., and Smith, A.F.M. (1993). A novel approach to non-linear and non-Gaussian Bayesian state estimation. *IEE-Proceedings F*, 140, 107–13.

Green, P.G., and Silverman, B.W. (1994). *Nonparametric Regression and Generalized Linear Models*. Chapman & Hall, London.

Grunwald, G.K., Guttorp, P., and Raftery, A.E. (1993). Prediction rules for exponential family state space models. *Journal of the Royal Statistical Society, Series B*, 55, 937–43.

Grunwald, G.K., Hamza, K., and Hyndman, R.J. (1997). Some properties and generalizations of non-negative Bayesian time series models. *Journal of the Royal Statistical Society, Series B*, 59, 615–26.

Grunwald, G.K., Raftery, A.E., and Guttorp, P. (1993). Time series of continuous proportions. *Journal of the Royal Statistical Society, Series B*, 55, 103–16.

Harrison, P.J., and Stevens, C.F. (1976). Bayesian forecasting, *Journal of the Royal Statistical Society, Series B*, 38, 205–47.

Harvey, A.C. (1989). *Forecasting, Structural Time Series and the Kalman Filter*. Cambridge University Press, Cambridge, UK.

Harvey, A.C. (2001). Testing in unobserved components models. *Journal of Forecasting*, 20, 1–19.

Harvey, A.C. (2004). A unified approach to testing for stationarity and unit roots. In D.W. Andrews and J.H. Stock (eds.), *Identification and Inference for Econometric Models*. Cambridge University Press, Cambridge.

Harvey, A.C., and Chung, C.-H. (2000). Estimating the underlying change in unemployment in the UK. *Journal of the Royal Statistics Society, Series A, Statistics in Society*, 163, Part 3, 303–39.

Harvey, A.C., and Fernandes, C. (1989). Time series models for count or qualitative observations. *Journal of Business and Economic Statistics*, 7, 407–17. Reprinted in Chapter 17 of this volume.

Harvey, A.C., and Jaeger, A. (1993). Detrending, stylized facts and the business cycle. *Journal of Applied Econometrics*, 8, 231–47. Reprinted in Chapter 9 of this volume.

Harvey, A.C., and Koopman, S.J. (1992). Diagnostic checking of unobserved components time series models. *Journal of Business and Economic Statistics*, 10, 377–89. Reprinted in Chapter 5 of this volume.

Harvey, A.C., and Koopman, S.J. (1993). Forecasting hourly electricity demand using time-varying splines. *Journal of the American Statistical Association*, 88, 1228–36.

Harvey, A.C., and Koopman, S.J. (2000). Signal extraction and the formulation of unobserved component models. *Econometrics Journal*, 3, 84–107.

Harvey, A.C., and Striebel, M. (1997). Testing for nonstationary unobserved components. Mimeo.

Harvey, A.C., Koopman, S.J., and Riani, M. (1997). The modeling and seasonal adjustment of weekly observations. *Journal of Business and Economic Statistics*, 15, 354–68. Reprinted in Chapter 12 of this volume.

Hodrick, R.J., and Prescott, E.C. (1997). Postwar U.S. business cycles: an empirical investigation. *Journal of Money, Credit and Banking*, 29, 1–16.

Johansen, S. (1988). Statistical analysis of cointegration vectors. *Journal of Economic Dynamics and Control*, 12, 13–54.

Kalman, R.E. (1960). A new approach to linear filtering and prediction problems. *Journal of Basic Engineering, Transactions ASME, Series D*, 82, 35–45.

Kalman, R.E., and Bucy, R.S. (1961). New results in linear filtering and prediction theory. *Journal of Basic Engineering, Transactions ASME, Series D*, 83, 95–108.

Kenny, P.B., and Durbin, J. (1982). Local trend estimation and seasonal adjustment of economic and social time series. *Journal of the Royal Statistical Society, Series A*, 145, 1–41.

Kim, C.J., and Nelson, C. (1999). *State-Space Models with Regime-Switching*, MIT Press, Cambridge, MA.

Kim, S., Shephard, N., and Chib, S. (1998). Stochastic volatility: likelihood inference and comparison with ARCH models. *Review of Economic Studies*, 65, 361–93.

Kitagawa, G. (1987). Non-Gaussian state-space modeling of nonstationary time series (with discussion). *Journal of the American Statistical Association*, 82, 1032–63.

Kitagawa, G. (1996). Monte Carlo filter and smoother for Non-Gaussian nonlinear state-space models. *Journal of Computational and Graphical Statistics*, 5, 1–25.

Kitagawa, G., and Gersch, W. (1996). *Smoothness priors analysis of time series*. Springer-Verlag, Berlin.

Kohn, R., and Ansley, C.F. (1989). A fast algorithm for signal extraction, influence and cross-validation in state space models. *Biometrika*, Vol. 76, No. 1, 65–79.

Kohn, R., Ansley, C.F., and Wong, C.H. (1992). Nonparametric spline regression with autoregressive moving average errors. *Biometrika*, 79, 335–46. Reprinted in Chapter 6 of this volume.

Koopman, S.J. (1993). Disturbance smoother for state space models. *Biometrika*, 80, 117–26.

Koopman, S.J. (1997). Exact initial Kalman filter and smoother for non-stationary time series models. *Journal of the American Statistical Association*, 92, 1630–8. Reprinted in Chapter 3 of this volume.

Koopman, S.J., and Harvey, A.C. (2003). Computing observation weights for signal extraction and filtering. *Journal of Economic Dynamics and Control*, 27, 1317–33.

Koopman, S.J., Harvey, A.C., Doornik, J.A., and Shephard, N. (2000). *STAMP 6.0 Structural Time Series Analyser, Modeller and Predictor*. Timberlake Consultants Ltd, London.

Koopman, S.J., Shephard, N., and Doornik, J.A. (1999). Statistical algorithms for models in state space using SsfPack 2.2. *Econometrics Journal*, 2, 113–66.

Kuo, B.-S. (1999). Asymptotics of ML estimator for regression models with a stochastic trend component. *Econometric Theory*, 15, 24–49.

Kuo, B.-S., and Mikkola, A. (2001). How sure are we about purchasing power parity? Panel evidence with the null of stationary exchange rates. *Journal of Money Credit and Banking*, 33, 767–89.

Kwiatkowski, D., Phillips, P.C.B., Schmidt, P., and Shin, Y. (1992). Testing the null hypothesis of stationarity against the alternative of a unit root: how sure are we that economic time series have a unit root? *Journal of Econometrics*, 44, 159–78.

Kydland, F.E., and Prescott, E.C. (1990). Business cycles: real facts and a monetary myth. FRB of Minneapolis quarterly review (Federal Reserve Bank of Minneapolis), 14, 3–18. Reprinted in *The New Classical Macroeconomics*, Vol. 3, 1992, pp. 514–29, International Library of Critical Writings in Economics, vol. 19, Elgar, Aldershot, UK.

Ladiray, D., and Quenneville, B. (2001). *Seasonal Adjustment with the X-11 Method*. Lecture Notes in Statistics, Springer.

Leybourne, S.J., and McCabe, B.P.M. (1994). A consistent test for a unit root. *Journal of Business and Economic Statistics*, 12, 157–66.

Lippi, M., and Reichlin, L. (1992). On persistence of shocks to economic variables. A common misconception. *Journal of Monetary Economics*, 29, 87–93.

MacNeill, I.B. (1978). Properties of sequences of partial sums of polynomial regression residuals with applications to tests for change of regression at unknown times. *The Annals of Statistics*, 6, 422–33.

Maddala, G.S., and Kim, I.-M. (1998). *Unit roots, co-integration, and structural change*, Cambridge University Press, Cambridge.

Maravall, A. (1993). Stochastic linear trends: modes and estimators. *Journal of Econometrics*, 56, 5–37. Reprinted in Chapter 10 of this volume.

Maravall, A., and Del Rio, A. (2001). Time aggregation and the Hodrick-Prescott filter. *Banco de España, Documento de Trabajo*, N.0108.

Meinhold, R.J., and Singpurwalla, N.D. (1983). Understanding the Kalman filter. *The American Statistician*, 37, 123–7.

Morley, J.C., Nelson, C.R., and Zivot, E. (2002). Why are Beveridge-Nelson and unobserved-component decompositions of GDP so different? *Review of Economics and Statistics*, 85, 235–43.

Nelson, C.R., and Plosser, C.I. (1982). Trends and random walks in macro-economic time series: some evidence and implications. *Journal of Monetary Economics*, 10, 139–62.

Nerlove, M., Grether, D.M., and Carvalho, J.L. (1979). *Analysis of Economic Time Series: A Synthesis*. Academic Press, New York.

Nyblom, J. (1986). Testing for deterministic linear trend in time series. *Journal of the American Statistical Association*, 81, 545–9. Reprinted in Chapter 14 of this volume.

Nyblom, J. (1989). Testing for the constancy of parameters over time. *Journal of the American Statistical Association*, 84, 223–30.

Nyblom, J., and Harvey, A.C. (2000). Tests of common stochastic trends. *Econometric Theory*, 16, 176–99.

Nyblom, J., and Mäkeläinen, T. (1983). Comparison of tests for the presence of random walk coefficients in a simple linear model. *Journal of the American Statistical Association*, 78, 856–64.

Ord, J.K., Koehler, A.B., and Snyder, R.D. (1997). Estimation and prediction for a class of dynamic nonlinear statistical models. *Journal of the American Statistical Association*, 92, 1621–9.

Pearlman, J.G. (1980). An algorithm for the exact likelihood of a high-order autoregressive-moving average process. *Biometrika*, 67, 232–3.

Pfeffermann, D. (1991). Estimation and seasonal adjustment of population means using data from repeated surveys. *Journal of Business and Economic Statistics*, 9, 163–75. Reprinted in Chapter 11 of this volume.

Pitt, M.K., and Shephard, N. (1999). Filtering via simulation: auxiliary particle filters. *Journal of the American Statistical Association*, 94, 590–9.

Pole, A., West, M., and Harrison, P.J. (1994). *Applied Bayesian Forecasting and Time Series Analysis*. Chapman-Hall, New York.

Proietti, T. (1995). The Beveridge-Nelson decomposition: properties and extensions. *Journal of the Italian Statistical Society*, Vol. 4, No. 1, 101–24.

Proietti, T. (1998). Seasonal heteroscedasticity and trends. *Journal of Forecasting*, 17, 1–17.

Proietti, T., and Harvey, A.C. (2000). A Beveridge Nelson smoother. *Economics Letters*, 67, 139–46.

Ripley, B.D. (1987). *Stochastic Simulation*. Wiley, New York.

Robert, C.P., and Casella, G. (1999). *Monte Carlo Statistical Methods*. Springer-Verlag, New York.

Rosenberg, B. (1973). Random coefficient models: the analysis of a cross-section of time series by stochastically convergent parameter regression. *Annals of Economic and Social Measurement*, 2, 399–428.

448   *Readings in Unobserved Components Models*

Rubin, D.B. (1987). A noniterative sampling/importance resampling alternative to the data augmentation algorithm for creating a few imputations when the fraction of missing information is modest: the SIR algorithm. Discussion of Tanner and Wong (1987). *Journal of the American Statistical Association*, 82, 543–6.

Schweppe, F. (1965). Evaluation of likelihood functions for Gaussian signals. *IEEE Transactions on Information Theory*, 11, 61–70.

Shephard, N. (1994). Partial non-Gaussian state space. *Biometrika*, 81, 115–31.

Shephard, N. (1994b). Local scale models: state space alternative to integrated GARCH processes. *Journal of Econometrics*, 60, 181–202.

Shephard, N. (1996). Statistical aspects of ARCH and stochastic volatility. In D.R. Cox, D.V. Hinkley and O.E. Barndor-Nielsen (eds.), *Time series Models in Econometrics, Finance and Other Fields*, pp. 1–67. Chapman & Hall, London.

Shephard, N.G., and Harvey, A.C. (1990). On the probability of estimating a deterministic component in the local level model. *Journal of Time Series Analysis*, 11, 339–47.

Shephard, N., and Pitt, M.K. (1997). Likelihood analysis of non-Gaussian measurement time series. *Biometrika*, 84, 653–67. Reprinted in Chapter 20 of this volume.

Smith, J.Q. (1979). A generalization of the Bayesian steady forecasting model. *Journal of the Royal Statistical Society, Series B*, 41, 357–87.

Smith, R.L., and Miller, J.E. (1986). A non-Gaussian state space model and application to prediction of records. *Journal of the Royal Statistical Society, Series B*, 48, 79–88.

Smith, R.J., and Taylor, A.M.R. (1998). Additional critical values and asymptotic representations for seasonal unit root tests. *Journal of Econometrics*, 85, 269–88.

Snyder, R.D. (1985). Recursive estimation of dynamic linear models. *Journal of the Royal Statistical Society, Series B*, 47, 272–6.

Stock, J.H. (1994). Unit roots, structural breaks and trends. In R.F. Engle and D.L. McFadden (eds.), *Handbook of Econometrics 4*. Elsevier Science, 2739–840.

Stock, J.H., and Watson, M.W. (1998). Median unbiased estimation of coefficient variance in time-varying parameter model. *Journal of the American Statistical Association*, 93, 349–57.

Tanaka, K. (1996). *Time Series Analysis*. John Wiley, New York.

Tanaka, K. (2002). A unified approach to the measurement error problem in time series models. *Econometric Theory*, 18, 278–96.

Tanner, M.A. (1996). *Tools for Statistical Inference*, 3rd edition. Springer-Verlag, New York.

Tanner, M.A., and Wong, W.H. (1987). The calculation of posterior distributions by data augmentation (with discussion). *Journal of the American Statistical Association*, 82, 528–50.

Tiao, G.C., and Xu, D. (1993). Robustness of maximum likelihood estimates for multi-step predictions: the exponential smoothing case. *Biometrika*, 80, 623–41.

Tiao, G.C., and Tsay, R.S. (1994). Some advances in non-linear and adaptive modelling in time-series. *Journal of Forecasting*, 13, 109–31.

Tunnicliffe-Wilson, G. (1989). On the use of marginal likelihood in time series model estimation. *Journal of the Royal Statistical Society, Series B*, 51, 15–27.

Uhlig, H. (1997). Bayesian vector autoregressions with stochastic volatility. *Econometrica*, 65, 59–73.

Vidoni, P. (1999). Exponential family state space models based on a conjugate latent process. *Journal of the Royal Statistical Society, Series B*, 61, 213–21.

Wahba, G. (1978). Improper priors, spline smoothing and the problem of guarding against errors in regression. *Journal of the Royal Statistical Society, Series B*, 3, 364–72.

Watson, M.W. (1986). Univariate detrending methods with stochastic trends. *Journal of Monetary Economics*, 18, 49–75. Reprinted in Chapter 8 of this volume.

Wecker, W.E., and Ansley, C.F. (1983). The signal extraction approach to non-linear regression and spline smoothing. *Journal of the American Statistical Association*, 78, 81–9.

West, M., and Harrison, P.J. (1989). *Bayesian Forecasting and Dynamic Models*. Springer-Verlag, New York.

West, M., Harrison, P.J., and Migon, H.S. (1985). Dynamic generalized linear models and Bayesian forecasting (with discussion). *Journal of the American Statistical Association*, 80, 73–97.

Whittle, P. (1983). *Prediction and Regulation by Linear Least Squares Methods*, 2nd edition. Basil Blackwell, Oxford.

Zivot, E., Wang, J., and Koopman, S.J. (2002). State space modeling in macroeconomics and finance using SsfPack in S+FinMetrics. Forthcoming in A.C. Harvey, S.J. Koopman and N. Shephard (eds.), *State Space and Unobserved Component Models: Theory and Applications*. Cambridge University Press, Cambridge, UK.

Author Index

Subject Index

Airline model, 189
antithetic variables, 400–401
approximating linear model, 395
ARIMA model, 90–91, 118, 121, 134–136, 161–162, 167, 180
ARIMA model based (AMB) approach, 172–174
ARMA model, 16, 29–30, 103
AR(1) plus noise model, 20–22
autocovariance generating function, 44, 79, 122, 154
auxiliary residuals, 10, 77–91

basic structural model, 81–82, 176, 202, 205, 227, 347
Bayesian inference, 343, 372, 392–394, 405–406, 420–421
Beveridge-Nelson decomposition, 118, 127, 132
best linear unbiased predictor (BLUP), 203
beta distribution, 322
beta-binomial distribution, 322
binary data, 323
binomial distribution, 321–323, 376
Bowman-Shenton normality test, 87, 88
business cycles, 120, 138, 152

calendar component, 227
canonical decomposition, 90, 121–123, 176–178, 183
canonical link, 375, 376
canonical factorisation of ACF, 37
closed loop matrix, 6, 25, 30
cointegration, 126, 258–259
common trends, 57–58, 258–259
continuous time, 106
controllability, 27–29, 37
control theory, 27–29
correlated components, 89–90, 118–119, 130

count observations, 316–336
Cramér-von Mises distribution, 253, 254, 258, 280–281, 282
cross-validation, 10, 13, 73, 105–106, 112
cubic smoothing spline, see spline
cyclical component, 117, 120, 128, 152–153

deleted residuals, 73
detectability, 6, 27–29, 36, 41
detrending, 126, 130, 152
diagnostic checking, 77, 85–88
Dickey-Fuller test, 253–254, 273, 288–301
difference-stationary processes, 15, 118
diffuse initialisation, 7, 50, 74, 97
Dirichlet distribution, 324
discrete filter, 351–352
disturbance smoothing, 10, 98, 312, 361
dynamic generalised linear models, 305, 426

EWMA, 22, 122–123, 317, 320, 323, 325, 326, 327
explanatory variables, 91, 326–329, 363–364
exponential family distribution, 368, 390, 397, 398, 426

filter, 120, 153, 155, 172, 184–185
filtered estimates, 131, 139
forecasting, 5, 16, 18–19

gamma distribution, 319
Gibbs sampling, 308, 309, 339–340, 343, 354

heavy-tailed distribution, 376, 398, 410–411
HEGY test, 273, 286, 288
Hodrick-Prescott filter, 119–121, 152–154, 166–167, 172, 177, 196, 235